OVERSIZE

362.1 Am3

America's health care crisis

S0-BWV-413

ACPL ITEM
DISCARDED

1833 02671 9805

**DO NOT REMOVE
CARDS FROM POCKET**

**ALLEN COUNTY PUBLIC LIBRARY
FORT WAYNE, INDIANA 46802**

You may return this book to any agency, branch,
or bookmobile of the Allen County Public Library.

DEMCO

AMERICA'S
HEALTH CARE
CRISIS

AMERICA'S HEALTH CARE CRISIS

An Editorials On File Book

Editor: Oliver Trager

Facts On File

Allen County Public Library
900 Webster Street
PO Box 2270
Fort Wayne, IN 46801-2270

AMERICA'S HEALTH CARE CRISIS

Published by Facts On File, Inc.
© Copyright 1993 by Facts On File, Inc.

All rights reserved. No part of this book may be reproduced in any form
without permission of the publisher except for reasonably brief
extracts used in reviews, which retain their copyrights.

Cataloging-in-Publication Data available on request from Facts On File, Inc.

ISBN 0-8160-2944-X

Printed in the United States of America

9 8 7 6 5 4 3 2 1

This book is printed on acid-free paper

Contents

Preface. 1

Part I: Health Care Reform 2
Catastrophic Care Plan Legislation, 1991 Medicaid Debate, 1993 Medicaid
Debate, Health Care Factors into 1988 Presidential Campaign, 1991 Senate
Health Care Bill Debated, 1992 President Bush Plan Presented, State Health
Care Plans Surveyed, 1992 Oregon Plan Debated, Hillary Rodham Clinton
Leads Reform

Part II: Families, Children & Health 56
1992 Family Leave Debate, 1993 Family Leave Debate, Infant Mortality Surveyed, Lead Poisoning Overviewed, Children's Vaccinations Debated, Disabled Rights Issues Gain Prominence, Elderly Issues Discussed

Part III: Disease in America 94
Blood Shortages & Contamination Confront U.S., Magic Johnson's HIV-Posi-
tive Announcement, 1991 Senate AIDS Bill, 1993 Senate AIDS Bill, 1992 Amster-
dam AIDS Conference, Tuberculosis on the Rise in U.S., EPA Releases Passive
Smoking Report, Heart Disease Surveyed, Breast Cancer Issues Overviewed,
Cancer Issues Surveyed, Alzheimer's Disease Research and Issues Discussed,
Mental Health Issues Surveyed

Part IV: Ethics & The Medical Profession 148
Medical Ethics Debated, Doctors Costs Discussed, Malpractice Issues
Overviewed, Pharmaceutical Drug Costs Surveyed, Hospital Practices &
Methods Debated, Nursing Profession Overviewed, Organ Transplant Issues
Surveyed, Breast Implant Sales Halted, FDA Curbs Breast Implants, Dr.
Kevorkian Brings Suicide Issues to a Head, Nancy Cruzan Death Raises Con-
troversy, Supreme Court's 1990 "Right-to-Die" Ruling

Index 206

Selected Bibliography

Califano, Jospeh A. Jr., *America's Health Care Revolution*, A Touchstone Book, Simon & Schuster, Inc., 1986

Consumer Reports Editors, *How To Resolve The Health Care Crisis*, Consumer Reports Books, Consumer Union of United States, Inc., 1992

Leichter, Howard M. (ed.), *Health Policy Reform in America*, M.E. Sharpe, Inc., 1992

Reagan, Michael D., *Curing the Crisis: Options for America's Health Care*, Westview Press, Inc., 1992

Sagan, Leonard A., *The Health of Nations*, Basic Books, Inc., 1987

Preface

Despite America's place as the planet's economic and political superpower, the U.S. health care system struggles to keep pace with the rest of the industrialized world. Medicine, like steel, oil and defense industries, has always made its presence felt on Capitol Hill and at the White House. However, the once-monolithic medical lobby has splintered as the number of major debates over medical issues proliferate and intensify.

As controversies and divisions plaguing the state of America's health system increase, a new Editorials On File book, *AMERICA'S HEALTH CARE CRISIS*, explores the issues that surround this vital topic and the questions they provoke: What is the future of Medicare? Has the medical establishment dealt properly with the AIDS crisis? Does the insurance industry need reform? How do malpractice issues affect the medical establishment's legitimacy? Should hospital standards be more closely scrutinized? Is there a cure for cancer on the horizon? Is suicide a viable medical and moral option for the terminally ill? Have medical ethics eroded? Is child health care improving? Are the costs of basic health care too high? Does the pharmaceutical industry need reform? Is enough importance placed on mental health care? Has the medical community dealt efficiently with the country's drug problems? Do the poor receive proper health care? Are preventative and alternative health care approaches given proper emphasis in our society? Are reform efforts eroding the quality of the U.S. health-care system?

In *AMERICA'S HEALTH CARE CRISIS* the nation's leading daily newspaper editorial writers and cartoonists examine the complicated issues informing this crucial subject.

Part I: Health Care Reform

Most people agree that every human being should have access to needed medical care, whether one sees care in terms of the individual's right to receive or in terms of society's obligation to provide. The question in the United States then becomes *how* can we best cure the "lack of coverage" disease that afflicts 34 million or more Americans withour basic medical insurance?

A bewildering diversity of proposals has been offered in recent years, and nothing approaching a consensus has yet emerged. But the abundance of schemes can be limited to a range of types for description and analysis.

The crux of the health care coverage reform debate turns on the appropriate mix of private and public elements. The critical questions are, "Who pays for health care, and how?" and "Who provides it?"

Currently, the U.S. system is nearly unique in its private, market-oriented, employer-dominated financing, with thousands of different payers and plans. The appropriateness of publicly financed health care is accepted for the elderly and, grudgingly, for the unemployed poor, but not for the bulk of the population. Our system is not unique, however, in its overwhelming use of the private sector to provide medical services. Most other Western nations combine public financing with private delivery of services. In examining the range of alternatives, there is a necessity to keep in mind the current ordinariness of this combination. However, since President Truman introduced his brand of national health insurance in the late 1940s, this union has been deemed "socialized medicine" and portrayed negatively in many quarters.

Health care reformers have con-tended that the term has been used to confuse government financing of health insurance with total government control of medical care, thus conjuring up the frightening prospect of Stalinist minions getting between patient and doctor and reduced quality overall. On the contrary, Truman's notion was to do for the entire population what Medicare has since done for the elderly: Take a major share of the health care financial burden off the shoulders of individual patients so that they could feel free to seek care as needed.

Traditional social science defines socialism as government ownership of the means of production. Using that definition, if doctors and hospitals are perceived as the health care system's "means of production," then any plan in which government's role is to pay private-sector providers on behalf of patients is not "socialized medicine." Whether a government-*run* (as distinguished from -*financed*) health care system can be effective is, of course, debatable. But the socialized medicine charge sometimes revived in the current health care controversy by opponents of any plan that is government financed is, according to its defenders, simply a red herring. They contend that it should not frighten us away from a dispassionate examination of the evidence concerning the more publicly oriented alternatives under discussion.

Ultimately, whether the financing is predominantly private or public tells us little about incentives to provide or withhold care or about the extent to which the payer does or does not intervene between physician and patient. The most important considerations – high quality medical care, equity, administrative and political feasibility, cost effectiveness, compatibility with patients' rights and physicans' professional responsibility – cannot be settled by ideological sloganeering. The need the need for open-mindeness becomes clear as the search for solutions continues.

As the Clinton administration charts its course in the rapacious waters of the health care debate, major congressional action on health care will take the form of enacting a specific, detailed legislative plan and will doubtless include a number of compromises to bring powerful interests on board – just as was the case with Medicare and Medicaid. Advocates on all sides of the health care reform debate agree that whatever emerges will be recognizable as embodying predominantly one or another of a limited number of policy models or "ideal types."

At one extreme end of the spectrum would be a national health service (NHS), in which the word "service" connotes government delivery of the services, as well as their financing. Next in degree of public-sector involvement are National Health Insurance (NHI) and Universal Health Insurance (UHI) systems.

NHI is primarily seen as a publicly (i.e., tax-) financed insurance plan to cover the entire population, whether financed and operated by the national government or jointly by national and state governments. Extending of Medicare to the entire population is an example of an entirely national plan. Canada's system, operated at the pro-vincial level, with dual financing from the national government and the governments of the provinces, exemplifies the intergovernmental type. Another definition of NHI is any health insurance system established by national law to cover the entire population that uses a mixture of public- and private-sector financing and operation. By terming this broader conception *Universal Health Insurance*, we can indicate the scope of coverage without necessarily implying governmental operation. Germany provides an example, as do the current "play-or-pay" proposals in the United States.

One aspect of the health care reform debate all advocates seem to agree on is the necessity to cut costs. There are, however, several real problems stemming from certain peculiarities of health care, especially the nature of its market, how it is paid for, and the uncertainties of its effectiveness. Additional trouble arises from the present weak economy and an increasing national debt.

Cost-cutting advocates argue that if reform methods commenced with medical rather than financial objectives, a great deal could be done to simultaneously improve the quality of care, use more effectively whatever we do spend, and sometimes actually save money. All of these approaches, they contend, are preferable to the emphasis on cost-shifting and cost-cutting of the economic model, which could turn medical care from a profession into a competitive bottom-line industry.

3

Deficit Bill Addresses Catastrophic Care

The House Oct. 5, 1989 passed a $10.9 billion budget reconciliation bill designed to reduce the federal budget deficit to its 1990 target of $110 billion. Congress was under pressure to meet an Oct. 15 deadline for avoiding automatic federal spending cuts under the Gramm-Rudman balanced budget act.

The tax-and-spending measure the House sent to the Senate was widely described as laden with accounting devices, as well as with controversial and extraneous programs.

Among the key provisions of the omnibus package were a reduction in the tax rate on capital gains, repeal of the federal catastrophic health-care insurance program just one year after it had been created and an expansion of federal funds for child-care services.

The House of Representatives Oct. 4 voted overwhelmingly, 360-66, to repeal an addition to the Medicaid program that had provided payment for "catastrophic" medical costs. The Medicare Catastrophic Care Act had been signed into law by President Ronald Reagan in July 1988.

The repeal proposal was an amendment to an omnibus deficit-reduction bill that was passed by the House Oct. 5.

The amendment was sponsored by Reps. Brian Donnelly (D, Mass.) and Bill Archer (R, Texas).

Los Angeles, California, January 13, 1989

Back in the early 1960s when the Medicare system was still just a gleam in President Lyndon Johnson's eye, doctors denounced it as "socialized medicine." They knew that if the idea of federally sponsored universal health insurance for senior citizens ever caught on, it was only a matter of time before somebody proposed universal health insurance for all — along with all the attendant oversight and cost controls on health-care providers that would imply.

Who would have dreamed that some 25 years later, such a once-radical call would be joined by no less than the New England Journal of Medicine, one of the most respected voices within the medical establishment itself? Yet, there it was. The Journal's current issue includes an editorial titled, "Universal Health Insurance: Its Time Has Come." which attacks "our disastrously inadequate health-care financing system." and urges doctors to join forces with the government and health-insurance industry to seek solutions.

The Journal goes on to offer two models of health-care financing. The more conventional of the pair, proposed by a Stanford University economist, resembles the plan just enacted last year in the state of Massachusetts.

It centers on increasing employers' responsibility for health-care coverage, requiring them to offer health benefits to their workers covering 80 percent of medical costs, as Medicare does. Employers would be charged an 8 percent payroll tax on behalf of any workers not so covered. The self-employed, retired and all others outside an employer plan would pay an 8 percent income-tax surcharge; those at or below the poverty line would pay nothing for their coverage.

A more avant-garde approach is advocated by a group of doctors called "Physicians for a National Health Program." They propose the United States adopt the Canadian model, where government becomes the health-care insurer of first, not last, resort. Under this system, those now paying health-insurance premiums would instead pay a tax to the government. The same state and federal agencies that now administer Medicaid health-care programs for the poor would presumably also handle the reimbursements for health care for everyone else.

It's too early to tell what these plans' financial impact would be, especially in light of our federal deficit problems. But the debate over universal health coverage has now taken an important new turn, and we look forward to seeing how Congress and the rest of the medical community responds.

FORT WORTH STAR-TELEGRAM
Fort Worth, Texas, January 14, 1989

As opposition mounts against the new Medicare catastrophic-cost health care program, Texas Sen. Lloyd Bentsen is preparing to stand his ground against the impending assault on Congress led by several organizations representing the elderly. Stand firm he should.

Much misunderstanding — fueled by much misinformation — has swirled around the issue for the last two months. The deepest misunderstanding, however, lies in a fundamental ignorance of the wedding of public policy to the principles of insurance: a pooling of risks against a probability of loss or injury.

Those two essential principles are at the heart of this issue.

First, the nation has made a social, therefore political, commitment to provide medical care for *all* elderly citizens of this country. Consequently, the program must be mandatory; optional Medicare, like optional Social Security, would crumble.

Certainly, Social Security met with opposition when Congress enacted it, as did Medicare in the mid-1960s. Healthy, pluralistic democracies will produce differences of opinion on matters of public policy. But the vehement opposition to Medicare 25 years ago has been replaced with a virtually universal sense of lawful and rightful entitlement to those benefits as a part of the social compact.

The second essential principle is that Medicare is an insurance program. Participants contribute to the system, thus pooling the risks of incurring illness and other medical infirmities. Medicare is not a simple compensation system by which all medical costs are socialized.

To assist in providing adequate benefits to all elderly, the federal government does socialize some of the cost through subsidies to Medicare participants. Be-

fore Jan. 1, that subsidy was 75 percent of the insurance premium. The catastrophic bill changed that with the new year.

Providing for a substantial increase in benefits, which the new law does, will cost billions more to fund. Who pays? Congress increased by $4 per month the basic premium for Medicare — now about $30 — and added a surtax on those whose incomes exceed $10,000 — up to a maximum of $800 this year. A couple would have to earn $70,000 before paying the maximum surtax, and even then taxpayers will be paying almost half of their total premium.

We agree with Congress that those who will receive the benefits — particularly those able to pay — should help to bear that cost, not future generations who would have to pick up the tab for current subsidies. Indeed, the surtax really is less a "tax" than it is a reduction of the subsidy.

Most of the hue and cry is coming from those who will see their taxpayer-provided subsidy decline from 75 percent to 40 percent — those elderly couples whose taxable income will exceed $70,000.

Others, who will not pay nearly the maximum surtax, oppose the new program by saying that they have worked and saved for retirement, do not want the program and did not ask for it. Public policy does not work that way. As a society, we have made the commitment to provide as much medical care for all our elderly citizens as we can afford. That is a morally right choice, as was the choice to have those financially able to pay more of their share in the cost of providing those benefits.

As the controversy intensifies, Bentsen will be on the receiving end of considerable political heat. But he has two things going for him: He has a persuasive mastery of the facts, and he's right.

House Ways and Means Committee Chairman Dan Rostenkowski, Senate Finance Committee Chairman Lloyd Bentsen and the American Association of Retired Persons are about to discover the risks of using one person's money to pay for another person's good intentions. America's elderly citizens have begun rebelling against a catastrophic health insurance bill that Sen. Bentsen, Rep. Rostenkowski and the AARP helped push through Congress last year because the measure makes senior citizens pay the cost of the politicians' good intentions.

The Washington Times
Washington, D.C., March 6, 1989

Senior-citizen protests have persuaded many members of Congress to take a second look at the catastrophic health insurance plan, which sailed through both houses of Congress last year. Sixty-five lawmakers are backing Rep. Bill Archer's proposal to delay implementation of some parts of the law for a year. Oklahoma Sens. David Boren and Don Nickles want to postpone things for two years. Nearly 40 members of Congress are co-sponsoring identical bills introduced by Democratic Sen. Harry Reid (a supporter of last year's catastrophic health insurance bill) and Republican Rep. Harris Fawell, who want to repeal the law and start over.

Such opposition hasn't impressed Rep. Rostenkowski or Sen. Bentsen, who refuse to hold hearings on the matter. "The biggest problem that we have," says Daniel Hawley, a former airline pilot from Las Vegas who's spearheading a nationwide drive to kill the bill, "is that Rostenkowski and Bentsen have become dictators."

At first glance, the catastrophic health insurance bill looks like a boon for senior citizens. It pays the hospitalization costs of Medicare beneficiaries after they have paid a single deductible, estimated at $564 this year. It helps pay the costs of prescription drugs from those who have spent $600 on medications in a year. It limits a patient's annual out-of-pocket costs to $1,370 for care by approved physicians and outpatient services. That cost-protection will rise each year by means of a formula that raises the deductible to whatever amount will hold to 7 percent the proportion of beneficiaries who pay the full deductible. The Congressional Budget Office estimates that this moving deductible will reach $1,900 by 1993.

The bad news comes with Congress's method for financing the plan. Rep. Rostenkowski and Sen. Bentsen have decided to put the burden on grandma and grandpa, even though more than 70 percent of America's elderly citizens have private "Medigap" insurance that pays for doctor and hospital costs covered by the catastrophic health insurance program. Meanwhile, the catastrophic program does virtually nothing to address the major health-cost problem seniors face, how to pay for the cost of long-term care in a nursing home.

Sen. Bentsen dismisses his critics as "wealthier people" who "want to be subsidized" by "other taxpayers." It just goes to show how being a multimillionaire and party bagman can distort a guy's world view.

Taxpayers who have reached their 65 birthdays will have to pay a 15-percent surcharge on their income taxes this year to pay for their catastrophic "benefits." This surcharge rises to 28 percent by 1993.

People of modest means could find themselves taxed virtually into poverty by the year 2000. The surtax on people with incomes of $21,000 a year could reach $1,400 a year by 2000, and the rate become steeper as people earn more. The effect would be to gut the cuts in marginal rates made in the 1986 tax reform legislation, and to impose a cruel burden on low- and moderate-income elderly.

President Bush, who supported the bill last year, has been silent on the repeal question. We hope that will change. The catastrophic health insurance plan mocks his visions of a "kinder, gentler" America and a budget that includes no new taxes. If Mr. Bush wants to serve the American people, and especially the elderly, he should seek the repeal of the catastrophic health insurance law, and suggest that Congress replace it with tax credits and incentives designed to expand the private Medigap market to reach those most in need.

Herald News
Fall River, Massachusetts, February 19, 1989

The Medicare Catastrophic Coverage Act of 1988, a complex and controversial law, demands careful study by the 32 million Americans who are affected by it.

Revolutionary changes are wrought by the law, which was passed by Congress in June, 1988 and signed by President Reagan in July of that year. Its first phase is now in effect.

The main intent of the law is to protect low-income senior citizens and their spouses from the staggering costs of acute illness. Medicare recipients of middle and higher income levels, who are also, in various degrees, vulnerable to the financial wipeout of catastrophic illness, will maintain a livable income, and a portion of their life savings, if their spouses become long-term, Medicaid-covered nursing home residents.

Most elderly advocates support the expanded benefits of the law, in terms of hospital care, physician care, prescription drugs, home health services, temporary skilled nursing facility care, and other benefits, implemented in phases.

New Medicare hospital insurance benefits, providing unlimited care after a deductible of $564, are now in effect.

The new system is estimated to cost some $30 billion over the first five years. The price of the new catastrophic benefits will be borne by those who receive the benefits, mainly retired people.

The Medicare Handbook, published by the U.S. Department of Health and Human Services, states, "The new catastrophic benefits will be financed by an increase in your monthly supplemental medical insurance premium, and by an annual supplemental premium that will depend on your Federal income tax liability."

Beginning this year, everyone enrolled in Medicare, except those under poverty level, will pay an extra $4 per month premium for Part B, covering doctors' bills. The amount is being deducted automatically from Social Security checks. Part B premium payments amount to $373 this year; they will rise to $428 in 1990, $500 in 1991, $529 in 1992, and $571 in 1993.

In addition, about 40 per cent of Medicare enrollees with federal income tax obligations will pay what the law terms a "supplemental premium," but is actually a surtax, based on their tax liability, for 1989 and beyond.

In the current year, for every $150 of the income tax they pay, retirees on on Medicare must pay $22.50, until the total hits a cap of $800 per person, or $1,600 for couples who are both eligible for Medicare and filing a joint return.

This "supplemental premium" will gradually rise until the cap hits $1,050 per person or $2,100 per couple in 1993. And some observers, foreseeing escalating medical costs, warn that the surtax may rise considerably by the end of the century.

Those who must pay the 1989 tax-related supplemental premium in April, 1990, should budget for it now, by increasing wage or pension withholdings, or increasing quarterly estimated payments. Persons with comfortable retirement incomes should consult with their financial advisers.

The premiums increases are already opposed by several legislators, including U.S. Rep. Barney Frank, who stated, "The new law requires senior citizen to bear too large a proportion of their health care costs." He advocates repeal of the Part B premiums and a freeze of the Part A surtax rate and cap at the 1989 levels, with an annual inflation adjustment. To compensate, he recommends doubling the cigarette tax, raising nearly $15 billion over the next five years.

Post-Tribune
Gary, Indiana, March 3, 1989

This country can't be very proud of the way it treats its elderly, particularly when it comes to easing their fears and worries about health care.

Medicare, although a major help, proves insufficient for most people. The Health Insurance Association of America estimates that at least 70 percent of those eligible for Medicare take out supplemental insurance to fill the gaps. The cost is a burden for many.

One of the saddest aspects, though, is that millions of older Americans are scared into buying more than one supplemental policy, wasting thousands of dollars annually. Since federal and state laws set a minimum level of benefits that a supplemental policy must pay, one policy is enough in almost every case.

It is a felony, under federal law, for an insurance agent to knowingly sell a supplemental policy that duplicates coverage a person already has. The law obviously isn't being effectively enforced. And there apparently are a lot of either unscrupulous or ill-informed insurance agents running around.

The whole specter of health care for the elderly, who normally require more health services than other adults, is another good argument for a national health insurance program similar to the one in place in Canada — where studies show that all age citizens are happier with their health care system than people in the United States and where the country, unlike the United States, has been able to slow the percentage of its gross national product spent on medical care.

Until the United States comes up with some kind of relief, the government and the insurance business should join together in a concerted campaign to educate people on buying appropriate insurance. Setting up a toll-free hotline and saturating the country with print and verbal advertisements urging people to call for advice before buying any insurance might be one approach that could help.

It would help the image of the insurance business, help the government enforce the law and help give people some peace of mind.

The Washington Post
Washington, D.C., April 22, 1989

CONGRESS STUCK to three important principles in the catastrophic health insurance bill it passed last year. The first was that the program should not add to the deficit, the second that the elderly beneficiaries themselves should be the ones to pay and the third that the better-off among the beneficiaries should be the ones to pay the most. The idea was partly to say to the elderly and to groups that so smoothly represent them here that they were going to have to let someone else go to the head of the line for a while—in particular, the nonelderly poor. The discipline would be that if the elderly and advocacy groups still wanted increased benefits, they would have to foot the bill.

The income surtax for the elderly that resulted—it is not called that, but a supplemental Medicare premium—has created an enormous stir. The people on whom it was imposed don't like it, and the politicians who so stoutly imposed it have now rushed to the head of the opposite parade to denounce it. The Senate recently adopted, 97 to 2, a resolution calling on the Finance Committee to hold hearings on the issue; a similar vote in the House was 408 to 0.

The chairmen of the tax committees, Sen. Lloyd Bentsen of Finance and Rep. Dan Rostenkowski of Ways and Means, had hitherto resisted calls for reconsideration. Now Mr. Bentsen has indicated he may relent. The basis is an estimate suggesting that the surtax will produce more revenue than previously believed. The elderly turn out to have higher incomes than first estimated; their tax liabilities are therefore also higher and a surtax yields more. If the Treasury concurs in the reestimate, it should be possible to cut the surtax by about a sixth and still pay for the program, Mr. Bentsen says.

The instant critics say that such a move would be premature, would add a billion dollars a year to the deficit and would bow too readily to a pressure group that, even with the surtax, is getting back more from Medicare than it put in. The program's costs may also have been underestimated, these defenders say, the costs of a new drug benefit especially; Congress should wait to cut the tax until it's sure it doesn't need the money.

We don't really care whether the tax is cut. (There is a provision in the law to begin adjusting the tax to costs in 1993 anyway.) Our concern is simply that Congress not stray from the bill's basic principles. If the beneficiaries don't like the tax, they should give up the benefits too. The elderly, thanks to the expansion of federal benefits in the past 20 years, are now less needy—have a lower poverty rate—than the population as a whole. The poverty rate among the young is almost twice that among the old. The next federal dollar should be spent not on the elderly but on the uninsured.

Birmingham Post-Herald
Birmingham, Alabama, March 2, 1989

Health insurance, it is widely agreed, is a good thing. Can one have too much of a good thing? You bet.

Nearly 6 million elderly Americans, worried about the ruinous costs of long illnesses, have bought two or more policies that supplement their Medicare coverage, a practice that is unnecessary, duplicative and costly.

The Health Insurance Association of America, the industry trade group, estimates that of the 32 million Medicare beneficiaries, 22.5 million, or 70 percent, have bought supplemental policies to cover the gap in costs not paid by the federal health insurance program for people 65 and older.

Federal and state laws set a minimum level of benefits that a private, so-called Medigap policy must pay, and honest insurers concede that one such policy is all virtually anyone needs.

Unfortunately, unscrupulous insurance salesmen exist who sell unsuspecting, frightened or confused elderly people multiple policies, costing some of them thousands of dollars a year.

James Firman, president of United Seniors Health Cooperative, a research group, said 20 percent to 35 percent of the elderly had some duplicative or wasted coverage. "If you have more than one policy," he said, "you're guaranteed to have some duplication, and millions of people have anywhere between two and eight policies.

"We have seen dramatic cases of people spending $5,000 to $7,000 on duplicative and unnecessary coverage. These are invariably people who can least afford it."

A 1980 federal law makes it a crime for an insurance agent knowingly to sell a policy duplicating coverage the buyer already has. No one ever has been indicted under the law. Some agents get around it by carefully not asking customers if they already have Medigap policies.

The House Energy and Commerce Committee plans hearings in April on the problems of duplicative policies. It could usefully amend the 1980 law to require agents to ask potential purchasers if they have supplemental coverage.

But more than that is necessary. State insurance commissions, better business groups, consumer protection agencies, advocates for the elderly and, above all, families must get the message across to those over 65: "Usually one policy is enough."

The Miami Herald

Miami, Florida, April 23, 1989

A STAMPEDE of lobbyists is charging toward the narrow crack that Sen. Lloyd Bentsen has opened in Medicare's fledgling catastrophic-illness program. The Administration, the House leadership, and Mr. Bentsen must take great care during planned hearings in both chambers to protect the program's sound financial premise from being trampled.

That premise rightly insisted that the cost of expanding Medicare coverage must be borne by Medicare's beneficiaries, and especially the affluent among them. The program therefore added $4 per month to every Medicare premium and tacked a surcharge onto the premiums of retirees who are wealthy enough to pay Federal income taxes. Most retirees pay only the $4. A couple with an income of $30,000 will pay about $321 in surtax this year.

Most retirees are willing to pay their own way, but not to support a bloated surplus fund in order to make the Federal deficit look smaller. That is the issue that Mr. Bentsen, the powerful chairman of the Senate Finance Committee, wishes to address.

Ironically, the unexpected surplus of $9.1 billion projected over five years has developed because more retirees are in the upper-income brackets than had been thought. If current trends continue, the

CATASTROPHIC-ILLNESS FEES

fund will have twice the $4.2-billion cushion that actuaries consider prudent. Senator Bentsen proposes to reduce the maximum surtax, perhaps to $500 from $800.

That is a reasonable step — *if* the line can be held there. Many, including House Ways and Means Chairman Dan Rostenkowski, fear that *any* reopening of the issue now will produce a raid on the Treasury.

Such a raid would be unconscionable. Retirees already are the best-insured age group in the nation, by far. In contrast, the most vulnerable are children: Some 20 million American children have no medical insurance at all, while millions more have only the welfare-level Medicaid program, which is far less generous then Medicare. A child with leukemia might bankrupt his working parents, but Medicare pays for grandparents' treatment.

No step can be tolerated that increases this existing imbalance. The Medicare surtax should not yield a windfall "profit" for the Government, but neither should the affluent elderly be relieved from paying their fair share.

Rockford Register Star

Rockford, Illinois, April 4, 1989

Rep. Bob Michel, the Peoria Republican, is Minority Leader in the U.S. House. He's also is a close friend and ally of Rep. Lynn Martin of Loves Park.

Last week, Michel earned another distinction —he joined a group of congressional leaders who now believe they won't have to reform a particularly bad piece of lawmaking "because the senior citizens have stopped complaining."

Although Republicans formed a study group to consider the issue, a spokesman for Michel now says, "I don't think that we Republicans are going to push for any changes."

That's a shame, because Michel and his fellow congressional Republicans had been in a position to try to shame the Democratic majority in Congress into reforms.

The issue involved, of course, is the federal government's new catastrophic health care program for the elderly — a plan designed to protect senior citizens from catastrophic medical bills. It sounds like a great idea, but it falls short on a few rather important points:

■ It provides no protection against the most catastrophic of all health costs — long-term care in or out of nursing homes.

■ It duplicates insurance protection many senior citizens already have earned for themselves as part of pre-planned retirement packages — and in the process replaces competitive private markets with a government monopoly.

■ It costs far too much and ignoring much less expensive alternatives.

■ It is financed in large part by a whopping income-tax surcharge on all senior citizens who have provided themselves with even modest retirement incomes. The National Center for Policy Analysis points out that, as a result of this surcharge and other Reagan-era taxes on senior citizens, "elderly taxpayers now face the highest marginal (income) tax rates ever imposed on middle-income Americans in the nation's history."

All of this, naturally enough, left senior citizens rather peevish last year as they learned the details. That anger led several politicians to come forward during the fall election campaign promising reforms.

But now, according to Michel and a few of his congressional friends, the anger is fading. The protests died down during the furor over congressional pay increases — and never revved up again.

So, these congressional leaders say, they really don't see any need to change the catastrophic health care law. What difference does it make that it is bad legislation, they seem to be saying. As long as the complaints have stopped, there is no reason for Congress to act.

That's absurd.

Pittsburgh Post-Gazette

Pittsburgh, Pennsylvania, August 4, 1989

As a practical matter, with the federal budget deficit being what it is, comprehensive catastrophic health coverage for the elderly never would have been made available by Congress unless the beneficiaries were to be required to pay the premiums.

Within that group, the payment formula was similar to the way income-tax responsibility is apportioned in the general population — those in a position to pay more were taxed more. The catastrophic-coverage surtax now has only persons with an income of more than $45,000 a year paying the maximum amount — $800 for individuals and $1,600 for couples. More than 60 percent of the 32 million Americans on Medicare pay nothing for the vastly expanded coverage.

Though some retiree groups endorsed the program as a good deal for millions of people for whom serious health problems spelled financial disaster, the fact that the cost of this additional protection wasn't being spread throughout the taxpaying population has been vigorously resented by many of those picking up the cost — so vigorously, in fact, that even some members of Congress who once stoutly defended the program's financing, such as Sen. Lloyd Bentsen, chairman of the Senate Finance Committee, have been worn down and are now ready to revise the payment program.

The House Ways and Means Committee last week decided to reduce the heat being applied to its chamber by cutting in half the amount those now at the maximum surtax level would be required to pay and transferring the burden to less-well-off Medicare participants. While pacifying one group of senior citizens, this approach seems likely to stir up another group. The committee also voted to make coverage voluntary, a step that would be sure to stampede those paying the higher amounts into dropping out and thus jeopardizing the fiscal viability of the program.

Some in Congress are hoping that it will be possible to reduce the surtax through surpluses in the program, but the difficulty is that no one is yet sure how much will be realized. Some estimates suggest a $5 billion surplus might be seen within five years in the program that had initially been estimated to cost some $31 billion during that initial period of operation. The Congressional Budget Office has said the surplus could be as much as $10 billion.

Sen. Bentsen's committee is hoping to have a surtax-reform plan fashioned by the end of the year, one that reflects the latest readings on financing requirements.

If the Senate panel can come up with a more equitable distribution plan, fine. If reliable surplus projections indicate a surtax reduction is possible, that would be even better. But such a program must continue to be fundamentally supported by those covered.

Providing this sort of additional protection to the elderly at a rate far lower than commercial policies cost is not going to be authorized by Congress in the present climate if it means throwing the budget further out of balance or hiking Social Security contributions. That is still the political reality of this issue.

Whatever is done to improve this program, will have to be accomplished within the framework of what it is actually costing to maintain and what the beneficiaries are able — and willing — to support.

The Washington Post

Washington, D.C., September 22, 1989

LLOYD BENTSEN was right to make the Bush administration take a stand on repeal of the catastrophic health insurance bill—and the administration took the right stand. Health and Human Services Secretary Louis Sullivan said repeal "would be a very serious mistake" because of the benefits that would be lost; that the best approach would be not to alter the year-old law at all; and failing that, that Congress should save as much as it can of both the benefits and financing scheme. That is what the House Ways and Means Committee has proposed and Sen. Bentsen's Finance Committee is also considering.

The objection to the plan, as ever in such things, has not been to the benefits, although not everyone thinks they are of major importance, but to the financing: who should pay. Congress in passing the bill wisely adopted the basic principle put forward by President Reagan that the elderly beneficiaries themselves should be the ones to pay; there are more important demands, beginning with deficit reduction, on the government's insufficient store of general revenues. Congress then went the president one better and said the better-off elderly should pay the most; the financing would be partly through the flat premium the president proposed, but partly also through an income surtax. The better-off elderly are now objecting to the surtax, and Congress is racing for safer ground.

It is craven of Congress to yield so quickly to a basically comfortable group for whom Medicare remains a good deal—they get back more than they put in—and good of the committees and administration to try to preserve as much as they can of the benefits and progressivity. (Among the side benefits are health care cost cuts for the poor. The catastrophic program would shift to Medicare some costs now borne by the state-federal Medicaid program; states would have to use these savings to help more poor.)

Repeal, if it comes, will also increase the short-term deficit because, to play safe, Congress had taxes under the catastrophic program start faster than benefits to build up a reserve. The fiscal effect is one of the things that has kept the administration in line. If the deficit is increased, there will be pressure to grant an exemption from the Gramm-Rudman process or otherwise to wink, and although there is already much fakery in this year's budget, the president's people fear the precedent.

The betting is nonetheless that repeal will be hard to stop. A question then will be whether to have the repeal remain part of the already too bulky reconciliation or deficit-reduction bill now moving to the House floor or split it off. It should be split. There are too many other important issues in reconciliation, and they ought not be trampled in the rush to placate those who do not want to pay the surtax.

THE BUFFALO NEWS

Buffalo, New York, September 25, 1989

FORTUNATELY, the Bush administration has joined congressional leaders' efforts to preserve the catastrophic health insurance plan for Americans on Medicare. Repealing this program, enacted only last year, would be a momentous mistake.

It is difficult to believe serious talk about repeal can even be circulating in Congress. In the near hysteria over how the program is financed, too many older Americans — and members of Congress — have forgotten the impressive benefits it provides.

The prevailing principle of the plan is not to pay all the health-care bills of those on Medicare. It is to protect the elderly and disabled from the heavy expenses caused by acute, serious illness that can devastate a family's lifetime savings in a very short time.

Under the program, the government will pay for unlimited hospital care after the beneficiary pays a single deductible. The plan includes extended hospice and home-care benefits. It contains coverage of mammography exams to detect breast cancer, expanded Medicaid services for the elderly poor and considerable help with drug bills when they exceed a certain amount ($600 or $800) in out-of-pocket costs for the patient each year. This last feature, however, could be eliminated in efforts to reduce the program costs.

Much of the current clamor against the program is coming from the more affluent elderly who will pay a new special surtax on their annual income tax. The surtax could rise to as much as $800 per person, or $1,600 per couple, on this year's income.

True enough, these figures look scary. But fewer than 6 percent of the beneficiaries, according to estimates by the Joint Congressional Committee on Taxation, would pay the maximum.

Those 6 percent would be the wealthiest Americans. For millions of others who will pay some tax, the actual bill will be much less, since the surtax is adjusted to income. "Next April 15, 94.4 percent of seniors will discover they're not paying anywhere near $800," said Sen. John D. Rockefeller IV, D-W.Va.

Responding to the pressure from affluent senior citizens, the House has already adopted modifications of the 1988 catastrophic insurance plan. The Senate is considering changes.

These differ in detail — some significantly — but given the political circumstances, there is good sense in their common purpose: to reduce the controversial surtax, as well as to trim program benefits in order to offset the reduced revenues, while preserving the core coverage.

This program is not perfect. It does not solve all the problems of health care costs for the elderly (nursing home care, for example, is not included). But that is no reason to repeal it. It is a progressive advance that will serve the nation's elderly well in the years ahead.

Those rashly pushing Congress for repeal should recheck the facts — and reconsider the benefits. For millions of Americans on Medicare, the 1988 catastrophic health insurance program is a bargain. It doesn't deserve to die.

The Pittsburgh PRESS

Pittsburgh, Pennsylvania, September 25, 1989

For Congress and the Bush administration, the Catastrophic Health Care Act of 1988 is quickly living up to its name: a government-sponsored health-care program with all the marks of a political and fiscal catastrophe.

Less than 15 months ago, President Reagan signed the act in a Rose Garden ceremony, with a bipartisan contingent of congressional leaders happily looking on. Now many in Congress are scrambling to undo what they congratulated themselves on doing last year.

Earlier this month, the Congressional Budget Office estimated that the catastrophic program, originally fixed with a price tag of $31 billion, will instead cost $48 billion through 1993.

This year alone, one of the planned benefits — increased access to skilled-nursing facilities — will cost a whopping 150 percent more than originally estimated. Those are overruns to make a Pentagon procurement officer blush.

What's more, a sizable portion of the nation's elderly — ostensibly the act's beneficiaries — are loudly letting their representatives know they didn't much want the bill in the first place.

Fully 85 percent are already covered for some or all of the program's benefits, through "medi-gap" or other forms of private insurance.

Nevertheless, 40 percent of the nation's seniors — those with higher incomes — will be forced to pay a hefty surtax for coverage they neither need nor want: up to $800 per taxpayer this year, increasing to more than $1,000 later.

Accordingly, a bipartisan group of congressmen, led by House Republican leader Bob Michel, is calling for repeal of the catastrophic bill and a fresh start in tackling the genuine health-care concerns of the elderly.

Some senators, including Pennsylvania's John Heinz, prefer only to reduce the surcharge rates but critics point out there would be no assurance the rates couldn't go back up in a year or two.

The Bush administration is reluctant to push for repeal because the surtax is expected to bring in surplus revenue this year — revenue that can be counted against the budget deficit and thereby help forestall unwanted Gramm-Rudman budget cuts.

But that's a shortsighted reason to stick with bad long-term policy. Congress appears on the verge of doing that rarest of things in Washington: acknowledging a mistake and correcting it. President Bush should encourage this healthy development, not stand in its way.

ARGUS-LEADER

Sioux Falls, South Dakota, October 14, 1989

Just last year, federal lawmakers were almost tripping over themselves in the rush to provide catastrophic health coverage for retired Americans.

Now, members of Congress are crashing around, undoing something they did right to appease influential and generally affluent senior citizens who opposed the health-care program.

EDITORIAL

Most likely, the losers will be the largely silent ranks of poor and middle-of-the-road seniors, many of whom do not enjoy the benefits of private insurance plans.

The most recent turn of legislative events began last week, when House members caved in to lobbying pressure and voted overwhelmingly to kill catastrophic health coverage provided under Medicare.

Senators responded more reasonably by voting to preserve some benefits but scrapping controversial funding provisions.

Now, the two chambers will have to work out their differences. Hopefully, representatives, senators and President Bush will eventually agree on a plan that retains much of the original philosophy of the Medicare Catastrophic Coverage Act of 1988. But don't bet on it.

The act was not perfect, but it was progressive and a step in the right direction. Under the program, costs would be imposed on those who benefitted, rather than all taxpayers. Under controversial income-tax surcharge provisions, seniors who are well off would have had to pay more than poor seniors. All participants would have had to pay at least a $4 monthly fee.

Senators voted to keep long-term hospital protection covered by the $4 fee, but they repealed such benefits as reimbursement for prescription-drug costs over $600.

Clearly, House members overreacted to the objections of well-organized opponents. The addition of catastrophic coverage had been the biggest and most welcome expansion of Medicare since 1965. Now, millions of elderly Americans may be left short of their needs for long-term hospital and skilled nursing home care and other services.

It's amazing how health-care coverage that was considered crucial as recently as year ago has fallen victim to the greedy mood that has swept the nation's capital and special interest groups.

Some senior citizens may come out ahead because of recent congressional action. But most appear destined to lose.

Rockford Register Star

Rockford, Illinois, October 11, 1989

Now that Congress is ripping up its ill-advised Medicare catastrophic health insurance program, there will be attempts to portray middle-class senior citizens as having been selfish in their opposition to the plan. That's absurd.

The congressional plan was a lot like asking left-handed bachelors to pay all the cost of subsidized child care: In neither case is there any logical reason for selecting the group selected to pay.

Congress was correct in recognizing the need for some catastrophic health insurance. It also was right in being concerned about handing too many bills to working Americans. It was wrong in handing the catastrophic insurance bills just to senior citizens who pay income taxes.

This group stood to benefit the least from the program — either now or in the future — because most of them already have their own insurance coverage. It also is most apt to be the group that can least afford a hefty new tax burden. Under those circumstances, they surely have not been selfish in objecting to the congressional scheme.

Asking all working Americans to pay a little bit would have been more logical, since at least some of them stand to benefit eventually.

But the best solution is to scale back the entire program to a more manageable level and target it more specifically to meet truly catastrophic needs. Once that is done, it shouldn't be too difficult to convince Americans it would be to their benefit to help provide the financing.

Congress Passes Medicaid Compromise

Both Houses of Congress Nov. 27, 1991 cleared by a voice vote legislation enacting a compromise reached between the Bush administration and the nation's governors on Medicaid funding rules.

The federal government matched between 50% and 83% of states' expenditures for Medicaid, the nation's health-care system for the poor. Pressed by spiraling health costs, many states were increasing their Medicaid spending – and thus the size of their federal matching grant – by collecting funds from hospitals and other Medicaid providers through either special "provider-specific" taxes or outright donations. Hospitals gladly cooperated, since they usually more than recouped their money through Medicaid payments.

The administration had characterized these techniques as bookkeeping tricks in effect designed to rob the federal treasury. On Sept. 10, it had announced regulations restricting the practices, sending states into a panic.

The House Nov. 19 passed, 348-71, a bill blocking the administration from putting the restrictions into effect until September 1992. The Senate Finance Committee Nov. 22 approved a similar measure.

SYRACUSE HERALD-JOURNAL
Syracuse, New York, November 14, 1991

Former Surgeon General C. Everett Koop, in his customary tell-it-like-it-is manner, astutely sums up the nation's health-care crisis this way: It's the final minute of the final quarter of a losing football game. Everyone in the huddle is shouting plays. The coach should be calling the plays. Alas, there is no coach.

The man billed as America's doctor is so right. The plays are being called by business groups, consumer groups, medical groups, labor groups, congressional groups, all with the same message: We've found the cure for what ails the sick health-care system. Yet trying to sort through the cures leaves the patients — the American public — feeling worse than when they last paid a major medical bill.

Not that the health reformers aren't well-intentioned or do not have valid ideas. It's just that they're all shouting plays at the same time, and rather than enlightening us, they've given us a migraine.

Here's what we mean:

On Tuesday, the National Leadership Coalition on Health Reform, honorarily chaired by former Presidents Jimmy Carter and Gerald Ford and made up of business, labor and medical groups, announced its support of a national health plan that combines private and public insurance.

The proposal would allow companies to buy private insurance for employees or enroll in a federal program, called Pro Health, that would also insure the poor and uninsured. A national review board, made up of members from the public and private sectors, would set insurance payment rates, approved by Congress, for all insurers.

In June, Senate Democrats announced a national health-care plan called AmeriCare. It would offer health-care insurance for anyone who did not receive employer-provided benefits, including Medicaid beneficiaries. A federal health expenditure board and state group — and businesses if they choose — could join together and negotiate with health-care providers to obtain better rates and services.

In March of 1990, the American Medical Association offered a 16-point proposal that included requiring employers to provide health insurance, while creating state risk pools for the uninsured and small businesses unable to provide health insurance.

In the same year, the Heritage Foundation proposed that tax reform was the answer to America's health-care problems. It suggested phasing in individual tax credits for the purchase of health insurance and mandating that families — not employers — be required to purchase coverage.

Frustrated with the helter-skelter manner in which health-care reform is being discussed on a national level, New York state decided to figure out its own strategies.

New Yorkers were asked at town meetings throughout the state — ours was held last month — to choose among four proposals: The state version of Pro-Health, supported by hospitals; UNYCare and New York Health, from the state Health Department and state Assembly; and a universal health-care plan from the Medical Society of New York.

It would be wonderful if the best features of all of these proposals could be combined into a health-care reform package that could serve all Americans. That may eventually happen, but for now we only see more proposals on the horizon — more players calling plays.

What makes the picture even more dismal is the fact that 1992 is an election year for the president and Congress. Election years bring grandiose speeches and many promises. Rarely do they produce any actions of substance.

It's the final quarter on health care and we desperately need a coach to tell us which plays are best, which ones are lousy.

But as Koop points out, "The only guy who can do it is the president, and he's disinclined."

We wish the president would become inclined. In doing so, he would prove to the American people that he is concerned about their health — and not just their votes.

THE LINCOLN STAR
Lincoln, Nebraska, November 14, 1991

The nation's health care problems are anything but simple. They are, in fact, a complex web of interdependent relationships.

Right now the focus is on basic access to health care.

As the cost of medical care and insurance soar, as more people find they are unable to afford insurance, there is growing public support for a national health plan of some sort.

Public debate currently is focused on the insurance side, the supply side of the equation. What national system for health insurance will best suit this country?

Politicians and labor groups and columnists are exploring the options. Do we want government to take over the health care system? Or do we want some kind of mix of our current private health insurance system and government intervention?

FEW OF the national leaders have yet begun to explore in public the relationship between cost and access. What kind of health care can this nation afford?

A recently released study on organ transplants adds another dimension to this debate. The nation's medical technology is years ahead of its ability to provide either the organs or the money for costly transplants, according to the three-year study.

Today 23,000 Americans are waiting for new hearts, kidneys, lungs, livers and pancreases, 10,000 more than were on waiting lists just five years ago.

There simply are not enough donor organs to meet this need.

But this shortage of organs also hides the true cost of this new transplant technology, according to the study.

CURRENTLY, RATIONING is based on the availability of organs instead of the ability to pay, said the researcher for the three-year study.

Improving organ supply may cause more economic problems than we have now, he said.

Transplants are expensive.

Few patients can afford the operations, which cost from $39,000 to $145,000 but can soar as high as $1.5 million. And many insurers are reluctant to pay for them.

In addition, many transplant patients remain chronically ill long after their operations, requiring medical care that costs an average of $10,000 a year — five times the per capita rate for medical care in the United States.

If organs become more available, the nation will be forced to make some decisions based on the costs of transplants.

The more familiar question — how we provide health care to all Americans — will likely be resolved first.

But the second question — how much care can we afford — will be tripping on its heels.

THE SPOKESMAN-REVIEW
Spokane, Washington, November 20, 1991

It won't cure everything that ails American health care — the system is far too complex for panaceas — but revolutionary new physician repayment rates for Medicare do promise to bring about some far-reaching, beneficial change.

Formulas and rules to implement the new rates were unveiled Friday by the Bush administration, and they had been awaited with considerable interest because a draft unveiled in the spring contained major flaws.

The administration repaired the worst flaws, in response to heavy pressure from the American Medical Association and congressional leaders of both parties.

Scrutiny and refinements must continue to ensure the reforms work as intended. But the successful struggle to implement them offers encouraging evidence that the nation's troubled health-care system can in fact be altered in fundamental ways to the public's benefit — even if the alterations take money from the pocket of powerful players.

The reforms, Medicare's largest ever, began with the simple recognition that physicians who perform specialized, high-technology services are overcompensated, while physicians who provide primary, diagnostic, preventive care are undercompensated.

This imbalance created financial incentives for the overuse of costly, high-tech procedures, and insufficient incentives for cost-saving preventive care. It led medical students to choose lucrative specialties over family practice. The ensuring shortage of primary-care physicians hit rural areas hard.

Reform meant cutting the pay of specialists in order to raise the pay of family doctors. That, in a nutshell, is what the rules and formulas unveiled last week will do. For example: Over five years, Medicare reimbursement rates for family and general practitioners will rise by 125 percent. But the fee for inserting a heart pacemaker will fall from $811 to $575.

The reforms appeared in jeopardy this spring, when the administration's draft rules set out to slash total Medicare spending rather than leaving total spending unchanged as Congress and the AMA intended when Congress ordered the reforms in 1989. The revised rules return to the original intent.

Now, it is expected that these revolutionary, standardized physician fees for Medicare gradually will be embraced by private insurance carriers as well. If private carriers did not follow suit, they would give specialists a chance to recover their pay cuts under Medicare through billings to everybody else.

Final results of the reforms await the verdict only experience can provide, but they do promise to lead medicine away from the technologists and mechanics and back toward early diagnosis, prevention and holistic care. And that is the right direction.

The Houston Post
Houston, Texas, November 21, 1991

FAST CONGRESSIONAL action is needed — before the Thanksgiving adjournment. It is needed to stop the Bush administration from abruptly changing the rules in midstream and leaving Texas and other states drowning in their efforts to pay for federally mandated Medicaid programs for the poor.

A temporary suspension of the administration's plan to change federal aid rules as of Jan. 1 is needed to give the states and the federal government time to work out a compromise that would help both. A bill that cleared the House of Representatives Tuesday would block the federal rules change until Sept. 30, 1992. But Gail Wilensky, administrator of the Health Care Financing Administration, says that would cost the government $10-12 billion it can't afford in aid to the states. Wilensky would urge a presidential veto of a postponement law unless Congress turns it into a two-sided moratorium in which states could not further increase the federal Medicaid cost.

Suspension of the rules change until next Sept. 30 would be too long. A shorter moratorium, suggested by U.S. Sen. Lloyd Bentsen of Texas, chairman of the Senate Finance Committee, seems a better idea. The National Governors Association and other state negotiators and the HCFA should reach a compromise during the moratorium to provide all states equal access to federal Medicaid funding while limiting federal spending.

During the 1992-93 biennium Texas stands to lose more than $1.3 billion in federal funding if the Bush administration-proposed rules change goes into effect Jan. 1. This is money the Legislature this year acted to obtain by charity-care expenditures by local hospitals as part of state matching funds.

A cutoff of the anticipated federal aid could force the Texas Legislature into a special session to raise more revenue or make crippling budget cuts.

Numerous other states more aggressive than Texas have already been maximizing their federal aid as Texas is trying to do so as to help finance Medicaid programs that have been expanded due to federal mandates. But because such maximization is costing the federal government a rapidly increasing amount, the Bush administration is trying to shut down this gravy train just as Texas gets on it.

The Post is sympathetic to both Washington's need to hold down spending and the states' need for the federal aid. Unfortunately, this is another case of Washington's mandating programs that it can't afford and the states are unable or reluctant to pay for. But the state governments should not be made to suffer for Washington's folly.

The Cincinnati Post
Cincinnati, Ohio, November 14, 1991

Political momentum is gathering for action on health care. But the politicians who see in recent election returns a demand for universal health coverage should not lose sight of another plea coming from voters: No new taxes.

To be considered responsible, any proposal for expanding access to health care must incorporate cost-containment features more effective than those currently in place. That rules out simple government-dictated fees, which have failed to prevent ballooning costs in Medicare and Medicaid, the taxpayer-supported insurance programs for the elderly, disabled and the poor.

Reliance on government price controls to hold down costs is a major drawback to the health insurance plan recently endorsed by former presidents Jimmy Carter and Gerald Ford and a coalition of big companies and unions. Fortunately other proposals would give both individual users and providers of medical care incentives to contain costs.

One such scheme was proposed by Martin Feldstein, Ronald Reagan's chairman of the Council of Economic Advisers, and endorsed by economist Alfred Kahn, an architect of airline deregulation in the Carter administration. The federal government would provide major-risk insurance to every household, and each household would pay a share of every medical bill up to an income-related ceiling.

Another plan designed by the Heritage Foundation and endorsed by The Economist magazine would require households to buy basic insurance coverage on the private market. Tax credits for health expenses would protect families against excessive medical costs. The plan, outlined Tuesday in a guest column on this page, would stimulate competition among insurers and encourage citizens to shop to suit their needs.

The details of those and other similarly sober proposals deserve serious study before a nation facing a $3.6 trillion debt and a $348 billion deficit next year assumes any new obligations.

THE BUFFALO NEWS

Buffalo, New York, November 25, 1991

WASHINGTON'S NEW FEE schedule for doctors performing 7,000 or so different procedures for Medicare patients may seem like pretty dull stuff. But think again. These are dramatic changes — positive ones.

They apply to 500,000 doctors across the country and to the 34 million elderly and disabled Americans insured under Medicare. And they represent the boldest fee revision since Medicare began in 1965.

Contrary to what one might expect, and possibly what might be desirable, the bottom-line here is not immediate cost savings.

The new schedule, due to take effect Jan. 1, does not reduce total payments expected from Medicare to doctors over the next five years. Now running at $27.3 billion, they will rise to $47.5 billion in 1996, a sobering 70 percent jump.

What's being rearranged is who gets how much of the money. Over the long run, that could slow the rise in fees.

More for preventive care

In deciding on what Medicare will pay for certain procedures, the revised schedule makes new basic judgments about the relative value of a physician's work, various medical procedures and physicians' overhead and malpractice expenses.

Rightly, it enhances rewards for general practitioners and internists who monitor the general health of patients. Naturally, those who will gain financially favor the changes. But the schedule downgrades relative fees for specialists, such as anesthesiologists, surgeons and ophthalmologists, and changes what Medicare will pay for the procedures they perform. This displeases them, but the reasoning behind the move is sound.

Take a specific example. On average, Medicare now pays $2,105 for a total hip replacement. Five years hence, it will typically pay just under $1,700. Coronary artery bypasses and cataract surgery will experience similar reductions.

Physicians who monitor the general health of elderly and disabled patients deserve the higher fees. These doctors offer basic access to health care. They can curb higher costs and serious ailments later on by monitoring and preventive care.

This is a direction health care *should* be taking, for Medicare and other patients, as America wrestles with medical costs that soar well beyond what other modern industrial societies pay.

Changing the incentives

The revisions will also rebalance the financial incentives for those aspiring to careers as physicians, prodding more to go into basic health care rather than high-priced specialties.

The rearranged incentives and judgments about medical care values are the foremost advantage of the new schedule.

But not the only one. The schedule, implementing a 1989 law, moves toward more uniform fees regardless of where the physician practices. Now, Medicare reimbursement rates may vary widely depending upon whether the work is performed in Buffalo or Phoenix or Peoria.

Uniform fees are fairer to those performing similar procedures. They diminish the risks of rip-offs compared with a system of widely diverse reimbursement tailored to individual communities or even physicians.

Because Medicare patients compose such a significant slice of the community requiring medical services, Washington's new fees may well nudge private insurers to follow suit. They should look in that direction. The changes are, on the whole, enlightened in terms both of cost and care.

THE TENNESSEAN

Nashville, Tennessee, November 25, 1991

CONGRESS, the White House and the nation's governors have little time left to save Medicaid coverage.

Medicaid, which provides health care for poor people, is paid for by both federal and state dollars. The more money the states put in, the more federal matching funds they get back.

A few years ago, the McWherter administration was searching for a way to pump more dollars into Tennessee's Medicaid funds without taking them out of general revenues. It devised a terrific plan where hospitals would make donations to the state's Medicaid pool.

And the idea caught on. Today, 39 states use some creative fundraising to pump up their Medicaid dollars.

The White House, however, said the fundraising methods are too much of a good thing. The Bush administration fears the creative financing is pushing Medicaid toward the point of being totally federally financed. And it wrote a regulation, which goes into effect Jan. 1, saying that a state must put its own money into the Medicaid pot.

That rule would deprive states of billion of Medicaid dollars. Tennessee would stand to lose $500 million in Medicaid funds. Given the matching formula, Tennessee would have to raise an additional $150 million in new taxes — not from health care providers but from general taxes — to get the federal money it will lose.

Last week, some progress was made on a compromise. The House and the Senate Finance Committee both passed bills delaying the rule's implementation. And the National Governors' Association and the White House agreed to a compromise that would allow hospitals to contribute to Medicaid pools, but those donations could be no more than 25% of a state's Medicaid money.

Before Congress signs off on this plan, it must be certain that the compromise with the White House doesn't compromise the health care of poor Americans.

The White House's position is understandable. Medicaid makes up 5% of the federal budget. And some analysts predict Medicaid costs will increase 31% this year.

But the states have budgets, too. The McWherter administration played by the rules. There was nothing at all in Medicaid regulations at the time the financing began that would prevent Tennessee from collecting money from the hospitals. And the additional money went to expand Medicaid to make more citizens eligible.

Some 27 million Americans depend on Medicaid. No one wants to pull the rug out from under them.

This latest crisis in Medicaid shows how desperate states have been to meet new federal demands on Medicaid coverage and keep up with rising health care costs. Tennessee taxpayers are just as interested as all the other taxpayers in controlling the federal budget. But states don't need to be penalized for searching for ways to expand Medicaid. What they need is a national health care policy. ∎

THE ATLANTA CONSTITUTION

Atlanta, Georgia, January 28, 1991

Who will pay for better health care for Georgia's poor?

Gov. Zell Miller, struggling to find funds to cover a Medicaid expansion, has suggested that recipients pay a small portion themselves — $1 to $3 for every doctor's visit or prescription. At first glance, the co-payments do not sound prohibitive. On closer scrunity, however, the proposal sets a bad precedent.

In one of its less celebrated achievements, the 101st Congress passed a bill that brought hope of better health care to poor children: Congress insisted that Medicaid be gradually expanded until children 18 and under are covered. Currently, states are only required to cover children up to the age of 6 in households that receive Medicaid.

Because the federal government funds only 62 percent of Georgia's Medicaid payments, Georgia must fund the other 38 percent. To begin the new coverage, which will start with 7- and 8-year-olds, Georgia will have to pay an additional $1.4 million in fiscal year 1992.

As the state covers more and more school-age children under Medicaid, the program, of course, will become more expensive. But the cost to the state will be even greater if it does not make an effort to keep its population well. If the state eventually needs more revenues to pay for Medicaid, it should consider a general tax increase.

While $3 may not sound like much to the man or woman with a professional salary, it can put a poverty-level household budget in the red. If the rent is due, the groceries have run out and an examination of that nagging chest pain will cost $3, the average man or woman would be tempted to see if it will go away without a doctor's visit. The next signal could be a fatal heart attack.

Mr. Miller says the small co-payments should discourage "frivolous" doctor's visits. What frivolous visits? The state has conducted no surveys nor collected any evidence that suggests large numbers of Medicaid recipients are seeing doctors too often.

Rather, the South is a region where the poor do not go to the doctor nearly often enough. Throughout this state and others in the region, the poor routinely die of diseases that could be easily treated if they could simply afford to see a physician.

Mr. Miller should drop his proposal for co-payments. As Medicaid coverage expands, other governors and other legislators would be tempted to raise the co-payments to $10 or to $20. Georgia cannot afford so many unhealthy citizens.

TULSA WORLD

Tulsa, Oklahoma, May 28, 1991

AS if further proof of the rampaging costs of medical care were needed, look at the dance federal and state governments are doing to dodge the tab on Medicare.

Medicare is a joint program in which the federal government matches money spent by the state — dollar for dollar in some states, more in poorer states. Over the years Congress has mandated that more people be included in Medicare, particularly pregnant women. But Congress sent no money. It just matched or sweetened whatever funds states came up with.

That the programs worked, there is no doubt. Alabama, one of the poorer states, had a 10 percent reduction in infant mortality.

But, this week the federal government plans to issue a new set of rules to curtail how states raise funds for the Medicare match.

A couple of years ago a mid-level Massachusetts welfare department official figured out a complex accounting shift to release another $200 million for the federal Medicare match. Other states caught on quickly and now about 40 states use the same method.

The feds say states are trying shift their financial problems to Washington. But in fact states are struggling to provide the mandated services.

Medical costs are escalating for the 27 million low-income people served by Medicare. Tragically, those millions are pregnant women, children and the elderly.

State and federal governments can play hot potato with the bill as long as they like, but until the rising costs of medical care for everyone are addressed, the problem will only escalate.

FORT WORTH STAR-TELEGRAM

Fort Worth, Texas, November 24, 1991

When the government recently issued its new physicians' fee schedule for Medicare, it broke new ground in how doctors are paid and made a positive shift in Medicare's emphasis from surgical procedures to preventive family medicine.

What it did not do was offer any ideas about how to contain Medicare's costs.

Indeed, the final fee schedule was a surrender to the American Medical Association and those who threaten that doctors would stop treating Medicare patients if payments were restricted.

Perhaps another time. Built into the new fee schedule is an annual 12-percent increase in payment for physicians' services, so that doctors will receive $27.3 billion this year, increasing to $47.5 billion by 1996.

Meanwhile, the annual Medicare deductible paid by beneficiaries will go up. And it is hard to see how the contributions of younger taxpayers to the Medicare system can escape future increases. It is an expensive system and one that is becoming more expensive, albeit of great benefit to Americans over 65 and to their families.

Other than that, this year's changes make sense. Family practitioners — by one definition, doctors who actually talk to patients — will be paid more. Specialists will be paid less. All medical activities and procedures will be charged according to a scale that is weighted toward primary care and health maintenance rather than state-of-the-art treatments.

All this is important for several reasons, first because we all pay the bill and are affected by Medicare but also because Medicare remains our most successful stab at a national health-care system. That is why it is a mistake to speak of Medicare as though it were somehow insulated and apart from the nation's overall health-care concerns.

Medicare is part of the rising tide of debate about how best to ensure proper — at least basic — care for all Americans and how to do it affordably. Medicare works, at a cost. So does Medicaid, at a cost. So does the private health insurance system, mostly underwritten by American business. And at a high cost. Yet some 33 million Americans are left "uncovered," at considerable public cost.

- The public policy debate about how to include *everyone*, including the federal government, in the health-care mix goes back many years. At various times, such plans have been opposed as socialistic and as anti-labor. Right now, much of the impetus is coming from business because the cost of underwriting workers' health plans is becoming a huge burden.

We may get there this time, if only because the nation has few alternatives. But there may be no way to expand health care and make it affordable for the nation without also limiting some options and making some hard choices about the extent of care and how much we, as a nation, will pay for it. Remember, Congress in 1989 had to repeal a catastrophic health coverage plan because it turned out the potential beneficiaries did not want to pay the bill.

Medicare could serve as a model for a federal health-care system — as a standard of basic care — just as its new fee schedule may become the model for private health insurers. But right now, it does not appear that Medicare will be a model for restraining cost increases in health care.

CHICAGO Sun-Times

Chicago, Illinois, November 25, 1991

Whew! Just in time, the White House and the nation's governors cut a deal that spares Illinois and many other states the immediate loss of hundreds of millions of dollars in Medicaid funds in their 1992 budgets.

They agreed on a plan to allow the states to continue for one more year fund-raising devices that the federal government wants to restrict under new rules, devices that have helped states qualify for more federal Medicaid money.

The agreement—subject to approval by Congress—would spare Illinois the loss of $640 million, and Cook County the loss of $120 million, in Medicaid funds. Neither the state nor county had any alternative funding plan to fill the gap.

The Bush administration initially sought to prohibit states immediately from using special taxes on hospitals to pay the state share of Medicaid, a method that the government called a scam. It allowed hospitals to get back much more than they paid in.

The first-year cost to the government would be $5.5 billion. After next year, the compromise would let states use revenue obtained this way to pay no more than 25 percent of the state share of Medicaid.

The Council of State Legislatures and a number of hospital associations are opposing the compromise partly because it leaves untouched other proposed rules that they regard as detrimental. Whatever the merits of that argument, the immediate problem of state and local funding was reaching crisis proportions, forcing swift readjustment of the key new rule. The compromise gets states and local governments past that hump.

As Gov. Edgar and County Board President Richard J. Phelan pointed out in lobbying for a compromise, an abrupt ending of present fund-raising methods would severely hurt the poor and indigent, those most dependent on Medicaid.

Those arguments prevailed, and rightly so.

LAS VEGAS REVIEW-JOURNAL

Las Vegas, Nevada, November 29, 1991

As if state officials didn't have enough budget problems, what with lagging sales and gaming tax revenues, they had to worry this week about the prospect of losing up to $25 million in federal Medicaid funds. As is the case with the tax collection shortfall, though, the Medicaid problem was self-inflicted.

Nevada, along with 42 other states, made it a habit of slyly employing loopholes to get around a federal law requiring states to pay 45 percent of Medicaid funding. By levying a tax on hospitals, using the money collected to obtain matching federal funds, then returning the tax, state officials pull in more from Washington than they're entitled to.

The Bush administration sought to end the game, which will cost the federal government more than $5.5 billion this fiscal year. At issue was whether the feds would dam the gravy flow all at once or gradually. The states, of course, including Nevada, panicked at the thought of going cold turkey. And despite the fact this controversy was ongoing for the better part of the year, the Nevada Legislature still insisted on basing its biennial budget on the dream that the feds would go away.

Luckily for Nevada and other states, Congress on Wednesday approved a compromise. Under the deal, states may continue their shaky hospital tax practices until late 1992, but the federal government would cap the amount of state tax revenues that could qualify for matching Medicaid funds.

The compromise is fair. It gives states some time to find new sources for the federal money that will eventually evaporate, and it allows the feds to close a few loopholes and save money. But why is it that states, including Nevada, choose trickery to extract more cash from the U.S. Treasury rather than relying on honest and responsible budget practices to fund the programs they deem necessary?

Clinton Orders Medicaid Streamlining

President Bill Clinton Feb. 1, 1993 ordered the federal government to make it easier for states to use Medicaid funds in innovative ways.

Medicaid was a program, run jointly by the federal government and state governments, that provided health care to poor Americans and disabled people. Medicaid was the fourth largest item in the federal budget, and its annual cost was skyrocketing. In 1992, the federal share of the program was $67.8 billion, while states spent over $50 billion.

The federal government controlled the disbursement of Medicaid funds through a complex code of rules. States could apply for exemptions from the rules in order to introduce new programs that would save money or cover new medical demands.

But obtaining a waiver required getting around red tape that Clinton called "Byzantine and counterproductive." For example, many states had encountered difficulty transferring money set aside for nursing homes and applying it to home care for elderly patients – even though many patients preferred to be treated at home, and such therapy was usually cheaper than nursing-home residence.

To make it easier for states to receive waivers. Clinton said that the Health Care Financing Administration (the branch of the Health and Human Services Department that managed Medicaid) would no longer be allowed to ask states for an unlimited number of additions and clarifications to their applications. Instead, the department could request information only once.

Clinton also instructed the agency to prepare a detailed list of innovative state programs that had already been approved. In that way, states that wanted to start similar programs could simply adopt them without having to write out the paperwork themselves.

The Phoenix Gazette
Phoenix, Arizona, February 4, 1993

President Bill Clinton's executive order giving states a freer hand to run their federal Medicaid programs offers a welcome ray of hope from Washington. At the minimum, it provides a flickering signal that the Clinton administration is finally getting its balance, learning to walk without stumbling and heading where it wants to go.

Medicaid, the massive $150 billion health care program for the poor, has always been an administrative nightmare for the states, with burdensome regulations adding costly expenses without significant health benefits to patients. For years, governors and state administrators have complained they could stretch federal and state dollars further if they could implement managed-care reforms and emphasize prevention over acute care. But Washington turned a deaf ear.

Until now. Monday, Clinton, a former governor active in the National Governors' Association, ordered the Health and Human Services Department to streamline the process for states seeking waivers and to allow waivers granted to one state to be automatically adopted by another.

The governors, whose states contribute about $65 million of the total cost this year, are ecstatic. Somebody in the White House is actually listening to them. Arizona's Dr. Leonard Kirschner, director of the Arizona Health Cost Care Containment System, a Medicaid alternative, relishes the prospect of not having to petition the feds every year for a waiver to keep running.

Clinton was not exaggerating when he said: "This will be one big step on the long road to giving the country the health care system it needs. States often believe they can provide more services at lower costs if we didn't impose our rules and regulations on them."

Public health advocates agree. The states are eager to look at innovation, at ways to redirect resources to preventive care and away from expensive care, including emergency room care.

Clinton seems to be willing to allow states to become laboratories of experimentation on health care policy, with the federal government setting standards and arranging financing and the states being trusted to deliver services in the most effective ways. Clinton is right. It is a big step.

THE BLADE
Toledo, Ohio, February 3, 1993

UNLESS something is done at the state and federal levels to control the costs of Medicaid in Ohio, "It is only a matter of time before there will be no money left for education or other important programs," Gov. George Voinovich warned last week.

The governor briefed Ohio editors on this and other issues following his State of the State message. In 1982 Medicaid, which provides health care coverage and long-term care for low-income elderly and disabled people, represented 19 per cent of the general revenue budget; 10 years later that percentage had jumped to 30 per cent. Primary and secondary education represented 29.8 per cent of the general revenue budget in 1982. A decade later education aid was down to 22.1 per cent.

President Clinton has told the nation's governors that he will cut red tape on Medicaid and try to make it easier for states to seek cost-effective alternatives for nursing homes. It will not be easy. In dollar terms Medicaid in Ohio has grown from $1.1 billion in 1982 to $3.9 billion, an increase of $2.8 billion, or 237 per cent during a time when inflation in the state grew by 47.9 per cent.

More than half of Medicaid expenditures go to care for only 6 per cent of the 1.4 million Ohioans eligible for aid. The great majority of Medicaid recipients, 90 per cent of whom are women and children, do not represent a heavy drain on the state.

The heaviest financial burden on the state is caused by chronically disabled people or those otherwise needing long-term care — for the most part older people. The Voinovich administration is seeking ways to expand alternatives to nursing-home care, and to put into place pre-admission screening, case management, and statewide selective contracting for medical supplies.

But the governor also let it be known he is concerned about people who spend down their resources before going to nursing homes so that they become public charges. It is a sensitive issue, which cannot be readily resolved. Most Americans wish to take care of their elderly relatives as best they can, even while shuddering over the prospect of one day having to enter nursing homes themselves. However, many people think it unfair that because of a lengthy illness people should be penalized for a lifetime of thrift, especially when economists berate us for not saving more.

It should not be necessary to spend oneself into poverty or to hand a lifetime of savings over to impersonal long-care institutions. Society must come to grips with costs of long-term disability care, by preventive medicine, by lower-cost options to nursing homes, and by making it more attractive to save money for long-term care.

President Clinton is on the right track in attempting to work with governors to rationalize Medicaid and ease the burden on states and individuals, of which Governor Voinovich spoke so forcefully last week.

The Hartford Courant
Hartford, Connecticut, February 6, 1993

As a five-term governor of Arkansas, Bill Clinton had plenty of experience with what he calls the "byzantine and counterproductive" paperwork required whenever his state wanted to experiment with more efficient ways to treat poor people on Medicaid.

As a White House resident of only two weeks, the president wasted no time doing away with the paperwork that daunts so many states considering deviations from the Medicaid rules.

Here's wishing Mr. Clinton success with his attempt to simplify the cumbersome system of waivers.

Mr. Clinton told governors this week that he is giving the Department of Health and Human Services only one shot at asking for additional information whenever a state requests a waiver from Medicaid rules.

And he has ordered the Health Care Financing Administration to make a list of state programs that have already received waivers, so other states may start the same programs without going through identical, time-consuming waiver applications.

Cutting the mountains of paper that Medicaid dumps on states requesting waivers won't save billions. But it will trim somewhat the expense of the federal medical program that cares for 30 million poor and disabled people.

And Mr. Clinton's changes will give states more leeway over programs that cost them billions of dollars, too.

Connecticut, for example, kicks in a staggering $800 million to Medicaid programs yearly. Yet state officials trying to curb Medicaid abuse among nursing home clients must apply for federal waivers that can take years to obtain.

The waivers would allow state officials to review the 5-year financial histories of nursing home clients. Currently, states can look back only 30 months to see if clients have transferred money, homes and other assets to relatives so they may qualify for Medicaid.

Waivers will also be needed to transfer Medicaid money from nursing home care to at-home care for elderly patients, a saving that Gov. Lowell P. Weicker Jr. is proposing in his new budget.

It took a former governor to understand how a federal bureaucracy can choke a state's will to save taxpayers' money.

THE PLAIN DEALER
Cleveland, Ohio, February 3, 1993

Liberating the states to be "laboratories of democracy," just as the theory of federalism intended, President Bill Clinton this week gave some good news to the nation's governors: In the Clinton era, Washington rulemakers intend to give the state capitals new flexibility to become partners in innovation. By streamlining Washington's rules for the most complex state-federal responsibility — the Medicaid program, which pays the health-care bills for 31 million poor and elderly patients — Clinton began to address the cost of medical care, the No. 1 concern of the National Governors Association.

If Clinton's Medicaid decision is any indication, the former Arkansas governor intends to adjust the state-federal balance of authority. Better still, it will help bolster the drive to "reinvent government" and deliver more cost-effective public services. Recalling his Medicaid struggle when he was in the Little Rock statehouse, Clinton knows that health-care financing is every governor's biggest headache. Clinton's directive to the Department of Health and Human Services should speed the approval of waivers from federal regulations, allowing the states to administer Medicaid with less micro-management from Washington.

Every state's budget is groaning under the burden of Medicaid, the health system's last-resort coverage for the poor and some of the elderly. The states now contribute $62.2 billion to the program each year, while Washington adds $82.5 billion more. "For years, the nation's governors have been arguing that the [Medicaid] process . . . is Byzantine and unproductive. They are right," Clinton told the governors. Clinton's Medicaid shift sensibly gives states added decision-making power: Ohio lawmakers may not make the same health-care decisions as their counterparts in Oklahoma or Oregon, but each state should have reasonable flexibility in managing its own Medicaid program.

Ohio expects to get a boost, worth as much as $300 million annually, from Clinton's Medicaid initiative. Since October, Ohio has been awaiting federal approval for a vital part of the state's health-care plan: the Hospital Care Assurance program, which reimburses hospitals for the cost of uncompensated care to the indigent. Ohio's Medicaid request was needlessly delayed within the federal Health Care Financing Administration during the presidential transition, but Clinton's action will clear the way for more federal Medicaid money for Ohio.

Clinton's plan won bipartisan support from the governors, including praise from Ohio's Gov. George V. Voinovich. Complaining that Medicaid has soared from 18.6% to 28% of Ohio's budget in the past decade, Voinovich hopes federal Care Assurance money will flow to Ohio within 45 days.

In addition, Clinton's directive will enable Ohio to expand its Passport program, which provides in-home care for the ill who don't want to be confined to costly nursing homes. Medicaid now pays an average of about $20,000 for nursing home patients. Under Passport, Medicaid would pay an estimated $4,000 to $8,000 annually.

But Medicaid reform is only one part of a larger effort that must be a top priority for Clinton: overhauling the nation's irrational system of paying for health care. By cooperating with the states on Medicaid, Clinton helped win the National Governors Association's endorsement this week of the concept of "managed competition," the market-based, government-guided effort to restrain health spending. Changing the way America pays for medical treatment will be a complex struggle, but Clinton's quick aid to the governors on Medicaid shows that he is eager to enlist the states as allies in the health-care reform effort.

THE DENVER POST
Denver, Colorado, February 14, 1993

VIRTUALLY LOST in the hailstorm of his young administration's political gaffes was Bill Clinton's announcement that from now on states will have more flexibility in running their Medicaid programs — a move that could relieve cash-strapped states like Colorado.

Seven years ago, Medicaid costs in Colorado totaled $364 million a year, of which the state paid half and Uncle Sam covered 50 percent. Today, Medicaid in Colorado costs more than $1 billion a year, with the state bearing $500 million and the federal government paying the rest. Medicaid has become the second-largest item in the state budget, ranking only behind elementary through high school education.

Most worrisome to state lawmakers, Medicaid's costs continue to climb, with no leveling off in sight. That's why, last year, the legislature adopted a desperate measure to completely withdraw Colorado from the Medicaid program, which pays the medical bills for low-income families. Romer wisely vetoed the proposal, saying that rejecting half a billion federal dollars wouldn't solve the problem of providing health care for the poor.

Instead, Romer suggested rolling Medicaid into a broader health insurance reform package. But to make Romer's plan work — or to make any number of health care reform proposals to work — the state would have to persuade the federal government to exempt Colorado from a host of federal Medicaid mandates. In the past, these exemptions were very difficult to get, and thus formed a formidable barrier to any reform efforts.

Clinton's policy, however, is to give states freer rein to experiment with Medicaid. That means federal agencies are more likely to grant the waivers, and perhaps it indicates that Clinton's team will side with state governments in trying to persuade Congress to roll back some existing mandates, or at least to avoid imposing new ones.

These changes give Colorado a chance to structure its health care plans to meet its citizens' needs, rather than being forced to build health care systems that respond solely to Washington's dictates.

The new policy may not reduce Medicaid costs, but it certainly could hold future increases to reasonable levels. It also won't solve the health care crisis, but it does allow reform to move forward. In sum, Clinton's new policy is the first step toward sensible reform.

The Courier-Journal

Louisville, Kentucky,
February 10, 1993

PRESIDENT Clinton took a respite from controversy recently and made a small change that should please everyone. He ordered bureaucrats to make it easier for states to experiment with Medicaid programs. The change is long overdue. Federal bureaucrats turn into barracudas when they get requests for Medicaid waivers. They gnaw every sentence, crunch every number and may let governors dangle for years.

Reviewing waiver requests carefully is essential — it helps ensure that proposed changes are appropriate, cost-efficient and structured to achieve the desired benefits. The problem is that the exceedingly detailed review process stifles innovation. Making it less stringent will give states more freedom to experiment with promising programs like the acclaimed Kentucky Patient Access and Care System. It has expanded access to care, increased preventive care and saved $296 million in state and federal funds. Some states that would like to copy it reportedly haven't done so because of the bureaucratic rigamarole.

President Clinton's order also may help Kentucky strengthen its Medicaid program. A waiver could let state health workers provide nursing-home style care to some elderly people outside an institutional setting. It may become easier to extend Medicaid benefits to more working poor.

The move also could have implications for Gov. Jones' health-care reform plan. At one time the governor ruled out making changes that hinged on waivers, but as Medicaid rules gain flexibility that may change. Also, President Clinton's order will make it possible for Kentucky to copy other states' approved programs without first obtaining a waiver.

No one would advocate giving states a blank check to alter Medicaid programs. Medicaid is a partnership, and every partnership needs balance. What this partnership also needed was trust, and now it has it.

The TENNESSEAN
Nashville, Tennessee, February 8, 1993

PRESIDENT Clinton freed the states last week from a lot of Medicaid red tape.

Breaking the stranglehold will not immediately free up money, but it does give state governments some leeway to devise innovative ways to save Medicaid dollars in the future.

Tennessee's Medicaid budget, which was $848 million just six years ago, has ballooned to $2.8 billion, burning more than 25% of the state's annual budget. Medicaid Director Manny Martins pushed health maintenance organizations earlier this year as a possible way to cut costs. By requiring recipients to seek care from a prescribed set of doctors, as private businesses do, the state figures to keep costs from getting out of hand.

The hurdles, as other states have learned, are byzantine regulations regarding waivers that state governments must get to even experiment with cost-saving alternatives.

No longer, according to the new President. As a former governor, he quickly spotted the problem: States can't rein in their sizable Medicaid bills without the freedom to seek different options.

Until the federal government comes up with new ways to handle all health care costs, the states have to do the best they can to keep their own costs in line. Freeing many of the restrictions gives them the tools to try. At the very least, they

Less federal red tape can only help

won't have to wait months for an answer to their applications.

States brave enough to take on the restrictions have devised some alternatives. Oregon's is by far by the most controversial, a form of rationed care. The Bush administration rejected the plan, but Oregon plans to re-submit it.

The fact, however, that Oregon and other states have been willing to make an effort to find cost-saving measures amply demonstrates their ability to use the loosening of the Medicaid restrictions productively. And who knows? States might come up with ideas that the federal government and other states can imitate.

Tennessee has a couple of state committees working on health care reform, centering on Medicaid. This state should take full advantage of the freer atmosphere to get more for its precious dollars.

Gov. Ned McWherter and other governors have long known their responsibility to hold down health care costs, but they haven't been given a chance to try. Not surprisingly, a former governor has given his former colleagues the opportunity to make changes. Governors can repay Mr. Clinton's confidence by giving Medicaid their best efforts. ■

The Des Moines Register
Des Moines, Iowa, February 4, 1993

There are Iowa lawyers who have made an art out of milking Medicaid, state health officials say. Their special talent is in showing the well-to-do how to shift their bills onto the backs of taxpayers.

The game is called "hide the assets," and it is played thusly: Grandma needs nursing-home care, but if she pays for it, her sons and daughters won't inherit as much money. So the children have grandma sign over all her property to them, making her poor and therefore eligible for Medicaid. She gets free nursing-home care, her children get her money, their lawyer collects a good fee, and everybody lives happily ever after.

Except, of course, the taxpayers. Grandma's care is part of the more than $200 million Medicaid pays nursing homes in Iowa every year. Iowans pay more than $70 million of that.

In an effort to fight back, the Iowa Department of Human Services sought the federal government's permission to check property transfers as far back as five years, in hopes of catching chiselers — in hopes, that is, of winning some of the hide-the-assets games on behalf of the taxpayers.

The policy would enable the DHS to deny a free ride to someone who transferred property for less than true value during the previous five years.

Under present federal policy, the state can only check 2½ years into the past — and Iowa remains bound by the policy because the federal government still hasn't

budged on Iowa's request for a waiver.

Iowa sought the waiver last summer, months after Oregon sought a waiver to

The policy would enable DHS to deny a free ride to someone who transferred property for less than true value during the previous five years.

allow it to limit Medicaid spending on high-risk, low-return medical procedures. Both were politically dangerous issues for the Bush administration to handle during the campaign.

This week, President Clinton promised governors more breathing room in setting Medicaid policy, in return for their support of his efforts to cut the budget.

That's a win-win situation for Clinton; most of the policy waivers sought by the states are to cut spending, and more than half of Medicaid's costs come out of the federal budget.

The only rationale for the combined federal-state financing and administration of Medicaid, as opposed to total federal financing and control, is to encourage innovation at the state level. Iowa, Oregon and others are seeking the chance to implement such innovations.

Tell your bureaucrats to approve the waivers, Mr. President. Time and taxes are a-wastin'.

TULSA WORLD
Tulsa, Oklahoma, February 11, 1993

THE funding crisis in Oklahoma's welfare system — the Department of Human Services faces an $87 million budget reduction next year and a possible shortfall of $120 million this year — is not a result of great increases in traditional welfare payments.

Instead it is the result of soaring medical costs, which mean huge increases in the amount spent for medical services for the poor, including Medicaid.

That's why it is so important for the state to keep a tight rein on medical expenses. State Sen. Bernest Cain, D-Oklahoma City, says controls on state-reimbursed drugs and medicines are far less than tight — DHS is paying for such things as hair restorers, diet pills, nicotine gum and over-the-counter, non-prescription drugs.

Cain says it amounts to a rip-off of taxpayers. He's introduced a bill that would tighten controls on approved drugs paid for by Medicaid. His bill would take certain optional medications off the approved list.

Potential savings, estimated at $2 million in state funds and up to $6 million when federal matching funds are counted, don't amount to much in DHS' $2 billion budget, and won't solve the system's funding woes.

But, as the late Sen. Everett Dirkson always said, a million here and a million there and soon you're talking about real money.

Cain is on the right track. Ultimately, what's needed is a priority list of Medicaid services similar to the system attempted by the state of Oregon to ensure the most efficient delivery of services to the needy.

FORT WORTH STAR-TELEGRAM
Fort Worth, Texas, February 3, 1993

President Clinton has taken commendable action by easing the bureaucratic headaches that hamstring states in delivering health care to the nation's poor. The key term is *easing,* however, not *eliminating.*

By granting the states greater flexibility in providing such services, Clinton has basically cut through some of the knots that federal bureaucrats have tied to state programs.

Now the states should be able to rely on their own experiences and inventiveness to find more affordable ways to treat more poor people through group HMO coverage, home services and outpatient care.

Medicaid, though, will persist as a major financial and social problem until the mother of knots — the U.S. healthcare system — is subjected to the sword of major reform.

Clinton's order only allows some breathing room for the states, most of which are grappling with rapidly rising costs for uncompensated federal mandates that drain precious resources from other needs such as education, criminal justice and transportation.

Texas is no exception as it faces a $1.8-billion 1993-95 budget shortfall for Medicaid, which now serves about 2 million people and costs $5.8 billion. The program has doubled in Texas since 1989 in the number of people served and in money spent — a growth trend showing no signs now of declining.

As appropriate as Clinton's executive order is for the country, Gov. Ann Richards and her constituents should face the harsh truth that much of the Medicaid budgetary discomfort in Texas is self-inflicted.

Medicaid is a matching program. Each state receives federal money in proportion to its own contribution. Texas has chosen to make relatively miserly contributions, so as not, we suppose, to encourage people to be poor, or at least not poor and sick.

Texas is among the most restrictive states in its Medicaid eligibility standards, which is part of a pattern of legislative behavior placing Texas 46th among the states and the District of Columbia in providing human services. Large states comparable in size to Texas serve about 90 percent of their poor; Texas holds the number down to 64 percent.

The Aid to Families with Dependent Children program, for instance, provides the greatest access to Medicaid. To qualify for AFDC in Texas, the eligibility standard is now 19 percent of the federal poverty level. In other words, a family of three must earn no more than $2,208 a year — *a year* — to be eligible.

State officials estimate that Clinton's order could save the state about $50 million, which sounds wonderful but represents a marginal one-half of 1 percent in a state Medicaid budget of $5.8 billion — which, recall, will fall an anticipated $1.8 billion short for 1993-95.

Clinton can provide some flexibility. Richards and the Legislature will have to provide the muscle — an inclination yet to be demonstrated in Austin.

Portland Press Herald
Portland, Maine, February 3, 1993

President Clinton has moved aggressively to give states greater flexibility in allocating federal Medicaid funds for health care.

Gov. McKernan should be equally aggressive in putting that new flexibility to work for Maine. Odds are that he will be. McKernan, by law, must balance Maine's state budget. That means cuts, painful cuts, even in social services.

Given that mandate, let's think carefully about how greater flexibility in Medicaid funding can best be used. It's vital that Medicaid dollars be focused on priority health needs.

Three areas, in particular, come immediately to mind:

1. Regardless of earlier budget plans, put Medicaid funds to work in every way possible to provide desperately needed community-based support services for the mentally disabled.

As Dr. William R. McFarlane, chief of psychiatry at Maine Medical Center, pointed out on these pages Monday, at least 7,000 persons with severe mental illnesses live in Greater Portland. Some have drifted out of treatment into homelessness. So have mentally retarded persons released from institutions without adequate support services. Portland has only half the health care professionals required to help them.

2. Target more Medicaid dollars to underwrite home health care for elderly persons still living independently.

While Maine has repeatedly promoted home-based health care for elderly citizens, Medicaid restrictions make it easier to obtain funding for nursing home beds. Yet home-based care is often more desirable, more effective and less expensive.

3. Use Medicaid money to improve rehabilitation of children in the state's juvenile corrections system.

So far, public discussion of Medicaid as it relates to the Maine Youth Center has centered on cutting costs. Let's use greater flexibility to target Medicaid dollars where they're really needed: to redirect young lawbreakers toward law-abiding adult lives. That means adequate programs at the center and expanded community-based services outside.

Last year, Maine spent $571.6 million on Medicaid services for more than 185,000 people. Sixty-three percent of those dollars came from the federal government. Greater flexibility can help us spend it better.

Neither Washington, D.C., nor Maine has any dollars to waste.

Health Care Seen as a Political Football in '88 Presidential Race

By Sept. 21, 1988, both presidential organizations – those of Vice President George Bush (R) and Gov. Michael S. Dukakis (D, Mass.) – were limiting campaign appearances by candidates to focus on briefing and rehearsal for their possibly decisive first televised debate on Sept. 25.

Dukakis Sept. 20 committed himself to seeking as president a system of mandatory employer-provided health insurance for all American workers. Although he did not spell out his plans in detail, Dukakis cited his achievement of a universal health-care law in his home state. The Massachusetts program was yet barely off the ground.

In a speech to nursing students at Western Kentucky University in Bowling Green, Dukakis declared, "Health care is a right, not a privilege, for every American, not just a privileged few."

Dukakis challenged Bush to "come out from behind the flag" and help working Americans who were uninsured. (More than 37 million Americans had no health insurance, according to estimates reported in the press, and the Dukakis staff said that at least 20 million of them would be covered under his plan.)

The Bush campaign dismissed the proposal as "a prescription for financial disaster" and "socialized medicine pure and simple."

Back home the next day, Dukakis Sept. 21 proposed a $100 million program to provide medical and nutritional care for expectant mothers not covered by insurance or Medicaid. The proposal was based on Massachusetts's so-called Healthy Start program, which, he said, had reduced infant mortality in the state by about 14% in 20 months.

Dukakis said the program was more than cost-effective. He cited one major study that calculated that every dollar spent on prenatal care saved $3 on postnatal care in the first year of a child's life.

Bush and Dukakis, met head-to-head for the first time in a televised debate Sept. 25.

Asked what he would do for the 37 million Americans not covered by either health insurance or Medicaid, the federal program of medical assistance for the poor, Bush replied with a reference to Dukakis's proposal for mandatory employer-proded insurance:

"One thing I will not do," Bush said, "is sock every business in this country and thus throw some people out of work. I want to keep this economic recovery going."

Bush suggested "flexibility in Medicaid so people at the lowest end can buy in there and get their needs covered," and "by everybody doing what they can do out of conscience."

Dukakis told of talking with a laid-off Houston father who could not let his son compete in Little League sports because he would not be able to pay the bills if the boy got hurt. Dukakis said Massachusetts had become "the only state in the nation to provide for universal health care," and that when he had proposed a similar program for the nation, Bush "or one of his spokesmen called it socialized medicine. The last time the vice president used that phrase, I suspect he remembers it. Don't you? It was in 1964 and that's what he called Medicare."

THE CHRISTIAN SCIENCE MONITOR
*Boston, Massachusetts,
October 3, 1988*

HEALTH care has been one of the many issues where the United States has stood apart, opting for rugged individualism over collectivism. Some form of what many Americans call "socialized medicine," such as Britain's National Health Service, is taken for granted in most of the West.

These systems are not without problems: Britain has over half a million people on waiting lists for elective surgery.

But America's system is an expensive patchwork – employer-paid health insurance for millions, medicaid for those on welfare, and medicare for the elderly. For the working poor, there is nothing. For many others, there is less than there could be. A short hospital stay can put a working-poor family onto the streets.

Now Michael Dukakis, the Democratic candidate for president, has committed himself to a proposal, modeled on a new Massachusetts program, requiring virtually all employers to provide health insurance for their employees. He also proposes to seek ways of insuring for those neither employed nor under the welfare/medicaid umbrella.

In a campaign often derided as "content free," this proposal is notable for what it's not: It's not a plan for a national health service. It would build on the existing reliance on employer-paid insurance, rather than instituting a new bureaucracy. It would not be a direct draw on the US Treasury or an excuse to raise taxes.

But mandatory health insurance would have its costs. The business community would perceive it, correctly, as a hidden payroll tax – specifically, on small business, since most larger employers already provide insurance. It would also burden employers of low-wage earners disproportionately and probably keep some employers from expanding their work force. Mr. Dukakis favors an exemption for the smallest employers, but hasn't spelled out details.

Continuing with the current patchwork would have its costs, too. In 1986 the US spent 11.1 percent of the gross national product on health care, nearly twice Britain's proportion. But on some measures of public health, such as infant mortality, the US ranks with parts of the third world. Ways to reduce infant mortality are often very simple – counseling women to avoid alcohol, tobacco, and drugs during pregnancy, for instance.

By expanding the access to health care in such cases, much could be done for relatively little. Big businesses already absorb indirectly some of the costs of health care for the uninsured.

If the working poor and others not covered by medicaid could receive the benefits of something like the community health services that have been well received in Britain (most of the problems have been in Britain's hospital-based services), much expense and emergency-room drama could be avoided.

The Dukakis proposal may not be what the US should adopt. Massachusetts, with its highly paid work force, may not be the best model for the rest of the country. And cost containment will surely have to be an element of whatever happens with American health care. But the governor deserves credit for raising the issue.

THE LINCOLN STAR
Lincoln, Nebraska, November 16, 1988

In the course of the political campaign, Vice President George Bush proposed in the first presidential debate a plan of health care for the poor. His proposal was that the poor be permitted to buy into Medicaid.

The idea is rather ridiculous when you think about it, and you never heard much more about it from Bush. Michael Dukakis' plan called for mandatory health insurance provided by all employers. That was about as impractical, for other reasons, as the Bush proposal.

Now, Congress has passed and President Reagan has signed a law granting families tax exemptions for income from U.S. Savings Bonds used to finance their children's higher education. While commendable, the program demonstrates the awesome nature of the parental challenge to encourage children to seek post-secondary degrees.

THE U.S. Department of Education has calculated that if the parents of a 2-year-old were to buy $2,000 in savings bonds each year until the child began college, the accumulated funds at age 18 would exceed $60,000 — the amount the department estimates a four-year public university education will cost by then. Unfortunately, hypothetical situations such as that are often far from reality.

What is the reality? The median family income in the United States is $30,853.

If the median-income family saved about 7 percent of its gross income, it would indeed put away $2,000 and have the $60,000 pot at the end of 16 years. But if it did that, it would be far and away above the average savings pattern of American families.

Is it logical to expect a family of three with $30,000 a year gross income to save $2,000? The answer depends upon your sense of values, but such a family would be very thrifty.

AND WHAT if the family had two children? Then the savings would have to climb to twice that, or about 13 percent of gross income.

That isn't thrifty, it's very nearly a practical impossibility, given any reasonable standard of living.

The U.S. Savings Bond program is fine, but it doesn't address the problems of most Americans. For most Americans, the cost of higher education for children remains a major concern and, to some, an unreachable goal.

Yes, there are scholarships, Yes, there are student loans and yes, there are jobs with which students can help pay for their own education.

But our guess is that the cost of education 16 years from now will be far more than the $60,000 estimated by the government. In the last eight years, public education costs have climbed 70 percent. At that rate, four years at a public university in 2004 easily could exceed $100,000.

And all of this fails to address the problems of families at income levels below $30,000 per year. The cost of higher education continues to be a concern of high priority on the national agenda.

The Register
Santa Ana, California, September 22, 1988

Has Michael Dukakis got a deal for you. He promises, if elected, to require all companies to give their employees health insurance. It sounds great at first: Shouldn't everyone get free health care? But we must always ask the price of such an apparent boon to the people. That price is heavy on two counts.

First, it removes the freedom of people to care for their health on their own, in their own way. What sort of health care is best? Physicians themselves argue about it constantly, not to mention the theories of such men outside the medical establishment as chiropractors and acupuncturists. In a free society each person should be allowed to make his own decisions on such matters. In contrast, Dukakis's scheme would impose a system that ossifies the current medical establishment in place.

Second, Dukakis's scheme would come at the cost of jobs. If you force companies to provide health care, many won't be able to afford it and will go broke. Dukakis's plan will favor big companies, which already have health plans, at the expense of small, new companies, many of which do not yet. These small companies, once established as successful firms, almost always institute health-care plans; they know how to keep good workers on the job.

Dukakis's plan, then, would prod people out of work, driving them into poverty and welfare. This, in turn, would lead to a call for comprehensive national health insurance, of the sort that has been tried, and has failed, in England. The British have discovered that when you make health care "free" for all, standards decline sharply. A hernia operation under Britain's national health care may require a wait of two years. Inasmuch as Dukakis's plan is being advocated in the Senate by Edward Kennedy, long a supporter of socialized medicine, where Dukakis's plan will lead is obvious.

And as William Buckley Jr. notes in a column today, a Dukakis edict requires all Massachusetts public safety employees to cease smoking, not only on the job but even in their homes. Will Dukakis also establish an anti-smoking Gestapo to enforce this law, spying on workers in their homes? A President Dukakis might impose, as part of a national health insurance scheme, such an edict on all American citizens — for the good of our health, of course.

Such an imposition would seem especially tempting when a national health scheme inevitably goes bankrupt. Forcing people to give up smokes would be seen as a way to save money on cancer operations, iron lungs, etc.

There's a better way to help improve Americans' health care than imposing socialist schemes and issuing dictatorial edicts. First, cut taxes sharply, so more people can afford better health care. Second, eliminate such agencies as the Food and Drug Administration, which retard the development and use of new drugs and techniques, while keeping costs high. Third, eliminate such socialized medicine as already exists — Medicare, Medicaid, and so on — which inflated doctors' bills hugely since their inception two decades ago.

Contrary to what Dr. Dukakis thinks, socialized medicine is the disease, freedom the cure.

The Washington Post
Washington, D.C., August 8, 1988

WHILE AMERICANS spend more of their income on health care than the people of any other country, their health—measured in the broad terms of life span and death rates—is not outstanding. It ranks somewhere around average among the world's industrial democracies. By one extremely important test, infant mortality, it is far below average. Some of the reasons for this mediocre showing have to do with the ways Americans eat, drink, use drugs, drive and, in general, choose to live. But some have a great deal to do with access to medical care.

The United States needs a system of universal access at least to basic care. That's going to be a compelling responsibility of the next president. The questions of how to provide access for everyone and how to pay for it are dauntingly difficult. But not many Americans like the idea that ambulances are sometimes turned away from hospitals because the person on the stretcher has no insurance card, or that a pregnant woman sometimes can't get prenatal care because she doesn't have enough ready cash for the doctor's fee. These incidents are becoming more common.

The number of Americans with no health insurance has risen over the past decade. Why? Manufacturing industry, in which fringe benefits are standard, has reduced its employment by more than a million jobs since 1980; the growth in employment is in the service industries, in which employers often do not provide health coverage. Another cause has been inflation. While Medicaid covers people on welfare, state governments have allowed their welfare eligibility limits to lag far behind inflation. The result is that Medicaid now covers fewer than half of the people whose incomes are below the poverty line.

But by no means all of the uninsured are destitute. Of the 37 million with no health insurance, a third are children—but of the adults, fully 60 percent are employed. The typical uninsured family includes someone working full time but never with enough money for visits to the doctor.

To cover these people, one possibility is to take the two existing systems—private insurance through employment and Medicaid for the poor—and extend them until they meet. That's essentially what Massachusetts has done under Gov. Michael Dukakis. The disadvantage with that strategy is that requiring companies to provide wider health benefits would drive up labor costs and generate unemployment. An alternative might be to require for uninsured workers a mandatory deduction from their pay, like the one for Social Security, sufficient to buy basic coverage. Any solution that works is going to cost a lot of money, and that cost will cause pain to the people who pay it.

But perhaps there's one more thing that you can say. What kind of a country do you want to live in? Not many Americans, we think, will be comfortable with a system in which most people get the best medical care in the world simply by showing a card while some, including 12 million children, have no claim on any medical care at all.

The Washington Post

Washington, D.C., October 9, 1988

WHATEVER THE FAILURES of this presidential campaign, it seems to be leading toward great improvements in health care for those who now get little or none of it. Vice President Bush, in his program for children, now proposes an important expansion of health insurance coverage for them. Gov. Dukakis brought out his health plan last month. This country's inability to guarantee basic medical care to all of its people is a moral lapse of substantial dimensions, and both candidates are now addressing it squarely and forcefully.

While Mr. Dukakis has explained precisely how he would provide health coverage for everybody who's employed, he remains vague about the unemployed and leaves them to a future commission. Mr. Bush's proposal would reach a much smaller number of people, but the most vulnerable—pregnant women and infants to begin with, gradually adding all children up to the age of 18.

Both, for reasons familiar to you, are anxious to keep as much of the cost as possible off the federal budget. Mr. Dukakis would put it on employers. Mr. Bush, using an expanded Medicaid system, would leave a lot of it with the states. He hasn't told you how he'd pay for the federal share, but that's true of all of the lengthening list of benefits that he's offering.

Putting aside the Adam Smith stuff, here Mr. Bush sensibly recognizes that if anything useful is to be done for the poorest and most isolated of mothers and their children, it will have to be done by direct government intervention. He goes farther and suggests an interesting innovation. At present there are the private insurance policies that cover the great majority of Americans, the federal-state Medicaid program covering a smaller number on welfare and some 37 million people in between with no protection at all. Mr. Bush says that the gap might be closed, at least for children, by splicing the public and private systems together with subsidized premiums.

An increasingly powerful national consensus lies behind the idea of broader health insurance protection, and in the two candidates' speeches you may well be seeing the first outlines of the next administration's greatest achievement in social policy. But there are a couple of pitfalls ahead.

As the insurance system becomes more comprehensive, the need for effective cost containment is going to increase. Neither candidate has touched that sensitive subject. The Bush plan, with its heavy emphasis on prenatal and natal care, will also have to deal with the soaring premiums for obstetrical liability insurance and the growing reluctance of doctors to practice that specialty particularly among poor women where fees are low and medical risks high. It's understandable that nobody wants to talk about that before the election. But voters need to keep it in mind that these good-hearted and welcome improvements in American health coverage cannot go forward without other, and bitterly controversial, reforms to accompany them.

BOSTON HERALD
Boston, Massachusetts, October 10, 1988

IF HE is allowed to take up tenancy in the White House, Gov. Michael Dukakis promises to push for a national health insurance law to cover the 37 million Americans who, he says, do not now enjoy such protection. After all, he pushed for one in Massachusetts, didn't he?

He sure did: the 1987 Health Security Act was the result.

At the time it was enacted, Dukakis confessed he had no idea of the new legislation's price tag. But the Pioneer Institute for Public Policy Research does. Its new study estimates that by 1992, when fully implemented, the law's net cost to the state's businesses will be an added $642 million per year — a figure more than 11 percent higher than previous estimates.

According to the Institute's detailed estimate, about 462,000 uninsured individuals and families will be covered by the law. But not all of them are poor — not by a long shot. In fact, the non-poor among them will outnumber the needy by a margin of 5-to-1.

"The mean family income of the non-poor uninsured population is over $34,000," the Institute's study says, "and about 16 percent of the uninsured come from families with annual incomes in excess of $50,000."

Those estimates support the suspicion that most of the beneficiaries of the governor's taxpayer-financed benevolence will be selfish, careless, or imprudent residents — not those who are down on their luck or impoverished.

The requirement that all companies with six or more workers either pay for their employees' health insurance or contribute to a state trust fund to cover uninsured workers will, by 1992, boost their annual cost of doing business here by $642 million. As a result, many small firms are faced with the choice of going out of business or moving elsewhere. Either way, the impact on the state's economy — in the form of jobs lost or jobs moved — is certain to be enormous.

Yet the governor now pledges that when and if he is elected president, he will provide basic health coverage for *37 million* Americans who, for one reason or another, don't have any. Only those who believe misery loves company — and wish to see the financial burden the governor's health insurance law has foisted on this state extend to the other 49 — will consider this a grand idea. For a nation that cannot now make ends meet, that will inevitably mean bigger-than-ever deficits, higher-than-ever taxes — or both.

Omaha World-Herald
Omaha, Nebraska, September 23, 1988

Michael Dukakis has apparently solved a problem that has plagued liberals for years. He has come up with a way for candidates to promise expensive new social programs and still be against the federal budget deficit. The Dukakis plan works this way: You have the federal government assume the responsibility but pass the cost on to somebody else.

That is the essence of the health program that Dukakis announced this week. He told an audience in Bowling Green, Ky., that "health care is a right, not a privilege, for every American." Dukakis would have the government take responsibility for the problem that too many Americans don't have health insurance, but his solution would be a law requiring that employers, not the government, provide insurance for all employees.

It's clever politics. If Dukakis had proposed a federally financed program, he might well have spent weeks being questioned about how much it would cost, who would be covered and how he could make such a proposal and still bring down deficit spending. His private-sector health insurance program attracted fewer questions, especially after aides refused to estimate the cost or elaborate, on the grounds that flexibility was needed to build a consensus.

Health care is only one of the ways in which the new Dukakis approach could be used. Think of the savings that could result if the government continued to order tanks and planes but required the defense contractors to pay the bill. Or if construction companies and food-processing companies could be required to pay for the government's highway and farm programs.

The deficit would become a thing of the past. Federal budgets would be instantly balanceable.

Medical care isn't free. Someone eventually pays the bill. Dukakis said his program would "make sure that, when Americans get sick, the first question they will hear will be . . . not 'How do you pay?' but 'Where does it hurt?' " The answer to Dukakis' second question is easy: It will hurt the consumers who eventually pay the cost through higher prices on goods and services which would be charged by the employers.

The question of extending health insurance coverage is a proper matter for public concern and action. But the question of cost, and who should pay it, surely deserves more consideration than was given to it in the Dukakis health insurance "plan."

THE ROANOKE TIMES
Roanoke, Virginia, September 21, 1988

WHILE THE candidates continue slanging at each other, they are slighting or ignoring most of the key issues that — as president — one of them will have to deal with beginning next January. Among these issues is health care: Its cost keeps rising and Americans keep demanding more of it.

Reasons abound for that. A steadily increasing proportion of America's population is 65 and older; these people require proportionately more health care, much of it the intensive kind that is so expensive. Medical technology makes new gains against disease, which prolongs lives but also adds to costs. Americans have come to expect the best of care, and their demands also put upward pressure on costs.

Why is this Uncle Sam's problem? He pays only about a fourth of total health-care costs, mainly through the Medicare and Medicaid programs ($117 billion in fiscal 1987); private insurance plans cover most of the rest. But the federal government sets standards that affect such costs across the board. When these costs rise — and they have outpaced the overall inflation rate since 1979 — people look to Washington to do something.

Mainly, what Washington has done is pay; Medicare and Medicaid are entitlement programs, which means that Uncle Sam is supposed to provide whatever they cost. The feds have also tried in various ways to hold down expenses. But the cost of health care has proved to be like a balloon: Pressed down at one point, it bulges out at another. After new Medicare rules were imposed in 1983 to put a brake on hospital bills, costs for outpatient services increased sharply.

Including both public and private outlays, the nation devotes about 11 percent of gross national product to health care — another proportion that has been rising. The figure would be higher yet but for the estimated 37 million Americans who lack any health insurance. Providing some kind of safety net for them has been a concern of national politicians for several years. The hope is that this could be done mostly through employers; two-thirds of those 37 million have jobs or are dependents of full-time workers. But when several million more people get increased access to health care, their added demand will also operate to drive up costs.

Part of the overall problem, some experts say, is that in a complex and rapidly changing health-care environment, those paying the bills — private insurers and the feds — don't know just what they and the patients are getting for the money. "We need to understand what the outcomes are of what we do," says Arnold S. Relman, editor of the New England Journal of Medicine. Continued inflation, he adds, is part of "the price we pay for a lack of hard, systematic evidence of the effectiveness of new technology and new drugs."

Uncle Sam can't provide all the answers; private responsibility and patient choice play parts as well. But Washington will be in the thick of whatever decision-making is done. What is the thinking of Bush or Dukakis? We need to hear more about that and less from each of them about how big a bum his opponent is.

Portland Press Herald
Portland, Maine, December 20, 1988

The notion of getting something for nothing has tremendous appeal. It's what keeps lotteries in business. That may be fine for get-rich-quick schemes but it's no way to run the nation's medical care programs.

Congress accepted that philosophy last year when, spurred by the nation's elderly, it approved a catastrophic health care program to be financed by a $4-a-month premium increase on Medicare and a 15 percent federal income surtax on the nation's 32 million Medicare recipients.

The elderly like the prospect of increased benefits. And with reason; the fear of a family's savings being wiped out by a lengthy catastrophic illness is a genuine one for many older Americans. But with the program due to be launched next month, they don't relish paying increased taxes. Some are pressuring Congress to rewrite the legislation.

Whatever it does, Congress should resist any effort to fund the program with broad-based general fund taxes. Granted, the catastrophic illness program isn't perfect. For one thing, it doesn't cover the cost of long-term nursing home care. For another, the income tax surcharge for Medicare recipients is capped at $800 a person. That means lower- and middle-income retirees face a higher percentage increase than wealthier Medicare recipients.

Nevertheless, both the Reagan administration and Congress agreed last year that the program should be financed by recipients, not all taxpayers. That's reasonable. Right now, the need to reduce federal deficits is paramount. If the elderly now want to reduce their costs, let it be done by cutting benefits.

Democrats Offer Health-Care Plan

Democrats in the Senate June 5, 1991 introduced a bill that would overhaul the nation's health-care system and guarantee basic health insurance for all Americans.

The bill would institute a system, known as "play or pay," in which employers could either provide health care insurance for their workers or pay into a fund that would finance coverage for the uninsured.

The bill's primary sponsors were Senate Majority Leader George J. Mitchell (Maine), Edward M. Kennedy (Mass.), Donald W. Riegle Jr. (Mich.) and John D. Rockefeller 4th (W. Va.).

"We must find a way to bring health-care costs under control," said Mitchell, "or we risk adding millions more to the rolls of the uninsured and ultimately face a total collapse of the health-care system." Mitchell estimated that there were 34 million Americans currently without health-care.

The "play-or-pay" plan and some other aspects of the bill had been included in recommendations made in 1990 by a bipartisan Congressional commission.

The fund to be created by employer contributions would help finance a program known as AmeriCare, which would effectively replace the current Medicaid program for the poor. People insured by the plan, except those under the poverty line, would pay premiums for coverage based on their income.

The legislation would also create a Federal Health Expenditure Board to set goals for cost containment and a system for negotiating rates between health-care providers and players.

Mitchell said that while the bill would cost $6 billion in its first year, the new system would reduce the nation's total health-care outlays by $78 billion over five years. Republicans criticized the plan for jeopardizing jobs by being too costly to business and for not specifying how the changes would be paid for.

THE ARIZONA REPUBLIC
Phoenix, Arizona, June 13, 1991

WHEN the U.S. Senate's Democratic leadership finally divulged its long-awaited legislative formula for national health-care reform, one might have expected loud hosannas in Washington.

After all, almost everyone — politicians of every stripe, doctors, businesses — agreed that America's medical delivery system was in need of intensive care. Even though the U.S. spends 12.5 percent of its annual economic output on health care — an estimated $670 billion this year — as many as 34 million Americans lack adequate medical insurance.

Yet the Democratic plan, when it was unveiled the other day, folded like a cheap card table. It offered no more than additional federal spending and additional bureaucrats to spend it. As John C. Goodman of the Dallas-based National Center for Policy Analysis put it, the Democrats proposed to "take a manageable problem and turn it into a major disaster."

Writing in *The Wall Street Journal*, Mr. Goodman described the program as no program at all. The Democrats propose a "pay or play" plan that would shift the health-care burden to the nation's businesses. Employers would be required either to provide employees with a federally mandated set of health benefits or pay a penalty to Washington, tentatively set at 7 percent of their payroll costs.

With health benefits estimated at more than 13 percent of payroll costs, most small firms —

those firms whose workers and dependents make up the bulk of the uninsured — would opt for the penalty. This would result in lower profits, lower wages or layoffs — hardly a bargain for the uninsured.

To make matters worse, the coverage — a modified form of Medicaid, called "Ameri-Care" — would be replete with the same woes that afflict the federal insurance plan for the poor, including huge cost overruns and a lack of participating quality medical providers. Add millions more people to the already overtaxed Medicaid rolls, and it does not take an accountant to figure out that the taxpayers would end up paying most of the cost.

America's health-care system is plagued by a number of ills, including the cost of medical malpractice and government mandates — more than 800 of them in the 50 states, requiring coverage for practices ranging from acupuncture to in-vitro fertilization — that have priced millions out of the market.

To their credit, some congressmen have proposed better solutions. Arizona's Sen. John McCain, for instance, is sponsoring a bill to offer tax incentives instead of tax increases as an inducement for small businesses to provide basic health coverage.

The Democratic leadership, in contrast, is offering the same old snake oil: more spending, more expensive mandates and more taxes to pay for them. This is a sure prescription for financial headaches and health-care disaster.

THE TENNESSEAN
Nashville, Tennessee, June 10, 1991

IT should be an embarrassment to this nation that 35 million people do not have health insurance.

Two-thirds of those 35 million people are workers or dependents of those workers. Most of them have incomes that exceed the poverty line and don't qualify for Medicaid.

Those Americans deserve to be covered by health insurance. A bill proposed in the United States Senate is trying to see that they receive it.

Senate leaders have proposed a plan where all Americans would be guaranteed basic health insurance. The plan calls for employers to either provide their own health care plan for workers or pay into a government plan that would provide it.

The move is due. Even small business organizations have seen merit in the legislation.

Adequate health coverage should be available to any American. It should not be limited only to those with the position or financial wherewithal to obtain it.

The bill before the Senate is likely to invite political posturing. Some may suggest it is a campaign tool for the Democrats in the 1992 elections. But the concept of providing adequate health coverage for Americans has been studied for years. Finally some workable legislation has come forward.

The bill is estimated to carry a cost of $6 billion in the first year, but sponsors of the legislation point to cost-containment aspects of the plan that allow savings of billions more. Among those cost-saving elements are proposals to eliminate unnecessary treatment.

The bill is still in its early stages. It may yet be refined and improved. It will, no doubt, bring some objections and substantial debate. But the premise is a solid one. The current system needs a cure. Millions of Americans are being left out of a fundamental need. And this legislation provides it. It should be allowed to move forward. ■

TULSA WORLD

Tulsa, Oklahoma, June 14, 1991

TESTIMONY before a U.S. Senate committee by Sand Springs resident Donna Johnson was moving.

Mrs. Johnson's son, Eric, 4, was born with cerebral palsy and epilepsy. Because of Eric's "pre-existing" medical condition, the family's health insurance was cancelled when her husband and Eric's father, Alan, changed jobs. The family is nearly overwhelmed by mounting medical bills that might wipe them out financially.

The Johnsons' story is all too common. An estimated 23 percent of all non-elderly Oklahomans do not have health insurance. Some, like Eric Johnson, are uninsurable because of medical risks. But most are without insurance because they are unemployed or their employers cannot afford to buy group health coverage for them.

It is estimated that more than a fourth of the typical medical bill paid by a patient or insurance company goes for unpaid services provided to uninsured patients.

Donna Johnson's Senate testimony was in support of Sen. Edward Kennedy's national health care plan, which would require employers to provide health insurance.

Kennedy's plan is not the answer. There are better ideas for extending health care to the uninsured without putting the entire burden on business. But uninsurance has reached a crisis stage and something must be done about it. That something will not be painless or cost-free.

THE DAILY OKLAHOMAN

Oklahoma City, Oklahoma, June 9, 1991

HEALTH care is almost certain to be a leading campaign issue in the 1992 elections.

Democrats already have started the pot boiling with a legislative proposal to guarantee basic health-care insurance for all Americans. Senate Majority Leader George Mitchell says his party will "push as hard and as vigorously as we can" to pass a measure before the end of next year.

Mitchell, Ted Kennedy and other Democrats have come up with a plan called AmeriCare, which would cost the federal treasury $6 billion the first year. It would give employers the option to "play or pay" — that is, they could privately provide basic insurance coverage for workers and their families or be required to contribute to the plan through a payroll tax in the range of 6 percent to 8 percent.

A coalition of labor unions and other groups is agitating for a full-fledged national health plan. Enactment of the Democratic leadership's proposal would open a wide crack in the door for a government-run system of universal health insurance.

There is wide agreement that health care reforms are long overdue. According to the Wall Street Journal, Americans spent about $670 billion on health care last year, or more than 12 percent of the gross national product. Yet while costs are spiraling, the nation's health status is not improving, and too many people are without affordable treatment for their ills.

Sen. John Chafee, R-R.I., who heads a Republican task force studying the problem, says the Democratic bill has little chance of passage. We hope he is right. Saddling businesses with additional costs — especially small employers already operating on the margin — would force many of them to shut down.

The Bush administration has taken a step toward cost control with a plan to place limits on court awards for medical malpractice claims. The White House is expected to present a broad health-care initiative later.

If the Democrat proposal gains too much momentum, it will be hard to stop. Those who oppose a Canadian-style government health care bureaucracy should be busy trying to head off this horrible possibility.

THE EMPORIA GAZETTE

THERE is no doubt in anyone's mind that America's health-care system is ailing. Costs are out of control and 35 million people are without insurance. The problem is how to cure it.

In their search for a solution, many Americans, and this includes lawmakers, have been fascinated with the Canadian health-care system. Under their system, all Canadians have access without charge to the physician of their choice. Most of the tests ordered by their physicians are available without cost, as are the services of specialists. Most surgery and hospital stays also are free. If this sounds like the perfect system, it is not.

The American Medical Association says that the Canadian system is "under-financed, overextended, and ill-equipped." It is true that when patients shoulder little or none of the cost for their medical care that there is often insatiable demand. This has forced the government to tighten regulations to control costs, which means that physician's fees are controlled, introduction of new technology is limited and certain services are unavailable. For instance, in some Canadian provinces the wait for a mammogram can be as long as 2½ months, and "urgent" surgery can be delayed four to eight weeks.

Waiting lists and a decline in quality care are not the only pitfalls in the Canadian system. The tight control that the government has over physician and hospital costs creates tension between heath-care providers and the government. This has resulted in strikes that can shut down health care in a given region.

While we think the United States should examine the Canadian system and utilize the best of it, much of it does not fit into our conception of an ideal medical system. There needs to be a definite means of controlling costs and the misuse or overuse of the system.

The Democrats are pushing legislation that would guarantee basic health-care coverage for all Americans. Like the Canadian system, it would vastly expand the role of government in economic regulation of hospitals, doctors and other aspects of medical care. It is known as "pay or play," and would dump much of the cost for insurance on business. Companies would have the choice of providing health insurance to their workers or paying a tax, expected to be 7.5 percent to 8 percent of their payroll. The plan would also revise and enlarge Medicaid and turn it into a new federal-state program to be called AmeriCare.

This plan shows some promise, but it could impose heavy costs on small- and medium-sized businesses. Democrats say that tax credits would be provided to small businesses with fewer than 25 employees to help reduce their costs. This does not take into account businesses that are twice that size, but which may already be operating at a loss. If they are not careful, overzealous planners may come up with a health-care plan that wipes out much of middle America.

The system needs reforming, but let us not get so caught up in politics that we forget that reform takes time and needs careful evaluation. With careful planning, we have a chance to come up with a unique system that is fair for everyone and does not penalize struggling businesses that are fighting to stay alive. — B.W.W.

THE TAMPA TRIBUNE
Tampa, Florida, June 6, 1991

"Without primary care for all of our citizens, the health care network in this country will continue to confuse us rather than to heal us."

A growing number of Americans would probably agree with that lament by Lois Nixon, chairman of the Tampa General Hospital board of trustees.

It's certainly confusing to many that the nation's health-care costs keep climbing when fewer and fewer people have health insurance, and thus have limited access to regular medical care.

But part of that increase can actually be attributed to the growing number of uninsured Americans. Without coverage to pay for doctor visits, the uninsured often forgo any contact with the health-care system until they're seriously ill. By then, their treatment costs are far greater than if they had been treated earlier.

This is particularly tragic because children and young adults are the largest groups among the 33 million Americans who have no health insurance. Those living in the South are at greatest risk.

But it's also tragic because the rest of Americans end up paying these bills for those who can't afford them. Hospitals charge patients with money or insurance a good deal extra to make up for non-paying patients, so insurance claims go up as indigent care goes up.

That's why a majority of Americans now understand that something must be done to remedy this problem. And why so many proposals have been written on what that remedy should be.

It's clear, though, that a national solution won't materialize soon. White House Press Secretary Marlin Fitzwater said this week he knows of no comprehensive health care proposal under development by the administration. Congress has reached no consensus on what to do. Even state governments have been slow to respond to this crisis, Florida included.

For that reason, elected leaders and public health officials in Hillsborough County are reaching for their own solution now.

They have obtained permission from the Legislature to allow Hillsborough County to enact a sales tax of up to half-a-penny to develop a health-care system to assist county residents who are uninsured.

At the core of that system would be a network of satellite clinics to treat the uninsured and help them avoid hospital visits. Pilot projects of this type in two sections of the county have already produced significant savings.

No new buildings would be erected; existing clinics would be contracted to provide the services. And only those who can prove they're county residents would be treated.

Yet to be worked out are the details of where those clinics would be located, what income level would make a resident eligible for subsidized care, and what medical and mental health services would be offered. Also unanswered is how much all of that would cost and whether a half-penny levy is needed or something smaller.

Those questions must be answered if the public is going to be sold on the need for a higher sales tax. The County Commission can establish the tax without a referendum as long as five of seven commissioners vote for it. But it would be foolish to take that step if there is widespread public opposition.

That's why the events of the next few months are crucial. Four citizen panels are working out the details of what this health-care delivery system would look like. Commission Chairman Phyllis Busansky wants them to take their final product on the road so the public will be familiar with those details.

"We need to treat this issue as if we were going to take it to a referendum," Busansky says. "To demonstrate to the public that we're trying to be open, thoughtful and honest. In the process, I hope they come to understand that this kind of health care system will give taxpayers relief in the long run."

If commissioners voted to hold a referendum on the issue, it couldn't occur until March. And it would cost money. So Busansky hopes enough public support can be garnered for the commission to make the decision on its own by October.

We urge the task force members, county staff members and county commissioners to make good on this opportunity. With the right proposal, Hillsborough County residents will support a higher sales tax. With the right proposal, this county could solve some of the health-care crisis on its own, without waiting for state and federal officials to get off their duffs.

The Phoenix Gazette
Phoenix, Arizona, June 10, 1991

The U.S. health care system has been pronounced sick and Congress is concocting a cure. As is so often the case with government remedies, the treatment is liable to have disastrous side effects.

Having spent every cent and more of the money collected from taxpayers, Senate Democrats now want to put the bite directly on business.

Under the Senate plan, companies would be forced to provide basic health insurance coverage or be taxed 6 percent to 8 percent of payroll if they don't.

The tax would fund a new federal-state "basic benefits" program called AmeriCare, which would replace Medicare and cover all those not covered by employment-based policies. Individuals under the poverty line would pay no premium, everyone else would pay premiums that would rise with income.

Shifting more of the costs of health care onto the shoulders of business is not a sensible solution. Mandating benefits would make it more difficult for American businesses to sell their products in the global marketplace. The added expense could well drive smaller firms to the wall, eliminating jobs and overloading the new indigent care system.

There is also reason to be dubious about the projected costs. The Democrats' plan is supposed to cost $6 billion the first year and go up to $20 billion to $30 billion a year after five years. Judging by how far off government numbers-crunchers were when they projected Medicare costs, it is more than likely that the program will exceed these estimates. The only question is, by how much?

Opinion polls indicate that the public is concerned about the more than 30 million people in America who do not have access to medical care. But is establishing the medical equivalent of the U.S. Postal Service the solution?

The plan calls for creation of a National Health Care Expenditure Board, which would establish voluntary targets, both at the national and state levels, for health care outlays.

Government regulation of medical care would be vastly increased with government aggressively defining what constitutes "unnecessary care."

It should not come as a shock if those definitions are driven more by the need to control spending than by medical necessity.

The cost of medical services runs at three times the cost of inflation because under our third party payment system, the connection between services and payments has been severed. The vast majority of Americans never question their hospital and doctor bills because they do not perceive that they are paying them.

Any reform of the health care system, if it is not to bankrupt us, will have to address that problem.

The Bush administration is right to want to proceed slowly and cautiously. It is clear that the Democrats are pushing us toward a national health-care system. It is not at all clear that is what Americans really want.

The Philadelphia Inquirer
Philadelphia, Pennsylvania, June 7, 1991

A gold star and pat on the back, please, for the Senate Democratic leadership, Edward "Mr. Deeply Flawed" Kennedy included. It has just changed the subject by putting a national health plan on the table. For a while there, it looked as if we were going to have a summer of "quota bill" rehashes, Millie's prognosis and musical promos for the Mother of All July Fourths.

It's not that the unraveling of America's health system has been a secret. Hardly. The blue-ribbon Pepper commission studied it to death. The American Medical Association only a couple of weeks ago hoisted its gown in near panic. And the captains of industry — Detroit's automakers, for instance — have been breaking with their old private-sector line: They're willing to take a close look at Canada's popular, government-run health system.

What's been missing is a political stand by anyone other then the usual interest groups — small business, big business, labor, organized medicine, the hospitals, the private insurance lobby. They've had no trouble speaking up, typically ascribing blame for the mess to the other guy. That's why it's refreshing that the Democrats, who have to appeal to a host of conflicting constituencies, are staking out a position — and a credible, thoughtful one at that.

Their plan would tax employers who didn't offer health benefits, reward those who do and begin charging workers as much as 20 perecent of the premiums. Businesses that didn't insure their workers — two-thirds of the 35 million Americans without insurance indeed have jobs — would pay a tax into a fund called Americare, which would largely replace Medicaid as an insurer of the poor and uninsured.

There would be cost controls, including treatment guidelines to discourage unneeded procedures. There'd be incentives for "managed care" approaches (such as health maintenance organizations), which have had success in holding down fees.

In short, the plan spreads the pain around: Non-insuring businesses, consumers, physicians all take a hit. (Insurance companies appear to have gotten a bye, but their sheer numbers contribute to the problem. Several recent studies suggest that billions could be saved by going to a Canadian-style system with a single insurer ruling on coverage, resolving billing disputes and doing paperwork. There are more than 1,000 in the United States.)

In boldly advancing a plan, Democratic leaders deserve applause on two scores. First, they give voice to the notion — lost during the Reagan administration — that health care is "not merely a luxury for those who have the economic means to purchase health insurance," to use Sen. Kennedy's words. Second, they're putting some beef on the table.

The suddenly quiet Bush White House, we're led to believe, would like to do the same. But it's having a few problems.

One is how to fashion a "market-oriented" plan that doesn't mimic the pitfalls of the market-driven system that's currently breaking down. Another, we suspect, is that the subject doesn't lend itself to the kind partisan gamesmanship Mr. Bush seems to prefer these days on domestic issues.

But the matter is too vital — and too costly — to ignore indefinitely. We'll soon see whether the President can get as whipped up about the challenge of rescuing a collapsing health-care system as he has been regarding "quotas" and campus free-speech.

THE TAMPA TRIBUNE
Tampa, Florida, June 10, 1991

Everyone complains about paperwork and bureaucracy but rarely does someone take the time to put a price tag on how much it adds to the cost of doing business. But the federal General Accounting Office has done just that, and the results are startling.

If the United States adopted universal health insurance coverage similar to Canada's, it would save about $67 billion in administrative costs, the GAO concludes. That's how much extra Americans spend on their patchwork system, which includes coverage by hundreds of private insurers, Medicaid, Medicare and special state government risk pools.

The administrative costs of the American health-care system are so substantial, in fact, that per-capita health care spending in the United States was $2,196 in 1989 compared to $1,570 in Canada.

But here's the most startling prediction: The GAO believes that $67 billion in savings would be great enough to pay for free universal health coverage for all Americans. In other words, everyone would have access to medical care without needing to pay premiums or co-payments.

Currently, nearly 33 million Americans have no health insurance and those that do usually pay substantial premiums and co-payments of between 10 and 50 percent of the cost of each medical bill.

The major complaint about Canada's system is that patients there have long waits for some medical services and procedures. So the GAO recommends that if the United States should move to universal health coverage, it should still make Americans pay for some of the costs and use some or all of the savings to beef up the system enough to avoid such long waits.

That's an excellent idea.

The question that remains is this: Will this report, which follows dozens of others from health researchers, be enough to spur President Bush and Congress to do something about this problem?

Bush promises to unveil some suggestions for reform by 1992. Congress is also studying the problem but so far has reached no consensus about what to do.

Meanwhile, billions of dollars continue to be wasted and millions of Americans continue to be locked out of the health-care system.

Arkansas Gazette.
Little Rock, Arkansas, June 14, 1991

How many more Americans will have to die needlessly because there was no dignified place for them in the nation's health care system? How many more American families will have to face financial ruin because of long-term or catastrophic illness?

These questions are more than rhetorical. They test national leadership, which falls woefully short. Had all those teeming masses that found their way to our shores stayed behind they certainly would not have to be worrying about receiving adequate health care regardless of station in life or the size of their bank accounts.

Reminders abound, but the one that caught our immediate attention this week was the news that Americans spent $666.2 billion on health care in 1990 although at least 33 million of them still lack health insurance coverage. And Bush administration spokesmen continue to brush off any suggestion that it address massive shortcomings in a system that cries for a national approach.

The administration has no quarrel with the fact that health care costs are much too high. Health and Human Services Secretary Louis Sullivan and White House budget director Richard Darman acknowledge that the costs are unsustainable. But they dismiss any suggestion that comprehensive reform is needed. A little fine tuning here or there, Dr. Sullivan indicates, would do just fine for now at least.

The fact is that 1990 was the third consecutive year that health care spending increased at double-digit rates. Last year's spending, according to HHS, was 10.5 percent more than the 1989 level. In 1989, spending rose 10.4 percent, and in 1988 it rose 10.5 percent.

Perhaps even more disturbing is the news that health care costs accounted for 12.2 percent of the gross national product, up from 11.6 percent.

This level of spending has produced the finest health care system in the world, according to many authorities, but it has shut out or severely limited access to millions of Americans. Something is wrong — bad wrong. Shrugging if off is not good enough.

Bush Unveils Reform Plan

President George Bush Feb. 6, 1992 unveiled a set of proposals that he said would ensure access to affordable health care for most Americans and keep down skyrocketing medical costs.

The plan was immediately greeted by a torrent of criticism from Democrats.

"Reform is urgent," said Bush as he introduced his plan in a speech in Cleveland. "Right now far too many Americans are uninsured, and those who are insured pay too much for health care, and we are going to do something about that."

Bush's plan would retain a market-based health-care system. The president attacked more sweeping proposals for reform that had been put forward by some Democrats: a national, single-payer system and "pay or play," in which businesses would be given a choice between providing health care for their employees or paying a payroll tax to finance coverage for those not insured through their job. He warned that a national system would raise costs and bring about "long waiting lists for surgery" and "shortages of high-tech equipment." Pay or play, he said, would mean lost jobs and higher costs.

One of the problems with the U.S. health-care system most often cited by analysts was the number of people who lacked health-insurance coverage. The Census Bureau in September 1991 had estimated that number at 34.6 million people, or 14% of the population.

To reduce the number of Americans lacking health-insurance coverage, Bush recommended providing poor families not on Medicaid with a voucher worth up to $3,750 that could be used to buy medical insurance. A system of tax deductions and tax credits would be instituted for middle-income people. Self-employed persons could deduct 100% of medical insurance premiums, an increase from the current level of 25%.

The administration said that its proposals would reduce the number of uninsured Americans to 4.9 million.

Bush also proposed reforms in the health-insurance industry, which, for example, would be prohibited from dropping the coverage of persons who developed costly conditions and from denying insurance to persons with preexisting conditions. Many workers felt unable to change jobs because they would lose their insurance.

Another impetus for those backing reforms in the U.S. health-care system was the drastic increase in the cost of the health care in recent years.

To contain costs, Bush's plan would offer incentives to foster the use of "coordinated care" such as health maintenance organizations, which kept costs down by closely monitoring the care given. In addition, small businesses would be encouraged to join together to form "health-insurance networks" when purchasing health insurance for their employees. Other steps would include encouraging states to overhaul malpractice laws, increasing federal spending on preventive care, and encouraging individuals to adopt healthier lifestyles.

The Bush administration estimated that the proposed tax credits and deductions would cost the Treasury $100 billion over five years. No specific financing mechanism was proposed. The administration said that its proposals for containing the costs of health care would partially offset the cost of the plan. Otherwise, Bush suggested capping spending on Medicaid, which was currently an open-ended entitlement program.

Democrats blasted Bush's plan as no more than an election-year gesture. "This is not a proposal to deal with the problem of health care, this is a proposal to deal with the perception that the president doesn't care about health care," said Senate Majority Leader George J. Mitchell (D, Maine) Feb. 6.

Bush was criticized for not being more specific on financing. Many Democrats said there was little chance that cuts in entitlement programs would pass.

The Charlotte Observer
Charlotte, North Carolina, February 9, 1992

President Bush's health care proposal includes some good ideas. But its financing is so sketchy, its coverage so limited and its impact on some major problems so minimal that it falls far short of meeting America's needs.

Mr. Bush's plan has virtually no chance of approval by the Democratic majority in Congress. The Democrats' plans have little chance of avoiding a presidential veto. The outlook? Business as usual in Washington: much self-serving talk, little or no action.

The good ideas in Mr. Bush's proposal include the idea that there's an urgent problem. That hadn't occurred to him until his former attorney general, Richard Thornburg, was trounced in a Pennsylvania Senate race by a Democrat who advocated a national health care plan. Now the president acknowledges, "In these hard times, we simply cannot accept the fact that one in every seven Americans is uninsured." That's progress.

Other good ideas include an effort to help low-income families buy health insurance, and heavier regulation of the health insurance industry to increase the likelihood that small businesses can afford it and people changing jobs won't lose it.

Mr. Bush's proposal, however, fails to adequately engage the toughest problems: controlling costs, financing universal care and determining who doesn't get what when the money runs out.

The problem is bad and getting worse. Between 32 million and 37 million Americans have no health insurance, and about 60 million others carry inadequate insurance. America's health-care bill last year was a staggering $738 billion, nearly 11% greater than in 1990. It consumes more than $1 of every $9 that Americans now spend, yet still left out a seventh of the population.

The current system of paying that bill is tolerable to the major interest groups: the insurance companies, the doctors, the hospitals and those patients whose bills are paid by insurance financed largely by their employers. It does not satisfy the growing number of people who have inadequate insurance or no insurance at all, or employers who see insatiable health-care costs gobbling up their profits.

To be an improvement over the present chaos, a health care plan must do four things:

1. Not over-burden business. If health care is a public necessity, private business shouldn't be squeezed to pay for it.

2. Cover everybody.

3. Control costs.

4. Provide a rational basis for providing — and denying — care.

President Bush's proposal may have solved his political problem of seeming not to care about Americans' health care mess, but it does little to clean up that mess.

The Republicans want to do too little. The Democrats want to do too much. The result: Washington does nothing. Inertia prevails, and the public is getting fed up with it.

The Sun
Vancouver, British Columbia, February 8, 1992

THERE IS a very good reason why President George Bush has joined the chorus of Republican senators and private insurance companies attacking Canada's medicare system: the issue of public health insurance threatens them all.

President Bush chose as his principal target the waiting list for coronary bypass surgery in British Columbia. Yes, there is one, although Mr. Bush's information is out of date: the average wait is now four months, not six. But it is surely better to be on a waiting list than to die because you cannot afford either surgery or insurance. That is the situation for 35 million uninsured Americans, and there are millions more who are underinsured.

The White House plan to give these people vouchers and tax credits of up to $3,750 a year is great news for the medical and insurance industries, but hardly anybody else. That won't buy much coverage, but it will be enough to drive medical costs even higher. Those are already 40 per cent higher per capita than in Canada.

Americans should not be fooled. While Canada's publicly funded, universally accessible health care system is far from perfect, and has cost problems of its own, it is one Canadians would not willingly go without. That is why a lot of people are arguing this weekend in Toronto that it should be entrenched in the constitution, so that no politicians can ever take it away.

The News and Observer
Raleigh, North Carolina, February 4, 1992

Americans desperate for help with health insurance can stop hoping for any from President Bush. The plan he will announce Thursday amounts to a campaign commercial and that's about it.

According to The New York Times, Bush will ask for tax credits and deductions worth up to $3,750 per family to help pay health premiums. The credits would go to the poor — including those too poor to pay income tax, who apparently would get federal checks — while everyone else, including the rich, would get deductions.

The first thing wrong with this approach is its $55 billion to $100 billion cost. The second is how Bush would fund it: by cutting payments to hospitals and doctors from the big government health programs, Medicare for the elderly and Medicaid for the poor.

What happens then? Providers would be faced with getting less for Medicare and Medicaid patients than they can get for giving the same care to privately insured or self-paid patients. So as usual, they would either require those latter patients to make up the difference, or they would stop treating patients on Medicare and Medicaid.

Economically, medically and politically, either result is a loser. That's especially so for the fast-growing senior population, who need a lot of health care and must rely on Medicare to pay for it.

Besides, the Bush people have short memories. Health insurance premiums were federally tax-deductible for years. The deduction was severely reduced in the Reagan-Bush era partly because it was thought to feed the health insurance cost spiral. If it fed it then, it would again.

The root source of the painful squeeze that health care has put on the national purse is costs and the so-far-unstoppable rate at which they rise. The Bush plan's fatal defect is its failure to come to grips with costs.

Of all the U.S. dollars there are, more than one in every eight now goes for health care: $666 billion in 1990, which is two and two-thirds times the $250 billion spent in 1980, and heading past $800 billion this year. The size of the bites has become ominous. In 1991 a North Carolina state employee paid $152 a month to insure one dependent; in 1992 he pays $216 a month, a 42 percent increase.

The unstoppable is becoming the insupportable. Finding ways to stop it has to be top priority, but Bush's plan finds no such ways. Because it doesn't, the plan itself is doomed to failure. Cost inflation would erode away in a very few years any early help from a fixed-amount tax credit or deduction.

That should worry the public plenty. It doesn't worry Bush, waging his last campaign and with no worries about his own insurance premiums. He will doubtless deck his Thursday pitch for this election-year gimmickry in the usual free-market slogans: as a plan that would allow everyone, but force no one, to choose and buy their own private health insurance.

The truth is, in an insurance market where rampant cost inflation is the name of the game, any plan that neither halts inflation nor flexes to allow for it is guaranteed to flop. This one flops.

ST. LOUIS POST-DISPATCH
St. Louis, Missouri, February 7, 1992

President Bush's health-care package, unveiled Thursday in Cleveland, fails to address basic problems that fuel medical inflation and send health-insurance costs beyond the reach of at least 34 million Americans. The president begins with the premise that what's ailing the system can be fixed primarily through tax laws. He's offering breaks ranging from $1,250 to $3,750 a year for individuals and families to offset private insurance premiums.

The breaks would be in the form of tax-credit vouchers for the poor and health-insurance tax deductions for families with incomes under $80,000 a year. Mr. Bush also promised to address waste and said he would encourage what he calls HINs, or Health Insurance Networks, as a way of covering more consumers at lower costs.

He also attacked national health insurance by reciting the standard litany of alleged shortcomings, including long waiting lists and less medical technology, claims which have been shown to be exaggerated. In fact, the centerpieces of the president's proposal explain why national health insurance is so much more preferable to his plan.

Unlike national health insurance, the tax-break approach would leave many families with far too many out-of-pocket health expenses. Families USA, a private health-care advocacy group, notes that families would still have to pay a large share of the cost. It notes that health spending per U.S. family averaged $6,535 last year. President Bush's maximum tax credit doesn't approach that amount.

How will he finance his plan, projected to cost at least $35 billion a year? That's $35 billion on top of what's already spent on U.S. health care. Mr. Bush says he would contain the costs of Medicare and Medicaid recipients, which, translated, means cutbacks in those programs. Medicare is a federal health insurance program for the elderly, and the federal-state funded Medicaid program covers the poor. These cuts could be devastating since care providers already complain about low Medicare-Medicaid reimbursement rates.

Yet the president takes pity on the forces that really drive up the price of health care. His HIN plan seeks to expand private insurance with no restraints on costs. Administrative expenses for Medicare and Medicaid run about 3 percent. For private insurers, those expenses average 15 percent. These expenses alone add billions of dollars to the price of health care, money consumers wouldn't have to spend under a single-payer, national health insurance system.

The fundamental issues — affordability and accessibility — are largely overlooked by Mr. Bush. This nation spends enough now on health insurance to finance a world-class national health insurance program with plenty of cost controls. These would include negotiated payments for providers, a single payer system to reduce administrative expenses and less high-tech medicine. Mr. Bush hasn't addressed any of these issues. He required Americans to wait more than two years for a plan that's a disappointment, even to some members of his own party.

The Star-Ledger

Newark, New Jersey, February 7, 1992

President Bush's long-awaited national health care plan is critically flawed by ambivalent implications. While it addresses some of the financial concerns of 35 million Americans without health insurance, it would have a devastating impact on the nation's elderly and indigent who are dependent on Medicare and Medicaid.

The major components of the President's five-year-plan health proposals call for vouchers and tax breaks to aid poor and middle-class Americans to purchase health insurance. There is, however, a critical problem with the deleterious impact of the proposed funding on existing government-supported health care programs.

About two-thirds of the $100 billion cost would be diverted from Medicare, which provides health care for 34 million elderly and handicapped persons. The remainder would come by imposing limits on Medicaid, a federal-state program that helps 30 million poor Americans obtain medical care.

What the President's plan does, in effect, is to shift the funding emphasis from the elderly and the poor to help underwrite the medical cost needs of middle-income Americans who don't have health care coverage. Besides, there are questions whether the vouchers and tax breaks would provide enough money to cover the soaring medical costs for uninsured persons.

For severely strapped urban states like New Jersey and New York, the Bush health plan would have a highly negative impact by capping the federal share of the $73 billion Medicaid program. Twenty percent of New Jersey's budget is for health care.

Gov. Jim Florio criticized the President's funding formula as constituting "cost-shifting," with states having to take on a larger share of medical costs. "To ask the state taxpayers to pick up the cost of a national health care plan misses the point of what we should be doing, which is containing costs," the Governor said.

For months, the President has been criticized for failing to come up with a national health care plan. Now it becomes apparent that he may face strong adverse reaction to the program he has proposed to fulfill the nation's medical care needs.

In a presidential election year, health care figures to be an issue of primacy. It will be an issue that the majority Democrats in Congress already are deploying for tactical advantage with several medical care proposals they have drafted. The partisan pressures for political gain could provide the incentives for enacting a national plan that would universally address the medical care needs for all Americans. But the Bush plan just doesn't get the job done.

The Hutchinson News

Hutchinson, Kansas, February 10, 1992

Although the big news was that President Bush had a national health plan in mind, the bigger news is that the nation is heading in the right direction.

While the merits of the handful of various existing plans will be debated at length, the focus of the current presidential campaign may finally come to roost on one of the most important issues in these times — making affordable health care available to all citizens.

Health has been a central national issue since the nation's beginnings when Congress created what would become the U.S. Public Health Service in 1798. The following year the government acknowledged the federal goverment's role in protecting a citizen's health by passing the first national quarantine act, which mandated that federal officials should aid states in enforcing health regulations.

A national health benefit is not a concept to be denigrated as some form of socialism. It would seem more likely to fit comfortably by the promise and by the spirit embraced in the phrase "life, liberty and the pursuit of happiness." Such a goal is difficult to seek when an American has been physically crushed by illness or by the financial inability to pay for decent medical care.

President Bush did not create the concept of guaranteed health care, nor did the members of Congress serving today. Harry Truman attempted to create a compulsory insurance program back in the 1940s, but the American Medical Association opposed it.

The question now is how does the nation pay for it, and what is it that we are paying for? Both employers and employees have become overburdened by health premiums, and the jobless and the poor carry their own unique burden of problems.

But one thing is crystal clear. There is something wrong with a nation that cares for the medical, dental and mental health of its incarcerated murderers, rapists and thieves, and denies the working stiffs of the nation and their children the same benefits.

One plank of any public health plan should be to accelerate subsidized schooling for medical students who pledge a term of public service work in return for their education. The world needs more doctors and nurses.

Those citizens who can afford it should be able to purchase whatever medical care they wish. But those who can't afford it should be guaranteed an acceptable level of affordable or subsidized quality care.

This is no time for the skeptics to dominate the national debate.

President Bush's plan is but one of many. The important point is that national health care is being discussed. Even a partial or temporary solution is better than no solution at all. The genie is finally out of the bottle. That's where this issue should be forced to stay.

FORT WORTH STAR-TELEGRAM

Fort Worth, Texas, February 4, 1992

The least that can be said for President Bush's health-care initiatives is that the administration has finally weighed in with proposals on one of the primary political issues of 1992.

Unfortunately, that is also the most that can be said.

The president is absolutely right to decry the enormous cost of the nation's health-care system, expected to exceed $800 billion this year. Even so, nearly 40 million Americans have no health insurance, and about 35 million others are underinsured.

Bush, however, proposes to arrest the costs by granting a $3,750 tax credit to lower- and middle-income taxpayers so that they can purchase health insurance. He would finance the cost by increasing Medicare premiums to upper-income retired persons and reducing expenditures on Medicaid services for the poor.

That amounts to shifting the financial burden, not addressing fundamental reform, and even some Bush supporters in Congress say they cannot make the arithmetic work.

Actually, the proposals among the Democratic presidential hopefuls are widely diverse and for the most part place the burden of providing insurance on employers, which is strongly resisted by the administration.

Nevertheless, all the recommendations reflect a lack of consensus on what the American people want when they talk of health-care reform. Everyone agrees that the system is too costly, but little agreement exists on how well and how efficiently the present expenditures contribute to better health in American society.

Many studies indicate that the system is fraught with waste and redundancy for those who are insured, but with nearly 40 million people lacking any insurance at all, the efficiency standard is moot on its face.

That is the system President Bush would retain. That is the system that must be fundamentally reformed if national health policy is to have any meaning at all.

Rockford Register Star

Rockford, Illinois, February 9, 1992

For all of its shortcomings, and there are more than a few, President Bush's newly unveiled health care plan is a welcome — nay, a historic — contribution. This nation has turned a corner and now is on a political path that inexorably leads to federal guarantees of decent health care for virtually of all of its citizens.

It's a development that validates the editorial observation of months ago in the Journal of the American Medical Association that "an aura of inevitability is upon us." It's just a matter of time now.

Philip S. Birnbaum, a professor of health administration at the George Washington University Medical Center, said it best: "This is the first time that the president of the United States, his party and the leaders of the opposition party are saying health care is a problem that has to be addressed by the nation. Now the debate evolves from 'shall we do it' to 'what is it we shall do.'"

What, indeed! This being an election year, the partisan divisions on specifics of a health care plan are going to be sharp. Democrats already are blasting Bush's plan as inadequate, while the president, in turn, raises the specter of socialized medicine if the Democrats have their way.

But then, if this were not an election year and Bush were not in trouble in the polls, this historic opportunity might not have yet presented itself. Stay tuned for a vigorous national debate on health care.

TULSA WORLD

Tulsa, Oklahoma, February 7, 1992

ALL of this year's presidential candidates have promised some sort of national health care plan. Unfortunately, none has explained in precise detail how his particular scheme would be paid for. This includes President Bush, who unveiled his proposal Thursday. The Bush proposal, while containing some sensible ideas, appears to have been hatched in some haste, more as a campaign document than a serious, detailed plan. It calls for tax vouchers and credits of up to $3,740 for lower and middle class families to buy their own health insurance. Bush would pay for the $100 billion program, in part, by cutting back on Medicare and Medicaid programs to the elderly and poor.

Restricting health services to the poor (Medicaid) to pay for health insurance tax credits for the middle class is unwise. And while the $3,750 credit for a family of four might approach a realistic cost for insurance, the proposed $1,250 for individuals would not come close.

A growing problem in Oklahoma, and presumably nationwide, is that some employers are unwilling or unable to provide group health coverage for their employees. Would the availability of tax credits to pay for middle class workers' coverage encourage more employers to drop their insurance?

These and other concerns give Bush's announced program a half-baked look. But this seems to be the fashion. With the possible exception of Nebraska Sen. Bob Kerrey, none of the Democrats appear to have given the issue much more thought than the authors of the Bush propos-

RAPID CITY JOURNAL—

Rapid City, South Dakota, February 7, 1992

The routine is becoming familiar.

President Bush unveils a plan for alleviating a domestic problem. Most, but not all, Republicans hail its merit. Democrats immediately assail its lack of merit. And many Americans, despite Bush's statements to the contrary, see such proposals as maneuvering toward re-election.

The economic recovery proposal outlined in his State of the Union address last week left middle-income Americans searching for some real benefit for them. And, as has become a trademark of Bush's presidency, his economic plan seemed to pay nothing but lip service to the problem of huge federal debt.

Thursday, Bush unveiled his plan for solving problems in the country's health care system. The plan, while outlined only broadly, leaves questions about funding and cost containment.

The heart of Bush's plan would create vouchers, tax credits and tax deductions for providing health insurance to low- and middle-income

The Journal's view

Americans. In concept, that part sounds like it could be of some help, although there is doubt whether the amounts — $1,250 a year for individuals, $2,500 for couples and $3,750 for families of three or more — would cover the cost of insurance now, let alone after future increases in health care costs.

And what about paying for these vouchers, credits and deductions, at a cost of $100 billion? Bush proposes to cap federal Medicaid payments to states and increase Medicare premiums for high-income people. It's difficult to see that those steps can raise $100 billion, let alone keep the plan from adding even more red ink to the federal budget.

Bush admitted that details are still to be worked out. Health and Human Services Secretary Louis W. Sullivan said the administration would ask Congress to choose from a 38-page list of financing options — which sounds suspiciously like passing the buck.

And what does this plan do to control health care costs to the consumer? If more people are insured, that should cut down on the number of uncollected bills and perhaps lower costs. The president's plan also provides for the publishing of a "blue book," similar to those used for auto sales, to help guide consumers in deciding fair market prices for various medical procedures.

But it hardly seems like enough to stem, much less, reverse this crisis. Improving access to health care is needed, but if health care costs are not controlled, the price of insurance will only continue to rise.

As Bush noted in his State of the Union address, America's health care crisis is illustrated in the rising amount Americans spend on health care — about one dollar in every eight in 1990.

It's hard to see where this plan does much to change that.

And as with Bush's economic plan, a closer look at the health care plan reinforces the view that Bush is unwilling to alter, even slightly, the current distribution of wealth. The suspicion is that Bush's plan would grant health insurance for low- and middle-income Americans at a price paid primarily through their own taxes or in cuts in other services they benefit from. Insurance and health care professionals would continue to reap their same profits. Bush has not done anything to cause anyone to suspect differently.

Last week the president emphasized that 60 percent of the people who benefit from his proposed cut in the capital gains tax earn less than $50,000 a year. But an analysis released Thursday by the non-partisan Joint Committee on Taxation found that 70 percent of the tax reduction would go to people with incomes over $100,000 per year, with average cuts of $8,500 for the richest half-million Americans. Meanwhile those with incomes under $50,000 a year would get an average of $263, and 10 percent of the total reduction.

It sounds all too familiar.

States Take the Lead in U.S. Health-Care Reform

Between 1965 and 1990 health care costs in the U.S. increased from $41.9 billion a year, representing $206 per person and 5.9% of the gross national product, to an estimated $666.2 billion representing $2,665 per person, and about 12% of the GNP. Furthermore, annual health cost increases in the last decade have been more than double that of other goods and services; overall inflation from 1980 to 1989 was 4.7 percent, while medical costs increased 10.4 percent. The increase in Medicaid costs for the federal government from fiscal year 1991 to fiscal year 1992 was the largest of any major national program.

Explanations for the explosion in health care costs are familiar. They include an aging population; overall inflation; costly advances in medical technology; a fee-for-service, third-party payer financing system; over-doctoring and defensive medical practices in response to a malpractice insurance crisis; and the failure of Americans to adopt more prudent lifestyles.

While no sector of the health care economy has been immune from the escalation of costs, the public sector has borne a considerable portion of the burden. Public sector spending on health care services increased from about 25% of all spending in this area in 1965 to over 40% today. The reason for this substantial increase was the introduction in 1965 of Medicaid and Medicare. State general fund spending on Medicaid, the largest and costliest health program run by the states, is one of the fastest growing items in state budgets. When it was first introduced, Medicaid comprised about 5% of state general fund expenditures. By 1990, it was up to around 11% and was predicted to go as high as 15% by 1995.

In response to the growth in Medicaid spending, the states have adopted one or more of three strategies. First, they have eliminated benefits. Oregon did this in 1987 when it ended state funding of organ transplants, a decision that set in motion the events that led to that state's basic health services act. Second, states have redefined eligibility and, consequently, thrown people off the Medicaid rolls. The Children's Defense Fund has estimated that there were 200,000 fewer children served by Medicaid in 1986 than there were in 1978, despite lower poverty rates in that earlier year. In fact, the proportion of poor people in general who are covered by Medicaid has declined from a high of about 65% to less than 40% today.

Third, states have reduced reimbursements to providers, a strategy rendered more difficult by a June 1990 Supreme Court decision that upheld the right of hospitals and other health providers to sue the states for higher Medicaid reimbursements. In 1989, for example, Oregon's hospitals were reimbursed by the state for only 78% of the actual cost of providing services under Medicaid. Oregon was one of the states in which a lawsuit by providers seeking increased reimbursements was pending when the court issued its ruling. One consequence of under-re-imbursement to providers has been that physicians and hospitals have increased the fees they charge private patients or their insurance companies to cover their expenses.

The Medicaid problem facing the states is partly a consequence of recent changes in the law that have mandated that additional health services be covered by the states. Beginning in the mid-1980s, Congress made it easier for pregnant women and young children, and people making the transition from welfare to work, to qualify for Medicaid. It also increased the health services available to these groups.

State policymakers will confront other major health problems that will stretch both their resources and their ingenuity. These include the care and treatment of the mentally ill, the aged, and people with chemical dependencies. Unlike many of the health problems that faced the states at the turn of the century, such as tuberculosis, influenza, measles and other infectious or contagious diseases, these problems will neither be episodic, as epidemics historically have been, nor lend themselves to a "magic bullet" solution. Instead, state governments can expect to find pressing health issues high on the policy agenda for decades to come, even if a cure for AIDS is found tomorrow.

Los Angeles Times
Los Angeles, California, April 1, 1988

More than 100 Californians, gathered under the sponsorship of the American Assembly, have called on Gov. George Deukmejian and President Reagan to become more involved in the problems of health care. Their report supports the recommendation.

Like the national American Assembly on health care in November, 1986, this regional assembly affirmed the right of each person to basic health care, asserting that this is a responsibility of the federal government, which should either finance the care or mandate the financing. That is important. Much of the recent erosion in financing appropriate care, and the fact that more than 30 million Americans are without any health insurance, is the result of a failure in Washington to strengthen federal programs and to require employers to protect employees with basic health insurance.

The need for greater involvement by both governor and President is evident. The American Assembly called on Deukmejian to convene "an appropriate panel at the earliest moment." A state commission on health problems could play a useful role in addressing the immediate crisis in such areas as dwindling Medi-Cal support that has crippled the crucially important prenatal program. The assembly called for the establishment of regular White House conferences on health care modeled after those that already address the problems of children, drug abuse and aging. The record of those conferences is mixed, their usefulness heavily dependent on the willingness of Presidents and Congresses to implement recommendations. But they at least serve as an effective way to focus national attention on problems.

The regional assembly coincided with the release of a new SRI/Gallup poll on California health care that showed satisfaction with the system by a large majority, but also reflected concern about weaknesses. About 70% of respondents affirmed medical care as a right rather than a privilege. A surprising 74% favored development of some form of national health insurance by the federal government. And 88% supported the necessity of maintaining trauma centers; some have had to close in Los Angeles County because of funding problems.

Those attending the regional assembly shared many of the concerns of the public at large, as reflected in the poll results. For all, the spiraling costs of health care and the need for cost containment were major concerns.

Once again the institution of the American Assembly has proved to be an effective tool in involving citizens in difficult public-policy questions. The assembly was established by Dwight D. Eisenhower at Columbia University in 1950 as a nonpartisan sponsor of such meetings. There have been 74 national assemblies and hundreds of regional assemblies since then. The most recent regional assembly for Californians on health care was in Newport Beach. Its value will now be measured not only by its effect on the participants but also by the willingness of the governor and the President to implement its constructive proposals.

The San Diego
Union-Tribune.
San Diego, California, March 31, 1988

When Gov. Deukmejian vetoed legislation last year that would have clamped down on those companies that prey upon senior citizens by selling them duplicative supplemental health-insurance policies, he said he wanted to wait a year and see if existing laws solved the problem. They haven't; and the governor should approve AB 4317, which contains many of the same provisions that were in the previous bill.

The revised measure, sponsored by Assemblyman Lloyd Connelly, D-Sacramento, would prohibit the unnecessary sale or replacement of medigap policies. It would prohibit a company from misrepresenting itself either as a government agency or a senior-citizen organization for the purpose of selling such policies. It would also increase the penalties against insurance companies and agents who engage in deceptive and unfair practices. And it would guarantee that seniors receive a reasonable return for each premium dollar paid.

Missing from AB 4317 is the requirement that a special unit be established within the state department of insurance to investigate complaints by the elderly concerning medigap policies. Nor would the bill limit large first-year sales, an earlier provision designed to remove the incentive for dishonest agents to replace policies willy-nilly.

We believe both provisions should have remained in the bill. But politics remains the art of the possible, and Gov. Deukmejian would not countenance an intrusion into the state insurance commission's authority to regulate medigap policies. Moreover, the National Association of Insurance Commissioners recently approved regulations and guidelines that address many of the problems raised by the previous bill. Finally, some of the insurance companies themselves are amenable to working with Assemblyman Connelly to eliminate some of the more glaring abuses that currently exist in the industry.

Last year, California senior citizens squandered an estimated $300 million on duplicative medigap policies because of high-pressure and dishonest sales techniques. This scandalous situation can be dealt with best by a state law that prompts the insurance industry to police its own ranks. The Connelly bill would be such a spur and it should be approved.

Los Angeles Times
Los Angeles, California, February 1, 1990

Gov. George Deukmejian is to be congratulated for putting aside his pride and personal irritation in settling the dispute over crucial family-planning funds. The governor did not sign the bill passed by the Legislature to restore $20 million to family planning programs, but he didn't veto it, either. That means state funding is again available for birth-control counseling, pregnancy testing and cancer, AIDS and venereal-disease screenings for half a million poor and uninsured women.

The family-planning fight had degenerated into a sometimes ugly battle between anti-abortion and pro-choice advocates and between alternately nervous and self-righteous politicians. But the governor managed to rise above it. In his message to the Legislature, he wrote: "I am willing to yield to the majority of the Legislature on this bill to relieve them of a potentially prolonged and difficult process and to continue to maintain the spirit of cooperation between the Legislature and the governor . . . ."

The family-planning fight has also been a prolonged educational process for many. Pro-choice advocates underestimated the discomfort the governor and some conservative legislators felt about some family-planning agencies and the possibility that the state was paying for "abortion counseling." By the same token, some anti-abortion advocates did not seem to understand that family-planning counseling, by law, must inform a woman of *all* her options, but that state-funded family-planning clinics never were in the business of abortion.

In the end it may not have been the sensible arguments for family-planning services that settled this controversy but the political realities. After the bills to restore family-planning funding received overwhelming support in both houses, it was not clear that a gubernatorial veto could be sustained. Many Republicans were nervously eyeing pro-choice public opinion polls and taking phone calls from supporters who saw the politically ill-advised stand against family planning as an anathema to those who want alternatives to abortion. U.S. Sen. Pete Wilson, a moderate Republican who hopes to succeed Deukmejian as governor next year, was also not shy about applying political pressure.

Still, in the end, the call was the governor's, and he could have stubbornly put his shoulder to the door and tried to keep it shut against the oncoming crowd. Instead, when he saw the crowd coming, he opened the door. And that was the wise thing to do.

THE SACRAMENTO BEE
Sacramento, California, February 2, 1990

So, after seven years of resistance to the family planning program that he once said he supported, Gov. Deukmejian yielded to overwhelming odds and allowed funding for the program to be restored.

A lot of damage has been done in the meantime, both to clinics and services that were shut down — clinics whose staffs will be hard to reassemble — and to countless poor women who have gone without the medical care and the counseling that, for them, this program alone provided. No one knows how many additional abortions will take place this year and how many unwanted babies will be born because those women could not easily get contraceptives or other family planning help, but it's hard to believe that there won't be a good many.

What's really been ironic about the governor's stance is that while he was resisting the family planning program because it used state money to provide abortion counseling, the state was paying for thousands of abortions through Medi-Cal. The most promising thing the state offered for reducing that number — and for preventing venereal disease and any number of other serious medical problems — was precisely this program.

The governor was correct when he said that his responsibility is to "act on an agenda of issues affecting the greatest number of our residents rather than establishing the highest number on a gubernatorial scoreboard." But that wise conclusion seems not to have hit him until he confronted the certain embarrassment of either suffering his first veto override or of exposing his Republican loyalists in the Assembly to the need to defend something so illogical that it bordered on the indefensible. For seven years his administration has been trying to harass, undercut and finally kill what, by general acknowledgment, is one of the most humane and cost-effective programs that the state offers. That this campaign now seems to be over is to be welcomed; that it took all this time, and caused so much damage along the way, is inexcusable.

The Oregonian

Portland, Oregon, October 25, 1990

Oregon knows about hunger. Year after year, 400,000 of its residents must reach out a hand for emergency food. Half of them are children; most of the rest are the working poor.

This picture of hunger in the state was produced by a survey conducted by the Oregon Food Bank, in conjunction with Oregon State University and its extension service, Linn Benton Food Share and the Portland St. Vincent de Paul Society, at 18 locations where emergency food is provided.

The problem is persistent. The need stays about the same regardless of general economic conditions. But supply has slipped. A huge drop in federal emergency food is the reason. While private donations have climbed from 6 million pounds to 9 million pounds in just three years, federal contributions sank by 8 million pounds. The Food Bank and its partners have less food now than they did three years ago to combat a problem of the same size.

That much is known about hunger in Oregon. But Oregon does not know enough about hunger.

In a step that was both practical and compassionate, the 1989 Legislature created a task force to study hunger and recommend a state policy to overcome it. But in a less practical and compassionate follow-through, the same Legislature did not give it the money needed for the sort of thorough survey that enabled the state of Washington to fashion a hunger strategy.

The assessment of needs announced by the participating organizations recently should be helpful to the Legislature. It shows the number of requests and the amount of food needed to meet them.

But the Legislature also ought to know the needs not met, requests not made, malnutrition that falls short of outright hunger. It should analyze the effect of rising housing costs on food supplies, for the rent may be paid at the expense of groceries.

The Legislature still needs a statewide survey before it can develop a statewide policy that will put adequate food on all tables in Oregon.

Portland, Oregon, March 20, 1991

The Oregon Health Sciences University has undertaken a commendable effort to open its doors to some dental, nursing and medical students who have health-care experience but don't fit the mold that faculty admissions committees tend to prefer. One of the first persons chosen by this non-traditional acceptance procedure was Elizabeth Hatfield Keller, daughter of Sen. Mark Hatfield, R-Ore.

Was this selection two years ago coincidence or preferential treatment for the daughter of a political benefactor?

The question arises because of the recent disclosure that the former president of the University of South Carolina gave Hatfield $9,300 worth of gifts and arranged a scholarship from a special fund for one of Hatfield's sons while Hatfield was chairman of the Senate Appropriations Committee.

Keller, a nurse, and three other medical school applicants with health-care experience were chosen outside of the normal admissions-committee process under a policy formulated by OHSU President Peter O. Kohler and agreed to by the deans of the medical, dental and nursing schools. The purpose was to broaden the student body base to include older students with health-care experience, especially those interested in rural health care.

University officials say that that had been one of Kohler's stated objectives even while he was under consideration for the presidency and a policy he was quick to push when he arrived on campus. That's a valid goal; even within the medical professions, there are worries about an overemphasis on technical prowess and shortages of medical professionals in rural areas.

OHSU's problem, however, is that in bypassing the established faculty admissions committees, the university opened itself to allegations of preferential treatment — whether or not it existed. The situation looks the same either way, and the university, at the least, looks insensitive to appearances. Every applicant rejected for medical school that year probably assumes now that the selection process — always somewhat subjective — also was rigged.

The university now can do little to correct that impression. The lesson for the future, though, is that where valid considerations dictate bypassing the normal selection process, clear and public criteria are needed to remove any doubts that the result is fair and merit-based. That's doubly true where any allegation of favoritism could arise.

Although procedures need to be clearer, OHSU should retain its interest in diversifying its student body and in addressing medical needs of Oregon's rural areas. It would be a pity if one controversial admission or procedural shortcomings undercut that effort.

Portland, Oregon, November 14, 1990

When legislators return to the unfinished business of a state policy on hunger, they will find that they do not have to devote scarce money to creating a system for getting food to the needy.

A thorough distribution network already exists, courtesy of the private sector.

The Oregon Food Bank is the central agency of a structure that includes 19 regional coordinators and 600 local helping agencies reaching out to the hungry in all 36 counties. If it has food on hand and knows where the hungry are, the network can get food to anyone in need anywhere in Oregon.

For the most part, it has food, although the cutback in federal emergency supplies has made the task a difficult challenge at times. Nonetheless, the system gets more than 15 million tons of emergency rations each year to 400,000 hungry Oregonians.

The food bank succeeds because of individual support of food drives and the cooperation of many corporations and business associations. Grocers and restaurants make surpluses available. Farm groups provide commodities. Canning and freezing facilities are donated. Flour is mixed with other ingredients for easily prepared meals.

Legislators will find all of this in place, along with food stamps, school lunches and breakfasts and a program for mothers and infants, before they have designed a state policy on hunger.

The 1989 Legislature had the right idea when it created a task force to study hunger and recommend a program. But it was not given money to do the job.

The food bank can tell the Legislature a great deal about the needs that are met. Not known are the needs unmet because people do not seek help. Inadequately understood is undernourishment that falls short of hunger. Food needs also should be anticipated when economic changes threaten.

It should not take much for the Legislature to complete analysis of need as a necessary step for legislation. It will find most of the elements of an effective system already working, just waiting for a policy to go with them.

TULSA WORLD

Tulsa, Oklahoma, August 7, 1992

OREGON, the first state to try to get a handle on rising Medicaid expenses by rationing services, may have been handed another first. It may be the first state to run afoul of the Americans with Disabilities Act.

The Secretary of Health and Human Services rejected Oregon's rationing plan because he felt the rankings were based on the premise that "the value of the life of a person with a disability is less than the value of a life of a person without a disability."

Oregon went through an agonizing and highly politicized process of devising a list of 709 medical procedures according to their costs and benefits. Those ranking below No. 587 would not be covered by Medicaid.

In general, illnesses not covered are those that generally improve on their own or are better treated at home and extremely expensive procedures such as incurable cancer, liver transplants for alcoholics, the final stages of AIDS and extremely low birthweight babies.

Oregon's plan would allow the state to add 120,000 uninsured people to its Medicaid rolls.

The HEW secretary has the authority to grant exceptions for experimental projects which do not conform to Medicaid law requirements, hence Oregon's petition.

Through leadership and political will, officials had made tough decisions to spread the budget to cover the maximum number of people. No one liked the rankings, but at least the process acknowledged that funds are limited and priorities had to be set — a difficult political process.

Oregon was trying to tackle a serious health care delivery problem. It deserves to be allowed to pursue the experiment. We all might learn something.

The Philadelphia Inquirer

Philadelphia, Pennsylvania, August 19, 1992

The Bush administration's rhetorical promotion of states as laboratories for social reform came to a screeching halt recently in Oregon.

After years of debate — and with amazingly broad consensus — the state had proposed rationing some kinds of medical care. Realizing that its public health dollars were not unlimited, it proposed to halt high-expense, low-benefit procedures, and use the savings to provide basic care to some 450,000 Oregonians who had no health coverage at all.

The plan would have ruled out heroic measures for extremely low-weight infants (under 18 ounces), or patients in the final stages of AIDS or cancer. It would not have paid for a kidney transplant for an alcoholic who hadn't stopped drinking. The program sought to ensure, on the other hand, that treatments with proven effectiveness — such as care for expectant mothers and newborn babies — was widely and easily available.

Since the plan involved Medicaid, which is federally funded, it required a waiver from the federal government to cut some services. But since there hadn't been any audible negative rumblings from the White House during the five years the plan was being formulated, state officials, including Gov. Barbara Roberts, figured they would get waived.

Then, a few months ago, Sen. Al Gore, who would become the Democratic vice-presidential candidate, criticized the plan. The Children's Defense Fund was soon to follow; then the Roman Catholic Church. That combination made the Oregon experiment a hot potato, but it was still a surprise when the plan was summarily rejected by the Bush administration on the dubious grounds that it would violate the new Americans With Disabilities Act.

The result was that a courageous experiment that had been the subject of lengthy public examination was stopped dead in its tracks, while angry state officials prepared to reargue their case. The plan's provisions *are* controversial; dealing with such matters honestly and openly will inevitably be controversial. But they can't be wished away.

Critics ask good questions. Why ration by procedure instead of by individual case? Why not restrict the profits of care providers, instead of the care provided? The answer, we suppose, is that *this* was how Oregon chose to shape its coverage — with bipartisan political support — and the White House doesn't have a better plan.

If the national health care debate is to move beyond the crude name-calling stage, the country is going to have to grapple with the limits that Oregon's plan confronts. There will be organized interests and advocacy groups that will feel the pinch, and who will scream. But in the end, it will be necessary to face the twin problems of unrestrained costs and unevaluated care.

That will take a president — a *national coach*, in the words of former Surgeon General C. Everett Koop — who rolls up his sleeves to build the critical political mass that can stand tall to the opposition.

Mr. Bush's cowardly retreat from the Oregon challenge is hardly cause for confidence that he is that man.

The Hartford Courant

Hartford, Connecticut, August 22, 1992

Oregon's pioneering health-care rationing proposal, although not perfect, ought to be tested as part of a broad effort to solve America's health-care crisis. The Bush administration, which rejected the plan recently, fortunately has asked for a revised version.

Under the Oregon plan, Medicaid would be expanded to include everyone in that state below the poverty line. The plan also would cover some high-risk people without insurance and would require private employers to provide health insurance to uncovered workers.

To pay for the 50 percent expansion of the Medicaid rolls, the plan would rank 709 medical conditions and treatments in terms of their costs and benefits. Oregon would have enough Medicaid money, under its revenue projections, to pay for the top 587 conditions.

The ranking was based, in part, on public opinion. It's supposed to take into account the quality of life after treatment as well as the cost of care. Expensive cancer treatments that add a few agonizing months of survival would not be covered, for example, while childhood immunizations would be.

Predictably, the rationing has drawn protests. Critics say the plan devalues the lives of some newborns and disabled people by limiting treatments for them. They object to the fact that treatment of extremely low-weight premature babies or some people with severe brain injuries would not be covered by Medicaid. Advocates for the disabled oppose any scheme that downgrades long-term care of permanently disabled people.

This imperfect attempt to set limits displeased the Bush administration. The White House claimed the plan would violate the Americans with Disabilities Act. Some rankings, it feared, would put more value on the life of someone without disabilities than someone with them.

Oregon cannot reform Medicaid by itself because the federal government pays half the costs of the program, imposes standards and requires approval for changes proposed by states. But Oregon deserves credit for trying.

Medicaid, whose costs have skyrocketed in every state, is only one slice of a health-care system. Other parts of the system also need reform.

In asking for a rewrite of the plan, President Bush appears to be putting off a final decision until after Election Day. There is no easy way to control costs. The key lies in fair and reasonable limits on everyone, including those on Medicare.

The Detroit News
Detroit, Michigan, August 7, 1992

Nearly everybody agrees that the U.S. health care system is a mess, desperately in need of reform, with costs soaring out of control and tens of millions of people lacking basic health insurance.

Yet when Oregon carefully drafted a difficult reform plan for Medicaid — with remarkable agreement among Democrats and Republicans — the plan was rejected this week by the U.S. Department of Health and Human Services on the grounds that it violated federal law. The ruling makes no sense and may have dealt a serious blow to other state attempts at reform.

Medicaid, a federal-state partnership, is supposed to help the poor, the elderly, the disabled, and children from low-income families. In actual practice, it covers fewer than half the poor and even those it covers do not get all necessary medical services.

Utah and other states wrestle constantly with this problem of trying to provide increasingly expensive medical care to growing numbers of uninsured poor people without breaking the state budget.

The Oregon plan sought to cut back some medical services to the 230,000 Oregonians covered by Medicaid so that the remaining 120,000 not covered could also get basic Medicaid benefits.

In order to allocate dollars to cover all the poor, Oregon officials did a cost-benefit analysis of 709 medical procedures and ranked them according to their effectiveness, cost and quality-of-life factors. Only the top 587 services would be covered.

Highest priority was given to those medical services involving primary care, preventive care, prenatal care,

life-threatening conditions, injuries, heart bypass operations and most organ transplants. Lower priority was given to those treatments where medical success is least likely but often enormously expensive. These included severe brain injury, end-stage AIDS, liver transplants for end-stage alcoholics and all-out efforts to save premature babies weighing less than 18 ounces and born before 23 weeks of gestation.

The state said it would go as far down the list for all the poor each year as was possible with the available money — in effect, a rationing system. But everybody was covered for the basics.

Opponents argued that treatment distinctions inevitably would be based on judgments about a patient's future quality of life and that care would be rationed for poor people but not others.

The federal government apparently bought that argument, saying that the proposed reform would violate the Americans With Disabilities Act by discriminating against some kinds of ailments.

In other words, everybody on Medicaid must have access to the latest and best medical treatment, without regard to their chances for recovery. Since Oregon — like every state — cannot afford that, the 120,000 uninsured poor will likely remain outside Medicaid coverage.

If cost-benefit analysis cannot be taken into account in using scarce Medicaid resources, then the only other alternative is for coverage to be cut for everybody — exactly the opposite of what Oregon was trying to accomplish.

With that kind of federal "help," no wonder the health care crisis just keeps getting worse.

The Providence Journal
Providence, Rhode Island, August 4, 1992

America must reform its health-care system — for the sake of public health and for the nation's international economic competitiveness. And next year will probably see a big push in that direction, regardless of who wins the White House.

Meanwhile, the states are the laboratories. Hawaii, Vermont and Oregon provide the most dramatic examples of new ways of providing coverage. We need to see how their plans work. That's why the Oregon experiment deserves a waiver of federal Medicaid rules, which it needs to get underway.

But a stumbling block has just appeared in the form of the Americans with Disabilities Act. Gail Wilensky, President Bush's health policy adviser, says that the White House has asked the Justice Department to determine whether the Oregon program, which would expand health care for the state's poorest residents, but limit certain procedures believed to be particularly cost-ineffective, might illegally discriminate against people with certain disabilities.

So now Washington is expected to either withhold the waiver of the Medicaid regulations until legal defects are corrected, or grant approval conditioned on steps to remedy potential legal problems. We hope the White House chooses the latter. The Oregon plan richly deserves a tryout.

The Bush administration believes that patients shouldn't be denied care simply because their treatment is expensive or because an anonymous official has decided that their lives are not worth saving. Apparently, the President has been deeply affected by such people as Robert Powell of the National Right to Life Committee, who asserted in a meeting with Mr. Bush a few months ago that he would be dead if the Oregon plan had been in effect when he was born; Mr. Powell had a malignant tumor that attacked

his spinal cord when he was five months old. The President, for his part, lost a young daughter to leukemia.

The Oregon plan has adopted a list of 709 procedures that would be paid for by the state, ranked by priority. This obviously involves rationing, especially when it comes to the refusal to finance some expensive treatments for seemingly terminal illnesses.

Mr. Powell's concern is understandable. But to complain about rationing is disingenuous, to say the least. The fact is that rationing on the basis of the ability to pay, and on age, is already pervasive. Since no economy can provide every sick or injured person everything he or she wants or needs, rationing is always inevitable.

Oregon's health planners have decided it would be fairer to provide basic health services to everyone below the federal poverty line, while ranking procedures in order of maximum benefit at the least cost. The rankings range from the most urgent, in which a single treatment prevents death and returns a patient to full health, to the least urgent, in which it is unclear if treatment does any good. And the Oregon approach commendably attaches much importance to preventive care — which helps reduce the number of such painful choices.

The program takes some big steps toward providing many currently unprotected citizens with basic health care, while applying some reasonable cost controls. The White House ought to approve the plan for now, while watching carefully that groups do not suffer illegal discrimination. The point is that it's better that many people have access to good medical care than that a relatively few people have their every medical wish fulfilled.

THE LINCOLN STAR
Lincoln, Nebraska, August 14, 1992

If the nation is to find a road to adequate health care for all citizens, our leaders will have to show more courage than did the Bush administration this month when it rejected the Oregon plan.

That rejection guarantees that this politically charged issue will be delayed until after the November election. That kind of timidity will not cure the nation's growing inequities in health care.

In fact what we need are more experiments, bold experiments like the Oregon plan.

States could become testing grounds for the plethora of national health care ideas. Then we could see the results in real life and understand the trade-offs in concrete human terms.

Oregon did its homework. Beginning in 1983 the state assembled doctors, businessmen and labor leaders for marathon discussions about how to distribute the state's limited resources.

They built elaborate computer models to help rank medical procedures by cost effectiveness.

They held 47 town meetings to thrash out the rules by which medical priorities would be set.

OREGON'S PLAN was a calculated trade-off. The plan required most businesses to insure permanent employees and dependents.

Medicaid (the system that provides health care for some low-income Americans) would cover the rest. In fact Ore-

gon wanted to bypass federal rules that make 120,000 Oregon residents ineligible. These are mostly women and children who earn too much to qualify for Medicaid coverage, but who have no insurance.

To pay for that expanded coverage, Oregon proposed to limit what Medicaid would cover.

At the heart of the system is a list of 709 medical conditions ranked in order of seriousness and responsiveness to treatment for bacterial pneumonia (1) to anencephaly (709).

The state determined how much it could afford, then drew a line — at 587 (inflammation of the esophagus.) The state Medicaid program would cover everything above that line and nothing below it.

THE PLAN had its flaws and its critics, from the Roman Catholic Church to the Children's Defense Fund.

Medicaid would pay for breast cancer treatment but not reconstruction after a mastectomy. It would cover a liver transplant due to cirrhosis unrelated to alcohol but no liver transplants for alcoholic cirrhosis. It would provide expensive life support and life-saving care for premature infants weighing 1.1 pounds or more but only "comfort care" for smaller preemies, with the least chance of survival.

The president backed off in the face of criticism of this experiment.

That timidity did nothing to help Americans face a future of tough choices. Rationing is inevitable unless we intend to spend the bulk of our national gross product on medical care.

Today we ration by circumstance. The insured get the best and most expensive medical care in the world. The uninsured, and particularly those who don't meet Medicaid rules, scrounge for health care.

Oregon's thoughtful approach to rationing is one alternative for the future. Oregon should be allowed to experiment.

St. Petersburg Times
St. Petersburg, Florida, August 6, 1992

The Oregon Medicaid reform plan is unacceptable for at least three reasons: It targets only one class of Americans, the poor. It forces residents of one state to accept a degree of control over medical decisions not experienced by other U.S. citizens. It fails to assure the disabled that their hard-won access to equal services would be fully protected.

The Bush administration Monday withheld permission for the Oregon experiment, and rightly so. Medicaid was designed as a federal/state cost-sharing program to help equalize access to health care for the poor, not to make it more unequal. To do less would be to create a population of medically needy migrants.

Under the Oregon plan, for instance, aggressive treatment for metastasized cancer with less than a 10 percent survival rate is item 688 on the state's list of 709 medical conditions. Since the Oregon Legislature has only budgeted money for the first 587 items on the list, a Medicaid patient with such a condition would have to establish residency elsewhere or do without.

The White House has already made a serious mistake in this direction by approving a New Jersey experiment that will deny aid to new children born into a family on welfare. Benefit levels vary enough from state to state without excluding whole categories of citizens by accident of birth, illness or disability.

That said, Oregon officials should be commended for trying hard to stretch an inadequate umbrella over all who need protection. That's a tougher challenge than either side in the presidential debate seems ready to face. The Oregon plan would place demands on insurers and employers, something President Bush, for one, has been unwilling to do.

The Oregon reforms would offer more preventive care to more people, but there would be cutbacks elsewhere. In a recent report, *Times* medical reporter Carol Gentry summarized the typical conditions that would be excluded:

"Gets better whether you treat it or not

> **Any plan for health care reform that is both equitable and realistic will require a radical rethinking of costs and goals.**

(the common cold, mononucleosis, the flu.)

"Can be treated just as well at home (hives, diaper rash, sprains, canker sores.)

"Does not present a threat to health (infertility, benign skin tumors, goiters, scars, crooked teeth, varicose veins, the absence of a breast after cancer surgery.)

"Won't get significantly better with medical or surgical treatment (severe brain injury, obesity, end-stage AIDS and cancer.)" Under the new guidelines, patients with end-stage AIDS or cancers with less than a 10 percent survival rate would be treated in non-aggressive ways aimed at easing pain.

Critics of the Oregon plan are overwhelmed by the ethical implications of such decision-making. Under the current system, however, even people with expensive insurance plans are often required to get second opinions and to accept the fact that certain procedures are simply not covered.

At the same time, many terminally ill but well-insured people are subtly coerced into trying just one more treatment; the popularity of living wills demonstrates how many fear being placed on life support when there is no hope of recovery.

Studies show that the dollars spent on extreme measures in the last year of life often outweigh the sum of earlier health care expenditures. Most Americans favor some form of national health care plan. Any plan that is both equitable and realistic will require a radical rethinking of costs and goals.

Pittsburgh Post-Gazette
Pittsburgh, Pennsylvania, May 9, 1988

With Gov. Michael Dukakis well on his way to the Democratic presidential nomination, the recent passage of a universal health insurance bill under his leadership in Massachusetts should attract more attention than ever.

The bill that made Massachusetts the first state to guarantee health insurance to all residents was aimed at the 600,000 of Massachusetts' 5.8 million residents who are uninsured. The measure would gradually introduce, over the next four years, health coverage for those who are uninsured, both the employed and the unemployed.

Uninsured citizens would be required to pay for their insurance based on how much money they earn. While the new law does not require an employer to offer insurance, its provisions make refusal to do so expensive.

An unemployed person with any kind of income would pay on a reduced basis. But no one would go uninsured. The cost to the state is estimated at $600 million through 1992, but some studies indicate the cost would be much higher.

Gov. Dukakis has been making universal health insurance a part of his presidential campaign. The Massachusetts plan will be closely watched to see if it can be replicated in other, less prosperous states, let alone at the national level. A bill introduced by Sen. Edward M. Kennedy last May that would mandate that employers with 11 or more workers provide a minimum level of health insurance is awaiting action by the full Senate.

But what seems to be developing is an alternative to a government-run national health insurance system — the "socialized medicine" that was defeated 30 years ago in Congress by a coalition led by the physicians in the American Medical Association. (The United States and South Africa are the only major industrialized nations without a government-operated health insurance plan.)

Instead, over the years businesses, often prodded by unions, and the medical and hospital professions have developed private insurance plans that cover a large proportion of Americans. Government plans — Medicare for the elderly and Medicaid for the poor — also partially fill the gap.

But, according to a 1985 Census Bureau estimate, there still are 37.2 million Americans without health insurance. It is on behalf of this group that the Dukakis and Kennedy initiatives are intended.

A curious twist is evolving. Business groups in general long have inveighed against more government programs, with socialized medicine a particular phobia. They have urged privatization in many spheres. Now they may become hoisted on their own petard, despite their protests at the added costs the Massachusetts law and the Kennedy bill will mean, especially for small business.

For, in reality, the Dukakis and Kennedy initiatives are moves away from government medicine and toward letting the private sector carry more of the burden. The Reagan administration's enthusiasm for cutting the amount of money available for domestic programs may unwittingly accelerate the process.

That is, legislators increasingly may find ways to push more of the burden for programs demanded by the public directly on the private sector, rather than indirectly through taxes. That is why the passage of the Massachusetts universal health insurance bill is so significant.

The Boston Globe
Boston, Massachusetts, April 21, 1988

Massachusetts sets a new course for the nation at noon today when Governor Dukakis signs into law the first health security act that grants basic health insurance to everyone in the state.

Though it will take four years to take full effect, as various groups gain coverage on a time-phased schedule, the law marks a turning point in the way this state – and in time the entire country – offers people insurance against ravaging medical costs and against the indignity of medical begging.

Already the staff of Senate Ways and Means chairman Patricia McGovern, the principal architect and guardian of the bill, is deluged with calls from other states inquiring into the law's specifics. Should Dukakis win the presidency, he has pledged to give top priority to a national version of health insurance.

His campaign championing of such a program strikes a responsive chord across the country. After decades of delay and bitter experience with the historically haphazard pattern of health insurance – lost when a job is lost or unavailable on the job – Americans are saying that they want universal, uninterrupted coverage. And they want it now.

Massachusetts' model of universal health insurance is exceptionally sound and reasonable.

It spreads an umbrella of coverage over 600,000 Bay Staters who previously have been shut out. They are largely the working poor, low-income, self-employed persons or those working where no health insurance is offered; disabled adults, and children in families who cannot afford to take jobs because they would lose their Medicaid eligibility; unemployed workers; and college students whose coverage usually ends at age 18.

A new state agency, the Department of Medical Security will act as a broker – the conduit through which applicants can buy into a basic health plan at group rates. Premiums can be subsidized by the state for those who cannot afford full price.

DMS also will act as an overseer of the program – evaluating plans, bargaining for low rates, monitoring usage. The agency also will study the state's experience, as each succeeding group is covered, to apply the lessons learned to the next group.

The costs of setting the plan in motion begin at nearly $8 million this year and stretch to $104 million by 1992. While there is some uncertainty about what the cost of maintaining the program will be, wisely there are cost-adjustive mechanisms built into the bill.

To encourage businesses to offer employees health insurance for the first time, tax benefits are also offered for the first two years. Companies that still resist making health insurance available by 1992 will pay a surcharge of 12 percent of the first $14,000 in wages of each employee – or $1680 a year – to counterbalance the cost of a basic family health plan for that employee through the state program.

Small businesses with fewer than six employees are exempt, thought it is felt marketplace competition for workers will influence their acceptance of insurance as a job benefit.

Large-scale containment of cost is addressed in a key section of the law that will help close unneeded hospitals which have a low volume of patients. Operating these excess facilities has been long known to be financially wasteful.

A commission will be established to help communities where these hospitals are located to determine their health needs and how they can be met. The commission also will help communities decide what better use could be made of the hospitals – housing, nursing homes, day care or a mixture of such uses.

No one can yet foretell the long-range benefits that may come from Massachusetts new health security act. No one can estimate the monetary savings or the health gains when good medical practice, prevention and early treatment, replace the current medical services used by those without insurance – irregular and impersonal care on the most expensive terms at emergency rooms.

Of all the industrialized nations, only the United States and South Africa have not assured their people health insurance. Massachusetts must now show the rest of the country, that it can be done, it can work, and work well.

The health security act is more than a step of historic significance; it is that most important of all steps for social progress – the first one in a new direction.

Los Angeles Times
Los Angeles, California, April 15, 1988

Massachusetts has set a constructive example for the nation with its adoption of legislation mandating basic health insurance for virtually all workers in the state.

Under provisions of the new law, all employers with more than five workers will be required to provide basic health-insurance coverage or pay a premium on their wages that will be used by the state to ensure the protection. The plan will be phased in, to be fully operational in 1992. When it comes on line, its net cost to the state for the first year, including some special funding for hospital improvements, will be $195 million, a small fraction of a total state budget of $11 billion.

In Massachusetts, an estimated 10% of the population is without health insurance. That is lower than in many states, including California. As in most states, the majority of those without insurance are employed, but at low wages, or are the dependents of the working poor. A particular advantage of the Massachusetts plan is that it is expected to encourage employment for people on welfare, who now cannot afford to take low-wage jobs because they would lose the health insurance available to them on welfare.

The action in Massachusetts has taken on national implications because of the presidential candidacy of the state's Democratic governor, Michael S. Dukakis. The bill is the handiwork of a leading Democrat, Patricia McGovern, chairman of the Senate Ways and Means Committee, but it has been strongly supported by Dukakis. Indeed, because of his close association with it, Republicans in the state senate who had earlier supported the measure voted in opposition on the final vote.

It is the second significant universal health-care proposal to emerge from Massachusetts. A similar measure to mandate health insurance on a national basis has been introduced by Sen. Edward Kennedy (D-Mass.) and has passed its first committee hurdle in the U.S. Senate. Both measures address an extraordinary gap in the American health-care system that has left more than 30 million persons without any protection. Recognition of the problem is growing in Washington, fortunately, for the best solution would be a national program rather than attempting, state by state, to solve the problem.

The Massachusetts legislation uses as its insurance base ·a cost of $1,680 a year, thought to be enough to ensure basic family health-insurance coverage. Employers who fail to provide health insurance would be taxed at 12% of the employee's first $14,000 in earnings, equal to $1,680. If the employee earns less, the tax would be 12% of the actual earnings, with the state making up the difference from the general fund to meet the basic insurance cost. Employers paying for costlier programs would not have to pay the surcharge.

Opponents have argued that the program will be catastrophic, ending the economic boom that Massachusetts is now enjoying. Sponsors of the legislation argue the contrary, confident that the new benefit will help attract even more people to meet labor shortages created by the boom. We think the sponsors are correct.

The Record
Hackensack, New Jersey, April 17, 1988

Massachusetts, a leader in welfare reform, has now emerged as an innovator in providing health insurance. A legislative vote this week made Massachusetts the first state to guarantee that every resident, employed and unemployed, be insured against health-care costs. It's a bold and commendable experiment. If it succeeds, it offers other states a way to deal with one of the most serious social problems facing America today.

The Massachusetts plan also offers some insights into Gov. Michael Dukakis's support for national health care if he's elected president. It would cover all 600,000 state residents who now lack insurance. Companies with six or more employees would have to offer coverage or pay a surcharge of $1,680 per employee. Employers providing coverage could deduct the cost of coverage from the surcharge, which would be a boon to companies presently offering health insurance. The unemployed as well as workers in companies employing fewer than six would be guaranteed coverage by the state; those with income would pay part of the cost.

The present health insurance system, in Massachusetts and in other states, is widely recognized to be intolerable. Across the country, as many as 37 million Americans have no health insurance to cushion the cost of a hospital stay, a visit to the doctor, or a trip to the dentist for their kids. Two-thirds of these people have jobs or are dependents of workingmen and women.

The failure to provide affordable health insurance makes no sense financially. It exerts a constant pressure on people in low-end jobs such as sweeping floors to quit work and go on welfare, which would qualify them and their families for health coverage under Medicaid. Government winds up paying much more. A National Academy of Sciences study estimates that every dollar spent on prenatal care for pregnant women saves $3 in medical costs for babies born with mental and physical defects.

The basic policy of forcing all but the elderly and the very poor to depend on the willingness of private employers for insurance no longer makes sense, if it ever did. More and more Americans are contract or part-time workers not covered by employer policies. A quarter of all women of child-bearing age have no health insurance. That helps explain why America's infant mortality rate is one of the highest in the industrialized world.

There are certainly a lot of unanswered questions about the Massachusetts experiment. It imposes a new cost on small employers, who will have to choose between a surcharge of $1,680 per employee or an insurance program that could cost that much or more. If small businesses start closing down or leaving Massachusetts, the program will have to be modified, which would probably require more state money. And the overall costs of the program are hard to calculate. Estimates for total cost over the next four years vary from $550 million to $1.2 billion. A prediction by one legislator that the program will bankrupt the commonwealth seems frivolous. But costs could go high enough to force the program to be redesigned and scaled down.

Some health-care experts say, however, that there's an excellent chance the program will do what it's supposed to do. And if Massachusetts can produce an affordable program that means no one will have to do without medical care, it will be a splendid achievement indeed. State governments are supposed to be, in the words of the late Robert La Follette of Wisconsin, laboratories for change. Massachusetts is turning out to be an unusually productive laboratory.

Newsday
New York City, New York, May 2, 1988

Like one end of a tottering seesaw, health problems inevitably shoot up when health insurance coverage goes down. Thus the more than 37 million Americans who aren't covered are less apt to see a doctor, more likely to die early, and their babies have a slimmer chance of surviving through the first year than those born to insured mothers.

Massachusetts has taken a significant step toward flattening out that tilted slide into bad health. Under the leadership of Gov. Michael Dukakis, the Bay State became the first in the country to guarantee all residents health insurance. By 1992, most private employers will have to "play or pay" — either insure their full-time workers or contribute to a statewide fund that will help subsidize insurance premiums for those not covered.

Uninsured workers from the 49 other states should hope that progress not only marches onward, but southward — to Washington, D.C. There, Sen. Edward Kennedy (D-Mass.) and Rep. Henry Waxman (D-Calif.) have introduced legislation requiring most private employers to provide health coverage for all employees who work at least 17½ hours a week. This would take care of 23 million people who are too poor to afford insurance but still don't qualify for Medicaid.

Although the Kennedy-Waxman plan wouldn't add one cent to the federal deficit, the mere mention of a measure of universal health insurance still gives some conservatives the shakes. Yet the U.S. is the only democracy that fails to provide its citizens with health insurance. Such neglect is not only nasty and brutish but expensive. Uninsured families often delay visits to the doctor, which allows their health to deteriorate and makes care more difficult and expensive. And as distressed as some small businessess may be by the added cost of insuring workers, larger firms are fed up with rocketing medical bills, higher insurance premiums and taxes that result from absorbing the costs of charity care.

Higher payrolls may cause some firms to *initially* cut back on minimum-wage workers, but such trimming should fade over time, says the Congressional Budget Office. Besides, bringing new people into the health-care system will surely create new health-care jobs.

Congress should follow Massachusetts' lead and begin treating the problems of America's uninsured by passing this bill.

The Boston Globe
Boston, Massachusetts, June 22, 1991

The social programs instituted in Massachusetts in the early 1970s are often hailed as models for less restrictive treatment of the mentally ill and retarded, and of juvenile offenders – hailed, if not always copied.

Now, one of the most dramatic reforms of that era – the closing of the state's training schools for juveniles and their replacement with a network of community-based treatment programs – is to be adopted in the Soviet Union.

One of the architects of the social reforms instituted under former Gov. Francis W. Sargent, was his chief secretary, Albert Kramer, who is now judge of the Quincy District Court. Last week, Kramer brought officials from the Soviet Ministry of Internal Affairs to Quincy to see the court's treatment and counseling programs for juvenile alcohol and drug abusers.

The Soviet Union has 4.5 million alcoholics, many of them juveniles. At present, the juveniles convicted of alcoholism are sent to child-labor camps, a practice that the Soviets want to change.

"The most special thing we have is our children," said Gen. Boris Voronov, who headed the delegation. Rehabilitation, he said, "is more humane than throwing people in prison."

"When you punish a youngster," he said in a comment that could have been made by such Sargent-era reform heroes as Kramer or Youth Services Commissioner Jerome Miller, "are you punishing him for not being an adult?"

While in Quincy, the Soviets signed contracts and agreements with a number of treatment and counseling programs to provide expert help in setting up similar programs. "They want to unlock the doors of their labor camps into a system like ours," Kramer said.

And as Massachusetts edges toward bringing back the juvenile-training schools, there may be some people from the community-based programs available to help the Soviets head in the other direction.

St. Paul Pioneer Press & Dispatch
St. Paul, Minnesota, May 15, 1988

One thing's for sure about the Massachusetts experiment with universal health insurance, described in last Sunday's Focus section: It's going to be an extraordinarily useful model.

It's plain wrong for 37 million Americans to be without health insurance protection. Something can and should be done about it; as that consensus builds, this first statewide program is bound to prove instructive.

The Massachusetts plan, recently signed into law by Gov. Michael Dukakis, requires all but the smallest employers to choose between providing health insurance benefits for their workers, or paying into a state insurance pool. The pool offers affordable insurance to uninsured workers and helps the unemployed buy coverage for themselves.

As the program is put into place over the next four years, the development of insurance-plan options attractive to small employers may well prove pivotal to success. New options are badly needed, because small businesses now pay up to three times as much for health-insurance benefit packages as their giant corporate neighbors.

It makes good sense to give incentives for businesses with few workers, or workers who are in low-paying or part-time jobs, to offer an insurance plan rather than pay into the pool.

■ It would keep most of the insurance business in the private sector, building on a familiar, existing, ongoing system.

Alex Leary/Staff Artist

■ It would hold down the size of the state pool. Keeping the number drawing from the pool as small as possible is important, since employer contributions will need supplements from tax money to ensure stability. More than two-thirds of Americans without health insurance are either employed, or dependents of the employed.

■ It would give virtually every business in the state a stake in keeping health-care costs within bounds.

One of the most attractive aspects of health insurance for everyone is that it gives a powerful work incentive to a sizable number of people: those who rightly fear losing Medicaid or Medicare if they begin an entry-level, no-benefits job. Think, for example, of the sense of worth and dignity employment would bring to the disabled, or to those with a disabled child.

Do problems lurk in the Massachusetts plan? Yes, at least one hefty one: It will raise the annual cost of hiring every worker. That could have a dual effect. It could mean a cutback in jobs or hours for some. It could mean that the state would lose a competitive edge with its neighbors if the rise in the cost of doing business in Massachusetts were not offset in other ways.

That competitive point makes a strong argument for an eventual nationwide health insurance plan.

Sen. Dave Durenberger, D-Minn., is a strong believer in universal access to medical insurance. He prefers to achieve it in logical pieces, rather than by statewide mandates like the Massachusetts initiative. One bill he has pending, for example, would guarantee health care to poverty-level pregnant women all over the country — a measure that makes enormous humane and economic sense, since it would help lower the incidence of high-risk, low-birthweight babies.

What matters is that, one way or another, the nation is inching toward health care for all its people.

A half-century ago, Supreme Court Justice Louis Brandeis said, "It is one of the happy incidents of our democracy that a single, courageous state may, if its citizens choose, serve as a laboratory for the rest of the nation."

Let that serve as benediction on the unfolding Massachusetts plan.

The Evening Gazette
Worcester, Massachusetts, January 13, 1989

Fiscal and political realities are catching up with the "first-in-the-nation" universal health insurance scheme that was a cornerstone of the Dukakis presidential campaign. The Legislature should move quickly to kill the ill-conceived plan and send it back to the drawing board.

In the heat of the presidential campaign last year, Gov. Michael Dukakis managed to hammer together a coalition of support for the insurance plan by loading on enough goodies to satisfy just about everyone. The only exception was the Massachusetts taxpayer, who was kept in the dark about its ultimate price tag.

The sweetener for the hospitals was Dukakis' promise to pick up about $100 million they would be losing over the next two years due to federal Medicare cutbacks. He also promised that the state would pay the cost of the hospitals' "free-care pool."

The state's precarious finances have made that impossible, and industry officials are irate about having been duped. Says the president of the Massachusetts Hospital Association: "The entire hospital community shares a sense of betrayal."

The perplexing explanation Human Services Secretary Philip Johnston gave for reneging is unlikely to placate hospital officials. "It's not that we won't make the payments," he said. "It's that the money doesn't exist."

Tangled rhetoric aside, however, Johnston is right. Closing the state's $600 million budget gap for the rest of this fiscal year has become the Dukakis administration's top priority, as well it should be.

The implications for the universal health insurance scheme are clear. The plan, hastily slapped together and passed without benefit of fiscal analysis, should be scrapped by the Legislature at once. Politically, that is becoming easier as broken promises erode the plan's support — and as public demands for fiscal responsibility grow.

The problem with political pipe dreams is that they usually go up in smoke when confronted with reality. The goal of extending health insurance to as many residents as possible is an admirable one, but the Dukakis plan clearly is not the answer. The justification for continuing with it is becoming wispier with each passing day.

THE ARIZONA REPUBLIC
Phoenix, Arizona, October 19, 1991

THE push in Washington and elsewhere to revamp America's ailing health-care system along the lines of, say, the Canadian model, got a seemingly significant boost recently from an alarming report issued by the Department of Health and Human Services.

HHS estimates that by the year 2000 as much as one-sixth of America's total economic output — $1.6 trillion — will be consumed by ever-rising health-care costs. In 1965, by way of comparison, the cost of health care amounted to a mere one-sixteenth of the U.S. gross national product. Despite such enormous outlays, more than 30 million Americans still lack adequate health-care insurance.

Canada often is extolled as having a model plan. Along with its universal "free" coverage, one of the purported advantages of the government-financed system there is its cost-efficiency. Total health-care spending in Canada consumes significantly less — around 9 percent of GNP. The Canadian plan seems almost too good to be true.

In fact, as noted by Michael Walker of Canada's Fraser Institute, the successes of the Canadian model are greatly exaggerated. The system controls costs not through efficiency, he says, but by rationing health-care delivery. Such controls have created "long waiting lists and chronic shortages of equipment and services in many regions," particularly for diagnostic and acute-care procedures.

Moreover, the comparative numbers are illusory. A recent study by the Washington-based American Legislative Exchange Council found that real per-capita health-care spending has increased more rapidly in Canada than in the U.S. — at an average rate of 4.58 percent per year from 1967 to 1987 vs. 4.38 percent. The difference in the GNP-health care ratio is due to the fact the Canada's economic growth rate was nearly twice that of the U.S. — 74 percent compared with 38 percent.

When adjusted for the different GNP growth rates, the ALEC study calculates that Canada's outlay for health care is "virtually identical to that of the United States." In fact, when other factors are added to the health-care spending equation, a case can be made that the Canadian system is less cost-effective.

The U.S. population, for instance, contains a significantly larger proportion of the elderly, who require more health-care services. Canada also devotes considerably less of its health-care resources to medical research and development, relying instead on new technology and procedures developed in the U.S.

All of this is not to say the Canadian model is devoid of good ideas. Canada's administrative costs amount to only 13.7 percent of each health-care dollar spent, as compared with 22 percent in the U.S. The tort system in Canada, which caps malpractice awards, all but eliminates the huge costs of "defensive medicine," which contribute substantially to medical costs in the United States.

The U.S. system has its problems, to be sure. However, a Canadian model that contains 11 open-heart surgery centers for the entire country (as against 793 in the U.S.) is not a system most Americans would want to mimic. As one HHS official puts it, the country does *not* need a medical delivery system "with the compassion of the IRS, the efficiency of the post office, at Pentagon pricing."

the Charleston Gazette
Charleston, West Virginia, August 4, 1988

INSIGHT magazine is produced by the Moonie-owned *Washington Times*, an ultraconservative outfit not usually sympathetic to collectivist ideas such as "socialized medicine."

But the magazine's current issue has kind words for the once-hated concept. It says:

"When Canada adopted its system of free health care for all citizens in 1971, the country and the United States spent roughly equivalent proportions of their gross national product on health care: 7 percent.

"Since then, spending on health care in the United States has grown to more than 11 percent of GNP, while in Canada it has held relatively steady, now at 8.6 percent.

"In spite of this, Canadian health care is widely considered equal to the U.S. system in terms of technology and quality."

America has become "the spendthrift of the world" in medicine, *Insight* says. U.S. medical spending leaped to $1,837 per capita in 1986 — while many advanced nations with free care spent less than $1,000.

Ironically, even though America outspends other societies, it fails to provide care for millions of families and individuals who don't have medical insurance and can't qualify for welfare. In other nations, this callous abandonment of people doesn't happen.

Newsweek recently reported that socialized medicine in Europe is in a money crisis. But, crisis or not, those nations have greater cost-efficiency than America does. Great Britain, for example, spends just $600 per person on health care — one-third of the U.S. rate.

How can Canada provide free, top-quality care for everyone at less cost than America's partial care? Evidently it's because America's for-profit medicine requires expensive armies of billing and insurance clerks to determine payments. Canada doesn't waste money on this overhead.

Democratic presidential nominee Michael Dukakis wants to establish complete medical coverage in America, as in other countries.

Why not? America is the world's richest nation. Surely it can provide for its people as well as Canada does.

If even far-right voices such as *Insight* are speaking well of government-funded medicine, the time finally has arrived for America to join the rest of the world.

The Phoenix Gazette
Phoenix, Arizona, July 8, 1988

According to a recent *Wall Street Journal*/NBC News poll, Americans are sick of the inequities of the current U.S. health care system and want a government remedy.

Sixty-nine percent of respondents favored adoption of a universal, government-paid health-care plan, similar to Canada's system.

But judging by news from the north, a Canadian system would be importing problems, not solutions.

Hospitals in Ontario, Alberta and Newfoundland, hammered by federal funding cuts, are unable to replace out-dated equipment or to keep all their beds in service. The provinces can't make up the shortfalls without increasing taxes or cutting services, or both.

In short, the Canadian system is foundering on the hard rock of reality: Unlimited demands cannot be met by limited resources.

The state of Oregon is proposing a solution: If government is going to pay for medical care, it will decide what care to pay for.

Oregon is seeking a Medicaid waiver to extend health care coverage to 450,000 uninsured Oregonians. A list of 709 treatments has been drawn up and the state will pay for 587 of them.

The state will not cover numbers 588 and above. Private employers also would be required to cover the magic 587, but could do as they please about the rest.

The theory is that treatments considered less effective would be sacrificed to extend care to the uninsured. For example, if you are a 588 and need surgery for a slipped disk, forget it.

However, the state senators who approved the plan voted against applying the 587 cutoff rule to their own health insurance plan.

Apparently, the theory is fine as long as it applies to someone else. The poll also shows that most Americans are unwilling to consider rationing as a way of extending coverage and holding down costs.

Fans of national health care might keep that in mind before they endorse a Canadian model that will do covertly what Oregon wants to do overtly.

The Phoenix Gazette
Phoenix, Arizona, June 13, 1991

The release of a General Accounting Office endorsement of a Canadian-style national health care scheme is adding fuel to the political engine of federalized medicine that is picking up steam in Congress.

According to the GAO study, a government-paid health care system would save more than $75 billion a year, enough to cover all Americans who are uninsured.

Such grandiose claims need to be put under the stethoscope of skepticism. Twenty years ago it was the British system of socialized medicine that was all the rage among federal social planners. Now it's Canada that Washington spenders want us to emulate.

Proponents like to compare Canada's spending of 8 percent of GNP on health care to America's 12 percent as proof of the efficacy of the Canadian system.

But the difference is less a miracle of efficiency than a function of rationing. The provision of "free" services, not surprisingly, has created a boom in demand. Canada holds down health care expenditures the only way it can: by spending less on research and technology and rationing services.

That is why Canadians who find themselves on long waiting lists often come to the United States for procedures not immediately available at home.

The assertion that Canadian-style health care would be more cost-effective contradicts experience with other government monopolies. It is more likely that initial savings would be absorbed by the inefficiencies of government administrators freed from competitive pressures and the pork-barrel politicking of congressional micromanagers.

The Canadian system, though very popular now, is still evolving. Over time, economic pressures are likely to erode access and quality.

The goal of broadening availability of health care is a worthy one that U.S. policy-makers should pursue. Remedies are needed for what is admittedly a wasteful system that spends more on health care than any other nation but leaves some 35 million Americans without coverage.

The Canadian model, however, is not the panacea the GAO portrays it to be.

The Gazette
Cedar Rapids, Iowa, January 21, 1991

AMERICANS DISTURBED over the rising cost of medical care might take a moment and ponder a snippet of information published the other day in the New England Journal of Medicine.

Point No. 1: Doctors in the United States are sued five times more often than are their counterparts in Canada. Those are Canadian numbers, not American. The question was researched by a team from the University of Toronto.

Point No. 2: Malpractice insurance premiums in the United States are about nine times larger than those paid by physicians in Canada.

Points No. 3, 4, 5, etc: Canadian courts rarely grant punitive damages, and compensatory awards typically are in the $200,000 range; malpractice cases usually are tried before a judge, not a jury; the Canadian legal system discourages frivolous lawsuits (and Canadian lawyers usually don't accept cases for a portion of the settlement).

So, what's an office call to your doctor cost these days?

The Washington Times
Washington, D.C., January 21, 1991

One of the reasons Americans still enjoy the best health care in the world is because enough of the free market still exists to ensure nearly everyone access to whatever medical care he needs when he needs it. But costs are rising, and congressional Democrats, as Warren Brookes reported in two columns last week, are doing everything they can to smash what remains of American medicine in the name of "controlling costs" that are rising as a result of government intervention in the first place. Meanwhile, Democratic presidential candidates have been stumping for health-care Canadian style to control costs. A better idea would be to stop politicians from practicing medicine without a license.

To begin, Canada's example is not one we should follow. As the Heritage Foundation's Ed Haislmaier reports in Policy Review, the last thing American medicine needs is the "Maple Leaf Drag." Its main attraction is its low cost, much lower than ours, proponents say, but like so much of what is reported about the glory of modern medicine up north, it only appears to cost less. Between 1967 and 1987, Canada's GNP was growing faster than ours, 74 percent per capita there compared to 38 percent here. "Canada," Mr. Haislmaier reports, "has done no better that the United States is controlling the growth of health care costs. ... The introduction of a government-financed health system in Canada generated no measurable change in the real rates of Canadian health care spending relative to that of America."

Nor does the Canadian model control what doctors charge, contrary to popular belief. The government pays Canadian doctors a fee per service according to a schedule negotiated between the government and provincial medical associations. Because consumers don't purchase medical care directly, they have no incentive to question certain medical procedures, leaving "doctors free to compensate for reduced government-set fees by increasing the volume of service they provide." In short, a lot of unnecessary testing is done. When Canadian provinces cut fees 18 percent between 1972 and 1984, billing claims rose 17 percent.

The third problem isn't monetary. It's medical. In the United States, doctors are using some 2,000 magnetic resonance imaging (MRI) machines to diagnose their patients. It is a valuable and sometime critical tool. In Canada, all patients have access to only 15 MRI scanners, all of them in hospitals. Somewhere in Canada right now, a person with a brain tumor is awaiting an MRI scan he could get immediately if he walked across the border.

Yet another kind of rationing involves the kind of patients doctors are willing to take. All over Canada, cancer victims, dialysis patients and heart surgery candidates are waiting months for procedures performed every day in the United States, while relatively healthy people fill Canadian hospital beds because it costs less to treat them. Sometimes, it's impossible to get on a waiting list for serious procedures at all. In Toronto, patients must bring their own pillows to the hospital, while hospitals in Montreal are so short-staffed that nurses make elderly patients wear diapers because they don't have time to help them go to the restroom.

Which brings us back to the United States. As Mr. Brookes concluded in his two-part series on the subject, "The only way the government could afford a national insurance scheme would be deliberate rationing of care," a process that's likely to begin soon if someone doesn't stop these efforts to wreck the practice of medicine. Much of problem stems from the Medicaid program, which has driven up health-care costs by leaps and bounds. But what may be the most devastating government intervention in medicine hovers on the horizon.

In January, doctors must begin charging fees based on a "relative value scale" concocted by a social scientists from Harvard, which would assign arbitrary "relative value units" to certain medical procedures. According to a former assistant health secretary, "its bureaucratic complexity looks like it was imported from Romania," and Romanian medicine is probably what we're going to get. All doctors, no matter how talented they are, will have to charge certain prices for certain procedures, meaning that mediocre and even incompetent physicians will be subsidized by Uncle Sam. All prices being equal, bad medicine will flourish.

American medicine is on the brink of disaster. It's time for some politicians to find the courage to join the debate on the other side.

Los Angeles Times
Los Angeles, California, May 16, 1988

The World Health Assembly now under way in Geneva is an embarrassment for the United States as the United Nations World Health Organization struggles to implement its campaign of "Health for All by the Year 2000." The campaign enjoys widespread support and virtually unanimous praise. But it remains handicapped by the continued failure of Americans to pay their share.

This particular assembly has much to celebrate, including the 40th anniversary of the founding of WHO. The organization has earned a reputation for efficiency and effectiveness, praised in almost every capital of the world. That has not spared it, however, from budget slashing in Washington, with the United States, the richest of the members, the only nation in substantial violation of its treaty obligation to pay its assessments.

There was, in the opening week of the assembly, an announcement by an American representative that the United States was finally going to pay up what it owed for 1987—a total of $20 million. But that left unpaid an additional $18 million owed from previous years, and it included not a penny toward the $74 million owed for this year. So the gesture did more to expose the meanness of the American position than to demonstrate generosity.

Fortunately, the U.S. contribution to the AIDS program at WHO is funded from discretionary foreign-aid funds. Voluntary contributions from member nations are being used to meet the extraordinary costs of the AIDS program, with a separate budget of $66 million this year. The U.S. Agency for International Development has promised full American support.

The conspicuous failure to meet obligations to the World Health Organization and other elements of the U.N. system is the result of three factors: the Reagan Administration's lack of interest in multilateral diplomacy, the current federal budget deficit and a campaign—led by Sen. Nancy Landon Kassebaum (R-Kan.)—to bludgeon the international organizations into more frugal operations by withholding U.S. support, even though that support is a treaty obligation. So much for the efforts to piece together a global rule of law.

Other nations are not impressed with the apologies from Washington, for most of them also have budget-balancing problems but generally have met their obligations to the international organizations. The arrears to WHO is particularly unseemly, for that body is one against which there have been no charges of extravagance or poor management.

The American share of 25% is reasonable—actually less than a fair proportion, based on gross national products of member nations. Until recent years the United States has provided that support enthusiastically, and with it strong leadership for WHO. That was not an entirely charitable decision. Clearly it is in the national self-interest to support a vigorous global public-health program, for, as the AIDS pandemic has shown most recently, no nation can isolate itself from the health problems of all nations.

Dr. Halfdan Mahler, the distinguished Danish physician, is stepping down in July as the director general of WHO. The election of Dr. Hiroshi Nakajima of Japan as his successor has been confirmed. Ahead lie programs of urgency—including renewed vaccination programs targeted at childhood diseases and polio, and the effort to extend basic health care to every corner of the world by the end of the century.

Congress and the Reagan Administration are placing at risk the promise of health benefits to be shared by every nation. Washington cannot afford to meet its treaty obligations, we are told. If not, who can?

ST. LOUIS POST-DISPATCH
St. Louis, Missouri, August 23, 1992

Both proponents and opponents of national health insurance usually point to the Canadian model as the one that would either salvage or destroy the U.S. health-care system. Benefits of the Canadian program are well-known. Access is guaranteed to all, and medical inflation is kept low through a single-payer system.

But there is another notable model, in Germany, where private insurance and public insurance groups compete. All but the very wealthy in Germany prefer the public system of paying premiums to what is known as sick funds. These are non-profit organizations that are managed jointly by business and labor groups. Premiums for employees are paid in part by employers and are based on salaries. Premiums for the jobless are paid from national and local unemployment funds, and premiums for the retired and disabled come from various pension, sickness and national government funds. Patients are permitted to choose their health-care providers.

Doctors in private practice are obliged to treat everyone and, like German dentists, are paid prenegotiated fees. Doctors who work in hospitals are paid salaries, just as nurses and other medical employees are. German health plans, moreover, are portable, remaining in effect even if the participant loses a job, becomes disabled or retires. Yet Germany spent less on health care — $1,232 per capita in 1989 — than this nation, which spent $2,354 per capita and still left millions with no insurance.

As the health-care issue continues to heat up, Germany's model is being discussed, though President Bush hasn't seen fit to mention either it or the Canadian model. He prefers to set aside too little money in an untested voucher program to help people buy private health insurance. Democratic presidential candidate Bill Clinton has praised the German system but favors letting small businesses and individuals negotiate the costs of premiums and services with insurance firms and health-care providers.

States, meanwhile, are taking the lead in health-care reform, as Oregon did, when it proposed a flawed but well-intentioned universal health insurance system. Variations of the German system are being discussed by other states. Vermont is debating whether to shift to the German plan or the Canadian model. And California officials are debating whether to copy parts of the German plan by allowing businesses and workers to pay premiums to a regional fund, then use the money to bargain with health-care providers on the pricing of medical service.

This nation eventually will adopt some form of national health insurance. Polls show that Americans favor it. The United States stands almost alone among industrial nations in lacking an affordable, accessible national health-care program. It makes sense for Washington to take the lead in building a better system by incorporating the best elements of successful national health insurance programs elsewhere.

The Oregonian
Portland, Oregon, July 6, 1988

A new book describing widely differing medical practice in the United States, France, Great Britain and West Germany should feed the important and growing debate about medical ethics in this country.

Lynn Payer's "Medicine and Culture" underscores the need for policy-makers, doctors and patients to weigh the value of evolving medical practice in medical, financial and ethical terms.

"Only about 15 percent of all contemporary clinical interventions are supported by objective scientific evidence that they do more good than harm," writes Dr. Kerr L. White, the retired deputy director of the Rockefeller Foundation, in the book's introduction.

And the good or harm of a medical procedure is often determined not by results or ethics or cost, but by the cultural values both of doctors and of patients.

Just how divergent is medicine as practiced in the four countries?

• In America, known for its aggressive medicine, a woman is two to three times more likely to have a hysterectomy than in England, France or West Germany.

• The Caesarean section, performed in more than 20 percent of births in the United States, is far more common here than in Europe even though neonatal deaths are lower in Europe.

• Because of economic constraints, the British practice minimalist medicine and have set higher thresholds in defining disease. As Payer points out, ". . . you can't be diagnosed as having hypertension if nobody ever takes your blood pressure."

• West German doctors are paid a little for each act they perform, so they perform as many as quickly as they can.

Payer's book points out the need for medicine to make comparative studies of various treatments and their results. Far too often a procedure is used here because it is new or aggressive or well-publicized or high-tech. Far more important factors should be considered in determining our medical care.

White House Rejects Oregon Health Plan

The Bush administration Aug. 3, 1992 rejected Oregon's controversial plan to ration health care, saying the proposal was "tainted by discrimination" against disabled people.

The aim of Oregon's proposal was to expand Medicaid coverage to all individuals living below the federal poverty line. The change would sharply increase the number of people on the state's Medicaid rolls, to some 350,000 from the 231,000 at present.

In order to pay for the additional patients, the state wanted to ration medical treatments. To do that, it ranked 709 medical procedures in descending order according to their cost and bearing on the patient's "quality of life." Procedures below number 587 on the list would not be covered, even if the state had paid for them in the past.

The list gave preference to preventative and primary care. Among the illnesses that would merit treatment (and their rank) were pneumonia (1), tuberculosis (2), AIDS (158) and spina bifida (510).

Procedures that would receive no coverage included therapy for viral hepatitis (597), breast reconstruction after mastectomy (600), liver transplant for alcoholics (690) and treatment for AIDS when the patient had only six months to live.

Oregon needed to obtain the White House's approval because the health-care plan broke legal requirements of Medicaid, which was jointly funded by states and the federal government. The health secretary could grant waivers for experimental projects.

Announcing the Bush administration's rejection in a letter to Oregon Gov. Barbara Roberts (D), U.S. Health and Human Services Secretary Louis W. Suillivan said there was "considerable evidence" that the rankings were based "on the premise that the value on the life of a person with a disability was less than the value of a life of a person without a disability." Such an assumption, Sullivan wrote, violated the Americans With Disabilities Act, parts of which took effect July 26, 1992.

THE SUN
Baltimore, Maryland, August 10, 1992

It is conceded within the Bush administration that the most important experiments in health care reform will take place at the state level. So the administration's decision last week to deny a crucial waiver to the state of Oregon for a far-reaching reform of its Medicaid coverage came as a surprise.

As columnist Neal R. Peirce notes on the page opposite, Oregon's plan would rank medical procedures on a cost-benefit basis in order to extend coverage to 120,000 more poor people. The state would cover only the first 587 procedures on a list of 709; it would pay for fewer kinds of medical treatment but for more people.

Supporters of the Oregon plan are calling the administration's move cynical and politically motivated. Yet even Sen. Al Gore of Tennessee, the Democratic vice presidential nominee, urged the Republican administration not to approve the plan. Just as Oregon's proposal to ration Medicaid coverage has drawn bipartisan support in many quarters, it also has elicited bipartisan criticism.

The Bush administration's objections are based on legal opinions that in denying coverage for certain procedures — in particular those that are deemed not to contribute to a high enough quality of life — the Oregon plan would violate provisions of the 1990 Americans with Disabilities Act. That statute, which the president supported, forbids any discrimination in government-funded benefit programs against individuals with disabilities.

Rationing is a scary word, but the current system in which millions of Americans lack access to care is itself a form of rationing. Oregon officials describe their plan as a way of setting priorities rather than rationing. But the effect is the same.

Some critics argue the federal rejection proves that the hard choices in health care reform are too politically risky to gain widespread support. But Oregon's plan has its defects. To cite one, it makes no provision for minimum coverage. It would give short shrift to the need to ensure basic medical coverage for all women and children — two groups lacking much political power that almost always end up shortchanged by public policies.

Those concerned with equity issues in medical care can take heart that the administration has now gone on record in favor of the idea that equal access to health care is a civil right for at least some Americans — the disabled. The only thing lacking is to extend that concept to all Americans.

The failure of this plan to pass federal muster is not the end of attempts to ration health care. Nor should it be. Only by working for a more rational way of allocating health care dollars will this country achieve a medical system that is efficient, effective and fair.

FORT WORTH STAR-TELEGRAM
Fort Worth, Texas, August 5, 1992

The Bush administration has never been really serious about resolving the growing dilemma of providing health care to all Americans, and that attitude was clear in its rejection this week of Oregon's revolutionary proposal to reform the health-care program for that state's poor people.

Ostensibly, the proposal was denied because it would illegally discriminate against those with existing disabilities. The point is not entirely without merit, but it is more an emotional appeal that ignores the vast, complex substance of the debate over basic health care in this country. The federal response is no more than the practice of politics by avoidance.

All health care in the United States has grown enormously expensive — as many as 40 million Americans lack medical insurance — and is increasingly out of reach for many working families, but the hard-strapped states are especially suffering from the burdens imposed on them by the federal Medicaid program for the nation's poor. Encouraged by the administration to experiment with alternatives, Oregon did just that, proposing to establish a system of rationed care.

Rationing explicitly requires making choices: What can be treated, what should be treated, what will not be treated? Oregon drew up a priority list of 709 medical procedures, their costs and benefits. Those procedures ranking below No. 587 would not be paid for, such as liver transplants for alcoholics and therapy for AIDS patients diagnosed to be in their final six months of life.

Those are hard choices, but fiscal limits impose hard choices on society. At least Oregon had the courage to decide, through a rational and reasonable public process, to curtail some treatments in favor of expanding coverage for more people.

Administration officials, seeking some political cover to continue avoiding the hard decisions on cost control, latched onto the argument by advocates for the disabled that the Oregon plan was "tainted with discrimination."

That argument, however emotionally appealing, will offer little consolation for the more than 120,000 additional working poor Oregonians who would have received health-care coverage and now, thanks to administrative "discrimination," will not.

Clearly, what this country has been doing in health care is not working and is only getting worse. Oregon proposed an alternative that deserved to be tested.

Los Angeles Times
Los Angeles, California, August 8, 1992

The Bush Administration refused last week to issue a federal waiver so that a health program with proposed health care rationing could go forward.

The objection, said Secretary of Health and Human Services Louis W. Sullivan, was that the plan would wind up discriminating against Americans with disabilities, certainly something no government should countenance. That's the easy part. But what the Administration failed to do was deal with the hard part. If not the type of rationing that Oregon proposes, then what?

Anyone who has ever worked in, or even visited, a hospital emergency room knows full well that the silent rationing of health care services goes on daily.

The current hodgepodge health care system works very well for those who are insured, works worse for those who are underinsured and poorly and sometimes not at all for the uninsured.

As one emergency room physician put it in the Op-Ed pages of this paper recently, the besieged public health care system can lead only to more "uneducated, unimmunized, malnourished, homeless children, not likely to acquire acceptable family values. Our mentally ill will act out even more bizarrely when they can't get medications at their clinics. Our county hospitals will be overwhelmed. . . . AIDS and tuberculosis patients will die for lack of medication, and hospital, nursing or hospice care. People with acute curable illnesses will suffer and die for lack of services." The physician, Dr. Brian D. Johnston, likened this state's health care system to "a very sick horse"— that, if it were a horse, would be shot to humanely end its misery.

Oregon proposes to expand Medicaid, the largest government program financing health care for the poor. An additional 120,000 working poor would have been covered by the plan.

But in order to afford it Oregon would have cut back on the variety of medical services covered, giving high priority to preventive care and treating illnesses that respond well to treatment and giving low or no coverage to procedures deemed medically useless or extraordinarily costly for the benefits produced. That formal priority list and a "quality of life" assessment are what got it in trouble with advocates for the disabled and others who said the plan would discriminate against them.

The Oregon plan, watched closely across the nation, no doubt needs some revisions. But credit that state with doing more than the federal government to face up to the existing unfairness and haphazard rationing that already occur as physicians, nurses and counselors scramble to try to decide who gets health care quickly, who waits and who, by default, gets none at all.

The Oregonian
Portland, Oregon, August 5, 1992

The Bush administration, in rejecting Oregon's innovative health-care plan, has reinforced a growing suspicion: This president is an invertebrate when dealing with controversy.

The best hope for national-policy progress in health care may lie in a change of administrations.

The turndown of Oregon's effort to increase cost-effective health care to the poor is disappointing and frustrating here. It is also perplexing and insulting nationally.

The message to Americans is: Sure, use your state as a "laboratory of democracy" for health-care delivery to the poor. Remember, though, in applying your limited resources, you must (1) disregard the effectiveness of the services you pay for; (2) disregard community values on such things as restored health, functional independence and quality of life in choosing health care that may be included or excluded; and (3) not engage in any priority-setting among disabilities, diseases or afflictions or it will be regarded as discrimination.

In other words, federal approval is possible if your plan doesn't make choices, if it is indifferent to medical and financial results and if it dodges all controversy.

These core-issue evasions are exactly why medical hyperinflation persists and why so many Americans, including the working poor, are bereft of health-care protection.

Louis Sullivan, secretary of health and human services, issued the rejection for the administration. (Sen. Bob Packwood, R-Ore., said Sullivan wanted to approve the Oregon Reform Demonstration, but was overruled for political reasons.)

Sullivan said he looked forward to approving Oregon's plan when the state reworked it to conform to the Americans With Disabilities Act, which went into effect last month. However, his analysis and the state's subsequent discussion with federal attorneys revealed abundant barriers and no inclination to be helpful. In fact, said Jean Thorne, director of the state's Office of Medical Assistance Programs, the state was never consulted on the perceived difficulties, making state-federal collaboration an illusion. This simply was not an administration trying to say yes.

So, Oregon and the nation are left with difficult ironies:

1. Rejection of the Oregon plan will stifle all states' attempts to spend health-care money effectively. Therefore, federal Medicaid expenses will get no relief.

2. As states strive to balance their budgets, they will cut non-required categories of care (prevention, education, shelter) and ultimately raise their own costs through elevated use of hospital care.

3. An administration that wants states to accept more authority has discredited its rhetoric about states being "laboratories of democracy."

4. A federal administration that says it is concerned about the lack of health coverage to the working poor cuts the ropes of the safety net Oregon would place under them.

Don't look for help from the Bush administration.

Newsday
New York City, New York, August 8, 1992

After years of saying good things about Oregon's groundbreaking state proposal to overhaul health care financing, the Bush administration says now it can't OK the plan because it conflicts with the new Americans with Disabilities Act.

But Oregon shouldn't quit now. Its proposal is an important experiment in controlling medical spending and in extending health insurance coverage. If modest revisions would satisfy the new disabilities act, they should be made. Or if the act itself is unreasonable, that must be made clear.

In any case, Oregon will probably fare better in Washington after the November election, when controversy will no longer threaten President George Bush's re-election chances.

Under Oregon's proposal, the state would require businesses to offer employees a basic, state-designed health insurance package. Poor families would get similar coverage under the state-federal Medicaid program.

The key to controlling costs — and the current hangup — is that medical services that are not cost-effective would not be covered. For example, Medicaid would not pay for an expensive treatment that doesn't significantly improve a patient's condition. Some advocates for the disabled claim that the way Oregon calculated cost-effectiveness worked against treatment for disabilities.

Advocates of the plan — which amounts to a reasoned way of rationing health care — say that any conflicts with the disabilities statute are overblown. That won't stop disabled groups from going to court, though. If their concerns can be resolved and a suit forestalled by adjusting its plan, Oregon should try.

Fending off a suit may be difficult, however, because the disabilities law is so vague and sweeping that its reach is hard to assess. In that case, it may be the law — not the Oregon plan — that should be changed.

Oregon's health care proposal isn't necessarily a terrific thing, but it is a carefully and conscientiously thought-out effort to both extend health care coverage and control costs. It deserves a try.

LAS VEGAS REVIEW-JOURNAL

Las Vegas, Nevada, August 13, 1992

All our troubles, if it be not blasphemy to cite the old spiritual, soon be over.

Blasphemy because the relief promised in the song was to come from a somewhat higher authority than our self-appointed saviours in Congress, who appear ready to cast off the last vestiges of Constitutional restraint so carefully forged by the founders, and simply announce their readiness to make every decision in America.

You think private companies need personnel executives?

Nonsense! The Senate will resurrect a bill requiring employers to grant 12 weeks unpaid leave anytime there's an illness or even an adoption — an adoption! — in the family.

No need to leave employers any flexibility. No, a Labor Department bureaucrat in distant Washington will doubtless know best. Take Linda Froehlich, for example. The owner of a small firm in Dayton, Ohio, Froehlich wrote in the Wall Street Journal Aug. 7 that the Labor Department threatened her with a levy of $20,000 in "retroactive overtime" if she continued to allow women with children to take half-days off without pay, under an unwritten "interpretation" that this practice changes a salaried worker into an hourly worker.

It may not make either the employer or the employee happy, but Washington knows best.

And the Senate's reapproval of the family-leave bill only accelerates a Washington power-grab which has reached such a frenzy that it overflows new territory each day.

It was only Monday that Health Secretary Louis Sullivan refused the necessary waiver for Oregon's new state health insurance plan.

Think what you will about the Oregon plan — and in fact we find its compulsory elements to be anathema — it was passed by a bipartisan coalition of state legislators after years of public debate hammered out a prioritized list of what medical treatments the state would pay for.

Though we would oppose such a plan if proposed here, the whole notion of federalism is that the individual states should be left free to attempt different solutions to common problems, with the federal government acting only as a referee to make sure no state infringes on the rights of another.

But as Dr. Kevin Concannon, director of the Oregon Dept. of Human Resources, wrote in The Washington Post on Monday: "Oregon gasps in stunned reaction to the denying of (its) Medicaid reform application.

"We took the administration at its word. It has an oft-repeated policy encouraging state innovation and reforms."

Unless, of course, they run afoul of such edifices as the politically correct new "Americans with Disabilities Act," cited by Secretary Sullivan in turning down Oregon's plan since Oregon specified that unreformed alcoholics — who rarely live long even with new livers — could be turned down for state-funded liver transplants, a forbidden form of "discrimination."

"Repeated surveys among people with disabilities have shown that their highest priority is their desire to work and hold a job," responded Dr. Concannon. "The biggest barrier to that is the fear of losing health-care benefits. . . .

"The very kind of slavery that the administration rails against when talking of public welfare had a couple of shackles refitted last week for people with disabilities."

Ah, but Dr. Concannon: Washington knows best.

The Washington Post

Washington, D.C., August 6, 1992

IN REJECTING Oregon's pioneering plan to "ration" health care for the poor under Medicaid, the Bush administration did the right thing, but not for the strongest reason. The plan, though well-intentioned, threatened one of the most important social accomplishments of the largely barren past 12 years.

Medicaid has never covered all the poor—it now covers fewer than half—nor provided even all of those it covers with all medically necessary care. In a series of underpublicized enactments in the 1980s, however, Congress decreed that at least it should begin to provide all necessary care to all poor children. The phase-in won't be complete until the turn of the century. But the Oregon plan would have breached the principle before it could be applied; the precedent would have been more damaging than the plan itself. It was too high a price to pay for the plan's supposed advantages.

Ironically, the goal of the proposal was precisely to extend care to all the state's poor. The problem, as in expanding access to health care nationally, was how to finance it. Oregon proposed to increase the Medicaid budget but also to limit the Medicaid benefit package. The limits meant that to some extent the poor already on the rolls would bear the cost of extending care to the poor who were not. That's the wrong place to look for financing.

Benefit limits are nothing new; every state has them. Most tend to be fairly crude; the state will pay for only so many days of hospital care, for example, no matter what the illness. Oregon said that, in spreading its dollars to cover all its poor, it was simply creating a new and more rational system for allocating scarce resources. It divided all medicine into about 700 procedures, ranked them according to their supposed efficacy and said it would go as far down the list for all the poor each year as it had money for.

The obvious winners would have included the older poor children not yet covered by Medicaid. But children would have been losers as well. The elderly whom Medicaid also serves would not have been subject to the new benefit limits until later. Nor were the limits proposed for the plan's first year a floor. Doctors and hospitals were guaranteed minimum fees if the budget tightened in future years, but recipients weren't guaranteed minimum benefits—and the Oregon budget, like many state budgets, is in bad shape.

The administration referred to none of this in rejecting the plan. It said instead that in ranking the 700 procedures, Oregon violated the Americans With Disabilities Act by seeming to place more value on life without a disability than on life with one. Critics say that this was only a smokescreen and that for all its supposed deference to state and local decision-making, the administration simply flinched when confronted with a controversial plan (that right-to-life groups joined in opposing) in an election year. That may be so, but the disabilities act does present a genuine problem not yet resolved if health care is to be explicitly rationed. That's because it suggests that procedures can't be readily judged by the quality of life it is thought they will produce. How else then to judge them?

But the main lesson of this plan is that the health care system is too compartmentalized to be reformed a state or a program at a time. Reforms all create both winners and losers. If the losers are going to be in the same population group as the winners—the poor, for example— reform is always going to be pretty much a wash. It ought to be better than that.

The Register-Guard

Eugene, Oregon, August 4, 1992

President Bush invited states to experiment with new ways of controlling medical costs and expanding coverage, but when Oregon responded the administration bolted the doors and drew the shades. On Monday Health and Human Services Secretary Louis Sullivan denied the federal waivers that would have allowed Oregon to expand the reach of Medicaid services. The rejection is disheartening, shortsighted and unfair.

Sullivan said the White House believed that Oregon's health care plan would violate provisions of the Americans with Disabilities Act. This new and belated concern — the act was approved two years ago, and no one has raised the issue of a potential conflict until recently — arises from a fundamental misunderstanding of Oregon's experiment and of the system it would replace.

States currently provide comprehensive medical care to poor people through the state-federal Medicaid program. Neither the federal government nor the states have the money to care for all low-income citizens. About 120,000 Oregonians with incomes below the federal poverty level of $10,857 for a family of three are not covered by Medicaid. That's more than a third of Oregon's low-income population, and the situation is worse in many other states.

Oregon proposed to spend its Medicaid dollars to provide the most important medical services to all low-income Oregonians. The state devised a list of 709 medical procedures and ranked them in order of effectiveness and cost. No one on Medicaid would have received the most costly, least effective treatments, but all would have qualified for the 578 most vital procedures on the list.

No conflict with the Americans with Disabilities Act was identified in exhaustive reviews by the General Accounting Office and the Office of Technology Assessment. The administration declined to seek an authoritative legal opinion on the issue. Nor were state officials given an opportunity to respond to the administration's concerns.

Had the White House been willing to listen, Oregon officials would have pointed out that the administration's objection ignored the fact that many disabled people who currently receive no health care would qualify for the most needed services under the Oregon plan. The administration also failed to consider the fact that some disabilities would be prevented through treatment of medical problems that are currently not covered.

A deeper concern emerged from the use of quality-of-life criteria in formulating the list of medical services that would be covered. Sullivan objected to the state's use of a poll in which the public was asked to rate the "net benefit" of medical treatments by assessing the effects of disabilities on people's quality of life. The poll, Sullivan said in his letter to Gov. Barbara Roberts, allowed room for bias against disabled people.

The quality-of-life criteria, however, played a smaller role in the development of the list than the Bush administration seems to believe. The effect of the poll results on the final list of treatments was neutral. Oregon's real sin was in making quality-of-life judgments in the open, rather than secretly or implicitly as is usually done. And it's stunning that the final, fatal objection to the Oregon plan stems from a fine procedural point, rather than from any defect in the result.

The implication that disability is an undesirable outcome in medical treatment, however, was inescapably a part of the Oregon plan. For instance, the plan did not disguise its preference for preventive care over aggressive treatment of terminally ill patients. If it is discriminatory to prefer health over illness, or to spend limited funds to buy health for many rather than prolonging the illness of a few, then the Oregon plan was guilty as charged.

The current system, of course, is guiltier yet. A system that won't treat one person's appendicitis while it pays for another's hemorrhoidectomy, all because of a few dollars' difference in income, can't be described as fair. The Oregon plan would have ended such absurdities by facing the hard choices the existing system is designed to avoid.

No major changes can be made in the Oregon plan without legislative approval. Senate President John Kitzhaber, the architect of the plan, is retiring from the Legislature and won't be back for the 1993 session. Unless the administration reconsiders or will accept the plan with only minor changes, the entire effort is dead. The Bush administration's flimsily reasoned decision is a cause of sadness and anger.

The Seattle Times

Seattle, Washington, August 5, 1992

President Bush praised Oregon's health-reform proposal in the past as a good effort in tackling medical spending.

Yet in a bizarre turnabout, the White House has decided to block Oregon's reform, charging the plan violates anti-discrimination provisions in the Americans with Disabilities Act.

The administration's new position has little to do with fair treatment for the disabled. The fact is, the current system discriminates against all people — including those with disabilities — who can't afford private health insurance or aren't poor enough to qualify for public assistance.

Oregon legislators worked for four years to craft a comprehensive reform plan. They waited a year for a federal waiver from Medicaid regulations to implement the reforms. Now the administration's blithe rejection puts the welfare of Oregonians on hold. It's uncertain whether the state can revise the plan to the administration's satisfaction.

To provide basic health care to nearly 450,000 uninsured people, the Oregon plan would extend publicly funded Medicaid to all people living below federal poverty level (under current rules, a family of three earning more than $616 a month makes too much to qualify for Medicaid) and require all employers to provide insurance for permanent workers and their dependents.

The only way the state can afford to add 120,000 poor people to the Medicaid rolls is by limiting medical services. A public commission, after hearing hundreds of hours of public testimony, ranked 709 services by medical effectiveness, cost, and quality-of-life factors. Only the top 587 services would be covered by the state's Medicaid program.

Preventive, primary, and prenatal care are given highest priority. Treatments for life-threatening conditions, injuries, heart bypass operations, and most organ transplants are included. The only services that Oregon Medicaid would not fund are for conditions that get better without treatment, conditions that get better with "home" remedies, and conditions where treatment is generally futile.

The last category includes simultaneous kidney-liver transplants, surgery for lower back pain, severe brain injury, end-stage AIDS, and aggressive medical treatment for infants born weighing less than 18 ounces and before 23 weeks of gestation.

Right-to-life groups and advocates for disabled people oppose a ranking system because it involves subjective judgments about a patient's future quality of life. And children's advocates oppose the plan because rationing would affect poor people on Medicaid, but not others.

The plan is not perfect. But the unreformed system is crueler — it rations on the basis of wealth and leaves hundreds of thousands of people without any care at all.

Until Congress and the White House tackle health care at the national level, states are forced to invent their own solutions. Oregonians have decided that limited government funds should be spread among more people, setting a "floor" of health care below which no one should fall.

Not all states will employ a rationing model. But every state contemplating reform, including Washington, will have to decide who receives care and at what cost. Other approaches may be equally painful to implement.

Oregonians crafted a plan they believe to be fair and efficient. Critics in the Bush administration offer no solutions; they seem to say: If the uninsured poor can't get every service, let them get nothing.

Hillary Clinton to Head Health Panel

Incoming First Lady Hillary Rodham Clinton, in a conspicuous break with tradition, would set up her office in the West Wing of the White House, which was usually reserved for senior staff members and policy makers, the White House announced Jan. 21. First ladies had traditionally had their offices in the East Wing. White House spokeswoman Dee Dee Myers said President Clinton wanted her there "to work . . . on a variety of domestic policy issues." Most prominently mentioned was health-care reform, one of Clinton's central priorities and an issue on which he was said to be dissatisfied with his staff's progress to date. Clinton had promised to introduce legislation within his first 100 days in office to guarantee health care for all Americans while controlling costs.

President Clinton Jan. 25 named his wife as head of a new commission to devise a plan for reforming the U.S.'s health-care system.

The job was the most influential ever awarded to a first lady. Health-care reform was considered one of the most difficult issues confronting the Clinton administration. Mrs. Clinton, 45, was expected to be at the center of a fierce political debate. (As required under laws against hiring relatives, the position would be unpaid.)

The main goal of the panel, named the Task Force on National Health Care Reform, was to find ways of providing medical coverage to all Americans and of halting the soaring costs of treatment. To this end, it would meet with experts and try to generate public support for its plans. It would also attempt to forge a consensus with Congress and powerful lobby groups.

THE KANSAS CITY STAR
Kansas City, Missouri, January 31, 1993

In Hillary Clinton, the nation finally has a powerful executive for health care reform.

The committee that will put together an administration proposal to equalize health care for Americans starts on an optimistic note with President Clinton's appointment of his wife. For a change, it has an outside chance of succeeding.

She has power, by virtue of being first lady — a long partnership with the man who is president. She has the wit and training. She has had experience in turning competing interest groups' agendas into a working program. The fact that she is not a health care expert may be an advantage — she has no bias for or against any of the major components of the complex and warring health care industry.

Clinton gave the committee the task of having a proposal to reform the health care system ready for Congress within 100 days of his inauguration. Other members include Carol Rasco and Ira Magaziner, White House domestic policy advisers; Judith Feder, head of the president's health care transition team; Donna E. Shalala, secretary of Health and Human Services; Leon E. Panetta, director of the Office of Management and Budget, and other cabinet secretaries.

It will be a formidable task to finish in less than three months, even for a fast-track panel headed by Hillary Clinton. Special interest groups admitted they "had no idea" what might emerge as the administration proposal.

Nonetheless, they were accumulating lobbying packets for their versions long before the inauguration. Honest differences of opinion exist about whether employer-paid insurance, managed care, a fee for service or some combination best serves patients in addition to less honest schemes driven by greed. National health insurance should not be ruled out as an option.

Over the past few years, in addition to the many congressional proposals, most professional groups, business organizations and consumer associations involved in the field of health care have circulated their own initiatives for reform. Somehow, the new panel must meld their best ideas, offend no one and fill President Clinton's orders to control costs and ensure care to all Americans.

The administration plan is expected to try to set an annual limit on public and private health care spending and devise a way to cover the nearly 37 million Americans presently without public or private insurance.

This is certainly the issue, as well as the time, for breaking new ground in Washington. So the less debate about the appropriateness of giving this job to the first lady, the better.

What's important is giving the health care system back to American citizens. If Hillary Clinton can marshal that, she can be Socks' veterinarian. What difference would it make?

The Globe and Mail
Toronto, Ontario, January 27, 1993

IT has long been clear that Hillary Rodham Clinton will be a different kind of First Lady of the United States. A successful lawyer and a nationally recognized campaigner for children's legal rights, she is unlikely to be content with cutting ribbons, leading kindergarten sing-alongs and taking tea with Naina Yeltsin while Boris and Bill talk business in the Oval Office. But should she have a leading policy-making post in her husband's administration?

Those who defend Mrs. Clinton's appointment as the head of a national health care task force make two arguments. The first is that Mrs. Clinton is qualified to do the job. As Bill Clinton was at pains to note this week, she held a number of public posts while he was Governor of Arkansas, including chair of the Arkansas education standards committee and member of a task force on infant mortality. Mrs. Clinton, says Mr. Clinton, is "better at organizing and leading people from a complex beginning to a certain end" than anybody he knows. This may be true.

But her chief qualification is that she is the wife of the President of the United States. She would not have been considered for the job otherwise. This is usually called nepotism, and its exercise by a President who says he is committed to the highest ethical standards sends a highly dubious message to other public officials. If Mr. Clinton can make his wife a top policy-maker, why shouldn't the Secretary of Defence give his well-qualified nephew a job? More concretely, how will the new health care task force work with the President's wife as its head? Will members feel free to debate with vigour, even challenge the chair?

The second argument for Mrs. Clinton is a practical one. Like it or not, the accomplished First Lady is going to be influential in the White House. Why not be up-front about it? Why not channel her energy into useful public endeavour, rather than confine her to the kind of backstairs role played by some First Ladies, notably the Svengali-like Nancy Reagan?

One answer is that there is a line between unofficial influence and official power. Arlene Perly Rae may, for all we know, exercise much influence over the Premier of Ontario, but most Ontarians would not want to see her become the head of a government task force. Another is that the Clinton camp has never been particularly up-front about Mrs. Clinton's influence in the past. After Mr. Clinton ran into trouble with his "two-for-one-deal" pitch early in the presidential campaign, his advisers repackaged Mrs. Clinton in a gauzy wrap of motherliness and wifely loyalty. Only since his election has the real, more assertive Mrs. Clinton re-emerged.

And so she should. Let Mrs. Clinton do all she can to remold the archaic role of First Lady. Let her put herself forward as a role model for girls and young women who might hesitate to use their minds and exercise their independence. Let her speak out openly on the power of feminism and the virtues of education. But, after her 100-day health posting is over, let her do it outside the official ranks of her husband's administration.

The Detroit News
Detroit, Michigan, April 28, 1993

The Big Three want some relief from their rising health care costs, but UAW President Owen Bieber promised Monday that the union would strike if the companies tried to touch retiree health benefits. So the domestic automakers appear to be turning to government for a bailout. The idea is that Uncle Sam would put the muscle on auto buyers to subsidize the benefits of the Big Three's workers and retirees.

A real problem does exist. The Japanese transplants have a $500 to $800 advantage per car over the Big Three because of health care costs. The transplants have much younger workforces than the Big Three and virtually no retirees. In fact, Richard O'Brien, GM vice-president of corporate personnel, says there are more retirees than employees actively at work at GM — and that doesn't even count dependents.

So the Big Three are lobbying President Clinton and his health care task force for the formation of an auto sector health care "cooperative" that would socialize health costs. The government would impose a 1-percent to 1.5-percent tax on each car, including those from the Japanese and emerging German transplants. The tax revenue would be redistributed mostly back to the Big Three, however, to eliminate their cost disadvantage.

The OPEC oil cartel couldn't have designed it any better. The tax might be called a "premium" and imposed on automakers, but consumers would end up footing the bill because taxes invariably are passed along in the form of higher prices. The auto companies simply want Washington to take the heat for the higher prices that will result from their unwillingness to bargain costs down.

The "transplants" have committed no crime. They are the result of the U.S. industry's challenge to stop importing so many cars. They are building them here, providing wages and benefits for tens of thousands of American workers. To Detroit's distress, however, this hasn't solved the domestic industry's competitive problem. Instead, it has exposed the inefficiencies accumulated by the Big Three when they had the market all to themselves.

It seems unlikely that the American public is going to want to help the Big Three out of their bargaining difficulties, especially if there are no concessions by the UAW this summer. The union doesn't like to admit that it is part of the problem and doesn't improve matters by advocating its own disastrous bailout plan, a single-payer national health care system.

The last thing the economy needs is another tax that discourages growth, even if it does hit the transplants harder than the Big Three. After all, if the auto industry can wangle subsidies from Washington, so can other industries. The result will be to take so much money out of taxpayers' pockets that nobody will be buying any cars, domestic or foreign.

Detroit and the UAW should press Washington to cut the costs of doing business, including relief from nutty environmental, safety and other regulations, as a way to level the playing field. And if health care benefits are making the Big Three uncompetitive, then they should solve that problem the same way it was created: at the bargaining table.

The Phoenix Gazette
Phoenix, Arizona, April 22, 1993

If Arizona lawmakers can brag about one bill they have passed, it should be Senate Bill 1109.

SB 1109 is arguably the most substantive measure of the legislative session, the one with the most positive impact on Arizonans. It advances the prospect of expanded and affordable health care coverage for workers and their families through the responsible private sector.

The measure sets the ground rules for health care insurers in Arizona to compete, establishing a level playing field by protecting all families, but also removing the governmental obstacles — politically inspired mandates and the like — from the market.

SB 1109, Accountable Health Plans for Arizona, has been endorsed by health care advocates, managed care associations, insurers, physicians, labor unions and business organizations. Interestingly, it was one of the few significant legislative achievements on which both Democrats and Republicans participated and agreed. And it faced a determined, resourceful opposition in Golden Rule Insurance and its lobbyists.

Practically every feature needed for responsible private insurance coverage is included in SB 1109 — and no more. Despite intense pressure from interest groups, there are no legislative mandates for chiropractors, optometrists, podiatrists or other specialized services. To do business in Arizona, a health care insurer need only offer a basic health care plan. Extra coverage can be negotiated by individual employee groups. Arizona consumers will be able to compare and shop for health policies intelligently because they will operate on a similar base.

There is a portability feature for employees changing jobs. There is a "guaranteed issuance" provision, meaning that some employees can't be excluded from coverage because of pre-existing illness in the family. Underwrite the risk; don't avoid it.

The system offers incentives for managed care and provides some state oversight of prices.

Gov. Symington will probably be subjected to intense lobbying pressure, the same kind heroic lawmakers such as Sen. Ann Day, Reps. Susan Gerard and Pat Blake, all Republicans, and Sen. Cindy Resnick, a Democrat, resisted.

Opponents will float bromides like "free market" to argue against this measure — and keep intact the current highly regulated, uneconomic system that protects corporations without conscience and specialized health care providers who have long benefited by legislative fiat.

Don't be fooled. This reform helps private enterprise work for the benefit of the public and its health. Sign SB 1109, Gov. Symington, and do so with pride.

The Wichita Eagle-Beacon
Wichita, Kansas, April 17, 1993

Health-care reform is on the minds of many Americans. But is there still the strong consensus for universal-health insurance that there was before the 1992 presidential election? Are people as committed to controlling medical costs and providing medical access for all as they were just a few months ago?

If the Clinton administration's forthcoming reform plan costs too much, limits physician choices and doesn't cover every conceivable health need, a fickle public could easily persuade Congress to dump the whole thing. Remember catastrophic health-care coverage for the elderly? Older Americans said they wanted a program to protect them from poverty-inducing long-term illnesses. Congress gave it to them. When those same older Americans figured out that they would have to help pay for such a plan, they marched on Washington and made Congress to reverse itself.

The specter of that time should hang heavily over the heads of the president's task force that is working on a health-care reform proposal. A recent survey suggests that Americans are still willing to pay higher taxes for the security of cradle-to-grave health insurance. Ah, but here's the deja-vu part. The survey also shows that they want to choose their own doctors and to have no restrictions on what is covered. Does that mean that they are all for it but if — like that catastrophic legislation — it isn't perfect, then they will change their minds?

Well, no health-care insurance package is going to be everything for everybody. It will cost a lot of money. Eliminating fraud and paperwork won't pay the bill. It is more complicated than that. And the big price tag will be for *basic* care only. Anyone who thinks an affordable health-reform package will evolve that includes everything from cataract surgery to immunizations, from acupuncture to nursing home care, from prenatal care to kidney transplants and from drug rehabilitation therapy to tummy tucks had better think again.

That's it. That's the way it is. Americans may still want a national health plan. That's fine. The Clinton administration wants to give them one. And Congress might just go along with that plan. But if the public starts getting upset with what's covered and how much it costs, it might not happen.

The prescription for successful health-care reform calls for a large dose of reality. Otherwise, the consensus that put the issue on the national agenda can disappear very quickly. And that would be too bad. Because there is little doubt that a plan is needed. It just may not be a perfect one.

The TENNESSEAN
Nashville, Tennessee, April 17, 1993

A value-added tax to fund health care reform is one trial balloon the Clinton administration should puncture quickly.

President Clinton stumbled earlier this year when he seemed to suggest a VAT, which is similar to a national sales tax, as a way to change the nation's tax structure. The idea was quickly dismissed.

The President's retreat, however, didn't stop Health and Human Services Secretary Donna Shalala from telling reporters this week that the VAT might be an option for funding health care.

Shalala's remarks sent Mr. Clinton's aides scrambling to stave off embarrassment at the seeming reversal. They should blush. The mere mention of a VAT wasn't a good political move for an administration embattled with Congress over an economic stimulus package. And, VAT simply isn't a good tax option.

Other presidents have toyed with the idea of a VAT or a national sales tax as a revenue source. Former President Nixon floated the idea 20 years ago to face his deficit problems. The Bush administration flirted with the tax.

The VAT is certainly a way to raise

pay virtually all of it as manufacturers pass on the cost.

But a VAT would also hurt those the administration wants to help. Tennessee and other states that already struggle with high sales taxes know how much they unfairly burden low- and middle-income families.

And sales taxes are particularly unreliable. When spending falls as it did during the recession, the revenue isn't there.

Funding health care reform represents a daunting task for the administration. So-called sin taxes on cigarettes and alcohol can help, but they can't raise the amounts the administration needs to fund a wide-reaching health care program.

If Shalala's comments were a way to gauge reaction, that's fine. But the Clinton administration doesn't need a trial balloon to know that this nation's low-income citizens — not only the poverty stricken but the working poor — are hurting. They are the ones most burdened by health care. They shouldn't be the ones most burdened by a national sales tax of any kind. ■

money. It taxes goods at every stage of production. A 5% tax would raise an estimated $47 billion, and consumers would

THE LINCOLN STAR
Lincoln, Nebraska, April 16, 1993

An open letter to Hillary Rodham Clinton:

Welcome to Nebraska and to Lincoln, its capital city.

We are honored by your visit.

This is our chance to listen, up close and live, to some of the national voices in health care in this two-day forum.

We hope you will also have time to listen to some of the Nebraska voices.

Most of us have health care protection. About 90 percent of all Nebraskans have health insurance or participate in Medicare or Medicaid. And we are generally satisfied, often pleased, with the care we get from our doctors and our local hospitals.

But there is an undercurrent of unease. We worry that we are one bad decision, one piece of bad luck away from not having adequate health care.

We could lose our job and with it our family's insurance coverage. We could develop a disease and get cut off of insurance.

WE ALSO WORRY about the exorbitant cost of hospital stays and the ever-escalating costs of insurance. We see a growing number of jobs without insurance benefits. We wonder what our children and grandchildren will do. How will they afford health care?

We, too, wonder about what is appropriate and responsible care at the very end of life.

Most of us are quite lucky.

We have exceptional health care choices. We can choose our doctors, our hospital. We still participate actively in the decision over what procedures to use in treating diseases.

We value those choices and would like

to retain that control.

We also have some unique problems in Nebraska, problems that managed competition simply will not address. In rural Nebraska, which is most of the state, we need more doctors and nurses. We need strengthened cooperation, not competition.

A national health care system cannot be one size or else it will certainly not fit us. We need the flexibility to adapt health care to our own open, spacious state.

WE ARE GENERALLY considered a Republican state, based on presidential voting patterns and reflecting voter registration.

But at heart we are a state that doesn't pay a lot of attention to partisanship. We have non-partisan local elections, a non-partisan single house Legislature. And we see health care not in partisan terms, but in very personal, human terms.

We hope that the solutions developed through this period of broad national discussion will become a bipartisan issue when it moves to Congress. We hope that our elected leaders will look for valid solutions rather than try to score points.

We also want to thank you for offering your time and your talent, to help our country come to some understanding of this very complex issue. You certainly picked a tough job.

We value your leadership capabilities. We share your great concern about America's children. We agree with your assessment that we must all take personal responsibility for our own behavior and also work together to develop socially responsible solutions.

We even like the headband.

The Boston Globe
Boston, Massachusetts, April 22, 1993

Even if President Clinton's economic stimulus package wins congressional approval and the funds for childhood immunization remain intact, the battle to ensure that every American child is fully vaccinated will be only half won. The next step will be to get the vaccines to the children who need them most.

Because schools require that children be vaccinated before they enroll, most youngsters are immunized by the age of 5. But far too many preschoolers are left at risk for preventable diseases like measles, mumps and diphtheria. For various reasons, including poverty and lack of access, they do not receive the battery of vaccinations that should begin shortly after birth.

Three of every 10 of the nation's 2-year-olds fail to get timely vaccinations. In some of the nation's urban centers, the immunization rate is as low as 40 percent.

That is why National Preschool Immunization Week is so important. The week, which begins Saturday, is designed to raise awareness about the need for preschool immunization and also to provide free vaccine to children in several cities across the country.

The Boston Immunization Coalition, which comprises more than 80 organizations and programs, will participate in the national campaign by sponsoring various activities during the week. This morning Mayor Flynn will hold an advance kick-off rally at City Hall at which he will be joined by more than 250 youth volunteers who will be knocking on doors next week providing information on available vaccination services.

The coalition's goal is to ensure that 90 percent of Boston's children are immunized by their second birthday. In order to reach that goal, the technology must be in place to keep track of children's immunization status. Funds and services are needed for an ongoing information campaign.

Boston's business community can help by contributing to this effort and also by reminding their own employees to have their children vaccinated.

The Hutchinson News

Hutchinson, Kansas, April 16, 1993

Viewing it from a distance, the death of Hillary Rodham Clinton's father, Hugh Rodham, will not be in vain, despite the loss to his family.

As Mrs. Clinton put consideration of the nation's health-care problems on hold, the recent weeks-long vigil at the hospital, the observation of medical services and, ultimately, the eventual cost of her father's hospitalization put her right at the center of the debate over a national health plan.

When her 82-year-old father suffered a debilitating stroke, Mrs. Clinton was transported from abstract analysis of an enormously complex puzzle to traveling through a concrete experience of how the system works in the case of one insured individual. She will find that the health-care system works fairly well for those lucky enough to have insurance. It also will give her a perspective on how Americans without insurance might have fared under similar circumstances.

Mrs. Clinton can take her own family's private tragedy and apply it to the public health-care issue.

Mrs. Clinton now is wholly sensitized to the health-care dilemma from a personal perspective, and while she endures the significant loss of a parent, the timing of her father's death can only clarify the necessity of an efficient and caring national health-care plan.

Whatever plan Mrs. Clinton and her task force evolve, she must ask herself the question, "How would Dad have fared under this proposal?"

The question is valid and is at the core of the task-force deliberations.

The Salt Lake Tribune

Salt Lake City, Utah, April 20, 1993

The Clinton administration's proposal to promote childhood immunization by providing free vaccines at government expense is only part of the answer to universal immunization, but it is an important part. So, the Clinton plan, or something like it, is an idea whose time has come.

The administration wants government to spend $1 billion to buy a national supply of vaccines and distribute them free to health-care providers. Vaccinations then would be free to parents, except for a nominal administrative fee that providers could charge.

The drug companies which make the vaccines oppose the plan for several reasons. One of their arguments is that lack of health-care access and parent education, not the price of vaccines, is the biggest impediment to childhood immunization. So, the companies say, the Clinton plan would be misdirected and wasteful.

The drug companies are partly right. In fact, both the price and distribution issues must be addressed.

Neither side disputes that childhood immunization rates are unacceptably low, especially for children under age 2. Though most children have received the necessary immunizations by the time they enter school, a 1991 study showed that 63 percent of Utah's 2-year-old children were underimmunized. In some urban areas of the United States, 90 percent of children in that age group are underimmunized.

There also is no denying that the cost of vaccines has risen dramatically in the last decade. A full set of vaccinations, purchased at the reduced price available to the federal government, cost $7 in 1982. In 1992 it cost $129.

The cost to a private physician was $23 in 1982; in 1992 it was $244. Private physicians must pass these charges on to patients, and only about half of private insurance plans cover them.

Medicaid is the only health insurance available for one quarter of the nation's preschool children, yet Medicaid reimbursements are inadequate to cover private physicians' immunization costs. So more private doctors have been sending their patients to overburdened public health clinics where vaccinations are free to those unable to pay. In some areas of the nation, public clinics have not been able to keep up with the demand.

The result is that immunizations increasingly are available only to the children of parents who can afford them. However, in the 11 states where free vaccines already are available to public clinics and private doctors, immunization rates are higher.

No one can make a final judgment on the Clinton plan until the administration answers remaining questions about how the federal government will determine the prices it pays vaccine manufacturers and how the program will be funded. Drug companies are worried that in a government-controlled monopoly market, they will not be able to demand prices high enough to recoup research and development costs and ensure a reasonable profit.

It is certain, too, that simply providing free vaccine to public clinics and private physicians will not be a panacea. Even if vaccines are plentiful and free, parents still must be educated and persuaded to make sure their children are immunized.

What's more, some centralized record-keeping system to keep track of a child's immunization history obviously would be very helpful. That is part of the Clinton proposal. More funds also could be used by public clinics to follow up on vaccination programs with individual patients.

Nevertheless, universally available vaccines are part of the answer to raising childhood immunization rates in this nation. At least the Clinton administration has got that part of the puzzle right.

The Hartford Courant

Hartford, COnnecticut, April 24, 1993

Several state governments are not waiting for the Clinton administration to develop a national health-care policy. They are working on their own plans, as well they should.

Letting states set some of the details of health-insurance coverage would allow various approaches to be tested in the marketplace, among them networks of purchasing cooperatives and so-called single-payer systems that would place everyone in one insurance program.

The Florida Legislature has approved some major reforms whose focus would be universal coverage, a choice among at least three health plans for consumers, and cost controls through a network of 11 regional group-purchasing alliances.

Maryland is considering a proposal to provide health coverage to 600,000 uninsured residents and to clamp down on costs. Tennessee, Hawaii, Oregon, Vermont and Minnesota are working on their versions of reform.

The Clinton administration is busily working on a national plan, of course. To be meaningful, that plan would have to establish the goals of universal access and cost controls for every state. But experimentation at the state level is a wise approach toward national reform.

Although no sweeping overhaul is on the Connecticut legislative agenda, several modest ideas are being considered. Most important is designing new $300-million-a-year health-insurance coverage for the state's 130,000 workers, retirees and their families.

Fierce competition among some insurers, hospital groups, unions and other interests delayed the project and may dilute its effectiveness.

Another idea is being promoted by State Comptroller William E. Curry Jr., who endorses the managed-competition model being promoted nationally by many large insurers. Mr. Curry wants the state to sponsor a network of providers, who would then open their program to municipal workers and, eventually, employees of small businesses.

The states should exercise their freedom to experiment with cost controls and insurance coverage. The United States is not likely to find a single solution for several years — if ever.

3-31-93 THE PHILADELPHIA INQUIRER. UNIVERSAL PRESS SYND.

The Seattle Times

Seattle, Washington, April 26, 1993

WHEN backers of Washington's sweeping health-care reform first introduced their legislation, they were quick to admit passage would not come easy. What an understatement that turned out to be.

Before passing reforms, lawmakers spent months haggling over numerous details in the 186-page bill. They huddled in closed-door sessions, reached consensus, had second thoughts, reached agreement again, then suffered more reservations.

Lobbyists on all sides were out in force last week, stirring images of thumb screws being applied to squeamish senators. One reform-backing senator was essentially held hostage in Olympia, unable to visit her ailing mother in Iowa.

All of which prompts congratulations to Gov. Mike Lowry, state Sen. Phil Talmadge, D-Seattle, state Rep. Dennis Dellwo, D-Spokane, and their staffs who had the gumption to fight for these breakthrough reforms. They worked tirelessly to extend coverage to thousands of uninsured residents and to rein in skyrocketing costs that hurt everybody.

That said, the plan is flawed. It needs even more work. Opponents now should work constructively with the soon-to-be-created, five-member health-care commission to fine-tune the reforms and make them better.

For example, in the original bill, doctors who charge too much or use unnecessary procedures were to be weeded out of the new health plans that will take shape.

But a troubling clause added to the bill could, under some interpretations, allow all licensed providers to participate until proven too expensive. This sets up an obvious administrative and legal nightmare — one that could hamper the competitive intent of the reforms.

Opponents who felt left out during the legislative fight should work now to assure that their interests are represented on the new commission and that it has a strong commitment to make the health plans truly competitive.

Lawmakers worked hard to ease the transition for owners of small businesses, who fear mandatory coverage for their employees by 1997 (and employees' dependents by 1999) will bankrupt them. Many small-business owners still have legitimate concerns. But they have years to try to work on them.

Indeed, everybody involved should take a well-earned break before moving to the next stage, which is to improve on these intriguing but untested proposals.

The Idaho STATESMAN

Boise, Idaho, April 26, 1993

State Health and Welfare officials are charging fees to help single parents collect unpaid child support, and many people don't like it.

Some struggling single parents, mostly women, fear they are being penalized, even discouraged, from trying to collect child support.

But the Idaho Department of Health and Welfare has devised a fair payment system that should not discourage anyone from pursuing a non-paying parent.

Health and Welfare will try to collect the fee from the parent who isn't paying child support, not the parent who is struggling to keep the kids fed and clothed.

And the fees will be used for the services of private attorneys that the agency has to hire, not for its own staff or computer time.

Unfortunately, the program is growing more rapidly than its budget. Taxpayers can no longer continue to shoulder all the costs of the collection service.

The higher costs come partly from federal rules that say the state can't discriminate as to who receives help. That means a wealthy person can ask the state to help him or her collect child support the same as someone who is poor.

In fairness to taxpayers, parents who can help support the program should. It makes little sense for taxpayers to continue paying the costs of collecting child support for someone who can afford to hire his or her own attorney.

But it does make sense for taxpayers to help collect child support for poor parents. Health and Welfare says its collection service will continue to be free for parents who qualify for welfare or Medicaid.

Everyone wins — especially the children — when both parents live up to their family obligations.

That's why it's important to keep the state's child support services in business, even if that means charging fees to some.

The Courier-Journal

Louisville, Kentucky, January 29, 1993

HILLARY CLINTON — no, make that Hillary *Rodham* Clinton — may be the perfect symbol of women in these times. One moment she's the hard-nosed lawyer, the next she's standing five respectful steps behind her husband with a look on her face that says, "Isn't he wonderful? Maybe I'll make his favorite meat-loaf tonight."

She's playing a balancing act that many women play these days, but, unfortunately for Mrs. Clinton, she must do it so visibly. Living, as she does, under the scrutiny of the press, the props of each role are so transparent. The headband is on when she sits at her desk, but then — *zip* — it disappears when it's time to play the traditional First Lady role.

These days Mrs. Clinton — a hero to professional women, a threat to women *and* men who fear the change she represents — is taking heat again. This time it's for her new appointment: head of the President's committee on overhauling the nation's health care system.

There's no debate over whether she's qualified for the job — her role in Arkansas' education reform efforts and her prominence in legal and children's issues prove she's the right person for the job. Debate has centered on ridiculous side issues, like this: Doesn't this put the President in an awkward position, since he'll have trouble firing her if she does a bad job?

Well, Mrs. Clinton is not going to do a bad job. Already she has pushed back her hair and is hard at work, displaying those skills for organization and bringing people together that are so rare, and that any solution to the health care problem will require.

But her intelligence goes even beyond that. Asked for details on what she plans to do, the Hillary without a headband smiled and told the press, "Whatever my husband asks me to."

Wow. Now there's a First Lady to admire.

DESERET NEWS

Salt Lake City, Utah, January 28, 1993

By putting his wife in charge of drafting legislation to overhaul the nation's staggering health-care problems, President Clinton is taking a calculated risk.

If this effort succeeds, it will set a precedent for giving major policy-setting roles to future first ladies and could open the door to the eventual election of the first woman president of the United States.

Of more immediate importance, if Hillary Clinton and her high-powered task force succeed, their work could have an impact far beyond health care. It's hard to see how the bloated federal deficit can be reduced without curbing the soaring costs of medical care and health insurance. Likewise, unless the deficit is sharply curtailed and eventually eliminated, the economy won't be nearly as robust as it can and should be.

But if Mrs. Clinton fails, doors are likely to be slammed in the faces of future first ladies, millions of Americans will continue to suffer, and the voters are not likely to treat her husband kindly the next time he seeks election.

At this point, the Clintons certainly deserve credit for candor. This unpaid appointment simply formalizes the role Hillary Clinton has long held as her husband's closest and most trusted adviser.

What's more, some of the criticism being directed at Mrs. Clinton's appointment is exaggerated. "How does a secretary of health and human services or a budget director tell a president that his wife's idea is half-baked?" one critic asks. The answer is simple: The same way an HHS secretary or a budget director tells the president himself that his own idea is half-baked. Namely, by using more tactful language but still being frank. Presidential ideas, after all, are discussed all the time in Cabinet meetings. Though Cabinet meetings are a far cry from free-for-all discussions a la the McLaughlin Group, they're no rubber stamps either.

Despite Hillary Clinton's impressive credentials as a lawyer and her notable track record in leading a task force that reformed Arkansas' school system, President Clinton has done his wife no favor by assigning her to spearhead health-care reform.

She will have to buck resistance from the 59 percent of Americans who, in a U.S. News & World Report survey just before the inauguration, objected to Hillary Clinton's becoming "a major adviser on appointments and policy."

And she will have to overcome the resistance of some highly powerful interest groups. Physicians, insurers, pharmaceutical firms, hospitals — each views health-care reform differently. Yet each group has purchased a voice in reform with big financial contributions to the 1992 presidential and congressional election campaigns.

To her challenging new assignment, Hillary Clinton is said to bring a unique gift for cutting through complex issues and forging consensus. All Americans have a stake in the reform effort. If the job is done right, it will not only extend health coverage to the uninsured but also rein in the skyrocketing cost of medical care. Let's all join in cheering for the first lady to succeed.

Newsday

New York City, New York, January 26, 1993

She's brilliant, unflinchingly loyal, and the president can trust her above every living soul on this planet. Nonetheless, President Bill Clinton is making a potentially grave political error in appointing his wife Hillary to head his task force on health care revision.

There is no doubt she is competent, tough and skilled at intricate negotiations. But everything Hillary Clinton does as the nation's health policy czar will be obscured by the long shadow cast by her role as first lady. Stripped to their essentials, the problems are these: He can't fire his wife. And who can be totally honest with — or about — the boss' wife?

Revamping the health care system is a defining task of Clinton's presidency. If he extricates the nation from this morass of runaway cost, systemic waste and horrifying coverage gaps, he will have helped fix the deficit and solved many social problems. The health care conundrum has so many competing constituent groups, so many lobbyists already jockeying — and so much sacrifice ahead for middle-income Americans who will end up paying more for less — that there is no other issue with higher stakes.

Putting his wife in charge gives Clinton certain loyalty. But it also gives him no political cover. If things go wrong, as they inevitably will at some point, he can't dismiss her. In a capital that thrives on finding scapegoats for every misstep, in a system where — rightly or wrongly — the person on top one moment can be wallowing at the bottom the next, it's a political necessity to be able to throw someone overboard who's perceived to have erred.

Short of being humiliated if the Clinton health plan founders, Hillary Clinton will face inevitable sniping about every decision she and the president make. Having suffered the indignity of being skewered for such inanities as her headbands and her hat, she may welcome such substantive criticism. And in giving her a highly visible role, the Clintons have eliminated the possibility that the first lady will be portrayed as a dark, behind-the-scenes force a la Nancy Reagan.

If Hillary Rodham Clinton and her husband succeed in solving the nation's health care crisis, as we hope, they will have redefined the very idea of the first lady. If they fail, the ignominy will be doubly deep, for it will be personal as well as political.

The San Diego Union-Tribune.

San Diego, California, January 30, 1993

Who elected Hillary Rodham Clinton? The answer, of course, is that no one did. But, then, no one elected any other member of Bill Clinton's senior staff or Cabinet.

It always has been a president's prerogative to choose his White House advisers. Thus it's entirely legitimate for Clinton to appoint his wife to a prominent staff position and give her an office in the West Wing.

And that's the point. It is the president who ultimately will be held accountable for solving America's health care crisis, the mission which he has just deputized Hillary to tackle.

Mrs. Clinton indeed may become the most powerful First Lady in American history. But at least her policy role will be aboveboard, unlike the dealings of such influential predecessors as Edith Wilson, who ran the executive branch behind closed doors after her husband had a stroke in 1919.

Hillary's considerable talents are not in dispute. In Arkansas, she skillfully managed a committee that pushed through a string of education reforms.

And she has had a much smoother first week in the White House than the president. That said, assigning the First Lady such a high-visibility role entails enormous political risks.

One obvious danger is that many Americans may resent her top-level involvement in the extraordinarily difficult issue of health care reform. A recent poll shows voters are split right down the middle on whether the president's wife should have a say in major policy decisions, with 47 percent supporting the idea and 45 percent opposed. If Mrs. Clinton's participation becomes a controversial matter itself, it will only complicate the president's efforts to straighten out the health care problem.

And what will happen if the recommendation from Mrs. Clinton's task force is one the president does not want to embrace? Will it be difficult for him to reject publicly his own wife's proposal?

If, in the end, Mrs. Clinton fails to deliver on the high expectations imposed by her new position, the responsibility will rest not with her but with the occupant of the Oval Office. As always, the buck stops on the president's desk.

LAS VEGAS
REVIEW-JOURNAL
Las Vegas, Nevada,
January 28, 1993

To a great extent, the discomfort level over the high profile Hillary Clinton will enjoy in her husband's administration reflects a lingering confusion over the gender roles in modern marriage in general.

The reassuring matronliness of Barbara Bush only postponed the inevitable. It simply is not reasonable to expect this or any first lady born and raised after 1945 to restrict herself to high teas and flower arrangements.

In fact, the change is not so sudden. Not only were insiders aware that a word to Nancy Reagan (or her astrologer) could get quick action a decade ago, some cynics even contend Mrs. Reagan was capable of taking care of the matter first and telling Ron about it later. And tales of first ladies conducting the nation's affairs during a presidential illness date back at least to Warren Harding's time ... probably a lot further.

Far from pretending any outrage at Mrs. Clinton's taking up her own office in the White House's West Wing (the hub of actual business), even the lady's philosophical detractors should rejoice that her role as newly-appointed "Health Czar" brings her out of the shadows where her activities are subject to public scrutiny.

On the bright side, Mr. Clinton proves he means to take health care seriously by handing the task over to his "better half" — this is one report that won't sit unread on the window sill — and the first lady's extramarital career leaves little doubt she is both quick and competent.

THE BLADE

Toledo, Ohio, January 27, 1993

WHETHER it is criticizing her choice of headgear or publicly fussing about her possible role in public affairs, Hillary Clinton already seems to be fair game for the critics. Why not cut her a little slack?

During almost the entire presidential campaign Mrs. Clinton was largely seen and not heard. After her gaffe about staying home

Hillary Clinton has the intelligence and certainly the right to play an important role as an unpaid official in her husband's administration

and baking cookies — still viewed as an honorable American activity even though most people buy theirs at the store — she adopted or was counseled to adopt a policy of strategic silence. Marilyn Quayle, also a lawyer and every bit as abrasive as Hillary Clinton was deemed to be, was quite active during the campaign, speaking at the GOP convention and working at rehabilitation efforts after Hurricane Andrew tore a destructive path through the Gulf states.

Mrs. Clinton wore a bright blue saucer-shaped hat for the inauguration, which is her business. She wasn't elected and is not being paid from public funds. Within the law and the ethics regulations already announced by the Clinton administration, she is free to pursue her own interests. It appears also that she will have an office in the West Wing of the White House — heavens, the men's policymaking wing! — and has been appointed to lead the group that

will draft a Clinton health-insurance proposal.

Some critics say Mr. Clinton should have a health plan drafted already. The appropriate rebuttal to that is the health-care plan is being delayed because it is so terribly complex. Many people are beginning to wonder if the federal government, having botched the administration of medicare, is the appropriate party to administer a more comprehensive health-insurance plan for Americans.

Mrs. Clinton is not known as an expert in this field; yet she contributed a good deal to the development of her husband's education program while he was governor of Arkansas. She cannot be paid under a law passed after the late President John Kennedy appointed his brother as attorney general. So there should be no problem there.

Many people still have problems adjusting to the fact that husbands and wives have separate careers and that even the President's wife has a right to lead a life and career of her own, even if it leads her into the caverns of the Clinton policy wonks in the West Wing of the White House.

Eleanor Roosevelt was in many ways a pioneer among wives of presidents who aspired to play an active role in the White House — in part because her husband was disabled from the effects of poliomyelitis. So there is ample precedent for the wife of a president to play a prominent part in her husband's administration. Moreover, a woman may well be elected president at some point, and suppose her husband were skilled and willing to be an unpaid official of her administration. Would he be subject to the same criticism that Mrs. Clinton has endured? Mrs. Clinton's critics should chill out a little.

The Washington Post

Washington, D.C., January 27, 1993

THE TWO great issues in health care reform point in opposite directions: One is extending protection to the one-seventh of the population that is without insurance at any one time; the other is controlling costs. As a society, we tend to be better at the first of these tasks—providing benefits—than at the second one of imposing discipline. It's always more pleasant to say yes to a lot of people than it is to say no, and we've provided health care insurance on a mass basis before, as in Medicare and Medicaid. We more or less know how to do it. There are plenty of problems associated with broadening coverage or making it universal— what mechanisms to use, the array of benefits to provide, how to pay the cost—but those are well within the bounds of normal political experience and expertise.

It's the second half of the problem that makes reform so hard; it is not within those bounds. Health care costs are now about 14 percent of gross domestic product and rising. They represent about $1 in every $7 that Americans spend and are the great budget busters for businesses and families as well as government, crowding out other expenditures. There are all sorts of theories about how they can be controlled. Some suggest the system has so many layers of fat that costs can easily be cut without diminution of the quality of care. Others say not, or not that much—that sooner or later, serious cost controls mean limits on care as well. Some say costs can be controlled by changing the incentives in the system so that providers have to compete for business on the basis of price. Others doubt a competitive model will ever be strong enough to do the job and think that government will ultimately have to intervene to hold down costs directly.

How large a cudgel to give the government,

along with what kind, is perhaps the hardest question the planners have to resolve. The simplest way of gaining control over costs, or at any rate the most direct, would likely be to federalize the basic health care system—have the government be the buyer for the entire population in more or less the way it already is for the elderly and the disabled under Medicare. But there are disadvantages to creating so large a role for government, and probably that is a bigger step than the country is prepared to take. The likelihood is that the planners, for good substantive as well as political reasons, will start trying to achieve cost control with as little direct government involvement as possible. At some point in this business, the dividing line between a private and public system begins to blur, but we would guess they are likely to try a system of "managed care" first (which the government would structure even though it would be privately run), and turn to a more direct government role in the form of fee schedules, more or less binding budgets and the rest, only if that failed.

That might be the right way to proceed, but it ought to be explicitly done. The first step should leave open the possibility of the second if the first fails. Our own sense is that managed care is too frail a reed and won't stem the costs, but perhaps that's wrong. Here again, Medicare is precedent if not quite model. In deference to the medical profession, it was set up with minimal controls over practice and cost. Now, in an effort to control costs, the government dictates not just price but, through the device of price, many aspects of practice as well. Even in health care, he who pays the piper ultimately calls the tune; it just takes longer. And that's the lengthy process in which, on behalf of us all, the administration and Congress are now engaged.

HILLARY CLINTON has always worked closely with her husband, both in government and politics. He and she both wanted it to be that way again in the White House. The plan they've come up with—appointing Hillary Clinton as head of a committee that will oversee health care reform legislation—is straightforward and audacious. It will make the president's wife publicly accountable for the large imprint she was going to make on public policy, whether or not she officially took on another title besides First Lady. It is hard to imagine a more difficult assignment than health care. The precedent Mr. Clinton invokes here is Hillary Clinton's role in helping to get education reform in Arkansas. That reform turned out to be his greatest source of pride during his tenure as governor. The president clearly expects that his wife will do a similar job this time around.

Hillary Clinton has been carrying a heavy burden over the last year. Americans have spent three decades or so in a free-form argument about the roles of men and women, husbands and wives, fathers and mothers. There's been a considerable shift in opinion. When pressed, few people (including few who call themselves conservative) want women to be forced back into the roles that had been defined for them in the 1950s. But the country is still divided and uncertain about many of the questions at stake.

Mrs. Clinton, as the quintessential transitional figure, thus has found herself at the center of many arguments that were not really about her at all. The issue was sometimes muddied by her husband's own campaign, which wanted simultaneously to use her to appeal to feminist voters

and to reassure the tradition-minded that she was really much more old-fashioned than supposed. But the truth is that she has always been more than a one-dimensional figure, that she does represent, in her outlook on life, her interests and activities, vast numbers of women who cannot be pigeonholed as homemakers vs. working women. She *is* First Lady, with all the duties that go with that role. She also now has a big policy job within the administration. She should be judged by how well she does each—not by whether she should be performing either set of duties or what is fitting for her to do and so on.

And judged she will be. For starters there are bound to be some difficulties inherent in Mrs. Clinton's West Wing role. This is a built-in risk of those who have spouses working for them along with others. Will members of Congress master the art of mixing respect for the First Lady with candor about the matter at hand? Will it be possible for other aides and subordinates of the president to stand up to his wife, or even to challenge her work to him, if they think they should (and as they would with any other person in her job)? With luck it won't come to that, but it is a hazard both Clintons should be mindful of. In fact, we suspect the president's aides would always be able to get any discontent across to him through the wonders of a free press and its obligation to protect sources. More important is that having taken line responsibility, Mrs. Clinton will have to accept the costs of being involved in controversies that revolve not around her "role," but around the public issues at stake. We don't think she'll have a problem with that at all.

The Register-Guard

Eugene, Oregon, January 27, 1993

Health care reform is near the top of the new president's agenda, just as it was one of the main issues on which he campaigned. Bill Clinton affirmed the seriousness of his interest this week by appointing his wife, Hillary, to chair the task force that will prepare a reform plan to submit to Congress.

This is no honorary job. Hillary Clinton will lead the new committee and be a full participant in its work. While she is not a health care expert in the technical sense, she has long worked in policy fields dealing primarily with children and secondarily with health. Her knowledge of those related subjects is well established.

It will be an advantage to the committee to have Mrs. Clinton at its head. The only way the group could acquire more clout and visibility would be for the president himself to act as chairman, which is not practical given his other responsibilities.

While there will be some critics, this type of role seems perfect for the new first lady. She is too capable and interested in issues to serve as merely a decorative White House hostess. Yet common sense — and a statute passed after John Kennedy named his brother Robert as attorney general — prevent her from serving in the Cabinet or in any other regular federal executive capacity.

Between those two roads, one unappealing and one blocked, lies a third involving hard, satisfying work as an unpaid, volunteer, high-level appointee on the kinds of ad hoc committees presidents often use to shape major legislative proposals. The health care group is only the first of what is likely to be a series of such appointments for the career woman who is now first lady.

In announcing her appointment, Clinton said his wife is "better at organizing and leading people from a complex beginning to a certain end than anybody I've ever worked with in my life."

She will need to live up to that praise to lead the health care task force successfully. Few issues are more complex. Everyone endorses the president's general goals — adequate health insurance coverage for all, at reasonable cost, without significant loss of quality. But there is no broad agreement on the means, the specifics of a plan that could accomplish those and other ends.

Yet the pressure for reform is greater than ever, thanks in part to expectations raised by Clinton's own campaign. So the new task force has a better chance than any predecessor to hammer out a plan that can be passed by Congress. Its chances of success were enhanced by Hillary Clinton's appointment.

LURIE'S WORLD

HIS

HERS

K/6 Jan. 24 '93

©1993 International Copyright by CARTOONEWS Inc., N.Y.C., USA

The News and Observer
Raleigh, North Carolina, January 24, 1993

President Clinton's choice of Hillary Rodham Clinton to head the drafting of his health care plan is two kinds of good news.

First, it tells Americans that giving health reform the top-priority urgency too long denied it is one campaign promise this president means to keep.

It also lays to rest, at the earliest possible moment, the tiresome speculation about this first lady's role. No, she will not retreat to a pretty East Wing desk and spend her formerly high-priced hours arranging state-dinner seating charts. None of Clinton's other smart, effective campaign wheelhorses has been expected to do that. Why should she?

Her experience both in legal practice and as a governor's wife and teammate have taught Mrs. Clinton plenty about the responsibilities of power. She may not know the kitchen as well as some, but she knows better than most that it's not the only place that generates heat, and she's prepared to take it.

On health care, no doubt she will have to. Her task force's plan will have to pass three very tough tests.

The plan must offer sound, prevention-oriented basic coverage to every American, from the pre-schoolers whose shameful public-policy neglect has been Mrs. Clinton's abiding concern to the senior citizens whose medical bills are our most intractable health-cost problem.

It must employ brakes strong enough to halt a cost spiral that has proved harder to stop than a 747 at full takeoff power. Cost containment was the Achilles heel of Clinton's campaign health-care proposals. No plan that leaves this weakness uncured will be worth his, his wife's or Congress' time.

Last, the plan must be politically do-able. That's a daunting stipulation, given the influence of a health care industry dripping with dollars and clad in the near-magical aura of respect and faith our society still accords its healers.

The Clinton campaign's "managed competition" pitch was to cover all citizens through employer taxes. Private insurers would bid competitively for the managed-care business of giant pools of supposedly cost-conscious customers.

But so far, most competition in the industry has aimed not at cutting care's price but at increasing its quantity and quality — or its technological intensity, which isn't always the same thing. Costs thus are pushed up, not down.

Until now, Clinton could get by with failing to lasso the health-cost bull because nobody else was even whirling a rope. Now, trying is no longer enough. For reasons both fiscal and humane, the stop must be made.

No one can say a president who has tapped his closest teammate to mobilize the effort isn't trying. No one in his right mind would envy Mrs. Clinton her new assignment — let alone grudge her the right to tackle it.

The Chattanooga Times
Chattanooga, Tennessee, January 23, 1993

So the first lady will have an office in the West Wing of the White House and serve as a key domestic policy adviser to her husband. Good.

Hillary Rodham Clinton, as she prefers to be called, is a woman with much to offer this country. She should not be shuffled into the traditional first lady's role just for appearances.

The first first lady who is a career woman, Ms. Clinton is blazing her own trail through this generational change in White House leadership. Millions of American women and girls look to her as a role model, and she has a responsibility to herself, her husband, her country and to them to put her talents to the highest use possible.

Other first ladies have wielded considerable influence on their husbands, but pains were taken to keep that influence behind the scenes — to avoid offending public sensibilities about meddling wives and the like. But times have changed.

President Clinton has made it very clear that he actively seeks his wife's advice on important decisions and has done so for years. Her expected role in overseeing development of his top-priority, national health-care policy demonstrates the level of confidence he has in her.

And, as Vice President Al Gore said during a pre-inaugural interview, "One of the things new with this generational change you see with this inaugural is a different kind of dialogue between husbands and wives about the kinds of issues that presidents have to deal with."

The vice president went on to stress the caliber of the contribution Ms. Clinton can make to this administration. "Hillary Clinton is a force for good, and she has excellent advice," he said. "If people knew the full range and value of advice she brings to the table they'd wonder why he (President Clinton) doesn't rely on her more."

The Miami Herald
Miami, Florida, January 24, 1993

IF THERE were embarrassing skeletons rattling in Hillary Clinton's closet, a year on the campaign trail ought to have revealed them. In fact the worst the gossips could do was sneer at her cookies and affirm that she is among the best and brightest lawyers in the nation. Were she not married to President Clinton and subject to anti-nepotism laws, she may well have been named attorney general. Instead the president has assigned her to develop a national health plan, arguably a more important role to many Americans.

She is eminently qualified to tackle this issue, which is atop the nation's list of domestic priorities. There is no doubt among the American people or in official Washington that Ms. Clinton speaks both to and for the president. The Clintons forged their "working partnership" in Arkansas, where she was instrumental in building coalitions among disparate interests to support public school reforms.

Coalition-building is a vital political skill, especially in dealing with an issue as amorphous, costly, and difficult to resolve as health care.

It's rare that a first lady gets an *official* role as a presidential adviser, though of course first ladies wield considerable influence unofficially. Eleanor Roosevelt, FDR's "eyes and ears," may come the closest to having had such a portfolio before. Hillary Clinton — focused, determined, accomplished — may create her own portfolio.

Still, there are cautions to be raised: Short of divorce, President Clinton can't just fire the first lady as an adviser, should things go awry and her advice prove faulty. Her *faux pas*, if any, will be his. Upon setting up shop in the West Wing of the White House, Ms. Clinton will be a key political player in formulating policy. That makes her as subject to criticism as all the other players. She has to accept those rules.

Already understood is that well over 30 million Americans have no health insurance at all. Millions of others live in dread of an illness that will consume a lifetime of savings. Health care's cost and accessibility have a wide-ranging impact on almost every other area of life, from education and crime to insurance rates and employment.

Hillary Clinton not only has the president's ear, but his heart and his trust. She has taken on a crucial new role for a first lady. By her performance, however, the president himself will be judged.

The State
Columbia, South Carolina, January 30, 1993

HILLARY RODHAM CLINTON has one of the toughest jobs in her husband's new Administration: Produce a comprehensive plan to reform American health care.

President Clinton placed health care reform high on his list of priorities during the campaign. Now his wife and her task force have 100 days to come up with a way to extend health care coverage to all Americans at a price the nation can afford. It's a tall order.

Besides giving her a real job, the assignment puts her role in the Administration out front, at least until this job is finished. Recent First Ladies' involvement in White House business has been less evident, although their behind-the-scenes influence has been substantial.

The nation will know what Hillary is up to as she settles into her new West Wing office. She is likely to be out among the people, holding hearings and gathering information, said Arkansas political scientist Roby Robertson, who watched her technique as she molded education reform while Clinton was Governor. President Clinton's job description for his wife is that she will be a consensus builder, not a power broker.

There are, of course, legitimate concerns about whether the President's wife should be a major policy maker, particularly if she stumbles in her mission. "Who's going to tell the President his wife's doing a lousy job," said Sheila Tate, former press secretary to Nancy Reagan. "What's to prevent her from abuse of power?"

Some observers fear that Hillary Clinton will tilt her decisions in favor of her long-time passion for children's interests and away from the needs of elderly people. She must take care to balance the needs of all Americans.

Another concern is that she might be little more than her husband's puppet. That's unlikely, given what we have heard and observed about the stiffness of her spine and independence of her mind. Still, it would be foolish to believe she would veer sharply from her husband's articulated ideas about health care reform. Indeed, he chose his wife to head the task force after he concluded last week that his health care advisers were not "in sync" with what he wanted, *The Los Angeles Times* reported. Coherent leadership in the executive branch is essential if progress is to be made on health care reform.

President Clinton has always been up front about his intention to rely on his wife's intelligence and abilities. He said in a *Newsweek* interview his wife's role was an easy question for him. "It's my duty to the American people to take advantage of the most talented people I can find. She certainly qualifies there, and I would be derelict in my duty if I didn't use her in some major way within the confines of what is proper," he said.

The job he has given her is proper — and challenging. The image is of a husband and wife working together, with mutual respect for each other's abilities. That is a role model for American families that few people could criticize.

DAYTON DAILY NEWS
Dayton, Ohio, January 28, 1993

If there were any doubts that Bill Clinton was serious about reforming the nation's health-care system, the assignment of Hillary Rodham Clinton to the task must remove them.

After all, the idea that *he's* just messing around could be reasonably entertained. The idea that *she* is messing around is just too silly.

The appointment has another meaning, of course: It is an historic development in the history of the first ladyship.

One can imagine a time — if not in this administration, then someday — when playing a major, acknowledged, substantive role in a presidential administration could lead to the first lady becoming a credible candidate for president.

Why not? An enormous percentage of presidential nominees are former vice presidents who put that fact forth as their major qualification.

And it certainly looks as though Hillary Clinton will have a larger role in the Clinton presidency than any vice president has ever had. Besides her assignment to specific tasks, she will certainly be advising and hearing out her husband on all manner of matters.

When the George Bush campaign attacked Hillary Clinton, it was widely criticized for changing the subject away from Bill. The Bush people responded that Bill Clinton had said that if you elect him, you get both of them, that they were a team.

That response is looking somewhat more powerful now than it did then.

Still the criticisms of Mrs. Clinton were silly, referring, for example, to obscure documents that supposedly painted her as some sort of anti-family radical.

The simple truth is that if she didn't make her husband a radical governor, there was no reason to believe that she'd make him a radical president.

At any rate, the president's deployment of his wife on substantive matters cannot be fairly criticized. She is a person of independent accomplishment, having been rated an exceptional lawyer. And she has much experience in dealing with public issues. And she has his confidence.

Indeed, it is better — more honest — for the president to give his wife this formal, acknowledged role than to proceed as if her influence is some sort of embarrassment or secret.

Part II: Families, Children & Health Care

Family health care is an important public policy issue in the United States. First, and foremost, its effectiveness is a considered reflection of the overall well-being and conscience of the nation. As two of the most vulnerable goups in American society women and children should receive appropriate quality medical treatment. The extent to which women and children are actually shielded from preventable and unnecessary medical problems tells us a great deal about the value priorities and moral commitment of the country.

The issue is also important for pragmatic reasons because, simply, family health care is cost effective. With an immediate impact on the health care status of all family members, especially pregnant women and children. In addition, there are long-range societal consequences. Healthy mothers, for example, are more likely to deliver healthy babies. Healthy babies have a better chance of becoming healthy children. And healthy children do better in school and are more apt to grow up to become productive citizens. By improving the health care status of mothers and children, we are able to deal with a host of important social issues.

Health care in relation to the family unit is also a symbolic and politically expedient issue. Most Americans believe that "mothers," "babies," and "children" deserve special care and treatment. Therefore, it is relatively easy to focus public attention on this area. It is also much easier for public officials to push for government-sponsored maternal and child health care programs. No one wants to be *against* providing services to pregnant women and infants.

This, in turn, helps to legitimize and stimulate governmental activity.

In order to understand governmental involvement in this area, it is necessary to focus on the role of the states. State governments have always played a role in America's maternal and child care system. During the 1980s, however, they became more actively involved in this policy area. The states helped focus national attention on the problems faced by poor women and children and they served as the testing grounds for major policy initiatives aimed at alleviating these problems. In essence, the states became key actors in the development of maternal and child health care programs in the United States.

Another area to which a dramatic reconsidering of our research and practical priorities will be devoted is aging and disability. As people live longer, the length of time during which they need help in the tasks of daily living increases. The astronomical cost of confronting this dependence has sent tremors through Congress and state capitals, and has drained the savings and psyches of far more American families than catastrophic illness.

Most nursing-home residents and millions of elderly living at home need help with the basic activities of living – bathing, dressing, using the toilet, and eating. Of the 1.3 million nursing-home residents, almost two-thirds suffer from dementia, mental disorientation, or loss of memory. Most suffer from difficulties in walking, often due to rheumatism, arthritis and, particularly for the 90 percent of women over 75 who suffer from osteoporosis, disabling injuries due to falls.

It has often been suggested that we need a massive effort to reduce and, for many of the elderly, eliminate the chief threats to their independence. What the elderly and the disabled want most is independence. Is there any son or daughter who would rather spend money to keep parents in a nursing home than to keep them living independently? Is there any disabled person who would rather be at the mercy of their dependents than be self-reliant? The more independent the elderly and disabled are, the less expensive nursing and institutional care they require. The payoff of a project aimed at making these Americans more independent could be enormous.

Critics of the U.S. health care system as it has funtioned for decades charge that politicians, as well as patients and physicians, need to exercise some self-discipline. They suggest that a cynical cycle of legislatively induced health care inflation too often marks the actions of Congress.

These advocates point to two primary goals in rectifying the health care system as it currently stands in regard to the traditional family structure. First, they urge the recognition of the best health care system and to build on it. Most Americans, about 140 million out of a population of 235 million, have some health care coverage through their employment relationship. The reformers suggest simply requiring that each employer subject to the minimum wage law assure its employees of a minimum level of health care: physician treatment, hospitalization, preventative services for the employee and his or her family. The employer could provide that care however it wished: through insurance, a health maintenance organization (HMO), preferred provider contracts, or directly. Under this plan, if the employer did not choose to pay the extra expense, the employee would

have to pay the difference. This would encourage competition in the marketplace, and press employers and workers to seek the best plan at the lowest cost. For the small employers and the self-employed, a government-sponsored corporation could be set up to provide competitive group rates and access to health maintenance organizations and preferred providers. All employers would of course remain free to provide greater health care benefits, and unions would have the right to bargain for them.

Second, the government would provide health care coverage for the poor, the elderly, and the temporarily unemployed. Supporters aregue that to reap the full benefits from a reoriented, truly competitive health care system, it is imperative for government to fulfill this repsonsibility. As corporate and other big buyers of health care press providers to be more efficient, there will be little maneuvering room to provide comprehensive care for the needy. Competitive forces would signal an end even to well-intentioned cost shifting to pay for the poor, the elderly, and the unemployed by charging the well-insured more for physicians' services and hospitalization.

It may be corporate America's aggressive pursuit of lower-cost quality health care that holds the best hope of getting the system to the level of efficency needed to provide care for all at a reasonable cost. Most Americans agree that social justice requires us to provide care for all at a reasonable cost and to offer comprehensive health care benefits to the average American family. There are more than 34 million Americans without health insurance coverage; no other industrial nation has such a gap. With America's affluence, health care reformers are united and adamant about one thing: There is no excuse for this offense to social justice.

Bush Vetoes Family-Leave Bill; Congressional Override Fails

President Bush Sept. 22, 1992 vetoed legislation that would require large employers to grant unpaid family and medical leave to their workers. The veto was sustained in the House Sept. 30.

The House had approved the final version of the bill, 241–161, on Sept. 10, following its passage by the Senate in August. The Senate Sept. 24 voted, 68-31, to override the veto, marking the first time in eight tries during Bush's term that the upper chamber had overridden the president.

In the House, however, Democratic leaders failed to muster support for an override among opponents of the bill within their own party. The 258–169 vote against sustaining the veto was 27 votes short of the two-thirds majority needed to thwart the president.

The legislation was almost identical to a measure vetoed by Bush in 1990. It would have required businesses with 50 or more employees to allow most of their full-time workers up to 12 weeks of leave for care of newborn or adopted infants, or for personal or family medical emergencies. The bill would have affected about 5% of all U.S. businesses and about 50% of all workers, according to the *Wall Street Journal*.

In a written veto message issued by Bush in Memphis, Tenn. during a six-state campaign trip through the South, Bush asserted his support for family-leave policies, but he restated his opposition to government interference in business practices. The president's statement asserted that the current bill would "stifle the creation of new jobs."

Bush Sept. 16 had announced a family-leave bill of his own that would offer tax credits of up to $1,200 per worker to businesses with under 500 employees that voluntarily provided family leave. The plan was introduced too late to see action in the current congressional session, however.

The veto, Bush's 32nd, quickly became a point of debate in the presidential campaign, where Democrats and Republicans had repeatedly sparred over "family values" and economic relief for working parents.

The Record

Hackensack, New Jersey, September 20, 1992

GEORGE BUSH'S solution to some of America's most pressing problems is tax credits.

He has proposed personal tax credits so that people who can't afford health insurance can purchase it. Now in place of the Family Leave Act, which he is expected to veto shortly, Mr. Bush is proposing business tax credits to give companies an incentive to provide family leave for workers.

In both cases, tax credits are not enough. People need thousands of dollars each year to buy adequate health insurance, and if they get that much money in tax credits, the tax credits are helping the wrong people. The working poor don't make enough money to get sizable tax credits.

Similarly, tax credits may encourage some companies to allow their workers up to 12 weeks of unpaid leave for the birth of a baby, the adoption of a child, or to care for a sick family member, and to hold their jobs for them until they return. But why leave something so important to the whim of the company?

And if the president believes so strongly in this supportive family policy, then why did he wait four years to introduce his version of it? The answer is that he is faced with the embarrassing task of vetoing the Family Leave Act at the same time that he has made family values a central theme of his campaign.

Mr. Bush should sign the family leave bill.

Mr. Bush should drop his tax credit substitute, sign the real Family Leave Act, and do something good for the families of America. There are certain minimum safety and health standards that workers are entitled to, and an unpaid leave for personal or family emergencies should be one of them.

American workers should not have to choose between their jobs and their families. Right now, too many of them do.

THE BUFFALO NEWS

Buffalo, New York, September 16, 1992

THE FAMILY-leave bill that made it through the House of Representatives last week faces a veto by President Bush. Votes are lacking for an override. The result will be a hot partisan issue for the presidential campaign but nothing more.

The gain for working women who need to recover from giving birth and for working families stretched by conflicting responsibilities will be zero.

That is to be lamented. The political process has failed in an area of very personal significance to many Americans.

The bill sent to Bush requires firms with 50 or more workers to grant up to 12 weeks of unpaid leave for childbirth or adoption of a child and for emergency medical reasons — to care for a sick spouse, child or parent. Workers would not face the prospect of losing their jobs if they had such critical family responsibilities.

Democrats are ready to maul Bush with the issue, saying it rightly puts him to the test on "family values." After all, what's more family-oriented than a bill that lets new mothers regain their strength and family members care for each other in hard times without losing employment? Bush and his team pushed "family values" into the campaign in the first place, so there is a good measure of rough justice in what the Democrats plan. They can say, "Prove yourself, George."

Republicans, on the other hand, can argue that the Democratic-controlled Congress is merely playing election-year politics, that it deliberately waited to bring the bill to the floor as the campaign peaks. It's true that the basic bills passed both houses last fall and differences were compromised in a one-day conference many months later.

Now the Bush team, as if to save its bacon, has suddenly produced a new position after all these months. Bush claims to support family leave, but says he doesn't want the government to force it on business.

Instead, the idea being floated by the White House is to provide tax breaks to companies with up to 500 employees that voluntarily adopt family-leave provisions. At least it gives Bush something to talk about if the Democrats back him into a corner and pound away. But because it is still voluntary, it provides no guarantees to workers. And unlike the Democrats' bill, it would cost the government money.

All the political fodder isn't going to help a new mother who may lose a job she badly needs if she stays home for a few weeks to recuperate and care for her new child.

In fact, the family-leave bill might have had a better chance of passage if it had concentrated on the basic issue of leave for mothers of newborn children. Such a simple bill should have had fewer foes. A new mother should have an uncontested right to restore her health and get her child off to a good start with loving care.

Washington may have a different political spin next year. The election could substantially change the outlook on many issues. But whatever the November results, there should be renewed efforts to get a family-leave bill on the books.

The Des Moines Register

Des Moines, Iowa, September 18, 1992

Instead of grumbling about President Bush's Johnny-come-lately alternative to the family-leave bill, the bill's supporters should take it and run with it.

It may be something of a ploy, not entirely unlike the Democrats' ploy of springing the family-leave bill on Bush shortly before the election, but the president's proposal has some merit. Not enough to be acceptable without substantial change, but enough to be a basis for a compromise.

The family-leave bill would require that businesses with more than 50 employees provide them up to 12 weeks unpaid leave annually, to care for their own illness, for a sick family member or for the birth or adoption of a child.

Job security would be guaranteed and health-insurance coverage continued as usual. But the highest-paid employees may be exempted by employers. And, realistically, many Americans could not begin to afford a long, unpaid leave, so the bill is only marginally beneficial.

Bush's plan would give businesses with fewer than 500 workers a tax write-off of up to $20 a day for as many as 60 days of leave annually per employee, or a maximum of $1,200 per worker. Strictly voluntary, it requires employers who participate to offer "reasonable employment or benefits protection to employees while on family leave." It is estimated to cost the federal government between $400 million and $500 million.

And that is the basis for compromise. If the government requires leave, perhaps the government should help businesses shoulder the cost of granting it.

The cost of the family-leave bill is not entirely clear, though a survey of four states with similar laws, by the Families and Work Institute in New York, found only a small percent of businesses reported sizable cost increases. With regard to training, only 4 percent indicated there was a significant cost increase, just 6 percent with regard to administration and just 2 percent with regard to unemployment insurance.

Whatever the extra costs, it may be reasonable for the public at large to share them with businesses. After all it would benefit everyone if there were a fair family-leave program in the United States — mandatory for employers — and available to everyone. Bush's alternative could help move the issue in that direction.

If those who support the bill and the alternative are really interested in family values, not just political opportunity, they will work toward a decent compromise.

The Washington Times

Washington, D.C., September 18, 1992

Bill Clinton doesn't like George Bush's proposed alternative to the family leave bill that Congress plopped into the president's lap last week. Mr. Clinton joined with congressional Democrats Wednesday to complain that Mr. Bush "has no idea how he'll pay for it." The bill sent down from Capitol Hill, by contrast, doesn't seem to cost anything. At least, there aren't any costs that lawmakers and presidential candidate Mr. Clinton care about. This is not only the heart of the Democrats' family leave bill, it is the core of how the Democratic Congress finances its adventures in social engineering: Use other people's money. Make somebody else pay for a program, and presto, social policy is free!

The family leave bill that legislators sent to Mr. Bush, hoping to force a veto out of him that can be portrayed in this election season as callously insensitive to "family values," would require businesses with more than 50 workers to extend up to 12 weeks of unpaid leave each year to employees giving birth or adopting a child, or those caring for a sick child, spouse or parent. Medical benefits would stay in force during the leave. Mr. Bush vetoed a nearly identical mandated-leave bill back in June 1990. The alternative the president has proposed to the new and unimproved bill is to give significant tax breaks to firms that grant their workers leave.

The president's plan might cost the government as much as $2.7 billion in lost business tax revenues. Sensibly, Mr. Bush has proposed that the shortfall be covered by spending cuts rather than tax increases. This is what Mr. Clinton and Democrats in Congress — who seem to have difficulty even conceptualizing spending cuts — call having "no idea" how to pay for a program.

The Democrats, after all, know how to pay for their programs, and they better, because their mandated-leave plan will no doubt cost far more than the president's proposal. But don't expect Congress to cut spending or even increase taxes to pay for the bill. Congress, in fact, won't have to do anything to pay up because lawmakers have hidden the costs. In doing so, Democrats have not made the expense any less real, only less fair. Middle- and lower-middle-class workers least able to afford it will be sneakily stuck with the bill.

Working-class people will be hit hard, first with the loss of jobs. Twelve weeks of leave will cost employers nearly $2,000 per worker, and, according to figures from Republican staff at the congressional Joint Economic Committee, the first response of businesses will be to cover that cost by cutting back on payroll to the tune of some 60,000 jobs. Has the Democratic presidential candidate asked how the loss to the treasury of 60,000 taxpayers, or the cost in unemployment payments will be paid for? Hardly.

Working-class people will also be stuck paying the tab when their hard-pressed employers forgo giving raises. On top of it all, these least fortunate workers will not even get to enjoy the benefit of taking family-crisis leave. A family with a joint income of $25,000 a year can't afford to go without one salary for three months — especially with a new baby in the house, or a sick relative who may be incurring medical bills. So the only ones who will benefit from the leave are the blue-collar workers' better-paid yuppie colleagues who need the time off to go shopping for hardwood Scandinavian cribs and to interview nannies.

Most workers who don't get their raises or who lose their jobs will be unable to trace their suffering directly to Congress' family leave bill. The lawmakers will have hidden not only from the cost of the laws they pass but also from the fact that they engendered those costs.

Congressmen do know what those costs really are, however, and know how to avoid them in dealing with their own employees. How else to explain the fact that members of the House of Representatives have exempted themselves from the enforcement procedures of the bill? No jury trials and punitive damages for representatives if they make new mothers put their noses to the grindstone — just a trip to the laughable House Fair Employment Office, where wrist-slapping is de rigueur.

The Bush proposal has the virtue of being voluntary — employers are not told what to do, they are given incentives. But the most important virtue of the president's plan is that it is honest in its accounting. It is only when the costs are up front that the taxpayers will know to ask the crucial question, "How are we going to pay for this, anyway?"

The Augusta Chronicle

Augusta, Georgia, September 17, 1992

When President Bush vetoed the family leave bill two years ago he explained that companies which could afford such policies were already implementing them, and those that couldn't shouldn't be forced to by government. The resulting closures and job losses, he said, would hurt more families than it would help.

The president did, however, use his "bully-pulpit" to urge business and industry to ease their employees' family burdens whenever possible.

Last week a key segment of corporate America answered the call — and none too soon. The Democrat-controlled Congress had just passed a new leave-bill, designed to embarrass Bush on the "family values" issue.

The measure, very similar to the one he successfully vetoed in 1990, requires high-paid workers — the only ones who can afford it — be allowed to take up to 12 weeks of unpaid leave to care for newborns or ailing parents.

This contrasts with the $25 million project announced by 11 of the nation's top companies and more than 100 small- and medium-sized businesses. They will pool their resources to help finance day care and elderly care in 44 cities.

The companies' sensitivity to the changing work force is far superior in scope to the legislation on the president's desk. He can cite their example as one which should be expanded or emulated throughout the private sector, as it becomes feasible. If the government interferes now, these innovative private initiatives will come to a screeching halt.

Mandates require conformity, not innovation. Besides, the government should stay clear of problems that are already being dealt with elsewhere.

Bush was right to veto family-leave the first time around, and given the progress under way, he'll be even more right to veto it the second time.

The Oregonian

Portland, Oregon, September 16, 1992

President Bush faces a real-life family-values test as he decides whether to veto or sign the family-leave bill Congress has sent to his desk.

This eminently sensible bill would require private businesses to provide up to 12 weeks of unpaid leave per year to employees to care for a newborn or a seriously ill child, parent or spouse. The law would apply to employers with 50 or more workers, to state and local governments and to Congress. About half of American workers would be covered.

Oregon already has a similar law. A parental-leave law took effect in 1988, and a family-medical-leave law took effect this January. Employers fought the parental-leave bill, arguing it would increase their costs and force them to trim their work forces or scale back on other worker benefits. A followup state study two years later showed that nine out of 10 employers experienced no increased costs because of the new law.

Making it easier for workers to care for a seriously ill child or spouse at home may help businesses hold down their health-insurance costs in the long run by reducing the number of days a dependent must spend in the hospital. Companies that already offer parental leave have found it to be more cost-effective than permanently replacing employees.

For their part, employees appreciate the recognition that they should not have to give up their jobs in order to deal with life-and-death family crises. The loss of wages during a leave period provides plenty of incentive for workers to use family leave rarely.

Oregon's congressional delegation, except for Rep. Bob Smith, has been supportive of this legislation. Bush has vetoed family-leave legislation before and has said he will veto this latest bill.

Reinforcing family obligations is an appropriate role for the federal government. Voters looking ahead to this November's election should remember family leave when considering what kind of family values they want their leaders in Washington, D.C., to uphold.

The Hartford Courant

Hartford, Connecticut, September 16, 1992

Less than three weeks after the Republicans sanctified "family values" at their presidential nominating convention, Congress sent to the White House the Family and Medical Leave Act.

Mr. Bush has vetoed similar legislation before, and he is likely to do the same again. By resending the bill, and doing so in the middle of an election campaign, congressional Democrats no doubt wanted to cast public doubt on the White House's commitment to family values.

Connecticut, whose U.S. Sen. Christopher J. Dodd has championed the federal bill for years, has experience with a state family leave law. It's no cure-all, but it has worked reasonably well during its two-year existence. At least 10 other states also have family leave laws.

The measure on Mr. Bush's desk would let workers at companies of 50 or more people take up to 12 weeks of unpaid leave to care for sick children or a spouse or to bear or adopt children.

Mr. Bush argues that the issue of family leave should be decided between employers and employees; government should not interfere. His rationale is challenged by, among others, conservative Republican Rep. Henry R. Hyde of Illinois, who says that government already requires employers to guarantee job security for people on jury duty and in the military reserves.

And if Connecticut is any example, workers haven't rushed in droves to take unpaid time off just because the law says they can under some circumstances. Indeed, some financially stressed companies may wish more workers would take unpaid time off.

Family leave may save the government money. A working mother, for example, may not have to sacrifice her job and fall back upon the public dole in the face of a temporary domestic crisis.

But the best reason for a family leave law lies in its recognition of realities in the workplace of the 1990s.

Family leave seems only fair for that segment of society expected to serve as family caretaker and bring home a paycheck. Women make up 42 percent of the full-time labor force in the United States, according to the Women's Bureau of the U.S. Department of Labor. But the role of caring for babies and sick family members still falls, usually, to women. A society that expects a worker to carry out two jobs should assure that one of the jobs is protected while the worker tends to the other.

THE SAGINAW NEWS

Saginaw, Michigan, September 16, 1992

The pressure of the election season apparently has persuaded President Bush to do what he should have done with the family-leave bill two years ago: Offer a sensible compromise.

Democrats in Congress, with backing from some Republicans, have revived a bill that Bush vetoed in 1990. The measure would require employers with at least 50 workers, along with state and local governments, to grant up to 12 weeks of unpaid "family" leave.

Two things to remember:

This is, to repeat, *unpaid* leave;

The goals go to the heart of the GOP posture on "family values."

The leave most often would go to the mother of a newborn. But it also would cover care for a seriously ill child, spouse or parent.

Some who term this "yuppie" legislation contend it would primarily help employees who could afford to take time off work. That's undoubtedly so.

But it would also help workers willing to sacrifice during a family emergency, but who could absolutely not afford to lose their jobs.

Bush again has the votes to sustain a veto. But this time he offers some middle ground. He says business tax credits to offset the costs could win him over.

And costs are involved. Even the most zealous advocates of family leave can't deny that a company would incur a burden either in finding a substitute worker for up to 12 weeks, or in overtime to other employees taking up the slack. Businesses also would have to maintain health insurance during the leave time.

In the give and take, Democrats have done the giving so far. They agreed to exclude the 95 percent of U.S. companies that have fewer than 50 workers, acknowledging that a small shop is far less capable of adjusting to an employee's prolonged absence.

For his part, Bush estimates the cost of tax credits at no more than $500 million. That's not bad to cover half of America's work force.

In many cases, business is compassionate enough, and aware enough of the value of employee morale, to grant family leave on its own. Tax credits would support that attitude.

Republicans accuse Democrats of using family leave to put Bush on a partisan spot. Democrats, meanwhile, say they simply are reviving a proposal that almost succeeded two years ago. If so, they can prove their sincerity by accepting Bush's tax credits as a buffer for business costs.

Government need not remain in gridlock during an election. A compromise on family leave could offer a win-win for both sides, and most important, for the strength of the family structure.

THE DAILY OKLAHOMAN
Oklahoma City, Oklahoma, September 16, 1992

TYPICAL of Democratic efforts to embarrass President Bush with political legislation in an election year is the family and medical leave bill.

Democrats claim his threatened veto belies his "family values" rhetoric. But the president has good sense on his side, not to mention concern about the bill's economic effect.

Although the measure, as it came out of the Senate last month, would exempt more than 95 percent of all employers from its provisions, it is emotionally symbolic. It would require any business with more than 50 workers to give all but its top employees up to 12 weeks of unpaid leave for the birth or adoption of a child, or for the serious illness of the worker or an immediate family member.

Under a version worked out by Sen. Christopher J. Dodd, D-Conn., and Sen. Christopher S. Bond, R-Mo., the bill would exempt the highest-paid 10 percent of an employer's work force and restrict eligibility to employees who have worked at least 25 hours per week for the previous 12 months.

While the bill would guarantee job protection for the worker granted the unpaid leave, it is silent on the fate of the person hired to fill in for that employee. Apparently he or she would be shown the door.

The Senate passed the conference report Aug. 11 and the House followed suit last week. Democratic leaders concede they don't have the votes to override the president's veto. That makes the bill fair game in the presidential campaign, and that suits the Democrats.

Even Republican Bond laments the president's opposition, saying Bush is missing an opportunity to show concern for family values. But Senate minority leader Bob Dole, R-Kan., has a more logical view: The issue is not whether family leave is good, but whether government knows best how to spend everyone's benefit dollars. He argues that, if the leave were required by government, businesses would cut back on other benefits.

At a time when government regulation already stifles business and costs jobs, Congress could show more compassion for families by refraining from imposing yet another economic mandate.

LEXINGTON HERALD-LEADER
Lexington, Kentucky, September 25, 1992

Everybody agrees there is gridlock in Washington. So who's to blame?

President Bush would have us believe that the obstinance of the Democrats who control Congress is the sole reason that Washington isn't acting on the nation's problems. But the president set a dubious record this week that suggests he bears considerable responsibility, too.

With his successful veto of the "motor voter" bill Tuesday, Bush topped Lyndon Johnson's previous record of 30 consecutive vetoes from 1963 to 1968. Bush's string of killed legislation includes bills that would have extended unemployment benefits, cut taxes on the middle class and broadened federal job discrimination laws.

There's no sign that he's content with the 31 victories he's got, either. Wednesday night, Bush quashed the family-leave bill, just as he promised he would. The Senate overrode it yesterday, but it's doubtful the House will muster the votes to do the same. Bush also has marked the cable television bill on his desk for a veto, although Congress appears to have the numbers it needs to override him.

Don't mistake our point here. No doubt, the Republicans are right when they talk about congressional gridlock. Politics take precedence over good government too often on Capitol Hill.

But the president's veto record shows that a number of times, he's also used politics to bog down the legislative process. It takes two to tango in Washington, and this president is no better a dancer than this Congress.

The Washington Post
Washington, D.C., September 30, 1992

THE HOUSE will have an opportunity today to break a record and enact a popular and much-needed law. The record is the president's: He has vetoed more than 30 bills during the last four years, and not one has been overridden. But his veto last week of the Family and Medical Leave Act has already been overturned by the Senate, and the final test will be in the House today. The bill is a good one; it is tied to the Republicans' theme of family values. The predictions are that there are not enough votes for an override. You would have thought that on this particular issue in this political season, a good family leave bill such as this one could draw the votes. It should.

No one, after all, can dispute the fact that as women have entered the work force in overwhelming numbers, problems that older generations did not face have arisen. The most difficult are those involving the need for some adults to stay home temporarily to care for a newborn or sick child, or a close family member who is ill. Many employers are both understanding and cooperative about granting unpaid leave in these situations, but some are inflexible and harsh. Workers are often faced with a choice between family responsibilities and keeping a job they may have had for years. The legislation at issue simply requires businesses with more than 50 employees to grant up to 12 weeks of unpaid leave for these emergency situations. Health insurance coverage would have to be continued, but the law wouldn't apply to the highest paid 10 percent of the work force, who might be difficult to replace.

The bill is not without cost to a business, but in the long run it is estimated that money would be saved because permanent replacement workers wouldn't have to be hired. The goodwill and loyalty engendered by such a family-oriented approach should also provide benefits. The president proposes, as an alternative, that tax credits be provided to businesses that voluntarily grant unpaid family leave. But that is a last-minute offer, made only last week, that has no chance of enactment this year. The House should not be distracted by this gambit.

Notwithstanding party affiliation, members should have the confidence to override this veto. Working families need this law as other generations of workers needed minimum wage, health and safety regulations and Social Security. The president should not be allowed to get away with turning his back on them.

Family-Leave Bill Signed by Clinton

President Clinton Feb. 5, 1993 signed legislation that would require large companies to provide workers up to 12 weeks of unpaid leave for family and medical emergencies. The bill, the Family and Medical Leave Act, was the first legislation to be passed under the Clinton administration and represented a symbolic end to gridlock in the Congress. President George Bush had twice vetoed similar family-leave legislation.

The Senate Feb. 4 had passed the bill, 71-27, as 16 Republicans joined all but two Democrats in voting for the Democratic proposal. Later that day, the House had approved the measure, 247-152. The House Feb. 3 had voted for a nearly identical bill but had to take a second vote because the Senate version contained a declaration backing Clinton's Jan. 29 order to the Defense Department to study the issue of homosexuals in the military and a plan by Sen. Sam Nunn [D, Ga.] to hold hearings on the issue.

Vice President Al Gore, who presided over the Senate as the legislation was passed, Feb. 4 declared, "We are seeing in just two weeks what a difference Bill Clinton makes."

The family- and medical-leave bill allowed workers to take up to 12 weeks' unpaid leave in any 12-month period to deal with the birth of a child or an adoption, or a serious illness that affected either themselves or an immediate family member. Employers would have to provide health-care benefits during the leave, and guarantee that the worker could return to his or her old job or an equivalent position at the conclusion of the leave.

The provisions of the bill would cover workers who had been employed for at least one year (and averaged 25 hours of work a week) at companies with a staff of 50 or more, or who were federal, state or local government employees. Overall, the bill would pertain to about half of the nation's work force, and it would become operable on Aug. 5, six months after Clinton signed the measure.

The bill stipulated that a worker on leave would be ineligible for jobless benefits or other government aid. It also permitted a company to deny leave to a salaried employee who was among the highest-paid 10% of the company's staff if such leave caused "substantial and grievous injury" to the company.

While supporters of the bill argued that it allowed workers to meet emergency needs at relatively low cost to employers, some of the bill's critics maintained that it would strain small businesses and pave the way for paid leave for employees.

The Senate, by a vote of 67-33, Feb. 3 had rejected a Republican alternative proposal to provide companies with tax credits to cover the cost of family leave. The Senate that same day also turned aside Republican proposals that workers be required to give employers a 30-day written notice prior to taking family leave and that arbitration procedures be instituted to resolve disputes over leave.

Nationwide, 11 states and the District of Columbia had family- and medical-leave policies similar to the federal bill, and 14 other states had some type of comparable legislation.

The General Accounting Office had estimated that the federal legislation would cost companies an average of $9.90 per worker in annual benefits, it was reported Feb. 5. That sum was relatively insubstantial compared with the roughly $3,500 in medical benefits per employee that companies paid each year.

The Washington Post

Washington, D.C., February 8, 1993

THAT WAS QUITE a party President Clinton threw at the White House Friday to celebrate the signing of the Family and Medical Leave bill and the breaking up of the dread gridlock. "The decade of gridlock has ended," pronounced Senate Majority Leader George Mitchell. "The decade of progress now opens before us."

Wouldn't that be nice? Gridlock was the explanation for how government got so stymied when Democrats controlled the Congress and Republicans held the White House. For a while, of course, it seemed like a fine situation for all concerned. Blame could be shifted up and down Pennsylvania Avenue without anyone's taking responsibility. The electorate seemed to like it, too. In the famous formulation of Charles McDowell of the Richmond Times-Dispatch, voters sent Democrats to Congress so they'd get what they wanted and Republicans to the White House so they wouldn't have to pay for it. True, for a time divided government did manage to produce some useful legislation and policy. But by last year, things really were at a standstill. It was time for somebody to go, and the voters decided it should be Mr. Bush.

Now we have unified government, which means that voters can figure out whom they should punish if things go badly and reward if they go right. The Democrats have no cover and lots of responsibility. So President Clinton and his party colleagues on Capitol Hill have a mutual interest in cooperation, not just on popular things like family leave but also on the hard things that may be in store later this month when Mr. Clinton announces his economic plan.

But despite Mr. Mitchell's hopes, there are obstacles to overcoming gridlock. In the first place, Republicans will not have much political interest in helping the Democrats through these next few years. Mr. Clinton does have a real possibility of building coalitions with moderate-to-liberal Republicans—such as the 36 House members who voted for the family leave bill—and he should pursue them as energetically as Ronald Reagan sought out the conservative Democratic Boll Weevils 12 years ago. As a party, though, Republicans have every reason to want Mr. Clinton to fall on his face. Democrats have to realize that.

Moreover, politics, human nature and the separation of powers being what they are, congressional Democrats could quickly see their interests diverge from Mr. Clinton's. Sen. Sam Nunn, Mr. Clinton's fellow Democrat, was not exactly helpful to him on the issue of gays in the military. Many Democrats shouted loud and clear objections when the Clinton camp leaked the possibility of curbing Social Security cost of living increases. That was a warning sign, and here's another. The last time Democrats controlled both the legislative and executive branches was during Jimmy Carter's administration. By the end of Mr. Carter's term, the two ends of Pennsylvania Avenue were barely speaking to each other. Democrats don't need to be reminded of what happened next. If Mr. Clinton and his congressional allies have the same gridlock problem this time around, the voters will have no trouble figuring out which party to blame.

THE
DENVER POST
Denver, Colorado, February 9, 1993

FAST AND tidy — that's how Congress pushed the Family and Medical Leave Act into law once the threat of a presidential veto vanished with Bill Clinton's election. Clearly, the primary reason the proposal hadn't become national policy in the seven years since U.S. Rep. Pat Schroeder of Denver first introduced the idea was opposition by the Reagan and Bush administrations.

This time, feeble attempts by Republicans to stop the measure, or to attach completely unrelated provisions dealing with gays in the military, simply were brushed aside. The swiftness with which Congress moved on this issue shows that if the GOP intends to make progress on any of its proposals in the next few years, it will have to reject the politics of confrontation and relearn the art of compromise.

That change will be good for America, since it breaks the partisan gridlock that has dominated Washington for four years. But it also puts the onus on the Democrats to deal with the nation's woes because there is no one else to blame for failure.

On a practical level, however, passage of the family leave law will benefit millions of working Americans by ensuring that they won't have to choose between earning a living and caring for their loved ones.

Even though the law doesn't take effect until early summer, businesses with more than 50 employees ought to start getting ready to implement the new national policy. For example, employers need to review their insurance plans to see how they will meet requirements that workers retain health-care benefits while on extended leave.

Despite these administrative headaches, the family leave measure likely will aid the economy. For one thing, it could make available many temporary positions, thereby returning unemployed people to the work force.

Public costs also may decline, since people who have to step away from their jobs won't be forced onto welfare or Medicaid.

What's more, the United States may get a more productive work force — after all, America's strongest international competitors have had similar family leave laws for years, and the results have been more loyal employees and social stability.

Simply put, the Democrats in this instance put their majority clout to work in the best interests of common citizens. The real test, however, is whether they can continue this positive momentum on even more contentious issues, such as how best to cut the national debt and reform federal election campaigns.

The Miami Herald
Miami, Florida, February 6, 1993

SO, THE family leave bill is finally law. A majority of Congress backed its rhetoric about family values with votes, and President Clinton signed the measure yesterday. Good. It was too long in coming.

The vote was the first victory for the new administration, a victory to be savored by workers across the country. It is, too, a well deserved, often desperately needed victory. No longer will men and women, already stressed by an emergency, also face losing a job to attend to family responsibilities. The new law assures 12 weeks of unpaid leave for medical emergencies, births, or adoptions.

President Bush vetoed the measure twice, and its passage was hardly assured the third time around. House and Senate Republicans tried to tie the anchor of gays in the military to family leave in order to sink both. They failed when Democrats compromised with the president on how to handle lifting the ban on gays.

Among the responsible lawmakers willing to separate the two issues and support family leave were Miami Republican Reps. Lincoln Diaz-Balart and Ileana Ros-Lehtinen. Ms. Ros-Lehtinen backed it from the outset, despite Republican colleagues' pressure to vote No, because she thought the bill was right. It was, and she is.

The No vote of Rep. E. Clay Shaw, a Republican whose new district spans Dade, Broward, and Palm Beach counties, was a disappointment. Though he consistently opposed this bill, he insisted in last fall's campaign that he could be depended on to protect families and the rights of women. He failed his first test in the new Congress.

Dade County commissioners actually led the way on family leave, enacting the nation's first local ordinance to require it. That law now is said to have wide support in the business community, which has found that it costs less than initially feared. Experience elsewhere shows that when employees feel a sense of job security when faced with a family emergency, everybody benefits — employee, employer, work product. That portends well for the nation's new family leave law.

THE ATLANTA CONSTITUTION
Atlanta, Georgia, February 6, 1993

Those Americans who wanted immediate change from the Clinton administration can mark off the first sign of progress on the domestic front: The president has signed into law the family leave act, which will provide 12 weeks of unpaid leave for workers in large and medium-size companies who need time off to care for ailing family members or new babies.

To be sure, passage of the act was no big deal for the Clinton team. Congress had passed it twice before, but President Bush had vetoed it twice. All Mr. Clinton had to do was keep a campaign pledge to sign the bill when it was passed a third time.

But the act *is* a big deal for all those families who desperately needed its provisions. During the campaign, Mr. Clinton spoke of several parents he had met who had lost their jobs because they had to take extended time off to care for a sick child. He noted that all other Western industrialized nations already provide family leave, and he argued that America could do better. He was right.

Nowadays, 61 percent of mothers with children are in the workplace. Parents should not be forced to choose between their sick children and their jobs.

Besides, the family leave act is good for families *and* employers. Workers are more productive when they believe their jobs will be protected if they ever need emergency leave. In Florida, where a state-mandated act has been in effect for nearly a year, many businesses say leave has been less expensive to provide than they had feared. Further, business executives say, it enhances employee loyalty.

Vice President Al Gore touted passage of the family leave law as a sign that the gridlock in national policy-making is finally broken. Mr. Gore may be overly optimistic. But the bill's swift journey through both houses of Congress does suggest that lawmakers understand the public is weary of the internecine policy disputes that have kept important issues unattended for far too long.

Republicans, for example, had little success with their rebellion over allowing gays and lesbians to serve in the military. Senate Republicans tried to attach an amendment making the military ban permanent. The amendment drew little support.

President Clinton will probably confront no greater obstacle than when he moves, in six months, to formally lift the ban. Americans are up in arms over the notion of allowing gays and lesbians to serve their country honorably. Instead, a nation that voted for change wants its president and its Congress to concentrate on solving the complex problems.

The Des Moines Register

Des Moines, Iowa, February 6, 1993

It's entirely fitting that the first piece of legislation passed by the 103rd Congress, and signed by President Clinton, involves families.

Just about everybody is talking about increased pressures on families these days, and many people cry out that family members ought to take more responsibility — and the government less — for care of their young and their older relatives. The Family and Medical Leave Act will allow more of just that.

It is a tepid piece of legislation. To benefit you must work for a company with more than 50 workers; only 40 percent of American workers do. Though you will continue to receive benefits while off work, you won't get paid, which means many middle- and lower-income Americans won't be able to afford to take advantage of the legislation.

But it is a worthwhile, if only marginal, step. Only the United States and South Africa, of the industrialized countries, lack national family-leave policies. The new federal law will mean that more and more Americans will have the opportunity to stay home with a child who has a major illness, or to attend to an ailing parent.

Won't family leave cause many mid-sized companies to reduce payroll to under 50 workers to avoid having to comply with the act? Won't all companies find their costs increasing because of the need to hire temporary replacement workers? And won't that mean an ultimate loss of jobs?

Good questions. There's no doubt that family leave doesn't mean much if a person doesn't have a job in the first place.

But many, many American companies already offer family-leave policies that are far more liberal than what is provided by the federal legislation. Those companies know the value of reducing stress on workers, and of reducing turnover. Ultimately, business will benefit, as well as employees.

Besides, those same questions were asked when the 40-hour work week was required by law, when the minimum wage was established, and when workplace-safety standards were imposed. The vast majority of Americans — including many in the business community — now value those regulations.

So it will be with family leave.

AKRON BEACON JOURNAL

Akron, Ohio, February 7, 1993

Congress' passage of the family leave bill is indeed a victory for the Clinton administration and perhaps thousands of families who will benefit. The bill itself stands for family values. And even many opponents now agree that it won't impose the terrible burden on companies that former President Bush warned of when he vetoed two earlier versions.

In places around the country, where there are already family-leave policies, fears that employees would abuse the privilege and that large numbers would go on leaves have proved unfounded. Some managers have even found family leave helpful, as employees have returned to work with greater loyalty to the company.

The truth is that even with the new law, not everyone will be able to take a leave. The law will simply make it possible for *some* to take time off, without pay, to care for a newborn or handle a family emergency.

Many won't be able to take advantage of a leave, even when they need one, because they can't afford to lose wages. Still others work for companies with fewer than 50 employees and will not be covered by the law.

Despite its limitations, the new legislation is a step forward and reflects the views of a majority of Americans.

No one should have to choose between losing a job or caring for a new baby or a sick, loved one. At the very least, the law sets the right course for public policy on families.

The Phoenix Gazette

Phoenix, Arizona, February 6, 1993

Family leave is the easy vote of the session for Congress, and the easy path for President Clinton to show immediate results to the public.

The idea that employees should be able to take up to three months off for the birth of a child or caring for a sick relative is appealing, but calling passage of this legislation an end to the dread "gridlock," as Democrats proclaimed Friday, is a fairly large reach.

What's wrong with the bill? First, it's Congress and the administration mandating programs they won't pay for, shoving the costs onto the very part of the economy that can least afford it: small business. Many big businesses, such as IBM, already provides paid family leave. Small business is where federal mandates will have the most negative impact.

"It was America's families who have beaten the gridlock in Washington to pass family leave," the president said, portraying the legislation as a major social program, which it is not. What it could lead to, however, is a major concern.

One of the reasons small business fears this approach is that unpaid leave is only a start. It is not hard to envision legislators coming back next year with proposals to enlarge the scope of the law to require paid leave, raise the number of weeks allowed and impose severe penalties on employers for failure to keep detailed records of who is present each day, so enforcement can proceed.

Certainly, paid leave is what backers of this law have in mind for the future, since few workers have enough savings to support themselves comfortably without income for three months. The bureaucratic process will be in place to make such matters mandatory.

One of the first casualties to such an approach is flexibility. Employers will be less likely to allow creative solutions to family leave problems when there is a federal law in the middle of the issue.

Anyone having a baby should have time off from work, with the prospect of returning after a reasonable period. Any person with a sick relative should be allowed some compassionate time off. But the details ought to be a matter between the individual and the employer, based on the requirements of the business and the employee.

What happens, for example, after an employee has cared for a sick relative for 12 weeks? Theoretically, the employee returns to work. But elderly sick relatives don't always get well in 12 weeks or 12 months; will there be an amendment coming next year to lengthen the period?

We cannot imagine things working more smoothly with a federal mandate interposed, nor can we imagine how the president hopes to create more jobs while pushing legislation that will force some of the most struggling companies to reduce jobs.

As we said, family leave was an easy shot at creating an image of important social change driven by the federal government. It doesn't measure up to that, and it might well encourage more costly intervention into business in the future, at the ultimate cost of the very jobs the president says he wants to create.

The Register-Guard
Eugene, Oregon, February 6, 1993

By passing and signing into law a family leave bill, Congress and President Clinton have set aside a misconception held by the Bush administration. Bush vetoed family leave legislation twice, acting on the mistaken notion that it would unfairly burden business. He could have looked to Oregon, where a family leave law has been on the books for a year, to find that his concern was misplaced.

The new Family and Medical Leave Act requires businesses with more than 50 workers to give employees up to 12 weeks of unpaid leave to care for a newborn infant or a sick spouse, parent or child. Leaves may be taken only once a year. The new federal law affects only 5 percent of the nation's employers but covers 44 percent of American workers. The only significant cost to employers is the cost of carrying medical insurance during the employee's leave period.

Oregon's law is tighter, covering employers with more than 25 workers. Ten percent of the state's businesses are affected, and two-thirds of the state's work force is covered. The legislation allowing unpaid leaves to care for ill relatives expanded upon a parental leave law that took effect in 1988 and a pregnancy leave law that took effect in 1990.

Anyone familiar with the realities of families and the workplace should never have feared that these laws would be disruptive or burdensome. Few families can afford to have their working members take extended periods of unpaid leave. Most employers already have formal or informal policies allowing employees to take time off for a family emergency. And when an emergency arises, workers will put their families ahead of their jobs no matter what the law or their employers say.

Family leave laws are needed to cover the relatively rare cases in which particularly hardhearted or inflexible employers force workers to choose between their jobs and their family responsibilities. Forcing such choices is not only cruel, it's shortsighted — according to the federal Small Business Administration, it costs as much as $3,152 to recruit and train a new employee, an amount that exceeds the cost of insurance during a leave.

Only half a dozen employers have complained to Oregon's Bureau of Labor and Industries about the state's family leave law. The Association of Oregon Industries has heard few negative comments. This is not surprising. Family leave legislation grants a right that will be seldom exercised, but when it's needed the need can be desperate. Most employers are humane enough to recognize the need already. Similar recognition by the federal government is long overdue.

The Birmingham News
Birmingham, Alabama, February 9, 1993

Consider Congress' naked hypocrisy on the first bill it passed this session, the family leave bill, signed into law last week by President Clinton.

What slipped by practically unnoticed amid the chest-thumping over the great victory for families was that Congress exempted itself from the law.

That's scandalous, but not unusual.

Congress exempts itself from many of the laws it expects the rest of us to follow, including the Occupational Safety and Health Act, the minimum wage laws, the equal pay laws, the Freedom of Information Act, the Americans with Disabilities Act, civil rights acts and others.

The standard rationale for this institutional hypocrisy is that the separation of powers bars the executive or judicial branches from enforcing such laws against Congress. Baloney.

The result is that congressional employees are specifically prohibited from taking their unfair labor practice claims to court under many laws, including the new family leave bill.

Instead, complaints are referred to an "Office of Fair Employment Practices," which is made up of members of Congress who serve as prosecutor, judge and jury, and whose proceedings are secret.

Such a system effectively eliminates complaints, considering there's little hope for impartiality.

It also gives Congress an artificial view of the kind of red-tape and inconvenience it requires American businesses to endure through its laws.

One of the best things Congress could do to really get in touch with what it's like to live outside the Beltway is to put itself under the same laws the rest of us follow. That would give the honorables some perspective they're not use to.

There's been a lot of talk about congressional reform in the last few years. A special House-Senate committee, in fact, started the year by holding hearings to look into ways Congress could improve the manner in which it operates.

The committee is considering everything from eliminating committees, to changing the role of chairman of the appropriations panels to reforming the ethics process.

The committee says it wants to make Congress more accountable to the people it represents. Even longtime incumbents are talking a good reform game.

With many of the more than 120 new members of Congress elected on reform platforms, it looked like reform might actually become a reality.

But where making itself abide by its own laws is concerned, talk of reform in Congress is cheap. All but one of the newly elected Democrats in Congress voted to continue Congress' exemption from the laws the rest of us have to follow.

The Chattanooga Times
Chattanooga, Tennessee, February 12, 1993

President Clinton's trouble finding an attorney general whose child-care history was spotless didn't prevent him from persuading Congress to pass the Family and Medical Leave Act, which President Bush vetoed twice, unencumbered by irrelevant amendments. In the end the passage was virtually effortless, a testimony to bipartisan support for the legislation.

The only substantive obstacle — a Republican-sponsored amendment to retain the ban on gays in the military — died a swift death. And other GOP-sponsored amendments, such as tax credits as incentives for businesses to provide leave, had trouble even attracting Republican support.

Still, the bill was a compromise. It provides up to 12 weeks of *unpaid* leave for family and medical emergencies, unlike the practice in other industrial countries, where such leave is paid.

Moreover, relatively few workers will be eligible since companies with fewer than 50 employees are exempted; so are employees who have been with a company for less than a year, or who work fewer than 25 hours weekly.

The restrictions mean, according to Labor Department estimates, that the bill will apply to about 5 percent of companies nationwide and roughly 40 percent of the U.S. work force. Even so, it's a welcome start.

Critics have charged that the bill poses a threat to American businesses, but companies that have already adopted leave policies report they have proved extremely successful. Businesses save training costs involved with replacing experienced employees and benefit from higher morale and a greater sense of company loyalty among employees who appreciate the security of having the leave policy.

Companies' criticism of family and medical leave is similar to the hand wringing that accompanied demands years ago for abolishing child labor, passage of a minimum wage, and equal pay for women. And criticism that the leave law could put American companies at a disadvantage with their European trading partners ignores that most countries there have had *paid* family leave policies for years — and their economies are booming.

Family leave is important because it enables business and industry to adjust to changes in families over the past 25 to 30 years. The most important change is that, especially in the last decade, families have found they need two paychecks to make ends meet.

The criticism notwithstanding, there's no substantive reason to fear that the cost of family leave will be prohibitive. Whatever direct cost is incurred should be offset by the policy's social benefit, and the expected return to companies whose employees will no longer have to put their jobs on the line just to attend to a family emergency.

That's worth a lot.

The Grand Rapids Press
Grand Rapids, Michigan, February 4, 1993

The family leave bill rolling through Congress will leave many families wishing they'd never heard of it. They'll be the ones living on unemployment checks or having their job fringes curtailed as employers try to cope with a very naive law.

The bill is not a plus either for most families or for the economy. Calling it "pro-family" is a veneer. Only affluent families are likely to benefit. Few people on modest incomes will be able to afford the 12 weeks of unpaid leave the legislation provides.

But the bill is on a fast track to adoption because that veneer looks good. The Democratic majority in the House passed it on Wednesday. All of West Michigan's representatives voted no, except Paul Henry, R-Grand Rapids Township, who was absent. The Senate will soon follow and the president is in support. The same bill was passed twice during the Bush presidency and was vetoed each time.

With Mr. Clinton's signature, employees will be guaranteed up to 12 weeks a year of unpaid leave to recover from illness; to tend a sick child, parent or spouse; or to spend time with a newborn or adopted child. Employee insurance benefits will continue during the leave period. On returning to work, the employee will be entitled to the same or a comparable job. Most part-time employees will be exempt, as will employers with fewer than 50 employees.

How could anyone be against this? The notion that people should be able to take time out for family emergencies seems like basic decency — and it is. Helping employees in such ways also promotes job satisfaction and better performance. Where possible, employers should allow such leave as a matter of course. Many of them, mostly larger corporations, already do. On their own, or in bargaining with their unions, they settle on what is affordable. Sometimes the leave is one of a number of benefits from which employees may choose.

But there is a huge difference between that free-market approach and the required benefit being pushed through Congress. This is a much more generous leave policy than is common among employers. In mandating that, government will be adding to labor costs — costs which already are high in relation to costs abroad. There is particular expense in the requirement that health insurance be continued while the employee is away and doing no work.

The effect will be cost-cutting somewhere else: reducing other benefits or trimming pay increases. For sure, it won't stimulate new hiring and will do nothing for the unemployed. Instead, family leave will be another incentive for employers to cut full-time jobs. If it causes them to reduce their domestic payrolls by even 1 percent, the loss would be between 50,000 and 60,000 jobs. No one should doubt that risk. Over the last 20 years, pressure to reduce labor costs has put millions of workers on the street.

Even the exemption for small businesses — those having 49 or fewer employees — will hurt. Which of those employers will want to add a 50th employee, knowing that such an addition would trigger a new layer of federally-imposed rules and costs? Also, those businesses will have a harder time holding onto good workers, who will be attracted to the leave option at larger shops.

This is a popular bill, especially with suburban and upper-income earners, and its "pro-family" label gives it the look of benevolence. But low- and middle-income families will pay a price. For them, there will be nothing "pro-family" about it.

The Gazette
Cedar Rapids, Iowa, January 31, 1993

WITH A DEMOCRATIC Congress now aligning with a Democratic White House, the previously vetoed Family and Medical Leave Act is a cinch.

So be it. The legislation is flawed on numerous counts, including its tilt toward relatively well-off workers, those who can afford to take off up to 12 weeks without pay. But let it go. This is popular legislation. No doubt it will remain so until people realize the law makes virtually no allowances for individual preferences or problems.

Still, it is unsettling to see Congress and President Clinton approve the family leave bill without rethinking the cut-off between small and larger businesses.

Generally speaking, the law will require companies with more than 50 employees to grant 12 weeks' leave to an employee for the birth or adoption of a child or the care of a seriously ill spouse or parent. The leave would be "unpaid," but the employer will be required to continue paying in the form of so-called fringe benefits, including health insurance. Businesses with fewer than 50 employees would be exempt.

The bill's sponsors should be ready to justify that exemption. What's fair for one business should be fair for all. If a company with a staff of 40 can't afford to arrange family leave for one or several employees, what makes social engineers think an employer of 60, 80 or several hundred could?

An honest answer could dim lawmakers' and President Clinton's enthusiasm for the family leave bill. What would be bad for small businesses could be bad for middle-sized and large businesses — their employees, too. Money spent on temporary workers or lost through reduced productivity does not simply represent reduced profits or smaller dividends for fat-cat stockholders. It is money that can't be spent for higher pay or for fringe benefits employees might prefer over unpaid leave.

But, as we said earlier, let it go. Somehow, government-enforced family leave looks good when displayed on Washington's drawing board. Maybe it takes a real-life run to expose the drawbacks.

The Record
Hackensack, New Jersey, February 7, 1993

THE United States is joining the rest of the industrialized world in adopting a national family leave policy, which President Clinton signed the morning after it was passed by Congress. The measure grants workers in companies of 50 employees or more up to 12 weeks of unpaid leave for birth or adoption, or a family member's illness.

When the law takes effect in six months, employers will have to continue health care benefits and guarantee workers their old job or a comparable one. Only workers employed for at least one year and 25 hours a week will be covered.

Former President George Bush vetoed a similar family leave bill twice, despite wide congressional and public support, on the grounds that it would hurt business. The opposite may be true, however.

In places where some form of leave policy is already law, including New Jersey, reports have been favorable for both businesses and workers. "I know that men and women are more productive when they are sure they won't lose their jobs because they are trying to be good parents," Mr. Clinton said.

The Seattle Times

Seattle, Washington, February 7, 1993

TWO weeks into the Clinton administration, the tone of government has changed noticeably for the better with the swift passage of the family-leave bill.

After a few days of politicking, the measure passed the House and Senate late Thursday. President Clinton moved quickly the next morning to sign into law a bill that will make a real difference in the lives of American families, particularly those led by single parents or with both parents working.

The law allows workers to take up to 12 weeks of unpaid leave to cope with a family sickness, childbirth or adoption. Companies with fewer than 50 employees are exempt.

President Bush twice vetoed family-leave legislation, despite overwhelming public sentiment in favor of it. His intransigence helped illustrate how out of touch he was with the problems of working people.

Clinton campaigned on a promise to make government more sensitive to modern families. And he delivered.

The demographics clearly were on his side. Sixty-seven percent of American women with children under 18 are in the workforce. In Seattle, the figure is even higher — 71 percent.

Far too often, women and men are forced to make a gut-wrenching choice between their job and caring for a new baby or an ailing parent. The family-leave bill eliminates this particular dilemma of everyday life. Employees will be guaranteed a return to their same job or an equivalent one.

U.S. Sen. Patty Murray, D-Wash., gave compelling first-person testimony in favor of the legislation.

The Washington delegation, except for Speaker Tom Foley, who traditionally abstains, and the two Republicans, voted for the bill. Sen. Slade Gorton and Rep. Jennifer Dunn voted against it on grounds that a mandatory measure places an unfair burden on businesses already struggling in difficult economic times.

Nationwide, 25 states, including Washington, have some type of family-leave legislation.

In 1991, Dade County, Fla., became the first county in the country to adopt family-leave legislation, a law that closely resembles the new federal law.

The experience of the 2,500 companies covered there is instructive. Many firms now say the law is less expensive than anticipated and has the benefit of increasing worker satisfaction and productivity.

This is one new law that resonates in the hinterlands — and resonates favorably.

The Oregonian

Portland, Oregon, February 10, 1993

Part of the price family-leave supporters paid to pass their bill was the exemption of businesses with fewer than 50 employees. Yet one well-known national employer will never be hauled into federal court for violating the act President Clinton signed into law last week.

This employer's 12,000-plus workers will never be able to take their cases before a judge or jury, seeking back pay or benefits as a result of their boss' failure to abide by the Family and Medical Leave Act.

A tale of Capitol Hill intrigue and influence-peddling? A brewing scandal?

Hardly. The favored employer is Congress, and, alas, Congress' practice of exempting itself wholly or partially from the laws it writes for everyone else is business as usual.

In the case of possible family-leave violations, Congress said that its employees can take their beefs to the Office of Fair Employment Practices.

How nice. The members of Congress, of course, control this office, and only the final decisions in any case are public information. Other large employers no doubt favored such cozy in-house enforcement provisions, but Congress had other plans for them.

In fact, when Rep. Harris W. Fawell, R-Ill., tried to give legislative branch workers the right to appeal Office of Fair Employment Practices' rulings in federal court, the House rejected his amendment, 175 to 253. That's too bad for Congress' employees and for Congress' tarnished image, though don't blame Republican Rep. Bob Smith. He was the only Oregon member to vote for the amendment.

In offering his motion, Fawell said, "Indeed, it appears to me that Congress would exempt itself from the law of gravity if they felt they could get away with it." Maybe so. But at least we know that, for all the talk of change, the laws of inertia are working just fine on Capitol Hill.

Rockford Register Star

Rockford, Illinois, February 7, 1993

It isn't only the gridlock in Washington that American families have beaten by gaining a president's signature — finally — on family leave law.

The victory is about more than politics and a Democratic Congress and president working together. It's the victory of a modern-day labor mentality over the thinking that would ultimately only set businesses back.

> **U.S. business will be more competitive now, not less so.**

The bill that President Clinton signed into law Friday mandates 12 weeks of unpaid leave for workers who need to cope with family sickness, adoption, or birth of a baby. It's the realization, one administration removed, of a pledge George Bush made in Rockford four years ago to assure job security for people who have to take time off to care for their families.

That promise —which Bush broke twice with vetoes of family leave bills —is grounded in good business sense. When 58 percent of all adult American women are in the workforce, companies must adjust to the shifting realities to stay competitive. In the final accounting, family leave doesn't come down to being nice or moral or right —it comes down to retaining skilled workers and building loyalty.

It also comes down to saving money. A 1990 study by the Institute for Women's Policy Research said that taxpayers pay an additional $4.3 billion a year for public benefit programs when a parent loses his or her job after a family-related absence. Companies, too, pay dearly to replace workers.

And, as Beverley Kingsley of Rock Valley College's Small Business Development Center found when she informally polled companies about family leave last year, "The best people they had were the ones who were going to want to look after a new baby or their parents. The most responsible worker is at risk here."

It's a risk that, thankfully, many American workers will no longer have to take.

U.S. Infant Mortality Rate Stirs Heated Controversy

The infant mortality rate had become embroiled in politics in the last decade. Although overall life expectancy in the U.S. had increased, the health gap between black and white Americans had also increased, according to a Department of Health and Human Services study released March 20, 1990. The study, titled "Health United States," had examined data from 1987, the latest year for which statistics were available at the time, and reported that the infant mortality rate had improved slightly to 10.1 deaths per 1,000 live births, down from 10.4 in 1986 and 20 in 1970. The rate for blacks was 17.9 per 1,000 in 1987, compared with 8.6 for whites. The overall rate placed the U.S. 22nd on a list of industrialized nations.

The National Center for Health Statistics reported April 5, 1991 that the infant mortality rate in the U.S. had dropped in 1990 by the largest amount in nearly a decade. The decline was to 9.1 deaths per 1,000 live births in 1990 from 9.7 deaths per 1,000 in 1989.

Although infant mortality has improved as medical care has advanced, progress against infant deaths began to slow in the early 1980s and the United States lags behind many other industrialized nations in this basic measurement of health care. However, the drop in infant mortality in this century has been one of the most striking statistics in medicine. In 1915, 99.9 infants died for every 1,000 live births in the U.S. By 1940 the rate was down to 47 for every 1,000; by 1970 it was down to 20 and by 1988 it was down to 10 per 1,000.

The National Commission to Prevent Infant Mortality April 23, 1991 released a report recommending that prenatal care, nutrition and other services be provided to pregnant women at single sites across the U.S. The commission, which had been established by Congress in 1987, said the current system contributed to excessive infant mortality by confronting women with a bureaucratic "obstacle course" as they sought prenatal care.

The Houston Post
Houston, Texas, January 30, 1989

IT IS BOTH A SHAME and a disgrace that a city can rank No. 1 in saving the lives of babies, and at the same time, have an infant mortality rate in its inner city that is as high as the rates in some of the world's poorest countries. That disparity can be changed as we see in Robert C. Newberry's column opposite this page.

Nationwide, the infant mortality rate is nine deaths per 1,000 babies. In Houston, that rate is 11 deaths per 1,000 and, get this, Houston's inner city rate is 20 deaths per 1,000. That's more than double the national rate. And most of these deaths can be prevented.

Lan Bentsen, a member of the executive committee of the Texas Gulf Coast Chapter of the March of Dimes, said correcting the problem "is a matter of political will." He said the problem will be solved by politically active people urging a city to provide adequate health care for its poor. We know what must be done, so let's get to work on bringing down the death rate of our babies.

THE INDIANAPOLIS STAR
Indianapolis, Indiana, February 13, 1989

Statistics reportedly showed that in 1984 Indianapolis had the highest black infant mortality rate among 22 cities with significant black populations. An estimated 24 out of every 1,000 black babies born here in 1984 died before they reached their first birthday.

The indictment was first published in the spring of 1987 by the Children's Defense Fund, a Washington-based lobbying and advocacy group. The mortality figures, though five years old continue to dog the city and are being used to rally support for additional prenatal care services and funding.

One rallying point is a $5.6 million plan devised by a health care task force appointed by the City-County Council. The plan was approved 4-0 recently by the council's Community Affairs Committee.

Committee members have urged the full council, Mayor William H. Hudnut and the task force to join forces in "selling" the plan to public and private funding sources.

It will be an expensive proposition. Among recommendations are a multi-faceted educational approach, more extensive and more accessible prenatal care for the poor and coordinated prenatal and newborn services. Some funding might be realized through the expansion of Medicaid, as proposed in a bill now before the state legislature.

Even if infant mortality figures have improved, even if they were distorted in the first place, the most economical approach is prevention: preventing teen-age pregnancies, preventing the malnutrition and alcohol and drug abuse that too often cause premature birth and underweight babies.

Babies weighing less than 5½ pounds are 20 times more likely to die during their first year. Yet many "preemies" that 20 years ago would have died within minutes are now being saved through the marvels of critical care nurseries — but at an estimated cost of $1,000 a day.

Some remain hospitalized for months, eventually growing into healthy children. Others suffer from chronic disabilities that can bankrupt families and drain government budgets.

The credibility of the CDF statistics has been challenged. And no doubt there will be challenges to the cost and directions of the plan awaiting the attention of the City-County Council.

But one aspect is beyond dispute. It is financially sound to assure all babies a healthful start in life, from the womb through the critical early years of development.

Not just dollars are saved, but lives and lifelong heartbreak.

The State
Columbia, South Carolina, October 5, 1991

SOUTH CAROLINA has the highest infant mortality rate in the nation. Teen pregnancies, substance abuse, inadequate prenatal and postnatal care are among the many reasons why almost 12 of every 1,000 babies born in this state do not see their first birthday. But thanks to a new federal grant program, South Carolina has a chance to reduce that tragic toll.

The "Healthy Start" program will provide five-year grants to 15 areas across the country that have high infant mortality rates. In South Carolina, $50 million will go to six Pee Dee counties that have an infant death rate of 16.1 per 1,000 live births.

Those counties — Chesterfield, Dar- lington, Dillon, Marion, Marlboro and Williamsburg — have developed a comprehensive plan that will be coordinated by the United Way. Strategies include reducing teen pregnancies, providing easy access to medical care, creating new jobs in "enterprise zones," improving nutrition, reducing alcohol and drug abuse and educating communities in good health practices.

The ambitious goal is to cut the area's infant mortality in half over the next five years. Equally important, as Governor Campbell pointed out, lessons learned from the program could be applied statewide to give more babies a healthy start in life.

ST. LOUIS POST-DISPATCH
St. Louis, Missouri, March 17, 1991

Federal funds for medical care that determines which children survive their first year of life shouldn't be limited to a few areas of the country, but that's how the Bush administration wants to allocate millions of dollars to help reduce infant mortality. It wants to concentrate on only 10 cities and rural areas and ignore the national scope of the problem.

The administration's approach defies common sense for a second reason. Its funds to fight infant mortality in the 10 locations would be taken from other crucial maternal-child health programs. In St. Louis, for instance, medical services that 16 health centers provide for poor pregnant women and newborn children would be cut to make room for the administration's infant-mortality initiative.

John M. Silva, who heads the Family Care Center of Carondelet on the South Side, rightly points out that the administration should give more money to community health centers in place of its more limited and ill-defined approach to the problem. For years now, community health centers have been at the front line of the infant mortality battle. Cuts in

funding for these centers certainly would cause infant mortality to rise overall even if the administration succeeded in reducing it in 10 targeted cities and rural areas.

St. Louis and 17 other cities that don't want to lose out are competing for a portion of the estimated $54 million in federal grants for the new infant mortality initiative. But there's no guarantee that St. Louis will get any of the funds, since it ranks 11th in infant mortality among major cities. The possibility that St. Louis and some other deserving cities may get no money points up one big drawback in the program.

The administration's strategy also overlooks the fallacy of having a cutoff point that misses a good part of the infant mortality problem in black communities, a number of which have higher infant death rates than some Third World nations. This fact, along with the concern that health centers would actually lose money under this program, makes the case for Congress to reject funding for this misguided and narrow infant mortality initiative and to do more instead to attack the problem nationwide.

St. Petersburg Times
St. Petersburg, Flordia, August 28, 1991

It's no secret. Florida health officials know how to reduce teen-age pregnancies and infant mortality. It can be done with better sex education, better health care for poor young people and school-based health clinics. What's hard is persuading communities to deliver those services in a way that will make a difference.

Gov. Lawton Chiles also knows how to attack this problem. "I would like school-based clinics in every town," he told a meeting this week of Healthy Start, his program to increase prenatal care to poor women. In all of Florida, 15 schools now have clinics. State health officials are working on creating 62 more. Every high school should have one.

Because there is organized religious opposition to the clinics, especially when they provide birth control services, strong leadership will be required to get these health services to the young people who need them. It still seems uncertain how hard Chiles will push. Clearly, he knows what is needed for success. But one comment to the Healthy Start group sounded rather low-key: "I would not try to tell any community that they have to have a

school-based health clinic. (But) I would sure encourage them to have it."

Secretary Bob Williams, of the Florida Department of Health and Rehabilitative Services, gave the conference some statistics that demonstrate the need for better family planning education in Florida. He said that 56 percent of Florida births are unintended. Twenty-six percent of children born in the state are unwanted. "The root of almost all problems is unintended and unwanted pregnancies," Williams said.

Yet the school clinic issue is still controversial. Former Gov. Bob Martinez turned down a clinic offered to Dade County schools by a private foundation. He moved the successful clinic at Shanks High School in Gadsden County off campus. (Chiles moved it back.)

That clinic at Shanks High shows how effective the clinics can be. After it was opened, two things happened. School attendance rose significantly. Pregnancies in the high school fell by 75 percent.

With strong leadership from the governor on this issue, every high school in Florida could show similar results.

The Phoenix Gazette
Phoenix, Arizona, January 5, 1991

It's Friday night, after the high school ball game. And teenagers from Deer Valley to Mesa are headed for the weekly drinking party. And danger.

The tragic death last Saturday of a 19-year-old Phoenix youth is certainly not typical. But it exemplifies the kegful of problems that can arise when hundreds of youths congregate for drinking bashes.

"Party hardy," the flyers promise. By charging a $3 or $5 admission, the hosts — usually youths not much past the legal drinking age themselves — can "earn" several hundreds of dollars in profits.

Within a few hours, either the beer runs out or the police break it up. The teenagers head for somewhere else, maybe a restaurant, maybe home.

Maybe. But the keg parties combine routinely dangerous ingredients: Alcohol, automobiles, youthful passions. Fights are commonplace. Sexual assaults and robberies have occurred. Do we need to remind anyone of the threat intoxicated drivers pose on city streets?

The shooting that killed Garrett Bardwell, 19, a non-drinker who merely accompanied his friends to the party, was not an isolated incident. Guns are adding another volatile element to this already explosive mix.

Underage drinking is already against the law. Stronger enforcement against the hosts, with penalties, might offer a stronger deterrent. The keg parties are becoming too dangerous.

ALBUQUERQUE JOURNAL
Albuquerque, New Mexico, August 16, 1991

Heightened awareness of the need for prenatal care and the availability of improved prenatal care had a significant impact on New Mexico's infant mortality rate during the decade ending in 1988. That encouraging news should be the basis for improving such care even more.

The Children's Defense Fund provided statistics showing the state's infant mortality rate declined a whopping 29.1 percent between 1978 and 1988. New Mexico Health Department statistics for 1989 — the most recent statistics available — show even more improvement. In 1978, the state recorded 14.1 infant deaths per 1,000 live births. In 1988, the number had dropped to 10 deaths per 1,000 live births, one-tenth of a percent below the national average for that year. In 1989, the statistic was 8.5 deaths for each 1,000 live births.

The statistics reflect the positive impact of increased legislative support on prenatal care and infant mortality programs. This year, the Legislature added funding for county councils that will help determine what health services — such as family planning, adolescent pregnancy programs, access to prenatal and pediatric care — are needed.

The statistics appear to show that New Mexico has been moving in the right direction to reduce its infant mortality rate. Let's hope the good work will continue.

THE ANN ARBOR NEWS
Ann Arbor, Michigan, May 16, 1991

The latest set of statistics from the Michigan Department of Public Health underscores the high priority that should be attached to the well-being of the state's children.

Infant mortality figures should shock us out of any complacency that we are living in the best of all possible worlds. The infant morality rate for Hispanics was 8.7 deaths per 1,000 births in 1989; the rate for white infants in 1989 was 8.2 deaths per 1,000 births.

The real shocker was the death rate for black infants: 22.6 per thousand births. Not only is that figure appallingly high, but also the disparity between black and the whites/Hispanic rates is unacceptable. We need to pinpoint why so many black babies die and why the black infant mortality rate is so disproportionate.

For that, the state needs to find a working model and then begin to pattern its own programs and policies after the model. Some things we know already; it's just a matter of targeting our resources in better, timelier ways.

For example, we know that the high number of low birth-weight babies could be reduced with better nutrition and early medical care. We also know that a comprehensive strategy for children at risk must follow efforts to reduce Michigan's high infant mortality rate through better outreach programs. The poor showing among blacks could be improved dramatically if strong efforts were made to break the cycle of substandard housing, unemployment and school dropouts.

Many of the problems associated with infant mortality are interrelated, which also argues strongly for strategies which follow children after they leave infancy. There is no question that poor prenatal care could be improved with better targeting of women in need and access to medical care.

CHICAGO Sun-Times
Chicago, Illinois, August 8, 1991

Too many babies are dying in Illinois, despite the tentative decline in infant mortalities touted last week by state health officials.

They estimate the infant mortality rate for 1990, for which only partial data are available, at 11 deaths per 1,000 live births. To put it another way, more than 2,000 babies—one of every 100—born in Illinois last year won't live to see his or her first birthday. And babies born to black women are twice as likely to die in that first year. For them, the rate is expected to level off at 22 per 1,000 live births, worse than in many Third World countries.

The available data would indeed constitute a kind of progress, if borne out by the final tallies, which are not yet in. The actual figure for 1989 was a grim 11.7 per 1,000 live births statewide. And that was the second time since 1986 that the death rate in this state went *up* instead of down.

But Illinois' halting and intermittent progress contrasts sharply with the steady declines in infant mortality elsewhere. The national infant death rate, always lower than our own, dropped to 9.1 in 1990, in what experts say is a direct response to beefed-up prenatal care in other states.

Quality prenatal care from the onset of pregnancy can spell the difference between a high-risk pregnancy and a safe one, between an underweight or developmentally impaired infant and a healthy one, between life and death. But poor women, who tend to be disproportionately black, are less likely to have any prenatal care at all, for reasons that range from lack of health insurance to hospital shutdowns and 3-to-9-month waits for appointments at Chicago public health clinics.

To Gov. Edgar's credit, he has increased spending for prenatal programs at a time when many others are being cut back. But there can be no letup when so many babies are dying, when there's such a long way to go.

The Clarion-Ledger
Jackson, Mississippi, March 15, 1991

Although state officials can point with pride to the strides being made to improve Mississippi's infant mortality rate, it is a long-term effort.

In Mississippi, infant mortality dropped 38 percent from 1979 through 1989, according to preliminary findings of the state's Infant Mortality Task Force.

That may bring Mississippi from near bottom up to 42nd among the states.

The improvement was a herculean effort. Only through better pre-natal care and greater education for impoverished mothers was the improvement made.

Yet, in order to continue to make strides in decreasing the infant mortality rate, much remains to be done.

Greater efforts must be made to aid young and unwed mothers. More prevention and outreach programs to keep kids from having kids must be provided.

Cutting the infant mortality rate is not a one-shot effort. It requires steady, long-term programs. The state can't just say, well, that's fixed, and shut them down.

Mississippi and other Southern states have traditionally lagged near bottom nationally. In 1989, 498 infants died before age 1, a rate of 10.8 per 1,000 live births.

That's still too high.

These are not mere figures, but human beings.

When state officials look at the bottom line for such services, they should ask: What is the cost of a human life?

TULSA WORLD
Tulsa, Oklahoma, April 2, 1991

PRESIDENT Bush was on the right track when he asked Congress to finance a campaign against infant mortality in 10 cities.

The problem was in his method. He wanted to divert money from other health programs that already serve pregnant women and poor children across the country.

In its budget request to Congress in February, the administration recognized the tragically high infant mortality rates in many American cities and proposed taking $33.7 million from the Maternal and Child Health Block Grant and $23.7 million from community health centers.

Congress said no. It wisely kept the original program intact but gave the president an additional $25 million in new money for his program, far less than the $57 million he requested.

Infant mortality is a serious problem and one in which America lags behind several industrial countries. Congress had it right. We need to solve it but not at the expense of successful programs making a difference to women and children in more than the ten selected locations.

America cannot pit one region's babies against another's or urban babies against rural ones.

The health of our smallest ones is a matter of national concern. The means must be found to see that proper nutrition and medical attention give infants the proper start in life to become healthy, productive Americans.

RAPID CITY JOURNAL—
Rapid City, South Dakota, October 6, 1991

Infant mortality rates are generally accepted as indicators of overall community health. The infant mortality rate for the United States is about 10 deaths per 1,000 births. Among the Native American population in South Dakota, it's more than twice as high. On the Pine Ridge Indian reservation, it's more than three times higher, above 33 deaths per 1,000 births.

In other words, family health among Native Americans represents a significant problem.

A project now in its developmental stage hopes to reduce — by 50 percent in five years — the infant mortality rate among Native Americans in the 17 tribes and two organizations represented by the Aberdeen Area Tribal Chairmen's Health Board. Along with the Oglala Sioux tribe at Pine Ridge and the Rapid City Indian Health Advisory Board, other South Dakota groups involved include the Standing Rock, Cheyenne River, Rosebud, Lower Brule, Crow Creek, Yankton, Flandreau-Santee and Sisseton-Wahpeton tribes.

The goal is ambitious. Yet even if attained it will be only the start of bringing family health among Native Americans in South Dakota to an acceptable level.

The project, one of 10 in a U.S. Health and Human Services pilot program dubbed "Healthy Start," will be funded by a federal grant expected to exceed $65 million over the five-year period. The federal expenditure for the entire Healthy Start program for fiscal year 1992 will be $171 million.

In other words, a lot of money.

The federal government is notorious for throwing large amounts of money at problems, often without solving them. This case appears different. This program holds promise for making a difference in the lives of many people.

The reason has to do with the design of "Healthy Start" and the local commitment that will be required.

According to Cynthia Smith, director of "Healthy Start" and associate director of the North Dakota Center for Rural Health, the key will be in diversity. Each of the 19 groups will have its own coordinator who will be responsible for developing a program that meets the particular needs of that group. The programs will emphasize two primary areas: direct medical services and education.

"It has so much potential," Smith says, "especially if the tribes take ownership."

And, although each group will develop its own program, plans call for groups to share methods. A central advisory board will oversee the program and should be able to ensure that methods proven effective for one group are available to others.

In addition, the intent of the program is not to duplicate existing programs, but to foster and facilitate them. A requirement of the program is that collaboration with existing programs be demonstrated. In fact, a key component will be to increase awareness of existing programs and to get pregnant women receiving already available prenatal care they would not otherwise receive.

Just over a year ago, world leaders gathered at the United Nations for the World Summit for Children. Out of the issues addressed at that gathering came a commitment to reduce infant mortality. Healthy Start represents significant movement toward that commitment, and in such a way as to address major problems experienced by Native Americans in South Dakota and neighboring states.

•

On Monday (National Child Health Day), the Journal's editorial will take a broad look at the status of commitments made at the World Summit for Children one year ago.

THE INDIANAPOLIS STAR
Indianapolis, Indiana, April 18, 1991

Behavior is the main cause of the nation's shockingly high rate of infant mortality, says an outstanding U.S. authority on nutrition and pediatrics.

For years malnutrition was blamed, and in many quarters it still is.

The malnutrition theory explains the popularity and fierce protection of WIC, the government financed program for the feeding of mothers-to-be and their babies.

But its validity should have been proven during the 19 years of WIC — the Special Supplemental Food Program for Women, Infants and Children. WIC costs the federal government about $2.5 billion a year and the states additional sums.

Behavior, not nutrition, is a major factor in high infant mortality rates.

Yet nutritional factors play a very small role in prematurity and low birth weight, which account for 60 percent of the high U.S. infant mortality rate, says Dr. George E. Graham, a professor of nutrition and pediatrics at Johns Hopkins University.

Even though advances in intensive care for newborns have boosted survival rates and the quality of life for very-low-birth-weight babies, "they continue to be disproportionately likely to suffer brain damage and other permanent medical problems," Graham explains in the April 2 *Wall Street Journal*.

What is the root-cause of high U.S. infant mortality? Graham writes:

"Studies of whites, blacks and Puerto Ricans all suggest that low-birth-weight births and very-low-birth-weight births in the United States correlate strongly with behavior, not nutrition, and especially with smoking, drug abuse (particularly the abuse of crack and other forms of cocaine), previous abortions, stress and infections of the genital tract and of the membranes surrounding the unborn baby, which often result from sexual promiscuity . . .

"Even extensive prenatal programs do little if expectant mothers fail to take advantage of them. Superhuman efforts in the District of Columbia to seek out and help high-risk pregnant girls have produced discouragingly meager results . . . It is their devastating climate of violence, drugs and sex that too often leads children to replicate the depressing fate of their parents . . . "

Behavior is obviously a far more complicated matter than malnutrition or a lack of medical care. It can cause malnutrition. It can prevent medical care. It can cause premature birth, low birth weight, brain damage and other permanent medical problems.

Aside from confinement and around-the-clock supervision, the only cure for bad behavior is a moral cure. For the sake of her unborn child, the mother-to-be must forgo drug abuse, promiscuous sex and other damaging behavior. The best means of persuading her to do so is debatable. What is not debatable is the need for responsible behavior, no matter how distasteful this may be to the foes of morality and self-control.

Unless means are found of motivating pregnant girls and women to behave in ways that will not threaten the lives and health of their unborn children, the nation can continue to spend more and more money on the infant mortality problem without making any progress toward the real goal of saving lives.

THE DALLAS TIMES HERALD

Dallas, Texas, March 10, 1991

Given the bipartisan criticism leveled at President Bush's proposal to fund a campaign to reduce infant mortality, we hope the administration gets the message that it's time to rethink the idea.

Granted, infant mortality is a national tragedy: Nearly 40,000 babies die annually in the United States before they are a year old. Dr. Louis Sullivan, the Secretary of Health and Human Services, rightfully called that figure "almost obscene" for a nation with so many resources.

We have no quarrel with the objective of the president's program; we do, however, question how it should be funded.

Mr. Bush is seeking to combine the $24 million now earmarked for community health centers and $34 million in block grants for maternal and child health care and put that money toward the infant mortality project, which will target 10 cities, as yet to be named.

Dr. Sullivan says such a strategy would not diminish resources but would instead refocus them.

The money taken from the approximately 550 centers would be concentrated rather than disbursed among the centers "where there is not enough to make a difference," Dr. Sullivan says.

We find that argument difficult to believe. As Sen. Pete Domenici, R-N.M., said last week, the centers have been a very efficient way to provide health care services, especially for people without health insurance.

In fact, Mr. Domenici, the ranking Republican on the Senate Budget Committee, said Congress is much more likely to increase funding for such centers than to agree to cut or transfer center funds.

Sen. Tom Harkin, D-Iowa, feels the same way. He has told Dr. Sullivan that Congress probably would fund the infant mortality program as a separate item, leaving intact the funding for the existing projects.

The nation's community health centers provided services for nearly 6 million clients in 1990.

While combating infant mortality is a commendable and critical objective, it's not one that ought to be achieved at the expense of adult Americans unable to afford health care.

The Philadelphia Inquirer

Philadelphia, Pennsylvania, September 23, 1991

As it has inched unrelentingly upward, Philadelphia's death-rate for newborns has overwhelmed each preventative effort set in its way — the good-hearted, but tiny mother-visitation projects, the high-tech nurseries, the erratic pamphleting, the episodic, after-school pregnancy-avoidance efforts. Today, in some neighborhoods of West Philadelphia, it is double the slowly *descending* national rate, which means that on average 23 babies out of every 1,000 die before their first birthday. In Japan, the rate is *four*.

There have been hearings on the matter, but few attend. There has been hand-wringing, but not the wave of emotion attending, say, a quarterback's injury. In many cases, too, there has been heroic, sometimes dangerous, work by dedicated health workers and pediatricians. But there has been neither broad political will, nor bulging wallet.

Until last week, that is.

As a result of a nationwide competition for federal funds to design a full-bore assault on infant mortality, the city's Health Department — hardly a usual pet of the Bush administration — could receive as much as $10 million, even $15 million, a year.

The money — which needs congressional approval — for the "Healthy Start" program means breathtaking new opportunities, from putting clinics in churches and housing projects to, more fundamentally, trying to change self-destructive lifestyles that contribute to the problem. It could also mean that America is one step closer to reaching consensus on a nationwide effort (like England's) to ensure basic, continuing prenatal care for all women.

Today's lack of consensus is born of a variety of factors. The high death rates are among the black and poor of the inner cities, American Indians, those underserved in remote rural areas — the sort of people who don't rank high on the political priority list. There have been disputes, too, over just what the main problem is — simply making more care available (having evening hours, for instance) or educating and motivating often troubled, sometimes drug-addicted, young women to act responsibly?

Indeed, Philadelphia's winning application — the work product of the department's indefatigable Harriet Dichter and a team of 50 community volunteers — addresses both problems, striving for user-friendly, well-advertised services, while trying to help women overcome the distractions, ignorance and isolation that lead to baby-damaging behavior.

If, ultimately, that combination can be shown to work (as it has on smaller scales), if demonstrable benefits follow the new federal dollars, the city and its 14 co-recipients may, at long last, show the way to common ground. If *that* comes to pass, the Healthy Start effort may do for infant health what Head Start did for early education — break the political ice.

FORT WORTH STAR-TELEGRAM

Fort Worth, Texas, July 27, 1991

Steps to combat infant mortality in Fort Worth may not be moving as quickly as all who are involved would prefer, but the important thing is that progress is being made and it is following a careful strategy.

Within a reasonable time, that approach should show helpful results.

Various studies have shown Fort Worth has an infant-mortality rate that is too high, one that is linked to prematurity and low birth weights. But what has not been readily known is how much drugs, alcohol and other lifestyle factors are involved. That information is necessary if causes are to be aggressively targeted.

Although the infant-mortality rate has been known to be high for some time, a comprehensively organized effort to counter it has come comparatively recently. That is why the local group now has applied only for federal funds to plan an attack against the problem and has delayed until later seeking federal money for programs to counter infant mortality.

Besides, some local government money could be available for that purpose in the 1991-92 fiscal year. Also, some services, such as prenatal clinics and the state's Supplemental Food Program for Women, Infants and Children, are already available.

If received, the federal planning money will permit the Fort Worth anti-infant-mortality organization to determine what needs to be done and how to accomplish it. Then, before long, federal money can be sought for programs aimed at reducing infant mortality.

Together, the local, state and federal funds and efforts should achieve what everyone seeks — healthier mothers and babies and fewer infant deaths.

The Register-Guard
Eugene, Oregon, October 13, 1991

The simple truth that women who receive adequate medical attention during pregnancy have healthier babies is generally acknowledged. Less widely understood is the fact that prenatal care actually saves money. Both the medical and financial benefits of good prenatal care have now been strongly borne out by a study in Lane County. Local investments in prenatal' care have paid handsome dividends, and opportunities exist for still further gains.

The two-year study of Lane County women found that those who received inadequate prenatal care gave birth to babies that weighed an average of nearly half a pound less than those born to women whose care was adequate. Low-birthweight babies — those weighing less than 5½ pounds — were nearly three times as common among the group receiving inadequate care. Congenital abnormalities occurred more than three times as often. Fifty percent more scored low on a test of newborn infants' vitality.

Babies born to women who received inadequate care stayed twice as long in the hospital and were nearly twice as likely to require admission to neonatal intensive care units. Thus medical costs for these women and their babies averaged $4,975.

For those who received adequate prenatal care, the cost was $2,163. When the cost of their prenatal care was added, the total came $4,250 — or $725 less than the bill for women whose care was inadequate. When total costs and reimbursements were considered, the final accounting showed that Sacred Heart General Hospital saved an average of $422 on each woman who had the benefit of medical care during pregnancy.

These findings underline the importance of programs like Lane County Comprehensive Pregnancy Services, established in 1987 by Sacred Heart, doctors, midwives and the county public health office. The program's goal is to provide prenatal care to every woman who needs it, regardless of her ability to pay. In 1987, 11 percent of women in Lane County received inadequate prenatal care. Today the percentage is slightly more than 6 percent, below the state and national averages.

This improvement is partly attributable to changes in Medicaid policy that favor improved prenatal care and to a general widening of public awareness of the importance of care during pregnancy. But the fact that Lane County's figures have improved so dramatically shows that the comprehensive pregnancy services program has had a profound impact. And now the study has found that the benefits to women and their children have been shared by the medical community.

Further gains are possible. The study went on to discover that women who don't receive prenatal care often have problems with transportation and lack information about where to go for medical help. Many don't understand the value of prenatal care, are living under psychological stress of various kinds or don't know they're pregnant until it's too late for adequate care. These women need to be reached.

Prenatal care offers a happy confluence of economic self-interest and the greater good of society. The Lane County study should help persuade governments and the health care industry locally and nationwide that medical care during pregnancy saves money and improves lives. Communities without universal access to medical care during pregnancy should ask themselves not only why they're compromising the health of the next generation but also why they're wasting money.

Chicago Tribune
Chicago, Illinois, April 9, 1991

Overall, the news is good, unexpected, welcome. Infant mortality in the United States, says the National Center for Health Statistics, declined at more than twice its usual, slow rate in 1990, down to 9.1 deaths per 1,000 live births, compared to 9.7 for 1989.

That means thousands more families could celebrate a birth and cherish a new life rather than mourn a baby's death last year.

The reasons for the gratifying gain aren't completely clear, according to analysts. As much as half of it may be due to the new drug surfactant, which helps a premature infant's lungs respond effectively to the need to breathe air weeks before they would normally be developed well enough to do so. Respiratory problems are a major reason why babies who are born too soon and too small do not survive, some after months of neonatal intensive care.

But scientific miracle drugs are rare, and new ones can't be counted on to keep infant mortality declining steadily in the future. The fact that these sad tolls are more than twice as high among blacks as whites helps point up the fact that this is a socioeconomic problem as much as a medical challenge.

High infant mortality is linked to poverty, to inadequate prenatal care, to unmarried teen pregnancy, to alcohol use, drug abuse, poor nutrition, poor health, AIDS and other health problems found disproportionately in poor areas. Efforts to reduce these disadvantages and to change personal behavior that may hurt unborn infants have already helped some high-risk babies to be born safely.

Government spending that aids these efforts is as smart fiscally as it is humane. For example, the Committee for Economic Development, a national coalition of business and academic leaders, calculates that every $1 spent in the prenatal component of WIC, a federal food program for women, infants and children, saves $3 in hospital costs.

Such programs are doubly important because many conditions linked to infant mortality also produce a high proportion of the children with learning disabilities, neurological handicaps and health problems. The improving infant mortality rate is a good indicator of progress in helping high-risk babies to be born healthy.

Much of what still must be done, however, lies beyond the power of scientists, doctors, social workers and legislators to change. They can keep putting out the urgent message that teenagers should not become pregnant until they are mature enough to be parents, and that women must start taking care of unborn babies right from the start of pregnancy.

They can—and must—make sure that prenatal care and education are easily accessible, that ample food is available to all. But they cannot relieve individual women from their vital responsibilities to give every baby the best start possible.

SYRACUSE
HERALD-JOURNAL
Syracuse, New York, October 14, 1991

We were saddened by the latest report from the state Health Department that showed 66 Onondaga County infants died last year. That put the death rate per 1,000 births at 17.1 — only slightly lower than it was three years ago when Syracuse's rate was the nation's seventh worst.

Only warm tears can express what those cold numbers mean in human terms — especially to the families involved. But, to county social workers trying to battle this problem, the numbers are an important and useful reminder. There is much work to be done. And they need to keep pushing hard.

The good news is the efforts county workers already have directed at reducing infant mortality are showing results:

■ The half-million federal dollars the county won for a program to help prevent common causes of infant deaths — short gestation and low-birth weight — should produce a health clinic at Gifford and West streets by February.

■ The federal government also is giving local private and public agencies $342,000 to improve care for babies and pregnant mothers in downtown Syracuse.

We look forward to seeing what these additions will do — and to the day when the annual state infant-mortality report brings better news.

Poor Children Ordered Tested for Lead

The U.S government was ordering that all children on Medicaid, the public health insurance system for the poor, be screened for lead poisoning, according to a *New York Times* article datelined Sept. 12, 1992.

The move was the result of a new consensus among health officials that levels of lead once thought to be safe could lead to mental retardation, learning handicaps, hearing impairment, stunted growth and behavior problems in children.

The new guidelines came from the Federal Health Care Financing Administration, which supervised Medicaid. They stipulated, "All children aged six months to 72 months are considered at risk and must be screened for lead poisoning." The screening involved both verbal questions about a child's exposure to lead, and blood tests. In all, more than six million children aged 72 months and under were on Medicaid.

Lead poisoning was one of the most prevalent health problems for children in the U.S. According to a calculation by health officials in 1984, it harmed three million to four million youngsters, or one out of every six children under six years of age. Low-income children faced the biggest risk because they often lived in dilapidated old homes that contained lead paint and lead plumbing. But the government emphasized that "no socioeconomic group, geographic area or racial or ethnic population" was invulnerable to lead poisoning.

Some physicians criticized the new directive because it allowed states to screen children with a lead test that was considered outmoded. The procedure, known as an erythrocyte protoporphyrin test, had been widely used since the late 1970s. But new evidence showed that children could be affected by extremely small amounts of lead, and the test was not sensitive to those amounts.

The Hartford Courant

Hartford, Connecticut, September 21, 1992

Lead, in paint that children find tasty, can damage a young child's brain, stunt growth and cause deafness. Lead poisoning afflicts one in six children under 6 years old, according to the federal government.

Yet many states have been slow to attack the menace or have had to play catchup with research showing that even very low amounts of lead can harm children.

After years of debate, the Legislature's Regulation Review Committee last week approved lead-paint rules. Connecticut is now ahead of many other states in testing, reporting and undoing the damage of lead. But the regulations also duck the threat in many ways. A few examples:

• The regulations require loose lead paint to be removed or covered, but they don't require testing for lead until a child is discovered to be poisoned.

• Local health officials are supposed to test dwellings whose young residents have high lead levels, but there is no mention of fines or other penalties. Thus, the policing problem is dumped on municipalities without the financial means to enforce the law.

• Lead inspectors don't have to be certified or licensed.

• Homeowners may do their own lead cleaning, although the amateurs among them may spread more lead dust than contain it. State health officials prefer that only professionals do the job, but don't require it.

• The legislative committee that adopted the regulations removed the provision that dwellings be tested for lead paint at the time of sale. In its place, Realtors have offered to note on the Multiple Listing Service whether properties have lead paint or whether the owners don't know.

• Home inspections are required by the regulations only when a child's lead level measures 20 micrograms per deciliter of blood or more. But the U.S. Public Health Service has reported "overwhelming and compelling" evidence that children are damaged by lead in concentrations as low as 10 micrograms.

So the rules help, but they fall short of the commitment needed in Connecticut, where nearly 40 percent of the housing stock contains lead paint. Two-thirds of New Haven's homes are believed to contain lead paint. Hartford Health Director Mark A. Mitchell estimates up to half of the city's children have harmful lead levels.

Connecticut is avoiding tougher standards because removing or covering lead paint is expensive. The job at 59 public-housing buildings at Bowles Park in Hartford, for example, will cost the state $1.7 million, or $28,000 per four-family building.

But dealing with lead poisoning could get even more expensive in years to come, for the state's health system, for local schools and for the families of the children rendered retarded, deaf and hyperactive by the tasty flakes on the floors and window sills.

THE DENVER POST

Denver, Colorado, September 21, 1992

ONE PROBLEM with the federal government's new plan to screen low-income children for lead poisoning is that the most commonly used test isn't sensitive enough to detect the low levels now considered harmful. But an even greater problem is that children on Medicaid, who are to be tested under regulations that go into effect this month, represent only about a quarter of all the youngsters aged 6 months to 6 years who ought to be checked.

Granted, poor kids may run the highest risk of exposure, since they tend to live in old, inner-city houses where lead-based paint may be peeling from the walls. But as the government noted in mandating tests for welfare recipients, "no socioeconomic group, geographic area or racial or ethnic population" is immune.

Of particular concern are the preschool children of young professional couples who renovate or remodel homes built before lead-based paints were outlawed in 1960. Such projects can generate toxic dust that often may not be discovered until the family cat goes into convulsions.

In view of the learning disabilities, behavior problems and hearing losses that even small amounts of lead can cause in children, it seems obvious that lead screenings ought to be included in all routine well-child checkups, as the American Academy of Pediatrics has long recommended.

Even verbal assessments — in which a nurse might ask a mother, for example, if her toddler attended a day-care center in an older home with peeling paint — could help head off thousands of potentially tragic cases of lead poisoning.

But to really protect children from this hidden menace, public health authorities should begin requiring that kids be screened before they can be enrolled in preschool — just as they must now be inoculated against measles, mumps and whooping cough before entering first grade.

State-of-the-art blood tests, which can detect lead poisoning while it's still treatable, don't come cheap. At $15 to $60 per test, they're far more expensive than immunizations for infectious diseases. But this may be a bargain compared to the lifetime costs of dealing with the metal's crippling impact on the young.

The News and Observer
Raleigh, North Carolina, September 17, 1992

North Carolina may find it costly to comply with a new requirement that every child on Medicaid who is between the ages of 6 months and 6 years be tested for lead poisoning. But the state has no choice — and not just because this is a federal directive. It can pay now. Or it can pay a lot more later.

The rule results from increasing recognition of the harm done by low amounts of lead in the blood. Levels once thought safe turn out to cause retardation, learning disabilities, stunted growth, and hearing and behavior problems.

Doctors in county health clinics will have to test about 150,000 children under age 6 — the sooner, the better. They now screen about 30,000 youngsters a year, so new laboratory workers and equipment will be needed. The state recently bought an $80,000 device for analyzing blood tests and will require at least one more like it to help meet the increased demand.

Little will be accomplished, though, until the screening method also is changed. The test now most widely used does not accurately measure small concentrations of lead in the blood. North Carolina prudently is requiring county clinics to switch to a more sensitive, although more costly, method. Strangely, the more accurate test is not called for under the new Medicaid rule — an oversight the federal government ought swiftly to correct.

To have a lasting impact, moreover, the new round of screening must be followed up with better measures to get at the source of children's exposure to lead. It is self-defeating to screen a child for lead and then send him back to a contaminated environment.

North Carolina has only one part-time inspector working on lead poisoning cases, and that inspector lacks the legal clout to compel landlords to remove lead-based paint, dust or other lead-tainted materials often found in older homes. The state Division of Environmental Health is going to ask the General Assembly for $1.1 million to hire new inspectors. When it does, the legislature should also take the opportunity to strengthen a law requiring owners to clean up contaminated property.

North Carolina's burden would be lightened by a proposal in Congress to increase federal funds for state screening programs. But the state cannot wait for the feds to put their money where their mandate is.

Lead poisoning can be treated if it is discovered early enough. Undetected, the damage may be irreversible. Compared to the likely price of remedial education, health care and job training, the bill for testing and inspection seems positively puny.

The Providence Journal
Providence, Rhode Island, September 25, 1992

"There is no medical cure for lead poisoning. The only thing you can do is prevent it." These words from Dr. Bela Matyas, chief of disease control for the Rhode Island Department of Health, sum up the reasons for the state's new drive to raise awareness of the dangers and prevalence of lead poisoning in young children.

We hope all Rhode Islanders, but especially parents, join in this campaign against a preventable pathology.

Launched by a coalition of public officials and private donors, and led by Lt. Gov. Roger Begin, the campaign realistically emphasizes, as Dr. Matyas says, going for "lead-safe rather than lead-free." There are large amounts of lead in any houses, in the ground and in the air from many years of pollution from lead paint and lead in gasoline. Both sources of lead have long been banned, but their residue remains.

We must deal with that reality. For instance, rather than covering or removing lead-contaminated (perhaps from old paint chips) soil, you can keep your child out of the dirt and buy a covered sandbox with a bottom. And rather than replacing old windows, which can produce lead dust when you open or close them, you can put obstacles, such as furniture, in front of them, so that your children can't reach them. And wash windowsills and floors frequently.

Here we should note that the problem of lead poisoning is often associated with youngsters in poor neighborhoods. But in fact, says Mr. Begin, the wide distribution in Rhode Island of old houses with lead paint on, in, or around them poses a peril to children of all races and economic backgrounds.

And it is difficult to overstate the seriousness of the problem. Dr. Matyas estimates that half the state's children under six years old have levels in their blood now considered unsafe. Their immature physiologies and tendency to crawl in lead-laden places makes the nervous systems of these very young children particularly vulnerable to injury, which can include brain damage that does incalculable harm to the individuals and to society.

Even low levels of lead can decrease IQ by an average of five points, Dr. Matyas says. While that might be distressing, it is manageable for an individual; but the implications for society are severe: "It means a shift down for the whole bell curve.... You have twice as many people with learning problems and half as many who are extremely bright."

A 1991 state law requires lead-screening tests for children and sets standards for lead inspections and lead removal. That statute should alleviate this public health menace. But it can't do nearly as much as can concerted efforts by parents and other adults to keep children out of harm's way. We hope the new campaign will inspire those efforts.

The lead around us will persist, but there is no excuse for more lead-poisoning cases.

For more information, readers may call a toll-free number 1 (800) 367-2700 for a copy of a brochure (in English, Cambodian, Spanish and Portuguese) describing ways to avoid exposure to lead.

ST. LOUIS POST-DISPATCH
St. Louis, Missouri, September 19, 1992

Lead poisoning in children is a serious problem, but the federal government isn't taking it seriously enough. A new policy will require states to screen almost all young children on Medicaid, to see if lead levels in their blood are high enough to harm their health. Unfortunately, federal officials are allowing use of a test whose results are generally not precise enough to find the lead levels that cause difficulty.

Statistics from Washington estimate that one in every six children under the age of 6 suffers from lead poisoning — between 3 and 4 million youngsters. The problem is primarily confined to children in low-income families, who are more likely to live in the run-down, inner-city buildings that have outmoded lead-based paint peeling off so kids can eat it.

With its order that states conduct blood tests to check for lead levels, the Federal Health Care Financing Administration could go a long way toward early diagnosis and treatment of lead poisoning and the problems it causes, including mental retardation, learning disabilities and stunted growth. But those problems can show up when lead is present at levels as low as 10 or 15 micrograms per deciliter of blood. The test that the government is allowing states to use is not that sophisticated and may not detect the presence of lead at less than 25 micrograms.

Federal officials who said they want to give states flexibility note that the less-sophisticated test is also less expensive: between $1 and $15 for each test, compared with between $15 and $60 for the better test, depending on how and where it is performed. Such flexibility generally is welcome, but only if all allowable methods can achieve the desired results. In this case, states using the cheaper test will not find all of the lead-poisoned children out there, leading to future health problems and a false sense of security that the problem is less common than it really is.

Experts on child health say if the less accurate blood test is used, the federal government's good intentions will be undermined. Good intentions are not enough to protect children who deserve a more determined effort to preserve their health.

Vaccines for Children Debated; Hepatitis Experiment Successful

Despite suspicion in recent years, there was little evidence linking two common childhood vaccinations with problems such as chronic nerve damage, aseptic menangitis, anemia, hyperactivity, learning disorders, and sudden infant death syndrome, according to a July 3, 1991 report by the Institute of Medicine, an affiliate of the National Academy of Sciences. The report's conclusions were based on a compilation of previous studies relating to the two shots, for DPT (diphtheria-pertussis-tetanus) and rubella.

An experimental vaccine had been found to halt the spread of hepatitis A, a potentially deadly liver infection, according to a study in the *New England Journal of Medicine* Aug. 13, 1992.

The drug was tested on a community of Hasidic Jews in Monroe, N.Y. that suffered from a high incidence of the disease. Of the 1,037 children who received injections, roughly half got the vaccine and half a placebo. None of those who took the vaccine developed the illness. The vaccine was manufactured by Merck & Co., Inc.

WORCESTER TELEGRAM.
Worcester, Massachusetts, September 16, 1988

Schoolchildren, who often pass communicable diseases around the classroom, have some good news this semester. Cases of measles, which increased in number for three years, are finally declining.

Younger students, vaccinated since 1980, probably stand the best chance of avoiding the common childhood disease. About 28 percent of the measles cases reported to the national Centers for Disease Control last year were considered preventable because they occurred in children who had not been vaccinated. Most of the rest of the measles cases were among older children, even college students, who were vaccinated more than eight years ago.

The measles vaccine was first used in 1963, but earlier versions may have worn off in some individuals. Newer vaccines are more effective and last longer. The CDC recommends revaccination for older students when a measles outbreak begins.

The CDC is also pushing to make sure all children receive their pre-school vaccination shots. Most states, including Massachusetts, require vaccinations before children start school. Some parents still neglect their children's shots, in the upheaval of moving or homelessness, so children go to school without being protected.

Urban school administrators may have difficulty tracking down vaccination records or may fear that sending the non-vaccinated children home will discourage attendance, so measles cases are more numerous in inner-city schools.

Every effort must be made to vaccinate all children as early in childhood as possible and to keep the pressure on until measles is eradicated. That goal was almost met in 1983, but then there were new outbreaks each year until 1987.

Measles can be a serious disease. With the better vaccines now available, we hope the time will come soon when the threat of this disease is finally overcome.

THE INDIANAPOLIS NEWS
Indianapolis, Indiana, July 5, 1988

Fear of lawsuits may be retarding the development of new vaccines, drugs and potential life-saving technology, according to the American Medical Association.

Many pharmaceutical companies have gotten out of the business of producing vaccines associated with lawsuits. Others are holding back development of new drugs.

And with reason.

From 1974 to 1985, the average jury award in product liability lawsuits soared from $494,580 to more than $1.8 million, according to a report to the AMA in Chicago last week. The number of lawsuits filed against manufacturers of a vaccine to prevent diphtheria, tetanus and pertussis increased from an average of about 33 a year from 1982 to 1984 to 110 in 1986.

"Product liability is having a profound negative impact on the development of new medical technologies," said the AMA report. "Innovative new products are not being developed or are being withheld from the market because of liability concerns or inability to obtain adequate insurance."

Dr. Lonnie Bristow, an internist and an AMA trustee, says some companies may be moving more slowly or holding off on the development and marketing of new vaccines for treating AIDS because of fear of spawning new litigation.

Ironically, the lawsuits may have an inverse effect on promoting the safety of vaccines. By reducing the number of firms producing a widely used vaccine, there is reduced competitive incentive to produce a purer or safer product. Drug prices also increase.

The House of Delegates approved a resolution urging state and federal governments to limit the amount of money awarded in product liability lawsuits involving vaccines.

Coincidentally, the AMA action comes the same week that the U.S. Supreme Court held that the estate of a Marine pilot killed in a helicopter accident cannot sue the manufacturer for design defects if the product was built according to government specifications.

Justice Antonin Scalia wrote in that decision, "The selection of the appropriate design for military equipment to be used by our armed forces often involves not merely engineering analysis but judgment as to the balancing of many technical, military and even social considerations, including specifically the trade-off between greater safety and greater combat effectiveness."

Perhaps something of the same legal doctrine should apply with respect to vaccines approved by the Federal Drug Administration.

The AMA policy acknowledges that those who are injured by the side effects of medical products deserve some compensation. Companies certainly should be held liable for vaccines that injure when negligence is involved in the manufacturing process.

But, if life-saving vaccines are to be developed and produced in this country, pharmaceutical companies need to be inoculated against soaring jury awards.

RAPID CITY JOURNAL—
Rapid City, South Dakota, November 18, 1991

While America struggles with resolving a crisis of escalating health care costs, South Dakota has come up with a plan that represents a small but significant step of progress.

State and federal officials were in Rapid City last week to unveil a pilot project of the Infant Immunization Initiative which aims to immunize 90 percent of South Dakota children under age 2 against a variety of dangerous diseases. Rapid City was one of six target cities selected for funding under the federal program. State officials who developed the plan want to implement it statewide, according to Ken Senger, director of the South Dakota Division of Public Health.

Currently less than 60 percent of South Dakota children are fully immunized by age 2, although almost all are immunized by school-age. By achieving a higher rate of immunization earlier in children's lives, society can realize health care cost savings by preventing diseases in children between the infant and school years. As an example, Senger explained, the cost associated with one case of congenital rubella syndrome, a disease that will require lifelong treatment, will exceed the cost of immunizing the entire state against the disease.

Officials at Health and Human Services, the federal agency administering the program, selected Rapid City — along with urban areas Phoenix, Dallas, Detroit, San Diego and Philadelphia — for pilot funding for the program. According to Senger, the South Dakota plan contains aspects of immunizing rural populations that make it attractive as a model for other areas of the country.

Any strategy for containing rising health care costs must include elements of prevention. South Dakota's infant immunization plan represents a step in that direction.

The Philadelphia Inquirer
Philadelphia, Pennsylvania, March 15, 1991

As the deadly measles outbreak continues its sweep though Philadelphia, the Bush administration is wondering aloud if it's time that welfare parents be required to show they've had their children immunized before getting benefits. It's a sorely tempting proposal, one that even overwhelmed public health officials — some of them, at least — aren't willing to dismiss out of hand. After all, if parents don't have their children inoculated after all the publicity about youngsters dying of measles, after special free-clinic days, after badgering, reminding and darn near pleading, what better way to get their attention?

Well, we've got a few ways, though they, too, accept parents' key role. It is mothers and fathers, in the end, who owe it to their children to protect them. And they owe it, as well, to the community at large. That's why there are laws — highly effective ones, in fact — that say children can't enter elementary school without shots against contagious childhood diseases.

Still, being clear about parental responsibility doesn't absolve government from its duty to get smarter and act quicker. For instance, since mothers applying for nutrition supplements often show up toting unvaccinated children, why not have a Health Department worker standing by to give a shot? (Indeed, bureau-cratic inertia appears ready to give way on just such a plan.)

Likewise, it's crucial to ensure that clinics routinely have user-friendly hours in the evenings and Saturdays and that it doesn't take long waits to get a shot — a not uncommon frustration before the epidemic. (The Bush administration might reflect on whether federal funding has kept pace with even *current* demands on big-city health clinic staff and resources.)

Other strategies include sending postcards to parents notifying when shots are due, more federal support for vaccine campaigns and enforcement of new laws requiring up-to-date immunization for entry into day care.

Those approaches make old-fashioned sense. They treat poor mothers and children more like customers than a burden. They appreciate the value of advertising, convenience and drive-through efficiency. Taken together, they ought to dramatically boost immunization rates, which are worse in parts of West Philadelphia than in parts of the Third World.

If they do not, Mr. Bush's proposed "no-shots, no-benefits" policy will have two things going for it that it doesn't have now — evidence that less-punitive strategies don't work and the moral authority to say that government has extended its hand, and parents need an extra prod.

THE INDIANAPOLIS STAR
Indianapolis, Indiana, January 11, 1991

State officials are convinced that vaccination laws must be changed to protect children from suffering preventable diseases.

The weakness in present law became evident last year when local health boards reported 412 cases of measles to the state.

This was four times the number in 1989 and the most since 1983 when 406 cases were reported.

Proposed legislation that has been reviewed by the executive committee of the State Board of Health may be introduced during the current session of the Indiana General Assembly.

The proposal comes in the wake of a federal report filed this week by the National Vaccine Advisory Committee that blamed the 1990 measles epidemic on a breakdown in the country's vaccination system.

The report said barriers in the nation's health care system keep parents from having their children vaccinated against easily preventable diseases including measles, polio, diphtheria, tetanus, whooping cough, rubella and mumps.

The State Board of Health proposal would make parents or guardians responsible for obtaining vaccinations for children and would eliminate provisions in the present law requiring local health departments to provide the shots if parents cannot.

Local health clinics will continue to offer immunization programs but increased vaccine costs could use up resources quickly, said Mary Lou Fleissner, State Board of Health expert on disease spread.

Meeting federal Centers for Disease Control standards for public clinic immunizations in Indiana through 1991 will cost $3.3 million, of which the state would pay about $958,000. A necessary second round of doses in 1992-93 will increase the state's share to $2.8 million.

Funds are likely to run out, and the proposed legislation, if introduced, should include provisions for sufficient funding, Fleissner said.

This makes sense. In the long run, it would be cheaper than a pound of cure.

CHICAGO Sun-Times
Chicago, Illinois, March 28, 1991

The federal government needs to stanch the resurgence of preventable childhood diseases that once were nearly wiped out in this country.

And health officials say the biggest step toward stopping outbreaks of these resurfacing diseases (such as measles, rubella, whooping cough and mumps) is to make it virtually mandatory for parents to get their children immunized in their first two years of age.

While immunization rates are more than 99 percent for children entering elementary school (a law in most states), it is during a child's first 24 months that most routine vaccinations should be administered, and at this age level the United States has been said to fall short of all Western Hemisphere nations except Bolivia and Haiti in immunization of kids.

The Centers for Disease Control says that nationally, only about 70 percent of 2-year-olds have had a combination vaccine against common childhood diseases, and this plunges to about 50 percent in inner cities. Those statistics indicate the greatest effort should be directed toward educating inner-city parents on the crucial need for preschool vaccinations.

It is fairly easy to trace the surge in childhood diseases to lack of parental knowledge about preschool immunization programs and their (perhaps unwitting) negligence of children's health care at this age. There is no shortage of vaccine or access to it.

The Bush admiministration is weighing a proposal that parents be required to prove children have been immunized before they can become eligible for welfare. That may seem drastic, but even more serious has been the revival of children's diseases.

The Seattle Times

Seattle, Washington, March 28, 1991

RUBELLA, a mild childhood disease with serious consequences for pregnant women and the unborn, has made a dramatic return.

The federal Centers for Disease Control report the highest number of cases in nine years, a 60 percent increase through September. This statistic is another benchmark of the nation's woefully low vaccination rate.

Rubella, or German measles, can cause birth defects, but the disease is preventable with a vaccine that has been around since 1970. The problem is that women of childbearing age are not being vaccinated and they are exposed to toddlers who likewise are unprotected.

Measles and rubella are two of a host of diseases that can be checked in childhood but have flourished because infants are not being immunized early enough.

Washington state has been lucky this year, or, more precisely, made its own luck. Aggressive public-health campaigns have checked measles and rubella outbreaks.

Rubella cases this year are up 60 percent, to mirror national figures, but the cases were isolated. Measles cases are down dramatically from 1990, but the diseases made a point about the spectrum of vulnerability. Last year preschool children were hit hardest, and in 1991 older children and adults have suffered.

Mindful of the nationwide epidemic, state law was changed to require a second measles vaccination for sixth-graders to attend school this fall.

Last year the Legislature acknowledged but failed to act on the gaps in immunization programs. General agreement was reached that impediments to vaccinations — fees, clinic hours, language barriers, and public education — must be addressed.

Immunizations are a cost-effective public-health investment. Each dollar spent saves $10.

TULSA WORLD

Tulsa, Oklahoma, October 30, 1991

NEAR eradication of some once-feared diseases has lulled many Americans into a false sense of security. Diseases like polio and rubeola, or hard measles, were all but wiped out but rebounded in recent years because many parents failed to have their children immunized against them.

That's why the "Due by Two" campaign led by Oklahoma first lady Rhonda Walters was so important. Following a couple of weeks of publicity and public appearances by Mrs. Walters, some 13,000 children received 37,000 immunizations at clinics throughout the state on Saturday. That effort significantly raised the immunization level among Oklahoma children, which previously stood at about 33 percent. The campaign's goal is to immunize 90 percent of Oklahoma's children by 1994.

Immunizations given at the clinics included oral polio vaccine; MMR, for measles, mumps and rubella; DPT, for diphtheria, pertussis and tetanus, and Hib, or haemophilus Influenzae type B, for childhood meningitis. Children should receive these vaccines by the time they are 2 years old.

The "Due by Two" campaign is a good step toward ensuring a healthy future for Oklahoma and its children.

Seattle, Washington, February 24, 1991

A NATIONWIDE epidemic of measles has provided brutal evidence of the fatal gaps in delivery of vaccines for preventable childhood diseases.

Legislation that would give local immunization programs a booster shot is in the Senate Health and Long-Term Care Committee. Failure to act will touch thousands of lives.

No one disputes the problem, but a perception persists in Olympia that health-care bureaucrats are lukewarm to responding. That lack of enthusiasm could be lethal.

Supplies of vaccine are not the issue; rather, the breakdown comes with missed opportunities to get the vaccine to the children who need it.

A federal study released in January found that more than 80 percent of the measles cases from 1989 through 1990 among children aged 16 months to 5 years could have been prevented by timely vaccination.

Measles cases in Washington are soaring along with the statistics for the rest of the nation. In 1983, 1,497 cases were reported in the entire country, according to the National Vaccine Program. In 1989, the figure was 18,000, and in 1990 the number went beyond 25,000.

The greatest increase has been among children under 5 years of age. Immunizations need to start early.

"The principal cause of the epidemic is failure to deliver vaccine to vulnerable preschool children on schedule," according to the study.

Minority children are disproportionately affected, with black and Hispanic youngsters in urban areas seven to nine times more likely to suffer from measles than white children.

Federal experts consider measles, the most infectious of the preventable diseases, a good indicator of an overall failure of the vaccine-delivery system. That means children who don't receive immunizations in a timely fashion may also be susceptible to pertussis, poliomyelitis, mumps and rubella.

Even though parents are often blamed for not getting their children immunized, the National Vaccine Program said the health-care system must assume substantial responsibility for failure to vaccinate.

A major gap involves children who have contact with health-care providers but the need for immunizations is not assessed or the vaccinations are not offered.

For example, the study recommends that immunization status should be routinely checked for persons enrolled in the Women, Infants and Children program and Aid to Families with Dependent Children. Vaccinations ought to be offered on-site, or scheduled with a planned follow-up.

Failure to vaccinate children enrolled in public-assistance programs suggests that potential gains from expanded coverage in Medicaid eligibility may not be realized if preschoolers are not protected, according to the National Vaccine Program.

This state has a chance not only to protect its young children but to provide national leadership. Senate Bill 5540 offers creative solutions to known delivery problems.

THE DENVER POST

Denver, Colorado, October 22, 1991

JUST A FEW years ago, most childhood diseases seemed on the verge of extinction in this country. Now they're making a comeback, thanks mainly to the rising cost of vaccines and alarming weaknesses in the immunization laws.

In Colorado, the state health department estimates that fewer than 60 percent of the children are fully immunized by the age of 2 years, as recommended by medical authorities. This means thousands of preschoolers are vulnerable to potentially serious diseases like measles, mumps, meningitis and whooping cough.

Worse, many of these youngsters remain open to attack until they enter public schools, when vaccinations are required for enrollment. That's because their parents may not be able to afford — or recognize the need for — proper immunizations, and the children may not attend licensed day-care centers, which are legally obligated to see that they've had all their shots.

The situation cries out for rectification — and not just because these preventable diseases cause such terrible pain and suffering. As public health officials are fond of pointing out, inoculations are highly cost-effective, saving $5 to $10 in hospital bills for each dollar spent on vaccine.

One remedy would be to remove the legal obstacles that prevent private physicians in Colorado from buying vaccines at the discount rates paid by public health clinics. This would enable parents to get their kids vaccinated by their family doctors at lower prices.

Another, more far-reaching approach would be to require insurance companies to pay for this kind of preventive care, just as many now pay for mammograms and other such procedures.

Still another antidote would be to make immunizations available at public clinics at least one night a week, to accommodate working parents. Alternatively, vaccines could be routinely administered by school nurses, or by public health workers stationed in the schools for a week or two each year.

All of these strategies — and more — may have to be tapped to keep today's healthy babies from becoming tomorrow's ailing boys and girls. This high-tech society simply can't ignore the need for such basic, simple and supremely humane precautions.

The Des Moines Register
Des Moines, Iowa, August 22, 1991

A resurgence of measles around the nation is occurring because children are not being immunized. Iowa is among the states that are affected. Free vaccinations are available throughout Iowa at more than 100 sites, which means it should be easy to manage the serious, sometimes deadly disease.

Nationwide, more than 26,000 cases of the highly contagious viral illness were reported in 1990, with 4,079 cases already logged this year. In 1983, only 1,497 total cases were recorded.

In Iowa, 26 cases were reported in 1990, with 15 so far this year, most of the latter in children under age 5. As recently as 1987, the state recorded no measles cases. Between 1981 and 1985, only one case was reported.

Ideally, youngsters are immunized for measles, with a combined measles-mumps-rubella inoculation, at age 15 months.

Some parents don't have children vaccinated because they lack a regular health-care provider, or they don't have health insurance and worry that the vaccination is too costly. Other parents mistakenly think it's wise to toughen up kids by exposing them to measles, even though it can cause serious complications such as pneumonia and encephalitis. Or parents simply may not make the time to schedule an appointment.

New public health department rules, effective this coming school year, should help counter the measles resurgence. Kindergartners will be required to show proof that they've received a second measles vaccination — in addition to the the one typically given at 15 months — since the first dose isn't always 100 percent effective. If kindergartners never have been vaccinated, they'll have to get two doses, one before starting school and a second one a month later. Religious and medical exemptions will be made.

Parents should check the vaccination records of their children. Measles is no longer the threat it once was, but it hasn't gone away. The best way to prevent it from becoming a widespread problem is for parents to make sure toddlers are immunized.

THE ROANOKE TIMES
Roanoke, Virginia, March 4, 1991

MEASLES, a highly contagious disease that can be deadly, has reached epidemic proportions in some areas of the country in the last couple of years. Thus far, Virginia has been lucky not to have had a major outbreak of the disease, such as that seen in Philadelphia (where six children recently died from it) and in several other areas, including in Maryland and North Carolina.

But the centuries-old malady, which many thought had disappeared after a vaccine became available in 1963, is coming back. Virginia parents should take steps to protect their children, especially at-risk preschoolers.

In 1990, there were 27,000 reported cases in the nation (up from 1,500 in 1983) and 65 measles-related deaths. In Virginia, there were 86 cases (fortunately, none fatal), up from 20 in 1989.

State health officials say there have been no reports of measles in Virginia this year. But, at the urging of the federal Centers For Disease Control, they asked the General Assembly to enact a bill requiring that children receive a second dose of measles vaccine prior to entering kindergarten or the first grade of school. (A single dose fails to provide lifelong immunity from measles in some individuals.)

That bill now awaits the governor's signature. The CDC will make about $500,000 in federal funds available to Virginia to pay for the second dose.

But the legislation is no substitute for parental responsibility. Current state law requires that every child be immunized against measles, mumps and German measles (rubella) before the age of 2. But, practically speaking, the law is unenforceable during a child's early years. Only when a youngster is ready for school must parents show documentation of required immunizations.

As a result, many postpone vaccinations until school time, leaving young children vulnerable to disease. Health officials say this is a key factor in the recent epidemics.

Because doctors are seeing increased cases of measles among those in their teens, the American Academy of Pediatrics believes a second dose of the vaccine would be most effective given at age 12. Ideally, health officials say, follow-up doses should be given at about the ages of 5, 12 and 18. But public funding hasn't been made available for multiple repeat doses.

Meanwhile, parents can help prevent a measles epidemic in Virginia by adhering to the law and seeing that their toddlers are immunized. The vaccine is available from private physicians or at local health departments, where there is no charge for it, regardless of parents' ability to pay.

Children deserve to be protected from this preventable disease.

The San Diego Union-Tribune.
San Diego, California, July 17, 1991

San Diego is one of six cities that the federal Centers for Disease Control will visit this fall to assess the breadth of the nation's measles problem. The White House indicates that it will defer action to stem the possible epidemic until the CDC reports its findings.

This does not set well with many public health officials who feel that President Bush should act now to avert a repeat of last year's measles epidemic, the worst in more than a decade. Health experts note that measles outbreaks follow a three-year cycle, which means that last year's crisis would recur in 1993.

For 1990, federal health officials confirmed 27,672 measles cases, a 52 percent increase over the previous year. Measles also claimed the lives of 89 pre-school-aged children, the highest such death toll in three decades. California was particularly hard hit by last year's measles epidemic, accounting for about 45 percent of total cases nationwide. Here in San Diego, local health officials reported 985 measles cases, three of which resulted in deaths of infant children.

Reports of measles outbreaks are understandable in poor Third World countries, but it should be unheard of in a nation as prosperous and medically advanced as the United States. Indeed, the development of an effective measles vaccine in 1963 by American researcher John F. Enders virtually eliminated the disease within two decades. In 1963, a half million measles cases were recorded. By 1983, there were only 1,497.

The key to preventing measles is of course universal immunization of young children. This was generally accepted public-health policy during the 1960s and 1970s, but toward the latter part of the 1980s increasing numbers of pre-school children from largely lower-income families were not getting measles shots.

There are several explanations for this lapse, but the most significant may be the escalating cost of child vaccines since 1963. Consider that a dose of measles vaccine with a syringe cost as little as 14 cents in the mid-1960s. The same dose now costs a whopping $15.32 for government agencies that buy in bulk quantities. Private physicians may pay $10 to $15 more.

Poor and working-class families increasingly find the price of immunizing their young children beyond their means. This portends a recurrence of such epidemics as whooping cough, rubella, diphtheria and other preventive diseases that most Americans had thought extinct. President Bush should embrace plans to provide sufficient funds to ensure that children of lower-income families are properly immunized.

THE ARIZONA REPUBLIC
Phoenix, Arizona, January 5, 1992

A few generations have come and gone since epidemics of childhood diseases such as polio swept through cities and towns with unmerciful vengeance. The fear those illnesses struck in the hearts of mothers and fathers is only a faded memory today, but what about tomorrow?

Barriers to vaccines against childhood diseases and the failure of parents to safeguard the health of their children are giving new life to preventable diseases that for a time were on the verge of eradication. A tomorrow for some families may bring clear, startling suffering and death that could have been avoided with an effective series of vaccinations.

The nation is seeing an upsurge in preventable diseases that can kill and cripple. According to the Robert Wood Johnson Foundation, a health-care philanthropy, 1983 saw only 1,497 cases of measles in the United States; 27,786 occurred in 1990. The number of reported cases dropped to fewer than 10,000 in 1991, but outbreaks continue to alarm public health officials. In Maricopa County, only half the children under 2 are vaccinated — an inexcusable figure inasmuch as the inoculations are provided free at county health clinics.

The danger presented by the lapse in vigilance against these diseases is widely recognized. Congress has held hearings on the vaccination issue; the Centers for Disease Control is trying to create a program that overcomes barriers to vaccines; and President Bush has set as a goal the immunization by the year 2000 of 90 percent of all children under 2. (Programs are being tested in six cities, including Phoenix, to reach that objective.)

Arizona's push to stave off senseless tragedies includes a new law requiring parents to show proof of immunization when they enroll their children in school. In the past the state took the word of parents that their children had been properly immunized.

The barriers to vaccines include costs for those wanting care from a private physician, access for families in outlying areas and ignorance and apathy on the part of some parents regarding the potential ravages these preventable diseases are capable of producing in large populations of unprotected children.

California Rep. Henry Waxman, chairman of the House Energy and Commerce subcommittee on health, said it best: "We cannot allow children to die of diseases that should never occur, and we cannot afford to treat children for crippling conditions that we can prevent."

Los Angeles Times
Los Angeles, California, August 10, 1992

Measles, whooping cough and other illnesses that debilitate and even kill children should be things of the past. Instead they keep cropping up in epidemics, and it's no wonder. Only 42% of 2-year-olds in Los Angeles and only half in Orange County are fully immunized against childhood diseases. Obviously, additional efforts must be made to increase the numbers of children who are protected.

One thing that would help would be for the Legislature to adopt—and Gov. Pete Wilson to sign—a bill by Assemblyman Tom Umberg (D-Garden Grove) that would require health insurers to cover the cost of routine immunization for children under 18. Currently, nearly every health maintenance organization (HMO) covers immunizations for youngsters, but only about 45% of other private insurance companies do so.

The measure would extend immunizations to more children. But it would also end up giving some relief to county health departments, which frequently sponsor programs to immunize preschool children.

Many middle-class families take advantage of these free programs when their own insurance coverage won't pay for immunizations, because private physicians generally charge $300 to $500 for a full set of shots—some of which must be given at intervals in order to be effective. By age 5, of course, nearly every youngster is immunized because California law requires it before a child can enter school.

Umberg's bill will not address the many other problems involved in achieving full immunization for children, many of whom come from families with no health insurance coverage at all. But it would make a clear statement to insurance companies that, at least in California, immunizations are something they must provide as a routine part of pediatric care.

Umberg's bill has passed the Assembly and is awaiting action in the Senate, which would do well to provide the votes needed to put the measure on Wilson's desk. That would give the governor, a strong supporter of preventive health programs, especially for children, another chance to show he is serious about that commitment.

The New York Times
New York City, New York, September 11, 1992

Three years ago measles, which had been reduced to very low levels in the United States, started making a comeback. It has since infected tens of thousands of young victims, many of them in New York. The epidemic has been caused by an unconscionable failure to vaccinate the most vulnerable children. But starting today, health authorities should be able to turn the tide.

The State Department of Social Services, working with the state and New York City Health Departments and the Human Resources Administration, is launching a campaign to reach the chief victims — poor children under 5 who are neither immunized nor connected to a primary care facility. Posters and brochures listing information and an 800 number to call for referrals to clinics and physicians will be broadly distributed. Next summer free vaccines will be distributed to the 4,000 physicians who vaccinate children enrolled in Medicaid. And 11 community organizations have received grants to help widen their outreach to families eligible for these services.

Three different approaches will be tested, in the Bronx, Brooklyn and Manhattan. They'll use nurses, caseworkers and health clerks respectively to contact and follow up on the immunization and health care referrals.

Which approach will be the most effective is impossible to predict. But these initiatives can make a welcome difference in poor children's lives.

copyright © The New York Times 1992

ST. LOUIS POST-DISPATCH
St. Louis, Missouri, January 5, 1992

The outbreaks of vaccine-preventable diseases during the late 1980s offer ominous signs that this nation is falling behind in immunizing and protecting children from illness, disability and needless death. Government indifference to this problem is such that a health-care philanthropy, the Robert Wood Johnson Foundation, has decided to take the lead.

The foundation is committing $9 million to programs to help immunize preschool children. Federal law requires that children be immunized before they start school, and most of these children receive vaccines. But over a million children under the age of 2 receive no vaccines, according to the foundation.

The intent of the foundation's program is to help overcome barriers, such as transportation and long waits for service, that discourage poor parents from seeking immunization of children in the under-2 age group. The federal government and states haven't been innovative in making vaccine programs more readily available. One answer is for states to set up one-stop social service centers where the poor could receive numerous services at a single location. Missouri is trying to move in this direction. There is no reason that food stamps, heath clinics, public aid and other social services couldn't all be under a single roof.

As matters now stand, the United States ranks 56th in immunizing minority youngsters against childhood illnesses and 17th in protecting children against preventable diseases. This nation began to lag behind during the 1980s. In 1983, there were only 1,497 cases of measles in this country. By 1989, the number had jumped to 18,193, and by 1990, there were 27,672 cases of measles, mostly among children, as well as 89 deaths.

The Johnson Foundation is to be commended for its five-year program to help tackle this issue. The shame is that the federal and state governments haven't done more to address it on their own. After all, effective immunization programs are relatively cheap compared to the public cost of treating diseases that vaccines might have prevented.

The Seattle Times

Seattle, Washington, August 27, 1992

THIS election, as in no prior campaign season, candidates are expected to be conversant in the lingo of the nation's health-care crisis.

Fast and furious discussions use a simple shorthand — pay-or-play, employer-based or universal — to describe reform plans for a $800 billion industry.

Lost in the complex schemes are some of the less dramatic, but effective ways to rein in costs and keep citizens healthy.

One example is early vaccinations for such deadly childhood maladies as measles. Providing timely immunizations is not inexpensive, but it is vastly cheaper than treating a sick child in a hospital emergency room or providing intensive care for an infant who is gravely ill.

Poor and low-income families without health insurance have turned the nation's emergency rooms into their family clinic. This is the most expensive form of medical care, and those costs all get passed along to patients with insurance.

Keeping people healthy with preventive medicine will lower our national overhead. Early immunizations are part of an early, cost-effective start on a healthier life.

As the politicians work on the larger puzzle of health-care provision, they should not overlook how the little pieces fit together.

The Hartford Courant

Hartford, Connecticut, September 10, 1992

The question of how much to spend on other countries' children could hardly have come up at a worse time. The United States faces a $20 billion cleaning bill from Hurricane Andrew's visit. Hartford teachers have taken a raincheck on raises. Nearly half of New Hampshire's school districts have cut kindergarten classes because they can't afford them.

So members of the Senate Foreign Operations Subcommittee will be sorely tempted to cut back on foreign aid pledged for vaccinating children against measles, providing antibiotics for diarrhea and supplying Third World countries with Vitamin A to keep children from going blind.

The subcommittee ought to resist the temptation, because the cost of neglect is high. Some 44,000 children die daily from preventable diseases. That death rate is unconscionable in itself. But it also encourages population explosion. The more children die in countries where the only social security lies in the family, the more and more children are conceived, partly to increase the odds that some children will survive, partly because a child's death means the end of breast-feeding, a natural contraceptive.

The matter of health and education money for children in other countries comes before the subcommittee this week as a small component of a large foreign aid bill. The U.S. House has already approved a $13.8 billion aid package that would allocate $275 million for child survival and $135 million for basic education — $100 million below the share that the United States pledged at the 1990 World Summit for Children.

Now it's up to the Senate subcommittee to recommend restoring that $100 million and paying for the pledge with money cut from the military side of the foreign-aid ledger.

THE KANSAS CITY STAR

Kansas City, Missouri, August 9, 1992

The near elimination of common childhood diseases in the United States has been one of the finest achievements of modern medicine. Within it, however, lies the seed for a potential disaster.

The trouble is that today's parents of young children have no experience with the horrors of polio, diptheria, whooping cough, perhaps even measles and the mumps. They and everyone around them were vaccinated. They were safe.

Whether they forget to have their infants immunized, postpone the task, downplay its importance or misjudge the risks of disease compared with a remote possibility of vaccine side effects, a large and growing minority have left their toddlers without protection against deadly disease.

The Mid-America Immunization Coalition will sponsor a free immunization clinic Aug. 22 at five church facilities, from way north of the Missouri River to way south, with several locations in the central city. Call 451-9389 for information and clinic addresses.

Every parent who has a child two months of age or older who has not been immunized should make a strenuous effort to get to one of these clinics. The benefits are high. The risk of doing nothing can be fatal.

Because of state laws requiring immunization before attendance, many people believe the schools are on top of the issue. Several factors, including the reduction or elimination of school nurses, reduce this backup.

Children are in danger of contracting the diseases long before they start elementary school. And with so many in day care and other communal pre-school arrangements, they share diseases at younger and younger ages.

Children's Mercy Hospital, the Kansas City Health Department, Cigna Healthplan of Kansas City and other major partners in the coalition putting on the clinics are making a real push at preventive health care. They deserve the city's thanks. But what they really want is for thousands of parents and their children to show up Aug. 22. It's the way to ensure a healthier next generation.

TULSA WORLD

Tulsa, Oklahoma, August 24, 1992

ONCE thought to be all but wiped out, measles, an infectious childhood disease that can kill, is rebounding in the United States. Public health officials say they are stunned by an epidemic of 55,000 cases in three years.

The inner cities, where immunization rates are low, have been hardest hit. Many of the 166 measles deaths in the United States since 1989 were inner-city preschool-age children.

The terrible thing about this epidemic is that it is easily prevented. From the early 1960s, when the measles vaccine was introduced, until the recent epidemic, there were 2,000 or fewer measles cases a year nationwide. In Oklahoma, too, has had recent problems with measles. Reported cases went from four in 1987 to 174 in 1990, with the first measles death in more than 10 years. Although that number receded in 1991, the threat remains.

Oklahoma law requires that in most cases school children be immunized against measles and other infectious childhood diseases. State health officials estimate that about 99 percent are immunized.

But it is estimated that only a third of the state's children under age 5 are immunized, despite the fact that full immunizations are recommended for all children by age 2 and can be completed by 15 months. It is among these younger, unimmunized children, that many of the new measles cases occur.

State and county health departments are working to increase immunization rates among preschoolers. But for such efforts to work, parents must cooperate.

Legislative Gains Made by Disabled Americans

The House May 22, 1990 approved legislation that would prohibit discrimination against disabled Americans in employment, housing, and public accomodations and transportation. A similar measure had been passed by the Senate in September 1989.

The House bill, which was passed by a vote of 403-20, would extend to people with mental or physical handicaps the protections of the Civil Rights Act of 1964. The legislation would cover individuals with AIDS as well as alcoholics or drug abusers who had undergone treatment for their addiction.

The major difference between the House and Senate versions was a provision in the House bill that would permit employers to transfer workers with contagious diseases out of food-handling. The House had approved the amendment, offered by Rep. Jim Chapman (D Texas), May 17, by a vote of 199-187. Lawmakers said the amendment was aimed at workers infected with the virus that caused AIDS.

The Senate July 13 voted, 91-6, to give final approval to a landmark bill that would prohibit discrimination against people with physical or mental disabilities.

President George Bush July 26 signed into law a landmark civil rights bill that prohibited discrimination against people with disabilities.

"America welcomes into the mainstream of life all of our fellow citizens with disabilities," Bush said. He added, "Every man, woman and child with a disability can now pass through once-closed doors into a bright new era of equality, independence and freedom."

The bill was expected to affect an estimated 43 million Americans with disabilities.

The Bush administration Jan. 21 and Feb. 21, 1991 proposed new federal regulations concerning accommodations for disabled persons in buildings and businesses open to the public. The rules were designed to implement the Americans With Disabilities Act of 1990.

The Bush administration announced March 14, 1991 that it would reconsider the cases of more than 400,000 children denied Social Security disability benefits since 1980. In 1990, the Supreme Court had struck down the criteria used by the Health and Human Services Department to judge whether children were entitled to benefits. The court ruled that the criteria were too restrictive, noting that they did not include such disorders as AIDS, Down's syndrome or muscular dystrophy. The court had ordered the government to make individual determinations based on the "functional capacity" of each child, just as it did for adults who sought Social Security benefits.

BOSTON HERALD
Boston, Massachusetts, December 12, 1989

When President Bush signed a bill last week that will provide benefits for severely disabled children and their families, he was reacting to what he had learned by listening to people like the Mulligan family of Methuen.

Kaleigh Mulligan suffers from Down's syndrome and its related medical problems. Her parents wanted only to care for their daughter at home. But a few years ago, existing laws made it incumbent upon them to institutionalize their child if they wanted financial assistance from the federal government and the state. Mulligan's salary was $3,200 above the Medicaid limit of $22,800. His choice was to keep his child home and pay for her care himself, or institutionalize her and let the government pick up the tab.

Massachusetts waived these rules for Medicaid in November 1987, allowing families who could show that home care for their children costs less than institutional care to be covered by Medicaid. This was a smart move: It costs thousands of dollars less to care for a disabled child at home than in an institution. The federal law signed by President Bush, cosponsored by U.S. Sen. John Kerry and U.S. Reps. Brian Donnelly and Chester Atkins, now extends Supplemental Security Income benefits to families whose severely disabled children live at home. In 47 states, these children will be eligible for $30 a month in SSI benefits they would have received if institutionalized, but had been denied if living at home.

The extra money the families of disabled children will now receive will help their families cope with burdens none of us would wish to bear. The new legislation makes economic and moral sense: It will make possible better and more loving care for disabled children while easing the financial strain on overburdened taxpayers.

Newsday
New York City, New York, March 12, 1989

In his zeal to present a budget that has all the trappings if not the reality of spending restraint, Gov. Mario Cuomo has tossed overboard much of the compassion once heralded as the hallmark of his administration.

Among the most vulnerable state clients Cuomo wants to dump, as he plows through this year's raging fiscal storm, are 2,500 severely handicapped children who get their educations at 11 special proprietary schools. New York's relationship with these schools dates from the 1800s and a 1947 law formalized its obligation to support them.

The governor's proposal to transfer to local school districts the $148-million cost of educating these youngsters would help balance his 1989-90 fiscal plan. But it also would threaten the stability of a model educational structure that until now has worked just fine.

Cuomo claims the restructuring would not hurt the children: The school districts would pay for their placement in the special schools, and the state would *partially* reimburse the district the following year. The additional burden on school-district taxpayers would total $46.9 million. Schools would also have to shoulder new administrative burdens and the cost of borrowing upfront funds.

Youngsters who attend these schools have severe physical and emotional disabilities which preclude their placement in public classroom settings. They are appointed by the commissioner of education to attend any of the 11 schools, where intensive educational programs are designed to compensate for their severe handicaps.

By itself, the suddenness of the state dumping its traditional responsibility onto the local school districts is likely to result in distortions in the way these youngsters are placed. Financially pressed school districts may choose to save money by inappropriately mainstreaming these children in home schools.

Ultimately, this is all part of the governor's attempt to balance his budget at the expense of defenseless children. But the instant question is whether cutting them adrift is worth the minimal savings for the state.

Chicago Tribune
Chicago, Illinois, August 27, 1990

If the new Americans with Disabilities Act works, thousands of people who have been blocked from mainstream life will have the chance to become productive. Employers won't be able to discriminate just because they don't want disabled workers. If the disabled need to get to a job, public transportation will have a way to get them there.

But when Congress passed the law, it forgot to open a checking account for the private businesses and public agencies that will foot the bill. It's going to be a hefty price, particularly for local public transit systems. The cost to the Chicago Transit Authority and Metra alone could approach $400 million.

The law will allow the disabled to open doors for themselves to new opportunities for social contact and employment. The federal government might have to spend less on benefits to the disabled if they can work. But no one has suggested that the money the federal government saves will be handed over to local governments to pay the costs of access.

The likely cost to Chicago area transit is staggering. It's not too late to temper that cost as federal agencies draw the guidelines for carrying out the law.

Public transit has to be affordable. A $400 million price tag will mean a bigger bonded debt, which will translate into higher state and local taxes. It also likely would mean higher fares. The stiffer the fare hike, the more people will find other ways to get to work, jamming the already overcrowded highways and increaing the pressure for more road money.

The U.S. Transportation Department and other agencies are drafting guidelines for the law. Congress showed little concern for the cost of handicapped access, but the agencies must. They will determine how many train stations must be accessible, how extensive the alterations must be to rail cars, and how much paratransit systems such as Dial-A-Ride must expand.

For instance, the cost of the CTA's Dial-A-Ride could double to about $30 million annually unless the Transportation Department takes a reasonable approach to what is an "undue" financial burden on local agencies.

The CTA and Metra face higher costs, in part, because they gambled and lost. Rather than accept guidelines proposed for Amtrak, they counted on an amendment to the disabilities law that would have required only one car on each train to be accessible to the handicapped. The amendment was stripped from the bill and they were left with much more stringent requirements. Local riders shouldn't have to pay for the way the shell game worked in Washington.

Raising the question of costs sounds like a curmudgeonly response to the plight of people who need help to get into mainstream society. Metra and the CTA shouldn't expect to get a break on the costs if it comes at the expense of those who have been waiting a long time for the public to recognize the rights of the handicapped. The task is to make public transit physically accessible to the handicapped while keeping it financially accessible to everyone.

The Miami Herald
Miami, Florida, November 24, 1990

BRIAN ZEBLEY is 12 and suffers from brain damage, mental retardation, eye problems, and delayed development. But the Social Security Administration didn't consider him disabled.

Social Security had a list of disabilities that qualified for payments to disabled poor children, and young Brian's disability didn't fit the paper pigeonhole. Although adults with impairments could ask for individual assessments of their ability to function, children could not.

Not fair, said a Philadelphia legal-aid service. It fought the issue to the U.S. Supreme Court over a six-year period and won decisively in February. So what has happened since? Zip. Zilch. Zero. The Government is writing rules . . .

Sure, there's a lot of money involved. No one knows how many children would be affected. Perhaps 300,000. Perhaps 500,000. It would depend on how far back into time that eligibility would extend, using which legal benchmark, which translates into retroactive payment of Supplemental Security Income (SSI). There is little doubt, though, that the Government is facing a bill of many, many millions.

Yet on a human scale, the prospect of small checks meant big help to the very poor, whose lives are made ever more complex by the severe disabilities of a child. A family typically would earn less than $15,000 to qualify and would receive $300 to $400 in SSI help. Significantly, qualifying for this help also means automatic qualification for Medicaid too.

Washington's caution with a dollar usually is a welcome surprise. But this case follows the pattern of the Reagan Administration's radical pruning of disabled adults from Social Security, and the Government's tardy action to reinstate the deserving after court orders to do so.

Picking on those who are both crippled and poor may save a buck — but at what a horrid human cost. Surely the Bush Administration can do better. It can get these rules written fairly — and without further delay — so that these children at last get the help that the Supreme Court says is rightfully theirs.

The Dallas Morning News
Dallas, Texas, November 28, 1990

When the U.S. Supreme Court speaks, people listen — unless they happen to be government bureaucrats, that is. In February, the court struck down a system the Social Security Administration had followed in distributing benefits to children with disabilities. Yet nine months later, many of the handicapped youngsters still have not received any financial assistance.

Yoo-hoo! Is anyone in the bureaucracy at all bothered by such a long delay in abiding by the Supreme Court's decision? As one frustrated lawyer who has handled children's disability cases complained, "I know there are good people at the Social Security Administration trying to create humane regulations. But it does not translate into helping the children I see day to day."

The court found that the government had violated the law by paying Supplemental Security Income benefits to only poor children with specific handicaps, such as deafness or severe mental retardation. The arbitrary criteria, the justices said, had unfairly excluded many others with other disabilities, like Down's syndrome, muscular dystrophy and spina bifida.

Although the Supreme Court ruling was seen as a major victory for the handicapped in February, it is becoming a hollow one for hundreds of thousands of youngsters with disabilities. The Social Security Administration still has not issued any new permanent rules for evaluating childhood handicaps. An Aug. 31 deadline for issuing those rules has come and gone.

As would be expected, the bureaucrats in charge of carrying out the court's mandate explain that they face overwhelming administrative problems and that the ruling will be costly. No doubt the Supreme Court decision will require some extra work. But the longer the government shuffles paper, the longer hundreds of thousands of poor youngsters will be denied justice.

The ruling will indeed have financial consequences, as the government makes payments to children who once had been denied help. But the law is the law. Simply put, the Social Security Administration cheated the youngsters out of their money for 16 years. Now that it has been reprimanded, the government should be doing everything it can to make amends promptly.

The Boston Globe

Boston, Massachusetts, February 16, 1991

Hundreds of disabled people in Massachusetts have moved from institutions into homes of their own, thanks to a network of nonprofit groups praised in a report released this week.

These groups are just the sort of small-scale entrepreneurial endeavors that appeal to Gov. Weld. They deserve the support of the administration as they struggle with money troubles brought on by the recession.

"A stable, safe and independent home" is vital to a disabled person's well-being, the Citizens' Housing and Planning Association concluded in the report. The association defines disability broadly because people with AIDS or in wheelchairs often have as much trouble finding suitable housing as the mentally ill.

Amid the difficulties, successes stand out: Foundations Inc., which provides apartments for the mentally ill in Holyoke; St. Helena's House in the South End, with apartments for the elderly and younger people with disabilities; and Bay House, a residence in Winthrop for deaf people who are mentally ill.

These small, independent groups have thrived over the past decade because the state has subsidized part of the disabled tenants' rents.

Weld wants to cut $17 million from the Section 707 program, one of the most important subsidies. Legislators need to protect as much of this as possible, despite the budget crisis.

The Housing and Planning Association believes that the administration can do much, at little cost, to nurture these groups through hard times.

■ The number of disabled people in need of housing is uncertain. The state should compile a count from the several agencies that deal with parts of this problem.

■ Housing and support services could be adapted to the changing needs of the residents. The governor should form an advisory group, composed of government officials, service providers and the disabled, to make the system more flexible and responsive.

■ Small, private groups need reliable information on the sources of money to build and sustain housing. The state should provide a clearinghouse where this information could be speedily obtained.

Without a stable funding source, coordination and information will be for nothing. Like all entrepreneurs, housing providers need steady sources of capital and income, which is best obtained from state government.

St. Petersburg Times

St. Petersburg, Florida, March 4, 1991

St. Petersburg has taken an important step toward becoming an accessible place for disabled citizens, a city in which they can live, work and enjoy their leisure time the same as everyone else.

The city has hired Gregory Phillips to be its coordinator for disabled services, a new position intended to help make St. Petersburg sensitive toward the needs of the disabled community. The selection of Phillips, who has a degree in social work and solid experience in that field, was made after a thorough screening process that included oversight by Abilities Inc. of Florida, an organization that provides job training, placement, rehabilitation and other services to physically impaired people. City Manager Robert Obering made the decision with advice from the city's advisory Committee for the Assistance of the Physically Impaired (CAPI).

As well as a resume and a knowledge of the local community, Phillips brings to his new job the personal perspective of a person who uses a wheelchair. All these elements will prove invaluable in his role as liaison between the city administration and citizens with complaints or problems with access and related issues.

Unfortunately, St. Petersburg has a rich history of such problems. The most recent example is the new Florida Suncoast Dome, which was allowed to be built with several design flaws that limited wheelchair accessibility, including insufficient number and variety of handicapped seating positions. Original guidance from CAPI was ignored throughout construction.

St. Petersburg officials no doubt were motivated by the passage of the Americans With Disabilities Act, federal legislation that requires sweeping public accommodations and other civil rights protections for impaired people. Nonetheless, the new position is a welcome indication that the mood of City Hall is changing.

Officials are considering CAPI for the valuable resource it is. Plans for necessary changes at the stadium, albeit the result of a settlement of an advocates' lawsuit against the city, are under way. Representatives of Bay Plaza, the city's downtown developer, have met with CAPI about making sure its new construction meets barrier-free standards. With a contribution from CAPI, money generated by volunteers policing violations of the city's handicapped parking ordinance, the recreation department has purchased a telecommunications device for the deaf.

Hiring a coordinator will not in itself transform St. Petersburg into a disabled-friendly city, but it should serve as a significant catalyst. Phillips started to work last Monday, and spent the latter part of the week attending a conference in Miami about the new federal legislation. "I as well as the rest of the city administration expect to be sensitized by what he does," said Herb Polson, city director of intergovernmental relations.

With such an attitude, and with a supportive commitment by the City Council, St. Petersburg's track record for the disabled can only improve.

The San Diego
Union-Tribune.

San Diego, California, February 22, 1991

Should there be a 90 percent reduction in the fines imposed by the state Department of Health Services against residential care centers that neglect or abuse patients who are developmentally disabled?

Assemblywoman Carol Bentley, R-El Cajon, believes so. She has proposed a bill that would subject these centers to only the more lenient fines levied against facilities supervised by the Department of Social Services. Under the Bentley bill, cases involving deaths or life-threatening injuries, which now can result in $25,000 fines, would be limited to $2,500 fines.

Although the Bentley measure is flawed, it attempts to redress an inequity in the law that should be be corrected.

Seven years ago, California authorized a 300 percent increase in the maximum fines against nursing and residential care homes that mistreat patients. This was in response to a report by the Little Hoover Commission detailing patient abuse.

Unfortunately, the fine structure makes no distinction between the different missions of skilled nursing homes and centers that care for people seriously afflicted with cerebral palsy, epilepsy, autism or other neurological disorders.

Because of their frailties, nursing home patients normally require custodial care. The developmentally disadvantaged, on the other hand, are being encouraged to become more self-sufficient. Because these centers are by definition training facilities, the residents are prone to accidents and other risks associated with learning to be independent.

State inspectors have been known to cite centers because residents who were learning to do their own laundry dropped clothing on the floor. Another center was fined because a resident making a peanut butter and jelly sandwich forgot to put a lid on a jar before putting it back in the refrigerator.

Such nitpicking is counter-productive. The purpose of the fines is to protect defenseless people against being abused. But steep fines are nonetheless necessary for serious infractions. Absent economic sanctions, the state would have no other recourse except to pursue criminal proceedings against major violators.

Instead of fiddling with the fee structure, as Bentley proposes, the law should be amended to reflect the differences between skilled nursing homes and care centers for the developmentally disabled. This may require relaxing some of the most stringent regulations now applied to centers for the disabled.

If the state expects these centers to fulfill their training function, it should establish rules consistent with that wider responsibility. In doing so, however, California must retain the power to impose severe fines against those facilities that negligently endanger persons under their care.

CHICAGO Sun-Times

Chicago, Illinois, February 22, 1991

The Loop will be more accessible for the disabled, thanks to the city's decision to set aside metered parking spaces for handicapped motorists.

There can be no quarrel with that. But what about all the downtown lots and drivers who ignore the state handicapped-parking laws? What good does it do to create new handicapped spaces if there's no enforcement?

People with wheelchairs and others who qualify for handicapped parking privileges should be able to count on spaces reserved for the disabled—the ones in lots and the metered ones set aside by the city.

Beginning next month, the city will reserve 140 of the 7,000 metered parking spaces in the Loop for handicapped parking. By summer, that number will increase to 200.

That move follows a city survey of 130 downtown parking lots, which found that about 85 percent are ignoring state handicapped-parking laws.

"The problems run the gamut," said Larry Gorski, head of the Mayor's Office for People with Disabilities.

Some lots don't have elevators or sufficient parking spaces. And some lots don't have proper signs directing the disabled to where they should park.

Besides creating additional spaces for handicapped parking, the city should make sure there's more compliance with the state law, beginning with the city-owned parking lots. That means educating lot owners about the requirements and handing out $50 fines for illegal use of handicapped parking spaces.

SYRACUSE HERALD-JOURNAL

Syracuse, New York, March 21, 1991

The Albany crew should have been at our editorial board meeting Tuesday with parents of developmentally disabled children and advocates for services provided to such families by the state.

Lawmakers could have listened to parents, who want to keep their children at home, ask how state officials could be so penny-wise and pound-foolish. The state plans to slash funds, by 50 percent in some areas, that support programs to keep disabled children at home.

They could have listened as parents pleaded for officials, not moved by compassion, to be moved by fiscal realities: The state is spending about $24 million each year, through the Office of Mental Retardation and Developmental Disabilities, on family service programs. Those include providing respite workers for parents so they can do such simple tasks as shop — or such critical ones as hold down a job. The money also is used to equip homes to handle the needs of disabled children.

What family services does essentially is assist parents — give them the supports — so they can keep their children out of institutions.

It's far cheaper to do so. It can cost more than $50,000 a year to institutionalize children. Yet in the Syracuse area alone, nearly 2,000 families are helped by the $800,000 allocated for such services. If the cuts become reality, $400,000 will be slashed.

That means that some parents may have to give up jobs because there will be no worker available to care for their children. Others who care for their children 24 hours a day, seven days a week, will break under the pressure and be forced to seek institutionalized care for young ones. That's where the penny-wise and pound-foolish notion comes in. Parents who

don't work go on welfare. And institutionalizing children is outrageously more expensive than keeping them at home.

The Albany crew — Gov. Mario Cuomo and every lawmaker and bureaucrat — should have been at that meeting. They should have sat across from the parents, looked them squarely in the eye and explained:

■ How Sen. Tarky Lombardi, R-Syracuse, a well-off businessman, could ride around in a taxpayer-paid, chauffeur-driven car, while parents beg for services for retarded, disabled children. Not a lot of services, mind you.

■ How former Assemblyman Bill Bush, a funeral director, could accept a $50,000 job from Assembly Republicans to be "intergovernmental affairs director" at the same time services for families will be cut by 50 percent.

■ How Assemblyman Mel Zimmer, D-Syracuse, could keep adding family members to his staff — his daughter was recently hired as "media coordinator" for $24,000.

■ How Assembly Speaker Mel Miller, D-Brooklyn, and Senate Majority Leader Ralph Marino, R-Long Island, can have upwards of 200 people each working for them. How this can happen at a time when barely-more-than-minimum-wage workers who care for disabled children may be laid off.

■ How lawmakers can pay themselves extra for working on committees.

■ How Gov. Cuomo, who speaks almost tearfully of the family of New York, can brush off legitimate budget complaints as "whining."

■ How elected officials dare treat themselves like members of royal families, while real families are paralyzed by incomprehensible budget decisions. Decisions that conservatives and liberals can agree will cost the state far more in the long run.

If lawmakers had been at that meeting, maybe they would have been ashamed to face parents asked to make unreasonable sacrifices — while they can't find the will to make reasonable ones.

AKRON BEACON JOURNAL

Akron, Ohio, July 11, 1991

The wheels of government turn excruciatingly slowly, it must seem to thousands of disabled children denied medical benefits under the Supplemental Security Income program from January 1980 to February 1990.

In deciding the children's claims, the Social Security Administration had not taken into account the effects of their disabilities on such activities as walking, eating and dressing themselves. Disabled adults didn't have it so hard. The agency assessed their benefits on the effect of their condition on their ability to work.

Last year the Supreme Court restored a sense of fairness to the agency's procedures, ruling the standards tougher than those for adults and ordering broader SSI eligibility standards for disabled children.

It's taken some time, but the agency finally is cranking up the action: It began Wednesday sending notices to more than half a million children who are eligible under the broader standards. We hope the process of review moves reasonably fast to make the lives of these children a little easier.

THE TAMPA TRIBUNE

Tampa, Florida, October 12, 1991

Half of all disabilities in children can be prevented and another third substantially minimized if certain medical and educational programs were provided to all teens, pregnant women and newborns.

But those programs are costly and have generally gone unfunded in favor of more traditional government programs, like those to imprison criminals, build roads and fund universities.

A new cost-benefit analysis, however, shows the error of neglecting these prevention and early intervention needs. A net savings of $4 billion could be realized over a lifetime, for instance, if those needs had been met in children born between 1989 and 1993, according to Anita Zervignon-Hakes, a researcher at Florida State University.

Teen pregnancy prevention, prenatal care, early intervention for children with established conditions and developmental delays, and pre-school for at-risk children could accomplish these savings, said Zervignon-Hakes, who is executive director of FSU's Center for Prevention and Early Intervention Policy.

These needs probably will continue to go unfunded another year, given the state's dire budget crunch. But her research once again emphasizes that the longer Florida delays bolstering prevention and early intervention programs, it will continue paying an escalating price.

LAS VEGAS SUN

Las Vegas, Nevada, August 22, 1990

A sizable group of fellow countrymen – 43 million of them – received a long-overdue break last week when President Bush signed into law, in an emotional White House ceremony on the South Lawn, the Americans with Disabilities Act.

"Every man, woman and child with a disability can now pass through a once-closed door to a bright new era of equality, independence and freedom," Bush said on signing the measure.

The law bans discrimination against the disabled. Bush said the "historic" document is the "world's first declaration of equality for people with disabilities." He said the new law is a "sledgehammer" for breaking down the wall separating the disabled from the "freedom they could glimpse but not grasp."

The Americans with Disabilities Act is designed to bring disabled people into the mainstream by giving them equal access to jobs, transportation and public facilities.

Equal access is to be provided anyone with physical or mental impairment that substantially limits a "major life activity" – such as caring for oneself, performing manual tasks, walking, seeing, hearing, speaking, breathing, learning and working. Almost anyone perceived as having a disability is covered, including people with AIDS. Excluded are current users of illegal drugs and several other categories based on certain sexual or compulsive behavior.

All businesses with 25 or more employees will be covered in two years, and with 15 or more in four years. Businesses must provide facilities for the disabled and may not reject applicants or fire present workers on the basis of disability. The only exemptions would be creation of undue financial hardship, decided on a case-by-case basis.

Generally within 18 months, hotels, restaurants, theaters, auditoriums, stadiums, doctors' offices, retail stores, transportation terminals, museums, libraries, parks and zoos all must be made accessible to disabled patrons.

All new buses and rail cars must be made wheelchair accessible.

All telephone companies must provide relay services for hearing-impaired and speech-impaired customers within three years.

Talk about breaking down a wall – some, including Bush, have compared the new law to tearing down the Berlin Wall, an historic impetus on the road to freedom for East European nations. Others have called the document the most important piece of human rights legislation since the Civil Rights Act of 1964.

Congress is to be commended for passing the far-reaching bill, after nine months of debate and final compromises between the House and the Senate.

And Bush is also to be praised for pushing for passage of the law. Now if he had only displayed the same understanding and compassion and not vetoed the family leave bill, which most in Congress favored but still could not get the necessary votes to override the veto. Congress has promised to give him another chance, however, both in this session and in each successive year of his presidency.

The News Journal

Wilmington, Delaware, November 20, 1990

People who park in fire lanes at malls and other locations endanger thousands of people's lives. Those without handicapped stickers who take the precious few spaces allocated for those in need are lower than low.

The Delaware State Police have begun a crackdown on drivers who ignore fire lane restrictions and those able bodied people who unfairly — and illegally take spaces for the handicapped.

The need for fire lane restrictions should be obvious.

They must be kept open so emergency vehicles, such as fire engines or ambulances, can get through. If they can't, there is a potential for loss of life.

But the need for clear fire lanes isn't obvious to everyone. Last weekend, the state police issued 90 tickets to people who parked in the fire lanes. There must be a lot of dim-witted or just plain lazy people out there.

It takes nerve to drive into spots reserved for people with handicaps. But there must be a lot of people with a lot of nerve. The police also issued 40 tickets to cars illegally parked in handicapped spots. Five motorists parked in handicapped spaces had their cars towed away.

Common sense and common courtesy are all that's needed to guide a driver in a big mall lot. Sure, it's tough having to walk a little to get to the stores. But if drivers consider how illegal parking endangers themselves and their fellow shoppers on the one hand, and causes great inconvenience to handicapped people on the other, we're sure they'll do the correct thing.

And if they don't, give them the hook.

THE TENNESSEAN

Nashville, Tennessee, August 18, 1990

FOR most Americans, the recent signing of the Americans with Disabilities Act at the White House was cause for celebration.

The act literally opened the doors of businesses, public transportation and restaurants to 43 million handicapped Americans. It was written affirmation that no one be prevented from full participation in American life because of physical impairments.

The White House didn't consult the Social Register when it made its guest list for the signing, and neither should the Christian Life Commission of the Southern Baptist Convention.

Mr. Richard Land, head of the commission in Nashville, fired off an angry letter to President Bush, complaining that the White House "betrayed" constituents by inviting gay representatives for the occasion. Mr. Land then went even further, comparing the invitation to asking "drug dealers" to the official residence.

Congress has passed no bill favorable to drug dealers, nor is it likely to. Of course, gays were there. The landmark legislation, which President Bush himself described as a "declaration of independence" for the handicapped, included guarantees prohibiting discriminating against victims of the deadly virus known as AIDS. Gay rights activists were among many groups fighting for those provisions as well as the entire bill.

The disabilities act was a remarkable achievement precisely because there was such widespread agreement on its merits. It passed the Senate by a vote of 91-6. Sen. Orrin Hatch, R-Utah, spoke movingly in support of the act by recalling his own brother-in-law's long struggle with polio. Sen. Tom Harkin, an Iowa Democrat and chief Senate sponsor of the bill, used signing to tell his brother, Frank, the approval was his "proudest day in 16 years in Congress."

The White House felt the same way, lending its support for the provisions.

People from all parts of society participated in the bill's passage and ceremonial signing because they realize that handicaps don't discriminate. AIDS is a case in point.

The virus is not a "gay men's" disease. The deadly complications of AIDS, like any affliction, can strike heterosexuals, black or white, old or young. It afflicts adults as well as new-born babies. AIDS can visit any household regardless of race, sex, wealth, age — or religion. ■

THE ATLANTA CONSTITUTION
Atlanta, Georgia, January 19, 1990

Georgians with disabled dependents often face a dilemma. Their financial burden would be unbearable without government assistance to help meet the cost of their dependents' care. Yet they want to provide what they can for the dependents' future. But doing so can mean the loss of that essential government aid.

State Sen. Charles C. Clay and Rep. Jack Vaughan have come up with legislation that could help correct this cruel Catch-22. The Cobb County Republicans want to create a state-administered Self-Sufficiency Trust Fund for Mentally Disabled Persons so private money can be set aside for the mentally disabled without affecting their eligibility for government benefits.

The proposal is modeled after a program that originated in Illinois in 1986, was copied by Maine a year later and is being studied by other states. Besides protecting a mentally disabled person's government benefits, the trust fund creates a pool of money to earn interest that would go back into the trust.

In addition to a private fund that would allow families to put money in specifically for their dependents, there would be a charitable fund to accept donations from individuals, corporations and other sources to supplement benefits paid to low-income mentally disabled persons.

Establishing the trust fund won't lessen the state's responsibility for helping meet the needs of the mentally disabled. If anything, that role must grow, especially with regard to encouraging the creation of group homes or similar facilities to allow the mentally disabled to lead as independent and productive lives as they are capable.

What the Self-Sufficiency Trust Fund would offer is a chance for families and others who are concerned about the mentally disabled to contribute to making their lives a little better. It is a good idea that deserves support. It's so good an idea, in fact, that it should be expanded to cover others who have disabilities that require long-term care and who qualify for government aid.

ST. LOUIS POST-DISPATCH
St. Louis, Missouri, August 27, 1990

Television may be a wondrous visual medium to most of us, but to those who have trouble hearing, it is "a sound-based medium with nice visuals to make it pleasant." So says King Jordan, who is deaf and is the president of Gallaudet University, the nation's only university for the hearing impaired. A bill in Congress that would change that significantly should become law.

At present, the hard of hearing can fully benefit from television only if they purchase a $160 decoder, which is wired to the television and provides captions at the bottom of the screen. That is, written words are provided for those programs that produce captioning — about 400 hours of cable-system programming a week, less on conventional TV. But a Senate-passed bill now awaiting action in the House would mandate that all TV sets sold after

July 1, 1993, have a built-in chip allowing them to display closed captioning at the push of a button.

A sound idea, of course, but should government really mandate it? Is it fair to require private manufacturers to provide a feature that demand has so far failed to justify? The answer is undeniably yes. One of the problems with being hard of hearing is that those with the ailment often seem hesitant to admit it. These same people then allow themselves to be gradually cut off from what goes on around them. They also don't like to buy unsightly decoders, which are expensive for some of them.

The Television Decoder Circuitry Act would resolve that problem, opening a highway to inclusion for the hard of hearing, not to mention providing help for the increasing number of bilingual Americans who want help with their English.

The Pittsburgh PRESS
Pittsburgh, Pennsylvania, October 13, 1990

The consequences of the recently passed Americans With Disabilities Act are already becoming apparent. The law, which was ostensibly meant to grant equal rights to the handicapped, represents a radical expansion of government power. It also offers considerable room for mischief.

In Baltimore recently, a building contractor named Donald Keister demanded that he be declared a minority for purposes of government contracts. The city sets aside 25 percent of its contracts for firms owned by "minorities."

Now, Mr. Keister is white, and male, but he's very big, tipping the scale at 640 pounds. Because his amplitude hinders him in his work

— he says he falls through floorboards whenever he visits construction sites — he has rightly declared that the disabilities act qualifies him as a minority. Ergo: Give him a contract.

As columnist Dave Barry says, we are not making this up. Certainly the city of Baltimore wishes Mr. Keister were kidding. But he's not. And what's more, thanks to the good intentions of President Bush and Congress, he may have the law on his side.

As soon as the lawyers and the professionally aggrieved realize the amazing potential of this flawed law, the Baltimore case will pale by comparison. But Donald Keister should forever be remembered as a true pioneer, the man who showed countless others the way.

Saginaw County's new Handicapped Parking Enforcement Team is designed to zero in on the able-bodied bozos who boorishly park in the designated spots, disregarding the needs of others.

But for the 21 deputized volunteers to perform that task effectively, the handicapped must cooperate.

Team members nailed 150 cars without windshield permits during their first two weeks on the prowl. More than 100, however, belonged to legitimate handicappers who neglected to display the permits. They won't get socked with the maximum $50 fine, but Magistrate Dennis W. Hall says he will make them shell out a few bucks "to help remind them that they have a responsibility."

The responsibility goes beyond the law, now that the Saginaw squad is at work. If a group of volunteers is concerned and conscientious enough to patrol parking lots, handicappers owe it to them to keep their permits properly posted.

Cases of undisplayed permits should decline as the team continues its work and establishes a reputation.

Coordinator Gail A. Sylvester, however, raises some points that are far more disturbing.

Some store owners complain that the parking-lot patrols are bad for business, she says, and some church ministers have complained about the scrutiny. That's sad to hear.

What's worse, Sylvester says the team actually has found evidence that a few people with permits have made copies and given them to friends.

In the case of able-bodied folks who don't see the need for handicapped parking, perhaps they could use some "sensitivity training." A possible lesson plan: Tape their ankles together on an icy winter evening, give them a set of crutches and invite them to head to the door from the rear corner of the parking lot.

As for a legitimate permit-holder running off copies for healthy friends, such a person has afflictions that are more than physical.

Nursing Homes and Elderly Care Come Under New National Scrutiny

The Department of Health and Human Services Dec. 1, 1989 published the results of the first annual government study of all nursing homes in the U.S. The survey found widespread compliance with health and safety standards but also noted that many homes failed to follow proper procedures in drug dispensing and food service.

The study, which was intended as a consumer guide to nursing homes, had examined conditions in 15,000 homes nationwide between January 1987 and July 1988. It had rated the homes on their performance in more than 500 categories, such as sanitary conditions, physician supervision and accounting of patients' personal finances. A summary of findings, based on 32 of the categories, was also released Dec. 1.

The study found that more than 25% of the homes had administered drugs without properly following a doctor's prescription. In addition, nearly 45% reportedly had prepared and served food under unsanitary conditions.

Both the nursing home industry and consumer groups attacked the study as flawed.

Paul Willging, executive vice president of the American Health Care Association, argued that "nursing homes are incredibly better than the impressions that might be left by this report."

Elma Holder, director of the National Citizens Coalition for Nursing Home Reform, said that that the study was "deficient and misleading" and that she did not think it was useful in selecting a nursing home.

A separate study released Nov. 25, 1988 indicated that many nursing homes used psychoactive, or mood-altering drugs, even when patients did not need them.

The study was performed by researchers from Harvard Medical School and published in the *Journal of the American Medical Association*.

The researchers had examined drug use in 12 intermediate-care nursing homes in the Boston area during a one-month period. They found that more than half of the 850 residents had received psychoactive drugs, such as sedatives and antidepressants. Twenty-five percent of the residents had received anti-psychotic drugs, even though only 15% had been diagnosed as psychotic.

Millions of poor, elderly Americans were unnecessarily paying insurance premiums because they did not know they were covered under Medicaid, a senior-citizens advocacy group said June 17, 1991.

Recipients of Medicare, the nation's health-insurance program for the elderly, paid a monthly premium of $29.90, a $100 annual deductible on any doctors' bills they might incur and a $628 deductible on hospital bills. However, of the 33 million Medicare beneficiaries, 4.2 million were also eligible for Medicaid, the nation's health-insurance program for the poor. Recipients of Medicaid could have that program pay for the Medicare premium and deductibles, but they had to apply for the benefit.

The advocacy group, the Families United for Senior Action Foundation (Families USA), charged that the government had not adequately notified eligible persons of the benefit. Families USA estimated that some Medicaid beneficiaries were paying as much as $1,000 a year in costs that the program would cover.

The Census Bureau Nov. 10, 1992 issued a report on the nation's elderly population. According to the report, which was based on the 1990 Census, there were 31.2 million Americans aged 65 years or over in 1989. Of those, 27.9 million (89%) were white and 2.5 million (8%) were black.

The report found that in 1990, the poverty rate among those aged 65 or older was 12%; for elderly whites it was 10%; for blacks, 34%, and for those of Hispanic origin, who could be of any race, the poverty rate was 23%. According to the report, 47% of the overall elderly population would have been in poverty without Social Security.

According to the report, 26% of non-institutionalized persons over age 65 considered their health to be fair or poor in 1989. About one in three of those aged 65 or older lived alone.

The Hartford Courant

Hartford, Connecticut, December 16, 1988

Any detailed evaluation of institutional care is likely to generate a high volume and wide range of criticism. Some will say the evaluation is too harsh, others will say it's too tolerant and the legitimacy of its methodology will be questioned.

All of this is happening with the federal government's first review of nursing homes, which was conducted by the Health Care Financing Administration, but that doesn't detract from the value of such studies.

Some 15,000 nursing homes — virtually all that are in the United States — are rated in the 75-volume published survey. Copies of all or part of it can be obtained for a fee from the Government Printing Office, Washington, D.C. 20402.

The findings, based on inspections from January 1987 to July 1988, ought to be of concern to all Americans, not just residents of the homes and their families. In such facilities, after all, millions of us are destined to spend significant parts of our lives, and taxpayers foot a growing part of the bill through Medicare.

Here, according to the survey, are a few of the worst failings of the nursing homes, considered as a group:

• The personal hygiene of residents wasn't adequately provided for in about 30 percent of the homes.

• In 29 percent of them, drugs weren't always given to residents according to written orders from their physicians.

• Food was stored, prepared, distributed or served in unsanitary conditions in about 43 percent of the homes.

The reliability of some of the findings is unclear. For instance, the survey found that only in 1.8 percent of the homes were residents physically or mentally abused, a figure that seems low in light of the large number of complaints of abuse.

But the apparent softness of the data is a reason to re-examine and, if necessary, refine the evaluation process, not to abandon it, and the Bush administration should ensure that such surveys continue. They aren't meant to be yes-or-no guides to the selection of nursing homes, but they can prompt important questions that otherwise wouldn't be asked.

The answers to those questions can make the choices of homes more rational, thus increasing the likelihood of satisfaction with those that are chosen. And just asking the questions may persuade operators of substandard homes to clean up their acts, figuratively, and, in some cases, literally.

Los Angeles Times
Los Angeles, California, March 19, 1991

Sacramento and Washington have teamed up to produce a theater of the absurd on the subject of new federal regulations covering nursing homes.

The plot is fairly devious. Sacramento gets to claim it has wiggled out of new rules that govern nursing home operations across the nation.

Washington's role is not to make too much in public of the fact that it agreed only to let Sacramento ignore some bureaucratic guidelines for imposing nursing care reforms, not the reforms themselves. The only reason Washington is on the stage at all is because it pays—through the program known in California as Medi-Cal—half the cost of maintaining 70,000 elderly patients in nursing homes. The state pays the other half.

What the new regulations ask is radical change. Patients will be helped to live at the highest possible levels of mental and physical health. That means hiring new therapists to work with patients rather than confining them with bed railings, straps or drugs, as is too often the case now.

Patients in California nursing homes will not find this state-federal public relations game amusing, any more than do 44 other states that are already operating under the new rules. What worries them is that California is dodging its responsibility to respect the rights of people too old or too ill to care for themselves.

Just how much more expensive California nursing care will be under the new regulations is a matter of dispute, but providers are sticking with an estimate of $440 million or more, with the state paying half.

A bill for $220 million in a state that already faces a $10-billion budget deficit with no prospect of an upturn in the economy clearly accounts for Gov. Pete Wilson's angry response to federal nursing home inspectors being sent into his state.

How do things like this happen?

One part of the explanation involves the evolution of the reforms. Congress said, as part of an omnibus budget bill in 1987, that the nation needs better rules for nursing homes, so it directed some experts to write them.

The second reason is that state government ignored for two years or more the 1987 budget act under which experts started filling in details of nursing home reform.

By the time Sacramento moved, it was too late. Nursing home associations nationwide had worked with officials of the U.S. Health Care Financing Administration on the new regulations and signed off on them. Only six states, including California, have yet to implement the rules.

In a decision circulated late last month, U.S. District Judge Edward J. Garcia in Oakland said he is bewildered by Sacramento's claim that it can ignore the law.

Two nursing home patients had asked Garcia to order the state to obey the law, and California said in its brief that it had a law of its own to improve the quality of nursing home care. It said the new federal rules change the focus but not the substance of nursing home law.

Garcia's decision addressed only the question of whether to make the state obey the law. Addressing the merits of the case will require a full trial. But the judge said it looked to him as if the plaintiffs probably would win on the merits as well.

Whether the state law, sponsored last year by state Sen. Henry J. Mello (D-Watsonville), would have produced improvements comparable to those of the 1987 federal act is something that may never be known. It would have added about $100 million to nursing care expenditures, instead of the $220 million that the federal law may require. And state negotiators came up with an amendment to the bill saying that the state law would expire if California agreed to comply with the federal law. It did so last month to avoid being in contempt of court.

In principle, when Washington raises standards, it should raise the money, too. In practice, 1987 was the year to bring that up. Ironically Wilson, then a U.S. senator, supported the reforms.

Besides, in principle and practice, the welfare of older people in nursing homes cannot be neglected.

The Hartford Courant
Hartford, Connecticut, April 27, 1991

Even the nursing-home industry agrees that something must be done about the out-of-control costs to the state of elderly Medicaid patients. But it dislikes the Weicker administration's plan.

The governor has proposed a $100 million cut in Medicaid payments to nursing homes for the fiscal year starting July 1. Doomsday warnings by the homes' operators are unconvincing.

After the $100 million cut, the Department of Income Maintenance still would be paying $604 million for this program. Next fiscal year, the payments are expected to exceed $800 million. Six years ago, the bill was $250 million.

Medicaid payments constitute the second largest item in the general fund budget, just behind education grants to cities and towns.

But since half of all Medicaid expenditures are eventually reimbursed by Washington, a $100 million cut would save the state only $50 million.

How bad would a $100 million hit be for the industry? Connecticut's nursing homes are among the most expensive in the nation, according to a study for the Legislative Management Committee by the accounting firm of KPMG Peat Marwick, which also found out that rates here are rising faster than inflation and that there are few incentives to hold down expenses.

Although Connecticut nursing homes showed small deficits in 1988 and 1989, they're mostly just paper losses, accountants and politicians say. Some homes use a system of interlocking ownerships, real-estate leases and tax and salary deductions to mask large profits. At any rate, the backlog of applications to build 4,000 more nursing-home beds is hardly a sign that business is ailing.

Some solutions advocated by nursing homes should be considered seriously. For example, the nonprofit nursing homes recommend a one-time assessment on the revenues of all homes — a kind of special tax — that could raise up to $15 million without crippling the industry. The revenue would be forwarded to the state in lieu of a cut in Medicaid payments. The state Health Department could save money by cutting out redundant regulations and inspections. In addition, the maximum state-paid per-bed rate could be lowered.

But if there are to be major and permanent savings, there must be long-term reform of the system financed largely by state and federal governments.

Most nursing-home patients initially are covered by Medicare, which pays only part of their bills. When they run out of money, they're put on Medicaid and continue to receive the same quality of care, but entirely at public expense.

Many patients are poor only technically. Before entering nursing homes, they transfer all their assets to their children. In short, Medicaid pays in too many instances when families could well afford to cover their loved ones' expenses.

Federal rules allow transfers of assets that are done at least 2½ years before the elderly person applies for Medicaid. This "look-back" period is far too short. The rules should be changed to make it at least five years.

In addition, Connecticut requires nursing homes to maintain a waiting list on a first-come, first-served basis. Thus, homes cannot reserve a percentage of their beds for private-pay patients who are able to buy extra services and willing to stay off Medicaid. The one-class, egalitarian system of nursing-home care is giving too many people of means a free ride, and must be changed.

The industry, the Weicker administration and legislative leaders claim they want a more flexible and affordable nursing-home system. The Legislature would make significant headway in 1991 if it approved state savings of, say, $40 million — by implementing the short-term reforms — and began overhauling the rate-setting and regulatory systems.

The Star-Ledger
Newark, New Jersey, February 17, 1991

A growing, but often ignored, segment of society is what has come to be known as the "sandwich generation," a population consisting mostly of women in their 40s trying to maintain a regular family life while caring for an elderly relative without resorting to nursing homes. These are the people seeking state support for adult day care programs.

Adult day care is an alternative to premature institutionalization of the elderly, and aids families in coping with caring for a dependent relative. An Assembly subcommittee is currently compiling information to develop legislative solutions to care for the elderly and the people who give that care.

The subcommittee hearings have increased the awareness level of the need for an expansion of adult day care services. It is expected to release its findings in May.

Proponents of such programs have made some good recommendations, among them that corporate tax incentives be allowed to subsidize services, that income tax credits be allowed for people contributing substantial time and money to the care of a relative, and the regulation of a uniform funding scheme for adult day care throughout the state.

Also recommended was state funding for senior transportation, a state-mandated and reasonable "sliding scale fee," and estblishment of uniform financial assistance for day care to assure it does not become "the upper-class option."

Day care allows the elderly to maintain a sense of independence that some experts say is often curative both phsyically and mentally. It also allows them to remain with the family without placing an undue burden on their time for work and other responsibilities.

One of the major problems facing continuance and growth of day care operations in the state is the rising costs of maintaining the programs, as more people are forced to turn to them. Subcommittee testimony also found a lack of public funding, transportation and coordination of the state's numerous senior services to be among the problems.

The information being gathered by the subcommittee should lay the groundwork for a greater state commitment to provide care for New Jersey's elderly. Legislation suggested by adult care advocates represents a reasonable approach to the problem.

TULSA WORLD
Tulsa, Oklahoma, June 26, 1991

ELDERCARE, a program to oversee services for elderly Oklahomans, reports subtle changes in the state's senior population from the 1990 census.

Oklahoma's senior citizens are growing in numbers, and they are not staying put. Many are leaving rural towns for larger cities.

The shift is not surprising. Small towns cannot deliver the services for seniors to remain in their homes or the medical care they require. Many leave longtime homes to live in cities and suburbs nearer their children.

This is a trend that is not likely to be reversed and Oklahoma's larger communities are struggling to deal with the growing problem. Statewide, the older population is up 10.79 percent and the over-75 category (which needs the most services) grew 24.89 percent.

The migration of elderly reflects a troubling population pattern for the whole state. Roughly, counties west of Interstate 35 lost senior citizens and those east gained.

Cleveland County posted the largest over-60 gain, a whopping 55.22 percent. Others with big increases included Canadian and Rogers counties, both up by 37 percent, Tulsa and Oklahoma counties with 21.10 percent and 18.41 percent respectively, McClain County (part of metropolitan Oklahoma City), Wagoner, and Delaware and Cherokee counties, which contain lake retirement communities.

Eldercare is pointing out the problem. Solutions are not easy. Those left in rural counties may find their circumstances even more difficult, while cities struggle to cope with rising numbers.

It's a problem that demands statewide help.

CHICAGO Sun-Times
Chicago, Illinois, March 29, 1991

Here's a piece of news for self-satisfied adults to chew on: Despite all the criticism of young Americans as self-centered and frivolous, a new survey shows they may be more generous than adults in volunteering to help the poor, elderly and others in need.

A recent poll by the Gallup Organization found that about 58 percent of teenagers said they did volunteer work in 1989, compared with 54 percent of adults. A similar, earlier study showed that people in their 20s, another group maligned as apathetic and lazy, also contribute slightly more volunteer hours than do Americans 30 and older.

Possibly the only bad news is that these hardworking teens and young Americans will grow up and become like the rest of us.

THE ARIZONA REPUBLIC
Phoenix, Arizona, January 28, 1991

TWO bills in Congress could provide measurable relief to senior citizens in need of extra income to help pay the bills. Known as the Older Americans' Freedom to Work Act, they would raise the lid on the amount of outside income retirees are allowed to earn before they begin to lose their Social Security benefits.

Strongest support for the legislation is coming from Republicans in Congress. The cap on earnings is "age discrimination of the worst kind," argues Sen. John McCain, who introduced the measure in the Senate. Rep. Jay Rhodes, sponsor of the House bill, likens the limit to an outmoded "Depression-era law."

The Arizonans make convincing arguments for repealing the Social Security earnings limit for those who work after age 65. The cap "severely penalizes seniors for attempting to be productive citizens," says Sen. McCain. "There's nothing kindler and gentler about a country that takes productive people out of the workplace," notes Congressman Rhodes.

Under the present system, Social Security keeps a tight rein on the outside income Americans between 65 and 70 are permitted to earn before their government benefits are reduced. For every $3 earned over this year's cap of $9,720 — up slightly from last year's

$9,360 — seniors lose $1 of their Social Security benefits.

The earnings test poses a serious threat to the welfare of low-income seniors — people in many cases who need to work because of inadequate fixed incomes. This is especially true of individuals without private pensions.

The trouble is that, once the earnings cap has been met, a person with a job paying just $5 an hour would find the after-tax value of his wages dropping to only $2.20. This adds up to a tax rate that, as Sen. McCain noted in introducing the bill, exceeds that of any other age group in the country. Not the least of the issues raised by this penalty is that of fairness.

Figures supplied by Sen. McCain show that 83 percent of all men and 92 percent of all women 65 or older are completely retired. The Labor Department reports that this represents an increase in the retirement rate of 40 percent since 1970.

Surely it is poor social policy to maintain disincentives to productive labor, and surely it is self-defeating to allow a vast pool of expertise to drain away simply because of an arbitrary limit on earnings. The nation would be better served by allowing experienced workers who wish to return to the work force to ease back into harness.

Omaha World-Herald
Omaha, Nebraska, February 28, 1991

The plight of the elderly poor in rural parts of the Midlands is shocking and sad. Finding ways to lighten their burdens may not be easy. But society should continue to try.

Stories by Gabriella Stern in The Sunday World-Herald described the problem. She wrote about independent-minded folks who live in parts of rural Nebraska. They were in their 70s or older. Some of them had no indoor plumbing. Medical attention was non-existent or difficult to obtain. One man cooks and even sponges himself off with bottled water because the structure in which he lives has no running water.

While elderly people living in more heavily populated areas might have a hard time of it, too, particularly if they don't have enough money to provide for the necessities of life, those living in rural areas have the added problems of isolation and distance.

The nearest doctor can be 50 miles away, the nearest specialist 250 miles away. Neighbors are often beyond walking distance.

Rural living has rewards. For elderly people who have chosen to grow old in the area in which they lived most of their lives there are often relatives or friends who help with transportation, errands and company.

In some rural areas, an informal network of farmers and gardeners sees to it that the needy receive a box of sweet corn or tomatoes, a roast from the slaughtered steer, a fresh-butchered chicken, groceries or fresh fruit in season.

But being elderly and poor in the country brings special problems. Few social service agencies are nearby. Some people go for years without knowing of their eligibility for programs designed to help people in their situation, such as Supplemental Security Income and Medicaid, or special programs for the blind.

Of those who do know, some are so proud and independent that they refuse the help to which they're entitled.

There is no sit-com solution to the difficulties these elderly Midlanders face, no quickie answers to tie up their lives neatly and prettily in 30 minutes. It is a continuing fight against the ravages of time and poverty, and the only soldiers — doctors, nurses and other health professionals and social workers — are already on the front lines.

Friends and neighbors help. In the best traditions of frontier neighborliness, they keep an alert eye open to what is happening in their communities and lend a hand when needed. The elderly themselves often work out arrangements in which they check on each other, reassuring and cheering each other up. The importance of a friendly word can't be overestimated.

Easy answers don't exist. That hasn't stopped compassionate Midlanders from seeking to help. May their numbers grow and become more effective.

The Wichita Eagle-Beacon
Wichita, Kansas, Ocotber 4, 1991

A new study released this week by the Centers for Disease Control in Atlanta shows that for every 1 million people over age 65 in 1980, 178 killed themselves. By 1986, the number was 215.

Males account for much of the increase in suicides among the elderly. Eighty percent of the older men who took their own lives had symptoms of depression.

Dr. Garry Porter, medical director of psychiatry at St. Joseph Hospital in Wichita and founder of the Living Improvement for the Elderly — LIFE — unit at the hospital, notes suicide has always been higher among white males than any other group.

"Depression in older white males most often begins with a loss," he said. "They lose people, jobs, power, bodily functions. They aren't talking about their feelings; they are not very self-nurturing."

He believes "gerontophobia" too often keeps people, including some health-care professionals, from recognizing the symptoms of depression. "We start seeing older people as fixtures, not people. They make us uncomfortable because we see our own futures. We don't want Grandpa to have problems, so we ignore them."

Most men born 60 or more years ago found their primary self-identity in their work. After retirement, they begin to feel like nobodies. Since they were taught that real men don't cry or show their emotions, they don't always send clear signals, let alone discuss openly their loneliness and their fears.

If, as Dr. Porter says, American society has a phobia that leads us to deny problems of the elderly, then we aren't listening as closely as we should to their cries for help. Men more than women, it would appear, muffle their cries for help, which makes it even harder to hear them.

Dr. Porter believes we must be much more aggressive in identifying depression among the elderly. "If he is not seriously ill, if he has good social time, good quality time left, he can be helped."

Welsh poet Dylan Thomas admonished his father and other older men: "Do not go gentle into that good night, old age should burn and rave at close of day; rage, rage against the dying of the light."

The sad truth is, however, when elderly men are depressed they have lost their ability to rage against death and then it is up to those who know and love them to help them find meaning to life, so they will indeed "not go gently into that good night."

Herald News
Fall River, Massachusetts, February 19, 1991

The experience of depression in our elderly population is often ignored and even accepted as part of the aging process. Yet that is far from the truth, according to Dr. Albert J. Stunkard, professor of psychiatry at the University of Pennsylvania School of Medicine.

Depression is not a normal reaction to aging. In fact, depression in the elderly is a very treatable disorder. This age group, however, is particularly vulnerable to depression as a result of the many losses suffered with declining years.

Being forced to go into a nursing home is especially painful because of the severe loss of independence. Those suffering from chronic disabling diseases can easily fall victim to depression. The loss of functional ability, as well as frequent, sometimes constant, pain is a common precipitating cause of depression in older people.

Yet with advances in the treatment of this disabling condition, depression is easily and often successfully treated. Anti-depressant medications can be very helpful. The new antidepressants have fewer toxic effects and can be taken safely by the elderly under a physician's or psychiatrist's supervision. Counseling, too, is a mainstay of the treatment of depression, as it assists the person through the crisis or stressful event.

Part of the problem is that this condition is frequently underdiagnosed. At times, physical symptoms can mask the emotional disorder.

All of us can assist our elderly by realizing that depression can easily occur, and we should all be on the alert for it. As Stunkard says, "Real improvement will not occur until elderly Americans, families and physicians stop viewing depression as an inescapable part of old age. It is not inescapable, but it will continue to blight the final years of many of our parents' and grandparents' lives until they get the treatment they need."

THE LINCOLN STAR
Lincoln, Nebraska, September 24, 1992

Americans and the experts agree on the definition of the major problems facing our health care system — soaring costs and inadequate health care coverage.

But the two groups disagree on the reasons behind these problems, according to research conducted by the Public Agenda Foundation and several polling organizations.

Americans do not understand the reasons behind the growing health care costs and the pending health care crisis. Ordinary Americans often blame high costs on unnecessary tests, overpaid doctors, wasteful hospitals, profiteering drug companies and greedy malpractice lawyers. Greed and profits are the problem, they believe.

EXPERTS HOWEVER believe the problem is much more complex. It includes defensive medicine (too many tests). It includes highly paid physicians. It includes the overuse of malpractice.

But the problems also stem from the high costs of new technology (which save more lives and push health care costs higher at the same time), the unnecessary duplication of services and technology, and something no one wants to discuss — the growing number of elderly.

When asked to choose which of the three reasons (greed and waste, new technology, or a growing number of older people) is the most important explanation of increasing health care costs, the majority of Americans (57 percent) selected greed, waste and high profits. Only 20 percent selected aging as the most important reason.

But aging is also an important factor in the rising costs of health care.

Currently people over 65 make up 12 percent of the population, but account for more than one-third of the $750 billion annual bill for health care spending.

Nebraska's Medicaid problem (part of the reason for the special legislative session that began yesterday) is the increasing cost of nursing home care for a growing number of elderly.

All of us pay for health care costs — both through our insurance premiums and through our taxes (for the Medicaid, Medicare and county relief programs).

The growing costs of nursing homes and of health services for older Americans is eventually passed on through taxes primarily.

But it is uncomfortable to talk about this fact.

MEMBERS OF focus groups asked to discuss health care issues were reluctant to consider the implications of the higher health costs for older Americans.

One Washington woman said: "It is true, but you shouldn't say it."

Many participants in the focus groups feared that any discussion of the high medical costs of the elderly was a prelude to urging some cutback in services or benefits for the elderly.

It is obvious from the polls and the focus groups that younger Americans had a genuine concern for the elderly. But genuine concern should not preclude honest discussion.

There is no way to determine what our ultimate choices will be in the health care area. But the discussion must include all the facets, including the growing senior generation.

Whether or not we discuss aging as a factor in the health cost crisis, demographic realities will remain central to the problem.

The Hartford Courant
Hartford, Connecticut, August 24, 1992

Many of Connecticut's older residents are angry and confused about recent changes in Medicare supplement insurance, which is known as Medigap. Some of the changes were mandated by Congress; others were imposed by Blue Cross-Blue Shield of Connecticut, which writes about 80 percent of the supplemental coverage in this state.

The elderly, through the advocacy group United Seniors in Action, have been asking state Insurance Commissioner Robert R. Googins for months to hold a public hearing on the changes. He should, even though his department can't solve many of the seniors' complaints.

One set of problems stems from the federal effort to force a standardization of Medicap insurance. As of Aug. 1, all new policies must fit one of 10 models, each of which must cover a specific scope of services and have a specific set of benefits. States had to rewrite their own regulations to fit the federal requirements.

In the past, the elderly had trouble sorting out the overlaps of policies from different companies and comparing prices. Standardization was supposed to end that waste and confusion.

But the smorgasbord approach has been just as confusing. Policyholders ask: Which one is best? Why will my premiums be higher even though the option I want offers less coverage than my present Medigap policy? Can I keep my current policy?

The insurance commissioner holds public hearings on proposed rate increases every autumn. But hearings are not required for new policies such as the 10-option plan. In fact, he didn't have the statutes, regulations, policies and rate cards in hand much before the July 31 deadline set by Congress to put the changes in place. So why didn't he postpone the new program until he conducted public hearings? Because Congress ordered federal officials to take over the programs in states that missed the deadline.

But now the deadline has passed, and the changes have been put in place. About two dozen national insurers are preparing to sell Medigap policies in Connecticut, compared with the nine that were in the marketplace before August. It's time for some informational hearings to hear the complaints of the elderly.

SYRACUSE
HERALD-JOURNAL
Syracuse, New York, November 15, 1991

One of the first things young visitors to Florida notice (once they leave Disney World, at least) is that, "Gosh, there are a lot of people like Grandma and Grandpa here."

As a matter of fact, about a fifth of that state's population is 65 or older.

Now, imagine Syracuse's population as that "gray." And picture every other city and state in the nation as having that percentage of older people.

You've just envisioned the future as it will be in about 30 years. By 2020, the Census Bureau projects about 17 percent of the U.S. population will be 65 or older; by 2030, more than a fifth will be. The "grandparent boom" will have replaced the baby boom that occurred between 1946 and 1964.

That's why we were pleased to see Syracuse University is taking a leading role in the research essential to help Americans age gracefully. The U.S. Department of Health and Human Services has chosen SU as the host institution for its National Academy on Aging.

SU had an unbeatable combination that won it the academy and a federal start-up grant of $1.1 million. It had both the Gerontology Center and the Maxwell School of Citizenship and Public Affairs. The academy's purpose is to bring the nation's top experts on aging and its major public-policy makers together for serious discussions.

That makes sense. And the timing is reasonable. With careful planning now between these key players, the nation can expect the kind of thoughtful public policy it will need. By the time today's middle-aged population bulge starts to retire, we hope the Syracuse-based National Academy of Aging will be looked upon with respect and gratitude.

It has been handed a huge responsibility and marvelous opportunity. Certainly, planning ways to handle the health, housing, transportation and other needs of a mostly older population won't be easy. But it already is reassuring to know that special efforts are under way to deal with these challenges.

Directing the academy will be Vernon Greene, who heads SU's Gerontology Center. We wish him and his colleagues well as they lead our country into this new frontier for our society.

How very different the 21st century promises to be. Consider that when the current century began, only one in 25 Americans was 65 or older.

The Times-Picayune
New Orleans, Louisiana, August 2, 1992

In an effort to raise public consciousness about the large number of malnourished elderly Americans, nutritionists attuned to their needs are reaching out to them through a promising approach called Nutrition Screening Initiative.

The emphasis of the screening program is on preventive medicine. "Our role is to help people take charge of their nutritional health and keep themselves out of hospitals and nursing homes," said Nancy Wellman, a nutrition professor who works with the initiative project as a representative of the American Dietetic Association.

But finding the at-risk elderly is the crucial first step. After two years of research, the initiative recently released a nutrition screening checklist intended to be a quick way for older adults to assess their risk of malnutrition.

Copies of the checklist are being distributed to social service agencies, dietitians, nursing homes, senior citizens organizations and other groups across the country. A more detailed screening is available for doctors and other health professionals.

The large number of elderly people whose poor diets adversely affect their quality of life are those nutritionists call the "hidden hungry." Their plight has received less attention than the serious nutrition problems of infants, children and pregnant teen-agers.

For a variety of reasons, including poverty, isolation, disease, poor eating habits, physical limitations and tooth and mouth problems, many elderly are prone to malnutrition. The Nutrition Screening Initiative estimates that of 30 million older Americans 6 million are at high risk of malnutrition. An additional 1 million are malnourished.

Undoubtedly, poverty is the biggest problem. More than 25 percent of older Americans have household incomes of less than $10,000 a year. People in this group may have to choose between food and medicine or food and rent.

But advocates for the elderly rightly point out that the issue is larger than just food. Other important factors are nutrition education, food-stamp information, transportation, cooking help, adult day care, home repair services, and a visit to the dentist.

In alerting health care professionals and others who deal with the problems of the elderly, the screening checklist is an important educational tool. In many geriatric cases, the doctor must also be a teacher.

A recent national survey showed many oldsters are ignorant about healthful eating. Only 6 percent believe they're at risk of malnutrition, and 36 percent said they don't worry at all about proper diets.

The initiative program is a timely wake-up message as well as an encouraging reminder that the lives of the at-risk group can be improved markedly by caring assistance from professionals who understand their needs.

The News and Observer
Raleigh, North Carolina, July 23, 1991

Perhaps, if North Carolina continues to toughen the fines against nursing and rest homes that repeatedly break rules, other violators will get the message. That will serve to protect the elderly residents of homes who often have only rules and regulators to stand for them.

A dramatic increase in the size of fines against offenders is a good sign that David T. Flaherty, secretary of human resources, has begun to straighten out a system that let too many rule-breakers off easily. Fines most recently approved by the state were the highest in many months, including one for $5,000.

Mr. Flaherty deserves credit for recognizing the gaping flaws in a system that often let homes off the hook with small financial penalties even though they were clearly neglecting patients. Often, when fines were considered, the home's past record of violations wasn't even reviewed. Mr. Flaherty has corrected that flaw, and others that allowed perpetual violators to stay in business and repeat their mistakes.

The worst problem, of course, was that those mistakes translated into literal torture for elderly residents — medication mishandled, medical care denied, sanitation inadequate. That would be bad enough if those affected could defend themselves, but so many of them are without families or their remaining family members are far away.

The state has for too long neglected its duty to be their "families." The increased fines are evidence that things are changing for the better.

The Hartford Courant
Hartford, Connecticut, October 10, 1992

All unused medications prescribed for nursing-home patients are destroyed, as a state law now requires, instead of being salvaged for redistribution. A legislative task force is looking into ways to halt what seems, on the surface at least, to be big-time waste.

But it may turn out to be more trouble and expense than it's worth to salvage the unused pills safely.

The true cost of this apparent extravagance is unclear. The state's 18,000 Medicaid patients in nursing homes receive an average of about $1,000 a year in prescription drugs. The state's total drug bill at nursing homes is about $17 million. But no one has totaled the value of what's thrown away when a patient dies or has a change in medication.

The idea of recycling unused drugs sounds simpler than it is. Most hospitals now use what is called the unit dose, in which individual quantities of medication are sent up from the in-house pharmacy to patients on a daily schedule. But nursing homes, which use community druggists, mostly employ a "unit use" system. The pills for Mrs. Jones, for instance, are sealed in individual plastic bubbles. The drug store sends over sheets of these "blister packs," which represent several months' worth of daily doses.

Druggists are paid $4.10 by the state each time they fill a Medicaid prescription. To save money, some welfare officials push doctors to order larger and larger supplies at a time — 60 or 90 days' worth of medications for Mrs. Jones instead of the typical 30-day order. It saves that dispensing fee, but can lead to wasting large quantities. As a partial solution, the state also permits small orders, such as a five-day supply, under special circumstances.

The do-not-reuse consumer protection laws were written when nursing-home patients received individual bottles of pills. The laws prevent such problems as mixing or tampering with returned drugs or using outdated, contaminated or recalled medications.

If reuse is allowed, how much should the pharmacist be paid to take the pills back and check them? The returns would have to be separated by lot number and expiration date for safety's sake. Paperwork to assure refunds would also be required.

Perhaps nursing homes — at least the larger ones — should set up their own in-house unit-dose dispensing systems. But that might be just as expensive. The task force has lots of issues to explore.

Part III: Disease in America

All cultures create their own theories of disease and death. Although there are variations, theories generally fall into two categories: Those that emphasize behavioral factors (health-oriented theories) and those that emphasize the importance of environmental factors (disease-oriented theories). During the thousand years prior to the modern period, Western medicine focused on behavior. Illness was seen as evidence of a disordered physiology, which was in turn seen as the result of unhealthy or immoral behavior. Even as recently as the nineteenth century, cholera epidemics, which affected the poor almost exclusively, were viewed as divine punishment of those who were considered slothful. Consistent with this individual person-oriented theory of disease, physicans prescribed diets, medications, or a change in location to restore health.

As medical attention largely moved from the individual to the environment as the source of illness and disease, a major emphasis was placed on external agents of disease, somewhat at the expense of the behavioral factors involved.

In contrast with our notions of health, which is perceived as at least partly a matter of personal responsibility, disease is seen as striking at random – the patient is viewed as victim. Just as with other external enemies, we make "war" on disease: a "war" on cancer, a "fight against multiple sclerosis," a "March of Dimes." The conquest of deadly infectious diseases such as malaria and typhoid through environmental control is seen as the glory of medical science and the model for our attack on most modern diseases. The decline in mortality rates is viewed as the result of a decline in disease rates rather than an improvement in health. Are those lower death rates the consequence of a better environment, or are they the result of our having become better animals – that is, healthier?

Physicians reach conclusions regarding health when they find that disease is absent. Health, then, is a diagnosis by exclusion. For example, patients undergoing a yearly checkup are likely to be told that they are in excellent health if their weight, blood pressure, electrocardiogram, and so on are normal and there is no anatomical evidence of disease. If no evidence of disease is found, a physician is likely to reassure the patient complaining of symptoms of illness.

While the absence of disease may be necessary to good health, clearly health implies more than an absence of disease. Most would agree that an element critical to health is a sense of subjective well-being, happiness, joy or exuberance – in other words, health is not an objective entity but a highly subjective one, reflecting the individual's cultural and personal values. Such entities are difficult to define and measure.

The World Health Organization (WHO) of the United Nations defines health as "a state of complete physical, mental and social well-being and not simply the absence of disease or infirmity." This definition provides a useful starting point, particularly in its emphasis on health as a positive and meaningful entity that has dimensions of its own.

In examining the role various factors have on the development of modern life expectancy, the objective is to understand whether each of these is or is not an important antecedent – that is, something that "causes" good health.

The underlying assumption is that each specific disease is the result of exposure to a specific agent: "one germ, one disease." These criteria have been recognized as being far too rigid and simplistic. The Epstein-Barr virus (EBV) is known to be associated in the United States with a rather benign disease common to college students, infectious mononucleosis. In Africa, the same virus is associated with a malignant tumor of children known as Burkitt's lymphoma. In China the same virus has been identified with the otherwise uncommon nasopharyngeal cancer. In addition, many people carry the virus without evidence of harm, a pattern not unique to EBV. Most infectious agents produce this same chameleon effect, appearing in each person in a different guise and often being present harmlessly. The virus may be necessary to the development of a particular "named disease," but it alone will not be sufficient to produce that disease. Obviously the notion of "one germ, one disease," is inadequate. More appropriate is the notion of a "web of causation" in which multiple factors, personal and environmental, interact to result in disease.

New information makes it appear that AIDS fits this same pattern. The virus is not transmitted easily. Multiple exposures are required and personal behavior patterns (sexual practices, drug use) strongly predispose to infection. Still, many people are apparently carrying the virus harmlessly – that is, they are infected, yet they do not have the disease. Among those with the virus who do become ill, personal or other characteristics will combine, in the presence of the virus, to produce a wide spectrum of individual diseases. The final appearance of disease, then, is a reflection of all of the individual's past experiences, exposures and genetic predisposition.

Public health policy in the United States is based on a biomedical model that assumes that disease, both acute and chronic, results largely from environmental agents and that, just as infectious disease was "conquered" during the past century through improvements in sanitation, the future of disease eradication in this century and the next will also result from improvements in the environment rather than changes in human behavior. We annually spend tens of billions of dollars on environmental improvement based largely on the hope that through such means we shall reduce cancer and other chronic diseases thought to result from contamination of the environment. Such a strategy ignores the fact that life expectancy rose in the United States most rapidly during the early decades of this century, when environmental contamination was most intense. In fact, just as with the medical care system, the enormously expensive environmental movement of the past few decades was initiated largely after the major improvement in American health had begun to plateau.

While results of proposed research will be useful to future health planning, most experts agree that the health of Americans will depend upon more than good research and information. Improvements in health will fundamentally depend upon a new vision of human health and its determinants. That new vision of health will have far broader dimensions than the present narrow concept. The unit of health must be broadened beyond the individual to include the entire social network on which the health of the individual depends; a healthy nation is more than a collection of healthy individuals. Just as no person is entirely self-contained, so too does the health of each of us depend upon those around us, upon the family, and also upon the larger network of a caring and nurturing community. Both the family and the caring community appear to be in decline in the United States, a trend that health care reformers say must be reversed.

U.S. Blood Supply Becomes National Concern

The board of directors of the American Red Cross May 19, 1991 unanimously voted to overhaul the organization's system of blood centers.

The American Red Cross handled half the U.S. blood supply. The organization included 2,700 U.S. chapters and 53 regional blood centers.

The Red Cross said it would replace the 10 different computer systems currently in place with one centralized system. Blood testing, currently performed at each center, would be shifted to a few centralized sites. Uniform collection and testing procedures would be instituted nationwide, and employees would be trained in the new standards.

The action came in a context of rising public fears over the safety of the blood supply. Mismanagement at regional centers had been periodically reported for several years. The Food and Drug Administration April 17 had threatened to shut down a blood collection center in Portland, Ore. after violations of procedure were discovered there.

Red Cross and government officials cited in news reports May 20 attributed many of the problems to the growing complexity of the blood collection process. Due to the AIDS epidemic and a rise in hepatitis cases, the number of tests that had to be performed on a unit of blood had increased by seven in the previous decade, they said. Red Cross officials also said that while the level of public fear was higher than ever before, the blood supply was safer than ever.

The Houston Post
Houston, Texas, May 27, 1991

AMERICANS HAVE always been keepers of the faith when it comes to expecting — and getting — the very best in health care. That is, until recently. Cries of a health-care crisis, dire warning about AIDS and fears that the nation's blood supply might not be completely safe have brought on severe attacks of national worry.

The country can rest easier about one concern, at least. The American Red Cross is beginning a massive reorganization of the way it collects and handles blood. Elizabeth Dole, president of the Red Cross, announced that there will be new national collection and handling procedures for blood, and that all employees at the organization's 53 blood centers will be retrained in these procedures.

"All our blood facilities will meet exacting standards of quality, or they will not collect blood," Dole said. The Red Cross will revolutionize blood banking, she added. Dole, who has been head of the organization for only three months, emphasized that the steps are preventive rather than corrective.

A grateful nation thanks you, Mrs. Dole. Although Red Cross officials maintain that the blood supplies from the centers are the safest ever, the federal Food and Drug Administration had threatened to close the Blood Collection Center in Portland, Ore., after 51 proce-

dural violations were found. It was not shut down, and apparently no contaminated blood left the center.

Even if the errors were clerical in nature, it is not the sort of thing that promotes a good night's sleep. As Dr. Jeffrey McCullough, senior vice president of the Red Cross, told a congressional subcommittee, "more must be done. Some people dismiss the problems we are having as just clerical. They are. But it is clerical error that can kill people in this business if we don't do it right."

America wants it done right. The Red Cross collects about half the nation's blood supply. The rest comes from independent centers, which is the way blood is collected in Houston. Countless people would die without such services. Because the deadly shadow of AIDS now falls across the country, "right" is the only way it can be done. Because we are human, there will always be the chance of mistakes, but the Red Cross restructuring is a positive step.

Blood must now be tested for AIDS and the hepatitis B and C viruses. As a result, the Red Cross blood centers had to carry out about 100 million more tests from 1985 to 1990 than in the previous five years.

It is a monumental task, but the Red Cross has reacted forcefully and courageously. The nation will be able to rest easier.

The Des Moines Register
Des Moines, Iowa, May 29, 1991

The American Red Cross will spend $120 million to revise its blood-collection system in hopes of reducing the chances of infecting unsuspecting people with AIDS.

The organization collects half of the blood used in transfusions in

Work at some centers is sloppy

this country. It has handled that vast undertaking through 53 collection centers, some of which have been plain sloppy, even though lives were at stake. Some of the mistakes were "clerical," but as Dr. Jeffrey McCullough, a senior vice president of the organization, said, "It is clerical error that can kill people in this business" — as when the Red Cross approved an AIDS-tainted blood unit for shipment to a hospital. A Food and Drug Administration official discovered and headed off that mistake.

It's said that the blood supply is safer than it's ever been. But what should bother the Red Cross is that the FDA has issued hundreds of citations against Red Cross centers over the span of a year without any red flags going up until now. After issuing 51 citations to a Portland, Ore., center, the FDA finally had to threaten to close it down. Not only did the federal regulators discover errors, they found further that the Red Cross was not properly reporting the errors that its own investigations uncovered.

As long as six months can elapse between the time a person is infected with the HIV virus — precursor to AIDS — and the time he or she tests positive for the virus. Thus some contaminated blood inevitably will escape detection. Officials estimate the chances at somewhere between one pint of contaminated blood out of 40,000 and one out of 153,000. Those are long odds. But if one in 40,000 is contaminated, you're 320 times as likely to get AIDS from a transfusion as to win the Lotto America jackpot.

The public may accept that risk with equanimity. What the public cannot and should not excuse is multiplication of that risk through carelessness and incompetence on the part of the Red Cross.

The Honolulu Advertiser
Honolulu, Hawaii, May 22, 1991

The Blood Bank of Hawaii is not part of the American Red Cross, so won't be involved in that organization's major revamping of its blood system.

But anyone who might travel on the Mainland and need blood due to accident or illness should be relieved the Red Cross will modernize equipment, update computers and centralize testing for its 53 blood centers across the country.

Congressional investigators and the Food and Drug Administration — which is required by law to make unannounced inspections of every blood center annually — have found that Red Cross blood and blood products were shipped for transfusion even though contaminated by viruses that cause AIDS and hepatitis.

But the Red Cross, which handles half the nation's supply, insists no truly HIV-positive blood was given to patients.

Hawaii's blood bank already has implemented stringent safety procedures and officials are confident everything that can reasonably be done to insure safety is being done.

In a way, our small size is a plus, allowing careful manual checking in addition to computer controls before each unit of blood is released. Total dependence on faulty software got the Red Cross in trouble.

Giving blood is always safe. Receiving blood involves a certain danger that is usually outweighed by the risk from the accident or illness requiring the transfusion.

The advent of incurable AIDS has upped the ante. Tests check for HIV antibodies, which may take weeks or even months after the virus enters the system to show up. That leaves an unfortunate "window of vulnerability."

The best way to shut that window is a personal interview with each donor about behavior that makes one susceptible to AIDS — and each donor's ability to confidentially prevent use of blood even after it has been given.

That interview, followed by medical testing and careful controls, is the Blood Bank of Hawaii's first line of defense.

The TENNESSEAN
Nashville, Tennessee, May 25, 1991

THE American Red Cross may have embarked on its biggest rescue ever Monday with the announcement of a sweeping reorganization of its own operations in the handling of blood products.

By saving itself, the Red Cross can continue to be in a position to rescue the millions of disaster victims and others on whom it has staked an enviable and deserved reputation over the years.

As announced by Red Cross president Elizabeth Dole, the organization plans a major overhaul in its blood supply centers. Workers would be retrained. State-of-the-art equipment would be employed to better handle the dispersal of blood supplies. New procedures would be established to help detect blood products tainted by the AIDS virus or hepatitis B and C viruses. A major shift would be from 10 different computer systems in the country to one national system.

Fear of AIDS has put the Red Cross and other smaller blood suppliers in a precarious, often embattled, position. The Red Cross supplies over half the nation's blood products. Because of its volume, the organization has also seen hundreds of citations from the Food and Drug Administration for improper procedures. While most of the citations were for minor clerical errors and failure to follow strict federal policy, a big concern centered on reports that the organization failed to report oversights to authorities.

Deserved or not, the impression left with the public is of a Red Cross that failed to lead as it should have on the issue of protecting blood supplies.

The Red Cross' own internal investigation showed that in one six-month period of six million blood products collected, 2,400 were improperly released. Notably, however, some 575,000 others were properly tested and destroyed because of contamination.

Under the specter of AIDS, any breakdown in procedure threatens the organization's public credibility.

The Red Cross' decision to dramatically change directions may inspire other blood supply groups to make their own needed changes. But the change for the Red Cross won't come easy. While centers are undergoing retraining and reorganization, they will be closed down on a schedule for up to eight weeks. That means that those centers operating elsewhere will be asked to donate 10% more for distribution than they normally would.

And it's also going to require money. The Red Cross plans to pay for its estimated $100 million reorganization through cuts elsewhere in its programs, loans and fund-raising.

The Red Cross' bold, if belated, decision to deal more aggressively with its blood supply program should help restore the confidence of potential gift-givers. This country needs a safe, effective blood supply. But it also needs the Red Cross. A reorganization that meets both goals surely deserves support from everyone. ■

The Washington Post
Washington, D.C., May 22, 1991

UNTIL A few days ago, a lot of people assumed that medical technology had taken care of the problem of AIDS transmission through organ transplants and blood transfusions. Since the development of a test for the virus's antibodies in 1985, there had been no reported cases of infection by transplant and only 15 cases, out of 6 million procedures a year, involving blood transfusions.

But late last week, two news stories raised fears that that confidence had been misplaced. On Thursday it was revealed that a Virginia organ donor who died in 1985 had been infected with the virus. Some of the dozens of people who received his organs and tissue transplants have contracted AIDS. Then, the Red Cross, which processes half the blood donations made each year, announced a major reorganization of that work, in the process creating an impression that significant problems had always been present.

These anxieties need to be addressed. Part of the problem with AIDS is that it cannot be detected for the first six to 12 weeks after infection. The Virginia man was probably infected shortly before he died, and in spite of the fact that his remains were tested twice, in two different laboratories, his condition was not detected. The accuracy of AIDS tests has increased since 1985, but the mechanism for reporting AIDS infection in organ recipients was ineffective in this case, so transplants of tissue continued for years after the first case developed. Improvements must be made in this system, though some small risk will remain. For recipients to whom a transplant is a matter of life and death, it will probably be worth taking.

The problems with blood also involve early AIDS infections not revealed by test. There is no record of error where blood, tested and identified as contaminated, has been used and has infected a recipient. The combination of testing and screening donors has been effective. Nevertheless, as both the Food and Drug Administration and Rep. John Dingell's investigative subcommittee found out, there have been problems in the operation of the Red Cross blood program. Clerical errors and computer snafus had increased, record-keeping and training suffered, and errors were not consistently reported. The organization's 53 blood centers were uncoordinated and poorly supervised.

The steps announced by Red Cross President Elizabeth Dole Monday—temporarily closing down blood centers on a staggered basis for reorganization, retraining and revising computer systems—are designed to correct these errors. Mrs. Dole says this country's blood supply is safer than ever—the safest in the world. But it is not yet as safe as it can be. The errors have been the Red Cross's responsibility and so is the obligation to fix them.

San Francisco Chronicle
San Francisco, California, January 9, 1991

THERE IS an acute shortage of donated blood and blood products in the Bay Area. Such a situation constitutes cause for concern on a variety of scores.

The possibility exists, for one thing, that all but emergency surgery could be curtailed in Northern California hospitals. Blood for transfusions is already being rationed to medical facilities in Marin and San Francisco counties and supplies are dwindling faster than the Irwin Memorial Blood Banks can replenish them.

The shortage is caused in part by the crisis in the Persian Gulf, but present reality also means that some local centers are simply unable to keep up with the needs of the military.

THE GOVERNMENT cannot step in and make these banks whole, as it has been doing with our fractured monetary institutions. What is wanted is that gift of self each healthy, mature human can offer. Surely the Bay Area can provide the donors that are so desperately needed.

SYRACUSE HERALD-JOURNAL
Syracuse, New York, May 22, 1991

The American Red Cross deserves credit for acting decisively to restore confidence in its blood distribution program. An effort that has meant life itself to millions of Americans over the years cannot function properly without that confidence.

Red Cross President Elizabeth Dole announced this week that the organization's 53 blood centers would be closed in rotation over the next two years to install a new computer system and train staff on new procedures. The aim is to improve testing of donated blood to guard against the passing of infections — especially AIDS — through transfusions.

The $120 million overhaul is in response to concerns that management of the blood supply has been lax in many instances around the country. Adding to the pressures faced by the Red Cross — which handles half the nation's blood supply — is a huge increase in the number of tests that must be performed on donated blood.

Everyone is frightened by the prospect of contracting AIDS, which is always fatal. This kind of anxiety is the last thing people need when they have medical problems serious enough to require blood transfusions. The sweeping changes announced this week should do much to assuage those fears. It's impossible for the blood supply to be made 100 percent safe, but the reorganization should reassure Americans that all that can be done is being done.

The Red Cross has been traveling over a rough patch of road lately. But let us not lose sight of the fact it is a remarkable organization. The services it performs are absolutely vital to the health of the nation, yet it depends largely on the generosity of Americans — donors of both money and blood — to keep going.

Under the leadership of Dole, who formerly headed the federal Labor and Transportation departments, the Red Cross should emerge from this episode with renewed momentum to continue serving Americans for generations to come.

The Clarion-Ledger
Jackson, Mississippi, May 21, 1991

The American Red Cross is right to take the drastic action of totally revamping its blood supply system, in the wake of potentially harmful mishaps to the public.

The decision to close centers in rotation to purge each region of inadequate ones is long in coming. The Food and Drug Administration has found that the Red Cross:

■ Released blood contaminated by hepatitis.

■ Failed to follow safety procedures against the use of AIDS-contaminated blood.

■ Repeatedly neglected to report errors and accidents.

Drastic action was needed to reassure the American public that its blood supply is safe.

This move should serve to help quell such unease.

The Des Moines Register
Des Moines, Iowa, October 5, 1991

People whose blood contains high levels of high-density lipoproteins seem less prone than most to develop heart disease. The evidence has long been obvious, but the explanation has not. Is it cause and effect or coincidence?

Now it's sort-of-official: cause and effect. The HDLs, natural enemies of LDLs (low-density lipoproteins), are on your side.

Experimenters in California engineered some mice to have bloodstreams armed with HDL. Then they loaded them up with LDL. The HDL won, carting off the LDL and dumping it into the liver, where it was chopped up and sent packing to the bladder.

By feeding to some of the mice cookies laced with heavy doses of cocoa butter, the researchers managed to overwhelm the HDL. Fat streaks grew in the arteries of the cookie-monster mice — but not near as much fat as was deposited in the arteries of the mice fed those too-rich cocoa butter cookies without any HDL.

The confirmation of HDL's benefits should shift the emphasis of some pharmaceutical research. At present, cholesterol-control medication will lower both LDL and HDL. New research should be aimed at raising HDL and lowering its bad-news cousin.

All of which confirms what the nutritionists have long been telling you: Cook with corn oil and olive oil, avoid coconut oil and palm oil. Pick lean cuts of meat, avoid whole-milk dairy products and bakery goods. Vegetables, fresh fruit and whole grains are in; egg yolks, cashews, macadamia nuts and avocados are out.

The Hutchinson News
Hutchinson, Kansas, May 22, 1991

The American Red Cross is undertaking its most ambitious overhaul of the nation's blood centers, and it's none too soon.

The numerous horror stories of patients' receiving tainted blood has sent a shudder through the nation. And it's not just in the U.S. Thousands of hemophiliacs in England are suing the National Health Service there after being exposed to hepatitis through NHS blood transfusions.

The $120 million, two-year revamping of the Red Cross blood centers, which handles half the nation's supply, is as important to the overall health of Americans as competent medical care.

In recent years, though, the confidence in the all-important blood supply has been seriously diminished by an abundance of errors involving incompetence and mismanagement.

AIDS and hepatitis have been transmitted to blood recipients in recent years, and officials state that even with a revamping of the testing procedures, the blood supply can never be wholly guaranteed.

That conclusion calls for more ambitious screening procedures and makes a clear case for official action in identifying AIDS patients in order to prohibit them from providing tainted blood.

Currently, Missouri is attempting to define its role and responsibility to the patients of an AIDS-infected dentist, whose condition was made known only after his death. Missouri wonders if it should contact the dentist's patients and inform them that their doctor was infected.

The Red Cross' inability to guarantee an absolutely safe blood supply should inspire greater measures to be undertaken along with revamping testing procedures.

LAS VEGAS SUN

Las Vegas, Nevada, January 15, 1991

*T*he threat of war in the Persian Gulf has added to the concern of blood bank officials who already are coping with the usual shortages brought on by the annual slump in donations each January.

"Although there have been no requests by the military for blood at this time, under agreement with the National Blood Exchange Program we will be required to accommodate such requests that are made of us," said Susan Baker of United Blood Services in Las Vegas.

"Our concern is that we don't endanger the local supply."

It is indeed a concern as, in the event of a war in Kuwait, the local blood bank could be required to turn over to military officials up to 50 percent of its current supply.

Last year in Las Vegas, 40,000 pints of blood were required for use and reserves. Without war, Baker said it is estimated that 45,000 units will be required this year to meet the needs of local hospitals.

Currently, United Blood Services is receiving 70 percent of its required donations of blood, Baker said, adding that 30 percent is being imported from other sources.

Baker said that anyone who wants to donate blood can give at 810 S. Casino Center Monday through Friday 9 a.m. to 6 p.m. or Saturdays 9 a.m. to 4 p.m.

TULSA WORLD

Tulsa, Oklahoma, May 22, 1991

THE American Red Cross is changing the way it tests and handles blood.

Elizabeth Dole, the new Red Cross president, outlined a plan to merge most of its 53 blood centers to a more manageable, standardized ten. The long-overdue revamping will begin in 1992 at a cost of some $120 million.

The change was unavoidable. Blood centers have been struggling to keep up with an enormous increase in tests performed to ensure a pure blood supply for Americans, particularly in light of the deadly AIDS virus.

But each center followed its own procedures and booking systems with different computer programs. Clerical errors were slipping in.

The new system will have uniform procedures and computerized record keeping. New oversight boards will be set up and workers retrained.

But no system is foolproof. Human error will always be a factor, in blood tests a deadly factor. And there is a brief period before AIDS antibodies show up indicating infection when that blood could be taken and distributed.

The Red Cross, through a dedicated network of volunteers and professionals, has given America the purest supply of blood in the world. Under the deadly threat of AIDS, the Red Cross is taking a necessary but expensive step to maintain that supply.

Risk will always be present, but the Red Cross is doing all it can to ensure the human factor is reduced.

AUGUSTA HERALD

Augusta, Georgia, May 22, 1991

The nation's blood supply can never be 100 percent safe, but it should be as safe as technology and medical research can make it. This is why the $120 million the American Red Cross will spend over the next two years to further protect the blood supply is a welcome investment.

It should improve the management of the nation's blood banks, which has come under heavy fire in recent years. Streamlining the computer operations of the 53 blood centers will reduce the mountains of clerical and paperwork, and thus the likelihood of lab or communications errors which sometimes cause sickness or even death.

Unfortunately, cleaning up management deficiencies won't help to identify the fatal AIDS virus which hides from existing testing techniques for several weeks or months soon after a person is infected. But Red Cross officials, like other blood centers such as Shepeard Community Blood Center in Augusta, are doing the best they can to weed out high-risk donors — drug users, homosexuals and persons who engage in promiscuous sex.

It is useful to remember as one reads about the problems blood banks are having that the chance of getting AIDS or other infectious diseases are remote — about one in 40,000.

Blood centers' most serious problem is getting enough qualified donors. As more people from high-risk groups are excluded, the need for healthy donors increases.

THE ANN ARBOR NEWS

Ann Arbor, Michigan, May 24, 1991

The decision by the nation's leading blood suppliers to revamp systems for testing donated blood and to improve monitoring of collection procedures is comforting news.

The American Red Cross announced Monday a sweeping reorganization that will cost about $100 million and take about two years to complete. Red Cross will close most of its 53 testing laboratories and replace them will six to eight regional, standardized laboratories to improve monitoring and testing operations. Computer systems will be updated and centralized, and workers will be retrained. Local oversight boards will be established.

In addition, the American Association of Blood Banks also said that it planned to make major procedural changes to improve safety in its blood units, collected by 2,400 independent blood banks across the nation. Specifics have not yet been detailed, but AABB expects to begin implementing them next year.

Red Cross and the independent blood blanks are responsible for nearly all of the nation's blood supply.

The changes are being made in conjunction with the federal Food and Drug Administration, the U.S. Department of Health and Human Services and congressional health leaders. They are intended to ease the minds of people whose concern about the nation's blood supply has grown in recent years because of AIDS.

It should be noted that the chances are extremely slim that patients needing blood transfusions will contract AIDS or other diseases. From a pool of 12 million units of donated blood collected each year, only 15 cases of AIDS has been attributed to blood transfusions since health officials began tracking the disease. Only 0.2 percent to 0.5 percent of 4 million Americans who received blood transfusions each year contracted a form of Hepatitis.

Nevertheless, there has been reason for increased public concern, and the blood banks do deserve criticism. The FDA, which monitors blood banks, have shown instances in which sloppy procedures have resulted in blood units being mislabeled and shipped to hospitals, including an alleged mislabeled shipment to University Hospitals from an independent Texas blood bank. In one case, the FDA found one unit of blood contaminated with AIDS had been mislabeled and prepared for shipment. FDA also said that Red Cross has failed to report all its procedural errors. Some blood banks have been closed by the FDA in recent months.

The changes to be made by the Red Cross and independent blood banks follow improvements made by the government last year. Health and Human Services has altered blood donor rules to improve screening of potential donors, and the FDA approved a new test that is expected to cut in half the number of blood units contaminated with Hepatitis C.

The improvements ought to improve public confidence in our nation's blood supply. Subsequently, upgraded systems should help increase the number of citizens willing to donate blood. Donated blood has been in short supply recently.

Basketball Star Magic Johnson Announces He Is HIV-Positive

Los Angeles Laker guard Earvin (Magic) Johnson, among the greatest and most popular players in the history of the National Basketball Association, Nov. 7, 1991 announced that he had tested positive for HIV, the virus that caused the fatal disease AIDS.

Johnson, 32, said he did not yet have any AIDS-related illnesses but that on the advice of his doctors he was retiring from basketball immediately. One of Johnson's doctors Nov. 10 said that the basketball star would soon begin treatments with the drug AZT. The drug helped to slow the progression of the AIDS virus, which attacked the body's immune system.

The star athlete's announcement, and later assertions that he had contracted the virus through heterosexual relations, aroused a surge of new publicity about AIDS, which had killed more than 126,000 Americans so far. Johnson's announcement and its expected effects on the fight against AIDS received news coverage throughout the world and dominated the U.S. media for days. Telephone hot-lines reported being swamped with calls seeking information about AIDS.

(Among athletes who were reported to have died from AIDS-related causes were football player Jerry Smith, Olympic decathlete Tom Waddell, race car driver Tim Richmond, baseball player Alan Wiggins and boxer Esteban DeJesus.)

At a press conference in Los Angeles, Johnson announced that he had tested positive for HIV during a screening for an insurance policy.

Johnson said he would use his public prominence to become a spokesman for the fight against AIDS. He urged young people to practice safe sex and warned that contracting AIDS "can happen to anybody, even Magic Johnson."

Johnson, from Lansing, Mich., was drafted by the Lakers in 1979 after leading Michigan State University to the National Collegiate Athletic Association title as a sophomore. The 1979 NCAA final, against an Indiana State team led by forward Larry Bird, was the most-watched college game of all time, according to the Associated Press.

The friendly rivalry between Johnson and Bird, who joined the NBA's Boston Celtics, continued throughout their professional careers and played a significant role in the recent popularity boom enjoyed by the league.

THE SPOKESMAN-REVIEW
Spokane, Washington, November 8, 1991

Dr. Michael Mellman, team physician for the Los Angeles Lakers, pretty much summed up Magic Johnson's remarkable press conference on Thursday when he called it "a courageous act by a very special man."

Johnson, a 14-carat superstar on and off the court, is HIV-positive. On the day after learning for sure he has the virus which ultimately leads to AIDS, he bravely told the world he was retiring as a player — and he told why.

He said he found out through a routine physical exam for a life insurance policy. He said he's going to be around for a good long time yet. He promised he'll battle this new foe with the same competitive intensity that has made him a champion on the basketball court. And he said he's going to be a vigorous spokesman for the AIDS cause.

He said all this with the same positive outlook that has won him a level of admiration that transcends sports. One observer noted that in a room full of reporters, teammates and basketball executives, the friendly giant who had such chilling news to impart was the most upbeat person in the room.

Johnson is not the first celebrity to acquire the AIDS virus, nor the first to use his own experience to raise public awareness. But he is among a handful who have the credibility and respect it takes to deliver the warning effectively, especially among the disbelieving youth.

Johnson has always shown special interest in young people. Now he wants to stress to them the importance of safe sex. That won't please self-righteous folks who believe moral injunctions can override hormones. But in the real world a lot of kids, and adults, need to hear what Magic Johnson will be telling them, lest they make bad decisions even worse.

During Johnson's forthright meeting with reporters, the obvious question was ventured only once, tentatively: How was the virus acquired? Johnson deferred it to team physician Mellman as a medical question. Once Johnson had departed, Mellman later said Johnson "was infected through heterosexual activity."

In the meantime, Magic Johnson has managed to do something that seems impossible in a sports world so tainted by professional athletes' hedonism, greed and self-aggrandizement. On a circumstance that ordinarily invokes seedy inferences, he has put an almost wholesome face.

THE DALLAS TIMES HERALD
Dallas, Texas, November 9, 1991

The reality of AIDS is more than human beings can willingly confront. Once the confrontation has been forced on people, the reality of how to avoid AIDS is staggering. The only known ways to avoid AIDS require changes in one of life's most basic behaviors — sex.

It is entirely natural that human beings put up imaginary walls, shielding themselves from the reality of AIDS. People who are just beginning to understand this plague try to find ways to say, "It's not about me."

It's not about me, it's about homosexuals. It's not about me, it's about drug users. It's not about me, it's about a "high-risk population."

But the terrible truth is that AIDS is marching through the general population. There are no walls. It is about all of us.

Beyond simple avoidance, other issues and shoes will fall before mainstream society confronts the disease. There is the unfaithful partner who puts his or her unwitting full-time sexual partner or future children at risk. The disease obligates human beings to re-examine the very deepest roots of their own personalities and morals.

When word spread that basketball star Earvin "Magic" Johnson was HIV positive, the reflexive attempts to build walls around him began. Was he an intravenous drug user or a bisexual? The answers to both questions seem to be a resounding no.

Mr. Johnson's own discussion of how he contracted the disease has been a bit circumlocutory so far, but he must be allowed a certain margin for having dealt well, otherwise, with a painful event in his life. In the courageous role Mr. Johnson has chosen for himself now, as a spokesman and symbol for AIDS prevention, he will do the most good by being as candid as he can about how he got the disease.

One of the greatest impediments to AIDS prevention is to believe it cannot happen to you. If Magic Johnson can help reverse that, he will have accomplished a great good on Earth.

DESERET·NEWS
Salt Lake City, Utah, November 8, 1991

As the grim news about Magic Johnson spread Thursday, the reaction was always the same — and appropriately so: Initial incredulity, followed quickly by shock and sadness.

How incredible that the public image of a world-famous athlete evidently could be so much at odds with the kind of private life associated with the usual ways of becoming HIV-positive, which eventually leads to the always-fatal AIDS.

How sad that such a great athletic career has been cut short by an ailment that is bound to mar but cannot eclipse the memory of his remarkable basketball achievements.

Yet how admirable is Johnson's optimism in striving to cope with the effects of the virus — and how commendable is his frankness in openly acknowledging the nature of his ailment.

By going public, he has focused new attention on the stern fact that HIV is no respecter of social or economic class. He has stimulated awareness on how to avoid this dreaded ailment, the most certain ways being adherence to the norms of traditional morality, including the avoidance of illicit drug injections.

May his announcement also give new impetus to efforts to raise funds for research and treatment of HIV and AIDS.

The dimensions of the challenge keep growing alarmingly. When actor Rock Hudson died of AIDS in October of 1985, there were 13,611 reported cases of AIDS in the United States, 6,944 of the victims had died, and the case rate was doubling about every nine months.

As of today, an estimated 1 million to 1.5 million Americans are infected with the virus, and some 200,000 have come down with the disease. There are still no known cures for AIDS. But a growing number of drugs are available to treat AIDS-related ailments, and many people with AIDS can expect to live years longer than they might have only a few years ago.

When Americans look back on the amazing career of Magic Johnson, let them remember not just a long and impressive record of triumphs on the basketball court and the sad way it ended. Let them also remember with compassion the optimism and candor with which he helped heighten public awareness and concern about a deadly disease.

THE INDIANAPOLIS NEWS
Indianapolis, Indiana, November 12, 1991

Magic Johnson's admission to the world last week that he is infected with the virus that causes AIDS may end up inspiring some good developments for AIDS public awareness and research.

The 32-year-old Los Angeles Lakers basketball marvel announced to the press last week that a recent blood test for a life insurance policy had revealed the presence of the HIV-virus. On the advice of his doctors, Magic is quitting basketball.

News travels fast when its subject is a popular, world-class athlete. After Magic's public disclosure, phones at Indianapolis health clinics were ringing off the hook from callers fearing HIV exposure and registering to be tested.

The Indiana University Medical Center's Bell Flower Clinic, which specializes in the diagnosis and treatment of sexually transmitted disease, says its daily calls have more than doubled since Magic's announcement.

The American Social Health Association, which operates the National AIDS Hotline, reported that more than 7,000 people called within the hour following Magic's press conference Thursday night.

Newspapers in Australia, Israel, Italy and Japan published the story as front page news.

Although Magic and his wife are on a vacation, President George Bush has announced that he plans to offer Johnson a position as a member of the National Commission on AIDS. Certainly Johnson's acceptance of the post would bring issues of AIDS testing, research and public awareness back into the world limelight.

Belinda Mason, a former Indiana resident and the only AIDS-infected commission member, died Sept. 9 from AIDS complications.

Regardless of Magic's future plans, his skill on the basketball court will always be held in high esteem. So will his remarkable courage in the face of this personal tragedy.

But one point has been missing in all of the discussion and response to this shattering development.

So-called "safe sex" is not necessarily safe. The most sophisticated forms of protection don't always work. Plenty of studies have identified the continuing risks.

The safest approach is what is set forth in the Scriptures: abstinence until marriage. That is a high standard, rejected by Hollywood and the entertainment media, not always followed even by heroes in Scripture like King David.

But it is the standard that ought to be reasserted in the wake of the tragic news about Magic Johnson.

It also happens to be the standard set forth in Indiana for teaching family values in public education.

SYRACUSE
HERALD·JOURNAL
Syracuse, New York, November 10, 1991

So life is going to go on for me, and I'm going to be a happy man.

The words are Earvin "Magic" Johnson's. The character they depict remains the only thing more extraordinary than the poetry he made with a basketball.

Just when we thought no news could shock anymore, Johnson announced last week that he was retiring from the Los Angeles Lakers because he had tested positive for the virus that causes AIDS.

President Bush's first reaction got right to the point: "Oh, it's sad," he said. "Good man."

The depth of that goodness was never more clear than it was at Thursday's press conference. There Magic Johnson stood, all 6 feet, 9 inches of him. Just a day after learning that he had tested positive for human immuno-deficiency virus, he spoke about the worst news of his life in positive terms. He even managed the famous smile.

Lesser men would have bowed to self-pity and looked for a place to hide. Johnson charged before the press with the facts, just like he always had charged down basketball courts. And, not surprisingly, the player known for dishing off assists so teammates could score, spoke about assisting the AIDS cause, with speeches about safe sex across the nation.

Los Angeles Major Tom Bradley said Johnson's was the worst personal news for him since President Kennedy's assassination. "It was like someone hit me in the stomach with a 300-pound hammer." The comparison was apt. And we certainly felt our stomachs give when the wire services tapped out the words that our minds interpreted against the wishes of our hearts.

Johnson is a hero at a time when few remain. Why else would newspapers from England to Australia devote front-page headlines to his announcement. And the attention clearly had more to do with him as a person than a player. A Spanish story described him as "an upright, honest and human sportsman."

This is such a strange twist. We can only hope it will prove a turning point in the fight against AIDS. Certainly the disease never has had a spokesman of Johnson's stature.

"This tragic news is going to hopefully have an unprecedented impact on the invincibility and sense of denial felt by most Americans," said Dr. Mervyn Silverman, president of the American Foundation for AIDS Research. "I wouldn't wish this on anybody, but perhaps this will help some of our youth from ending up in the same situation."

So far, nothing has worked to stop this disease. A miracle might be needed. We hope Magic will be sufficient. His approach already speaks powerfully:

"I think sometimes we think, well, only gay people can get it, it's not going to happen to me. And here I am saying that it can happen to anybody. Even me, Magic Johnson, it could happen to."

THE
DENVER POST

Denver, Colorado, November 8, 1991

THE AIDS VIRUS respects no boundaries — not race, not income, not sexual preference. If you are exposed to it, you can get it.

Today the world understands that more clearly than it did 24 hours ago. It has prematurely ended the remarkable career of Earvin "Magic" Johnson, one of the three or four greatest players in the history of basketball.

Because Johnson has been idolized around the world by adults, teenagers and children of all races on all continents, news of his fate was flashed around the globe Thursday afternoon. And with the news came a heightened awareness of this awful disease.

As long as the disease is viewed by most people as a threat only to homosexuals, or only to drug abusers who use contaminated needles, or only to people who have sex with prostitutes, we will always be surprised that it strikes someone like Magic Johnson.

The stark truth is that if you have sex with multiple partners, you increase your chances of getting the virus. That's the simple, straightforward truth.

There is no absolute guard against getting the virus — not even so-called "safe sex" precautions — among promiscuous sexual partners.

If Magic Johnson's experience can help drive home that lesson, his personal tragedy will benefit untold numbers of others. As a spokesman for the AIDS cause, Johnson can do more for public education about the disease than any government program, any school-based campaign, any TV crusade.

But it's no longer just enough to talk about the importance of "safe sex," as Johnson did yesterday. He must also talk about responsible sex, and that includes more restrained attitudes about casual and promiscuous sexual practices.

Johnson showed tremendous courage and strength in his first public announcement. However, he needs to expand his message beyond the common definition of "safe sex" — primarily, the use of condoms — and talk just as forcefully about the risks of any casual sex.

As Johnson now knows, it can be a matter of life and death, and there is no magic immunity.

The Register-Guard

Eugene, Oregon, November 9, 1991

Sports heroes are role models, and none has played the part better then Earvin "Magic" Johnson. The NBA superstar's off-court charm and generosity have been as admirable as his dazzling athletic ability. Now Johnson will act as an example of another kind — an example of the fact that AIDS does not discriminate.

Johnson announced Thursday that he is retiring at the peak of his basketball career because he carries the HIV virus, which causes Acquired Immune Deficiency Syndrome. He said he would become a spokesman for AIDS prevention, and began by urging young people to practice safe sex.

In the United States, the HIV virus is spread primarily through unprotected homosexual contact or through the sharing of intravenous needles. Gays and drug users are marginal groups in American society, and a broad current of opinion holds that they deserve whatever fate befalls them. Those attitudes have attached a stigma to AIDS and have hindered rational discussion of how the disease can be prevented.

Johnson carries no such stigma. His great physical talent is universally admired. The riches, fame and glamour his ability brought him are envied. His sincere smile, his charitable work and his respect for his fans made him a genuinely likable hero in a world of spoiled celebrities. Now that this well-loved figure has tested positive for the HIV virus and has told the world about it, people should have a harder time scorning those with AIDS.

Johnson did not say at his news conference Thursday how he contracted the virus. As Johnson embarks on a campaign to warn people of the risk of AIDS, greater frankness about his own case would be helpful. AIDS is preventable — by taking sensible precautions or abstaining from risky behavior. Johnson can serve the cause of public health by telling people what kind of carelessness cost him his career and, unless a cure is found, will cost him his life.

People can, however, remain healthy for years while carrying the HIV virus. Johnson's new career as an AIDS educator could last even longer than his career in basketball. In that time he'll have an opportunity to save an untold number of lives. It's a big job, but by showing that no one — not even Magic Johnson — can ignore the risk of AIDS, he has already begun.

THE 〰 SUN

Baltimore, Maryland, November 9, 1991

Earvin "Magic" Johnson is not alone. The U.S. Centers for Disease Control estimates 1 million to 1.5 million Americans have the HIV virus. Officials from the Agency for International Development told a House committee over six million Africans have the virus, too — one out of every 40 adult Africans. Under the present state of medical knowledge, every one of them will get AIDS and die.

The AIDS epidemic is going to get much worse in this country before it can diminish. As of Sept. 30, CDC received reports of 195,718 American AIDS cases in a decade, and 126,159 AIDS deaths. That leaves 69,559 active cases, and roughly 20 times as many more Americans who have the virus and are fated to contract AIDS.

If Magic Johnson can get AIDS — and he will — anyone can. They don't make an athletic shoe that protects you from it. You can be one of the greatest players who ever graced the game of basketball, make the best passes in the world, play with amazing gifts, skill, intelligence, dedication and joy. You can make $3 million a year to do what you love, and three times as much to endorse harmless products. None of that can save you. A condom with spermicide probably would, or a sterilized needle.

In his announcement of retirement and doom, Magic Johnson brought the same positive attitude that made him a champion on the basketball court. It shocked a million young players in mid-dribble. But he is not slinking off. He means to go out of the world as he came into adulthood, a celebrity and genial instructor. Only instead of saying, "be like me if you can," he is saying, "don't do what I did."

Education has reduced the AIDS contamination among American male homosexuals and somewhat among drug users. Transmission from contaminated blood transfusion has largely stopped. Infection from a health practitioner is statistically infinitesimal. But in Africa, the main transmission is from sex between men and women. And in this country, the number infected through heterosexual sex is an estimated 10 percent of all cases compared to less than 3 percent five years ago. It is easier for men to give it to women than women to men, but 4,321 American men who have the disease got it from women.

Though Magic Johnson may not yet know when, he and the Los Angeles Lakers team physician implied that he contracted HIV from incautious heterosexual activity. So it is as an endorser of safe-sex practices that he will end his public career: "And here I am saying that it can happen to anybody. Even me, Magic Johnson, it could happen to." The safest sexual practice is abstinence, the second safest is faithfulness and the next safest after that is a condom plus spermicide. Magic Johnson is going to be the greatest condom salesman of all time. He is turning his tragedy into instruction, and as a cautionary tale he is fast-breaking into the safe-sex hall of fame.

The Times-Picayune

New Orleans, Louisiana, November 9, 1991

In announcing that he has tested positive for the AIDS virus and is retiring from basketball, Earvin "Magic" Johnson characteristically elected to share his personal tribulation with his large extended family of admiring fans.

The gifted athlete, whose life-affirming career is one of the brightest chapters in the history of the National Basketball Association, is widely respected and loved as much for who he is as for what he does.

And as every sports fan knows, what the Los Angeles Lakers superstar does is play the round ball game with surpassing skill and boundless enthusiasm. The charismatic point guard's ball handling and leadership on the court have carried the Lakers to five championships.

But Magic's appeal reaches far beyond his Los Angeles stomping ground. Around the world, children wear T-shirts bearing his image. Recently, he was mobbed by fans when the Lakers played in Paris.

At Thursday's press conference, Magic's trademark smile and sense of humor underscored his upbeat attitude. Although expressing his disappointment at having to hang up No. 32 permanently, the Lakers' consummate team player sought to reassure his admirers, saying, "I plan to go on living for a long time."

He added that he would become a spokesman in the campaign for safe sex.

Magic was accompanied by team physician, Dr. Michael Mellman, who said the Laker star doesn't have AIDS, only the virus that leads to it.

Television basketball analyst Al McGuire, a former coach at Marquette University, seemed to sum up the hopes of many that the pride of the Lakers will become a powerful crusader in the war against AIDS. "I wish that somehow, maybe this could push our research development quicker into possible answers for AIDS," he said.

Off the court, Magic was equally larger than life. The hats he wore with distinction were those of philanthropist, corporate spokesman and role model for young people. He has been a generous supporter of such worthwhile causes as the United Negro College Fund, Musclar Dystrophy, City of Hope and the American Heart Association.

Magic's exciting and unselfish style of playmaking is the stuff of basketball legends. The deep respect his fellow players have for him stems in large measure from their understanding that he would rather see them score and look good than make a basket himself.

Magic acted with typical courage and dignity in disclosing the nature of his condition. We join his many friends and fans in hoping that the closing of the door to one rewarding world will soon be followed by the opening of a window to another.

THE CHRISTIAN SCIENCE MONITOR
Boston, Massachusetts, November 14, 1991

HEALING demands compassion. And one problem surrounding the AIDS epidemic has been a lack of compassion in the mainstream of society for victims of the disease. The people afflicted with AIDS were too easily categorized as a separate segment of the population, distant from the heterosexual, non-drug-using majority.

That has long been an oversimplification. But Magic Johnson's dramatic announcement that he's infected with the AIDS virus should help put that perception to rest for good.

Here is a man who has personified many sound values – he's hard working and likable. While he, like many other NBA stars, may have succumbed to the fast life of the pro basketball tour, the Laker star set a standard for decency on the court and in his treatment of his fans.

Would he be someone to shun and isolate because he has been touched by this disease – the way victims ranging from homeless junkies to innocent schoolchildren have been shunned?

AIDS has generated fear, even hysteria, along with its suffering – fear that has kept people from getting the compassionate care they need.

Johnson's first impulse on learning of his infection was to commit himself to helping others protect themselves. "Safe sex" is the byword of AIDS prevention. It's a reasonable, practical path for many – a step toward greater responsibility for oneself and others. The message needs to be reinforced, and Johnson's words should help.

The message of abstinence before marriage and rejection of promiscuity must also be reinforced.

AIDS presents society with multiple challenges – social, medical, ethical. Each individual can take a step toward meeting those challenges by finding the compassion to recognize the worth of others regardless of their affliction.

THE RICHMOND NEWS LEADER
Richmond, Virginia, November 11, 1991

On Friday night's Arsenio Hall Show, Magic Johnson urged the audience "to practice safe sex, start using condoms, and be aware."

Johnson's courage and grace are extraordinary — and much to be admired. He defines champion in just about every sense of the word.

Yet better advice regarding AIDS comes from Vice President Dan Quayle, who — after praising Johnson — said:

"If there is something I can do, it is not to encourage young people to practice safe sex, but to emphasize abstinence. That's a sure [defense]."

It's the *only* way to prevent sexually transmitted AIDS.

The State
Columbia, South Carolina, November 12, 1991

THERE are very few athletes who transcend the narrow world in which they perform. The ones who do are special. One such is Magic Johnson, the legendary Los Angeles Lakers point guard and long-time goodwill ambassador for professional basketball.

Cruel circumstances thrust him into the limelight before TV cameras Thursday — a solitary figure of remarkable self-possession, conceding without a flinch that, yes, the deadly AIDS virus was in his system and he must retire from a sport to which he had given so much.

It was a dark moment, to be sure, but Magic Johnson was having none of it. Upbeat to a fault, he said he will be telling people, especially kids, about the dangers of AIDS and ways of preventing its spread. While declining to respond to questions about how he contracted the disease, it was revealed through a Lakers official that the virus was transmitted through a heterosexual relationship.

Mr. Johnson said the virus that has infected his system is a challenge against which he vowed "to come out swinging."

There have been few live moments on TV so poignant, so personal. It was quite simply a genuine profile in courage.

The Philadelphia Inquirer / TONY AUTH

Rockford Register Star

Rockford, Illinois, November 10, 1991

"It can happen to anybody, even me, Magic Johnson."

When those words were first spoken last Thursday afternoon, they instantly sent shock waves through American society. An icon of our popular culture, an athletic wizard with a winning personality and a broad smile, a good guy by anybody's measure, suddenly had declared that he had contracted the dreaded AIDS virus.

Then, as the disbelief that this could happen to Magic Johnson gave way to the reality that it had, the gravity of the man's universal message began to take hold in millions of minds: It can happen to anybody.

Incredibly, Johnson's grace in announcing this personal tragedy was every bit as great as that with which he played basketball for the Los Angeles Lakers for 12 seasons. It had been only one day since he first learned of the situation himself, yet he displayed not a trace of self-pity. Instead, he cheerfully dedicated himself to helping educate the public about AIDS and the virus that causes it.

As one of Magic's National Basketball Association colleagues put it, God could not have chosen a better spokesman for the cause of fighting AIDS and promoting greater public understanding of the plight of its victims. Amen.

The first lesson we all must draw from this tragedy is the one on which Magic Johnson already has lectured: It can happen to anybody.

AKRON BEACON JOURNAL
Akron, Ohio, November 12, 1991

The first shock waves at news of basketball star Earvin "Magic" Johnson's affliction are receding. As on other such stunning occasions, the extent of media coverage prompts many to wonder why it takes a celebrity to keep national concern focused on containing the spread of HIV, the viral infection that causes AIDS.

Reaction to the stunning news of Johnson's infection shows how far we've come in understanding AIDS and how it is contracted, how far we have to go collectively in finding a cure and what personal responsibility we have to prevent infection.

A number of signs stand out that we are making headway, but with the hopeful signs must go caution.

One significant point is news that tests of experimental AIDS vaccines may be two years away. The vaccines are to be tested on volunteers in Brazil, Rwanda, Thailand and Uganda. According to the World Health Organization, the trials on people will bypass the usual, lengthy testing on animals because health officials are discouraged by the inability to stop the spread of AIDS, with an estimated 11 million infected worldwide.

Pressing on with testing, in such demoralizing circumstances, is understandable. The same impetus to do something is behind the announced intention of the U.S. Food and Drug Administration to speed up its prescription-drug marketing procedures. Whether it is bypassing animal testing or streamlining procedures of drug approval, there is always the danger that inadequately tested vaccines or drugs could be used on desperate people. Hopes may be falsely raised, undercutting trust in medical products and processes crucial to containing AIDS.

■

Two other reports, perhaps trivial in comparison, demonstrate the value of celebrity impact. The coverage of Magic Johnson's HIV infection is bound to fall off soon. This is no cynical comment on Magic's personal tragedy or of the horror of AIDS. It's only a reflection of our hyperactive information world, which turns most events into three-day wonders. The hope is that before we move on to other interests, the intense focus on AIDS since Thursday would have made a lasting contribution.

Magic's celebrity coattails presumably are working already.

Monday's Wall Street Journal reported a boost in the stocks of manufacturers and biotechnology companies researching AIDS-related products. The stock market isn't an index of moral commitment, but it shows where the money is moving. If investors' instincts are accurate, AIDS-related research should have the capital for more work.

Advertisers are notorious for dropping spokesmen and women at the hint of any taint. But the Wall Street Journal reports that Converse, and other companies whose products Magic Johnson endorses, are planning AIDS-awareness campaigns in support of Magic's role as an educator. Corporate involvement in stressing personal responsibility adds needed weight.

THE BILLINGS GAZETTE
Billings, Montana, November 11, 1991

Who says America has no heroes?

We hear that complaint a lot, delivered with an unqualified, undebatable certainty, and there is some truth in it.

GAZETTE OPINION

We have few political heroes. Recent revelations show that politicians of both parties have clay feet all the way to their chins.

But we have military heroes. The Iraqi war delivered Gens. Colin Powell and "Stormin" Norman Schwartzkopf to us wrapped in red, white and blue bunting.

Certainly, we have sports heroes, sports heroes like Earvin "Magic" Johnson.

Johnson, slam dunker, dazzler, play maker, is "Magic" on the basketball court. He holds three Most Valuable Player awards. He is a team player with the league record for assists. That shows in the fact that Magic's Los Angeles Lakers have won five NBA championships.

Certainly, Magic Johnson is a YUPPIE hero. His salary is $3.1 million annually. He earns another $9 million in endorsements.

But Johnson is more. He has an intangible charisma. Something shines in him, on and off the court, something that makes Pepsi and and Kentucky Fried Chicken and others willing to pay $9 million a year just to stand in his shadow.

And now we find that Magic Johnson has the HIV virus. He doesn't have AIDS, yet, but it seems inevitable that he will.

He makes the revelation in public — that's appropriate, most of his life has been spent in public — and he does so with such class that people talk about him in whispered tones.

And he does something that no one else has been able to do. He makes us realize for the first time that all of us are susceptible to this dreaded killer, ordinary person and hero, heterosexual and homosexual, drug users and drug-free, alike.

Johnson says he will spend the rest of his life fighting this disease, trying to make America aware of the dangers it poses, trying to galvanize this country to action,

Magic Johnson was on five NBA championship teams. He is "Magic" on the basketball court and off. He is a bona fide American hero. If anyone can win this one, he can. God help us, if he can't.

CHICAGO Sun-Times
Chicago, Illinois, November 12, 1991

Yes, Earvin "Magic" Johnson should be named to the National Commission on AIDS, as Health and Human Services Secretary Louis W. Sullivan proposes.

The White House would be hard-pressed to find a more inspired—and inspiring—candidate for the vacancy created by the death of AIDS patient Belinda Mason.

The retired Los Angeles Lakers superstar has already galvanized the sports and political worlds with his announcement that he is infected with the AIDS virus.

Congressmen are trying to free more money for AIDS research, condom companies' stock prices are up and other athletes are offering to help Johnson get his message across. Teenagers are talking about using more "caution" in their social behavior.

Black ministers, long criticized for their reluctance to address the issue from their pulpits, broke their silence after hearing the news about America's engagingly courageous hero.

There is enormous potential here for making a difference with athletes and the very young, who tend to think of themselves as invulnerable and leave such worries to others.

"This could be the spark," as the Rev. Zan Holmes in Houston put it Sunday, "that will bring unity among the African American churches and wake people up to the dangers of AIDS."

A seat on the commission would provide a highly visible platform for Johnson, who has already said he would like to become a national spokesman for AIDS prevention.

If the magic man is willing, that seat should be his.

The Courier-Journal
Louisville, Kentucky, November 19, 1991

WHAT a tragedy. One can only hope that the superhuman sense of timing that told Magic Johnson when to shoot and when to pass will now tell his body how to conquer AIDS — or at least how to hang on until scientists find a cure. The possibility that he will triumph over AIDS isn't unthinkable. After all, the man has soared over every other kind of hurdle.

His retirement from the Los Angeles Lakers hits where it hurts — in the hearts of millions of fans. He is the world ambassador of basketball who does everything with class. Taking his final bow from pro basketball proved no exception. The courage with which he spoke out about AIDS on Thursday was stunning. Surely his candor and personal bravery will help shatter misconceptions about the disease and erase its terrible stigma. "[If] it can happen to Magic Johnson," he said, "it can happen to anybody." Indeed.

May his courage inspire others living with AIDS and their loved ones. May it also hasten the development of a cure for this terrible disease.

The Grand Rapids Press
Grand Rapids, Michigan, November 12, 1991

Though Magic Johnson is unlikely to emerge a winner over AIDS, he already has scored a significant victory over ignorance and apathy about the disease.

Part of that is in the simple fact of his fame, particularly his celebrity among young people. In saying that "It happened to me, it can happen to you," Mr. Johnson made a point like no other person has in this country's experience with AIDS. The fact that he seemingly contracted the infection through heterosexual relations helps to break down the common presumption that this affliction is transmittable only among homosexuals and drug users.

For those things he is due great credit. Mr. Johnson's candor and public grace about having the AIDS virus are nothing to take for granted. He could more easily have faded away quietly, without exposing his personal life to public scrutiny and discussion. Surely he had no obligation to take on a national campaign against AIDS, as he has committed himself to doing.

By remaining in the public eye and continuing to live in a near normal way, he also will help to teach that AIDS-afflicted people can remain useful in society. It will be apparent to many millions of Americans that an AIDS victim is not a monster, not a fit subject for discrimination or rejection, and isn't a danger to everyone else on the elevator or in the washroom. And in calling attention to how the disease is passed, he can emphasize how it is *not* passed – not by handshakes, sneezes, contact with toilet seats or any of the other common forms of interaction in workplaces and public buildings.

More attention to those facets of AIDS can relieve some of the public fear about its victims and perhaps prevent unreasonable bias toward them. Just as a rational society must be realistic about AIDS, a compassionate one must care for the disease's victims. Mr. Johnson can help the United States be both.

Senate Passes Medical Disclosure Bills

The Senate July 18, 1991 passed two bills that would regulate the work of doctors infected with the AIDS virus.

The first measure, sponsored by Sen. Jesse Helms (R, N.C.), would mandate criminal sanctions for health workers who knew they were infected with the HIV virus, which caused AIDS, and who performed invasive procedures on patients without informing them. It was passed by a vote of 81-18. The second bill, passed 99-0, would virtually require states to test medical workers who performed invasive procedures for AIDS, or risk losing federal health funding.

(Invasive procedures included surgery and other procedures that involved work in any of the body's cavities.)

The danger of AIDS transmission from health workers had become the subject of increasing media attention and public worry in the preceding months. The issue had been fueled by reports concerning the only known case of AIDS transmission from a health worker, in which a Florida dentist had infected five of his patients.

The Helms bill would mandate minimum sentences of 10 years in prison and fines of up to $10,000 for health workers who failed to inform patients of their AIDS status.

The second bill, which was put forward by Senate leaders, was originally presented as an attempt to replace the Helms bill, but it ended up being passed in addition to that measure. The leadership bill required states to adopt the guidelines for health workers set earlier in the week by the Centers for Disease Control. It would bar those who tested positive for AIDS from performing invasive procedures without the permission of both the patient and a panel of experts. The measure would also apply to those infected with hepatitis B, a potentially fatal liver disease.

Regardless of whether either of the bills was eventually signed into law, the Senate action was expected to impel hospitals to enact much stricter AIDS-safety measures, according to health officials quoted July 19 in the *New York Times*.

The Helms bill was widely criticized by health experts and AIDS activists as calling for a huge allocation of resources to a tiny source of danger, and for setting sanctions that could be counterproductive. "This is what happens when politicians decide that the way to respond to panic and fear among their constituents is with panic and fear among themselves," said Donald Goldman of the National Commission on AIDS.

But W. Shepard Smith Jr., president of Americans for a Sound AIDS Policy, said public concern was understandable. Most Americans "face their greatest risk of acquiring HIV only through blood transfusion and in the health-care setting," he said. "The least likely mode of transmission overall is, in fact, the most likely mode of transmission for most people."

The U.S. Centers for Disease Control July 15 issued a set of guidelines on health-care workers and AIDS. The recommendations said that dentists, doctors and others performing invasive procedures should find out if they had AIDS, but rejected calls for mandatory testing. In addition, the CDC said that health workers who tested positive should stop performing invasive, "exposure-prone" procedures unless they obtained the permission of a panel of experts and informed their patients. The guidelines also applied to hepatitis B.

CDC officials said there was no reason to restrict the practice of noninvasive procedures by AIDS-infected doctors, and that notification of patients of a doctor's AIDS-status was unnecessary in such cases.

The policy also recommended strict enforcement of standard precautions against infection, such as sterilization of instruments, the wearing of gloves, and proper disposal of waste.

The guidelines did not have the force of law, but they were expected to be influential among health workers and for policy-setters such as state medical boards.

The Atlanta Journal AND THE ATLANTA CONSTITUTION
Atlanta, Georgia, July 20, 1991

A good deal of the hysteria that initially surrounded AIDS has died down. But there is a sure way to make fear of the disease flare anew. Just put out the word that a doctor or dentist has AIDS.

Many communities have faced that situation. Just a few days ago, Georgia's Board of Dentistry suspended a dentist and began notifying his patients that he may have AIDS. The action was appropriate not only because the case involves AIDS, but because the board had reliable information that mental dysfunction undermined the dentist's ability to take precautions against infecting patients.

In the most notorious case yet — and the only one in which a health-care worker has been shown to transmit AIDS to patients — Florida dentist David Acer infected five of his patients. The incident brought emotional public calls for stricter safeguards.

The federal Centers for Disease Control (CDC), recommending guidelines for health-care workers, has avoided extremism in the face of public pressure. Unfortunately, the U.S. Senate has not, passing a Jesse Helms proposal to jail AIDS-infected health care workers who perform invasive procedures without first warning patients. This will only discourage doctors from taking AIDS tests.

The CDC guidelines call for voluntary AIDS testing for doctors and dentists who perform "invasive" procedures in which the patient might accidentally be exposed to the health-care worker's blood. A doctor or dentist who tests positive should refrain from performing such procedures unless permission is granted from a special medical review committee and the patient is informed.

The CDC errs on the side of moderation. It rejected mandatory testing of health-care workers mainly because the risk of transmission of AIDS to a patient is believed to be as low as 1 chance in 2.6 million. Yet it concedes that the risk is highest for certain procedures, and that testing in those disciplines is a good idea.

If that is so, mandatory testing for doctors who perform those procedures — and the patients who undergo them — also is a good idea. The credibility of the health-care system is at issue; its maintenance is worth limited mandatory testing for those in high-risk practices.

THE SUN

Baltimore, Maryland, July 24, 1991

Hysteria does not make for good medical policies. An unfortunate example of the hysteria surrounding the acquired immune deficiency syndrome, surfacing just as many in Congress prepare to face elections, is the Senate's recent passage of two bills concerning health workers with AIDS.

The first, backed by the leaders of both parties, would direct the states to require health professionals doing "invasive" procedures to submit to tests for human immunodeficiency virus infection. That bill, crafted with a close eye on the new guidelines published by the Atlanta-based Centers for Disease Control, also requires review by a panel of experts before an infected person can perform dental extractions, bone or abdominal surgery, obstetric and gynecological procedures, heart and blood-vessel catheterization or other procedures. Mandating action by state medical societies against practitioners who violate its guidelines, the bill puts teeth into what otherwise would be a tame rendition of a doctor's ethical responsibility to the patients. So it is not surprising that major professional societies and AIDS advocacy groups have either backed this bill or expressed no serious opposition to it.

The second, backed by North Carolina Sen. Jesse Helms, would vest the final authority for a doctor's decisions in the Justice Department. It would mandate prison terms of at least 10 years and fines up to $10,000 for health-care workers who knew they had AIDS but failed to inform patients on whom they performed invasive procedures. Passed 81-18, this is a bill many senators probably supported rather than face the fears and confusion many of their constituents express about AIDS.

With five confirmed AIDS cases stemming from the infection of Florida dentist David J. Acer before he died, members of the American public are anxious about the possibility of catching AIDS from a medical worker. And simply repeating that those five infections add up to a minuscule proportion of the 182,000 AIDS cases since the disease was identified in 1981 cannot reassure everyone. No one wants to be No. 6 out of 200,000.

But a hysterical hunt to find infected medical workers and slap "quarantine" restrictions on their activities is not the answer, even if it appeals to Mr. Helms. The better answer, expressed in the Senate leadership bill, puts a rigorous medical review in between the patient and any infected professional and mandates disciplinary action for those who fail to comply with its guidelines. The witch-hunt answer might warm Mr. Helms' heart, but it could drive people who suspect they are infected to illegal, dangerous attempts to hide the evidence. And it would add new misery to the lives of people whose term on earth is already foreshortened by this terrible disease. This is one piece of Senate business the House should reject summarily.

The Des Moines Register

Des Moines, Iowa, July 23, 1991

Despite the near-panic once generated by fears of the "drug menace," no one ever seriously proposed mandatory prison sentences for doctors who knowingly operate while under the influence of heroin or cocaine. But last week the U.S. Senate overwhelmingly adopted a law providing 10-year prison terms for a health worker who knows he or she has AIDS but fails to tell that to a patient prior to surgery or dental work.

The law was the brainchild of North Carolina's gift to the Dark Ages, Senator Jesse Helms, whose target, he said, was the "rogues in the medical community who have knowingly and callously exposed hundreds upon hundreds of innocent people to the AIDS virus."

In truth, the number known to have been thus infected is five, not "hundreds and hundreds," and all were patients of a single Florida dentist, not Helms' ghost platoon of "rogues."

The Senate also passed a more moderate and reasonable measure that forces states to require surgeons and others who could contaminate a patient's blood to undergo testing for AIDS. Those who test positive could not perform invasive procedures without approval of a health panel and informed consent of the patient. Failure to comply would mean discipline by a state licensing board.

Neither measure will solve the problem of medical transmission of AIDS; as with a few hundred other diseases, there are an endless number of ways the virus can get past inadequate defenses or careless guards, and the bills deal with only one possible contamination source. But the latter measure is a reasonable attempt to plug another avenue for infection. The Helms bill simply tosses a bone to the hysterical.

The nature of AIDS has made it unique among medical phenomena. The voices of politicians and moralists have all but drowned out the counsel of the scientists who are in the best position to understand it.

Chicago Tribune

Chicago, Illinois, July 21, 1991

How do you make sure that doctors, dentists and other health-care workers infected with the AIDS virus don't pass the deadly infection on to their patients?

You ask them nicely, the American Medical Association's policymakers said, in essence, in June. They voted that health-care workers who think they might be infected should have themselves tested, please, and those who are HIV-positive should voluntarily stop doing invasive procedures unless their patients are informed and consent.

Last Monday, the Centers for Disease Control, after stalling for months, also decided on an ask-nicely approach. The CDC recommended voluntary testing of doctors, dentists and other health-care workers who do what it calls "exposure-prone" procedures. Those found to be infected with HIV are urged to stop doing such work unless they have the approval of an expert review panel and their patients are notified.

But the U.S. Senate hasn't been in a mood to ask nicely. On Thursday, by a vote of 81 to 18, it approved a proposal by Sen. Jesse Helms to impose a prison term of at least 10 years and a fine of up to $10,000 on doctors, dentists and other health-care workers who know they are infected and continue performing invasive treatments without telling patients.

Senators then passed, by 99 to 0, a second measure, backed by Senate leaders, that would require states to adopt the CDC's guidelines within a year or lose millions of dollars in federal Public Health Service grants. Health-care workers who fail to comply would be subject to discipline by the state's licensing agency and could lose their licenses to practice. Bush administration officials support this bill.

So much for asking nicely.

The Senate tacked its measures onto a multi-purpose appropriations bill that the House has already approved without the AIDS provisions. A conference committee is expected to work out the differences.

The Helms penalties aren't likely to survive in the final version of the bill because the Bush administration has already agreed to accept the less stringent provisions. But legislators with their eyes on public-opinion polls know the vast majority of American people aren't willing to trust in voluntary compliance and, despite valid objections, want tight, mandatory controls on HIV-infected health-care personnel.

Opponents of non-voluntary regulations say that although 6,436 health-care workers are reported to have full-blown AIDS, only one—the Florida dentist who infected five patients—is known to have passed on the virus in the course of treatment. Scrupulous use of universal protective measures should prevent the virus from spreading, health officials insist—except, perhaps, in the case of accidental needle-sticks or scalpel nickings during invasive procedures. Besides, they add, testing isn't a total protection; a person may be infected—and infectious—for as long as six months before the standard HIV test registers as positive. It is not clear how often repeat testing should be required.

But a case can no longer be made for just asking HIV-infected health-care workers nicely not to take risks with their patients' health, while allowing them to protect their jobs and their privacy. Several cases have now been reported in which dentists and doctors who must have known they had full-blown AIDS have continued to perform invasive procedures. After they died from AIDS, their patients have been offered HIV testing—a sad substitute for the protection these patients should have had.

(The Illinois General Assembly this week passed legislation requiring the state to notify the patients of a health-care worker who may have exposed them to the AIDS virus—again doing nothing directly to prevent the danger of exposure. Health-care personnel are also to be warned about patients who have AIDS. But the state does not know the identities of people who are infected with HIV but do not yet have full-blown AIDS. So whatever protection this legislation provides will be very limited.)

The Helms legislation with its prison terms and fines is unnecessarily harsh. The compromise measure makes more sense. Revoking a health-care worker's license to practice is an appropriate penalty and does help protect patients.

Granted, the Senate has acted largely in response to public-opinion polls and exaggerated fears of the risks imposed by HIV-infected health-care workers. But politics and pressure groups have long interfered with efforts by public health officials to combat the AIDS epidemic. Maybe it's time politics provided some help for people who are not yet infected with HIV and are trying to protect themselves from it.

The Forum

Fargo, North Dakota, July 22, 1991

The problem with discussing AIDS is that in some quarters the disease is being treated as a civil rights issue, not a matter of public health.

The rights of AIDS virus carriers are important; but protecting the public from a fatal disease epidemic also is important. The dilemma is balancing the two. Add homophobia to the equation and balance is impossible.

Sen. Jesse Helms, R-N.C., is not interested in balance. He introduced and got passed in the Senate a homophobic proposal calling for a minimum 10-year prison term for health-care workers infected with the AIDS virus who treat patients without disclosing their condition. It passed because Helms frightened a majority of senators into believing that if they voted "no" the vote would be used against them politically.

The Helms measure will not cause infected health-care workers to reveal their condition. If anything, it will drive more of them to hide it. It's an unnecessarily punitive approach that Helms pushed because homosexual groups opposed it. Ever the demagogue, Helms used public homophobia as a political club over his colleagues' heads.

A second measure makes more sense. It would compel states to adopt Centers for Disease Control guidelines advising doctors and nurses who perform procedures involving exposure to blood to be tested for the AIDS virus. It has no harsh penalties, so is more likely to cause infected persons to identify themselves.

The hammer in the second bill is that states would have to adopt the guidelines or risk losing millions of dollars in federal public health grants. Doctors who fail to comply would risk discipline by state medical licensing boards.

So rather than punishing people who have the virus — as Helms would do — the bipartisan compromise would help identify infected health-care workers and then establish procedures to protect the public.

The passage of the unworkable Helms bill and the more sensible compromise reveals the Senate's lack of courage on the AIDS issue. The Helms bill should have been killed; it's an attack on people who are afflicted with a terrible disease, not a serious approach to protecting the public from the spread of AIDS.

Both bills now go to the House of Representatives. We hope the members of that chamber have enough backbone to embarrass Sen. Helms by killing his bill. Then they should pass the compromise legislation because it's humane and takes a strong step toward dealing with the AIDS disclosure dilemma.

TULSA WORLD

Tulsa, Oklahoma, July 22, 1991

THE U.S. Senate overwhelmingly approved measures to see that doctors and medical workers who might accidentally spread the AIDS virus are tested for the disease.

The senators passed a strong amendment offered by Sen. Jesse Helms, R-N.C., providing for a 10-year prison sentence for AIDS-infected health workers who perform risky treatments without telling their patients.

The Senate left for later negotiation with the House how to deal with AIDS-infected workers.

Sen. Helms' prison sentence is unduly harsh and probably of little effect. How many AIDS-infected doctors would live to serve out such a sentence? Or, for that matter, wouldn't they be in hospitals themselves?

Whatever the final form of legislation that comes out of Congress, it seems no longer possible to avoid the issue.

Patients have the right to be treated by doctors and health-care workers free of the AIDS virus. Doctors and health-care workers should not have to treat AIDS-infected patients without knowing the patients are infected. If it were not for the politically sensitive nature of AIDS, these questions would scarcely merit debate.

The final form of the testing law is yet to be determined. But the Senate is headed in the right direction. Patients and doctors alike should have all the information — and therefore protection — they can get in fighting this dread disease.

LAS VEGAS REVIEW-JOURNAL

Las Vegas, Nevada, July 22, 1991

Doctors who know they have full-blown AIDS, or the precursor to the disease, have no business practicing invasive medical procedures unless they inform their patients of the risks. In addition, doctors have a right to know whether patients whose treatment could potentially infect health care providers carry the disease. It's as simple as that.

Just ask 23-year-old Kimberly Bergalis of Florida, now near death after contracting AIDS from a visit to her infected dentist. Her tragic case attracted national attention and spurred the Senate to act last week on the issue of AIDS and doctors.

The results were mixed.

On the positive side, the Senate unanimously voted to urge doctors and other health care workers to undergo testing for HIV, which becomes AIDS. This makes sense from both a moral and ethical viewpoint. Let's face it: A doctor who shields from his patients that he is HIV-positive, and continues to perform invasive medical techniques, spits at the Hippocratic oath. Obviously some AIDS-carrying doctors, like Bergalis' dentist, continue to work because they realize admitting their condition will devastate their medical practices. As unfair as that may be, such doctors cavalierly elevate their own welfare above the safety of their patients.

On the down side, the Senate overwhelmingly passed a proposal that would jail for at least 10 years doctors who know they are infected but continue performing invasive procedures on uninformed patients. This asinine proposal — sponsored by North Carolina's Jesse Helms — represents classic overkill. Certainly, doctors who infect patients should be civilly liable, maybe even prosecuted for negligent homicide. But keep in mind the average convicted first-degree murderer serves less than eight years. In addition, an HIV-infected doctor prosecuted under Helms' draconian statute likely won't live anywhere near 10 years, so what's the point?

At this juncture in the AIDS debacle there's only one confirmed case of a doctor transmitting HIV to patients — Bergalis' dentist, who infected at least five people. There is no need for panic. But there is also no need for patients to be put at risk by doctors who selfishly value their practice more than the health of those who feed it. The House should back the Senate's efforts, but drop the ridiculous 10-year prison term provision.

THE SACRAMENTO BEE
Sacramento, California, July 25, 1991

Doctors and other health workers owe their patients a duty of care not to do harm. Thus it was appropriate for the federal Centers for Disease Control to tell medical professionals infected with HIV virus or hepatitis B not to perform procedures where there is risk of blood-to-blood contact, or to inform their patients before doing the work. The U.S. Senate last week sensibly voted to direct the states to implement those guidelines through their licensing boards.

But there was no sense behind the Senate's passage of a contradictory amendment by Sen. Jesse Helms, which would impose a 10-year prison term on a health worker infected with HIV who knowingly performed any invasive procedure. Such an irresponsible measure, which creates a new category of criminal law directed specifically at health workers, strikes at the trust without which medical care is impossible.

Ever since the nation learned that five people in Florida were infected with HIV at the office of a dentist who subsequently died of AIDS, there has been intense fear about catching AIDS at the clinic or hospital. Yet of the million people in this country infected with HIV, health officials have identified only those five as having been infected by a health worker in a medical procedure. Investigations point to the Florida dentist's use of unsterilized equipment and improper reuse of disposable items as the most likely cause of the outbreak.

Even one such case is tragic, but the overall risk to the public of catching AIDS from a health worker is remote, and far less significant than scores of other things that go wrong at medical offices and hospitals: unneeded surgery, alcoholic doctors, wrongly prescribed medications, botched diagnoses, procedures performed by inexperienced or undertrained personnel.

Why then single out AIDS and health workers for a new criminal sanction that does not even apply to the misconduct that apparently caused the Florida infection? Because the Senate, which styles itself the world's greatest deliberative body, behaved more like a herd of cattle in a stampede. Faced with Helms' threat to run campaign ads painting opponents as tools of the "homosexual lobby," most senators abandoned their courage.

Health workers have special reason to be angry at this performance. Hysteria among the uninformed is understandable, but lawmakers should know that by far the greater AIDS risk in the medical office runs not from health worker to patient, but the other way. Hundreds of health workers have been infected with HIV in the line of duty; thousands of others put themselves at risk every day to heal and provide solace to the sick.

Without their courage, and the public's trust in their judgment, the nation's medical system could not work. Treating health workers as if they were criminals and a worrisome source of AIDS infection is a sure way to discourage them from treating AIDS at all. Is that what the Senate wants?

FORT WORTH STAR-TELEGRAM
Fort Worth, Texas, July 20, 1991

Anyone smart enough to become a doctor or dentist is smart enough to know that "invasive" surgical procedures should not be performed by a person infected with the human immunodeficiency virus, HIV.

With that in mind, the federal Centers for Disease Control's statement supporting voluntary HIV testing for such medical practitioners is well taken.

Without constituting an invasion of privacy, voluntary testing would be at once professional and prudent. If — possibly a big if — every doctor or dentist involved with invasive procedures would see it as a professional duty to be tested, and, if testing positive, to stop performing such procedures, the public and the healing professions both would be well served.

Such responsible and professional behavior also would render this week's action of the U.S. Senate meaningless. Responding emotionally to public fears, the Senate approved fines and jail sentences for doctors and others who spread HIV through medical treatment, and mandated HIV testing of virtually all medical personnel. That degree of statutory heavy-handedness should not be necessary.

We wonder if the entire argument about testing of health care workers, particularly doctors and dentists, will not be solved soon by another agency, the free enterprise marketplace.

No medical professional can practice without insurance these days. Certainly no surgeon can afford to operate and no hospital can afford to provide surgical privileges to a doctor without insurance coverage.

Yet it will take only the threat of large malpractice settlements involving a lack of HIV testing of a surgeon or dentist, or a hospital's failure to *know* a physician's HIV status, for insurers to say, "No test, no insurance."

AIDS is 100 percent deadly. It is not something that the public, the politicians, the medical profession or insurance companies can fool around with. The issue may not be who is to be tested, or how, but rather who will require the testing, and how soon.

The Boston Globe
Boston, Massachusetts, July 24, 1991

Sen. Jesse Helms wants to imprison any doctor, dentist, nurse or health-care worker who is infected with the AIDS virus and knows it, but fails to tell patients – and continues to treat them. This punitive approach to preventing the spread of AIDS is likely to have the opposite effect – cause more cases rather than curtail any.

Of course, patients should be advised of AIDS infection in their physician or any other health professional caring for them. And AIDS-infected medical personnel should not perform procedures that might infect a patient.

But Helms' extreme punishment could be reason enough for some hard-pressed medical personnel to avoid being tested on the chance they would have to reveal they are infected. He also would apply the restrictions so broadly that even medical personnel who are not engaged in AIDS-risky tasks would be subject to heavy fines and prison terms.

Helms' timing on the proposal makes his strategy doubly suspect. He introduced his harsh proposal knowing that AIDS experts at the Centers for Disease Control had just released strict guidelines aimed at further minimizing the inadvertent spread of AIDS from health workers to patients.

Worse, Helms seems again to be deliberately fanning the flames of AIDS hysteria. Though only five instances are known of AIDS transmission by a health worker to a patient, Helms told the Senate, "To recklessly expose thousands of innocent Americans to this deadly disease and to create wholesale panic in countless communities is a vile act which should be rooted out and punished."

Helms knew that Sen. Edward Kennedy, along with the Democratic and Republican leadership of the Senate, had agreed to a bipartisan bill – quick implementation of new CDC guidelines – to safeguard patients from AIDS-infected medical personnel. Though both the Kennedy and Helms bills were approved by the Senate, a moderate version is expected to be worked out.

Adoption of the CDC guidelines by every hospital and medical worker in the country would accomplish more than would Helms' bill, which is almost certain to boomerang. Universal precautions in handling blood and medical devices, use of protective gloves and avoidance of invasive medical procedures by any health worker infected with the AIDS virus, as CDC recommends, is the best way to prevent infecting patients – and health workers as well.

As Kennedy noted, it is useless to pretend that patients will gain peace of mind by terrorizing health professionals who themselves are at risk caring for AIDS patients. Criminal penalties are not the answer to AIDS prevention.

Senate Votes to Retain AIDS Entry Curb

The Senate Feb. 18, 1993 voted overwhelmingly to retain an existing ban on immigration by people who had AIDS or were infected with HIV, the virus that caused AIDS. The move was seen as a rebuke to President Clinton, who had signaled his intention to lift the restriction. The measure provided for waivers to be granted to short-term visitors.

The vote was 76-23, with 34 Democrats and 42 Republicans in favor of the ban. Voting against it were 22 Democrats and a lone Republican, Sen. Mark Hatfield (R., Ore.). The measure was attached to a $5.9 billion spending reauthorization bill for the National Institutes of Health for fiscal 1994, which passed the same day by a vote of 93-4.

The prohibition on immigrants with HIV had been put in place under President Ronald Reagan in 1987 and was enforced by the administration of President George Bush. HIV infection was part of a list of diseases for which the government denied visas to carriers.

In 1990, a new immigration law passed by Congress allowed the secretary of Health and Human Services to remove HIV from the list of diseases for which visitors or immigrants could be excluded. The Bush administration had not lifted the ban, but President Clinton had given indications that he would. If the new Senate bill were passed by the House and withstood a possible presidential veto, the HIV ban could not be overturned by the president.

The vote was preceded by debate between Republicans, who portrayed infected immigrants as health risks and financial burdens, and liberal Democrats, who argued that the U.S. should show the same compassion toward AIDS patients that many other Western countries showed.

Sen. Don Nickles (R, Okla.), a sponsor of the measure, estimated that lifting the ban would cost taxpayers $100,000 for each AIDS patient. "I do not think it is compassionate to open up a sign that says, 'Come to America. . . we are going to take care of your medical expenses,' " he said.

Sen. Edward M. Kennedy (D, Mass.), who led opposition to the measure, presented a substitute amendment that would have kept the existing bar in place for 90 days and then allowed the president to remove it without approval by Congress. The amendment was defeated, 56-42.

The Clinton administration reportedly did not lobby hard against the measure for fear that the issue would explode into a social debate that would shift attention from the president's economic program. The administration apparently did not want a repetition of the furor that had surrounded its attempt to end the military's exclusion of homosexuals.

The White House had first publicized its desire to lift the ban on Feb. 4, when spokesman George Stephanopoulos said that Clinton "intends to move forward on removing" it. Stephanopoulos said he could not give a precise date for eliminating the rule because national security advisers were reviewing policy toward Haitian immigrants. (As of Feb. 5, about 270 Haitians with HIV were being detained at a U.S. naval base at Guantanamo Bay in Cuba. Although they had been cleared for political asylum, the AIDS ban was holding them up.)

Civil-rights groups, advocates for AIDS victims and many doctors criticized the immigration curb as discriminatory and medically superfluous. In 1991, organizers of the International AIDS Conference had relocated the 1992 event, scheduled for Boston, to Amsterdam in order to protest U.S. policy.

Portland Press Herald

Portland, Maine, February 20, 1993

The U.S. Senate's untimely vote to post a "Keep Out!" sign on America's shores for foreign AIDS sufferers complicates an already disastrous Haitian immigrant policy. The immediate result is that it places in even deeper limbo the 230 Haitian boat people with the HIV virus detained at the U.S. naval base at Guantanamo Bay, Cuba.

The Rev. Jesse Jackson has been undergoing a hunger strike to pressure the new Clinton administration to drop the ban on admitting these poor souls into the country. The Senate vote, the civil rights leader correctly says, is "a setback to America's credibility. To put up a kind of Berlin Wall to people just because they are sick is beneath the promise of America."

Now, given the more than 3-1 margin of the Senate vote to enact the ban into law — which Sen. William S. Cohen, R-Maine, thinks would be just fine — the president will be even more reluctant to force the issue. This comes on top of Clinton's having reversed his campaign position on Haitian immigration even before he took office. When Clinton was gigging former President George Bush on the subject, it was for the latter's "cruel policy of returning Haitian refugees to a brutal dictatorship without an asylum hearing."

Now that Clinton has outdone Bush, ringing Haiti with an armada of Navy steel to keep persecuted Haitians in, this "cruel policy" is suddenly all right.

The only flickering light in Haiti's long night is the arrival, beginning last weekend, of the first U.N. human rights monitors in a force expected to grow to 400-500 members within a few months. The idea is to give Haitian citizens a sense of security they have not had before, and to stop the flood of human rights abuses that has been sweeping over the nation. These occurred even when President Jean-Bertrand Aristide was in power before his ouster in a September 1991 military coup.

Placement of the monitors and the military government's allowing them free movement throughout the country, even in the vulnerable countryside, is a first step toward returning Haiti to the rule of law. The world will be watching to see how much freedom the monitors do have, especially if their presence leads the opposition to organize marches and other anti-military protests.

With a situation so fragile, the Senate shouldn't be mucking up whatever hope remains for a just and lasting solution.

The Honolulu Advertiser
Honolulu, Hawaii, February 22, 1993

It seems cruel and irrational to bar people who are HIV-positive from entering or remaining in this country if they are otherwise eligible to be here.

Over the years, U.S. immigration laws have sought to prevent people with communicable diseases from becoming permanent residents, out of concern for public health. Since 1987, the contagious-disease exclusion has been used to keep people with HIV — even those living and working here — from obtaining "green cards."

But in 1990, Congress directed the U.S. Public Health Service to determine which medical conditions are "communicable diseases of public health significance" and grounds for exclusion. The Public Health Service decided HIV was not one of them. But the Bush administration bowed to political pressure and left it on the list.

The Clinton administration was prepared to drop HIV infection from the exclusion list. Then, on Thursday, the U.S.

Senate pre-empted the move by passing legislation to keep HIV-infected aliens from being admitted or becoming permanent residents. They would not be barred from visiting relatives, seeking medical treatment or attending conferences or business meetings.

Senators who back the exclusion argue that people with AIDS incur astronomical medical bills and become public charges. Some proponents find it hard to believe the deadly disease is not a threat to public health.

Those who oppose it say the exclusion is rooted in ignorance and prejudice, not public health considerations. They note that many of the people affected already live and work in the United States. Immigrants with other potentially expensive diseases — cancer, for instance — are allowed in.

The latest flap indicates that lawmakers, like the Americans they represent, must learn more about AIDS. It's not enough to label it a plague.

DAYTON DAILY NEWS
Dayton, Ohio, February 23, 1993

President Clinton isn't the only one who has waffled about whether to allow immigrants who test positive for AIDS into this country.

In 1986, the Senate voted 96-0 to prohibit people with the AIDS virus from immigrating. The House agreed to the policy without a vote.

Public-health officials protested. This was the first time Congress, rather than public-health people, had decided what diseases would disqualify a person from immigrating.

Moreover, it's inconsistent to exclude people who will come down with AIDS, while not screening out, say, people with heart conditions or cancer. (Obviously, cancer isn't contagious, while AIDS can be spread, but treating cancer or heart conditions can be as expensive as medical care for people with AIDS.)

After squarely supporting the ban, Congress then reversed itself and directed the Health and Human Services secretary to review the list of exclusions and decide what conditions could prevent a person from immigrating. President Bush's secretary said only people with TB should not be allowed in. Louis Sullivan's recommendation, however, wasn't acted on by the Bush administration.

Now President Clinton is delaying lifting the ban, and the Senate is back to its original position (on a vote of 76-23) that people infected with AIDS shouldn't be allowed to immigrate.

The issue is urgent because close to 300 Haitians who have tested positive for

the AIDS virus are stuck in awful living quarters at Guantanamo Bay in Cuba. If they had not had positive HIV test results, they would have been allowed in this country.

The president has an awful choice. He can keep his campaign promise and do the humanitarian thing, all the while knowing that he's creating more burdens for an already overwhelmed system that provides medical care for people without resources.

Or he can say this country will treat people with AIDS differently than it treats others with serious and costly illnesses.

Some people want the president to keep the ban for the wrong reasons. Some have unreasonable fears about people with AIDS. Some resent immigrants generally, especially poor and black immigrants. But nobody believes these are the president's prejudices.

In refusing to allow the immigrants to leave Guantanamo — which is the effect of the delaying — the president is violating a law that says this country won't send back refugees who are likely to be persecuted if they're returned to their homes. But like a lot of other laws, this one espouses a just principle while leaving complicated details and money matters for another day.

What Mr. Clinton is struggling with is how to pay for doing the right thing. If that cost and safety risk prove too high, the United States at some point can defensibly say "no"

THE SPOKESMAN-REVIEW
Spokane, Washington, February 22, 1993

Bill Clinton will have enough trouble convincing Americans later this year to accept the higher taxes required for universal health insurance. Why he also would want to open his arms, and the nation's coffers, to AIDS patients from overseas is a puzzle.

Politics, unfortunately, explains what common sense cannot. When Clinton was a candidate, promises flowed freely from his lips, including promises to AIDS activists.

Now that he's president, he quickly has discovered some of his promises — including some whoppers, like the pledge not to raise taxes on the middle class — were easier made than kept.

Now that he has chosen to break his prominent tax promise to the largest constituency group in the country, Americans will find it peculiar if he insists on keeping his far less defensible promise to admit immigrants suffering from AIDS.

Current federal policy prohibits people with certain particularly dangerous diseases, including AIDS and tuberculosis, from immigrating permanently to the United States.

That policy may be politically incorrect as far as AIDS activists are concerned, but it is sound from the standpoint of protecting public health, conserving scarce tax dollars and containing the explosion in health-care costs.

The majority of people with AIDS get the disease by choosing to engage in high-risk behaviors. This demonstrated behavioral tendency, coupled with the contagious nature of the disease, means that AIDS sufferers as a group pose a challenge not to be ignored by policy-makers responsible for public health and immigration.

The inevitably fatal outcome of AIDS and the high cost of treatment — roughly $100,000 per patient — makes this challenge even more significant.

Health care reformers including Clinton have called, wisely, for disease prevention measures as an element in cost control. Immigration policy for many years has played a valid role in preventing the spread of epidemics.

Reformers also have called for ensuring that the U.S. health care system provides more uniform access to the care each AIDS sufferer will require. That is a humane, appropriate and very expensive proposition.

But it pushes generosity past the breaking point, to argue that U.S. taxpayers must volunteer to provide treatment for every AIDS immigrant on the planet who is lucky or ingenious enough to make his way here.

There is no good reason to treat AIDS carriers differently from the carriers of other diseases who are not allowed to immigrate. Clinton's effort to win the election with ill-considered promises is not a good reason; nor is the effort by AIDS activists to attach special political privilege to their particular disease.

This week the Senate voted 76-23 to cement current federal policy into law. The Senate's overwhelming statement doubtless reflects public opinion, as well as the nation's best interests.

The Washington Post

Washington, D.C., February 20, 1993

THE SENATE has voted decisively to fore-close President Clinton's options in dealing with entry into the United States of people infected by the virus that causes AIDS. During the campaign, the president had promised to lift regulations that now keep out HIV-positive immigrants and visitors. To prevent that, the Senate on Thursday, by a vote of 76-23, approved an amendment to a National Institutes of Health authorization bill offered by Sen. Don Nickles (R-Okla.) that would allow waivers for visitors with HIV to enter the country temporarily, but would continue the ban for immigrants and refugees, who are admitted for permanent residence.

The different treatment accorded visitors and immigrants reflects current medical opinion that AIDS, which is not casually transmitted, is not a danger to public health in this country. While some senators continue to argue this point, most of those who voted to keep the ban expressed concern about the cost of caring for AIDS patients. This is not a frivolous question, because caring for AIDS patients is expensive. Estimates begin at about $100,000 each, and the cost is increasingly being borne by the taxpayers. Even Sen. Edward Kennedy, the leading opponent of Thursday's decision, acknowledges that cost is a legitimate issue that ought to be examined. He would have continued the ban for 90 days so that a study could be done, but would have allowed the president to make a final decision after that. The strong vote for the Nickles amendment indicates, however, that while senators do want to get the facts, they want Congress, and not the president acting alone, to make any decisions on lifting the ban.

If the House accepts the Senate language, the ban should be treated as a moratorium, not a permanent restriction. In six months, the president will have to submit information on the cost of admitting HIV immigrants and refugees, an estimate of those likely to seek entry into the United States and a report on the feasibility, in the absence of an AIDS test, of enforcing that part of the immigration law that bars persons likely to become public charges. Once this information is at hand, Congress should reconsider the restriction. Meanwhile, waivers still available for the unification of families, the protection of refugees and other humanitarian reasons should be granted.

The Augusta Chronicle

Augusta, Georgia, February 22, 1993

Add Dr. Schwartz's voice — representing the 300,000-member medical association — to that of 76 U.S. senators who last Thursday dealt a stunning setback to President Clinton's plan to help allow every AIDS-infected refugee in the world into the United States.

The AMA's warning, and the Senate's surprisingly lop-sided 76-23 vote, comes amid rising concern that there's not even enough money to care for all domestic AIDS patients. And it comes at a time when there's talk about capping health care costs.

Clinton's Department of Health and Human Services earlier this month proposed lifting the Reagan-era ban on immigrants with infectious diseases such as AIDS and leprosy. Now, however, Clinton's press secretary admits the Senate vote takes the wind out of the administration's sails.

This is good news.

Sen. Don Nickles, R-Okla., underscores that medical costs could range upward of $100,000 per person with AIDS. And it is estimated that over half of Haiti's illegal aliens intercepted by the U.S. test HIV-positive. (There is even a documented case of a Haitian with the bubonic plague, the feared disease of the Middle Ages.)

But we'll give a Georgia physician who serves on the National AIDS Commission the last word. Says Rep. Roy Rowland, D-Ga.: "We already have an overburdened health system. It just doesn't make sense to let in more people who will become an additional burden."

The Evening Gazette

Worcester, Massachusetts, February 16, 1993

An eminent scientific panel has warned that winning the fight against AIDS requires a determined, conscious national effort. The reason: Most victims come from groups that are socially invisible — or looked down on by the majority population.

The report — from the National Research Council, a private, non-profit research organization affiliated with the National Academy of Sciences — restates the statistical fact that AIDS has primarily affected the poor, minorities, drug users and gay men.

That's reason enough to give top priority to eradicating it.

Moreover, the disease does not remain neatly confined to groups that tend to be isolated — or, in some disturbing scenarios, could *be isolated* — from the mainstream. It can spread without respect for social position.

The report warns that AIDS threatens to disappear from public consciousness — "not because, like smallpox, it has been eliminated, but because those who continue to be affected by it are socially invisible, beyond the sight and attention of the majority population."

Accordingly, the report concludes, keeping the epidemic high on the public health agenda will be difficult.

Beyond the humanitarian need to fight AIDS wherever it may be encountered, the premise of "invisibility," even if supported in the broadest measure by statistics, becomes shakier upon close scrutiny.

Every community in Worcester County now has at least one resident afflicted with AIDS, each with family and friends who will be touched by the ravages of the disease as it wears out immune systems and, inevitably, leads to death. Meanwhile, there are many persons who, knowingly or unknowingly, carry the HIV virus, predecessor to AIDS.

At the other extreme, fear-mongers have raised the specter of AIDS sweeping through the population — taking one in 10, one in 50, the figures vary. They do no service to the cause by scare tactics. A disease that at present is inevitably fatal is frightening enough.

A realistic balanced outlook — combined with compassion for anyone with the disease — should be sufficient to keep AIDS in the public health spotlight where it belongs.

AKRON BEACON JOURNAL
Akron, Ohio, February 22, 1993

In 1991, Louis Sullivan, the secretary of health and human services in the Bush administration, advised the White House that it should lift the ban preventing people infected with the virus that causes AIDS from immigrating to the United States.

Quickly, however, politics intruded, and proponents of the ban convinced George Bush to continue it.

Many of those same voices could be heard again last week as 76 senators voted to write the ban into law. The move was triggered by President Clinton's decision to pick up where Sullivan had been ignored.

The reasons for lifting the ban remain persuasive. AIDS is not easily spread, in the way, say, tuberculosis is. Yes, AIDS always kills, but it is not any more expensive to treat than many cancers or coronary diseases, as Canadian officials learned.

International health authorities have long vehemently condemned the American ban. What's troubling, too, is that those immigrants infected with the virus and already here, paying taxes and seeking permanent residence, would be forced, in effect, underground, for fear of deportation.

Isn't there room for a more humane approach, one guided by the public health officials who are best equipped to make such decisions?

THE ARIZONA REPUBLIC
Phoenix, Arizona, February 23, 1993

AIDS is a world player that affords the United States little advantage in competition. So formidable a foe is the disease that the United States, a superpower in most respects, shrinks from the possibility of engaging the enemy.

One way to control the casualties in the fight against AIDS is to reduce exposure by limiting the number of people who are host to the AIDS virus. That is why the United States, at least for the present, maintains a policy banning foreigners who have AIDS or who have tested positive for HIV, the virus that causes the disease, from immigrating to this country.

It is a difficult position to take, particularly for a nation that prides itself on being a leader in humanitarian causes — a nation that boasts of fostering inclusiveness, not exclusivity.

After jolting the nation with a proposal to lift the ban on gays in the military, President Clinton has touched another nerve with his stated intent to remove restrictions on immigrants with AIDS. The existing policy, implemented in 1987, has caused international boycotts by AIDS groups — a world conference last year was moved from Boston to Amsterdam — and AIDS activists denounce the ban as a clear indication that Washington lacks sensitivity and understanding with respect to AIDS. In fact, the policy merely exemplifies a prudent caution toward a fatal disease for which no cure is known. Despite some progress over the past decade in research and treatment, AIDS is still a mysterious killer whose victims die slowly, in the process drawing heavily on the available medical resources.

Already the president's effort to fulfill his campaign promise to admit infected immigrants has been rebuffed on Capitol Hill, with the Senate's overwhelming vote in opposition to lifting immigration restrictions.

While the House seems unlikely to resist the president's desire, last week's vote in the Senate, where 34 Democrats joined the Republican opposition to lifting the immigration ban, signals the long road the White House must travel to enact this portion of its social agenda. As with the issue of gays in the military, Mr. Clinton finds himself caught in the toils of a contentious social issue when he needs to apply his energy and political capital to consuming economic issues. Unless he can shift the focus, it is hard to see how he will have any chance of enacting his economic program, which is not without controversial elements itself.

Allowing people with AIDS to migrate to the United States, it needs to be understood, transcends politics. Important economic and public health questions have to be considered.

It is not enough to know, as health experts are quick to point out, that the disease is not transmitted by casual contact and poses a different sort of threat than, for example, tuberculosis, which is easily communicated. The question is whether the nation can afford to allow a possibly large number of immigrants to enjoy resident status, knowing that the costs of treating their disease — estimated at $100,000 per case — could cause the collapse of an already rickety public health system.

Until more is known about the disease, its cure, its cost to the nation — socially and economically — the existing ban should remain in place.

Minneapolis Star and Tribune
Minneapolis, Minnesota, February 23, 1993

If President Clinton wants to admit HIV-infected foreigners to the United States, he shouldn't count on the Senate to roll out the welcome mat. Last week the senators muddied the mat by voting 76-23 to bar permanent residency for HIV carriers. Though the mud-throwing isn't likely to be repeated in the House, it puts heavy pressure on the president. He should stand fast against the cold-hearted throng.

HIV carriers have been unwelcome on U.S. soil since the last days of the Reagan administration, when the government bowed to baseless fears that such immigrants threaten public health. President Clinton is anxious to reverse the discriminatory ban. But many senators, including Minnesota's Dave Durenberger, balk at that plan. Some still maintain that infected immigrants could pose a profound health danger — even though they would represent a minuscule fraction of the country's HIV-afflicted population.

Yet the most-often cited excuse for excluding HIV carriers involves not health, but money. Welcome such foreigners to our shores, the argument goes, and they'll soon be dying at our expense. Never mind that existing law allows denying residency to anyone likely to become dependent on welfare. In the Senate's view, the mere presence of the AIDS virus is reason enough to bar the door.

But if the potential for one disease raises alarms, why not others? A quick battery of tests could reveal whether a would-be immigrant might someday meet a premature end. It's hard to see why HIV carriers are inherently less desirable immigrants than people with cancer or kidney disease or multiple sclerosis or alcoholism — all progressive illnesses that require expensive and sustained care. For that matter, all foreigners who settle here are going to die sooner or later — and there's no guarantee that they'll do so quickly or cheaply.

Which points to the real motivations behind the Senate vote: prejudice and fear, not thriftiness. The federal government has a long and lamentable history of persecuting AIDS patients. It's shameful that so many senators want to continue it.

Eighth AIDS Conference Held in Amsterdam

The Eighth International Conference on AIDS was held in Amsterdam July 19–24, 1992. The event was attended by more than 9,000 researchers and public health officials from around the world, who heard over 4,875 reports on the deadly disease.

Few major scientific breakthroughs had been expected to be announced at the conference. However, the gathering was dominated by reports of a mysterious illness whose victims had the symptoms of AIDS but did not test positive for the human immuno-deficiency virus (HIV) that caused the disease.

Besides providing a forum for the exchange of medical findings, the conference brought to the fore questions about the social, ethical, and economic aspects of AIDS.

Past conferences had been disrupted by AIDS activists protesting what they regarded as inadequate government response to the epidemic and overpricing by drug manufacturers. Although such demonstrations continued in Amsterdam, the conference was the first in which activists took the podium as official participants.

The conference originally had been scheduled to be held in Boston, Mass. But organizers switched venues to protest the U.S. government's policy of excluding immigrants and visitors infected with the AIDS virus. The 1993 conference was to take place in Berlin.

(A Spanish citizen with AIDS who resided in the U.S. July 23 announced his intention to return to the U.S. to challenge the government's entry curb. The man, Tomas Fabregas, said, "I defy [U.S. President] George Bush to prevent me from returning to my home.")

In the opening speech, Jonathan Mann, the conference chairman, July 19 questioned why governments paid more attention to "the inflation rate" than they did to AIDS and other diseases. He suggested that just as environmentalists had formed "Green" political parties, so should health activists form their own "blue" parties.

Mann, citing figures from the Harvard AIDS Institute, which he directed, predicted that the number of HIV-infected adults worldwide would rise to between 38 million and 110 million by the year 2000.

Offering a lower estimate, Michael Merson, the director of the World Health Organization's AIDS program, July 20 projected the number of AIDS patients to reach 40 million by the year 2000. Currently, he said, a new person was infected by the AIDS virus every 15 seconds.

Merson July 20 noted that women made up the fastest growing category of AIDS patients in the U.S., although their infection rate did not equal that of men.

In the past, homosexual men had made up about two-thirds of those infected in the U.S. and Europe. However, Merson said, the lines between high-risk groups and the rest of the population were "becoming blurred" as more women caught the virus through intercourse with infected men. Merson said the scourge among women was even more pronounced in the Third World.

Anke Ehrhardt of Columbia University July 20 said that trying to change sexual patterns to slow the spread of AIDS was difficult in some male-dominated societies, where women could not force the use of condoms or control their partners' behavior outside the home. She urged swift development of the "female condom."

Ehrhardt also complained about "moralizing" religious groups that obstructed safe-sex education by stressing sexual abstinence. There was no evidence that sexually active youths would abstain if they were told to, she said, adding, "Programs on re-virginization will not work."

The furor over the mysterious AIDS-like illness began when the July 27 edition of *Newsweek* magazine (available July 20) reported that Jeffrey Laurence, a Cornell University Medical Center immunologist, had discovered six patients with classic AIDS symptoms—Kaposi's sarcoma (an otherwise rare skin cancer), pneumonia, and severely depressed immune systems—who showed no trace of HIV in their blood. Fueling concern was *Newsweek*'s suggestion that the syndrome was caused by a new virus that went undetected by normal HIV tests.

THE SACRAMENTO BEE
Sacramento, California, July 28, 1992

The Eighth International Conference on AIDS ended last week with little encouraging news. With no vaccine on the horizon, and predictions by some that AIDS may remain a common disease a century from now, prevention therefore takes on an even greater urgency.

The primary lesson of the conference was that the disease is even more elusive and complicated than previously thought, with researchers revealing new discoveries and trends that are more troubling than encouraging. One is a rare new disease with AIDS-like symptoms in patients who show no signs of any of the identifiable strains of the virus known to cause AIDS. Another is that women are now the fastest-growing subgroup among the infected.

At one time, AIDS was looked upon as a gay disease, a man's disease, a drug abuser's disease, a disease for the economic underclass, for the Third World. But AIDS has shown itself to be a straight disease, too, and a women's disease – with predictions that women will be its primary victims by the end of the decade. The AIDS circle is expanding, and what was once perceived as an affliction that strikes *them* must increasingly be seen as an affliction that strikes *us*.

Some hope can be squeezed from the scale of the conference: With more than 10,000 researchers and activists from 130 countries attending, it was the largest-ever gathering of minds for the AIDS fight. That has to be taken as a good sign, because anything less than worldwide attention to this global crisis would be unconscionably short-sighted.

As long as there is no cure, prevention is all we have. The proven preventatives – condoms, a well-monitored blood supply, sterilized needles for intravenous drug users, swift treatment of venereal diseases, which increase susceptibility to HIV, the AIDS virus, candor in our personal relationships and extreme care in our sexual behavior – must be pushed harder than ever before.

AIDS research is an issue that will continue to be hotly debated against other worthy causes such as cancer and heart disease, but political support for AIDS prevention and education can no longer be short-changed. More information must be given to children in school. Condoms and sterilized needles should be more readily available. And medieval attitudes that sometimes still treat AIDS and HIV-infected patients like lepers must become a thing of the past.

St. Petersburg Times
St. Petersburg, Florida, July 22, 1992

Over the past decade AIDS has moved swiftly from abstract scientific discovery to a routine coffee shop topic. Isn't it a shame about that young woman who was infected with AIDS by her dentist? Isn't it terrible about that boy who got HIV from a blood transfusion?

Yet looking the other way instead of treating AIDS as a crisis that can affect anyone has remained fairly easy for most Americans. Aside from fluke cases involving "innocent" people, the disease strikes others, people with undesirable lifestyles and careless habits, or so the rationalizing goes. Even news from Third World countries, at this point in far graver danger than the United States from the ravages of HIV, has not made a great impact, partly because the media haven't focused much of their AIDS reporting in places such as Africa.

It's not fair, though, to place all the blame on Americans for the comfortable "us/them" division between who gets AIDS and who doesn't. Americans have been taking cues from a national policy that has refused to commit resources for adequate research, treatment and education efforts, a policy that has been carried out by people whose prejudices against homosexuals and drug users have impaired their vision for the country's survival.

As the eighth International Conference on AIDS proceeds this week in Amsterdam, alarms to action should be sounding in public and private circles alike. What are politicians planning to do about the horrifying prediction that women will become the primary victims of AIDS, especially in the world's poorest countries where their subservient status makes them the least empowered to prevent unprotected sexual intercourse? What will be the nation's response to the frightening possibility of a new mutation of HIV that is undetectable by current testing methods, or the disease's link to highly contagious tuberculosis? What contribution can this wealthy nation make to Africa, where 80 percent of the hospital beds in some cities are occupied by AIDS patients?

One television image, a result of the disease's higher profile during the AIDS conference, sears the mind and heart: a young African boy, probably no more than 12, hammering nails into his mother's coffin. The reporter recounted the story of the mother's death from AIDS, which she contracted from her husband. Before the disease claimed her, she unknowingly had passed it to her newborn, who also died.

AIDS is on all our doorsteps. Americans should be far beyond dismissing AIDS as a new leprosy that can be shunned and quarantined. The first move is shedding our denial so that we are fully equipped to demand that the government address the deadly threat AIDS poses to all public health.

St. Petersburg, Florida, July 28, 1992

The eighth international AIDS conference ended Friday in Amsterdam, Netherlands, amid reports of a newly discovered AIDS-like illness of unknown cause. For many who had grown complacent about their low risks of contact with HIV, the 30 mysterious cases provoked renewed concern with the safety of blood supplies and other possible means of exposure.

The "new" disease may prove to be unrelated to AIDS; it may not be triggered by a virus at all. In the meantime, however, fresh urgency has been lent to the already critical worldwide effort to contain the spread of acquired immune deficiency syndrome.

AIDS isn't really an epidemic, it's a pandemic — a disease that already has spread over vast geographic regions. Americans, however, cushioned by their relative isolation from the rest of the world, still think in terms of "risk groups" such as gay men and needle users. The AIDS conference reflects our misguided faith in this line of thinking; it was nôt held in Boston as originally planned because U.S. immigration policy bars HIV-positive noncitizens from entering the country.

In contrast, last week's conference in Amsterdam was structured to bring scientists and citizen-activists together. As those who are committed to stopping AIDS well understand, the medical and behavioral aspects of HIV transmission cannot be divided. All sexually active adolescents and adults and all those who practice abstinence but hope to marry are potentially affected, as are their offspring.

Throughout most of the world, AIDS is already a family disease, transmitted heterosexually and passed to children in the womb or through breast milk. In poor nations, health officials have struggled to decide whether HIV-positive mothers should be encouraged to breast-feed their children. If they do, the children might develop AIDS. If they don't, the babies won't get the boost in immunity to other illnesses that is a major benefit of breast-feeding, and a major factor in surviving infancy.

Grim choices such as this make up the worldwide reality of HIV. The virus is remarkably adaptable; researchers have found that it mutates at an astonishing pace, developing increasingly virulent strains. Evolutionary changes that would take the human body a million years to achieve are accomplished by the human immunodeficiency virus in a single year. An accelerated research effort is needed just to keep up with this killer, let alone to find a vaccine or a cure. The virus also has the potential to resist drugs that are effective in keeping people healthy, prompting stepped-up research on new compounds.

A million people already have died of AIDS-related diseases. Some 80 percent of new cases are being identified in developing countries, where young families are devastated, health services are scarce and community life often grinds to a halt.

Despite the tragic loss of life in the United States and the mounting strain on health-care resources, American society has not yet begun to experience the full impact of AIDS. We are, however, a high-risk nation; for the average man, woman or child, ignoring the facts is the riskiest behavior of all.

The Detroit News
Detroit, Michigan, July 22, 1992

In recent years, there have been numerous calls in the United States for more presidential speechmaking and larger amounts of money to deal with the AIDS crisis. To critics it has appeared that the government has been ineffective in efforts to prevent or control AIDS and lacking in commitment.

With the 8th International Conference on AIDS convening this week in Amsterdam, there are opportunities to test that claim and to compare data from researchers and physicians from all over the world.

Unquestionably, the conference is necessary to inspire renewed commitment to cooperate in the fight against this rapidly spreading disease. Unfortunately, the world has grown complacent.

Clearly, this epidemic is not confined to the United States.

More than 130 countries are represented at the conference, which will feature nearly 5,000 scientific presentations. It has already been said that no major breakthroughs are expected in spite of discussions of new treatments.

One of the most important things for the world to grasp is that the current understanding of AIDS is outdated — that of a separate, unique and isolated health problem. During the opening session, Dr. Jonathan Mann, of the Harvard School of Public Health in Boston, asserted that the old interpretation of AIDS has "become a straitjacket."

Mann wisely said the disease can no longer be fought in isolation but only with integrated approaches. He called isolation inefficient and dangerous and called out for "dialogue, tolerance and solidarity" to facilitate finding new "pathways to more effective control and care."

He suggested the need for a bold approach organized on a global scale. He is right. Americans need to stop limiting their attention to what they regard as their own country's failure while joining with the world in finding the answers that might relieve the massive suffering engendered by this disease.

The AIDS epidemic has not disappeared. In fact, it is growing in even more dangerous ways. AIDS is no longer a "homosexual disease" confined mostly to males or to illegal drug users sharing dirty needles. While that may have been the core, the waves of expanding infection keep reaching a little farther into other people's lives. The disease is spreading rapidly among heterosexuals, including hundreds of thousands of women.

Concerned observers throughout the world need to start finding ways to combine tolerance and scientific ingenuity to find solutions. In short, concern about AIDS has to become everybody's problem.

ST. LOUIS POST-DISPATCH
St. Louis, Missouri, July 24, 1992

As the 8th International Conference on AIDS meets in Amsterdam this week, the 11,000 participants are struggling, once again, with the bitter facts of life — and death — about this disease. Just as scientific knowledge about AIDS is advancing, so, too, are the death toll and the disease itself.

The disease that once infected primarily homosexual men now is firmly entrenched among heterosexuals, as the appalling numbers from Africa and Asia all too vividly illustrate. The disease that once seemed concentrated in New York City and San Francisco can now be found in rural villages around the globe. The disease that once seemed the preserve of the rich, industrial nations is now running riot through the impoverished countries of the Third World, the countries least able to cope with the social and medical burden that AIDS represents.

It is this stark, unrelenting reality that accounts for the somewhat desperate, sometimes hyperbolic statements that often accompany these conferences. Calls for a new AIDS political party, for example, should be viewed as reflecting frustration more than good political sense. But other recommendations are as sober and somber as they come.

Money is of primary importance. The Bush administration can defend, without embarrassment, its billion-dollar-plus AIDS research budget. But spending on prevention, the only "cure" we have, has gone down to $480 million this year from $497 million in 1990. Making the AIDS prevention picture even bleaker is the administration's squeamishness about straight talk about sex and intravenous drug use.

The Bush administration's record does demand improvement, especially in the moral leadership department. But AIDS is also a global problem, and the situation internationally is far worse. In 1991, the AIDS program of the World Health Organization had less than $50 million, an unbelievably paltry sum to combat the disease in the Third World.

Unfortunately, the countries of Africa and Asia that are experiencing the greatest upsurge in HIV infection lack the national budgets and the healthcare systems to address their citizens' most basic needs.

Fighting AIDS, especially in the Third World, also requires a revolution in attitudes, particularly toward women. The pervasive exploitation of women and girls as prostitutes is one of the major reasons AIDS is spreading like wildfire in Thailand. The second-class status of African women who can't tell their husbands to use condoms — much less demand monogamy — is one reason for AIDS' prevalence.

No one can be complacent. Many fantastic predictions about AIDS that were made early in the epidemic did not come true. That doesn't diminish, though, the horror of the current reality of 2 million people worldwide with AIDS and 10 million people worldwide who are HIV-positive — or the need to do better in stopping the epidemic.

Rockford Register Star
Rockford, Illinois, July 24, 1992

At the international AIDS conference in Amsterdam this week, the spotlight unexpectedly has been thrown on a phenemenon that may or may not involve the dreaded disease. An early and reliable answer to that question will require the universal cooperation of AIDS researchers everywhere.

At issue are reports that some 30 people around the world have come up with AIDS-like symptoms, but have not tested positive for the HIV virus which causes AIDS. In California, a researcher says he has isolated a new virus in a woman suffering from AIDS symptoms.

Some people with AIDS symptoms don't have the HIV virus.

Whether all these cases involve the same thing, or whether some previously unknown virus is responsible, is not yet known. If there is, in fact, another virus causing AIDS, an uneducated reaction among the public might be to panic about the safety of blood supplies. But that would fly in the face of proof that the spread of AIDS through blood transfusions has declined sharply with the advent of blood screening.

In order for the mystery of the unexplained AIDS cases to be solved, it is incumbent on researchers to immediately share the data with other scientists rather than horde it for glory in future publication — as seems to have been the case in some instances.

Meanwhile, the public has no good reason to become greatly alarmed. It behooves us all to continue to observe sensible safeguards against contracting AIDS, to show sympathy and compassion for people who have the disease, and to push government for ever greater efforts to conquer this scourge.

The Idaho STATESMAN
Boise, Idaho, July 24, 1992

News from an international conference on AIDS dispels the myth that acquired immune deficiency syndrome affects only gay men or IV drug users.

Indeed, one expert said women around the world are now catching the HIV virus almost as fast as men.

Many of the women and children who are contracting the HIV virus live in poor, Third World countries. But women and children in the United States are vulnerable, too.

Here in Idaho, about 10 percent of the people infected with the HIV virus are women.

That's still a relatively small proportion, but the number of women and teens infected with the HIV virus is growing, according to John Glaza, supervisor of the state's STD/AIDS program for the Idaho Department of Health and Welfare.

As of July 15, 356 Idahoans (men and women) carried the HIV virus. The number increases exponentially every year. In 1986, for example, Idaho reported just 41 people infected with the HIV virus.

"I'm convinced that, in the state of Idaho, not everybody is armed and equipped with the information they need to stop the spread of the disease," Glaza said.

It's important to know the facts.

Condoms are no guarantee against transmission of the virus, but they can reduce the risk if used correctly.

Many of the people attending this week's international AIDS conference have called for more money for research. That will certainly help. But education and prevention continue to be two of the most effective weapons against this terrible plague.

The News Journal

Wilmington, Delaware, July 26, 1992

WHERE WE STAND
Education is the key to preventing the spread of AIDS.

Reports from the Eighth International Conference on AIDS show that women are contacting the AIDS virus almost as often as men, and will probably become the primary victims by the end of the decade.

About 111,000 women are among the one million Americans who are infected with the virus who do not show any major symptoms.

When AIDS came to world attention a decade ago, homosexual men and intravenous drug users were the primary groups infected. Since then, the disease has spread to heterosexual men and women.

The most worrisome thing now is that AIDS is among the five leading causes of death for women 25 to 44. Half of the women now sick with AIDS acquired the virus by injecting drugs, but 34 percent contacted AIDS through heterosexual sex. Among teen-age girls, 50 percent of those diagnosed with AIDS in 1990 reported contracting the virus through heterosexual contact.

As U.S. Surgeon General Antonia Novello says in an article on the previous page, women must stop taking chances and take charge of their lives: "We must take the initiative to protect our health, to shield ourselves and our children from all sexually transmitted diseases, including HIV."

An infected man is twice as likely to pass the virus to a woman than a woman is likely to pass it to a man.

It is time for women in the risk group to change their sexual behavior. Denial is an important reason why the AIDS epidemic has spread so far, so fast. Obviously women in the drug culture must stop injecting drugs and seek treatment, if the alarming numbers of AIDS cases is to decrease.

Abstinence and maintaining monogamous relationships can help. But education and the use of condoms must be reinforced in our homes, schools, and the media, if we are going to win the war against this dreaded disease.

Time is not on our side. There is no need to panic, but without firm resolve the spread of this disease could become catastrophic.

TULSA WORLD

Tulsa, Oklahoma, July 23, 1992

THE Eighth International Conference on AIDS meeting in Amsterdam, Netherlands, daily releases startling statistics on the fatal disease.

But the numbers fail to communicate the tragedy.

In the United States the Centers for Disease Control estimate 1 million people carry the AIDS virus. Worldwide as many as 10 million are infected. These are millions of people who are condemned to die. There is no cure.

But before they die, they infect others. In the 11 years since the disease burst onto the medical charts, the infection and death rate has steadily grown.

A sense of calm in industrialized nations, where the disease has leveled off, belies the numbers. According to a New York Times report, through March the CDC reported 218,000 cases of AIDS and 139,000 deaths. Allowing for underreporting the CDC believes 50,000 to 60,000 people in the United States will contract AIDS in each of the next few years. During the same period about 50,000 a year are predicted to die from the disease.

In industrialized nations, AIDS mainly spreads through homosexual sex and drug use. Education programs encouraging safe sex and lifestyle changes have made an impact. However, a small but growing number of women are being infected heterosexually.

But devastating as these numbers are, the real plague is worldwide where the World Health Organization estimates that 71 percent of the cases are spread heterosexually, made easier by the high incidence of veneral diseases that produce open sores.

A disease this deadly threatens all the world. The answer is a global effort at education and funding of research for a cure.

THE CHRONICLE-HERALD

Halifax, Nova Scotia, July 23, 1992

THE INCIDENCE of new AIDS cases appears to be levelling off in North America, but an international gathering of scientists this week in Amsterdam has made it clear it is no time to grow complacent about the fatal immune deficiency syndrome.

Indeed, the troubling trends in African countries — where the disease has the greatest foothold — appear to be emerging in other parts of the world. Once known as a disease of drug users and male homosexuals, AIDS is now spreading rapidly to women through heterosexual sex.

Dr. Michael Merson of the World Health Organization (WHO) told the conference women throughout the world are becoming infected with HIV, the virus which causes AIDS, about as often as men. This year about 500,000 women have been infected.

Further, "women's rising infection rates have been accompanied by a corresponding rise in the number of children born to them infected with HIV." The higher HIV rate among women, tragic in itself, is also increasing the numbers of AIDS orphans — the non-infected offspring of parents who have contracted the virus.

This trend is evident in Uganda, a country of 17 million people which has 1.5 million AIDS orphans, and another 1.5 million adults and children infected with HIV.

Today, about 11 million people are infected with the virus worldwide (including an estimated 600-800 people in Nova Scotia). By the year 2000, WHO estimates up to 40 million people will be infected.

Victims, at least those in rich Western nations, can take some hope from promising new treatments. British researchers say they have developed a compound (So221) 30 times more active and having fewer side effects than the leading AIDS drug, AZT.

Other medical experts have identified an AIDS-like syndrome in at least two dozen Americans who show no signs of HIV. Experts differed at the conference about whether an undetectable mutant microbe is responsible for this AIDS imitator, a disagreement which underlines researchers' limited understanding of the immune system and what causes it to go wrong.

In general, expensive AIDS treatments hold less hope for curbing the spread of the disease than prevention.

In 1986, Honduras and Chile had similar AIDS infection rates, a researcher at the Pan American Health Organization in Washington told the conference. Five years later, the rate among heterosexuals was 100 times higher in Honduras, which, unlike Chile, had no effective prevention programs for sexually transmitted diseases (STDs).

Several researchers said AIDS spreads more rapidly among those suffering other STDs like gonorrhea and syphilis, which cause sores which may allow HIV to enter the bloodstream.

Effective STD prevention programs then, and use of condoms and other safe-sex practices, are probably the best way to slow the spread of this tragic affliction.

Proper education and sensible public health policies are the first priorities, even in a small jurisdiction like Nova Scotia. In this light, Health Minister George Moody should quickly introduce his long-promised AIDS strategy. It was to be ready in the spring but is still under bureaucratic review.

Tuberculosis on the Rise Throughout U.S.

Tuberculosis (TB) was on the rise in New York City, and strains of the bacteria resistant to conventional drugs were spreading, the federal Centers for Disease Control reported Nov. 19, 1991.

TB was a lung infection caused by airborne bacteria that often spread through coughing. Symptoms included fever, sweating, weight loss, enervation, and a nagging cough that brought up blood. TB bacteria could remain dormant in the body for years.

Since the 1950s, federal agencies had worked to eradicate the disease in the U.S. by the year 2010. The number of cases nationwide reached a low of 22,201 in 1985. But in subsequent years, increases in poverty, homelessness, drug abuse, and the deadly disease AIDS had made TB resurgent. Inadequate screening of infected immigrants, whose countries had higher TB rates than the U.S., was also a problem. Another factor was the curtailment of a nationwide TB monitoring program in 1986 due to a lack of funds.

The problem was most severe in New York City. According to CDC figures, 3,520 new cases of active TB had been diagnosed in the metropolis in 1990, a 38% jump over the 2,545 cases in 1989. For the nation as a whole, TB rose 9.4% over the same period, to 25,701 cases from 23,495.

The CDC was especially concerned about the spread of TB strains that were unaffected by standard medications such as ioniazid or rifampin. Treatments for the new strains averaged $180,000, as opposed to $150 for ordinary TB, and needed to be used for up to 18 months.

The *New York Times* Dec. 10, 1991 reported that the AIDS virus (HIV) was hindering the detection of TB. For example, the standard TB test in which a tuberculosis protein was injected under the skin was supposed to cause a swelling if TB antibodies were present. But the immune deficiencies of HIV patients could lower their antibody count and cause the test not to register.

el diario / la prensa
Miami, Florida, November 20, 1991

The news last week that twelve inmates and one guard in New York state prisons had recently died of tuberculosis sent shock waves through our health agencies. According to commissioner Thomas A. Coughlin of the state Department of Correctional Services, there is plenty of cause of concern, given that the deaths of the inmates and the guard are the result of the emergence of a new, drug-resistant strain of TB.

As commissioner Coughlin said: "This new strain of TB has been identified in other parts of the nation, and is a new and deadly threat to all of us. It is an airborne bacteria that can be spread by acts as common as coughing...Inmates are public health sentinels. Their health problems reflect those that are faced by the community at large."

The parallel comparison with the now-rampant AIDS epidemic is obvious and disturbing. One of the first places where the AIDS epidemic was first detected at the beginning of the 1980s was as among the New York state prison population, due in large part to the great numbers of incoming inmates who had contracted the disease on the outside, usually by sharing infected drug needles. Those same type of HIV-infected inmates are the most susceptible to the new drug-resistant TB, because of their depressed immune system.

It would be a mistake, however, to think that only HIV-infected persons are susceptible to this new strain of TB. As the state Department of Health points out, the disease is highly contagious, even for persons whose immune systems are not compromised.

The Department of Health warns that TB among prison inmates is a microcosm of what is happening in New York state as a whole, where TB increased 31 percent from 3,202 to 4,186 cases in one year (1989-90). Much of the increase in TB in New York has been in African-Americans and Latino males, particularly among those between the ages of 20-44 years of age, and is associated with poverty, substance abuse and HIV infection.

Earlier this year, there was alarm throughout the city at the news of the increasing numbers of homeless persons being diagnosed with tuberculosis. Given the ease with which the disease is transmitted, and the emergence of this new strain of drug-resistant TB, the cause for alarm is very real indeed.

Arkansas Gazette.
Little Rock, Arkansas, August 19, 1990

"TB's all right to have if your friends didn't treat you so low-down," Leadbelly used to sing. People with disabilities today can get by surprisingly well when the non-disabled don't insist on making it hard for them. In Pulaski County, election officials have begun to treat disabled voters less low-down.

For years, the disabled have complained of a lack of access to Pulaski County polling places that made it difficult if not impossible for them to cast their ballots. In a recent meeting, Harry Tapp, coordinator of the county election commission, agreed to try to relocate some polling places to more accommodating sites. Other inaccessible sites may be made accessible by inexpensive modifications, such as temporary wheelchair ramps.

Volunteers will inspect existing polling places and look for alternatives. Their recommendations are due in mid-September. The election commission is required by law to select final polling places by Oct. 6.

The size of the problem is startling to anyone who hasn't experienced it personally. A 1987 survey estimated that 93 percent of Arkansas polling places are inaccessible to disabled people. The Pulaski County percentage is thought to be about the same. A spokesman for a group of disabled people estimates that for less than $250,000, Pulaski County could make all its voting sites accessible to the disabled. The county probably won't reach that goal in the coming general election, but it should remain the ultimate goal, and for the not-too-distant future.

The rest of the state too must work to make all polling places accessible to all voters. No one should have to be reminded, but some do, that the disabled are citizens too, with all the rights and duties that citizenship imposes.

DAILY ⊜ NEWS
New York City, New York, August 7, 1991

It is imperative that all new enrollees in city schools be tested for TB. That's not opinion — it's the rule. Under the Health Code, new students will be barred from class next month unless the tests have been administered. And that means children in all schools — public, private and parochial. The disease is not rampant in classrooms, but there has been a 40% increase among schoolkids.

There will be a citywide outreach campaign, alerting parents to the need for both the initial test and a crucial followup. Public service announcements and leaflets and mailings will be used. There also should be community group involvement, especially to reach all the new non-English speaking immigrants.

Free tests will be available at city-run clinics. In addition, tests will be given in 90 schools that have their own clinics. Logistical problems are cited as the reason for not conducting on-premise tests in all schools for all students. But if monitoring shows TB continuing to increase dramatically, such testing must be reconsidered — difficult logistics notwithstanding. Better safe than sorry.

THE SACRAMENTO BEE
Sacramento, California, September 16, 1992

A decade ago, it was easy to assume that medicine and antibiotics had won the war against mankind's oldest health enemy, bacterial infection. The tuberculosis sanitariums had disappeared and hospital beds once full of young patients suffering from typhoid fever, pneumonia and meningitis were devoted instead to caring for people with diseases of the old: cancer, heart disease, diabetes.

That easy assumption holds no longer. As Science magazine made plain in a recent special issue on antibiotic resistance in bacteria, microbes are on the counterattack. And they have caught the United States with its defenses weakening.

Since 1985, cases of TB have been on the rise in the United States; in 1991, one in seven of cases involved a bug resistant to one or more drugs. Doctors are seeing more hospital-acquired infections with organisms resistant to multiple antibiotics. And bacteria that cause more common diseases such as diarrhea, food poisoning, ear infections and sore throats are turning up with resistance. These hardier bacteria drive up the incidence of disease, make treatment more costly and cost lives.

Resistance is unavoidable, a product of evolution in action. It has been, unfortunately, speeded along by the use of antibiotics for non-bacterial infections, by doctors too often prescribing broad-spectrum antibiotics when a more specific one would suffice and by the overuse of antibiotics in livestock.

Worse, this unavoidable counterattack has yet to be met with an adequate response, the Science articles point out. Drug companies have slowed development of new antibiotics, seeing little profit in them. The federal government last year devoted only $8.8 million of its billions in health research to investigation of antibiotic resistance. Those priorities obviously need to change to assure new drug therapies to counter resistance.

But the largest, and growing chink, in our defenses is in public health, the vital complement to antibiotic treatment. The spread of resistant bacteria and TB comes at a moment when public health systems are sagging under the weight of budget cutbacks, rising numbers of uninsured people, and growing populations of groups – homeless people, drug users, poor children – most vulnerable to disease. In many major U.S. cities, TB patients are less likely to complete drug therapy than in Malawi or Tanzania. Instead of doing more to detect resistant diseases early, screen for infections and attend to the causes of outbreaks, public health authorities are faced with doing less.

There is no private retreat from the challenge of drug-resistant bugs. With infectious diseases that can be spread by breathing, touching or eating, the front line can be anywhere: on an airliner, in a day-care center, at a restaurant. We will either take on the challenge as a society, with public health measures that serve everyone, or all of us will be at greater risk.

AKRON BEACON JOURNAL
Akron, Ohio, August 17, 1992

In urban hospitals across the country, doctors worry about the rising number of tuberculosis cases and about new strains of TB resistant to traditional drug treatments.

They are keenly aware of the potential for a medical nightmare if resistant strains of this highly infectious disease spread in cities with populations of HIV-infected people whose immune systems are already weakened.

Scientists report finding a genetic clue why some strains of TB are resistant to the drug isoniazid, the standard TB medication. As the reports point out, the discovery is that a missing or defective gene is responsible for only some resistant TB.

The discovery comes as an immense relief, even with that careful qualification. The scientists suggest the discovery would enable researchers to develop diagnostic tests to identify isoniazid-resistant strains within hours instead of months, as is now the case.

Noting the increase in resistant TB, medical professionals have pointed to patients who quit taking their medicines before they are fully cured, contributing to new strains of the disease that are tougher to treat. If the genetic discovery leads to quicker and more sensitive diagnostic tests, that also may help reduce cases where resistant strains may be the result of improper use or prescription of medication.

The medical challenge is to eradicate TB or, at the very least, to keep it from becoming a widespread scourge. The genetic clue gives researchers a solid and very encouraging lead.

The New York Times
New York City, New York, October 16, 1992

"We have turned a disease that was completely preventable and curable into one that is neither," says Dr. Lee B. Reichman, a leading tuberculosis expert. "We should be ashamed."

Dr. Reichman was lamenting that TB, once headed for elimination in the U.S., has been allowed, through shortsighted public health cuts, to surge back in a more lethal form. Now the nation and its cities are scrambling for money and programs to cope with an epidemic that could have been prevented for a fraction of the cost.

The problems caused by this debacle were documented in a five-part series in The New York Times this week. The number of new TB cases nationwide jumped from 22,000 in 1985 to almost 27,000 last year — 3,700 in New York City alone. Worse yet, many of the new cases are resistant to one or more drugs used to treat TB. As many as half these patients will die of the disease, and many will spread their resistant strains to others.

The Bush Administration is spending tens of millions of dollars a year on TB control, but still far less than the $540 million called for by top health officials. New York City will spend more than $100 million next year, mostly for a prison TB unit and clinic improvements. And it is speeding the hiring of health workers.

But much more is needed, including a long-term care facility for very sick or uncooperative patients, housing for homeless TB victims, and more outreach workers to track down infected individuals and make sure they take their medicine every day. The resistant strains proliferate largely because many patients fail to complete the full 6-to-24-month course of medication.

These programs will cost money. But the sad history of this needless epidemic shows the folly of scrimping on disease control.

copyright © The New York Times 1992

EPA Issues Report on Passive Smoking

The Environmental Protection Agency Jan. 7, 1993 released a long-awaited report on the medical effects of second-hand tobacco smoke. It concluded that other people's tobacco smoke had a "serious and substantial public health impact" on nonsmokers.

Among other problems, the agency found that passive smoking led to:

■ Lung cancer in 3,000 nonsmokers annually.

■ Between 150,000 and 300,000 cases of bronchitis, pneumonia, and other respiratory infections in children up to 18 months of age.

■ A higher frequency of asthma attacks in 200,000 to one million asthmatic children, as well as an increase in the risk of developing asthma.

■ An accumulation of fluid in the inner ear, which could lead to an ear infection.

The report formally classified tobacco smoke as a Class A toxin, along with such carcinogenic substances as radon and benzene.

A first draft of the study had been released in 1990. The EPA had devoted the subsequent years to performing additional research and fending off attempts by the tobacco industry to dilute the report's conclusions.

The report was immediately denounced by representatives of the tobacco industry, who insisted that studies on the health risks of second-hand smoke were scientifically unsound.

The Providence Journal
Providence, Rhode Island, January 10, 1993

Tell St. Peter at the golden gate/That I hate to make him wait/But I've gotta have another cigarette

What was funny some 40 years ago — and "Smoke, Smoke, Smoke" led the Hit Parade when Harry Truman was in the White House — is not so amusing in retrospect.

The health hazards of smoking have been well known for decades: The Surgeon General issued his first official warning about cigarettes in 1964; indeed, snuff was believed to be carcinogenic as long ago as the 18th century. The movement to restrict smoking in public buildings, on airplanes and trains and in the workplace, has gathered momentum in recent years.

Now the Environmental Protection Agency is joining the parade. Last week, the EPA announced that second-hand cigarette smoke — known in the lung trade as "environmental tobacco smoke" (ETS) — causes lung cancer in adults, and significantly increases the risk of respiratory illnesses in children.

Of course, no one who has grown up around a smoker, shares living space with one, or has worked for any length of time in a smoke-filled environment, will be surprised by these findings. But what was once thought to be annoying can, it turns out, be lethal. It certainly makes sense: If smoke, in-haled directly from a cigarette, can lead to illness, there is reason to suppose that cigarette smoke, inhaled at a distance, can damage health as well.

This is basically an advisory opinion: The EPA has no authority to regulate indoor pollution. But it certainly deserves credit for wrestling with an emotional, contentious public issue, and reaching a conclusion that will anger many individuals, especially in the tobacco industry. For while the EPA cannot act on its findings, other institutions of government can be expected to do so. State and local governments, as well as the federal Occupational Safety and Health Administration, will surely give weight to the EPA's findings when designing and enforcing workplace smoking rules.

In the meantime, smokers — especially smokers with children — should take note of some facts: Second-hand cigarette smoke is believed to cause some 3,000 deaths annually from lung cancer. And it is disturbing to learn that thousands of cases of childhood respiratory illness, including bronchitis, asthma and pneumonia, are caused and sometimes aggravated by exposure to smoke.

It is one thing to harm oneself, but quite another to injure one's children. And why hasten that appointment with St. Peter in the first place?

Rockford Register Star
Rockford, Illinois, January 12, 1993

The tobacco industry has attacked the latest Environmental Protection Agency report on secondhand smoke as one more weapon in the war against smoker's rights. It just isn't politically correct to smoke anymore, the industry snidely observes.

But talk about political correctness and the rights of smokers has no place in the dialog about the health effects of secondhand smoke. Smokers have no right to threaten the health of other people. The discussion should focus on the health risks posed by passive smoking.

That's the issue that the EPA report attempts to address. The agency concluded that secondhand tobacco smoke causes the lung cancer that kills an estimated 3,000 non-smokers a year. Just as alarming are the documented effects on children. It's estimated that hundreds of thousands of kids suffer from respiratory diseases that stem from environmental tobacco smoke.

The EPA says secondhand smoke is killing people.

These are children whose asthma is made worse, who get fluid in the middle ear and ear infections, who get bronchitis and pneumonia — all because they are exposed to smokers, some of whom undoubtedly claim that smoking is an inalienable right on which they will tolerate no encroachment.

Such an attitude is shameful. Nobody's health should be chronically, perhaps terminally, threatened by another person's choice to smoke. It's incumbent upon the EPA now to explore in greater detail the risks run by varying levels of exposure.

Ironically, however, in the same week it released the passive smoke report, the EPA dropped tobacco from its studies of indoor air pollutants. The action effectively shut the door on further research on secondhand smoke — just as the debate was beginning to really heat up.

Maybe the flurry of lawsuits that likely will result from the report will convince agency administrators that the research must continue. Now that the battle has been joined, it's no time for the EPA to surrender.

Richmond Times-Dispatch
Richmond, Virginia, January 11, 1993

Last year a blue-ribbon scientific panel warned EPA Administrator William Reilly that much of the agency's science was "unsound" because the EPA lacked adequate safeguards to prevent its scientific findings from being "adjusted to fit policy." The EPA's report on passive tobacco smoke — bureaucratically known as environmental tobacco smoke (ETS) — is a case of fudging science to fit a politically correct, pre-determined policy result.

Since the link between smoking and lung cancer is well-known, many people naturally believe that ETS also must be linked to cancer. But the scientific evidence does not support that view. Some may dislike the sight and smell of tobacco smoke, but offensive does not necessarily equal hazardous.

A recent study by the National Cancer Institute — no tobacco industry lackey — reluctantly concluded there is "no elevated lung cancer risk associated with passive smoke exposure in the workplace," "no increased risk" from childhood exposure, and no increased risk among most non-smoking spouses of smokers. Spouses exposed to more than 40 pack-years (i.e., a pack per day for a year) of passive smoke showed a statistically insignificant 30 percent relative risk of lung cancer. That is less than the risk of miscarriage or cancer associated with drinking ordinary tap water. Epidemiologists generally do not worry about relative risks until they double or triple.

In pursuit of greater regulatory authority over indoor air quality, the EPA skewed its assessment of ETS. First, it included career anti-smoking activists on its ETS panel, while excluding some scientists who had published research questioning the risk of ETS. Then the agency started fudging. When it was discovered that ETS could not be classified as a carcinogen under long-standing scientific accuracy guidelines, the guidelines were changed. Bothersome data were averaged away through a questionable statistical averaging technique — employed by the EPA for the first time on ETS. The National Cancer Institute study simply was ignored altogether.

Even with all this fudging, the EPA cannot explain why its claim that ETS causes as many as 3,800 lung-cancer deaths per year — which would be a large percentage of lung cancers among non-smokers — is not supported by real case histories.

Such shoddy science raised eyebrows on Capitol Hill. When Congressman John Dingell, a Detroit Democrat known for his take-no-prisoners investigations, challenged EPA officials, they essentially answered that the agency needn't be scientifically careful because the subject is tobacco.

The implications of the EPA's ruling go far beyond tobacco. If it can skew science on ETS and get away with it, then what happens when another substance is deemed politically incorrect?

The Record
Hackensack, New Jersey, January 12, 1993

IN LIGHT OF THE damning evidence against secondhand smoke found in a report last week by the federal government, one observer noted that pretty soon there will be only two places where smokers can light up in peace — their homes or their cars.

Unless, of course, the smokers live in New Jersey, where they can go right on polluting restaurants, banks, and other public places. Incredibly, despite conclusive evidence that cigarette smoke is bad for everybody's health, New Jersey has pitifully lax smoking laws. Restaurants aren't even required to have a non-smoking area.

The Environmental Protection Agency's report demonstrates the folly of New Jersey's permissiveness. The EPA officially linked secondhand smoke to lung cancer and childhood pneumonia and bronchitis, and classified second-hand smoke as a human carcinogen, calling it more dangerous than asbestos or benzene.

The EPA also said that second-hand cigarette smoke increases the severity and frequency of asthma in children, causes as many as 300,000 cases of bronchitis and pneumonia in infants, and results in an average of 3,000 lung cancer deaths a year.

New Jersey has pitifully lax laws on smoking.

According to Dr. Alfred Munzer, a spokesman for a coalition that includes the American Cancer Society and the American Lung Association, the report "will motivate state governments . . . to enact further regulations limiting smoking in public places."

But Brenda Dawson, a tobacco industry spokeswoman, said the EPA report would have little impact: "Most places already have smoking and non-smoking sections." Dr. Munzer and Ms. Dawson obviously don't know Trenton.

St. Petersburg Times
St. Petersburg, Florida, January 12, 1993

Four years in the making, an exhaustive U.S. Environmental Protection Agency (EPA) study about second-hand tobacco smoke makes this formal finding:

Second-hand smoke is a Group A carcinogen that kills people.

The federal regulatory classification ranks it with such other cancer-causing agents as benzene, asbestos and radon, and the assessment of EPA Administrator William K. Reilly is even more chilling. Says Reilly: "The risks associated with environmental tobacco smoke are at least an order of magnitude greater than they are for virtually any chemical or risk that EPA regulates."

The public health implications are obvious, perhaps frightening. Among the report's findings are that: Second-hand smoke kills an estimated 3,000 non-smokers each year, it is responsible for 20 percent of lung cancers that are not already attributable to direct smoking, and the cancer risk for a non-smoking spouse of a smoker is one in 500. Worse, the risks escalate for children. The EPA found that children who are exposed to tobacco smoke are more likely to develop asthma, respiratory infections and ear infections.

Though the Tobacco Institute is still unmoved, it is likely that insurers, businesses and legislatures will be. Already, Sen. Frank R. Lautenberg of New Jersey and Rep. Richard J. Durbin of Illinois have announced they will introduce legislation to ban smoking in all federal office buildings and in places with federally supported children's services. One health activist group is already sending copies of the EPA study to 30 fast-food restaurant chains, urging those businesses to recognize the dangers to children and the legal liability the companies could face. In Florida, which strengthened its Clean Indoor Air Act last year, the law is comparatively tougher than in most states but still leaves too many children sitting next to smokers in restaurants.

The issue raised by the second-hand smoke report is not one of limiting smoker rights but of assuring non-smoker safety. The Occupational Safety and Health Administration forbids businesses from exposing workers to other health hazards, such as asbestos; it cannot defend a policy that would allow workers to be exposed continuously to a carcinogen that poses a greater health risk. Similarly, federal and state agencies that regulate the safety of buildings and exposure to such substances as radon can no longer overlook the daily, preventable indoor health threat from second-hand smoke.

Though Reilly seems content to leave the regulatory response to his successors, he did make one important policy distinction in announcing the study results. Said Reilly: "People who do not want to be exposed to environmental tobacco smoke . . . should have that right." That right, in essence, is the right to breathe fresh air.

The Virginian-Pilot

Norfolk, Virginia, January 15, 1993

Forty percent of American adults smoked in 1964, the year when the U.S. surgeon general first published a report indicting smoking as a cause of lung cancer. Roughly 27 percent smoke today, and polls indicate that 80 percent of these 50 million smokers want to quit.

Pressure to quit will intensify now that the federal Environmental Protection Agency has formally declared that environmental tobacco smoke (also known as "secondhand smoke," "ambient smoke" and "passive smoke") has "a serious and substantial public-health" impact on non-smokers.

Specifically, the EPA — relying upon a plethora of studies and rigorous review of research by a broad array of scientists — has proclaimed secondhand smoke to be a "class A carcinogen," as injurious to those who breathe it as benzene, arsenic and radon. The EPA's action clears the way for a near-total banishment of smoking from enclosed public spaces and workplaces, which should further improve the health of Americans overall.

The EPA has been persuaded by evidence that secondhand smoke causes an estimated 3,000 lung-cancer deaths annually in American non-smokers and between 150,000 and 300,000 cases of bronchitis and pneumonia each year in American children up to 18 months of age and leading to hospitalization of 7,500 to 15,000 of these. The EPA asserts that passive smoke worsens asthma symptoms in 200,000 to 1 million children and can increase fluid in the middle ear, triggering infection, which may stimulate a reduction in smoking in households containing young children.

The National Academy of Science and a succession of surgeon generals have long accepted the statistics damning secondhand smoke. But the tobacco industry — with notable assistance by Virginia Republican Rep. Thomas J. Bliley — fought hard against any EPA embrace of the data. Little wonder. The EPA's classification of secondhand smoke as a dangerous carcinogen to bystanders dramatically enlarges the stigma already attached to smoking.

The EPA's pronouncement is not smoking's death knell. But 70 percent of U.S. businesses now regulate smoking in the workplace. The possibility of lawsuits by non-smokers will compel most other employers, profit and non-profit alike, to do the same. More and more companies will refuse to hire smokers.

Smoking ceased to be chic in the United States at least a decade ago. Domestic airline flights are smoke-free and international flights are likely to be so before the year 2000. Forty-four states regulate smoking to some degree. The European Community is warring on smoking — even the French have outlawed it in workplaces and public spaces.

Anti-smoking forces are renewing their efforts to get the U.S. Occupational Safety and Health Administration to restrict workplace smoking nationwide now that the EPA has spoken. It surely will have to do so. But the guess in Washington and elsewhere is that the threat of litigation by non-smokers claiming harm from co-workers' smoke will make regulation barely necessary. And that conjecture could be right on the money.

Washington, D.C., January 7, 1993

Cigarette smoke doesn't just make non-smokers cough. It kills them.

That's a fact the tobacco industry has been trying to put a lid on. For almost two years, its political muscle kept the Environmental Protection Agency from releasing its study on the effects of secondhand tobacco smoke. But today the ugly facts come out: Secondhand smoke injures and kills.

The overdue EPA report estimates that secondhand smoke causes 3,000 lung-cancer deaths a year among non-smokers. It finds hundreds of thousands of children suffer pneumonia, bronchitis, middle-ear infections and asthma attacks from secondhand smoke.

And that's not the only toll.

The EPA report sticks to respiratory dangers; it doesn't go into the links of secondhand smoke to heart disease.

The American Heart Association last August concluded that between 35,000 and 40,000 heart-disease deaths a year are linked to secondhand smoke. That's more than are killed by murderers or by drunken drivers on the highway.

The EPA must study that threat and let the public know the full extent of tobacco's dangers.

But enough already is known for the Occupational Safety and Health Administration to protect workers from secondhand smoke. It does that now for other carcinogens, such as benzene and asbestos, by barring employers from letting them into the workplace air. Where tobacco smoke is a threat, it should be treated the same way.

State and local governments and employers can help clear the air, too.

Five states have no restrictions on smoking and many others only weak ones to protect people in restaurants, airports and other public places.

Three-fifths of schools, to which children must go each day, have yet to ban smoking. Two-thirds of businesses lack rules to keep the air safe.

With today's EPA report, there's no excuse not to enact smoking bans in confined spaces. Secondhand smoke is a killer. It can't be allowed to linger.

Herald News

Fall River, Massachusetts, January 8, 1993

The Environmental Protection Agency's report, released yesterday, concluding that secondhand smoke is more dangerous than previously thought should force all of us to reconsider the ever-burning question of smokers' rights.

The report found that secondhand cigarette smoke is a human carcinogen and causes about 3,000 lung-cancer deaths a year in non-smokers, EPA officials said Tuesday. It also concludes that secondhand smoke increases the risk of pneumonia and bronchitis in children.

Those smokers who have battled for the freedom to light up when and where they want to have argued that smoking only hurts the smoker — an essentially victimless habit, save the harm they inflict on themselves.

But as we are seeing, smoking indeed has its innocent victims. Most notably children of smokers, who have the least control over their environment and often must live in the fouled air of their parents' habits.

While outlawing cigarettes is impractical and charging a heavy user's tax, while useful, can only mitigate some of the problem, the idea of restricting where people can smoke is absolutely essential. Whether in public or private places, it is the non-smoker who should enjoy the right to protection. Smokers, who may be feeling the sting of public disapproval as smoking loses even more of its glamor, should expect more.

The facts are difficult to refute, and those who'd rather fight than switch should realize they threaten to take down a whole lot of others.

The Oregonian
Portland, Oregon, January 11, 1993

The Environmental Protection Agency's new report on secondhand smoke wasn't even officially unveiled before anti-smoking advocates across the land said there ought to be a law – a whole lot of laws. Such hell-bent law-proposing may be an addiction, and champions of government-enforced smoke-free bans might consider a program to kick their habit.

Not that the EPA's latest findings don't raise serious issues. They do. The document blames secondhand smoke for 3,000 lung-cancer deaths among nonsmokers each year, 1 million asthma attacks, hundreds of thousands of cases of pneumonia, bronchitis and other respiratory infections. It says secondhand smoke or environmental tobacco smoke is especially harmful to those suffering from childhood respiratory illnesses. Our bill for this comes due in needless hospitalizations and lost work time.

Nevertheless, calls for across-the-board smoking bans in the workplace and public areas are too sweeping — and probably unnecessary. The science behind the controversial report needs thorough scrutiny. After all, this was a study of studies. We should have the same (healthy) skepticism about this government report as we do about others.

Beyond the science and public-policy communities, the courtroom may be one of the best places to put the report's assumptions and conclusions under the microscope. Let the experts contend in this adversarial arena, as plaintiffs' lawyers bring environmental-tobacco-smoke cases.

For our money, businesses would be wise to create smoke-free environments if only to get out from under the legal costs and damage awards involved in such cases. The fact that the EPA has now listed secondhand smoke as a Class A carcinogen with the likes of asbestos and benzene will doubtless tilt the legal scales. Nonetheless, the tobacco industry and business defendants should have a chance to challenge the science and the prudence of applying these findings to particular circumstances.

There's another reason for letting the plaintiffs' bar rather than government regulators promote smoke-free environments through lawsuits (or threats of lawsuits). Last time we checked, most regulatory agencies in Measure-5 Oregon and elsewhere did not have the wherewithal to enforce laws already on the books. Is a secondary-smoke crusade really where cash-strapped states and localities want to spend their next enforcement dollar?

Adding such new prohibitions and paying for new smoke police — particularly when the science and necessity of these sweeping bans are still debatable — will do little to enhance the government's credibility and moral authority.

Wisconsin ▲ State Journal
Madison, Wisconsin, January 15, 1993

It has been more than 27 years since the surgeon general declared that smoking causes cancer, but even a generation's worth of compounded evidence and millions of printed warnings on cigarette packages have failed to do more than halve the smoking rate. So why are anti-smokers so convinced that the Environmental Protection Agency's declaration that "second-hand smoke" is a carcinogen will extinguish smoking in our time?

It won't, of course, but there is one real-world reason to believe the EPA's ruling will have a dramatic effect on smoking in the workplace, and it may be summed up in one costly word: lawsuits.

Business owners prefer not to leave themselves open to lawsuits if they can avoid it, but businesses that have failed to control workplace smoking may now be vulnerable due to the EPA's long-awaited finding that second-hand cigarette smoke can cause cancer. Sure, the risks of getting cancer from breathing someone else's smoke aren't high — even the spouses of people who smoke at home face no more than a 1 in 500 chance of developing lung cancer, the EPA says, compared to a 1 in 10 chance for smokers themselves. But now that the odds are set, many companies will choose the safest course.

"Prudent employers will, or should, quickly review their smoking policies, and limit smoking to isolated areas with independent ventilation systems to ensure that smoke migration does not reach non-smoking workers," said Jack Lohman, director of the Milwaukee-based Wisconsin Initiative on Smoking and Health.

Legal experts say the kinds of lawsuits that may be spawned by the EPA ruling include workers' compensation claims by non-smokers who say they became ill in a smoke-filled workplace; suits against tobacco companies by non-smokers who have been exposed, anywhere, to cigarette smoke; and damage suits by customers who experience adverse reactions, such as respiratory problems, at restaurants and other facilities that permit smoking.

So much the better, then, that the Madison City Council and city restaurateurs have fashioned a "smoke-free" compromise that will ease cigarettes out of most restaurants by 1995.

About 34 percent of the nation's employers have already banned smoking in the workplace, according to the American Lung Association. The latest EPA ruling won't push that figure to 100 percent overnight or, perhaps, ever, but it has given companies a new incentive to ban or significantly limit smoking in the workplace. Not only is it good for the health of their workers, it may be good for the financial health of the company, too.

The Chattanooga Times
Chattanooga, Tennessee, January 9, 1993

The Environmental Protection Agency certified this week what has been apparent for years. "Passive smoking," which is merely a diluted form of active, voluntary smoking, kills thousands of people and causes smoking-related diseases to hundreds of thousands more every year. That presents a public health issue to the Tennessee Legislature which, perhaps not surprisingly, has House Speaker Jimmy Naifeh backing up at a quick pace.

The question is whether the Tennessee Legislature now will pass a no-smoking law to apply to the state's many public buildings? The cowardly answer is: not very likely. The state's powerful tobacco lobby would probably kill any such effort, says the cigar-chomping speaker.

"I think, with Tennessee being the third largest tobacco growing state in the country, the 50,000 families who rely on that industry might be concerned about that," Mr. Naifeh explained to The Tennessean in Nashville.

The question was asked just after the EPA issued its long-awaited report. That report, and a new state Health Department finding that the number of smokers has risen recently in Tennessee, prompted discussions among several state officials about the need for a ban on smoking in more than 6,000 state buildings.

Such a ban would seem reasonable, even compulsory. The U.S. surgeon general has long required cigarette makers to warn smokers that smoking causes emphysema, lung cancer, heart disease, respiratory ailments, low-birth-weight babies and can be fatal. It's not surprising that research confirms that secondhand smoke does the same thing to involuntary smokers. Nor is it surprising that EPA researchers now officially agree with the heart, lung and cancer associations that secondhand smoke increases asthma, bronchitis and pneumonia in children and the elderly.

What is surprising is that, in view of the now-official health hazard, Mr. Naifeh would expose the state to the legal liability of tacitly condoning smoking in state buildings.

Tennessee and other governmental agencies, after all, impose strict rules governing other health hazards, such as asbestos removal and disposal of toxic wastes. By such standards, Tennessee can hardly afford to be negligent in addressing now-confirmed health hazards relating to secondhand smoke.

Employees and the public have a right to expect to be protected from involuntary exposure to such noxious fumes, and they are likely to press for affirmation of that right. That means lawsuits, delays, lawyers' fees, and possibly damage awards, and there is no sense in dragging out the issue or resisting the inevitable.

Neither is there any reason for Mr. Naifeh to defend Tennessee's tobacco lobby. Tobacco may be, as he says, Tennessee's third largest crop and one on which many families depend. But the Legislature probably would not support abolition of DUI laws to please the liquor lobby. Nor would it encourage the cultivation of marijuana just because it is the state's largest cash crop. So supporting the cancer-for-cash crop doesn't burst with overwhelming logic.

Tennessee deserves better than this disheartening example of upholding private interest over public policy.

St. Paul Pioneer Press & Dispatch

St. Paul, Minnesota, January 10, 1993

In the nation's heated, 30-year-old battle over smoking and the rights of nonsmokers, anti-smoking forces scored a major victory last week. The federal Environmental Protection Agency declared secondhand cigarette smoke to be a dangerous carcinogen and general health risk to nonsmokers.

The ruling is sure to have far-

> **We can't believe Constitution demands that felons be housed according to smoking preference.**

reaching impact — triggering lawsuits, inspiring new regulations on workplace and public smoking, kindling arguments. It may also complicate an already difficult case due to be argued before the U.S. Supreme Court Wednesday. The court's decision, in turn, may have sweeping effects on both the smoking debate and prison policy.

The odd issue before the court in *Helling vs. Mc Kinney* is this: Is compelling a nonsmoking convicted killer to share a cell with a heavy smoker "cruel and unusual punishment" as prohibited by the Eighth Amendment?

William McKinney's situation may well sound like torture to many nonsmokers. The Nevada murderer has often had chain-smoking cellmates, one of whom choked down five packs a day. But the issue before the court is not whether McKinney has a constitutional right to be spared such discomfort, but whether "passive smoking" is sufficiently dangerous to his health to trigger Eighth Amendment protection.

Obviously, the EPA's decision, coming atop much scientific evidence of health risks in secondhand smoke, would make it quite a stretch for the court to deny the risk McKinney is being forced to run.

But does the Constitution protect felons from such risks? If the court decides it does, on what principle could we reject inmates' demands for, say, less sodium in their food, or less "stress" in prison? Any number of credible studies show stress to be a killer.

Several American prisons have attempted to restrict smoking, with disagreeable results, so far. Corrections officials should keep trying. But with due respect to nonsmokers' rights, and to the importance of the Eighth Amendment, we can't believe the Constitution demands that all felons be housed according to their smoking preference.

THE DENVER POST

Denver, Colorado, January 8, 1993

THE PHRASE "Smoking or nonsmoking?" has become as familiar today as the letters "L.S.M.F.T." appeared to Americans a generation ago.

But it may be headed for extinction as a result of the Environmental Protection Agency's decision to formally classify second-hand cigarette smoke as a Class A carcinogen, or proven cancer-causing substance.

Simply put, the designation should prompt restaurants not merely to segregate smokers from non-smokers, as many already do, but to ban smoking altogether, rather than to expose themselves to liability lawsuits by subjecting their waiters and waitresses to such a life-threatening hazard.

Indeed, employers in general may need to review their smoking policies as a result of the ruling. Even the provision of separate smoking lounges now appears to be legally chancy, since such facilities expose workers to a substantial health risk — one that the EPA says is even greater than the risk that is posed by asbestos, benzene or radon.

True, smokers today may voluntarily accept t' e risk. But this should not excuse the employer from the legal obligation to provide a clean and healthful working environment, much less to fend off future lawsuits from former smokers.

In any case, the EPA's long-anticipated decision should give the Occupational Safety and Health Administration all the hard evidence it needs to justify an outright ban on smoking in the workplace — including bars, taverns and private clubs where the practice has long been condoned.

Realistically, it may take awhile for these traditional refuges to be declared smoke-free. In the meantime, OSHA should focus on schools, day-care centers and other facilities that cater to children, who suffer mightily from this sort of indoor air pollution.

Among other things, the EPA says second-hand cigarette fumes cause bronchitis and pneumonia in infants, worsen symptoms of asthma in older children, and even lead to ear infections.

Eventually, cigarettes may be outlawed entirely. But until that day arrives, non-smokers have a right to airtight protections against exposure to the airborne poisons which cigarette smokers generate.

Chicago Defender

Chicago, Illinois, January 9, 1993

It has been reported that the Environmental Protection Agency (EPA) may soon embark on a crusade against a popular target: the tobacco industry. If the crusade is successful, the likely result would be a ban on smoking in restaurants and the workplace to protect others from "secondary" smoke.

The Science Advisory Board (SAB) at EPA has recommended that the EPA administrator list secondary smoke, bureaucratically known as environmental tobacco smoke (ETS), as a Class "A" carcinogen. The board based its recommendation on a yearlong review of the EPA data on the subject. Unfortunately, the board's recommendation was not based on standard scientific methods. Instead, it was based on methods specifically devised by EPA to yield the desired result...that secondary smoke caused cancer.

The study on ETS has ramifications beyond the smoking controversy. This is the first major risk-assessment study conducted by the EPA since the agency issued guide-lines in 1992--and already the EPA is ignoring its own guidelines.

This sets the wrong precedent. And the likely result already can be predicted: Other products similarly will be tarred as "carcinogens" using the same politically correct procedures.

For instance, EPA is now looking into the carcinogenic effects of taking showers. The alleged culprit is the small amount of gas released from volatile organic compounds in shower water. Obviously, most people would be concerned, if not horrified, at the prospect of EPA regulating their showers. Yet the methods used for secondary smoke assessment will partly determine the likelihood of such a possibility.

One problem is the conclusions of the scientific advisory board may have been derived from incorrectly combining numerous disimilar studies. In scientific inquiry, large studies are now alway available to provide researchers with accurate reliable data upon which to form their conclusions. In such cases, scientists sometimes combine the statistical information from smaller studies to form a more reliable statistical picture. This process is known as met-analysis. However, meta-analysis is not an appropriate analytical tool unless the smaller studies are all similarly structured.

Other problems with the EPA secondary-smoke assessment include overeliance on exposure data drawn from people's recollection of their exposure to other people's smoke over many decades.

Specifically, the NCI study found "no increased risk of lung cancer was associated with childhood passive smoke exposure," and no link between cancer and exposure of a spouse for less than 40 pack years (one pack per day for 40 years or two packs a day for 20 years). The study did find a statistically insignificantly increase in cancer risk for spouses exposed for more than 40 pack years.

If science is to be credible and valuable to the public-policy process, it must pass the test of critical scrutiny whether we like the answers or not.

THE ATLANTA CONSTITUTION

Atlanta, Georgia, January 11, 1993

The tobacco industry has come out the loser in its efforts to suppress a federal Environmental Protection Agency (EPA) report on the dangers of secondhand tobacco smoke. That means the American public will come out the winners, if governments at all levels respond to EPA's warnings.

EPA for the first time has declared secondhand smoke a cause of cancer in humans, putting it in the same class with such dangerous substances as asbestos, benzene and radon. An agency advisory panel's survey of studies of passive smoking also blames passive smoking for the deaths of an average of 3,000 Americans a year and for increased risk of respiratory illnesses in children.

Tobacco industry lobbyists have attacked the "flawed science" used by the panel that wrote the report. Hmmmm. Who can be trusted on this one? A group of scientific experts, or the cigarette makers whose multibillion-dollar market shrinks with each confirmation of the dire health consequences of using their product?

A finding by a government agency that secondhand smoke is indeed a threat to the public health should close the debate over just how active governments should be curtailing smoking in public places. The government should no more sit by and allow people to be exposed to secondhand smoke than allow them to be exposed to asbestos.

The EPA has no power to enforce the smoking restrictions that are the obvious follow-up to this report, but its sister federal agency, the Occupational Safety and Health Administration (OSHA), does have the authority. OSHA has dodged requests that it get involved in regulating smoking in the workplace. It should dodge no longer.

If George Bush hasn't issued an executive order to ban smoking in all federal buildings by the time he leaves office, Bill Clinton should do so shortly after he is sworn in. State laws and local ordinances restricting smoking in public places should be going on the books around the country.

The tobacco industry for years has used smoke screens in attempts to obscure the health issues surrounding its products. It has called smoking simply a matter of choice, having consequences — if any — only for those who chose to smoke. That — as the EPA report makes clear — is untrue.

THE ⬛ SUN

Baltimore, Maryland, January 10, 1993

It took the Orioles less time in Camden Yards than it did the Environmental Protection Agency in its labs and offices to decide that cigarette smokers can kill others as well as themselves. The Orioles are going to prohibit smoking in ballpark seats next season. Anyone who still needs to know why need only read the EPA report on the dangers of second-hand smoke fumes also released Thursday. And then wonder how long it will be until smoking is banned in virtually all public places.

The EPA took much too long to publish its report on the damage done to innocent bystanders by people who smoke in public places. The study was ready nearly two years ago but was held up by tobacco industry politicking and bureaucratic nit-picking. Though the study was stripped of some of its more devastating statistics, it ranks cigarette smoke inhaled indirectly through the air with such cancer-causing substances as asbestos and benzene. Perhaps worst of all, smoking inflicts respiratory diseases and aggravates asthma attacks on hundreds of thousands of children each year.

Left out of the EPA report was additional evidence that other peoples' smoke kills even more non-smokers — tens of thousands a year, in fact — by contributing to heart attacks than are afflicted by fatal cancers. Leading health researchers concluded last year that non-smokers had a 30 percent greater risk of dying from heart disease if they are exposed to other peoples' fumes at home.

The tobacco industry and some of its captive experts will doubtless respond once more that the link between cigarette smoke and fatal illness is not scientifically established. Rubbish. From successive U.S. surgeon generals to the overwhelming majority of independent scientists, the poisonous nature of tobacco smoke and so-called smokeless tobacco is firmly established.

The tobacco industry fertilized the coffers of congressional candidates in the last election campaign with an estimated $1.7 million in contributions, according to one advocacy group. But it's a losing cause. More and more the owners or operators of public facilities like the Orioles are sending tobacco smoke the way of flaking asbestos — and for the same reason. It kills innocent people.

Studies of Heart Ailments Advanced and Debated

A new study published Jan. 14, 1988 challenged the widely held belief that aggressive behavior patterns led to heart attack deaths.

It had now been some two decades since the publication of a study by Dr. Meyer Friedman that reported a nearly two-fold difference in likelihood of heart disease between men with a pattern of hard-driving, aggressive, inwardly hostile personality traits – the so-called "Type A" personality – and those with the more placid "Type B." But in a follow-up study by Dr. David Ragland, of 257 of Friedman's original 3,000-plus patients, Ragland reported that the "Type As" turned out to be more than twice as likely to survive heart disease as were those who were less aggressive.

The study left the relationship between personality and heart disease muddled. Friedman contended that every patient in Ragaland's study who died must actually have been a Type A whom Friedman had initially misdiagnosed. "You can't get a heart attack before age 60 if you're a Type B," Friedman said flatly. Ragaland said Friedman was changing the rules after the fact.

Los Angeles Times
Los Angeles, California, April 7, 1988

The controversy over federal funding for a new drug, effective in the treatment of heart attacks, points to the kind of hard decisions that lie ahead as the nation tries to control the ever-increasing cost of health care. The case is all the more pertinent because it focuses both on the inflationary effect of new technologies and on their potential for reducing overall costs in some cases.

Under a new ruling, the Health Care Finance Administration has refused a request from hospitals to allow an add-on Medicare fee to cover the cost of Activase, a new tissue plasminogen activator (TPA) made by Genentech, reported to be the fastest selling new drug in prescription drug history. It is effective in reducing blood clotting that causes heart attacks when applied promptly after an attack. A single dose costs $2,332 compared with an average cost of $185 for alternative drugs, such as streptokinase. Medicare pays a flat rate for hospitalization with any given ailment; payments for acute heart attacks average about $6,500. Hospitals assert that the payment does not cover their costs when they use Activase.

Dr. William L. Roper, administrator of the Health Care Finance Administration responsible for both Medicaid and Medicare, concluded that neither the relative merits of the new drug nor the net cost of its use in hospitals has been sufficiently established to justify a special payment. Some proponents of Activase argue that its effectiveness will lead to shorter hospital stays, which could help off-set the high cost of the drug for hospitals.

We think Roper's caution is justified. He has not closed the door on later acceptance of additional funding for TPA. The drug is authorized for Medicare patients. But he has set a reasonable economic limit until the full story is known.

The economic impact on hospitals may not be as great as forecast. Almost half of the Medicare patients with acute heart attacks are 75 or older, a group for which physicians are instructed to weigh with particular care the risks of the new drug, including that of strokes, against potential benefits.

All health insurers, government and private alike, are coming to recognize that every treatment, every diagnostic tool, every surgical procedure cannot be made available to every person.

Some pharmaceutical manufacturers have helped ease the problem. Last year Merck & Co. made available without charge a drug it developed to prevent river blindness. Earlier this week, G.D. Searle & Co., made available all of its heart treatment drugs without charge to low-income persons.

Rationing is another means to control costs. Despite the resistance in principle to rationing of health care, it already is part of the American system for an increasing number of people. For some who have health insurance, the rationing is effected by requirements for a second opinion before surgery or the permission of a primary-care doctor to gain access to specialists. For more than 30 million Americans, the rationing is indirect: They have no insurance and therefore no easy access to the system at any level of care.

"We are rationing by default," according to the keynote address to the recent meeting of the California Medical Assn. House of Delegates. "It's guided by no social policy. It's not equitable. We are wasting millions of dollars and thousands of lives. The reason we are rationing implicitly as opposed to explicitly is because we don't want to come to grips with our own limits."

That keynote address was delivered by an emergency room physician from Roseburg, Ore., Dr. John Kitzhaber, who also happens to be president of the Oregon state Senate. Furthermore, Oregon is doing something about the problem, making sure at least that prenatal care is available for all before the state undertakes costly transplants for a few.

California state government has yet to take any step along the path to that sort of planning. Nor has the federal government. Problems, such as the supplementary funding for Activase, are certain to multiply. Their solution will only be made more difficult by delaying appropriate global planning for the use of public health-care funds.

The Cincinnati Post
Cincinnati, Ohio, June 29, 1988

In a welcome development, the American Heart Association has decided to seek out and endorse packaged foods that meet its dietary guidelines for fat, salt and cholesterol — culprits often implicated in heart attack and stroke.

According to the association, heart and blood vessel diseases are the nation's leading killers, claiming nearly 1 million lives in the United States in 1985, the last year for which complete statistics are available.

The medical group believes that dietary control is one of the most effective ways to reduce the danger of cardiovascular disease. Since 1961 it has been recommending a diet low in sodium, cholesterol and saturated fat.

Surveys show that many consumers are willing to make dietary changes to lower their risk of heart disease but often are uncertain about which foods to eat.

"As more and more foods are processed and contain all kinds of additives and fat, it is important for the consumer to have a label that they can believe in." said Dr. W. Virgil Brown.

"The American people need better nutritional guidance," he said. "This is really a clear statement that the American Heart Association is willing to take a gamble to achieve that end."

The gamble he spoke of is that the highly regarded American Heart Association will have to deal closely with food processors, often owned by tobacco companies, and may come under suspicion as a consequence.

Under the program, makers of packaged foods will be invited to submit their products for testing by an independent laboratory. Those meeting AHA guidelines for a healthy and prudent diet would be allowed to use its "heart-healthy" logo on their labels.

Many packaged foods now carry labels specifying how many milligrams of sodium and cholesterol they contain. The trouble is that few people know how many milligrams of either are safe to eat. Thus the AHA stamp of approval on supermarket shelves should be of considerable help.

The Providence Journal
Providence, Rhode Island, May 23, 1988

Considering the results of artificial heart implants — none of the five men who received the permanent device is alive; the longest survivor, William Schroeder, lived in ill-health for two fragile years — it is not surprising that the government has decided to discontinue funding for its research.

The announcement, made by the National Institutes of Health, pointed out the present incompatability of the artificial heart to man. "The human body just couldn't seem to tolerate it," said Dr. Claude Lenfant, director of the National Heart, Lung and Blood Institute. This reaction seems to indicate to scientists that the heart may have a ma-

jor role in the body beyond that of simply pumping blood — for instance, that of balancing the chemical make-up.

The government's decision to halt funding should not be seen as an abandonment of the idea of manmade hearts. For one thing, it does not affect private institutions, where, in fact, much of the artificial heart research has been done. Heart surgeon William De-Vries of the for-profit Humana-Audubon Hospital in Louisville, Ky., should still have permission to complete the series of seven transplant operations that the FDA originally approved.

Meanwhile, the government will continue to fund research on what is at

present a much more practical and promising invention — namely, left ventricular assist devices. Much less complex than an artificial heart, these devices work together with the heart to assist it in its pumping activity. They can be used to relieve faltering hearts, as well as — like the artificial heart in recent years — to keep patients alive until a donor organ can be found for transplant.

More important, some scientists believe that advances made with left ventricular assist devices may lead to greater knowledge on how to construct a serviceable artificial heart. It seems quite clear that this is the direction the research should now be taking.

Omaha World-Herald
Omaha, Nebraska, June 19, 1988

Everybody dies of something, it's true. But the object is not to die young, and the nearly 1 million deaths from cardiovascular diseases in the United States each year are cutting short a lot of lives prematurely, according to statistics released by the American Heart Association Sunday.

Once upon a time, many Americans died in infancy or childhood, or long before old age would normally have claimed them. Women died in childbirth; so did their newborns. Men died in industrial accidents because machinery wasn't as safe.

Smallpox took its toll, and influenza, and any one of dozens of deadly diseases that have been conquered — or at least shoved into the background — today. These days, more Americans are living longer and thus giving the

degenerative diseases of old age a chance at them.

But the cardiovascular diseases, heart disease and stroke, are the most responsive to lifestyle changes, according to medical research. Those who want to lessen their risk of developing these diseases, or delay their onset, can stop smoking and get their blood pressure and cholesterol level under control.

There are no guarantees in this life; heart disease has claimed even apparently healthy individuals who followed all the rules. But to improve the odds of dying as late — and as healthy — as possible, listen to the heart association's recommendations: Don't smoke. Keep your blood pressure under control. Consult your physician. Watch your diet to keep your cholesterol level down.

THE DAILY OKLAHOMAN
Oklahoma City, Oklahoma, November 18, 1988

JUST when a generation of well-fed Americans is looking forward to an orgy of holiday feasting, word comes from the medical lab that big bellies mean a high risk of heart attacks.

It's not enough to be weight-conscious, say scientists. How the pounds are distributed on your body could make a difference in your longevity.

A panel of researchers told the American Heart Association meeting that a series of studies in the United States, Europe and Canada have confirmed that those who had more fat around the waist than on the buttocks tended to have a greater number of heart attacks. The ones with big paunches also experienced more strokes and were more apt to develop diabetes.

Wonder if Santa Claus is aware of that?

The findings are of more concern to men than women because fat tends to go

to the hips and thighs in women. In other words, men are more apt to be apples and women pears.

One panel member, Dr. C. Wayne Callaway, said one reason belly fat is more dangerous is that it is more easily released into the bloodstream. His recommendation is, take off the fat and keep it off.

That's good, sound, life-saving advice and everybody ought to follow it.

But couldn't it wait until after Thanksgiving and Christmas?

The Boston Globe
Boston, Massachusetts, June 30, 1988

The nation's most famous and beloved heart specialist, the late Dr. Paul Dudley White of Boston, must be cheering from on high the American Heart Association's program to help people eat their way to healthy hearts.

An early champion of sound diets for the heart, along with dutiful doses of exercise, White, who remained lean and spry throughout a long and vigorous life, practiced what he preached. To encourage Americans to do likewise, the heart association has hit on a way to promote awareness of heart-healthy foods. It plans to give its seal of approval to packaged foods that meet AHA standards for low contents of fat, cholesterol and salt.

Consumers want accurate information about food, but find it hard to get. Labeling is variable, confusing and often misleading.

Before the AHA decided to allow food products that pass its tests to carry an AHA logo of approval, a Task Force on Commercial Product Ventures sorted through the ethical implications of the move. It developed guide-

lines that it believes make the move permissible, including a ban on profiting from the collaboration with food companies.

The benefit of the program is public education, the AHA asserts, not revenue generation. AHA market studies show that the majority of the public would buy brands approved by the AHA. An added boon is that the program should encourage suppliers to develop and market healthier foods.

"Many Americans have already adopted healthier eating habits," noted W. W. Aston, who headed the task force. By identifying heart-healthy food items, Aston says, the AHA is taking "a sensible step further," helping the public become better informed about the diet-heart disease connection and making better foods more widely available.

The AHA is putting the final touches on the program and expects that food designated as healthy for the heart will be on the grocery shelves by July 1989. The spirit of Paul Dudley White would heartily approve.

DAILY NEWS

New York City, New York, July 27, 1991

FOR TOO MANY YEARS, HEART DISEASE was looked upon, both by physicians and layfolk, as a "man's disease." It's not. Women die of heart attacks, too. Yet two new studies show that women still may not be getting the kind of treatment they require.

It's time for doctors to do a thorough examination of the guidelines they follow. And of their attitudes in general regarding female patients.

According to reports published in the New England Journal of Medicine, women complaining of severe chest pain were half as likely as men to be given a basic diagnostic test called cardiac catheterization.

Women were also less likely to undergo bypass surgery or balloon angioplasty. This, even though the women tended to have more advanced heart trouble.

There were certain caveats regarding the age groups involved. One must be cautious, for example, about comparing data on middle-aged men with data on older women. But the results cannot and must not be discounted. They should spur doctors to consider more appropriate treatment for women — and to raise the medical profession's consciousness.

There also should be more aggressive educational efforts directed at women – be it by medical and health groups or by individual practitioners. Women, as well as men, need to be told of preventive measures. They need also to know the early-warning signals. That "man's disease" label must be removed once and for all.

There's another factor at work here. Even in today's supposedly enlightened society, many women continue to complain that doctors — male and female — treat them like children. Talk down to them. Are less than forthcoming with important information.

It's impossible to prove the heart-treatment data have any link to this. But many women have their suspicions.

Chicago Tribune

Chicago, Illinois, August 4, 1991

It's not that women don't die of coronary heart disease. They do, with a U.S. toll of about 500,000 every year, more than from cancer, stroke or any other ailment.

It's not that women don't seek medical care for symptoms of heart problems and coronary artery disease. They do, just as men do.

But physicians don't take women with chest pain and other cardiac symptoms as seriously as they do men with similar problems, two major new studies show. The differences in care are big, significant—and sometimes fatal.

Doctors are much less likely to order major diagnostic procedures and treatment such as bypass surgery for women than for men, even when their symptoms are similar, the studies reveal. And because of such delay, women who do have heart surgery tend to have a more advanced stage of heart disease than do men—and, consequently, a higher rate of death.

Such deadly sexist prejudice is probably not deliberate, but so ingrained in traditional attitudes and perceptions that it goes unrecognized. Women are thought to complain about their health more than men do, so their complaints may be taken less seriously. And despite the grim mortality figures, many doctors are less likely to link chest pain to heart disease in women than in men.

It's also possible that men are considered—at least subconsciously—of more value than women and therefore worth more immediate attention and aggressive treatment, as earlier studies of health care have suggested. Another possibility is that men may tend to be more assertive in seeking medical help and less docile about having their symptoms brushed off as insignificant or emotionally based.

There are some completely valid reasons why men and women need different kinds of health care. These would be more clearly understood if more medical research involved women instead of the usual high preponderance of men.

But when men and women do share similar ailments, such wide discrepancies in their care as are reported in these new studies must be acknowledged and corrected—intentional or not.

THE ROANOKE TIMES

Roanoke, Virginia, March 6, 1991

SCIENTISTS have developed a tiny, diamond-studded tool that can be pushed into heart patients' arteries to tunnel through deposits clogging those blood vessels. The new procedure reportedly was tried on 315 people and succeeded in 95 percent of them.

Another medical marvel. Two cheers.

The third cheer let's hold until more people start taking better care of themselves — so that heart-repair surgery isn't needed as often.

Saving lives is good. So is using fast-expanding medical knowledge and technology to save more of them. But so, too, are preventive care and healthier lifestyles — and they're an awful lot cheaper.

Not everyone with heart trouble, or other health problems, brings it on himself or herself. There are genetic defects. There are congenital difficulties. There are ailments and disorders caused by accidents, by exposure to contagion or bad environment, by poor nutrition and inadequate health care in childhood, by the vulnerabilities of aging. The list is long. Those who need medical care should receive it, and society should be concerned if they do not.

People should not, however, overeat, drink to excess, smoke, drive recklessly and in other ways jeopardize their lives, limbs and general health — then expect medical science to kiss it and make it all well, and health insurance to pay for it. A big chunk of the nation's $600 billion annual health-care bill goes to repair, or try repairing, damage people heedlessly do to themselves.

You can bet that in a majority of cases where it's needed, the diamond-tipped cutter is routing out hardened deposits of fat that derive from bad diet or smoking or both. You also can bet that the technology cost millions to develop and will cost many thousands of dollars each time it's used. Technological wonders are one big reason the cost of health care jumps every year, far outpacing the annual increase in other living costs.

Whenever a new medical marvel is developed, patients want it. That's natural. But there's no way every life-saving medical technique can be made available to everyone who needs or seeks it. There aren't enough machines or hospitals or physicians for that, nor is there enough money. Choices will always be necessary. Do we spend $100,000 of our limited health-care funds to cure one person? Or do we spend $1,000 to make 100 people healthier?

Every life is valuable. That's why priorities are important. The well-off can always afford to take care of themselves. But when government or health-insurance funds are lavished on one person's ailment, it can deprive many other people of essential help. The nation needs a unitary system that assures a basic level of health care to everyone — and includes preventive care to head off the more expensive treatments.

Birmingham Post-Herald

Birmingham, Alabama, July 18, 1988

In a welcome development, the American Heart Association has decided to seek out and endorse packaged foods that meet its dietary guidelines for fat, salt and cholesterol, products that medical science has implicated in heart attack and stroke.

According to the association, heart and blood vessel diseases are the nation's leading killers, claiming nearly 1 million lives in the United States in 1985, the last year for which complete statistics are available.

The AHA believes that dietary control is one of the most effective ways to reduce the danger of cardiovascular disease. Since 1961 it has been recommending a diet low in sodium, cholesterol and saturated fat.

Surveys show that many consumers are willing to make dietary changes to lower their risk of heart disease but often are uncertain about which foods to eat.

"As more and more foods are processed and contain all kinds of additives and fat, it is important for the consumer to have a label that they can believe in," said Dr. W. Virgil Brown, an AHA director.

"The American people need better nutritional guidance," he said. "This is really a clear statement that the American Heart Association is willing to take a gamble to achieve that end."

The gamble he spoke of is that the highly regarded AHA will have to deal closely with food processors, often owned by tobacco companies, and may come under suspicion as a consequence.

Under the program, makers of packaged foods will be invited to submit their products for testing by an independent laboratory. Those meeting AHA guidelines for a healthy and prudent diet would be allowed to use its "heart-healthy" logo on their labels.

Many packaged foods now carry labels specifying how many milligrams of sodium and cholesterol they contain. The trouble is that few people know how many milligrams of either are safe to eat, and thus the AHA stamp of approval should be of considerable help.

The Pittsburgh
PRESS

Pittsburgh, Pennsylvania, February 27, 1991

As Pittsburgh marched through two spectacular brick-and-mortar renaissance periods over the past 40 years, it paid little attention to its regional flesh-and-blood lifestyle. The oversight apparently has caught up with the populace.

The Western Pennsylvania portion of a study being conducted throughout the nation shows that those who live in this region are running more risks of heart attacks than most people in the country. In this region, the study shows so far, more people have high cholesterol or are overweight than those screened in other areas.

More than 3,000 people have been studied in Western Pennsylvania so far and about 40,000 have been screened in 39 hospitals throughout the country. Before the study is concluded, 18,000 people will be checked locally, 500,000 nationwide.

During the first screenings at Mercy Hospital, it was found that 27 percent of the people were up to 40 percent above their ideal weight, compared with 26.2 per cent nationally. In cholesterol tests, in which a reading of 200 or below is desirable, 38 percent of those checked at Mercy had levels from 201-240. The national study so far shows that 33.9 percent of the people are in that range.

Although researchers have not pinpointed the cause of Western Pennsylvania's high numbers, diet has long been the prime suspect in heart attacks. That's where a third renaissance is necessary.

And it wouldn't take as long as the ones that transformed Pittsburgh. "We can change our health, and I think we can do it, 'boom,' overnight," said Dr. William C. Roberts, national director of the study.

He suggests a national campaign to reduce consumption of fat, much the same as the anti-smoking campaign has cut cigarette usage. He also urges people to quit eating between meals, cut down on desserts and reduce meat consumption.

Considering the benefits that could be derived from Dr. Roberts' suggestions, they can hardly be considered Draconian.

CHICAGO
Sun-Times

Chicago, Illinois, January 5, 1991

To a public made skeptical by frequent shifts among doctors on what is good or bad for your health, a study by the American Heart Association brings reassuring news.

The U.S. death rate from heart disease plummeted 30 percent during the 1980s, the study says, attributing most of the decline to general changes in lifestyle and diet.

Specific reasons for this remain officially a mystery due to the lack of hard data, researchers say, but they speculate that two-thirds of the reasons arise from less cigarette smoking, better blood pressure control and lower cholesterol levels.

Control of blood pressure was cited as most significant in the lower death rate from strokes (which fell 31.5 percent). Progress in preventing strokes, the study added, was the greatest it has been since the beginning of the century, when refrigeration eliminated the need to preserve meat in salt, leading to a lower sodium content in diets and, consequently, to fewer strokes.

All of this should satisfy Americans that the trouble they go through exerting self-discipline in lifestyle and diet does have a big payback. The emphasis on preventing heart disease, rather than treating it once it occurs, is proving to be well-placed.

The study's other main conclusion was also significant. It said high-tech medical advances did not seem to improve chances of survival after a heart attack.

Because much of the soaring cost of medical care reflects high-tech diagnosis and treatment, that conclusion could start a national debate on the economic merits of high-tech in medicine.

Newsday

New York City, New York, March 23, 1991

The track record of heart surgeons varies widely. Some keep all their patients alive. Others lose as many as 82 percent of the people on whom they operate.

So the state Health Department is properly interested in monitoring their performance. And with the help of surgeons and cardiologists, it devised a fairly ingenious way of monitoring each hospital's and each surgeon's record, taking account of patients' histories, the complexity of procedures they required and other risk factors.

But the Health Department failed to take account of something else — the public's right to know the results. Newsday needed a Freedom of Information request to pry loose the rankings, and, when it got them, the names of the state's 138 cardiac surgeons had been scratched out. This is censorship that raises the blood pressure to dangerously high levels.

The department's excuse is that making the names public would violate the state's personal privacy act. Nonsense. That act is designed to protect people from unwarranted snooping into strictly personal details of their lives. But it is not intended to shield state licensees from scrutiny of their qualifications and performance.

An even more feeble argument is that surgeons would refuse to operate on high-risk patients if they felt their reputations might be put in jeopardy. But this is a terrible indictment and an unjustified slur on the ethics of the medical profession. Doctors — most of them — don't decide that only the easy cases deserve their attention.

Patients have a right to facts on which to make informed decisions and the Health Department should make them available.

New York City, New York, October 24, 1991

Which heart surgeon would you rather have doing your coronary bypass?

Dr. A, who performed 110 open-heart procedures in a year without losing a patient? Dr. B, who operated 238 times with just two fatalities? Or Dr. C, who did 203 operations but lost three patients?

An easy decision? Not necessarily. For instance, according to the state Health Department, Dr. B's patients were much better risks for heart surgery than Dr. C's, so C's performance actually ranked higher than B's on a risk-adjusted basis. Those all-important risk-adjustments have already been factored into the Health Department's rankings of heart surgeons. One problem: State health officials have stubbornly refused to make the risk-adjusted rankings available to the public.

Although they first compiled the data on mortality rates for coronary bypasses by 30 hospitals and 126 surgeons in 1989, they've refused to identify the surgeons by name. They insisted that the information was likely to be misused or misunderstood, to the detriment of doctors' reputations, if made public.

Now a state Supreme Court justice in Albany has put the bureaucrats in their place. Ruling in a suit brought by this newspaper after reporter David Zinman was denied the names under the state's Freedom of Information laws, Justice Harold Hughes wrote, "The duty of administrators to release to the population the records of its government cannot be dependent upon the administrators' assessment of the population's intelligence."

The judge made the right decision. The Health Department should continue to monitor hospitals' and doctors' performance in open-heart surgery. And it should get over the idea that this information is suitable only for the eyes of health-care professionals when it could be a matter of life or death to patients.

Drugs Urged in Breast Cancer Therapy; Mammograms Before 50 Questioned

In a major policy change reported May 21, 1988, the U.S. National Cancer Institute was now urging that all women who had had breast cancer surgery should follow up with drug or hormone therapy whether or not there was evidence that the cancer had spread.

The advisory was based on three new studies that showed that women who received such therapies were much less likely to have a recurrence of breast cancer. The NCI had earlier advised that there was no need for such therapies after surgery unless there was evidence that the cancer had spread to the lymph nodes or other organs.

In what it said was an attempt to disseminate the information swiftly, the NCI announced the data in a letter to 13,000 physicians without waiting for the results to be published. But it released the results to the public only in a printed press release.

A study published March 10, 1988 questioned whether mammograms or breast X-rays, were worth the expense in women under 50 years old who had no special risk factors for breast cancer. Many health groups advised regular mammograms for women 40 and older.

The new analysis, by Dr. David Eddy of Duke University, was published in the *Journal of the American Medical Association*. Eddy noted that of the 130,000 cases of breast cancer per year in American women, only about 16% were in women aged 40 to 49. According to Eddy's statistical analysis, if 10,000 American women had annual mammograms throughout the decade of their 40s, the mammogram would make the difference between life and death for only 22 women. He questioned whether the outcome was worth the cost – some $250-$200 per mammogram, an expense often not covered by health insurance.

Eddy conceded, "For women aged 50 or over, the value of mammography is so great that everyone agrees that it is worthwhile."

Twelve health organizations June 27, 1989 endorsed guidelines calling on women to have a mammogram every one or two years beginning at age 40 and every year beginning at age 50, whether or not there were any signs of breast cancer.

Those endorsing the advisory included the American Cancer Society and the National Cancer Institute, which had recently issued similar guidelines, and the American Medical Association and various societies of medical specialists. The groups said the guidelines were intended to end confusion over conflicting recommendations.

Lumpectomy, or removal of a breast tumor, when followed by radiation therapy, continued to be as effective a treatment for breast cancer as was mastectomy, or removal of the whole breast. That was the conclusion of a large-scale study that tracked women for up to eight years after various types of surgery. The study was reported in the *New England Journal of Medicine* March 30, 1989.

A panel of experts convened by the National Institutes of Health June 1, 1990 endorsed lumpectomy plus radiation in early cases of breast cancer. The panel concluded that lumpectomy, removal of only the malignant tumor, when coupled with radiation therapy, gave the same "excellent" survival chances as mastectomy, removal of the whole breast, in cases where the malignancy had not yet spread to the lymph nodes.

A high-fiber diet could cut the risk of breast cancer by as much as 50%, according to an Australian study reported Dec. 5, 1991.

The study surveyed 451 women newly diagnosed with breast cancer and an equal number with no history of the disease. It found that those women least at risk ate about one ounce of fiber daily, twice the amount of those most at risk. It also said that fat and high caloric intake, long considered culprits in the disease, actually had little effect on its development.

The
Hartford Courant
**Hartford, Connecticut,
September 24, 1988**

Younger women and their doctors who question the benefit of having a mammogram to detect breast cancer should read a recent National Cancer Institute study.

The research focused on a group of women in their 40s who had confirmed cases of breast cancer. It found fewer deaths among those younger women who had undergone an annual breast-screening, including both a physical examination and X-rays by mammography machines, than a similar group without such checkups.

Among those screened, the reseachers found a 24 percent reduction in the deaths of women 40 to 49, as well as 21 percent fewer deaths in woman 50 to 64, compared with matched groups who had not undergone these yearly examinations. Early detection, when the tumor is small and more treatable, was credited for the improvement.

A decade ago, some people considered repeated mammography unsafe for all women. They argued that the radiation from the machines produced as much cancer as the equipment detected. After those criticisms were rebutted and the test was shown to be beneficial for older women, questions arose about testing women under 50. Skeptics wondered whether mammograms were worth it for women in this group. After all, the disease is rarer among these women, repeated X-ray exposure could cause trouble, the test costs money and sorting out cancer from non-cancerous lumps in young women adds to the expense.

The latest cancer institute study shows mammography carries the same clear benefit for women between the ages of 40 and 49 that it does for women 50 and older. The tests do cost money and can be uncomfortable. They also save lives.

The Miami Herald

Miami, Florida, July 3, 1988

CANCER. The word strikes dread and terror in the hearts of millions of Americans. And yet research over the last 20 years clearly demonstrates that cancer in some of its forms can be cured and in many more forms can be treated. That is certainly true of breast cancer.

Now the National Cancer Institute (NCI), American Cancer Society, and nine other health organizations jointly urge women to begin using mammograms to assure early detection and treatment. Women aged 40 to 50 should schedule mammograms — breast X-rays — biennially, and

women over 50 annually. The tests are simple, safe, and, according to the NCI, can cut the death rate for breast cancer by 30 percent. That could save as many as 13,000 lives annually.

To be sure, the tests involve some expense. The costs normally range from $35 to $70 for women with no symptoms, $100 to $125 for those with symptoms. For many, the cost is simply an investment in good health and peace of mind. So important are these diagnostic tests that Florida and 21 other states require health-insurance companies to pay the costs. Medicare

and Medicaid will begin reimbursing costs in January 1990.

Years ago, when X-rays became a vital tool for early diagnoses of tuberculosis — another great killer that sowed fear and dread — the state established traveling X-ray vans through its public-health clinics. The Legislature should re-establish the program to ensure that women who have no health insurance also have easy access to life-saving mammograms and treatment.

Cancer has touched untold numbers of Floridians. They have waged a personal struggle or watched the fight of a loved one. Cancer is an indiscriminate disease, striking seemingly at random. When the opportunity comes to strike back, it should be taken — by all the women of this state.

PORTLAND EVENING EXPRESS

Portland, Maine, June 29, 1988

In the fight against breast cancer — a disease with an excellent recovery rate if discovered early — nothing is more valuable than breast X-rays, or mammograms.

Therefore, the real tragedy is that relatively few women in the vulnerable age bracket of 40 to 49 get them. The reason appears to be cost: Insurance companies won't pay for screening mammograms — X-rays taken before there's any visible evidence of cancer — and charges run from $65 to $184 across the state.

Since 200 women die a year of breast cancer in Maine and 600 cases are diagnosed annually, the need is great.

A group of 11 national medical and research groups said Tuesday that women 40 to 49 with no symptoms should have mammograms every one to two years, and women over 50 should have them annually. But can they be made affordable?

The Department of Human Services, with the assistance of a financial grant from the

Centers for Disease Control, is working on a plan to improve the process. They hope to assist radiologists with quality assurance programs; advise doctors to recommend mammograms for their patients; help with financing for people who can't afford the full cost and educate consumers about the benefits of regular screening.

Since the cost is the big hurdle, the state is thinking about making insurance companies pay for screening X-rays. Seventeen other states require it. But mandated benefits in other areas are giving cost controllers fits and there's sure to be resistance, even though catching cancer early is the best way to cure it.

State subsidies for low-income women also are under study and the Medicare program will begin to pay $50 for screening mammographies starting next Jan. 1.

For women 40 and older, today isn't too soon to get that first mammogram.

ALBUQUERQUE JOURNAL

Albuquerque, New Mexico, June 19, 1988

Medical consumers and physicians alike should take note of an important study published Friday by University of New Mexico researchers in the Journal of the American Medical Association.

The study's authors wanted to know whether medical *research* translates into medical *practice*. They used breast cancer surgery as their subject, and found that, indeed, New Mexico surgeons have begun practicing breast-conserving procedures since clinical trials in 1981 and 1985 showed them to be effective.

That's good news for women. Breast cancer, a leading cause of death for women, will strike one out of 10. The dread of a diagnosis, however, has been eased somewhat by recent medical developments. One is the mammogram, a low-dosage X-ray that can detect lumps when they're still very small and thus more likely to be successfully treated.

A second step is the growing acceptance of breast-conserving lumpectomies that remove the lump but leave as much of the breast intact as possible. Many women find this preferable to a mastectomy because it is less physically — and emotionally — scarring.

But, there's bad news, too, in the UNM study. Researchers found that, while lumpectomies were becoming more common, a startling number of women were not receiving the follow-up radiation therapy proven to reduce chances of the cancer recurring.

Clinical trials in the 1970s and 1980s showed that excising the lump and irradiating the breast is just as effective as removing the entire breast for women whose cancers haven't yet spread beyond the breast. Yet, the UNM study found that from 1981 through 1985, a quarter of the women under age 65 and more than half of the women over 65 received no radiotherapy following lumpectomies.

Doctors, then, are adopting *some* findings from clinical trials, but not all. And the missing piece could prove fatal.

Why is the radiation treatment not being given? That question was not a part of the study, and cancer specialists familiar with the research can only speculate.

It's a question both breast cancer patients and their doctors need to address. This is one research project that definitely should lead to a change in medical practice.

THE BUFFALO NEWS

Buffalo, New York, September 1989

ANNUAL BREAST X-RAYS for women 50 years and older could save thousands of lives each year. Yet the American Cancer Society estimates that only 15 percent of such women follow its advice and get an annual mammogram test.

Now, however, better compliance with that sensible advice should get a boost from a bill just signed into law by Gov. Cuomo.

It requires all carriers selling insurance policies in the state to cover the costs of these annual examinations, for women 49 years and older, in both their individual and group policies issued or re-issued after next Jan. 15.

Thus, the bill makes it easier for women in this age group, the most vulnerable to breast cancer, to protect

their health against the leading cause of cancer among New York women.

One estimate is that 1,000 new cases of breast cancer and 350 deaths from it occur annually in Western New York.

Thus, as the governor said in signing the bill, this "should save lives."

The state Health Department stresses that mammograms are effective in discovering small breast cancers before they become clinically evident. And early detection is a key to successful treatment of the disease. Yet most health insurance policies, Albany says, don't include such coverage now.

The new law will mandate it in all group and individual hospital, surgical or medical expense policies. It is a good investment in better health for women in New York State.

MILWAUKEE SENTINEL

Milwaukee, Wisconsin, July 12, 1989

A recommendation by 11 medical and research groups that all women have a mammogram every one or two years beginning at age 40 is born of justified concern that ignoring this precaution against breast cancer will needlessly cost tens of thousands of lives.

Statistics showing that one in every 10 American women is stricken with cancer are frightening. But the situation could be devastating. Reports show that only about 15% of the women who should be getting mammograms are doing so.

Part of the problem has been that some medical groups differ on mammography guidelines.

The American College of Obstetricians and Gynecologists did not sign on to the recent report because that organization currently is revising its own guidelines. The American Cancer Society is recommending mammograms at 35.

These groups should try as best they can to explain their differences to women without making them uncertain about the reliability or safety of the test. Such a situation only reinforces the natural fear some individuals have about unexpectedly finding out bad news or confirming worst suspicions.

Where appropriate, counseling on financial aid for the test should be available to those who are not insured.

Ultimately, however, the responsibility for dealing with this killer disease lies with the women who are its victims and who must take the initiative in at least consulting their physicians about a mammogram.

As Charles P. Duvall, president-elect of the American Society of Internal Medicine, put it: "We know we can save lives using this technique. If you have cancer . . ., this is the one way you can detect it at a stage that is relatively mild."

Indeed, as far as potential breast-cancer victims are concerned, this is a case of the life you save being your own.

The Providence Journal

Providence, Rhode Island, July 3, 1989

The importance of mammograms in breast-cancer screening has long been recognized, but there have been conflicting recommendations from various health groups as to their use: Specifically with regard to the questions of when a woman should begin having them, and how often.

Because of this, the recommendations announced last week are especially welcome, having been formulated and endorsed by not one but a dozen health organizations. Included among them were the American Cancer Society, the National Cancer Institute (both of which had issued similar recommendations), the American Medical Association, and a number of radiology organizations.

The guidelines focus on women in their 40s, and recommend that they have a mammogram every one or two years. This takes in women at an earlier age than some of the groups had previously thought necessary.

The importance of targeting this age group is borne out by statistics, which show that one-third of all breast cancer occurs in women in their 40s. It does not mean, however, that earlier mammograms are to be discouraged. The American Cancer Society has recommended that women from 35-39 have a baseline mammogram, because comparing it with future X-rays can be of great benefit.

The real value of this new recommendation would be if it could convince women of the importance of breast cancer screening. It is estimated that only 15 percent of those who should be getting mammograms are doing so, even though early detection of breast cancer greatly increases the chances of effective treatment.

AKRON BEACON JOURNAL

Akron, Ohio, July 2, 1989

THE DEBATE has gone on for years about when women should start having routine mammograms to detect breast cancer. Some doctors question the value of yearly mammograms for women under 50, saying the cost is too great for the relatively few lives saved. Others argue saving even a few lives is worth the effort.

Now, for the first time, the American Cancer Society and 10 other medical organizations have reached a consensus on when the screening should begin: at age 40.

For women, this new agreement puts weight on the side of caution — where it should be. If detected early, breast cancer is highly curable. And while the number of lives to be saved is not great, it's not insignificant either. Last year, a major study by a Duke University physician found that among women between 40 and 50 who have routine mammograms, 22 out of 10,000 women could be saved over a 10-year period.

Of course, mammograms can be expensive, ranging from $35 to $125, meaning that some women in low-income families will be unable to afford them. The consolation is that the price is usually at the lower end at public health clinics, and for those who suspect they have breast cancer, public health workers also help arrange further treatment. For those on Medicaid and Medicare, coverage for mammograms begins in January.

However often a woman has a mammogram, she should examine herself regularly for lumps. About 70 percent of all breast cancer is detected by women themselves.

Still, mammograms can find cancers too small to be felt. The National Cancer Institute says if all women had routine mammograms, 13,000 lives would be saved each year.

Those are figures worth sharing with the women you care about.

St. Petersburg Times

St. Petersburg, Florida, June 30, 1989

Major medical organizations have settled on important advice for women that, if heeded, could be life saving: Women age 40 to 49 should have mammograms every one to two years.

The groups have reconciled contradictory guidelines about when women should begin to have regular screenings for breast cancer, a significant move that should help end confusion that may have kept women from obtaining the breast X-rays.

Unfortunately, even though mammograms are highly effective in early detection of cancer, the number of women who have them is relatively low. In 1987, only 37 percent of women over 40 had ever undergone the procedure.

The benefit of a medical consensus about the best time to begin mammograms would be even greater if there were political consensus about their importance as well. The X-rays can be costly, usually ranging from $50 to $150 in the Tampa Bay area, and insurance companies are required to pay for them in only 22 states, including Florida. Fortunately, a bill to exempt the group policies of small businesses from that law didn't get anywhere in this year's Legislature.

Of course, the law is worthless for women who are too poor to pay for insurance. Even women who qualify for Medicaid are out of luck for routine screening; Medicaid will pay for a mammogram only after a doctor suspects a problem.

And although Medicare will begin paying for mammograms next year for women 65 and older, it will do so only every two years. The National Cancer Institute and other health and research organizations long have urged yearly screenings for women over age 50.

The frightening prediction by the American Cancer Society is that one in 10 women can count on facing breast cancer; 142,000 cases are expected to be diagnosed in 1989. It is second only to lung cancer for causing cancer deaths in women, and 43,000 breast cancer victims are expected to die this year.

Those numbers are too serious to ignore. Lawmakers could help prevent more women from ignoring them by changing the rules that restrict reimbursement for mammograms.

CHICAGO Sun-Times

Chicago, Illinois, October 31, 1991

Stung by charges that it has ignored the impact on women of cancer and other diseases, the National Institutes of Health is finally targeting women's health problems. It is about to embark on the most sweeping women's health study ever attempted, ending its historic focus on men.

The NIH plans to spend $25 million this year to launch a study involving 140,000 female participants and another $50 million a year through the end of the century in what it candidly describes as "the first honest appraisal" of its kind.

"I don't think anybody would dare not fund it after we get this thing rolling," its new director declares. What a difference a woman at the top makes.

We refer to Dr. Bernadine Healy, the first woman to head the nation's largest and most influential consortium of health research institutions, who has ordered new clinical studies and surveys of heart disease, breast cancer and osteoporosis, all of them killers of more women than men.

These studies will examine the roles of hormone replacement therapy, low-fat diets, calcium and vitamin D supplements in prevention, especially among older women. This is gratifying news not only for those at risk, but also for their physicians.

Doctors have long known that women are more susceptible to some diseases and may exhibit markedly different symptoms and responses to treatment than men. But policymakers have been slow to include women in government research.

Such ostrichlike behavior is doomed by Healy's assault on the research gap. She could not have selected a more fitting target.

The News and Observer

Raleigh, North Carolina, November 15, 1990

These days a lot of people talk about preventive medical care and especially about early detection and treatment of cancer. But too few have been able to do anything decisive about it. Now, healthy changes are suggested in two actions aimed at finding and treating breast cancer at its most curable stage.

These are insurance and medical breakthroughs that could be a godsend for American women. Annually, this country has about 150,000 new cases and 44,000 deaths from breast cancer. The rate of death hasn't changed significantly in 30 years, in large part because too few of the nation's older women get timely breast exams and mammograms. (The mammogram, a breast X-ray, is used to find cancerous lumps before they can be seen or felt and before the tumors can spread.)

The good news in the fight against breast cancer came first from an unlikely source: the fiscal 1991 budget bill that Congress debated so bitterly. In a most unlikely development in its closing moments, Congress provided Medicare coverage for a mammogram every other year for women 65 and older. Estimated cost for the first five years: $1.25 billion.

The main reason women ages 50 to 74 give for not getting a mammogram is that they didn't know they needed one. The doctors of many of them still aren't recommending the test to them. But National Cancer Institute studies suggest that 10,000 lives could be saved each year if these women got annual breast exams and mammograms.

The Medicare change, though insuring only a biennial test, addresses cost as another reason too few elderly women get breast X-rays. Although the mammogram cost has dropped from $150 or so a few years ago to $50 in many locations, the expense is still a deterrent for many.

But there's a far more compelling fiscal consideration here: the many billions of dollars that can be saved through early detection. Huge outpourings of Medicare benefits come in the last year or two of life for patients whose cancer is found too late.

The hope of saving lives and money in treating breast cancer is reflected, too, in a decision by one-fifth of the member plans of the Blue Cross and Blue Shield Association. They will pay up to $10 million for the care of 600 breast cancer patients receiving bone-marrow transplants in an experimental program of the National Cancer Institute. This is the kind of transplant in which the patient's own marrow is removed and stored for use in future treatment.

(In North Carolina, Blue Cross and Blue Shield already covers bone marrow transplants for breast cancer cases — one of the few plans that do so. This treatment is offered at Duke Medical Center.)

To be sure, the decision by a substantial number of private medical insurers to pay for a promising experiment in the fight against breast cancer entails financial risk. But Medicare, private insurers, patients and their employers can save big money down the road with serious investment in preventive medicine, early detection and timely treatment. The two recent steps are a promising start.

The Star-Ledger

Newark, New Jersey, October 11, 1991

Modern medical technology can diagnose a problem and correct it. Of course, if that knowledge is not put to use, it's as useless as snake oil remedies.

New Jersey is a state that has been making serious efforts to address major health problems by making it easier for people at risk to consult specialists and find out if they have problems. For thousands of New Jersey women, the state has enacted legislation that will require health insurance coverage for mammograms.

Gov. Jim Florio signed into law a bill that means women 35 or older will no longer have to wait until a doctor finds something wrong before private insurance companies and health maintenance organizations pay for mammograms. The bill requires health insurers to pay for the screening before it is deemed necessary, something that will be a major benefit for many of the state's women.

In this case, the Garden State is not in the fore front. Thirty-three states already require coverage for mammograms, breast X-rays which use low doses of radiation to detect very early signs of cancer in the female breast.

Breast cancer is the most common form of the disease in women and the second-leading cause of cancer death. New Jersey has the third-highest breast cancer rate in the country, behind Delaware and Rhode Island, for both incidence and deaths.

Studies have proven that mammograms can reduce the breast cancer rate in middle-aged women by half, a factor which makes the state's new mammogram coverage requirement a significant medical advance. The new legislation is expected to make physicians feel more comfortable in encouraging women to get mammograms, where in the past they had to find an indication for a mammogram in order for women to get insurance reimbursement.

Assemblywoman Stephanie Bush (D-Essex), a sponsor of the bill, noted that with early detection, women can seek treatment and avoid mastectomies. The legislation is overdue. It is a sound measure that should go far in prompting women to get preventive screenings that provide early detection of breast cancer.

The Virginian-Pilot
Norfolk, Virginia, October 26, 1991

Kathy Gervais has advanced breast cancer. Kathy Gervais also has gumption, valiant not just in her battle against the disease but against impersonal, even imperious medical care, and the taboos about acknowledging cancer's emotional, physical and financial effects.

Enduring them personally must be difficult enough; sharing them with strangers to raise their consciousness — and to tempt their criticism — is more difficult still. The heart unmoved by reporter April Witt's recounting of this one woman's story could shatter concrete.

And this was one woman's story. Similar experiences don't lie ahead for every woman with breast cancer. If given treatments aren't always helpful and appropriate, they aren't always inappropriate and futile, either. Women's responses to this disease, their treatment, their doctors vary, as does the course of their battle.

The vast majority of the 175,000 women who discover breast cancer this year can find effective, even curative treatment in surgery, radiation, chemotherapy or a combination.

A smaller group of women — women with minimal metastasis (spread) and a demonstrated responsiveness to chemotherapy — may well benefit from autologous bone-marrow transplant. They will find ABMT safer than only recently: Mortality associated with the procedure itself has about halved, from 10 percent to 15 percent to 5 percent to 8 percent.

ABMT will not benefit every woman with breast cancer: Many will not have reached the stage of disease at which it is helpful; others will have passed it. And since no insurance funds are infinite, no patient can demand that others pay for any and every available treatment, no matter the expected effectiveness or the consequences for other patients and other ills. But as this treatment is refined both in procedures and in the profile of patients it will help, these patients should find more insurers ready to pay for it than do now.

Learning who benefits from what therapies and why — that takes research, and research takes money. So does answering fundamental questions answerable about other killers of women — lung cancer (No. 1) and AIDS (climbing toward No. 5) — but still unanswered about a disease that now occurs in one woman in nine, is the No. 2 cause of death in women: What causes it? And, that known, how to prevent it?

Given the number of lives it touches, and the number of lives it takes, breast cancer has been shorted on research funds. Of all the problems and difficulties associated with this disease, that should be the easiest remedied.

THE ATLANTA CONSTITUTION
Atlanta, Georgia, January 24, 1991

This year, more than 150,000 American women will discover they have breast cancer. About 44,000 will die.

Today's statistics are horrifying enough, but the future may be even worse. While other diseases are being beaten back by modern medicine, the breast cancer rate is soaring.

One woman in 10 will join the ranks of victims — that's up from one in 20 in 1960. The National Cancer Institute says the U.S. incidence shot up 32 percent just between 1982 and 1987.

The U.S. government, insurers and the medical establishment have been slow to respond to this crisis. A lack of dollars and coordination are making the problem worse.

For example, Congress finally has agreed, beginning this year, to allow Medicare to pay for one test every two years for women over 65. But Medicaid still won't reimburse poor women for the tests, which cost up to $200 each.

Nor is federal support for research adequate. The government is spending only $77 million a year on breast cancer research, while giving $1.1 billion to the study of AIDS. The point is not that Congress is spending too much to fight an infectious disease, but that it is doing too little to stop another major killer. Rep. Mary Rose Oakar (D-Ohio) is now pushing a bill to boost basic research on breast cancer by $25 million.

Congress also must look into the practices of insurance companies, which are trying to dodge the breast cancer issue. For example, insurers who routinely pay for bone-marrow transplants for victims of leukemia and lymphoma refuse to pay for the same procedure for women with breast cancer.

While studies show promising results for women getting such treatments, insurers insist the efforts are "experimental." The $150,000 price tag has something to do with their skepticism.

Even the price of a mammogram to detect a tumor early is too much to bear for most insurers. They refuse to pay for the expensive late-stage treatments and balk at reimbursing women for early detection efforts.

The medical establishment also has failed to respond adequately to the breast cancer crisis.

Nearly half of all women who never have had a mammogram say their doctors have never suggested they get one. In addition, many doctors fail to properly maintain their mammography equipment. Most facilities have never been certified by the American College of Radiology. No national guidelines exist for licensing the technologists who operate the equipment.

Physicians, researchers, technologists, insurers and government officials must pull together their knowledge and resources to develop better strategies for preventing and treating breast cancer. Ignoring the problem will cost far more — in lost productivity, growing medical expenses and human misery — than working together to attack it.

Atlanta, Georgia, August 5, 1991

The timing is pretty amazing: Just as a series of medical-journal articles indicates the male-dominated medical profession may be poorly serving women, President Bush has decided to veto a bill aimed at improving health care for women.

The articles clearly suggest that sexism gets in the way of medical care. According to two studies on heart disease in The New England Journal of Medicine, women routinely are being treated less aggressively than men.

One study, involving more than 2,000 male and female heart attack victims at 112 hospitals, showed that even when women had worse chest pains than men, they were far less likely to get an important test known as cardiac catheterization. As a result, the women were half as likely to have bypass surgery.

The second study, of 82,000 heart patients, found that women with heart disease lag in getting another treatment, angioplasty.

A third report, from the American Medical Association, found similar discrepancies in kidney transplants and lung cancer.

Now Congress is trying to undo some of the discrimination against women. A bill passed by the House would create the Office of Research on Women's Health in the National Institutes of Health (NIH). It also authorizes a $50 million increase in research for breast and ovarian cancer; gives $40 million to research osteoporosis and other diseases that strike women; encourages research into contraception and infertility; and requires that women and minorities be included as subjects in NIH research.

Despite overwhelming evidence that women are being studied less and treated less, Mr. Bush says he will veto the bill. He claims the bill would intrude on the NIH's ability to spend research money as it sees fit.

He also opposes a provision permitting research using fetal tissue obtained from miscarriages or abortions to save a mother's life. Mr. Bush fears abortions will increase if the moratorium on such research is ended, a worry that is, quite simply, nonsense.

Many in Congress were stunned that the administration would take such a hard line against research to benefit women.

Mr. Bush "opposes every one of the key enhancements for women's health in the NIH revitalization bill," Rep. Nita Lowey (D-N.Y.) said. "Women are sick and tired — sick because their health concerns are ignored and tired of inaction by the administration."

Top-quality health care will continue to elude women until attitudes change in the doctor's office, at the NIH and in the White House.

The Des Moines Register

Des Moines, Iowa, March 4, 1991

Senator Tom Harkin wants to expand Medicare to include one diagnostic procedure at an added annual cost of about $140 million. That's one-seventh of 1 percent of Medicare's $100 billion total cost — but it has implications far greater than its price tag would indicate.

Citing the significance of mammograms in the detection of breast cancer in women, Harkin wants Medicare to pay the cost of the diagnostic procedure for all woman over age 50, unless they have private insurance that will cover it.

The importance of early diagnosis of breast cancer is unquestioned, given the cancer's high incidence. Of the 3,000 Iowa women expected to die of cancer this year, breast cancer will claim 550 (second only to lung cancer's 560). Breast cancer will account for almost one-third of the 6,900 cancer cases expected to be diagnosed among Iowa women this year.

Harkin's idea could save tax money as well as lives. Treatment in early stages of breast cancer is far less costly than in advanced stages. Mammograms represent sound preventive medicine that should be encouraged.

But the Harkin proposal also represents a break with the policy that has governed Medicare throughout its quarter-century of existence. Medicare, financed in major part with income taxes and to a lesser degree by earmarked worker contributions, was designed to serve retirees and the disabled. In 1974, in a move little noticed by those not directly involved, the program was expanded to cover renal dialysis for kidney-disease victims of all ages — an expensive treatment necessary to their survival. Otherwise, Medicare has remained a benefit serving exclusively the elderly and disabled.

Harkin's proposal would extend coverage to a new age group — women over 50 — establishing a precedent that conceivably could open the floodgates. Medicare coverage would be sought for dozens of procedures for others who are neither elderly nor disabled. Is Harkin prepared to argue that other diagnostic procedures involving deadly diseases are of lesser merit, and hence should not be financed with public money?

Health care in America is approaching a crossroads. Its cost this year will hit $700 billion, equal to the nation's total gross national product just 25 years ago. With health care gobbling up a steadily increasing share of the nation's income, something has to give. Fee-for-service care could all but collapse, giving way to a national health-insurance plan that, in effect, extends Medicare-style benefits to all, while imposing some draconian controls on patient prerogatives.

Harkin's proposal helps demonstrate the inadequacies of the present system, inadequacies for which there may be no cure other than some type of national health insurance. If nothing else, the Harkin plan regarding mammograms should place more pressure on Congress to examine where health care falls short, and to work harder to ensure that all Americans get the care they need.

Newsday

New York City, New York
October 6, 1991

Some really good news for women: Follow-up treatment of early breast cancers with tamoxifen — a synthetic hormone that blocks the action of estrogen — can save lives. An Oxford University team analyzed the data on follow-up treatments of 75,000 women whose breast cancers had been surgically removed. The researchers concluded that women treated with tamoxifen, chemotherapy or (even better) both had a real edge over those who weren't: they lived longer and had fewer recurrences of the disease.

The Oxford study should persuade more women *and* their doctors to follow the National Cancer Institute's 1988 recommendations. The institute has urged all women with breast cancer — no matter how small the growth — to undergo hormone treatment and/or chemotherapy after the tumor is removed.

The Oxford team, led by statistical whiz Richard Peto, also found that the benefits of even brief treatments are long-lasting. But it'll take additional research to determine how long tamoxifen should be taken to maximize its benefits and whether it could help prevent cancer. With one in nine American women expected to get breast cancer, Oxford's study should help doctors provide more effective therapy — and women to lead longer lives.

The Duluth News-Tribune

Duluth, Minnesota, October 4, 1991

After her sister died in 1981 from breast cancer, Nancy Brinker could have stayed in her grief, hidden from the world. Instead, Mrs. Brinker began gathering information on who gets the disease, when, the symptoms and what could be done to save thousands of lives. Many women are grateful for her efforts, which became the Susan Komen Breast Cancer Foundation in 1982.

Over the past several years, the foundation has provided information to thousands of women nationally, offered low-cost mammograms to those who couldn't afford the fee and brought national attention to what was once considered a woman's issue. It's been a champion of women's rights, helped states change laws to force insurance companies to pay for annual mammograms and raised millions of dollars in research grants.

The American Cancer Society estimates more than 175,000 American women will be diagnosed with breast cancer and about 44,000 will die this year from the disease. The society says at least 12,000 of them might have been saved if they had followed early detection guidelines.

Worse yet, the American Cancer Society says the incidence has been growing steadily since the 1960s, when one in 14 women was expected to get the disease.

Unfortunately, too many women have placed their health care as a last priority — behind the spouse or children's health, behind the mortgage payment and car note. Sometimes, their health care is ignored. Or because they fear the unknown. If they know they have breast cancer, decisions will have to be made. No test, no decision.

The foundation's goal is to provide women with information so they can make informed decisions.

The Komen Foundation is joining with the National Cancer Institute to hold a series of breast cancer symposiums across the nation beginning next year. Special emphasis will be placed on the creation of in-house screening programs and the importance of early detection.

Early detection can be a matter of life and death.

Minneapolis Star and Tribune
Minneapolis, Minnesota, June 23, 1991

Much was made last week of the national Blue Cross and Blue Shield Association's decision to provide insurance for preventive health care, including regular mammogram screenings.

Maine women have a head start. As of March 1, health insurers in this state have been required to include non-diagnostic mammograms as mandated coverage. Medicaid already provides it.

That doesn't mean the screening coverage is now on line for every insured woman. Under the law, it kicks in on the day of the year that corresponds to a policy's renewal date, whether or not the policy is actually up for renewal.

Are you covered? It's worth finding out. Each year 200 Maine women die of breast cancer. Adequate mammogram screenings, experts say, could cut that deadly number in half.

Cancer Cases Rise 1% a Year

The number of new cases of most major forms of cancer in the U.S. was continuing to increase about 1% a year, according to the annual report of the National Cancer Institute, reported Feb. 2, 1988. Scientists had no specific explanation for the rise, though current speculation focused on environmental causes such as exposure to industrial wastes and industrial chemicals, radon gas, diesel exhausts, and various dietary factors.

Among other findings, the NCI reported that when lung cancer was excluded, the overall death rate from all other forms of cancer was down slightly from the previous year. Both the incidence and death rate from breast cancer were rising, however.

Deaths from lung cancer continued to rise sharply among American women, a new U.S. government study reported July 28, 1989. According to the Centers for Disease Control in Atlanta, lung cancer deaths among American women increased by 44% from 1979 to 1986. Although the overall number of lung cancer deaths among men was still much higher, the lung cancer death rate rose by only 7% among men over the same span. The Center said that 126,000 Americans, more than 40,000 of them women, had died of lung cancer in 1986. There was recent evidence that the rate of new cancers had leveled off or begun to decline among white men, though it was still rising among black men and women of both races.

The incidence of cancer in the U.S. continued to increase, but a greater number of victims lived at least five years from the time of diagnosis, according to a report released July 31, 1991 by the National Cancer Institute.

The report was based on studies of nine geographic areas representing 9.6% of the total U.S. population.

According to the report, the incidence of cancer between 1973 and 1988 had risen 16.8% among whites and 16.3% among blacks. Cancer among males rose 20.2%, while among females it increased 12.6%. However, cancer deaths among children had declined 13.8%, the study said.

The institute reported that 51.1% of cancer patients survived five years or more.

Lung cancer was the leading deadly cancer, according to the institute, which forecast that it would amount to 28% of all cancer deaths in 1991.

The Evening Gazette

Worcester, Massachusetts, December 26, 1988

It's far too soon to announce the discovery of the long-sought therapy that destroys cancer cells without damaging healthy tissue. But a report from the National Cancer Institute on a new biological therapy has renewed hope that — just maybe — researchers are on the road to finding that elusive "magic bullet."

Radiation therapy, chemotherapy and improved surgical techniques developed in recent decades have gone a long way toward convincing the public that a cancer diagnosis — particularly early diagnosis — is no longer tantamount to a death sentence. Yet these conventional therapies carry a danger, since healthy tissue often is damaged or destroyed along with the cancers.

The so-called "biological therapy" is designed to fight cancer by strengthening a patient's own immune response to the tumor. The therapy — a variation of an approach announced three years ago and still being tested — uses a potent immune-system hormone called interleukin-2, which spurs rapid growth of certain cancer-fighting white blood cells.

The results reported by the cancer institute were based on a small sample of 20 patients with advanced malignant melanoma — a deadly skin cancer. After a five-day course of treatment, widespread tumors shrank by more than half in 10 patients; the tumor disappeared completely in another patient, who has remained disease-free for 15 months.

There are serious drawbacks to the new biological therapy. It is even more cumbersome and expensive than the previous application. Despite the encouraging results in cases of skin cancer, it seems to be ineffective against other cancers, including lung cancer. It has potentially severe toxic side effects and can cause fluids to leak from blood vessels.

Whether the therapy will ever find its way from the laboratory to the hospital is an open question. Other, less elaborate "magic bullet" therapies might make interleukin-2 obsolete before the treatment is perfected. At the very least, however, the new therapy represents another small victory in scientists' continuing war on cancer.

Lincoln Journal

Lincoln, Nebraska, Spetember 12, 1988

One doesn't have to accept unconditionally the statement made by the director of epidemiology for the Dow Chemical Co. Nevertheless, there's a lot going for Dr. Ralph Cook's blunt comment:

"If you really want to prevent getting cancer, the best way to do it is to take a good look in the mirror. You'll be looking at the one person who has the most to say in whether or not you get the disease."

Corporations like Dow which manufacture industrial chemicals usually are hypersensitive to public concerns about the carcinogenic potential of their products in the environment. That's a big reason why Dow and like giants even have epidemiologists on the corporate payroll.

The Dow news release providing Dr. Cook's observations includes a summary of research done in 1981 estimating that "environmental pollution accounts for only 2 percent of cancer cases." The other cancer causes, according to that research:

Diet — 35 percent, tobacco — 30 percent, infections and viruses — 10 percent, reproductive and sexual behavior — 7 percent, occupation — 4 percent, alcohol — 3 percent, excessive sunshine — 3 percent, medicine and medical procedures — 1 percent, food additives — 1 percent or less.

That doesn't add up to 100 percent, but the central actors in the general cancer scenario seem sufficiently identified.

Even in the ever-threatening soup of industrial chemicals in which we swim, cancer risks can be minimized by not smoking, drinking alcohol only in moderation, avoiding too much sunlight and sticking to a balanced diet that is calorically reasonable, low in fat and high in fiber.

The Gazette

Cedar Rapids, Iowa, April 8, 1988

WHEN AMERICAN and Soviet physicians held their satellite-linked conference on cancer recently, a fascinating attitudinal polarity emerged: Majorities of Russian doctors and patients both favored patients' being *not* informed when they are diagnosed as having the disease. Majorities of U.S. residents and doctors both preferred the patients' knowing of it all the way.

A telltale contrast in societal devotion to reality and truth seems evident in that. Paternalism seems to father what the Soviets prefer. For us, a stress on individuality comes through. The most intriguing aspect is *why* citizens of the U.S.S.R. prefer their shielding from painful truth.

A solid hint of why they do turns up in an exchange of cancer-treatment data for both countries: The United States has 5 million cancer survivors. The Soviet Union, with 50-60 million more people, has 2.7 million survivors. Manifestly, treatments here produce distinctly more successes than do Russia's treatments. Hence the Russians' gloomy attitudes on cancer: People generally don't want to know because so many think that "cancer" automatically means death. Their doctors seemingly concur: Informing patients is taboo because it "burdens" them too much. Survivability is seen and known here much more vividly.

We can't claim overwhelming qualities of U.S. candor-practice even so, however. More and more Americans at heavy risk from AIDS reportedly are spurning tests for that because they just "don't want to know" if doom impends. But cancer's obvious survivability has made it something for Americans to face and fight head-on.

What Russia clearly needs are comparable skills and information to attack the cancer menace there. Early detection, preventive education, intensified research, ever-emerging advances in radiation treatment, chemotherapy and surgery — all these elements of U.S. work have made their mark. When Soviets know generally what our American majorities already know, their fright can turn to hope and confidence in due course, too.

Portland Press Herald

Portland, Maine, July 18, 1988

Nearly eight years ago, billionaire industrialist Armand Hammer, chairman of the Occidental Petroleum Corp., offered a million dollars to any scientist who could come up with a cure for cancer by 1991. So far, the prize has gone unclaimed.

But a subtle change has occurred all the same. From talk of a single dramatic breakthrough that will erase cancer forever, emphasis has shifted to what *can* be done right now, today, to encourage cancer's early detection, treatment and prevention.

Right at the top of the list, of course, are the most preventable of cancer deaths: those related to smoking. An estimated 320,000 smoking-related deaths occur in this nation each year, several hundred of them in Maine.

Yet not all forms of cancer are as clearly linked to personal habits. And for these the most potent weapon remains early detection and treatment. The National Cancer Institute believes aggressive use of knowledge and techniques available now could halve the number of Americans who die from cancer by the year 2000.

Surely that's worth shooting for. But it's a goal unlikely to be met if, as the National Centers for Disease Control reported this week, cancer detection tests continue to be underutilized.

Prime among underutilized tests is routine screening mammography, effective in detecting breast cancer among women years before it can be found by any other means. Unfortunately, the cost of such tests — ranging from $60 to $200 in Maine — frequently is not covered by health insurance. That's bad enough. Even worse, state-of-the-art mammography is widely unavailable in rural areas of this state.

Until science steps forth to claim Hammer's million-dollar prize, no weapon available to fight cancer should go underused by anybody.

The Houston Post

Houston, Texas, June 17, 1988

Congratulations to Dr. John Stehlin and the researchers at the Stehlin Foundation for Cancer Research. Their work on skin cancer has resulted in a treatment that dramatically increases the chances of survival for those suffering from advanced melanoma.

Stehlin's procedure, which combines heat and chemotherapy to combat cancer cells, has raised the five-year survival rate of those with advanced skin cancer from 20 percent to 74 percent. And this method is certainly preferable to the previous one: amputation.

The most intriguing part of this work is the possibility that Stehlin's treatment actually activates a patient's immune system to fight the cancer — a side effect which might pave the way to a vaccine. But whether that comes to pass or not, this is great work.

Portland Press Herald

Portland, Maine, June 1, 1988

Found and treated before it spreads, the five-year survival rate for breast cancer approaches 100 percent.

But women in various parts of the state aren't getting a fair shake at receiving the most likely means of detecting breast cancer early: X-rays of the breast, called mammograms, which at $60 to $200 are priced beyond the capacity of many poor patients to pay and unavailable at many smaller hospitals.

And worse yet, those women covered by insurance find their policies don't pay for "screening mammography," recommended by physicians every year or two once their patients reach middle age.

Insurance typically will pay for "diagnostic" X-rays, once a doctor suspects cancer is present. But that usually means first finding a lump considerably larger than one that would initially show up on an X-ray.

The insurers say routine mammography catches only a small percentage of breast cancers and their customers would find themselves paying premiums for many useless tests.

But they should take seriously the argument that finding cancers two to five years earlier through screening will save their clients more than the present policy of shortsighted cost-cutting.

More diagnostic units in more hospitals would also help rural women to get convenient tests. Hospitals have to re-evaluate their pricing policies to lower the cost of mammography as much as possible. And the state has to find some way to help uninsured women as well.

For as long as remedies are debated and not implemented, more women will needlessly die.

THE ANN ARBOR NEWS
Ann Arbor, Michigan, August 20, 1991

Zelenka's Nursery of Grand Haven will receive federal funds to promote growth of a rare ornamental shrub, the Pacific yew, from which the anti-cancer drug taxol can be extracted.

Taxol is an effective treatment for breast and ovarian cancers, and has been shown to inhibit or shrink tumors in one-third of the 500 cancer patients tested, according to the National Cancer Institute. Each year, ovarian cancer kills 12,500 women and breast cancer kills 45,000.

However promising taxol is, the production of it has been controversial. The yews grow naturally as trees in Northwest Pacific forests, which are also homes to the spotted owl, an endangered species. Because it takes the bark of 38,000 trees to produce about 25 to 36 kilograms of taxol, production of the drug threatens the owl as well as the environment. Zelenka's says it can produce 25 to 36 kilograms from the needles and twigs it clips from the yews.

The nursery will receive over $300,000 in federal grants to improve production of the shrub. It will work with Bristol-Myers, who won a contract from the National Cancer Institute to study and develop the drug.

This is a good use of our federal taxes.

Herald STYRACUSE American
Syracuse, New York, June 2, 1988

Say "cancer" and for a moment, the heart quickens and panic sets in.

You don't want to say it again.

That's how terrifying a disease it is — we don't even want to form the word that describes the illness — as if saying it out loud will jinx us and we'll get it.

We have good reason to be afraid. Cancer is expected to kill 500,000 Americans this year; another 1 million will be diagnosed with the disease.

What we don't hear about too often is the people who defy the dragon and live to tell about it. Six million of them — perhaps weakened from the battle with difficult treatments, with insurance companies over benefits, with a government reluctant to sanction experimental treatments and properly fund research, with the fear of reoccurrence — but alive.

Today is National Cancer Survivor's Day, the occasion set aside to honor their triumph. The survivors should help ease fears about cancer, while making it clear to those who have never had cancer that there is still no potion, no treatment that guarantees survival.

If only the government would commit funds to save lives as quickly as it does to destroy them, say cancer groups like the locally based Families Against Cancer Terror. They're right.

Cancer killed more people in 1990 than died in all U.S. wars in the 20th century. Yet, the money spent on one $850 million B-2 bomber is half of what is spent by the government on cancer programs.

The cruel reality is that most of us are more likely to die from a cancer-related disease than in a war against an undetermined enemy. The government would be hard-pressed to find a family in America that doesn't have a member who has or has had cancer.

With that truth in mind, the government should loosen its purse strings where cancer funds are concerned and should make sure that bureaucratic bumbling doesn't stand in the way of promising cancer drugs.

Then one day soon we can have a Cancer Cure Day and count the billions who survived a disease that people could speak of without fear.

Los Angeles Times
Los Angeles, California, March 7, 1989

IN a strong and welcome move, the 12 nations of the European Community have agreed to end by the year 2000 production and use of chemicals that destroy the Earth's ozone layer.

The EC action quickly caused President Bush to adopt the same goal. The two developments are important because Western Europe and the United States together account for more than two-thirds of world consumption of chlorofluorocarbons (CFCs).

The chemicals are used as coolants in refrigerators and air conditioners, as propellants in aerosol spray cans, as solvents and in foam products. They are as dangerous as they are useful, for they rise to the stratosphere where they attack the gaseous ozone that screens cancer-causing ultraviolet radiation from the sun.

If the ozone layer breaks down, scientists expect a sharp increase in skin cancer and harm to domestic animals, plants and crops.

Many industrial nations agreed in 1987 to reduce use of CFCs by 50 percent by the end of the century. That treaty has been signed by 31 countries, including the United States, most of Western Europe, Japan and the Soviet Union. It took effect last December. The EC agreement also calls for an 85 percent cut in production "as soon as possible."

Prime Minister Thatcher of Britain is not often thought of as an environmentalist. But she was educated as an industrial chemist and is taking the lead in seeking to lessen the CFC problem.

Britain has invited representatives of 112 nations to London, where it is hoped developing countries can be persuaded to join industrial ones in phasing out CFCs. The key is to get China and India, both large CFC users, to adhere to the Montreal treaty.

Scientists calculate that if the whole world stopped making the chemicals now, enough are rising toward the stratosphere to continue to deplete the ozone layer.

If that's true, human beings will have to demonstrate uncommon cooperation among nations to limit the growth of skin cancer.

Omaha World-Herald
Omaha, Nebraska, July 26, 1989

A new report from the American Medical Association's Council on Scientific Affairs makes it unmistakably clear: Tanning isn't good for human beings.

Tanning raises the risk of skin cancer, wrinkles and eye damage and can harm the skin's immune system. It offers no benefits beyond, for some people, the psychological lift that comes with a good suntan.

Similar reports, though few so unequivocal, have been released in recent years. Most tanners should know by now the risks they take.

But tanning is associated with fun. Heading for the lake or the pool is one of the pleasurable aspects of summer. A tanned complexion is, to some people, a sign of good health and attractiveness. That is a relatively recent part of American culture, and not only for young people.

But cultures can be changed and in this instance should be. People can still enjoy the beach while using a heavy-duty sun screen instead of ointments that help the sun darken the skin.

Despite the new report, a lot of people will still spend long summer hours seeking a tan. That doesn't mean that the AMA is wasting its time. Somewhere, someone may curtail his or her exposure to the sun because of these warnings. As the evidence accumulates, untanned skin could eventually become the norm.

The Hutchinson News

Hutchinson, Kansas, August 19, 1992

Sen. Bob Dole, R-Kansas, seems to enjoy his role as point man for the war on prostate cancer.

More power to him.

Prostate cancer doesn't know what's in store for it.

Daily, Americans are deluged with warnings about everything from the dangers of pigging out on bacon rinds to hearing the constant litany of precautions necessary to avoid contracting the AIDS virus.

A lot of those messages are lost in the course of a busy day, especially because many spokesmen are selling something along with delivering their message. They are raising money, selling books or simply promoting themselves and their own dark made-for-television tales.

With Dole walking point on behalf of the prostate message, chances are good that many American men will take notice.

Dole's personal close call with cancer resulted in a successful surgery and a zealous determination to get the word out.

As a self-made spokesman for the medical malady, Dole's visibility gives him an advantage over other spokesmen hyping messages that begin to sound like a disease-of-the-week television series.

He is not selling a book, an afternoon television weep session or a coming movie. He is merely spreading the message of good health.

While celebrating his political party's convention in Houston, Dole used the occasion to celebrate his own good fortune by telling his health tale to anyone who would listen. His office receives 200 phone inquiries a day from people concerned about prostate cancer, a measure of his effectiveness.

Unsparing diseases need more spokesmen such as Dole, whose wit, good humor and engaging message can be heard above the for-profit medical babble that has many Americans so tuned out they can't separate necessary health advice from those who would exploit disease for their own selfish motives.

The Detroit News

Detroit, Michigan, September 29, 1992

Pose this simple question to a schoolchild:

What makes more economic sense? To pay $125 for a screening test that could detect cancer and prevent the spread of the disease? Or to pay $60,000 for surgery and treatment after the cancer has spread?

The common sense behind prevention seems so obvious that it is almost embarrassing to debate.

Yet many insurance companies — including the government's Medicaid program — refuse to pick up costs for preventive screening tests, preferring to pay for "symptoms" and their costly remedies.

For instance, there is a procedure capable of fully preventing the spread of colon cancer that costs a little over $100. Suspicious polyps are detected with a scope and removed. Internists can't receive reimbursement from Medicaid for the preventive process, but they receive payment for expensive surgery later.

According to the U.S. Public Health Service's 1992 report, only 41 percent of insured adults have insurance coverage for preventive examinations, and only 69 percent of diagnostic tests are covered.

Simple things such as routine physical examinations that could save billions in health care in the United States frequently aren't covered by insurance.

In Utah, business leader Jon Huntsman participated in a series of tests at The Fitness Institute at LDS Hospital designed to determine overall health. Through a blood test, it was discovered Huntsman had symptoms of prostate cancer. He was scheduled immediately for surgery. In gratitude for the "lifesaving" tests, Huntsman donated a substantial amount of

money to the fitness program to educate the public about the merits of early detection.

Many cancers can be detected early. But it's only been within the past few years that insurance companies have been willing to pay for mammograms. That change in policy only occurred after the public and doctors united to campaign for the preventive tests.

A small percentage of insurers have not been willing to pay for health care services unless a symptom is diagnosed. That makes as much sense as waiting until a child gets the measles before getting a measles shot.

Blue Cross/Blue Shield announced nationally last year it would begin to pay for preventive services. This is a step in the right direction, but other insurance companies need to follow at an accelerated rate.

Obviously, it is imperative with skyrocketing medical costs to examine *any* proposal that could yield substantial savings.

But the savings of preventive health care goes beyond financial incentives.

Consider the quality of life of a woman spared the agony of breast cancer, for instance, because of early detection with a mammogram.

As Utahns we enjoy a healthy lifestyle that ranks our state in the top five percent in America. We ought to take the lead in maximizing our interest in responsible, healthy living by asking insurance companies to help us maintain good health.

Individuals should be responsible for taking care of their health through regular exercise, balanced diets and screening tests.

And for their own sake, insurance companies should be the catalyst in helping people take better care of themselves.

THE ARIZONA REPUBLIC

Phoenix, Arizona, October 14, 1992

THERE'S a new twist to the old argument about carcinogens. It is now suggested that nature may be as culpable as man in creating these substances.

Compared with the natural toxins that make up more than 99 percent of the cancer-causing substances we ingest, say researchers, the risks from pesticides and other synthetic chemicals are "quite insignificant." They're not talking about the so-called junk foods that Americans consume in such quantity, but such nourishing fare as broccoli, cauliflower and spinach.

"Our results indicate that many ordinary foods would not pass the regulatory criteria used for synthetic chemicals," say researchers at the University of California at Berkeley in an article appearing in the journal *Science.*

These researchers, according to a report in the *Boston Globe,* assert that regulatory agencies involved with protecting Americans from cancer risks should put considerably more emphasis on the dangers presented by naturally occurring carcinogens. Present policy focuses entirely on man-made substances, though these are consumed in only minute amounts.

"Our priorities aren't right if our goal is to prevent human cancer," says Lois Swirsky Gold of the Lawrence Berkeley Laboratory, one of the authors of the carcinogen study. The study, she says, is intended to correct the widespread notion that pesticides and other man-made chemicals, simply because they are synthetic, must be more dangerous than naturally occurring substances. This is the mistake of assuming that nature is in all respects benign.

While the Environmental Protection Agency and many scientists tend to agree on the need for testing natural food components, they point to a lack of legislative authority. Natural substances, notes Dr. Penny Fenner-Crisp of the EPA's office of pesticide programs, "have no regulatory constituency," and therefore Congress has left them alone.

In view of the Great Apple Scare of 1989, precipitated by fanciful, unsupported fears about alar, perhaps we should simply let nature take its course, rather than continually modify man-made chemicals so as to cleanse fruits and vegetables of carinogens, much like a dog chasing its tail.

Alzheimer's Disease Garners Attention Throughout U.S.

A California researcher acknowledged that there were serious flaws in his 1986 study that purported to show dramatic success with the drug THA (tetrahydroaminocrydine, or tacrine) against Alzheimer's disease. The admission was part of a consent agreement reported May 18, 1989 and signed by the researcher, Dr. William K. Summers, and the Food and Drug Administration. The agreement allowed Summers to continue limited testing of the drug. His initial report had sparked a clamor for the drug from victims and their relatives.

Scientists Sept. 14, 1989 reported finding a distinctive protein linked to Alzheimer's disease outside the brain for the first time. Alzheimer's was a degenerative disease characterized by loss of mental function. The discovery, reported in the British journal *Nature*, fueled hopes that a practical, definitive laboratory test for the disease could be developed.

The researchers were led by Dr. Dennis J. Selkoe of Harvard Medical School. Selkoe said the characteristic compound, an amyloid protein, had been found for the first time in tissues other than the brain in some Alzheimer's patients, though he did not know whether it could be located in all tissues.

The meaning of the finding was unclear, Selkoe acknowledged. It could mean that the compound was a marker for Alzheimer's disease that would be detectable in other tissues, or it could mean that the compound was produced in many organs or circulated throughout the body in the blood.

A new study published Nov. 10, 1989 concluded that Alzheimer's disease was more widespread than had been previously assumed.

The large-scale study examined and tested 3,626 elderly Boston-area residents. It found that the rate of incidence of Alzheimer's symptoms rose steadily with age. Researchers concluded that 10% of people over age 65 had some memory impairment or other mental problems for which Alzheimer's was the probably cause. More strikingly, they concluded that 47% of those over 85 had the disease.

Both figures were about double that of previous estimates. The study appeared in the *Journal of the American Medical Association*.

A widely prescribed drug for Alzheimer's disease, Hydergine (ergoloid mesylates), did not slow or cure the diesease and might actually accelerate the mental deterioration of sufferers, according to a study in the *New England Journal of Medicine* Aug. 16, 1990.

The reported death rate from Alzheimer's disease increased tenfold between 1979 and 1987, according to the U.S. Centers for Disease Control Nov. 8, 1990.

CDC officials emphasized, however, that while the number of cases of the disease might be rising, it was more likely that the statistical increase reflected the fact that doctors were more aware of the condition and were diagnosing it more often.

The disease was listed as the underlying cause of death for 46,202 Americans over the nine-year span. The death rate increased to 4.2 per 100,000 people in 1987 from 0.4 per 100,000 in 1979. For men the increase was 4.6 per 100,000 from 0.5; for women it rose to 3.9 per 100,000 from 0.3.

An elderly Alzheimer's disease patient who had been abandoned March 21, 1992 at a dog-racing track in Post Falls, Idaho was identified March 24, 1992 as John Kingery, 82, a retired automobile worker from Oregon. Police said Kingery's daughter, Sue Gifford, had checked him out of a Portland, Ore. nursing home about 10 hours before he was discovered. Kingery had been left at the track holding a bag of diapers, with all identifying marks removed from his clothes and wheelchair. A note pinned to his chest identified him as "John King," a former farmer who suffered from Alzheimer's disease and required 24-hour-a-day care. The plight of the unknown man had generated publicity as a possible example of the growing phenomenon known as "granny dumping," in which adult children abandoned parents they were no longer able or willing to care for. Such an act was not illegal in Idaho.

St. Petersburg Times
St. Petersburg, Florida, June 3, 1991

People with Alzheimer's disease are often restless, and safety can be a major factor in their care. Left alone, they may wander off outdoors, oblivious to their current surroundings and bound for destinations that can never be attained. They may be looking for loved ones who died years ago, or trying to be punctual for jobs from which they have long since retired. Despite their frailty, they can display great energy and persistence. Frustrated in their efforts, they sometimes become agitated, making their behavior even more difficult to manage.

One obvious solution is to keep the mentally confused elderly behind locked doors, in secured wings of nursing homes, for instance. Some Florida nursing homes do just that.

Last year, however, state rules changed in response to federal reforms that addressed patients' rights. Connie Cheren, former director of the Office of Licensure and Certification, which handles such matters in Florida, explained the shift this way: "It's like we locked up mentally retarded people in the 1950s. The families wanted it, everybody wanted it. But you won't find the mentally retarded locked up now without a court order that proves them dangerous. There was a time we thought it was okay. Now we look at it as archaic."

Cheren was fired in February, and her replacement, Lumarie Polivka-West, inherited a complex problem. While Cheren had cited and fined nursing homes that locked patients in, many continued the practice. The rule was not easy to enforce, and the nursing homes were not equal with regard to services. Some devoted special staff and facilities to caring for the mentally confused in segregated units. Others, unfortunately, simply locked the doors for convenience.

In late May, Polivka-West decided to stop the fines. "This is not a blanket approval of locked units," she explained. "But we are not going to be giving out citations just because a unit is locked."

Instead, a committee of experts will take three weeks to decide when and how the mentally confused should be locked up. The committee includes members of the nursing home industry, physicians, advocates and state officials.

Such standards cannot be drafted without addressing two underlying issues. First, does the practice violate patients' rights? These nursing home residents have committed no crimes, and most have not been granted formal competency hearings. Should a private institution be given the power of judge and jury over individual freedoms, even though the individuals clearly require constant supervision to protect them from harm?

Second, does confining patients address their therapeutic needs? Federal studies show that more than half of nursing home residents are labeled as mentally confused. Confusion can stem from many causes other than Alzheimer's disease, and many problems respond dramatically to the proper diagnosis and treatment. Should it become too easy to lock people away, those with treatable conditions will be robbed of their potential for recovery.

Alzheimer's itself is not fully understood, and there is some evidence to suggest that patients can benefit from increased freedom of movement. Many nursing homes have found humane ways to manage them without resorting to locked doors.

Three weeks seems a brutally short time to settle such questions and also fashion a workable standard for maintaining the highest quality of care. At stake is the issue of confining ill and elderly citizens — for life.

CHICAGO Sun-Times

Chicago, Illinois, March 31, 1992

It took the dumping of 82-year-old, wheelchair-bound John Kingery, who has Alzheimer's disease, at an Idaho dog racing track to open the nation's eyes to an increasingly serious problem.

As the nation ages, more elderly people suffering from disabling diseases and conditions like Alzheimer's are being abandoned by relatives no longer wanting or able to cope.

Kingery couldn't tell authorities his name or where he came from, but he was soon identified, thanks to nursing home operators back home in Portland who recognized his photo from news accounts.

Instinctively, most of us are horrified by the thought of secretly dumping a relative on someone's doorstep.

Yet, as the American Association of Retired Persons notes, it is a growing problem, aggravated by the recession and by an increasing number of baby boomers who now face the difficult problem of rearing children and caring for a disabled parent.

Beyond whatever judgment society makes of people who dump a relative or friend—either because of simple selfishness or because they are driven to it by the taxing job of providing around-the-clock care—lies the need for a national debate about the problem.

Should financial aid be provided for children who care for the infirm elderly? Should more in-home services be provided? What can society afford?

Whatever solution is developed, one thing is clear: Leaving helpless people all over the place, like unwanted bags of garbage, is not acceptable.

The Salt Lake Tribune

Salt Lake City, Utah, March 30, 1992

Insensitive city folks sometimes dump unwanted pets on rural roads to fend for themselves. Increasingly pressed for dollars, health-care facilities often push patients out into the streets before they can care for themselves properly.

Last weekend, somebody abandoned an 82-year-old retired autoworker at an Idaho dog-racing track with only a bag of diapers and a note identifying him as an Alzheimer's patient.

No wonder "Dr. Death" (Jack Kevorkian) could find customers for his suicide machine in Michigan. No wonder suicide rates for elderly Americans, after declining steadily for five decades, took a sharp turn back upward in the 1980s. No wonder most Americans, according to a survey last year by the Alliance for Aging Research, fear ending up in a nursing home more than dying a quick death from a sudden disease. People in this country apparently realize they can't count on humane care once they fall seriously ill.

Unfortunately, unless major reform occurs, conditions will only worsen as the elderly population expands and families fracture and evolve.

Of course the abandonment of John Kingery is just one incident. It's not even clear who left the Oregon resident at the Coeur d'Alene Greyhound Park or why. Alzheimer's is an insidious brain disease that sometimes allows victims to function almost normally and communicate coherently, sometimes not. Their actions can be difficult to supervise.

Nevertheless, it is obvious that Mr. Kingery became the victim of tragic circumstances or uncommon cruelty. Where there's one incident of this kind, there are similar, unpublicized cases in which society has fallen short of serving its most vulnerable citizens' needs.

In fact, the American Association of Retired Persons has identified abandonment as a small but "rapidly growing" problem most prevalent in retirement communities. An informal survey by the American College of Emergency Physicians last year found an average of eight abandonments a week among 169 emergency rooms across the country. In one case, an elderly woman was left sprawled in a hospital driveway as a car sped away. Another woman was wheeled into an emergency room with a note saying "Please take care of her" pinned to her purse.

Whether a symptom of overwhelming demands for health care, compassion fatigue, disintegrating families, a growing throw-away attitude or some combination of such conditions, this is an issue begging to be addressed.

The U.S. population is aging. In Utah, for example, the 65-and-older population will have increased 82 percent between 1980 and the year 2000. With most women working outside the home, fewer are available to care for elderly parents. Today's middle-age adults have smaller families and are more likely to experience divorce and live longer than previous generations. As they get older and start succumbing to diseases like Alzheimer's, these people may lack family resources for support and care. An already burdened, inadequate system of long-term health care cannot be expected to absorb the added pressure for assistance.

Better provisions must be made for dealing with catastrophic illnesses in this nation. Any health-care reform to come out of Congress must include accessible, high quality long-term care prominently among its measures.

Meanwhile, states must prepare for an onslaught of demands for services for the elderly. And Americans themselves must do what they can to plan for their own illnesses while watching out for their friends, families and acquaintances to ensure that no one else is forgotten or discarded like worthless refuse.

The Seattle Times

Seattle, Washington, March 30, 1992

THE abandonment an 82-year-old Alzheimer's patient made shocking headlines, but the act is common enough to have its own crude name: granny dumping.

Health-care experts who understand the ravages of the disease offer a partial explanation for these family tragedies: Sheer and utter desperation.

Providing care is so stressful that University of Washington researchers are studying links between the psychological toll and physical health.

Alzheimer's is a form of dementia, a progressive decline of intellectual function. Patients lose verbal skills, memory, attention, and ultimately literally forget how to walk and move.

The origins of the disease are not understood, and it is usually diagnosed by eliminating other medical maladies. Aging does not cause the disease, but the incidence of the illness increases with each decade of life.

Alzheimer's disease can strike in the 40s, with a progression toward death that takes from two to 20 years.

Common among all Alzheimer's patients is continual degeneration. A tragic result is a broad spectrum of communication failures between loved ones, family and the community.

Most Alzheimer sufferers receive home care from spouses or adult children. Unlike nursing someone who is frail or convalescing with a broken hip, the demands are incessant.

Husbands and wives, mothers and father become strangers who cannot feed, groom or dress themselves. Twenty-four hour supervision is required for the health and safety of a person who may only respond with agitation, hostility or violence.

> ## Caregivers become anxious and angry, upset by the personal abuse and resentful of the enormous, solitary burden.

Caregivers become anxious and angry, upset by the personal abuse and resentful of the enormous, solitary burden.

A spouse's embarrassing behavior may cause a caregiver to withdraw from friends. Fear that outsiders cannot cope with a loved one's needs or outbursts keep caregivers from even taking a break to putter in a garden or shop.

Casting a dark shadow over the intensive care and monitoring is the uncertain course of the disease, and the knowledge that the only outcome is decline and death.

Guilt keeps loved ones from investigating institutional care, and by the time the burden is too great, they discover a two-year waiting list for better facilities.

The myth, of course, is that placing an Alzheimer's patient in the best professional care automatically absolves a spouse or family of guilt.

If Alzheimer's disease has touched your family, ask for help. Financial assistance, emotional support and respite are available.

Here is a start: Alzheimer's Association of Puget Sound, 365-7488 or toll-free 1-800-848-7097, and Senior Information and Assistance, 448-3110 or toll-free 1-800-972-9990.

Mental Health Issues Debated Nationwide

A new study reported Oct. 7, 1989 weakened the evidence that manic-depressive behavior was linked to a specific gene, as had been asserted in a widely reported 1987 paper.

The original study had been hailed as the first to show a genetic cause for a behavioral illness not stemming from physical abnormalities in the brain. It had traced manic-depressive illness in 81 members of three generations of an Amish family, 19 of whom had the condition. By careful statistical analysis, the authors had concluded that a gene causing the illness lay somewhere on the 11th chromosome. When the new study added 40 new individuals to the analysis and reassigned three of the original subjects who had since developed the disorder, however, the evidence became considerably weaker.

The new study was reported by Yale University researcher David Pauls, who had participated in the earlier one. Pauls now said the evidence was "not up to the accepted or the conventional level of significance."

The Senate Aug. 2, 1991 approved by a voice vote a $3.87 billion bill reauthorizing block grants for state mental-health and drug-abuse programs.

Herald News

Fall River, Massachusetts, October 4, 1988

—"A Being darkly wise and rudely great" — so Alexander Pope summed up the contradictions of human nature in his "Essay on Man," which still offers tips for good living. Human nature hasn't changed since Pope published the verse essay, anonymously, in 1733.

During National Mental Illness Awareness Week, the public is urged to think of the mentally ill with new understanding. Professionals hope to correct misconceptions about the nature, causes and cures of mental illness. The National Institute for Mental Health has launched a $500 million fund raising campaign for research into a complex condition from which no segment of society is immune.

Most people will react with due attention, and some will contribute to the much needed funds, thankfully reflecting that mental illness is a disease that other people have.

But few will take the time to ask questions like "What is mental health? And how do I measure up on the sanity scale?"

Today physical fitness is much more in vogue. Enthusiasts pursue it with disciplined purpose, exercising their muscles and munching oat bran. They know it takes work to keep fit, and counteract the additives, pollutants and palliatives of modern life.

Yet the pressures that can erode mental health are more subtle, less recognized. Actually, to maintain a consistent level of mental well-being is very difficult, and also takes work. Healthy minds are intangible, but very real qualities. Society can't function without a goodly store of them.

Therefore, even people who feel they're coping fairly well with life shouldn't take their minds for granted, muddling along on the habitual tracks of temperament and inclination.

Moreover, it's impossible to be truly happy without being mentally healthy. And since the pursuit of happiness is an inalienable right, individuals are also endowed with the power to adapt their personalities to the demands of reality.

Alexander Pope offered a basic rule for those who seek to be as serene and as useful as possible: Accept human limitations, both in yourself and others.

To realize that we are, at best, "darkly wise" is an antidote to delusions of grandeur, self-complacency, name-calling, blame-shifting, rash judgment, and rationalization.

To realize that we are, at best, "rudely great" should restrain tendencies to paranoia, aggression, prejudice, obsessiveness, compulsiveness and perfectionism.

The factors that make for mental health can't be measured like blood pressure or cholesterol levels. As the ancients understood, the mind and the body work together. Good nutrition, for example, helps the brain to function well; and good attitudes can help protect the heart.

Omaha World-Herald

Omaha, Nebraska, September 25, 1988

Horrible crimes in New York and Chicago in the past few days are yet another reflection of the nation's failure to identify homicidal mental patients and either treat them or institutionalize them.

The deinstitutionalization of the mentally ill has reduced the population of America's mental institutions by about four-fifths over the last three decades. Thousands of those former patients are now living in the streets, often endangering themselves and others. And other people who are so deranged that they would have been hospitalized in an earlier age are left to fend for themselves without adequate supervision to protect themselves and the public.

The man who ran naked into St. Patrick's Cathedral and bludgeoned an usher to death had a history of arrests and mental breakdowns. The Chicago man who killed four people with a handgun had quit taking medication that he had been prescribed for a psychiatric illness, members of his family said. Now both men, and five other people, are dead.

Irrational killings seem to have proliferated in recent years. The pattern is often familiar. The person's problems were known but not adequately treated. He was in contact with the criminal justice system or the mental health system but slipped through.

The ease with which a person can obtain a handgun has merged with the ability of deranged people to avoid treatment, compounding the danger. There are too few shelters, halfway houses and community-based programs to take care of everyone who needs care or supervision. As for the mental hospitals, the courts and legislatures have made it difficult to institutionalize mentally ill people who might become dangerous unless those people volunteer for treatment.

It is disgraceful that the mentally ill are so shabbily treated and that the public is so unnecessarily endangered. Some of the old mental hospitals were horrors in themselves, but nobody is suggesting that they be recreated. The modern public display of sickness and misery on the streets has come about in part because of a patients' rights movement. What a horrible failure it was to have patients' rights lead to patients' misery, and worse.

The Boston Globe
Boston, Massachusetts, August 16, 1991

Persistent doubts among mental health advocates about the ability to reorganize the care and treatment system without penalizing those who depend on it must be carefully addressed by the Weld administration. The concerns expressed by organizations like the Alliance for the Mentally Ill are based on anecdotal but discouraging evidence that cuts in both community and hospital services have reduced the levels of assistance for those who suffer from long-term illness.

The focus of the concerns is a series of recommendations by a special commission that reviewed the system earlier this year. Its report and proposals, quite sound in broad outline, call for the closing of three state hospitals and a reduction of beds in remaining hospital facilities, with the patients moving to other hospitals or to lower-level, community-based facilities.

The report insisted that no patient be moved, and no facility be closed, until equal or improved care can be provided for each patient. The Weld administration and its secretary of human services, David Forsberg, endorsed that proposition.

Members of the AMI, however, remain skeptical about that commitment on the grounds that community services continue to erode under heavy budget pressure at just the time when they are becoming more essential to help deal with the needs of persons being discharged from hospitals.

Furthermore, their call for a slower pace of reorganization, to test its effectiveness in moving some patients to private institutions where they may qualify for Medicaid, seems appropriate in the light of limited experience with such policy.

Whatever the flaws of state-hospital services, the care, treatment and discharge of mental health patients were not heavily driven by financial considerations, which threatens to be the case in the new arrangements. Some evidence suggests that patients in such circumstances are in greater danger of relapse – scarcely a formula for cutting costs in the long run.

The commission's recommendations are promising and deserve exploration. Their success, however, depends on thoughtful implementation rather than haste. The victims of mistakes in the process, who have already suffered grievously, need no gratuitous injury from mismanagement.

The San Diego
Union-Tribune.
San Diego, California, March 8, 1991

California's community mental-health network, once regarded as a model for the nation, is in shambles.

In 1957, the Legislature enacted the Short-Doyle Act enabling the mentally ill to receive community-based treatment instead of being warehoused in state institutions. Regrettably, that humane idea has been frustrated by a lack of legislative oversight and chronic underfunding.

The mental health budget has seen its share of general revenues shrink from 2.5 percent to .25 percent during the last three decades. As a consequence, most counties cannot adequately care for poor people who require psychiatric help. The waiting period for a hospital bed in a state mental institution averages two years and an estimated 50,000 emotionally and mentally ill persons wander California's streets.

San Diego County has approximately 1,000 psychiatric beds to serve 10,000 mentally ill. Lacking proper medication, thousands are left to suffer, alone, the unwitting victims of flawed state policies.

The Legislature should give counties the authority and the means to care for their mentally ill.

To address this problem, Gov. Wilson has devised a plan to strengthen long-term funding for community mental-health programs.

Wilson has proposed that the state transfer fiscal and administrative responsibility for these programs to the counties.

To ensure fiscal stability beyond 1991, Wilson would provide mental-health programs with a permanent funding base that would have growth potential. This would be achieved through a 15 percent increase in annual vehicle licensing fees, coupled with a boost in alcohol beverage taxes. (A six-pack of beer would cost about 6 cents more, a bottle of wine 5 cents more, and a bottle of whiskey 26 cents more.) Counties also could impose an additional half-cent sales tax increase, provided it receives voter approval.

In 1985, the Legislature tacitly conceded the unfairness of mental-health funding per county by enacting an "equity" formula for the allocation of new monies. But the power brokers in Sacramento soon undermined that reform. Thanks to Assembly Speaker Willie Brown, San Francisco still gets a generous $62 per capita while San Diego County scrapes by with $19 per capita.

That disparity prompted San Diego County to file suit five years ago seeking to equalize funding levels. San Diego Superior Court Judge Barbara Gamer concluded during the early phases of the trial that San Diego has been illegally shortchanged by the state. But her final ruling, expected within the next several weeks, will almost certainly be appealed by the state. That could mean several more years before this issue ultimately is resolved.

The Legislature could cut through this legal thicket by giving counties the authority and the means to care for their mentally ill. That was the promise of the Short-Doyle law 34 years ago. It's time to honor that promise.

The State
Columbia, South Carolina, March 5, 1991

THE General Assembly has within its grasp the capacity to do something genuinely humane: pass a law that bars the execution of individuals who are mentally retarded.

Such legislation, identical to laws in place in four other states, is pending on the House calendar. It could be approved and passed to the Senate as early as this week.

Under South Carolina's existing capital law, the defendant's mental or emotional state is one of several mitigating circumstances to be considered by a judge or jury in determining whether the sentence imposed in a murder case should be death or life imprisonment.

Be that as it may, juries (and judges) are still free to sentence retarded offenders to death if one of several aggravating circumstances, such as rape or armed robbery, exists.

For that reason, there needs to be a clear policy against imposition of the death penalty on persons with an IQ of 70 or less and otherwise clearly defined under S.C. law as being mentally impaired. Regardless of actual age, no state in good conscience can sanction the execution of someone with the mind of an 11-year-old.

Eagle-Beacon
Wichita, Kansas, March 21, 1991

Thirty people with chronic long-term mental illnesses are embarking on a living option that up to now hasn't been available in Wichita — group homes that are new and well appointed. Built by the Mental Health Association of Sedgwick County with the help of a federal grant, the homes opened this week.

They should help bring stability to the lives of the residents, who've undergone repeated hospitalizations but are able to live in a community setting as long as they have some support. During the day, they'll take part in programs to help them cope with community life.

They'll return to the group homes at night, where home coordinators employed by the Mental Health Association will tend to their needs. Most important in that regard is making certain residents take the medications that make it possible for them to function in the community.

Once the group homes are running, says the association, the goal will be to bring residents to the point where they can live on their own. To that end, the association plans to apply for federal grants to build apartments for residents who no longer need group housing.

Too many mentally ill Kansans lead difficult lives, bouncing from state hospitals to jails to the streets. The Mental Health Association deserves the community's thanks for rescuing some of them, and helping them lead productive lives.

The Grand Rapids Press

Grand Rapids, Michigan, July 7, 1991

Michigan Mental Health Director James Haveman has made the right moves in his effort to bring sanity to the state's ailing mental health system.

When he took over as director earlier this year, Mr. Haveman discovered an array of problems from fiscal mismanagement to patient neglect. In his first months as head of the department, the Grand Rapids native and former director of Bethany Christian Services has quickly shown he means business in revamping a system that has rewarded the greed of a few foster home owners and too often neglected the needs of the disabled.

Among the financial abuses he encountered when he took over the department was the case of Shamshad Sabri, who heads Kent Care Corp., a Cascade-based firm which operates group homes in this area. State police believe Mr. Sabri fled to his native Pakistan after allegedly overcharging the state $430,000 for patient care.

The case of Kent Care Corp. is not unusual. A confusing mix of state regulations and lax accounting procedures has created a situation in which the state loses as much as $8 million a year in "improper and undocumented" charges.

Mr. Haveman is working to ensure that such expensive mistakes don't happen again. On Oct. 1 group home operators will pay a daily rate per resident, a wise approach. The current procedure of allowing operators to estimate annual costs and receive larger payments at the beginning of each month lends itself to problems.

There are other troubles with the state's overburdened foster care system. As the state has moved to house more mentally and physically disabled persons in residential settings, checks and balances on these homes have slipped.

There aren't enough workers to investigate complaints or systematically log concerns in the state's 1,700 small group homes. Such a situation is intolerable, placing society's least vulnerable persons needlessly at risk.

Mr. Haveman plans to strengthen the offices charged with investigating abuse and neglect complaints. This may require additional funding, but money saved by stopping the "improper and undocumented charges" to home operators might offset some of the cost. Currently, there is no statewide system that compiles complaints.

Finally, the director is pushing for more local control of all group homes. About half of the homes in Michigan are run by the state. Mr. Haveman is working to place these into the hands of local communities similar to what is happening in Kent and Ottawa counties. Homes here are monitored by local community mental health boards, which puts the power where it ought to be — in the backyards of those who live where these homes are placed.

Mr. Haveman's ability to sense problems in the mental health system and suggest meaningful solutions is laudable. But he must be careful; the state, for instance, must ensure that all communities are providing adequate care. Mr. Haveman has made the right diagnoses so far, but his patient — the state's mental health system — has acute problems. It needs plenty of attention before being given a clean bill of health.

The Des Moines Register

Des Moines, Iowa, June 3, 1991

An argument that developed in Iowa and other states regarding states paying for a new "miracle drug" was ended last month by the federal government. The feds ordered all states with Medicaid coverage of prescription drugs to pay. All states have Medicaid, and most cover drugs.

The new drug is clozapine (sold

Clozapine means new life for some schizophrenics
---

as Clozaril) and it could mean new life for some schizophrenics. The real issue is not whether states should pay for it when patients can't; its potential benefit is established. The question is how much.

Clozapine is a jackpot winner for Sandoz Pharmaceuticals Corp. of New Jersey. It has earned lavish praise since coming on the market 15 months ago. From the field come reports that sufferers of schizophrenia, one of the most intractable of mental illnesses, have shown definite improvement after clozapine treatment, usually after several other drugs have been tried and failed.

Clozapine has opened the doors of the mental wards for some and enabled them to function in society. The drug apparently works by binding itself to a protein found on brain cells.

Drawbacks include its price — close to $9,000 per patient per year when first offered, but dropping slightly — and some disturbing side effects. Clozapine can cause a sometimes-fatal blood disorder, for which the blood must be regularly monitored. Also, the first dose of the new drug can cause the patient to stop breathing.

Sandoz first charged $8,944 per patient per year for clozapine, including the cost of a blood-monitoring service. Various adjustments have brought that down somewhat. Iowa Medicaid expects to pay around $6,000 per patient per year, for about 625 patients, pushing the Iowa Medicaid program's cost for one drug close to $4 million. As with all other Medicaid programs, the federal government pays about five-eighths of the cost, Iowa three-eighths.

Clozapine is the first good news to come down the pike in years for thousands of long-term mentally ill. Sandoz gleefully predicts a market of as many as 80,000 Americans, meaning an income of half to three-quarters of a billion dollars per year from Clozapine. Sandoz will keep harvesting that bonanza for as long as it retains the exclusive right, under patent law, to synthesize and market the drug. That could keep those hundreds of millions of dollars flowing in for many years.

That also should help the drug makers retain their status as the top contributor to the runaway inflation in health-care costs. That, in turn, should raise questions about patent laws adopted to guarantee years of competition-free profiteering on new drugs.

And it should raise further questions as to how Sandoz can sell clozapine overseas for one-sixth the price it demands of U.S. taxpayers and the general public.

The TENNESSEAN

Nashville, Tennessee, October 12, 1991

THE unfair stigma of mental illness is not as bad as it used to be.

But it's still bad.

Information about mental illness, its many forms and the impact it has on millions of Americans can help alleviate misunderstandings about such disease. Providing that information is part of the reason for Mental Health Awareness Week this week.

Some people may be surprised to learn that mental illness is more common than cancer, diabetes, heart disease or arthritis. Others may not understand that mental illnesses are biological disorders, just like other organic diseases, and should be thought of in the same terms. Over 12 million Americans have experienced some sort of mental illness.

But just as mental illness deserves the understanding of all people, there are issues of practical application to be dealt with as well. A report from the Inspector

General of the Department of Health and Human Services says that almost half of the community mental health centers have failed to provide the basic services they should under federal contracts. In Tennessee, as beds in mental hospitals are reduced, some officials have warned that community services are not adequately in place to handle those patients.

It takes more than just an understanding of what mental illness is all about to deal with the problem. Proper services to aid mental patients must be available to all who need them. Otherwise, public understanding won't be of much help.

One family in four will be affected by mental illness. That means millions of Americans cope with it every day. But it takes maturity, concern and dedication from all Americans to see that it is understood, and that programs designed to address it are effective. ∎

THE ASHEVILLE CITIZEN
Asheville, North Carolina, November 11, 1991

Forsyth County District Attorney Thomas Keith isn't the only person who will be "astounded" to learn that the state has no secure facilities to house mental patients with a record of violence — killers included.

Keith recently visited Dorothea Dix Hospital in Raleigh to discuss the case of Michael Charles Hayes, who was committed to the hospital for treatment after being acquitted by reason of insanity on charges that he killed four people in Forsyth County in 1988.

"What I saw just astounded me," Keith declared after his visit. "Hayes can just walk wherever he wants to go."

It's little wonder that Keith and Donald E. Taylor, hospital director, are worried about security. There are no gates or walls at Dix. Guards carry no weapons. There are locked buildings, but patients kept on the more secure wards frequently are allowed to walk about for exercise and treatment. More often than not they are escorted by staff members, not guards. A patient intent on escaping would not encounter insurmountable difficulties.

There's an obvious gap in the state's provisions for dealing with the mentally ill.

Dix and its sister institutions are set up as hospitals. They are not, as Taylor noted, "staffed or physically structured to handle people who have a tendency to violence or are an escape risk."

> **There's an obvious gap in the state's provisions for dealing with the mentally ill.**

State prisons provide on-site mental health services for inmates. (All incoming prisoners are screened for mental problems, with the most severe cases being assigned to maximum-security institutions.) But judges can't imprison individuals acquitted of violent crimes by reason of insanity. Neither can they just turn them loose. So the offenders wind up in mental hospitals that are not designed to handle them.

Under such circumstances, the institutions cannot adequately protect their patients, staff members or the public. This was dramatically illustrated in May 1986 when a patient named Kerwin Wayne Coley was charged with murder in the beating death of another patient. (The charge was eventually dropped because Coley was ruled incompetent to stand trial.) A few months later, patient Robert W. Joyner, committed after being accused of killing his mother, walked off the Dix campus and enjoyed a day of freedom before being located and returned to the hospital.

The security problem could get even worse if state officials don't act to solve it. Budget cuts could result in staff reductions, meaning less supervision of patients. And a new law on insanity could increase the number of violent patients and the amount of time they spend in mental hospitals.

Previously, prosecutors had to prove that a patient still was mentally ill and a danger to himself or others. The new law shifts the burden of proof. Patients must now prove they are cured and are no longer a threat.

Although the North Carolina Alliance for the Mentally Ill and other groups have for years advocated separate, high-security wards for violent patients, state officials have made no move in that direction. One of the reasons might be that Dr. Walter W. Stelle, chief of mental health services for the state Department of Human Resources, disagrees with the proposal. He said similar attempts in other states have resulted in institutions that essentially are prisons. "These are patients, and treatment at such places is often not what you hope it might be," Stelle said.

Perhaps so, but North Carolina doesn't have to make the mistakes that other states have made. It is quite possible to design a secure facility while maintaining a hospital setting.

Perhaps there is a fine line between imprisonment and confinement in a mental institution, but semantics isn't the issue here. The issue is protecting the public — and that includes the mentally ill — from those known to be inclined toward violence.

As a result of the concerns raised by Keith, Taylor and others, Stelle has scheduled a meeting early next month with the directors of all state mental hospitals. He wants to find out how many patients acquitted by reason of insanity are in the institutions and how many are considered a threat.

Perhaps the session will result in steps to close the security gap. Let's hope so. To paraphrase a well-known saying, the life of a human being is a terrible thing to waste — especially if the loss can be avoided.

THE INDIANAPOLIS NEWS
Indianapolis, Indiana, September 30, 1991

Improve the delivery system for mental health services through coordination of service providers and expansion of residential facilities within communities.
— The News Proposes

Waiting lists can be deadly.

Steven A. Reinhardt was on a waiting list to get into Central State Hospital when he climbed into a 1987 Buick, drove onto I-65, crossed the median and crashed into another car, killing himself and Nick Eiserman, a 32-year-old man with two young children.

Had Reinhardt been in Central State getting his court-ordered mental health counseling, he and Eiserman might be alive today.

These unnecessary deaths exemplify the weakness of Indiana's mental health care system and how its failures impact the community.

The Indiana Legislative Services Agency recently documented the system's illness and some possible remedies. The findings suggest intense work for the next state mental health commissioner.

In its report, LSA acknowleges the national shift in caring for the mentally ill — the move from centralized hospital care to community-based care. But the agency does not let Indiana off the hook.

Quite simply, Indiana has not made the shift — physically or financially. As a result, those who depend on the state for help face a fragmented system of care that often forces them to find their own way by "piecing together their own treatment and support system."

Waiting lists often foul their plans.

It is not unusual for the institutions to have month-long waiting lists, and the problem isn't always that there aren't enough beds. Many times there simply isn't enough staff to take care of patients if all beds were filled. And much of the time, beds are taken up by patients who could be placed outside the hospitals if community centers and group homes had more funding.

By a 1989 estimate, roughly 1,400 persons, at any given time, wait about three weeks for non-residental treatment. At any given time, about 500 persons stand in line for community residental placement. At any given time, 110 individuals in community inpatient units wait to get into state hospitals. Another report shows that about 2,200 mentally ill Hoosiers are inappropriately housed in nursing homes.

To complicate matters, Indiana spends 54 percent of its mental health budget on state hospitals, only 17 percent on community mental health centers, and 9 percent for residential services.

The sad part is Indiana often knows what to do to make the system work. According to the report, "numerous demonstration projects and grant programs that prove to be cost effective and desirable for the state are often abandoned when the federal grant money runs out."

Furthermore, Indiana doesn't take advantage of the federal funds that are available. The report shows that Indiana draws only about 50 percent of the Medicaid dollars available to it, using state money to cover costs Medicaid would reimburse.

Overall, Indiana leaders, past and present, have allowed this state's network of mental health care to not only stagnate, but to degenerate. They may try to excuse themselves by pointing to the shift from institutionalization to community care, but no one should buy that ploy.

Indiana's system of mental health care has deteriorated not because of the shift in care delivery, but because caring for the mentally ill has not been a political point-getter. That, however, is beginning to change.

Those who seek political offices or desire to hold on to them should read the LSA report — cover to cover.

The Virginian-Pilot

Norfolk, Virginia, November 14, 1991

The death of Brian Heath raises angry questions but, so far, few helpful answers. There are no easy ones.

Mr. Heath was homeless, and reportedly mentally ill. He was killed in Virginia Beach last month, allegedly by two homeless men, one a convicted murderer on parole. Beach authorities are investigating not just his death but the last months of his life. Did the system designed to help Mr. Heath and others like him — to help them find shelter and other sorts of continuing support — fail? And if it failed, can the failures be corrected without creating worse problems for others?

We don't know; Mr. Heath's records, are confidential (but should be made available to investigating authorities).

But it is worth noting how easy it is to expect too much of government, and to second-guess professional decisions that seemed proper and wise at the time but had terrible unintended consequences. It is worth noting, too, how difficult it is by law to assist people the nature of whose illness can make them balk at getting help.

It is far from impossible to deprive the mentally ill of their physical liberty and other freedoms, but it is hard do that — for good reason: to avoid the horrors documented over centuries of institutionalization when the mentally ill were treated as second-class citizens, to be warehoused, without rights or recourse, or hope.

A mentally ill person may now be deprived of his liberty only if he is clearly a danger to himself or others as determined in a judicial proceeding instituted by his family or local mental-health or law-enforcement authorities. But what is clear danger to a layperson may not be to a professional — and vice versa. And although no danger to themselves or others, the mentally ill may be in particular danger from unscrupulous others.

That danger exists for everyone else, too, mental-health professionals point out; if that's reason enough to keep the unscrupulous off the streets — and to reassess the parole system that puts murderers back on them — is it also reason enough to curtail the liberty of the mentally ill?

Current investigations should reveal any specific lapses in Mr. Heath's case. But it illumines a larger issue, the other side of that slippery slope into Bedlam: If according the mentally ill the same rights as everybody else means many more productive lives, at times it means inadequate protections, and dire consequences: the right to refuse treatment — and hit bottom before help arrives; the freedom to move about at will — and die on the dunes.

The ideal is to give the mentally ill person as much care or as little as he needs, as he needs it. The ideal certainly runs up against limited resources, of families and society. Mr. Heath's case raises anew the question whether that ideal also is hampered by overreaction to past wrongs of institutionalization and mandatory medication, and current overemphasis on rights.

The Salt Lake Tribune

Salt Lake City, Utah, February 15, 1991

Public programs for Utahns with serious mental illnesses are inadequate and inefficient. It makes no sense to put off plans to solve the problem.

When Utahns experience psychotic episodes that endanger them and/or others, they ordinarily enter a local hospital voluntarily, and their crisis care is financed with private insurance. However, a significant number lack the means for such expensive services, and some refuse treatment.

Counties are responsible for dealing with these indigent and involuntarily committed patients while their acute illnesses are diagnosed, stabilized with medication and evaluated for further treatment. This emergency service, provided at such local hospitals as the University Medical Center, costs government agencies between $250 and $565 per patient per day.

Most of these patients can be discharged within 16 days and treated on an out-patient basis. However, a few need to be hospitalized for months and even years. These people ordinarily would be transferred to the State Hospital, which now houses about 145 seriously mentally ill adults a day at a cost of about $160 per patient.

Because of funding constraints and population growth, however, the State Hospital has become a bottleneck in this mental health system. There are never enough beds to serve patients who are ready to move in from acute-care hospitals, so some stay hundreds of days in the higher-priced facilities (at public expense). A bed shortage then develops in the acute-care hospitals, causing some patients, despite emergency needs, to wait in line.

Utah's growing tendency to fill new State Hospital beds with patients who have committed crimes and need heavy supervision contribute to this service crunch.

The State Mental Health Planning Council appointed a task force last spring to review the state's role in serving seriously mentally ill adults. That group has made some practical proposals, to be implemented over three years, for better meeting Utah's mental health needs.

The most dramatic is to establish a new level of service for patients who don't respond well to treatment and require constant supervision for an indefinite period. A 50-bed facility would be located at the State Hospital and, because of lower treatment levels, operate at a cost of about $100 per day per patient. A $2.2 million budget request would be made to the 1993 Legislature.

The task force also recommends that the 1991 Utah Legislature appropriate $540,000 to expand services to 25 percent of the state's seriously mentally ill (20 percent now are served). And the group requests $550,000 to serve an additional 25 chronically ill Utahns in so-called "intensive outplacement" programs, which are less restrictive, less expensive community facilities than hospitals (25 now are served).

These measures provide reasonable assurance that more of the Utahns who need help with serious mental illness would receive it, by both expanding public services and spending existing dollars more wisely. It's inhumane to make seriously mentally ill wait for health care, and it's financially irresponsible to keep chronically ill patients in the most expensive facilities longer than necessary.

The Wichita Eagle-Beacon

Wichita, Kansas, October 9, 1991

Neglect and abuse of mentally ill Kansans under state care prompted the Legislature to order reforms in the state's mental health system a little over a year ago, beginning in the eastern 22 counties. But reform is off to a rocky start.

Dave Ranney of the Harris News Service reported recently that some patients turned out of the Osawatomie State Hospital under the reform plan are being warehoused in nursing homes. The reform law requires the community mental health centers in the region served by the Osawatomie hospital to see to the care of patients whose illnesses don't warrant hospitalization. But some centers in Eastern Kansas haven't accepted that responsibility.

Mr. Ranney reported that patients may be worse off in the nursing homes than they were in the Osawatomie hospital. State inspectors found that mental patients in one nursing home engaged in homosexual acts, and that a female patient traded oral sex for cigarettes. Some patients in another home received incorrect dosages of medication while others didn't receive their medication on time. And so on.

Through it all, the leadership of the Southeast Kansas Mental Health Center in Chanute denies that it's responsible for seeing to these patients' care, saying it's up to the nursing homes to make sure patients' needs are met. That attitude contradicts the intent of the reform law.

Mental health reform was supposed to seal over the cracks in the mental health system so horrors of this sort no longer occurred. They still occur because a provision in the state nursing home licensing process allows hospitals to refer patients to nursing homes — even though the homes clearly aren't capable of caring for them. That provision, coupled with the refusal of some mental health centers to accept responsibility for patients who don't really need hospitalization (other centers, such as Johnson County's, are doing a better job), creates the very sort of crack that the law was meant to close.

As mental health reform moves across the state — it's scheduled to begin in the central counties, including Sedgwick, next year — Kansans can look forward to more such horror stories. The Chanute community mental health center likely isn't the only one that won't accept its legal obligation to make mental health reform work.

The Legislature must monitor the situation, with an eye to fine-tuning the law to encourage compliance with mental health reform. And the Department of Social and Rehabilitation Services should hasten a rewrite of the rules making it impossible for the mental health system to dump patients in nursing homes.

Until this crack is sealed, mental health reform will remain an empty promise to many of the state's mentally ill.

The Philadelphia Inquirer
Philadelphia, Pennsylvania, October 7, 1991

For years, there have been two ways to handle the touchy business of mental-health commitments in Pennsylvania — the Philadelphia way and everyone else's.

The way other counties do it is this: Before someone is committed, either a hearing is held to document the patient's dangerous condition or lawyers formally agree — stipulate, in legal language — to the facts. That way there's a record to refer to if, for instance, a patient suddenly demands release.

In the overwhelming majority of cases in Philadelphia, no such record is produced. Instead, in a process similar to "no-contest" plea, the patients agree to accept treatment without formally acknowledging the truth of allegations that form the basis for committing them.

Most of the time that process has worked. But in a handful of frightening instances, it has not. In 1989, a patient with a history of violent outbursts was released on his own request because no witnesses could be found to show why he was committed in the first place. His name was Derek Bey and he stabbed a SEPTA officer to death and was himself mortally wounded.

In another episode, a 2-year-old child was allegedly raped by a man who was released because there was no legally binding record to keep him committed. He has since been found incompetent to stand trial.

A new Commonwealth Court ruling ought to guard against such discharges. The court ruled last week that Philadelphia has to play from the same sheet music as the rest of the state — either holding hearings or producing a formal agreement on the facts.

That higher standard should create no problem in dealing with people who have demonstrated clear threats to themselves or others. They are committed relatively easily on evidence of their own making. But those who may be closer calls will now require more formal proceedings and higher standards of proof.

Legally, that seems appropriate. But under the more informal system, those troubled people could often be persuaded to agree to sign themselves up for a finite period of care that didn't allow them to walk away.

The court's higher standard implies three options: full hearings, which will totally bog down unless the city greatly expands its legal machinery; voluntary commitments, which won't work unless hospitals agree to accept and treat poor, problematic patients; formal stipulations of the facts, which is common in other counties.

But Philadelphia's chief mental-health defender, Ned Levine, balks at stipulations, saying they are a fraudulent way to represent clients. Does he think, then, that other counties are operating fraudulently? He says he is not familar with how commitments are handled elsewhere.

May we suggest that he familarize himself? The court has ruled Philadelphia's procedures out of step, after all, not the other way around.

THE ARIZONA REPUBLIC
Phoenix, Arizona, April 20, 1991

IT is hard to imagine a more responsible position than the one Gov. Symington has taken on funding for mental health services. With Arizona's fiscal house in disarray, a one-year moratorium on a funding increase indicates neither a lack of commitment, as some have charged, nor irresponsibility.

The record of the past four years has been one of great sensitivity to the plight of the seriously mentally ill and their families. While the initial nudge came from Superior Court Judge Bernard Dougherty, who ruled that the state had to provide a "full continuum of services," the executive and legislative branches also have contributed to bringing Arizona out of the Dark Ages.

Since 1987 the level of state funds has nearly quintupled, going from $11 million to $52 million. Services have been expanded, and there is every reason to believe that care has improved immeasurably. Whereas Arizona once ranked dead last among the states in mental health funding, its rise to 36th is strong evidence that the state's commitment to the mentally ill is in no danger of wavering.

Gov. Symington has affirmed his advocacy on two recent occasions. Two weeks ago in a letter to the Arizona Center for Law in the Public Interest, he wrote, "The additional funding I would like to commit to SMIs is not available. I will, however, do everything possible to maintain existing levels of services, as well as implement the portions of the court order that require no additional funding at this time."

The other day the governor's pitch to Senate Democrats sounded a similar note. "I'm in no way abandoning the issue," he said. "But I believe we have achieved great strides . . . and the program can well afford a one-year moratorium." Although he need not have, Mr. Symington underscored his position with a promise to add $15 million to the 1993 budget, no strings attached.

It is regrettable that those who oppose the governor have lost touch with the fiscal realities. Democrats have made it clear they were unmoved, and public interest lawyer Tannis Fox has vowed to take the case back to court, to seek appointment of a special master and to boost mental health outlays by $30 million.

Whether Judge Dougherty will be so foolish as to issue a contempt citation against the executive branch is anybody's guess, though stomping on the separation of powers doctrine did not seem to deter him earlier.

Mr. Symington feels strongly about judicial interference, and his inclination to resist is correct. Ms. Fox and her special interest lobby unfortunately show no signs of compromise, no sign of backing off as they should. They prefer the very grave risk of turning advocates into opponents of their cause.

There is a way out of this game of chicken, made necessary by the intransigence of some of mental health's principal backers. The Legislature could tighten the statutes so that mental health funding were contingent on a legislative appropriation, and this it should do.

THE DALLAS TIMES HERALD
Dallas, Texas, October 8, 1991

What did Abraham Lincoln, Isaac Newton, Patty Duke, Jimmy Piersall and Charles Dickens have in common? They all suffered from some form of mental illness, a catch-all phrase for related disorders of the brain that cause severe disturbances in thinking, feeling and relating.

This week through Saturday is Mental Illness Awareness Week, a chance to learn the facts — and dispel the myths — about this common disease.

Those afflicted are by all accounts of normal or even above-normal intelligence. Their mental illness, however, sometimes may make it difficult for them to perform even normal tasks. They are not to be confused with the mentally retarded, whose intelligence has been diminished since birth.

Mental illness afflicts one in 100 Americans and touches one in five families. But treatment can help most sufferers from this disease whose manifestations vary from schizophrenia (disturbances of thought) to depression (disturbances in mood). While mentally ill people are often feared as irrational, aggressive or violent, they are in fact more likely to be isolated, passive or withdrawn. They are often blamed personally for something that is biologically based. With treatment, many mentally ill people are able to cope successfully and lead full, productive lives.

The Dallas Alliance for the Mentally Ill is a locally-based organization composed of families and friends of persons with mental illness. The group provides support, advocacy and education for the mentally ill and their families. Anyone with questions is encouraged to call them at 960-0525.

Part IV: Ethics & The Medical Profession

In 1984 a grand jury in New York City issued a blistering report describing a hospital's "purple-dot system" designated which terminally ill patients should be resuscitated and which should not. In response, New York Governor Mario Cuomo ordered the state health commissioner to write guidelines establishing under what circumstances doctors could deliberately let such patients die. Eventually Cuomo agreed to send to the state legislature a recommendation from the commissioner and the Governor's Task Force on Life and the Law that would require doctors to document the consent of a patient or surrogate (in the case of an incompetent patient) before intentionally letting a terminally ill patient die. Cuomo also agreed to draft health department rules setting out the procedures to be followed and defining death as "the irreversible cessation of all functions of the entire brain, including the brain stem."

Such ethical dilemmas and actions involving matters of life and death have profoundly affected the medical profession in the last decade. Organ transplants, for example, that can make the difference between life and death have become one of the most obvious symbols of the ethics debate.

The questions that have been sparked have gotten harder to answer. Who gets the next available liver? heart? lung? Who gets intensive care for how long? Isn't a patient always entitled to live for as long as he or she can?

Health care reformers don't suggest that we can avoid these questions by tempering the advances of technology. Luddites in nineteenth century England, who invaded textile factories and smashed machines because of their desperate opposition to technology, solved nothing in their day, and their descendants will solve nothing in ours. But reformers insist that progress serve a decent human end, inform our scientific genius with morality, and recognize the moral dimension of our obligation to use our health care dollars effectively.

Reformers often suggest that we can learn from Great Britain's overall experience. They point out that the U.S. economy is far more productive than Britain's and contest that our nation can well afford to provide quality medical care to all if we have the courage to act and the stamina and persistence to eliminate the profligacy of our health care system in the face of economic special interests.

Reformers contend that if some sort of death control is to be an inevitable feature of U.S. society, then we must prepare for it. They say we need time to plan, to think through the incredibly perplexing ethical, religious, and social issues, to work and agonize our way to a system of dignity, justice, and compassion, to assure the primacy of the person over machinery and technology. An efficient health care system can provide that critical time.

No matter how wise or efficient we are, we still confront a host of ethical issues of the kind that lead moral theologians to thank God there's a God. Though our health care system remains dominantly a private one, the cutting edge of many decisions are likely to be faced first through government programs. As government has financed health care and biomedical research, it has become the center of bitter controversies over what it should pay for, controversies that involve questions about when life begins, when it ends, and the nature of human existence.

Reformers charge that America cannot tolerate a health care system that wastes as much as $75 billion a year, when tighter corporate and government budgets force choices that may result in life for some and death for others.

No modern society, not even one as wealthy as our own, can completely escape the issue of medical ethics. But we have the resources, if we apply them effectively, to keep government in its place, to make fewer hard choices necessary, and to concentrate our collective wisdom on those choices we truly cannot avoid. The tragedy will be if we continue to waste our health care dollars and resources by throwing them into a reimbursement system with little incentive for efficiency. The judgment of our parents, children and history could be harsh if we choose to squander our resources. The judgment could come in our lifetime, on our families, because the elderly are eventually ourselves and our children.

Medical Ethics Debated Nationally

The issues of who lives and who dies, and at what cost, are complex and confounding. We must think deeply and far-reachingly if we are to comprehend them and deal with them wisely. But the omnivorous appetite of the health care industry for our financial resources adds an urgency that demands action, under threat that our society will be torn apart by a debate over medical ethics and propriety.

The questions are becoming harder, not easier. Who gets the next available liver? Who gets intensive care for how long? Should government pay for all heroic life-extending measures? If not, when should it pay and when not? Does it make sense to allocate 30% of our multibillion-dollar Medicare bill to high-tech medical services for those who have less than a year to live?

The sagas of artificial heart recipients like Barney Clark and William Schroeder alert us to the probability that the geniuses of modern medicine and bioengineering will some day perfect a workable artificial heart. But who then decides who should be eligible to recieve such incredible, life-sustaining and no doubt astronomically expensive devices?

The Register-Guard

Eugene, Oregon, July 8, 1988

Ethical dilemmas often lend themselves to answers that are correct in principle but troublesome in practice. So it is with the American Medical Association's decision that physicians should warn the sexual partners of people carrying the AIDS virus that they are in danger of contracting the fatal disease.

The dilemma is an old one. Priests, lawyers and even journalists sometimes confront the problem of what to do with potentially life-saving information gained in a confidential setting. In the abstract, it's easy to argue that the human duty to save lives transcends the professional obligation to honor promises of confidentiality. The AMA's 420-member House of Delegates was on firm moral ground when it voted overwhelmingly to notify potential AIDS victims if there is no other way to inform them of the risk.

The presidential commission on AIDS dealt with the problem of notification in its recent report. Clearly, those who have been exposed to the AIDS virus need to be told so that they can be tested, receive counseling and alter their behavior to avoid spreading the disease. The commission's report stated that the infected person has the primary obligation to notify unsuspecting partners. But when people carrying the virus won't notify others who are at risk, the commission said, health care providers should do the job.

In the day-to-day world of treating AIDS victims, however, the AMA's decision to breach confidentiality is not so cut and dried. The absence of iron-clad confidentiality may deter some AIDS victims from seeking medical attention, thereby defeating the purpose of the AMA's notification decision. The new policy may also have saddled physicians with a new potential legal liability.

Cases in which any breach of confidentiality is needed will be rare. Usually, people who learn they carry the virus will inform their sexual partners themselves, or have someone — a doctor or public health worker — do it on their behalf. The occasional uncooperative patient exists, but in those cases it's difficult to find out who should be contacted. The AMA's policy permitting involuntary notification will seldom be needed, and when it is needed doctors will seldom know whom to notify.

At the same time, people who contract AIDS may now have reason to ask why they weren't notified that they were at risk. Physicians may find themselves in court trying to explain why they didn't go to greater lengths to discover the identities of a patient's sexual partners and warn them. To guard against this threat, doctors may resort to over-notification, contacting all their AIDS patients' friends and acquaintances. This would not advance efforts to fight the disease.

In principle, the AMA delegates voted the right way on the issue of notification and confidentiality. Paradoxically, in practice the new policy may cause more problems than it solves.

Pittsburgh Post-Gazette

Pittsburgh, Pennsylvania, March 7, 1989

In this day of record medical advances with their effects on thwarting death at every stage of life, it's little wonder that the field of medical ethics has burgeoned. When is enough enough in prolonging life? What about the new techniques in molecular biology and genetics as they affect human behavior?

It is fitting, therefore, that Pittsburgh, as an important medical center also is expanding its efforts in the field of medical ethics. The latest example is the decision by the University of Pittsburgh to offer a master's degree program in medical ethics. This interdisciplinary program will be operated by its departments of History and the Philosophy of Science with the cooperation of the three-year-old Center for Medical Ethics.

The outline for the program includes this rationale: "Decisions involving end-of-life care, resource allocation, truth-telling, informed consent, and complex ethical-legal interactions require specialized education. At present, there is an insufficient number of professions, trained in both ethics and clinical medicine, available to help health-care institutions deal with these difficult problems."

To give just one example of problems coming over the horizon, take genetic discrimination. This "bio-menace," as some critics call it, comes from the growing ability of geneticists to use DNA testing to track criminals but also to predict the potential for genetically caused disease in a person. DNA is the nucleic acid that carries coded genetic information and therefore is the basis of heredity.

Criminologists already have used the fact that the DNA is as different in each person as are his fingerprints to crack difficult cases, particularly identifying a serial rapist. Most citizens would applaud.

But the other side of this biomedical advance is the possibility that DNA testing will be used by companies and insurance companies to reject applicants.

The Washington Post in an article on the subject outlines the case of a mythical Frank, at 31 a healthy newlywed who decides to take out life insurance. Weeks later, after a routine physical exam, he is shocked by the insurance company's response. Sophisticated DNA testing has revealed in Frank's tissues a single missing anti-cancer element that suggests his chances of getting small-cell lung cancer by age 55 are triple the normal risk. His application is rejected.

What will be society's reaction to such uses of DNA testing? The Post points out that the U.S. Constitution protects citizens from government-inflicted discrimination on immutable characteristics such as race. What about the immutable characteristics in one's gene pattern?

Even though people such as activist Jeremy Rifkin want to halt certain kinds of gene research pending a more complete review of the social and ethical implications, sooner or later new territory inevitably will be discovered. Clearly, society will face some intriguing new questions in medical ethics.

Obviously, it is none too soon to be establishing programs to train people to aid health-care and other institutions in society to address them.

THE PLAIN DEALER
Cleveland, Ohio, April 20, 1991

Astounding advances in medical science carry with them sobering responsibilities. The more that is known about tiny, genetic differences that can determine health, length of life and even cognitive abilities, the greater the temptation to alter the biochemistry that today is destiny. Tomorrow, today's destiny might simply be another, curable illness.

The need for stringent new rules, and a tightened code of ethical responsibility as medicine and science follow these new paths is obvious.

Political bars are not the same as ethical codes. Yet that message has been slow to get through, particularly in the ticklish area of using fetal tissue to try to cure debilitating diseases that strike adults, such as Parkinson's, or to treat a rare genetic disorder afflicting children called Hurler's syndrome.

The Reagan administration imposed an unreasoned ban on federal support for fetal tissue research in the late 1980s, despite expert recommendations to the contrary. One of those experts, Dr. Bernadine Healy of Cleveland, now heads the prestigious National Institutes of Health. She still favors lifting the ban. That puts her squarely in the medical mainstream. Yet the Bush administration continues its opposition, and Healy will carry out orders — unless Congress intervenes.

Rep. Henry Waxman, a California Democrat, tried just that last year, but failed to get his measure to the House floor. He has reintroduced the bill this year. Hearings this week underscored the fundamentally anti-life, anti-progress, head-in-the-sand mindset underlying the government research ban.

Much of the testimony concerned a disorder that should be familiar to readers of this newspaper. Hurler's syndrome is the disease that is attacking Kourtaney Collins, 2, of Willoughby. The progressive, crippling syndrome is gradually killing her. Her only hope is that the enzyme deficiency that causes it can be overcome with the bone marrow transplant she just underwent in Iowa.

The disease is rare. Only 50 to 70 children a year in this country are born with Hurler's syndrome. Most won't know they have it until about age 1, when the first symptoms may appear. Those who suffer from it rarely live beyond age 10. It is regarded as incurable. Kourtaney's bone marrow transplant is experimental, and it's far too early to tell whether that will be the answer for her, or the others. Still it holds out hope.

There is another source of hope. If doctors know to look for it, Hurler's syndrome can be diagnosed before birth. That is what happened to Guy and Terri Walden of Houston, who testified bravely to Congress last Monday about their personal tragedies.

After the Waldens' first child was born with the disorder, the parents knew they were genetic carriers. Each additional child faced a 25% probability of being affected. The Waldens' second child was diagnosed in the womb. They chose to give her life. She died at age 6½. Their fifth child was also diagnosed in the womb. They chose to give him life, and also chance at a longer life.

This boy underwent an operation before birth. Healthy liver cells from an aborted fetus were transplanted into his developing body. The hope was that the healthy cells would get picked up in the boy's developing bone marrow and direct production of the life-saving enzyme. (Without this particular enzyme, one of hundreds in the body, harmful waste products build up in cells.) It is too early to tell whether the operation a year ago was a success. The boy is 5½ months old.

But his parents believe they have given their son, and others like him, more hope. They believe someone else's tragedy can give the gift of life. They are anti-abortion, but they are also pro-life. They know the two aren't synonymous.

A federal funding ban does not provide ethical guidance or protection. Fortunately, in the Waldens' case, the California hospital where the operation was done and the university connected to it understood their obligations. The proposal was reviewed by bioethics committees and administrations of both institutions. A board of health professionals, doctors and outsiders was created to oversee all such work.

But there is no substitute for the force of law. Waxman's proposal, part of NIH reauthorization legislation, spells out strict guidelines for use of fetal tissue and prohibits its sale. Fetal tissue from abortions would be covered by even more stringent rules, to discourage anyone sick enough to consider it from getting an abortion just to provide fetal tissue for research.

A law is what is needed. An all-encompassing, unthinking ban is not.

THE ASHEVILLE CITIZEN
Asheville, North Carolina, May 3, 1989

Doctors should not refer patients to labs and test clinics in which they own part interest. The practice leads to unnecessary tests, high prices and poor quality control.

The conflict of interest inherent in such arrangements should be evident enough, but apparently many physicians either don't recognize it or don't care. It will take federal legislation to keep them from doing what is unethical.

Kickbacks for medical referrals long have been seen as unethical, yet Congress had to proscribe these. Federal law says that doctors may not accept kickbacks from those to whom they refer Medicare and Medicaid patients.

Doctors have found a way to evade the prohibition. They own and operate commercial labs and services themselves, or they buy part interest in them through joint ventures and limited partnerships. Instead of direct payments or kickbacks, they receive profits from the venture. The more business the lab or clinic gets, the more doctor-owners benefit.

Congress last year ordered the Department of Health and Human Services to determine how prevalent the practice is. The inspector general's office released its findings last week. At least 12 percent of physicians who bill Medicare have ownership or investment interests in the services to which they refer patients.

It's encouraging that 88 percent of doctors abstain from such arrangements, but that's about the only good thing you can say. The other 12 percent of the profession create a field rife with exploitation and abuse.

One example: An X-ray and computerized scanning service in Pennsylvania promised physician-investors a five-year return of $111,000 for an investment of $10,000 — which they could borrow from the service if they wanted. What the service expected in return, of course, was referrals from each doctor.

Sometimes the initiative comes from physicians themselves. A handful of doctors will offer to set up a physical therapist or some other professional in business and share the profits.

This leads to unnecessary tests and treatment. The inspector general found that Medicare patients of physicians who own or invest in clinical labs receive about 34 percent more lab services than the average Medicare patient. The extra cost to the Medicare program comes to millions of dollars a year.

Excessive rates are another problem. Doctors have no incentive to shop for lower fees, or to hold down the cost of outside services, when they own a stake in the service to which they send patients. The incentive is to do the opposite — to overcharge. When Blue Cross-Blue Shield in Michigan, for example, reviewed claims submitted by the 40 clinical labs in that state, it found that labs with physician-ownership interests (one-half of the labs) were paid an average of 43 percent more per patient than labs without doctor ownership.

Quality control can suffer in the same way. When a lab or clinic does substandard work, doctors normally are free to send their patients and business elsewhere. This is less likely to happen when physicians own an interest in the service.

The House Ways and Means Subcommittee on Health has proposed legislation that would extend to physician ownership of outside services the same ban that applies to kickbacks. Doctors could not bill Medicare for referrals to businesses in which they share profits or income.

The bill provides adequate exemptions. Among others, it does not apply to services provided within a physician's office, to health maintenance organizations, and to sole providers in rural areas.

The American Medical Association opposes the bill anyway. It says that physician ownership poses no real problem and that a federal ban is not needed.

The record shows otherwise.

Rising Medical Costs Debated Nationwide

The average American doctor had earned $164,300 before taxes in 1990, according to the American Medical Association's annual review of social and economic aspects of the profession, reported May 21, 1992. That figure represented a doctor's net earnings after paying an average of $150,000 in office and business expenses.

Among the various specialists, surgeons earned the most ($236,400), followed by radiologists ($219,400), anesthesiologists ($207,400) and obstetricians and gynecologists ($207,300). Pediatricians made an average of $106,500 and general practitioners took in $102,700.

In general, rural doctors made one-fifth less money than their urban colleagues. Doctors in New England made less than those in other regions.

The percentage of the U.S. gross national product spent on health care had been higher in 1990 than in any previous year, according to an analysis by the Health Care Financing Administration released in the journal *Health Affairs* and made public April 23, 1991.

The report was based on estimates made from incomplete 1990 economic data. It also included final figures for health spending in 1989, which showed sharp growth.

According to the report, health spending in 1990 had totaled $671 billion, which accounted for 12.2% of the GNP, a measurement of the nation's total output of goods and services. The increase, from $604 billion (11.6% of GNP) in 1989, was three times as great as the average annual increase of the previous 30 years. Health-care expenditures had grown faster than GNP in all but three of those years, the report said.

The government statisticians also found that one-fourth of the growth in the 1990 GNP had been made up of growth in health-care spending.

The report concluded that the accelerated growth in health expenditures from 1988 to 1989 had been spurred by large increases in spending on home health care and nursing-home care. During the same period, growth in spending on physician and dental services, research, drugs, and hospital care had declined or remained roughly constant.

Health spending by federal, state, and local governments had grown to 14.8% of revenues in 1989, from 5% in 1965, the analysts found. In the same period, spending by businesses had grown to 8.3% of wages and salaries, from 2.2%.

Administrative costs accounted for up to 24% of health-care spending, according to a study published in the *New England Journal of Medicine* May 2, 1991. The report's authors, Steffie Woolhandler and David Himmelstein of the Harvard Medical School, concluded that the existence of more than 1,500 different health-insurance programs raised health costs by necessitating large numbers of clerical workers in hospitals and insurance companies. The report concluded that $100 billion could be saved annually if the percentage of bureaucratic expenditures were lowered to the Canadian level of 11%.

Spending on health care in the U.S. would total $738 billion in 1991, an 11% increase over 1990, according to a report released by the Commerce Department Dec. 30, 1991. That figure would represent 13% of the U.S. gross national product, a measure of the nation's total output of goods and services.

The report was based on data gathered through November, combined with projected spending levels for December.

Employment in the health-care industry grew significantly between 1988 and 1990, according to the report. The number of jobs in hospitals increased by 409,000 in that period, while 200,000 new jobs were created in doctors' offices, the report said.

The Boston Globe

Boston, Massachusetts, January 19, 1988

To gain time in which to reassemble support for an omnibus health-care bill, an interim agreement has been reached; it grants a substantial degree of relief for the state's financially distressed hospitals. At best, this is a temporizing strategy — necessary, perhaps, but still fraught with risk.

The state's 100-plus hospitals are indeed in financial trouble, especially the 40 that have long been underpaid.

The omnibus bill that was scuttled by the House leadership at the close of the 1987 session was crafted to deal with the whole hospital cost and reimbursement problem. A lesser bill to benefit only the 40 underfunded hospitals was pocket-vetoed.

Meanwhile, all of the hospitals have been operating since last October on 1987 payment rates that have plunged them deeply into debt. They are receiving less in federal Medicare payments and are being paid more slowly for Medicaid patients. Some hospitals border on financial crisis.

Furthermore, the system that subsidizes hospital care for patients with no source of payment is breaking down. With no law on the books since October, payments to this free-care pool have been solely voluntary for four months.

Without rate increases and hard put to meet their own bills and payrolls, hospitals have paid only 40 percent of the money they should have paid into the free-care pool since November. Less is expected to come in this month.

The hospitals were left in a financial limbo because of executive-legislative squabbling over another aspect of the omnibus bill: a plan to offer health insurance to the state's 600,000 residents who have little or no coverage. The strategy was to keep the two halves of the omnibus bill — hospital-payment rates and health insurance for the working poor — tied together. Pressure to keep the hospitals solvent was meant to spur action on the universal health insurance portion. But the hospitals' financial status became too precarious.

The agreement reached last week releases $40 million in overdue Medicaid payments and raises hospital-payment rates to 80 percent of what was specified under the omnibus bill. The underfunded hospitals get even more. To do this will require extraordinary cooperation by hard-pressed health insurers.

The shift in strategy was forced by 13 chairmen of House committees and 16 members of the Ways and Means Committee, who advised the governor they would not support his omnibus bill until he acted in behalf of the underfunded hospitals.

Instead, Governor Dukakis; his secretary for health and human services, Philip Johnston; the governor's top adviser, Hale Champion; and House Speaker George Keverian opted for the agreement that shores up all the hospitals. Its intent is to diminish the political obstacles blocking the omnibus bill.

The agreement is an administrative maneuver that buys some time. Yet few in state government understand the chaotic state of health-care funding here and across the nation — as dire for health insurers as it is for hospitals. State legislators, if they further delay coming to grips with the omnibus health-care bill, will not avert the problem of funding health care, but only prolong it.

The Des Moines Register

Des Moines, Iowa, July 11, 1989

A medical rite of passage has come to an end in New York, and other states are watching to see what develops in anticipation of similar policy debates.

Medical interns and residents in New York hospitals will no longer

New York law limits work hours.

be putting in the traditional 100-hour work weeks, with their grueling 36-hour on-call shifts. As of July 1, a new state law limits most student doctors to 24-hour shifts and 80-hour weeks.

It also increases senior-staff responsibility for supervision of student doctors' work.

And it opens the door to recognition of the vital roles nurses and technicians play in medical care.

These rules, the first in the nation, came to be, in part, after the 1984 death of 18-year-old Libby Zion while under the care of the night shift at a New York hospital. A grand jury investigated but did not file any criminal charges. Its report, however, recommended sweeping changes in a system in which patient care often was left in the hands of exhausted students.

The regulations were written a year ago by a commission of medical experts impaneled by the New York state health commissioner.

This sort of sanity is overdue in the training of student doctors, and Iowa should be among those watching closely.

The New York regulations are not without opponents. Although awareness has been increasing throughout the business world that fatigue is a major factor in problems ranging from productivity to worker health and safety, many in the health professions still argue that the long hours are necessary to hone medical skills in true-life situations.

Some doctors and medical educators even have argued that the new regulations could "get in the way of caring for patients" by not allowing student doctors to follow through on the treatment of individual patients they have admitted during their on-duty shifts.

Yet it is difficult to understand why a well-rested student doctor making clear-headed decisions for a variety of new patients is any less capable of good care than a tired student treating familiar patients at the end of a 100-hour week.

More telling is the financial argument: How to pay for the extra staffing required to cover shifts opened by the new time limits. The state of New York approved $65 million last month to hire more support staff — nurses and technicians especially — to fulfill regulated requirements.

Lawsuits filed as the new law was going into effect, however, challenge whether this is sufficient. The suits have been filed by the The Hospital Association of New York State and by Blue Cross and Blue Shield of New York.

What is being lost in the debate over how to implement these rules is the question of what is best for patients.

The course set for New York hospitals is the right one. The details can be worked out.

The State

Columbia, South Carolina, February 1, 1989

MOST doctors are both competent and ethical. But those who are not will soon have a harder time covering their tracks.

Under the federal Health Care Quality Improvement Act, hospitals will be required to report all substantial disciplinary actions against physicians to their state medical boards, which then must report them to a national databank. Hospitals will get certain legal immunities by following the reporting procedures but will lose that protection if they do not comply.

In addition, anyone — doctor, insurance company, hospital — who pays off a medical malpractice claim or verdict must follow the same reporting procedures or incur a $10,000 fine for each infraction.

The new reporting provisions will go into effect later this year when the databank becomes operative. Thus, unethical or incompetent doctors will find it harder to move from one hospital to another or one state to another, since hospitals and state medical boards will be expected to check the databank before granting licenses and staff privileges to new physicians.

The law also applies to dentists and eventually may be extended to include all licensed health-care professionals, including nurses and pharmacists.

South Carolina has similar statutes requiring the reporting of disciplinary and malpractice incidents, but these laws have no built-in penalties for non-compliance. The state should follow the federal government's lead and give these laws some teeth.

The Washington Post

Washington, D.C., March 22, 1989

SHOULD doctors be thought of mainly as scientists—people who rigorously apply their accumulation of factual medical expertise to the problem of a patient's illness—or should they be humanists, caring healers whose scientific expertise is just one more tool in the human encounter with the patient? In the past five years, after a long ascendancy of the more technical model, the consensus among medical schools has been moving back the other way. Last week a collection of the field's top authorities announced a giant step in that direction: they will revamp the dreaded Medical College Admissions Test, or MCAT. This does not alter the academic course work required for most admissions (usually biology, chemistry, physics and math), but it is a way of sending a substantially different message about what kinds of students medical schools want. In place of the test's six science sections, there will now be two science sections, a reasoning skills section and—wonder of wonders—an essay. The very notion should strike terror into the hearts of the stereotypical, totally science-focused premed student. It would even scare the stereotypical doctor. Then again, that's exactly the idea.

The doctors making the change point out that the scientific parts of medical training can be taught much more easily—and to people of more widely varying aptitude to begin with—than the far more subtle abilities to grasp what is bothering a patient and to give advice in the context of the patient's own concerns. They consider medical education to be casting a net too narrowly and, though taking in many people who are talented in broad as well as narrow ways, to be missing out on many more who would do the profession good. (The steady drop in medical school applications over the past five years, which mirrors similar drops in other science and engineering fields, gives such concerns a certain edge.)

All this makes solid sense. But altering the MCAT can only nibble a corner off the fearsome premed culture that prevails on most college campuses. That culture turns away many liberal-arts-minded students, not so much from the idea of studying medicine as from the boot-camp ambience of the required courses. That image of ordeal and trying-ground—as distinct from simple curriculum rigor—still marks medical education in general. Witness the controversy over whether medical residents ought to serve more-than-24-hour shifts on hospital wards.

Toughness in curriculum is of course crucial for doctors. But it requires no dilution of that toughness to pay attention also to those less quantified nonscientific abilities—to talk, listen, detect all dimensions of a health problem—that often get reflected in an essay test or in academic interests that go beyond science. The humanist-doctor of yore, even the poet-doctor, is a sentimental cultural figure of sorts; but the issues raised by decisions like this go beyond the image of the profession. Keep training rigorous, but by all means make it something that attracts not just the smart but the wise.

The Charlotte Observer

**Charlotte, North Carolina,
July 10, 1989**

The state of New York is running into some flak from the medical profession over its decision to cut back on the hours-per-shift and hours-per-week required of interns and residents.

Traditionally, those young doctors have worked 36-hour shifts and 100-hour weeks. New York, where 16% of the nation's doctors are trained, is now limiting shifts to 24 hours and the work week to 80 hours — still a back-breaking schedule — in order to reduce the risks of error by weary, sleepy doctors-in-training.

Instead of applauding the change, some doctors don't like it. Perhaps because they've already been through it, some established doctors don't want younger doctors to attain the same status without going through the same kind of ordeal. One doctor referred to the traditional schedules as "a rite of passage." That makes it sound as though medical internship and residency are supposed to be not only essential on-the-job training, but also a sort of hazing required before the apprentice can be admitted to some exalted fraternity.

Defenders of the tradition say the long hours toughen young doctors to the rigors of medicine and permit the same doctor to stay with a patient over an extended period.

The first part of that argument isn't without merit. Depending on the specialty, some doctors do need to be able to stay alert through long hours on the job, and their training should be rigorous enough to give them that kind of endurance. But 24-hour shifts and 80-hour weeks should be sufficient for that purpose. The second part of the argument makes sense only if the patient can be sure the intern or resident isn't too groggy to function.

Putting interns and residents on more reasonable schedules surely will reduce the incidence of mistakes caused by fatigue. Some hospitals and insurers point out that shorter schedules will increase costs, because more people will be needed. As important as it is these days to hold down the costs of medical care, exposing patients to doctors who have been on the job longer than anyone can be expected to stay alert isn't the way to do it.

THE TAMPA TRIBUNE

Tampa, Florida, July 13, 1989

Speaking of curative matters, one of the glaring ironies of the medical profession has been its insistence on making doctors-in-training work 36-hour shifts and 100-hour work weeks. This, despite the advice of many a doctor to his or her patient that good health requires moderation.

Some doctors say the marathon workload of interns and residents is good training for a future in medicine, because a large number of them will take jobs requiring alertness in emergencies no matter how tired they are. The long shifts also allow doctors-in-training to better track the progression of a patient's illness.

But closer to the truth is that interns and residents supply cheap labor to hospitals, so the embattled health-care industry has fought any change in the arrangement.

Still, it is changing. New York, which trains 16 percent of the nation's doctors, is the first state to crack down on these inhuman working conditions. And other states are expected to follow. New York now prohibits interns and residents from working more than 24 hours at a time or 80 hours a week. Not exactly a cushy schedule, but one that will leave them less prone to making fatal mistakes.

That, of course, is what finally forced some reforms — patients were dying or becoming sicker due to errors committed by exhausted doctors-in-training.

In 1984, an 18-year-old girl admitted to a New York hospital with an earache and fever died unexpectedly, and a grand jury blamed the death on shoddy care by overextended interns and residents.

This change will no doubt increase hospital costs. A greater number of interns and residents will have to be hired — or perhaps even more full-fledged doctors.

But this is a necessary cost. Asking individuals in charge of life-and-death matters to work 100 hours a week is not only poor medicine — it's tantamount to slavery.

SYRACUSE HERALD-JOURNAL

Syracuse, New York, March 15, 1989

American medical schools — troubled by falling enrollments — are changing their basic admissions tests to encourage applications from students of varied educational backgrounds. It strikes us as a good move.

Traditionally, the study of medicine has been considered an option open only to the "science dweebs." Undergraduates majoring in other areas have been disinclined to apply to medical school.

Beginning in 1991, admissions tests will try to balance the focus on science with thinking and writing skills. This is in response to the alarm med school officials have expressed over diminishing applications and declining levels of verbal skills among those who do seek admission.

"This is no longer a world in which a doctor can afford to be a narrow, poorly educated human being," Richard Behrman, dean of the School of Medicine at Case Western Reserve University, told The Washington Post.

Science is only part of what doctors do. They treat people, not merely diseases. A diverse educational background can only help them in developing the human side of their professional awareness.

The new standards will encourage undergrads who want to study medicine to get to know more of their world than can be seen through a microscope. It might just make them better doctors.

The Houston Post

Houston, Texas, July 6, 1989

LAST WEEKEND, New York state limited the number of hours medical interns and residents can work in hospitals, a move to save patients from being treated by exhausted new doctors. Texas would do well to consider such regulations.

There is a century-old tradition of 36-hour shifts and 100-hour work weeks for doctors-in-training. New York now limits that to 24-hour shifts and 80-hour work weeks. This is still nobody's idea of a picnic, but it beats what was.

Arguments for the longer hours include the idea it is a rite of passage to test residents' worthiness and that the extended hours are essential to proper training because to understand many diseases it is necessary to observe the patient over time. Also, it is a concession to economic realities.

But what of the patient seen in the 35th hour of the shift? Quality of care must be the overriding concern here.

The New England Journal of Medicine reported a sociological study of interns and residents that suggested long hours and other intense pressures of clinical training condition physicians to view patients as enemies.

Let's not let this go on. Another study showed the average interns had nine to 14 hours of free time a week — the only time they had for family, spouses, friends and taking care of errands.

The stress interns and residents suffer is appalling. There is always more work than time to get it done. Frequently they have a sense of inadequacy, and they have constant exposure to suffering, disability and death. And today, with the rise in AIDS cases, they are seeing more young people their own age die.

Let's give the young doctors a break — and hope they'll do the same for us.

The Orlando Sentinel

Orlando, Florida, July 28, 1991

'**I**t *stinks ethically when you see the patient as a big pork chop coming in the front door.*"

— **Dallas physician Ron Anderson**

Florida's doctors, like physicians all over the country, have to realize people are fed up with their practice of turning patients into tasty financial pork chops by devising new ways to profit from their illnesses.

Some doctors — an estimated 10 percent nationwide — buy into various kinds of medical clinics and service companies, then refer their patients to them.

Appropriately, the federal Department of Health and Human Services took a step last week that will help slow or even reverse this trend. It will limit doctors' ability to refer Medicare and Medicaid patients to health-care businesses in which the doctors have invested.

Among other things, beginning immediately, doctors can't own more than 40 percent of enterprises to which they refer patients. That will have a substantial effect, since Medicare and Medicaid represent such a large part of medical practice. But only a new law can bring broader change.

Too often, the evidence suggests, doctors' referrals are dictated more by greed than by patients' needs. Some examples:

■ A man with a back problem was examined by a doctor who charged him more than $100. The doctor then sent the man to a physical therapy clinic, where he ran up additional charges. The patient later discovered, quite accidentally, that his doctor is one of the clinic's owners.

■ Some doctors demanded a radiologist

sell them shares in his clinic, thus returning some of the profits from patients they sent him. Otherwise, they warned, they would start their own company and run him out of business. He sold them shares.

■ A hospital started splitting profits from its operating room with the surgeons who use it. Suddenly, the surgeons began performing a lot more operations than they had been previously.

Such examples also extend to some walk-in surgical clinics, medical testing laboratories, home health agencies, psychiatric hospitals, suppliers of medical equipment and other clinics and services.

A report by Florida's Health Care Cost Containment Board last January suggested that doctors own part of 40 percent of the state's health-care operations. Hundreds of physicians cut themselves in on the extra action, in what are euphemistically called joint ventures.

A major, unconscionable result of such double-dipping, here as in other states, is to push soaring medical care costs higher.

The cost-containment board will issue a second report soon, and it could be a blockbuster. It will give a lot more details on how joint ventures affect access to — and the use of — health care. And it will offer more information on how much joint ventures increase costs.

Let's hope the report will have a strong effect in Tallahassee and Washington. Efforts in both cities to curb medical joint ventures through laws have failed so far.

The general public's growing awareness of the problem is another plus. A concerted, louder national outcry will be needed to stop the smelly double-dipping.

The Miami Herald

Miami, Florida, August 12, 1991

WILL THAT recommended CAT scan of your innards do more for your health or for your doctor's wallet? A study for Florida's Health Cost Containment Board suggests that sometimes the wallet's health is the bigger concern.

In South Florida, doctors own or are investors in nearly every diagnostic imaging device. Here, far more scans are ordered than in Baltimore, where fewer machines are doctor-owned. The ratio was 20 scans ordered per 1,000 residents in South Florida, 12 in Baltimore.

Spokesmen for Florida doctors want to justify the numbers because of Florida's high percentage of older patients and of litigation. Even so, a study in Arizona also showed that doctors owning devices were more likely to order more tests and charge much more. A 1989 Medicare study in Florida found that patients whose doctors have such investments undergo 40 percent more tests and 12 percent more scans.

The new Florida study also tracked the costs for laboratory work. It found that doctor-owned labs had an average charge of $43 as against $20 for independent labs. The study also said that physical therapists at doctor-owned centers treat more patients each day and suggested that the quality of care is likely to be lower.

What are patients to do? Doctors do not have to tell patients of potential conflicts of interest other than any ownership of physical-therapy clinics or drug stores.

Of course, there are instances where owning testing equipment makes sense. An orthopedist would be handicapped without the ability to get X-rays quickly. But who is to say how many views are needed and what the appropriate charge is?

The Legislature refused this year to consider a bill that would restrict doctor investments and joint ventures. The Federal Government is pushing a rule that would limit the size of a doctor's investment in testing facilities and the number of referrals for patients covered by Medicare and Medicaid. Private insurers also are studying the issue; some have flexed muscle through preferred-provider contracts.

Physicians complain that they already are overregulated. But such strong evidence of hip-pocket medicine invites even more regulation, be it strengthened disclosure or strict control of investment.

Arkansas Gazette.

Little Rock, Arkansas, January 18, 1991

A layman would say that a public health clinic in an imperfect location is better than no clinic at all. Apparently they don't teach that way in medical school, because Dr. Joycelyn Elders, director of the state Health Department, says she'll oppose a $600,000 grant for the Pulaski Central Health Unit if local governments try to put it downtown.

Actually, a downtown location would not be all that imperfect, especially if it's available free, as is one Main Street building that has been offered. A downtown location would be closer and more accessible by bus to the low-income patients of the clinic than would a site in western Little Rock that Elders had approved, a site no longer available. County Judge Floyd G. "Buddy" Villines had recommended a lease on that property, at nearly five times the cost of the lease on the present clinic at 1115 Wolfe St. The clinic must relocate because the Arkansas Children's Hospital owns the building and has other plans for it. The owner of the West Side property gra-

ciously withdrew it from consideration after learning through the news media that a free building was available for the clinic. Dr. Elders, however, seemed to take offense at news coverage of the proposed lease on the West Side property. That's her right, of course. It's the people's right to expect her to perform her duties responsibly. She is not being responsible when she declares that she'll try to block the clinic entirely if it's located downtown. If Pulaski County needs the clinic, and we presume that it does, the county needs it whether it's downtown or out west. No good reason has been given for not locating the clinic downtown, where lots of space is available at a reasonable rent, if the free building is unsuitable. Dr. Elders has mentioned that a West Side clinic would be more convenient for the doctors who work at the clinic. That is not a good reason.

Dr. Elders is afflicted by obstinacy. Unless she improves, Gov. Clinton, who appointed her, may have to make a house call.

The Providence Journal

Providence, Rhode Island,
August 20, 1991

New federal rules that place limits on referrals by doctors of Medicare and Medicaid patients to health care businesses in which the physicians have financial interests are essential if spiraling medical costs are ever to be checked. These regulations, it is hoped, will curb the abuse by some doctors of these federal programs, which help pay the medical bills of elderly and poor people.

During the last ten years, many doctors have set up partnerships and joint ventures to provide expensive, specialized services such as X-rays, CAT scans and magnetic resonance imaging (MRI). These can be lucrative businesses, sometimes paying back five to fifteen times the original investment in a few years. Not surprisingly, doctors have referred patients who need these tests and procedures to centers in which they are part owners.

Unscrupulous practitioners have sent patients who did *not* need such testing or other procedures to their medical service businesses anyway, figuring that the taxpayers would foot the bill. A 1989 study, for example, found that Medicare patients whose doctors invested in clinical laboratories received 45 percent more lab services than Medicare patients in general.

Richard Kusserow, inspector general of the Department of Health and Human Services, has noted that some physicians were able to buy shares in these medical service centers at "a remarkably low price" on the assumption that the doctors would supply an ample number of patients to keep the enterprise going. Some outside physicians have even received kickbacks for sending patients to these centers, a clear violation of laws covering Medicare and Medicaid.

The Health Department's new regulations are entirely sensible. Doctors or hospitals that refer patients to a health care business may not own more than 40 percent of that business. No more than 40 percent of the revenues may come from referrals by investors. Profits paid to doctor-owners must be proportional to the amount invested, not to the number of patients referred.

Some physicians are irked by yet another layer of government regulation applied to their practice of medicine — as well as the implication that some members of their profession may be less than honest. However, the new rules are simple and straightforward. They allow doctors to continue investing in medical businesses, while clearly defining the situations in which they may send patients to laboratories or clinics in which they have a financial interest.

THE BUFFALO NEWS

Buffalo, New York, August 24, 1991

A REVEALING Florida study backs up enlightened government efforts to limit self-referrals by physicians. Those referrals — where doctors refer their patients for tests or other services at health-care businesses those same doctors own — pose a grave potential for conflicts of interest.

In these arrangements, referring physicians make money at both ends of the deal, in ordering and then supplying the ordered test or equipment.

The financial temptations of self-referrals, then, are obvious. That's the warning of common sense. It's also what a 1989 federal study suggested.

Now these scattered indications spotted earlier have received solid confirmation in a far more comprehensive Florida study that surveyed 2,200 health-care businesses. It reports that doctor-owned laboratories, for example, "perform more tests per patient, have higher charges and provide a lower quality of services" than those in which doctors have no investments.

The long-awaited study also confirmed the recent rapid growth of physician investments in joint-venture labs, medical supply outfits, imaging centers and other health-care businesses. Forty percent of the more than 18,000 doctors practicing in Florida own a piece of these businesses to which they refer their patients.

Thus, according to the study, it is not unusual for patients referred to joint-venture facilities to pay more and get less for their money. If that money comes from government Medicare or Medicaid programs, taxpayers and the public may foot bills more expensive than necessary.

Results of the study by the Florida Health Care Cost Containment Board strengthen the case for the more stringent regulations imposed last month on physician joint ventures by the U.S. Department of Health and Human Services.

The Florida findings also ought to add strength to reform efforts under consideration in this state. Months ago the New York State Public Health Council cited risks from these self-referrals and issued recommended changes that the State Legislature has not yet acted upon.

Some physicians object to any investment limits, and care must be taken to assure they are fair. But other doctors don't object to clear, fair guidelines.

One constructive approach governs the new HHS rules. They limit how much of a lab or other health-care facility can be owned by physicians who refer patients to it and also limit the volume of those self-referrals in the overall business the facility does. Ownership or self-referrals exceeding these limits (generally 40 percent of the totals) expose the businesses to possible legal prosecution and stiff fines.

Whatever the details, an urgent need exists for more strict legal constraints on self-referrals for all patients, not just those in the Medicare and Medicaid programs.

These constraints can invigorate competition. They enhance fairness in supplying and receiving the ordered services.

Above all, they minimize financial temptations that can soil the ethics of physicians, overcharge taxpayers and, if the Florida study offers any clues, even shortchange patients on the service.

The Washington Post

Washington, D.C., August 5, 1991

IN 1983 the Reagan administration suspended its campaign for federal deregulation long enough to join with Congress in taking away from hospitals the price-setting power under Medicare. The federal fee schedule published instead was a cost-cutting effort. It has been successful enough that in 1989 the Bush administration and Congress took a similar step with regard to the physicians' fees that are Medicare's other major component.

Now the American Medical Association, in the likely first of many battles as the new system is put in effect, says the government is breaking its promise as to the impact in the first year by cutting total payments to doctors that were to be held constant. The AMA is right on this one, the Department of Health and Human Services wrong, and the system too valuable to let the bureaucracy produce a result that no one intended.

The fee schedule for physicians seeks not just to control what they are paid—the total has been rising at well over 10 percent a year—but to change the pecking order among them. Fees for general practitioners are increased relative to those of surgeons and other specialists. The good idea is partly to encourage a different mix of medicine. There were to be winners as well as losers in the process.

Congress also pledged that the schedule would not itself be used as a cost-cutting device but would be budget-neutral; the total cuts and increases it

called for would match. To limit lost income in any one year, a five-year transition was set up as well.

The department, however, is now proposing to apply these provisions in such a way as to sharpen precisely the effects they were meant to blunt. Thus the Medicare actuaries expect that some physicians whose fees are cut will make up part of the loss per service by prescribing and performing more services. HHS says the budget-neutrality rule requires it to offset this likely increased cost by cutting fees across the board. The transition rules will likewise add to costs (among other things, they require that fee increases be ladled out faster than fee cuts) unless compensated for, the department says.

In some cases the department is thus proposing a lower fee structure for Medicare than even that which is already driving doctors out of Medicaid. The AMA alone is not alone in being up in arms. Leading members of both the House Ways and Means and Senate Finance committees have also written in protest.

But the protest has mainly been technical, and the argument needs to be lifted above that level. This is a powerful and still under-appreciated system likely to transform, by implication, not just the way doctors are paid under Medicare, but the way they are paid across the entire society. Sooner or later it will become a green-eyeshade system like all the rest. But for now it deserves to be thought of and dealt with at a higher level and in broader terms.

Rockford Register Star
Rockford, Illinois, August 21, 1991

■ **Useless PR:** Doctors need to concentrate less on public image and more on how they look to their own patients.

What a medical waste. The largest physicians group in the country recently announced it will spend close to $2 million to improve the sagging image of doctors.

Ask disgruntled patients anywhere what they think of such madness by the American Medical Association. They would say:

■ Forget the public relations campaign and the glossy ads in major news magazines. We don't care about the New York pediatrician who treats cocaine babies. Matter of fact, it only makes for frustrating reading as we wait and wait and WAIT for appointments. Many of us would be willing to forgive, though, if once we heard, "I'm sorry."

■ Forget resurrecting Marcus Welby and Dr. Kildare. We don't want a doctor who holds our hand, just one who doesn't have one hand on the door as we ask our final questions.

■ Forget being comforted by a survey that showed only 10 percent of people were unhappy with their own doctor. Look at the 69 percent who agreed that "people are beginning to lose faith in their doctors." Every doctor can benefit by heeding the early warning signs of trouble.

Most of all, today's patients want to know their doctors really do care. If something is wrong with the doctor-patient relationship, it won't be fixed in a magazine ad. Let the healing begin at home, starting with old-fashioned courtesy.

The Gazette
Cedar Rapids, Iowa, October 28, 1991

A CALIFORNIA CONGRESSMAN is planning to introduce legislation that would protect medical consumers from the excessive financial ambitions of some doctors. Rep. Pete Stark, D-Calif., has a gem of an idea. We hope he can find the necessary support in the House.

Stark wants to prohibit a doctor from referring patients to other outpatient facilities in which he has financial interest. In other words, if a doctor were part-owner of a clinic that offers physical therapy or radiation therapy or C-T scans, he couldn't refer any of his own patients to it.

What worries Stark is that doctors may be unnecessarily referring patients to their own clinics as a means of boosting profits.

It sounds unconscionable — and it is. But there's strong evidence doctors do it all the time. A study co-authored by Elton Scott, a finance professor at Florida State University, shows "significant negative impacts on access, significantly higher utilization and significantly higher charges" for clinical laboratories, diagnostic imaging and physical therapy services partly owned by doctors.

That kind of accusation, of course, makes doctors who own these types of facilities indignant. The profit motive isn't that important, they claim. What is important is improving medical care in underserved areas. By pooling their resources and sharing equipment, the doctors say they can provide quality health care at reasonable costs in rural, underserved areas. But that argument, too, is undermined by the Florida study, which shows that none of the state's doctor-owned clinics is located in medically underserved areas.

During a hearing on the matter, members of the House heard from Robert D. Carl III, president of Health Images Inc., the largest owner of free-standing MRI clinics in the nation. He said his company decided to buy out the shares owned by physicians because of the high percentage of negative MRI scans among patients referred by doctors who had financial stakes in the clinics. It indicated unnecessary referrals. Carl estimates that doctors owning a share of a center with 20 partners could earn as much as $51,000 per partner per year if each partner referred just four patients a week.

Says Stark: "We are quickly getting to the point where each of us is going to have to wonder if we are getting a service because we need it or because it would fatten our physician's dividend check."

Patients would have less to wonder about if the congressman is successful in banning referrals made by physicians who own shares in the clinics.

The Duluth News-Tribune
Duluth, Minnesota, January 7, 1991

Rural Texans are told they have difficulty attracting good doctors because rural areas can't compete with the cities in terms of the livings doctors can earn there. While there is an obvious content of truth in that analysis, we cannot help noticing countervailing indications from the countryside, from time to time. The Texas Attorney General's office was successful this month in bringing to settlement a 5-year-old case involving three doctors in San Angelo accused of violations of state anti-trust laws. The three doctors — Leslie K. Williamson, Allen Anderson and Brian Humphreys — agreed in the settlement not to violate antitrust laws in the future and to pay the state $90,000 in attorneys' fees and investigative costs.

The three — all ear, nose and throat specialists — were accused of conspiring to keep a fourth ear, nose and throat specialist from establishing a practice in their area. The investigation by Attorney General Jim Mattox, concluded by his successor, Dan Morales, found the three had threatened to withhold various forms of professional support and otherwise harass the newcomer in order to avoid economic competition.

Certainly this case is not a paradigm for the medical care crisis in rural Texas. But neither is this the first case of its kind to break the surface of the news in recent years.

In rural areas where resources are stretched thin, it is not difficult for doctors with established practices to shut out a potential competitor. The methods used in the case settled last week were relatively benign in comparison with other recent cases, in which doctors appear to have used peer review and accusations of incompetence to maintain their own medical monopolies.

The attorney general's staff is to be congratulated for having pursued the San Angelo case to a successful conclusion. The attorney general and the Legislature should take the case as an indication that an ongoing enforcement effort may well be needed.

Malpractice Issues
Affect Medical Practice

The Institute of Medicine, a division of the National Academy of Sciences, said Oct. 11, 1989 that a two-year study had found that increasing numbers of obstetricians were no longer delivering babies because of skyrocketing malpractice costs.

The study, conducted by a committee of doctors, lawyers, and educators, found that the problem was particularly severe for poor women or those in rural areas. The number of obstetricians, other doctors and nurse-midwives willing to assist with a normal delivery had dropped by 20% in rural areas over the past five years, the study said.

"The fear of being sued has caused many doctors and midwives to limit care, especially for women with high-risk pregnancies," said Dr. Roger J. Bulger, the chairman of the institute's study committee. "In urban areas, this often means that low-income women have been hurt the most by the lack of providers."

The committee noted that malpractice insurance premiums for obstetricians in some cities were more than $100,000 a year. Although the number of claims against obstetricians represented about 10% of all malpractice claims, the large size of awards to plaintiffs meant that obstetrical damages made up almost half of all malpractice damages awarded by the courts.

The report said that the increase in malpractice suits was partly responsible for a rise in the number of Caesarean births being performed in the U.S. because doctors feared being sued if anything went wrong during a vaginal delivery.

The study urged states to experiment with new methods of resolving obstetrical malpractice claims, such as binding arbitration or no-fault compensation for some conditions.

President George Bush announced Feb. 22, 1990 that he had asked his domestic policy council to determine what steps could be taken "to restore common sense and fairness to America's medical malpractice system."

Bush made his remarks at a ceremony in Baltimore, Md. marking the 114th anniversary of Johns Hopkins University, which contained one of the nation's foremost medical research centers.

The American Medical Association estimated that jury awards and doctors' malpractice insurance premiums cost the U.S. some $14 billion a year.

A White House spokesman said that the domestic policy council had been studying several possible options to ease the problem, including actions to encourage states to revise their malpractice laws by setting up special boards to handle malpractice claims.

A study by researchers at Harvard University had found that thousands of people in New York State died or were injured each year in hospitals because of medical negligence, it was reported March 1, 1990. The study was reported to be the most comprehensive examination of malpractice ever conducted in the U.S.

The study had been commissioned by New York State health officials. It had examined four areas: the number of injuries caused by medical treatment, the proportion of injuries that led to malpractice suits, the overall cost of such injuries and the impact of the threat of malpractice lawsuits on medical practice.

After examining the outcome of medical treatment on 30,000 patients at 51 hospitals throughout the state in 1984, the researchers found 1,133 adverse effects, ranging from patient falls to infections caused by surgery.

By extrapolating their findings to the 2.7 million patients hospitalized in New York in 1984, the researchers concluded that nearly 99,000 patients had experienced injury because of the medical treatment they received, with one-quarter of those injuries resulting from negligence. The panel estimated that negligence had contributed to the deaths of more than 13,000 patients. The incidence of negligence had been higher in hospitals run by state, county or city governments than in private or nonprofit hospitals.

Only a small fraction of patients injured by negligence had filed malpractice suits, the study found.

THE DAILY OKLAHOMAN
Oklahoma City, Oklahoma,
June 28, 1988

THE high cost of medical malpractice insurance threatens to deny many expectant mothers proper health care.

Because insurance is so expensive, large numbers of obstetricians and family doctors have stopped delivering babies.

A recent survey by the American College of Obstetricians and Gynecologists showed the cost of malpractice insurance jumped almost 240 percent in the past five years. The average annual premium for baby doctors rose from $10,946 in 1982 to $37,015 in 1987. In Florida and New York, the average is about $52,000.

As a result, the study revealed, more and more physicians are leaving obstetrics at the height of their professional ability. Those who continue their practice are beginning to limit their care of high-risk pregnancies.

Health and Human Services Secretary Otis R. Bowen told a medical symposium last week that the problem is becoming especially acute in rural and inner-city areas. Numerous counties or entire regions of some states report they have just one or two doctors to deliver babies, he said.

Nurse-midwives can't very well take up the slack, because they also are at risk for malpractice suits and must carry the high-cost insurance.

Something must be done to halt this runaway trend that is driving up the cost of maternal and child health care and making such care inaccessible to many who need it. The medical and legal professions need to work together to find a solution, or government will surely move in.

THE ANN ARBOR NEWS

Ann Arbor, Michigan, January 21, 1989

In what Michigan State Medical Society President Dr. Robert E. Paxton refers to as "the state's continuing medical liability crisis," it still costs Michigan physicians an arm and a leg for malpractice insurance. A medical society survey found annual insurance paid by Michigan obstetricians is more than $50,000, compared with $14,000 in Indiana and $18,000 in Ohio.

Gov. James Blanchard's special consultant on malpractice, former University of Michigan President Robben Fleming, has offered preliminary recommendations for reforms to help reduce the high cost of medical malpractice insurance in Michigan.

They include:

■ Limiting damage awards by handling medical malpractice cases much like workers' compensation cases, in which claims are resolved administratively, not in the courts.

■ Strengthening physician licensing laws to weed out the incompetents. This would include requiring doctors to take a licensing exam every five years.

■ Periodically publishing a list of hospitals with high levels of malpractice, in an attempt to prompt hospitals to reduce occurrences of malpractice.

Limiting the amount of awards will be tough to pull off because the vested interests of another powerful lobbying group — the state's trial lawyers — are involved. Fleming proposes definitions of the types of injuries that deserve damage awards and the amount of such awards, and the trial lawyers oppose further restrictions on claims.

Fleming and his assistant, health-care consultant Jay Rosen, are expected to offer a formal report in February. They have suggested an interesting combination of changes that offer a number of checks that cover problems in several areas. In particular, the concept of a medical malpractice claims compensation system similar to workers' compensation is worth further development.

THE BUFFALO NEWS

Buffalo, New York, January 8, 1989

THE CREATION of the nation's first centralized data bank to disseminate malpractice and disciplinary information on physicians and dentists is a logical step that should do much to protect patients.

The data bank, authorized by Congress three years ago, should be functioning by this summer to allow hospitals, state licensing boards and others in the health-care industry to get information on the background of physicians and dentists.

Some states already publicize the names of health-care professionals who have been disciplined. But that does little to protect patients in other states where officials may not have access to that information.

The new plan requires all U.S hospitals to consult the nationwide data bank when a physician or dentist applies for a staff position or clinical privileges. That hardly seems a bureaucratic hardship, given the stakes for patients. In addition, the hospitals will have to check the repository every two years to make sure those already on the staff or with privileges have not been deemed negligent or incompetent in that time.

Besides mandatory usage by hospitals, the data bank also will be available to health-care organizations — such as group medical and dental practices — and to state licensing boards, whose need for such information should be apparent.

The repository will contain all information regarding final action on malpractice suits, including out-of-court settlements, as well as disciplinary action by state boards and hospital or peer review boards.

As Health and Human Services Secretary Otis R. Bowen said in announcing the new program, "no longer will incompetent health professionals be enabled to move from hospital to hospital."

Instead, a record acquired at one facility will be known by officials at all facilities — even those in another state — who can then decide if the infraction or alleged incompetence warrants denial of a staff position or clinical privileges.

However, though the information will be available to hospitals and health-care organizations, it will not be available to the general public. That precaution seems sensible even though it has aroused some criticism.

As Bowen stressed, the settlement or loss of a malpractice suit is no guarantee that malpractice has occurred. A hospital or health-care organization checking the background of a prospective doctor has both the time and expertise to sift through the details of such a case — including hearing the doctor's side — to determine whether the physician or dentist actually poses a threat to patients.

By contrast, medical consumers who simply see a doctor listed in a data bank do not have the opportunity to make that kind of determination, and thus could be unduly influenced simply by the fact that a physician or dentist is listed. Bowen pointed out that patients have other means of checking on a doctor, such as consulting the local medical society.

Even so, patients should cheer implementation of the data bank. The fact that licensing boards and others in the health-care industry will have access to this information should mean fewer incompetent doctors to have to worry about.

THE SACRAMENTO BEE

Sacramento, California, January 4, 1989

No one knows how often it occurred, but there's no doubt that it occurred with some regularity: A physician disciplined for malpractice in one state would end up practicing — or continue practicing — in another where no one was aware of the disciplinary action. In response, the federal government has now established a central computer listing of disciplinary and malpractice information on the nation's doctors and dentists that ought to preclude that possibility. It's a welcome addition in encouraging responsible medical practice.

The data bank, created by outgoing Secretary of Health and Human Services Otis Bowen, will include information on final action on malpractice suits against all licensed health-care providers, disciplinary actions taken by state medical and dental licensing boards, peer review decisions in hospitals and health maintenance organizations and adverse decisions resulting from peer review by professional organizations.

Some states have been publicizing information on completed disciplinary actions against health-care professionals, but this is the first time the information will be available to hospitals, state licensing boards and physicians groups. The government will require hospitals to check the list whenever a physician wants to join the staff or receive clinical privileges and will require them to review the names of physicians already on the staff against the list every two years.

The list, unfortunately, will not be open to the public. In part, that's understandable since such things as malpractice settlements, or even malpractice judgments, don't necessarily reflect on a physician's dedication and ability; in part it no doubt makes it much easier to avoid opposition from organized medical groups. Still, information on official disciplinary actions, at least, is something to which consumers ought to have access and about which they should to be competent to make their own reasonable evaluations. Bowen says consumers can get adequate information from "neighbors or friends" — but that kind of information is as subject to rumor and misinterpretation as anything about malpractice in a data bank.

Nonetheless, the data bank ought to do a lot to keep the peripatetic charlatans off the road and out of the hospitals. When a doctor is defrocked in one state there is presumably good reason not to let him back into the operating room somewhere else.

THE INDIANAPOLIS STAR
Indianapolis, Indiana, January 7, 1989

Often a physician who has his license suspended or revoked in one state can just move to another and leave his bad record behind.

New employers and associates may not even check his background but instead assume he is a qualified practitioner of unquestioned good character and proper credentials.

By next fall there will be no need for assumptions. A contract has been awarded for a national computerized network to keep track of professional black marks.

The data bank, expected to cost $15.9 million over five years, requires medical authorities to report serious sanctions or disciplinary actions, including malpractice claims or settlements and expulsion from medical societies, hospital staffs and the like for incompetence, fraud, drug abuse, etc.

In turn, hospitals are required to consult the data bank before granting hospital privileges and to check staff doctors against accumulated data every two years. Though not required to do so, it is expected that licensing boards will routinely consult the bank.

Dr. Otis R. Bowen, outgoing secretary of health and human services, said there are no reliable statistics on malpractice and there are "hundreds, maybe thousands" of doctors with fake credentials now practicing medicine.

The data bank should improve medical care and bring down the cost of malpractice insurance, he said.

Though a welcome development, the data bank has limitations. Doctors start off with a clean slate. There will be no record of actions that predate the operation of the data network. Moreover, the public will be denied access. All information will be confidential and available only to the medical community.

Bowen said it wouldn't be fair to make the information available to the public. Dr. Sidney Wolfe of the Public Citizen's Health Research Group disagrees.

Wolfe said it is an outrage to deny consumers access to data which they are paying to compile and maintain. He noted that in many states patients must go to court to get information on a doctor's disciplinary status.

Wolfe seems to have the better argument. The medical profession is understandably concerned about confidentiality but it should not expect to secure it at public expense. If, as Bowen says, the data bank helps reduce the cost of malpractice insurance, there is all the more reason for the health care industry — not the public — to pay for it.

It seems the medical profession is getting to have its cake and eat it too. It will get a confidential way of policing its own ranks, a way that should make malpractice insurance less expensive, and it will have it courtesy of the taxpayers.

AKRON BEACON JOURNAL
Akron, Ohio, December 18, 1989

THE CASE of Dr. James Burt is extreme. Burt, a Dayton physician, performed controversial vaginal reconstruction surgery on hundreds of women, many without their consent, supposedly to heighten their sexual pleasure.

Doctors in at least four Ohio cities knew of complications resulting from Burt's surgery. Yet not one reported him to the Ohio Medical Board. The board finally learned of Burt's surgeries through a state senator's intervention.

Now, a bill introduced in the Ohio House would allow for stiff fines on doctors who fail to report medical malpractice. Many doctors are expected to oppose it.

However, doctors, more than anyone, know when patients have been wronged by other physicians. Those who fail to report medical abuses put other unsuspecting patients at risk.

To protect the public, the laws should be strict enough so that doctors fear the consequences of not reporting malpractice.

To be sure, the percentage of incompetent doctors is small. And it is understandable that some doctors fear penalties for not reporting every practice by another doctor that they question. In many cases, what is or is not malpractice is debatable.

However, a doctor's duty should be to report questionable practices and let the Ohio Medical Board decide whether the laws governing physicians have been violated.

That compares to Ohio's laws on reporting child abuse. A teacher, for example, must report suspected abuse to proper authorities. It is then up to authorities to handle cases from that point.

Currently, doctors have little incentive to report their peers. And few actually do. Of 1,061 complaints to the medical board in 1987, only 37 came from doctors. Figures for 1988 are similar.

The Ohio State Medical Association, which represents the special interests of doctors, argues that the current laws on failing to report malpractice are sufficient.

But in reality, the state medical board has never cited a doctor for failing to report. In part, that is because the board's only choice of serious punishment — the revoking of a doctor's license — is so drastic. Under the new bill, the board could impose financial penalties up to $50,000 for failure to report.

Also under the bill, a doctor convicted under criminal law for failing to report would face a maximum $25,000 fine, and possibly jail time.

When the hearings on this bill begin in the legislature, the doctors will have a chance to air their concerns. And, as lawmakers continue their work, they should take care to safeguard against frivolous investigations of doctors for failing to report.

The goal should be to make doctors more vigilant — and to compel them to come forward with information without facing the possibility of civil liability for reporting a violation. The bill introduced in the House is a good start toward that goal.

San Francisco Chronicle
San Francisco, California, August 22, 1991

TOO MUCH government money intended to provide medical care for the poor is being spent on malpractice insurance instead. Premiums have risen 30 percent to 40 percent in the last year — so much that many of the nation's 600 community health centers have been forced to cut back on the service they provide.

Insurance companies contend, with justice, that many of the clinics' patients are poor risks because they do not get in touch with doctors until their medical problems are acute.

BUT THE END result is that some clinics, like the Mission Neighborhood Health Center in San Francisco, refer obstetrics cases elsewhere because they cannot afford insurance. In rural counties, where acceptable alternatives may not exist, the elimination of services can result in severe hardship.

The solution is not to attempt to repeat California's unsatisfactory experience with Proposition 103, in which voters were promised arbitrary, market-stifling and unrealistic cuts in insurance rates that have yet to be delivered.

Instead, Congress must accept the challenge of setting reasonable limits on malpractice awards. Clinics and the doctors who dedicate their lives to serving the poor should not remain in financial jeopardy.

Nearly everyone knows what's wrong with the health care system in the United States. It costs more money than in virtually any other developed nation, yet covers on the average fewer people. Expenses have soared at an astronomical rate and millions of Americans have been priced right out of health care, lacking even basic insurance.

What they don't always know is what to do about the situation. That's because there is no single solution to this increasingly difficult problem. It will have to be attacked on many fronts.

The Des Moines Register

Des Moines, Iowa, January 9, 1991

Reforms control costs, but do little to resolve inequities

To lawyers who specialize in suing doctors, it's annoying enough that California's malpractice reform law works. Even more annoying for them is that it could serve as the model for nationwide reform sought by President Bush.

The California law, enacted in 1975, sets a limit of $250,000 on the amount juries can award a plaintiff for alleged "pain and suffering" sustained at the hands of an errant doctor. The sky's the limit in other states, and imaginative attorneys routinely reach for it. Given pliable juries, attorneys sometimes score awards that spell instant retirement.

The California law also takes a bit of the luster off that pot of gold, limiting slightly the lawyer's share of a jury award. President Bush has called for reforms that would limit punitive damages, but has not endorsed limiting attorneys' shares of awards.

California juries can award enough to compensate a victim for all medical bills, all loss of potential income, and any other actual loss to which a dollar cost can be attached. But since no such cost can be affixed for pain and suffering, juries are winging it when setting those damages. That's why California trial lawyers want that limit raised — meaning doubled, preferably tripled.

Allowing plaintiffs to recover some damage for pain is important. If they could sue only for actual damages, the retired elderly, in particular, might get only slight compensation for a gross injury since they would lose no income, and any handicap they suffered might be considered of little conse-quence, given their age and possible other infirmities.

But surely the possibility of a quarter-million-dollar judgment for pain — and the professional stigma attached to losing a malpractice suit — are sufficient to ensure against calloused or wantonly careless doctoring.

Before California enacted its reform law, the state's doctors paid the highest rates in the nation for malpractice insurance. Now their premiums rank 33rd. The average malpractice award fell from $566,000 in 1975 to $519,000 in 1988, despite inflation.

Applied nationwide, the reforms could significantly reduce "defensive medicine," the costly and wasteful practice of running un-needed diagnostic tests as insurance against a malpractice claim.

The reforms are important in containing costs. But they do little to resolve the basic inequities of malpractice — which overcompensates a lucky few and their attorneys, while leaving the vast majority of true malpractice victims adrift.

A Harvard University study completed last year showed that in New York State, only one out of 16 victims of medical negligence ever received compensation. Actual negligence was rare — occurring in eight out of 1,000 hospitalizations. But negligence does not necessarily determine whether a patient sues for malpractice, nor does it necessarily determine whether he collects.

No-fault is designed to channel compensation for negligence to the victims rather than to the lawyers and expert witnesses. It holds the potential to achieve greater equality while at the same time, reducing health-care costs.

Observers contend that no-fault may be years away from gaining acceptance. In the meantime, it makes sense to broaden application of the reform that has worked in California.

DESERET NEWS

Salt Lake City, Utah, February 22, 1992

One potentially promising attck is being pushed by Sen. Orrin Hatch, R-Utah, who is sponsoring a measure designed to reduce "defensive medicine" — the often unnecessary and usually expensive testing, procedures and consultations done by doctors to protect themselves against possible malpractice lawsuits.

The senator says the medical methods arising from doctors' fear of malpractice claims have inflated the nation's yearly health-care costs by 25 percent. That would be equal to a staggering $150 billion in 1989.

Hatch's bill would authorize $200 million a year to encourage states to develop ways to resolve medical malpractice disputes without going to court. The bill also would cap punitive damages at $250,000, limit attorney fees, and allow periodic instead of lump-sum payments for awards exceeding $100,000.

Trial lawyers are opposed to the plan. Though they couch their opposition in terms of concern for plaintiffs, they have a vested financial interest in seeing expensive malpractice suits continue to increase.

An average of 900 malpractice lawsuits are filed each day in the United States, and in cases that plaintiffs win, the average award is in excess of $300,000. Multimillion-dollar awards, once rare, are now common.

Arbitration seems to make more sense than litigation; it takes less time and is less costly. Arbitration has been adopted as an option in Michigan. In Canada, malpractice cases are heard by a judge instead of a jury, reducing the melodramatic appeals lawyers often use on jurors.

Canada also caps punitive damages at $200,000, which are rarely awarded in any case. As result, Canadian doctors practice less of the expensive "defensive medicine" and Canadian malpractice insurance costs only one-ninth of that in the United States.

Arbitration and caps on punitive damages aren't the only answers to the soaring cost of health care, but they are a good place to begin.

THE DENVER POST

Denver, Colorado, January 9, 1992

WHEN A policeman shoots a citizen, the officer is normally put on leave or otherwise taken off the streets until the incident can be fully investigated.

Similarly, when a schoolteacher is alleged to have molested a student, the accused individual is typically suspended with pay until the charge is resolved.

But when a doctor appears to have mistreated a patient, he may continue to practice for months or even years — possibly threatening the well-being of hundreds of others — before the question finally is settled.

Such slow-motion justice can be especially injurious in rural areas, where people may not have access to other medical professionals with more salutary records in the meantime.

Even greater harm might ensue, however, if physicians automatically lost their licenses while their charts were being reviewed. Some small towns could be deprived of even minimally adequate health care, which is arguably better than no care at all. Others might lose perfectly good doctors who couldn't sup-port themselves in other ways during the time it took to clear their names.

The solution here is not to deny doctors due process, but to speed up and improve the process of reviewing and resolving such cases.

The Board of Medical Examiners should be given sufficient funds to hire a large enough staff to investigate complaints in a timely manner, and the board itself should meet whenever it is necessary to take action on their findings.

In addition, the legislature should re-examine the state's medical practices law to ensure that second-rate doctors aren't being protected by legal or administrative barriers that make it harder to revoke a license than it really ought to be.

In many cases, the practice of medicine may be as much an art as a science.

However, it doesn't necessarily follow that licensing authorities can't readily distinguish between good care and bad care — or operate efficiently enough to keep patients from being unduly jeopardized.

Black Life Expectancy Low; Blacks' Heart-Surgery Rate Seen Low

The life expectancy of black Americans had decreased, while that for white Americans had increased in 1987, the National Center for Health Statistics said in a study reported Dec. 15, 1988.

The decline in black life expectancy was the second in two years. That statistic marked the first time in the 20th century that a consecutive decline had been reported among blacks but not among whites.

Harry Rosenberg, chief of the center's mortality statistics branch, noted that while both young whites and young blacks had experienced an increase in homicide rates in 1987, the rate had risen by 15% for blacks but only 5% for whites.

Other causes of death that had increased more among blacks than among whites in 1987 had been motor-vehicle accidents, AIDS and other infectious diseases.

Some officials attributed part of the problem to Reagan administration policies that, they said, had increased homelessness, cut health care and decreased aid to the poor.

Older white Medicare patients were three-and-one-half times as likely to receive a heart bypass operation as their black counterparts, according to a study published March 18, 1992 in the *Journal of the American Medical Association.*

The *JAMA* study was based on an analysis of more than 86,000 coronary artery bypass operations performed in 1986 under the Medicare health insurance program for the elderly. The study took into account racial differences in heart-disease rates and geographical access to hospitals.

The researchers found an overall bypass rate of 25.6 Medicare patients per 10,000 people. The rate for whites was 27.1 per 10,000 people and for blacks, 7.6 per 10,000 people.

The *JAMA* study found the highest white-black ratio of operations in Alabama, where it was about 8 to 1. The rate was nearly 7 to 1 in Mississippi, Louisiana, South Carolina, and Arkansas.

THE BUFFALO NEWS
Buffalo, New York, July 29, 1988

THE REAGAN Administration has slashed an important medical program that for 16 years has been supplying doctors to serve the poor in inner cities and rural areas.

The program, called the National Health Service Corps, pays the tuition of medical students who agree to serve a year in such areas for every year they receive tuition assistance.

The corps has been an outstanding success, enrolling 13,600 doctors since it was created under the Nixon administration in 1972. The program has made it possible for more people to complete their medical training, and it has brought first-rate medical care to clinics serving the indigent.

Now the program has been cut back to near the vanishing point, and clinics are facing a shortage of doctors. The figures tell the deplorable story. The budget of the corps in 1978, the peak year, was $100 million; this year it is $2 million. There were 3,347 new medical students enrolled in the program in 1978; this year, there were under 40.

The effect of the cutbacks will be magnified even more because about half of the corps physicians voluntarily stay and work in areas that are short of doctors after their service with the corps has been completed.

Critics of the program within the administration condemn it as a step toward socialized medicine — hardly something that one would think the Nixon administration would favor. They also say that the program is unnecessary in view of the increased number of doctors nationally. This claim is belied by the doctor shortage that still exists in 1,900 areas of the country.

Protests from such areas about the decline of medical care has stirred Congress to double the appropriation for the program for next year. But this will be still only $4 million, compared with the $100 million spent 11 years earlier.

The administration has been accused of being callous toward the poor, but it justifies this and other cutbacks in social welfare programs as necessary to reduce spending. And yet the cost of the corps medical program was, at its peak, less than half the cost of a single B-1 bomber.

Granted our national defense deserves top priority, but surely some priority should go to a program like the National Health Service Corps, which improves the medical training and the medical care of the nation at the same time.

Arkansas Gazette.
Little Rock, Arkansas, August 18, 1988

Nowhere has there been such a massive public investment in medicine as in the United States, but it has brought us to this point: This is the only advanced nation besides South Africa where the benefits of that investment, including life itself, may be rationed according to wealth.

Little Brandy Ellis of El Dorado is the latest to exemplify this paradox. Brandy, who is nine months old, needs a liver transplant to live, but she also must have $125,000 or the University of Nebraska Medical Center will pass her by for someone who has the cash. A medical bill of $125,000 will make paupers of most families, but Arkansas's Medicaid program, which is supposed to insure the poor, won't guarantee payment for Brandy's surgery and treatment for the good reason that if it pays the costs of liver transplants it must stop paying for the care of many other people whose treatment may also be life-saving. State governments decide the treatments on which they will spend Medicaid money so that they keep the total spending within the appropriated limits. The state has begun to pay for organ transplants, but it has agreed to pay only about a fourth of the costs of liver transplants.

Federal Judge G. Thomas Eisele, who heard a lawsuit by Brandy's parents, ruefully decided last week that the state was within its legal rights and that he was powerless to order it to allocate its limited money another way. Today, a panel of the 8th U.S. Circuit Court of Appeals will have its sorrowful shot at the case.

The court could conclude that the state violated equal protection in making a distinction in the kinds of life-saving surgery it would pay for. Liver transplants are no longer experimental, which once was the premise for paying for some transplants and not others.

However it rules will leave losers, though maybe unseen. Medical technology has advanced beyond our ethical and moral frontiers. As a guest writer to the *Gazette* observed wryly the other day, maybe now computers, which have a hand in every other decision, should tell us who will benefit from science and live and who will die.

The time is approaching when the United States will resolve the dilemma by insuring health care for everyone. Every industrialized nation in the world, except South Africa, does it and all at a much smaller aggregate expenditure for health care. Meantime, life must depend sometimes on these desperate appeals to the compassionate impulses of individuals or judges.

The Oregonian

Portland, Oregon, November 9, 1991

Evidence that non-white Americans receive a poorer quality of health care than whites has been given new emphasis in the past few days both nationally and in Oregon.

The status of blacks' health is worse by any measure than that of whites, reported Suezanne Orr, assistant professor in the Department of Health Policy and Management at Johns Hopkins University.

The average-life expectancy of a black male born in 1988 was 7.4 years less than for a white. For a black female it was 5.5 years less. Infant mortality was twice as great for blacks as whites, and blacks' rates of death from heart disease, stroke, cancer and AIDS all were markedly higher, Orr reported.

Similar information appeared in a report of a committee of the City Club of Portland, quoting studies of the Oregon Health Division. The figures showed poorer health conditions not only for blacks in Oregon but for American Indians and for Asian immigrants as well, compared with whites, with similar information on Hispanics still to be compiled.

The City Club committee also looked at spending on Medicaid, the federal-state program for medical services to the poor, and found that per capita it was higher for whites than for other groups.

Kevin W. Concannon, director of the Oregon Department of Human Resources, denied that the difference in figures shows racial or ethnic discrimination in the Medicaid program. His explanation is significant:

Per-capita Medicaid spending for adults is higher for whites, he said, because nursing-home expenses make up nearly three-fifths of the cost of Medicaid in Oregon. Minority populations tend to take care of their elderly at home or in community-based care, rather than use more expensive nursing homes. More important, he said, white Medicaid recipients on average are older than non-whites, and need more costly care.

Both reports converge on the same point: In the United States today, whites are living longer than people of other races. The reasons may be complex. They do not necessarily involve intentional discrimination. But the results are discriminatory, and disturbing.

The Wichita
Eagle-Beacon

Wichita, Kansas, January 9, 1991

Triage is the sorting of sick and injured people according to priorities aimed at maximizing the number of survivors. In allocating medical treatment to the poor, Kansas thus far has avoided making such painful life-or-death choices.

But during the 1980s, medical assistance costs spiraled out of control, putting a terrible strain on the state budget. That trend shows no sign of abating in the 1990s. That was one factor that prompted the Legislature last year to set up a task force to look into the Department of Social and Rehabilitation Services, with an eye to controlling welfare costs.

On Monday, the task force said it's time the Legislature launched a debate over triage as a way to contain medical assistance costs. The 1991 Legislature should take that recommendation seriously.

The recommendation is sure to be controversial because it implies that some sick people would be denied treatment that the state deemed too costly. But the current haphazard system of allocating medical costs entails far greater cruelties.

Because that system emphasizes treating people after they become ill, thousands of poor Kansans are vulnerable to ailments that a more enlightened system might be able to prevent. A task force member, Sen. Frank Gaines, D-Augusta, notes, for instance, that "there's a large percentage of youngsters that haven't been immunized."

The task force rightly says that SRS ought to be concentrating on programs that keep people from getting ill. The agency, says the task force, should de-emphasize expensive, high-tech medical procedures such as organ transplants.

There is a precedent for such a system. Oregon has developed a list of what medical procedures it will pay for. The task force rightly sees Oregon's work as a starting point for Kansas' studies into new ways of allocating medical care to the poor.

Regardless of how the Legislature may choose to broach the subject, it's important that ethics be a prominent feature of the debate. To limit debate to financial and political considerations would cause many a Kansan to suspect that legislators want only to abandon the most costly of the poor in order to keep down the taxes of the healthy, employed and insured.

To be sure, the healthy, employed and insured have a moral obligation to care for the poor — a duty they've performed admirably. But they can't be expected to pick up ever-rising tabs for a medical assistance system that indiscriminately funds virtually every procedure that comes down the pike. There's got to be a better way to handle medical assistance in Kansas, and it's the Legislature's duty to discover it.

THE ATLANTA CONSTITUTION
Atlanta, Georgia, May 23, 1991

Why doesn't America guarantee the basic right of health care to all, as most industrialized nations do? An editorial in a highly respected medical journal offers a provocative and yet thoughtful answer: racism.

Millions of health-care consumers are dissatisfied with a costly but yet patchy system in which even working citizens often cannot afford the medical care they need. Businesses are fed up with costs. Insurers howl about prices. President Bush has cited our chaotic health-care "system" as a major concern. Yet, no solution is forthcoming.

In the May 15 issue of the Journal of the American Medical Association (JAMA), editor Dr. George D. Lundberg wrote the following in an unflinching editorial:

"Access to basic medical care for all of our inhabitants is still not a reality in this country. There are many reasons for this, not the least of which is long-standing, systematic, institutionalized racial discrimination . . .

"It is not a coincidence that the United States of America and the Republic of South Africa — the only two developed, industrialized countries that do not have a national health policy ensuring that all citizens have access to basic health care — also are the only two such countries that have within their borders substantial numbers of underserved people who are different ethnically from the controlling group."

Health care is not the only social issue swept to the shoals of the public agenda by the undercurrents of racism, and America's failure to tackle social problems does not affect only citizens of color adversely. There are millions of white citizens, for instance, who cannot afford decent housing, a point often overlooked when the majority shies from a social issue because blacks would benefit disproportionately from the solution.

But our national failure to provide health care for all represents one of our greatest challenges. Perhaps the willingness of the medical community to tackle this awkward and difficult subject can help all of us overcome divisive ethnicity and get on with the business of providing a basic human service that will better the lives of individual citizens and boost the productivity of the nation.

Los Angeles Times
Los Angeles, California, Janaury 4, 1991

Mobile vans already are delivering health care to poor neighborhoods in Southern California through such projects as the Watts Health Foundation's mobile units for prenatal screenings and treatment for the sick homeless; St. Jude Hospital and Rehabilitation Center in Orange County runs a pediatric van. St. Jude's now also wants to create a "mom-mobile" to offer free prenatal exams to indigent women who may not have access to transportation or child care. Unfortunately, the good intentions are being choked by red tape.

The hospital plans to outfit a van with medical equipment and send an obstetrician and nurse to low-income neighborhoods. There's wide support for the idea, even from the people who say it can't be done now. The catch is that while services such as the Watts prenatal program are funded through other means, St. Jude's

wants authorization for Medi-Cal reimbursement to run its "mom-mobile." To do that, Washington must reinterpret bureaucratic language so that the program can fulfill its promise and serve as a model.

Under existing guidelines, Medi-Cal money cannot be made available for the van because that would amount to providing off-site hospital services, which are not authorized at present. This is an absurdity, given the need for such care among a segment of the population that has a difficult time getting to a hospital. And proper and early prenatal care for poor people, as a way of ensuring healthy mothers and babies, increasingly has become a national concern.

The regional administrator of the U.S. Health Care Financing Administration apparently agrees, and has vowed to push either for a reinterpretation of the regulations or for a

change in the rules. A decision that would allow the "mom-mobile" to start up its engine is expected this month. Clearly, the finding ought to come down on the side of this much-needed service.

The Fullerton hospital already has nine of its 12 obstetricians signed up to take turn in the vans. Orange County officials were so impressed with the idea that last summer they gave St. Jude's $250,000 from the new state tax on tobacco to start the project. State Medi-Cal officials have been interested enough to say that other California hospitals could be considered for similar vans.

But the problem remains with narrowly drawn federal regulations. A lot—including a future generation about to enter the world with the strike of poverty against it—is riding on an administrative guideline that ought to be changed.

ST. LOUIS POST-DISPATCH
St. Louis, Missouri, August 22, 1992

Does it take a dozen years of medical training to set broken bones, read X-rays, stitch cuts? The question is becoming more relevant as this nation seeks ways to boost competition in the medical profession and reduce the cost of health care.

Until the 1960s, it was unheard of to have anyone other than physicians perform these medical procedures. Now they're being handled by physician assistants, along with advanced nurse practitioners and nurse anesthetists. Their medical training might last only 15 months, but they are filling a void.

These new practitioners are responding to the shortage of physicians in urban and rural communities and the preference of medical students to specialize rather than become family physicians. The medical profession's objections to the growing use of physician assistants is only partly a quality-care issue. The real concern is that these junior practitioners are demanding that federal agencies and insurance companies pay them directly for services.

The difference in who is paid will make an enormous difference in your hospital bill. One owner of a nurse practitioner group in Cambridge, Mass., told *The Wall Street Journal* of how a nurse practitioner might charge $150 for a procedure that might cost $300 if performed by a physician.

Doctors brought this dilemma on themselves by choosing to pursue financially lucrative specialities rather than be family physicians. The latter earns an average of $102,700 a year, while a surgeon makes an average salary of $236,400. Physician assistants earn an average of $47,500 a year and nurse practitioners can expect to make $42,000. Doctors say they are forced to specialize in order to pay off medical school debts, which averaged $50,000 last year.

Meanwhile, physician assistants are the fastest-growing group of medical practitioners. They compensate for the dwindling supply of family physicians. They have the extra benefit of performing some medical procedures at less cost. There may be no valid reason they shouldn't be paid directly by government agencies and insurance companies that have an interest in keeping down the cost of health care.

THE INDIANAPOLIS NEWS
Indianapolis, Indiana, August 24, 1992

Right now the ratio of medical students from urban areas to rural areas in the state is about 3:1. We'd like to see that change to 1:1.
— Clyde Ingle, Commissioner Indiana Commission for Higher Education

The Indiana Commission for Higher Education wants to see students from the state's rural areas receive incentives to complete medical school and return home to practice medicine.

It also has been working directly with rural area high school guidance counselors, parents and students to impress upon high-schoolers that their communities need them and those who are up to a career in medicine should seriously consider it.

If students do not, there could be something even more serious to consider later — the fact that those who continue to live in those communities may not have adequate medical care available close to home.

Such is already the case. Many rural communities in Indiana do not have even one resident doctor. According to I.U. Medical School Dean Walter J. Daly, as of mid-August the school had not received one application for medical school from 23 Indiana counties, areas Daly noted were most in need of primary-care physicians.

The Indiana Commission for Higher Education has been studying the problem for months and will be discussing some of its recommendations at upcoming meetings at the school's eight regional centers. Tying state funding of I.U. Medical School to the number of graduates entering residencies in certain specialties and granting tuition forgiveness to students willing to serve primary-care residencies are some of the measures suggested to bolster Hoosier enrollment in

medical school.

There certainly is validity to such approaches. Short supply merits a higher price. There may well be a need, at least for a time, to "pay" more in terms of incentives for medical students who eventually open up practices in primary care medicine here in Indiana.

But more needs to be done, acknowledged Clyde Ingle, commissioner of the Indiana Commission for Higher Education.

"If high school teachers knew that there was an undersupply of med school applicants, they might take a bright student aside and tell him or her, 'Look, you would be an ideal candidate for medical school.' Right now, I don't think that's happening," Ingle told The News.

"But we do have in place a major outreach effort for ninth-graders, their parents and high school teachers," he said. "Through surveys and ISTEP score tracking, the Commission sends any one of a number of letters to students regarding their career aspirations, hoping to spur their interest in professional fields.

"For example, if we knew a young lady was planning to undertake a study of cosmetology, and she scored remarkably well on state math tests, we would send her a letter citing other opportunities — medicine or engineering, for example — available to her" — not to denigrate the field of cosmetology, Ingle explained, but simply to bring to light other viable options.

The Indiana Commission for Higher Education wisely has identified a problem area that could worsen in rural communities across the state if not addressed now. Resolving that problem in concert with I.U. Medical School, its subsidizers and local communities are steps in the right direction.

The Philadelphia Inquirer
Philadelphia, Pennsylvania, August 19, 1992

Let their teeth rot. That's what Gov. Casey said, in effect, when he proposed cutting off dental care (except for emergencies) for adults on general assistance. Now the Casey administration wants to do more false economizing by cutting the dental coverage of adults in all welfare programs, including Aid to Families with Dependent Children (AFDC) and supplemental security income for the blind and the disabled.

That's just one of many wrongheaded features of the governor's plan to save money on medical assistance for poor Pennsylvanians by limiting their doctors' visits and prescriptions. (There'd be a way to apply for exceptions to these limits, but it's unclear how well that would work because the administration hasn't yet spelled out the procedure.) Some prescriptions — including drugs for allergies, ear infections, skin infections and digestive disorders — wouldn't be provided at all for adults on general assistance.

Granted, it's incongruous and unfair that there's medical assistance for poor people on welfare, while many people who work at low pay have no health coverage. But that should be addressed by expanding health coverage, not stunting it.

There is some improvement in the latest version of this cutback plan: People on general assistance would still be covered for visiting an optometrist, a podiatrist or a chiropractor — services that at one point were going to be eliminated. But the plan remains penny-wise, and pound-foolish.

What's more, the savings from these cutbacks wouldn't amount to much. If they were implemented soon, they would save an estimated $20 million by next July. For a state with a $14 · billion general-fund budget, that's a pittance.

The changes are being implemented t¹hrough a sort of backdoor approach. Rather than wait for the legislature to approve such changes, the administration is going the regulatory route. This week, it will propose the cutbacks to the House and Senate committees that handle health and welfare, the state attorney general's office and an obscure panel that reviews state regulations. If any one of these bodies rejects the changes — and the House panel almost certainly will — then the legislature can pass a resolution rejecting the changes. Unfortunately, such a resolution could be vetoed, and the veto probably would stick.

So let's hope that sometime soon Mr. Casey relents in his crusade to give poor people second-class health care that makes it more likely they'll end up getting sicker and requiring more expensive care.

Lincoln Journal
Lincoln, Nebraska, September 23, 1992

A National Cancer Institute study documenting farmers' increased risk of cancer hardly comes as startling news.

As soon as Nebraska began keeping a cancer registry in 1986, preliminary evidence suggesting such a conclusion could be read. Even before that, researchers had closed in on parallel conclusions.

The particular value of the latest study, though, is that it involves a so-called "meta-analysis." More than two dozen independent studies around the world were examined mathematically. The objective was to determine whether common trends could be found. They were. Risks of various kinds of cancer are greater among farmers.

Set aside skin cancers attributed to extended exposure to ultraviolet radiation from sunshine; the others are being tied — if still relatively loosely — to chemicals used in contemporary agricultural operations.

Seven years ago, Dr. Dennis D. Weisenburger of the University of Nebraska Medical Center was saying something along the same line. Take a moment to review what Dr. Weisenburger reported in the August 1985 issue of the Nebraska Medical Journal:

"Residents of Nebraska, both males and females, have a significantly increased risk of death due to lymphoma and leukemia when compared to the national average. Males also have an increased risk of death due to Hodgkin's disease while females are at risk for . non-Hodgkin's malignant lymphoma.

". . . In a cluster of six counties in the Platte River valley of central Nebraska, the incidence of leukemia and lymphoma is twofold greater than the national average. In those same counties, the incidence of lymphoma is fourfold greater than in Wyoming.

"The factors responsible for the increased incidence and risk of death from lymphoid malignancies in Nebraska are unknown. Recent death certificate studies investigating the association between farming and cancer have indicated that Midwestern farmers have a higher risk of leukemia and lymphoma than other occupations. . . These findings suggest the recent changes in agricultural techniques and practices, such as the increased use of pesticides and fertilizers, may be involved.

". . . Clearly, the potential for health problems arising from the use of agricultural pesticides is great in Nebraska."

Farming always has been a physically dangerous occupation. Being around heavy machinery requires a special, constant alertness. The irony of the medical research is that elements of production agriculture considered essential for great crop yields and as defenses against organic enemies themselves can pose equal dangers.

THE ASHEVILLE CITIZEN
Asheville, North Carolina, August 4, 1992

 North Carolina's rural poor and elderly do not get adequate health care. There are not enough family practice physicians in 49 of the state's 100 counties to meet their needs – an increase from 44 counties that were so classified two years ago. The state needs at least 400 more general practice physicians spread among those underserved counties.

One doctor practices in Clay County. Swain County has only three family practice physicians. Only four doctors work in Graham, six in Madison and seven in Mitchell County. Rural Eastern North Carolina fares no better.

Clay and Swain counties are designated by the U.S. Department of Health and Human Services as shortage areas, labeling them below acceptable levels of medical service. Also included are the Hot House and Shoal Creek townships of Cherokee County and the migrant populations in Henderson and Polk counties.

The General Assembly took a modest step just before it adjourned. Lawmakers appropriated $300,000 for bonuses to entice medical students to practice primary care in rural areas.

> **One doctor practices in Clay County. Swain County has only three family practice physicians.**

Medical schools turn out fewer and fewer doctors who are interested in practicing general family medicine. And most of those graduates go to urban centers with large medical communities serving vast numbers of patients.

Rural practices require long hours and allow little time off for family and recreation. Job opportunities for spouses and educational horizons for children are limited. Housing choices and cultural outlets are few. Most medical graduates are reluctant to launch careers in such sparsely populated counties as Clay and Swain in the mountains, Hyde on the coast or Caswell and Montgomery in the piedmont.

Legislation sponsored by Sen. Jim Forrester, R-Gaston, and Rep. Robert Hunter, D-McDowell, provides one way to lure young doctors away from the big cities. Forrester, a primary care physician in Stanley, a small town in Gaston County, sought money to offer a $10,000 stipend to resident students (those serving a hospital residency) who agree to practice primary care medicine, internal medicine or pediatrics in rural areas for at least one year.

That certainly won't cure the problem, but it's a positive step that reflects the concern of at least a majority of the Legislature. Others in and out of the General Assembly, including the Area Health Education Centers, worked hard for the legislation.

Jim Bernstein, director of the N.C. Office of Rural Health, described what the bonuses can do. If made available on an annual basis – and he believes they will be – they will push doctors' incomes during residency to about $35,000. It was one of the recommendations in a 14-point plan by the North Carolina Hospital Association to improve rural health care.

This is good medicine for North Carolina. Coupled with the asset of having Area Health Education Centers around the state, it will provide incentive to medical graduates from across the country to come to North Carolina for their residency training.

Cost and Quality of Pharmaceutical Drugs are Topic of National Debate

Many pharmaceutical companies were circumventing a new law that required them to give Medicaid programs the same discounts for drugs that they gave to other big customers, according to a *New York Times* article dated Feb. 17, 1991. Instead of lowering drug prices for Medicaid programs, the article stated, the companies were raising prices for their other customers.

(Hospitals, family-planning clinics and other large buyers were able to negotiate with drug companies for discounts of up to 60% off wholesale prices. Under a law sponsored by Rep. Ron Wyden (D, Ore.) and Sen. David H. Pryor (D, Ark.), drug companies were required to give discounts of 12.5% to state Medicaid programs, or to charge them the lowest price they charged any customer. Lawmakers had hoped to save the federal and state governments an estimated $3.3 billion through 1996.)

The U.S. Department of Veterans Affairs, the Kaiser Permanente health maintenance organization and several other large drug purchasers had reported price increases since the law took effect Jan. 1. A VA official had been told by drug company representatives that the increases were in response to the new law, the *Times* said.

The Des Moines Register

Des Moines, Iowa, November 26, 1988

In the television ad, the customer enters the drugstore and asks for an antacid, a product that neutralizes stomach acids and is available without a prescription. The pharmacist advises the customer that she might better consult her doctor than buy any more of the over-the-counter drug; there's a new prescription antacid drug — whose name is not mentioned — that's all the rage.

The ad, which looks for all the world like a public-service announcement, is brought to you courtesy of Glaxo, a British pharmaceutical house. By no coincidence, Glaxo holds the patent on one of the hottest-selling new prescriptions on the pharmaceutical scene. It's Zantac, which is replacing Smith Kline & French Laboratories' Tagamet as the new kid on the "hydrogen antagonist" block.

The hydrogen ion is the cutting edge of an acid solution; ulcer-fighting drugs neutralize the acid by tying up the hydrogen ions. And if Glaxo can convince more Americans to give up their non-prescription antacid in favor of a far more expensive prescription drug, it will get even richer.

Not long ago, Glaxo bought out a small U.S. drug-manufacturing house in Louisiana to give it an American base of operation and launched Zantac here. The drug is already No. 1 on the Iowa Medicaid chart, meaning taxpayers spend more Iowa welfare dollars for it ($100,000 per month) than any other drug. Zantac ranks seventh in frequency of Medicaid prescription; while Tagamet has slipped to 14th (and $40,000 monthly).

If the general public in Iowa buys Zantac with the same frequency as do Medicaid recipients, Glaxo is doing a $20 million yearly business here. That will buy a lot of advertising. And because the drug's patent has years to run, Glaxo can reap the profits without fear of competition from generic forms of the drug.

Why not just be up front about it and mention the drug's name in the ads? To do that, Glaxo would be required by law to list all of the prescribing information, including possible "contraindications" — no-no's — associated with the drug. When prescription drugs are advertised in medical journals, a full-page ad is commonly followed by a full page of small type listing such warnings about drug reactions and interactions and various other side effects.

Advertising can help consumers make more educated choices, but a pharmaceutical crash course consisting of a TV ad can provide just enough information to cause patients to try to second-guess their doctors. (Trust them; your internist already knows about Zantac.)

The Zantac blitz is not unique. Also on the tube of late has been an ad in which a customer tells his druggist that his antihistamine makes him drowsy. There's a prescription antihistamine that won't, the druggist replies.

It's a come-on for the new money-maker of another pharmaceutical house.

DESERET·NEWS
Salt Lake City, Utah,
August 22, 1988

Here's hoping that the G.D. Searle & Co. pharmaceutical firm has started a trend.

A few months ago, Searle officials announced a policy of offering heart drugs free of charge to the poor.

Now Searle is receiving the sincerest form of flattery from a San Francisco company, Genentech Inc., which says it will give free doses of its genetically engineered heart-attack drug to patients who can't afford the high price tag.

"Our goal ... is to see that Activase is not denied to heart-attack patients based solely on their ability to pay," said Genentech's president, Kirk Raab. The company will replace, without cost, vials of Activase administered by hospitals to patients who earn less than $25,000 and have no insurance.

Human nature being what it is, there probably is more than altruism at work here. "It is a genuine attempt to take some of the pressure off the company with regard to its aggressive pricing of the product, which costs $2,200 per dose," one industry analyst told the San Francisco Examiner.

Sales have been sluggish as well, according to Scripps Howard News Service, partly because of questions about Activase's effectiveness compared with a cheaper drug known as streptokinase.

But whatever public-relations or marketing considerations may have moved Genentech, they don't negate the fact that a drug of proven worth will be more accessible to patients who couldn't afford it before.

The "medically indigent" — people who have no health insurance — number several million across the country. Many are poor or unemployed, while others are working at jobs that offer no significant health benefits.

Private health-care companies ought to help out. Taxpayer-financed medical coverage is a big source of income for these firms; in response, they ought to assist taxpayers in easing the plight of the medically indigent.

Searle and Genentech understand. Let's hope that more companies catch on soon.

The Houston Post
Houston, Texas, August 3, 1988

These days it is no longer certain that a physician who prescribes a drug for you is acting purely in your best interest. As noted in a recent story by Post medical writer D.J. Wilson, drug firms are offering such perks as free air travel and lodging to doctors who prescribe enough of the firms' products or attend their seminars.

For decades, pharmaceutical firms have provided free samples of new products to doctors. That's about as far as they should go. At least the samples cost the patients nothing and provide doctors with a way to evaluate the medicines' effectiveness. Now, the freebies go to the doctors, and the dollar-equivalents involved are not trivial.

Doctors and drug companies have always had an uneasy yet necessary relationship, but today's practices shift the balance too far. They, and others designed to nudge what ought to be objective judgment, should be banned forthwith by the American Medical Association. Stiff penalties should be set forth for violations. If the AMA doesn't act, Congress and/or state legislatures should.

THE ANN ARBOR NEWS
Ann Arbor, Michigan, October 21, 1991

The decision of a Grand Rapids hospital to cap the price increase it will pay for prescription drugs is one that should be considered by leaders of all medical institutions.

William A. Himmelsbach Jr., president and chief executive officer of Kent County Hospital, sent letters to six pharmaceutical companies earlier this month stating that the hospital would not deal with firms whose price increases outstripped the 9.8 percent inflation rate set by the Medical Consumer Price Index.

Himmelsbach is right. Prescription drug prices have skyrocketed in the last decade. While general inflation rose 58 percent in the 1980s, prescription drug prices increased 158 percent, according to a U.S. Senate report. At the same time, profits of the top 10 drug companies averaged 15.5 percent, three times that of the average Fortune 500 company.

Two weeks ago, we called for a congressional investigation of drug pricing because government money goes to pharmaceutical companies through tax breaks and funding for research.

But if a few more medical administrators stood up, like Himmelsbach has, to unreasonably high prices, it could produce a more effective curb on prices than a thousand government studies.

The Des Moines Register
Des Moines, Iowa, March 11, 1991

Physician assistants, like nurses, are underrated professionals. The title itself inadequately encompasses the PAs' medical role.

Lack of understanding of that role, and of the PAs' training and experience, contribute to a crucial limitation placed on their practice. PAs can't prescribe drugs without the specific approval of their supervising physicians, although they may be in a far better position to make the judgment. The rule can cause unnecessary delay and grief, or possibly threaten a patient's health.

Supporters are trying again this year to pass legislation allowing PAs to write prescriptions without contacting their supervising physicians. But a hangup over "controlled substances" — drugs with a potential for abuse — could scuttle the effort.

In the University of Iowa's 20-year-old PA training program, PA students take many of the same courses as med students, including pharmacology classes. Their test scores regularly vary from those of med students by no more than 3½ percent, said Denis Oliver, program director. In the field, PAs sometimes train M.D. residents in some of the technical skills involved in surgery, where the PAs' practice gives them expertise.

The PAs should more accurately be described as "physician associates," rather than assistants, Oliver suggested. Far from serving as aides who do prep work and clean up after their doctor-supervisors, the PAs conduct physical examinations, make medical diagnoses, treat illnesses and injuries.

Year-old figures indicate Iowa's 200 PAs see 2,500 patients daily. Some work in close proximity with physicians. For them, the issue of drug-prescribing privilege is moot. In fact, while the PA program is generally conceived as extending health care to rural areas, only half of Iowa's PAs are in towns of under 40,000, only one-quarter in towns of under 5,000.

The farther from the hospitals and clinics the PA works, the greater the need for authority to prescribe — but only 18 of Iowa's PAs work in satellite clinics in areas that otherwise would likely go unserved. Having authority to prescribe drugs might encourage more PAs to work in rural areas.

The Iowa Medical Society, representing Iowa doctors, favors allowing such authority except for the very narrow classification of drugs carrying serious potential for abuse, on the rationale that increasing the outlets for dispensing such drugs can only broaden that potential. That would still enable PAs to serve patients in need of any of the other 95-plus-percent of prescription drugs. Logic dictates that solution.

Unfortunately, the debate is skewed by a turf war involving a few doctors and PAs at odds over the ultimate responsibility for regulating PAs. That skirmish should not overshadow the issue of how best to serve the health needs of Iowans. Those needs are best met through the obvious compromise.

Herald News
Fall River, Massachusetts, February 17, 1991

In 1989, the federal government launched an investigation into the generic drug industry and discovered some disturbing facts. The special inquiry found that some of the generic drug companies had falsified records, and that their products were not up to standard.

The Food and Drug Administration was highly criticized for not disapproving the generics and a significant scandal occurred.

Now, "Congress wants a tougher FDA but it's not sure how tough," observes John Carey in *Business Week* (Jan. 14). He describes a reform bill that has been proposed by John Dingell (D.-Mich.) The bill would bar FDA approval on any pending drug if a particular company was found guilty of any fraud. The FDA could also bar the drug manufacturer from selling any of its current products.

Yet Senate disapproval barred the bill from passage last year. The main opponent, according to Carey, was Sen. Howard M. Metzenbaum (D.-Ohio), who believed that any disbarment bill should cover a wider range than the generic drug industry alone. The generic drug industry is less closely scrutinized than the brand name drug industry.

If a wider bill is proposed, brand name industries, medical device industries and the like could all be covered.

Opponents of disbarment feel that punishing a whole company for the actions of what may be a single employee is unfair. Others say that safe products could be removed along with the poor quality products, and then, in the long run, the consumer would suffer.

Congress, however, is less likely to accept any compromise bill in this area. Although studies show that the public has recovered from the generic drug scandal of two years ago, all still feel these products must be closely supervised.

One thing is for sure. Drug companies, generic and name brand alike, will be more conscientious in the future, with threats of disbarment over their heads. The public will be watching, too, as Congress proposes new legislation this year.

The Oregonian

Portland, Oregon,
January 4, 1991

A Senate hearing last month about the way pharmaceutical manufacturers promote their products should have stung the consciences of doctors.

The Senate Labor and Human Resources Committee heard testimony that in order to persuade physicians to learn about and try new drugs and medical devices, manufacturers have used techniques that in some cases have included:

• Offering "points" that were redeemable like green stamps for a variety of personal items, such as videocassette recorders, to doctors who bought a particular manufacturer's vaccine.

• Inviting physicians and their spouses on expenses-paid trips to such luxurious resorts as Monte Carlo and Tahiti in exchange for listening to lectures there on the manufacturer's products.

• Paying doctors $100 or $200 apiece to attend dinner meetings to hear talks about the manufacturer's drugs.

Physician witnesses before the committee acknowledged that industry-sponsored seminars and visits to physicians' offices by company representatives known as detail men can be helpful in keeping doctors up to date on new developments.

Their concerns, they said, were that the promotions add to the cost of drugs, which patients must eventually pay; and also, that in some cases doctors might be persuaded to prescribe drugs that cost more than suitable competing products or that might not even be appropriate.

Only a few days before the Senate hearings, the House of Delegates of the American Medical Association unanimously approved a list of ethical principles that recognized the problem. The Pharmaceutical Manufacturers Association announced that it endorsed the list.

The only gifts doctors should accept from the manufacturers, the new code said, are ones of "minimal value" and directly related to the physician's work, such as pens or note pads. Manufacturers may subsidize medical conferences, but the only physicians who should accept pay from the industry for attending are those who are on the program. No doctor should accept a gift if it comes with any strings attached.

Competitive pressures in the pharmaceutical industry ought not to affect a doctor's judgment. Physicians who put their patients' interests first should have no difficulty following the American Medical Association's guidelines.

THE ATLANTA CONSTITUTION
Atlanta, Georgia, March 13, 1991

Generic drugs are supposed to be the consumer's friend. In theory, customers should be able to purchase safe, reliable pharmaceutical products at a relatively low price only because the brand-name manufacturers' expensive patents have expired.

The purity of the drugs should not be affected by the label on the outside of the package — that is, if the Food and Drug Administration (FDA) is properly watching over the industry. Unfortunately, many generic drugs have become dangerous ripoffs because federal officials have been ignoring gross violations of regulations.

In a House subcommittee hearing last week, FDA inspectors testified that they knew of numerous incidents in which the agency refused to act on their recommendations, allowing generic-drug makers to repeatedly violate manufacturing rules.

For example, field inspectors at one company found that drugs were being contaminated by steel wool pads left inside blenders in which drug powders were made. In such cases, inspectors' recommendations for legal action were ignored or rejected by higher officials. At most, companies were given meaningless warnings.

Officers of some generic-drug companies have even pleaded guilty to giving payoffs to FDA officials to overlook wrongdoing.

During the 1980s, the FDA was hampered both by the Reagan administration's lax attitude toward government regulation of businesses as well as the agency's inefficient, multilayered enforcement structure.

The agency's new commissioner, Dr. David Kessler, insists enforcement is now a top priority. That commitment is an improvement, but the FDA's entire bureaucracy is due for an overhaul to give field inspectors greater power to punish wrongdoing.

The San Diego Union-Tribune.
San Diego, California, June 5, 1991

As many as 80,000 Americans with severe cases of schizophrenia will have a chance to lead normal lives because of a decision by the federal government to provide Medicaid coverage for a new drug treatment. The drug, sold under the name Clozaril, is extremely effective but also extremely expensive.

At present, Clozaril is available to only 9,000 patients. That's because most state Medicaid programs — including Medi-Cal in California — have not yet approved payments for the drug.

Clozaril is one of the most expensive medications on the market. It costs patients $172 a week. Most of the steep price, about $140 of the $172, is due to a blood-monitoring package that the maker, Sandoz Pharmaceutical Corp., sells with the drug. Patients cannot acquire the drug without also paying for the weekly monitoring.

Sandoz's reason for bundling its drug therapy and its monitoring package is that up to 2 percent of Clozaril patients develop a potentially fatal condition that causes depletion of white blood cells. At least 78 Clozaril patients have been taken off the medication because the monitoring system revealed their susceptibility to the deadly blood disorder.

Sandoz says it makes no money off of its blood monitoring system. Its object is to save money by avoiding future liability suits if a patient were to die from Clozaril side effects. Thus, 80 percent of the cost of using Clozaril — the portion that pays for blood monitoring — may be viewed partly as a liability premium for patients.

In coming years, Americans can expect to see such liability premiums increasingly included in the costs of promising new treatments for AIDS, Alzheimer's disease, heart disease and other afflictions.

Lawmakers at the federal and state levels need to take steps to limit the exposure of pharmaceutical companies to expensive liability lawsuits by the tiny minority of patients who might suffer harmful effects. Otherwise, the majority of patients that benefit from a medication will find it increasingly priced beyond their reach.

The Hartford Courant
Hartford, Connecticut, July 9, 1991

Prescription drugs in most European countries cost only a fraction of what they do in the United States. Governments there negotiate prices with pharmaceutical manufacturers instead of letting the companies write their own tickets. Washington should begin doing the same.

The price disparity is striking. Drug prices here are more than double the average in some other countries. In Europe, prices for 25 commonly prescribed drugs are about 54 percent lower than in the United States. Some differences are dramatic — $28 a month for a common Parkinson's disease drug in Italy, $48 in Austria, $240 in the United States.

The U.S. manufacturers claim that the high cost is based on research expenses, although the cost figures they submit are inflated, according to federal regulators. Critics also charge that Americans pay a disproportionate share of the research and development expenses for drugs because of the low government-negotiated prices paid by consumers in other countries. "We subsidize the world," says Harvard University economist Richard Zeckhauser.

Complicating matters is a law requiring drug makers to lower the prices of some products sold to Medicaid patients. Hospitals, insurers and their patients have reason to fear that the companies are increasing prices to them so the firms' bottom line would not be hurt by the price cuts to Medicaid. Drug stocks have been soaring recently.

Negotiated prices and increased excess profit taxes are under consideration by Congress. Manufacturers should be discouraged from setting outrageously low prices abroad that do not include a fair share of research and development costs.

The Providence Journal
Providence, Rhode Island, October 4, 1991

The Food and Drug Administration has found no link between the use of the anti-depressant drug Prozac and suicide or other violent behavior. Furthermore, it sees no reason to require a warning label on the widely prescribed Eli Lilly medication.

In a perfect world, this declaration would end the hysterical attacks on a drug that is said to have helped millions of Americans overcome debilitating depression. But since lawyers have filed over 50 suits claiming that use of Prozac made people kill themselves or others, the last chapter of this sordid history may not have been written. Perhaps the saddest spectacle in the campaign against Prozac was the parade of distraught individuals testifying before a recent FDA hearing that the drug made them (or a loved one) commit a violent act.

Prozac is a relatively new drug that has been used by five million people worldwide. It seems to produce fewer side effects than most anti-depressant drugs, although some users report nervousness or headaches.

Allegations that Prozac has caused unsocial behavior are hard to prove when you consider that it is administered to people already in the throes of severe depression. What would be more significant — but not easily measured — is how many people were deterred from suicide or other violence by the depression-lifting effects of the drug.

The Health Research Group, founded by Ralph Nader and headed by Sidney Wolfe, considers Prozac an "excellent" drug. But for reasons still unclear, Dr. Wolfe wants Prozac labeled to warn that some users have experienced violent and suicidal thoughts. Well, so have users of Velveeta cheese and Honda Civics, and by logical extension these, too, should be so labeled.

Of course, many tort lawyers would be delighted to see mandated labeling, especially those who have tried (unsuccessfully so far) to claim that Prozac made their clients commit crimes. A government-required warning that strange things happen to people who use the drug would certainly add weight to the "Prozac defense" in court.

Probably the most active opponent of Prozac has been the so-called Church of Scientology. This cult organization condemns psychiatric medicine in general, promoting instead its 'Dianetics' theory of mental therapy. We should point out that under Scientology doctrine psychological disorders are called "engrams," and can be cured (among other ways) by a creature called a "thetan" who travels through the galaxies.

Enough said.

With Eli Lilly selling close to $1 billion worth of Prozac a year, the target for carnival critics, or the fundamentally greedy, is a big one. Unfortunately, the real victims of the Prozac brouhaha are the depressed individuals themselves. Some may be scared away from seeking relief from their despair, and users could suffer the stigma of taking a drug that has been unfairly portrayed as a cause of mental instability.

Providence, Rhode Island, October 11, 1991

The British government surprised the American medical community recently when it banned the popular sleeping pill Halcion. The drug, whose generic name is triazolam, is associated with a higher incidence of memory loss and depression than others in its group. Halcion is the world's most prescribed sleeping pill, and last year was taken by some eight million Americans.

The US Food and Drug Administration will look into the reasoning behind Britain's action, but has no plans to follow suit and take Halcion off the American market. This approach seems eminently prudent, given the recent controversy over the anti-depressant drug Prozac. Claims that Prozac was linked to violent behavior were found to be unsubstantiated, and the FDA declined to restrict its use.

There is a dilemma in the fact that many effective drugs involve a trade-off between their ability to alleviate an ailment and the unwanted side effects they may cause. Particularly hazardous medications are kept off the market, but many others produce reactions that vary enormously according to the individual using it, the dosage prescribed, and other drugs the patient may be taking.

Aspirin, for example, is a non-prescription medicine that can cause life-threatening reactions in allergic individuals. Mixed with alcohol, aspirin can cause death. Certain foods that are utterly harmless to the vast majority of the population are known to produce serious reactions in some users.

When a drug like Halcion is used by millions of people, there are bound to be reports of side effects that may seem numerous, but not statistically significant, in light of the multitudes involved. The suggestion that a drug may cause certain reactions can, by itself, increase the number of people claiming to be so affected.

For this reason, some American medical researchers have taken a skeptical view of the British ban on Halcion, saying that it seems based more on anecdotal evidence than on new data. They also note that European doctors tend to prescribe far higher doses of Halcion, which could account for the larger number of reported problems with the drug in Great Britain.

Prescription drugs are strong chemicals that ought to be taken under a doctor's supervision. Physicians usually ask patients to report any adverse reactions to a drug, and can adjust the dosage accordingly.

Some doctors are concerned that patients worried about the British ban on Halcion will try to quit cold turkey, which can cause withdrawal symptoms, such as insomnia and anxiety. Halcion use should be tapered off, they say, under a physician's watchful eye.

THE SACRAMENTO BEE
Sacramento, California, July 15, 1991

Once upon a time, back when they were known as apothecaries, pharmacists actually mixed up medicines, brewed potions and even prescribed drugs. Today, making medicine is an industrial operation, and dispensing drugs is mostly a matter of counting out pills from big bottles and putting them in smaller ones. Yet state law still requires expensively trained pharmacists to perform the work.

That's a waste of pharmacists' skills and consumers' dollars. Routine packaging and dispensing of medicines can easily be performed at lower cost by medical technicians with a few months training. Indeed, pharmacy technicians already perform those duties under a pharmacist's supervision in California hospitals and at retail pharmacies in 40 states. It makes sense to allow the same thing in California drug stores, as the state Board of Pharmacy proposes in AB 1244, which will soon be heard before the Senate Business and Professions Committee.

Under new board rules, pharmacists will soon be required to counsel patients on appropriate use of their prescriptions and to check for potentially dangerous interactions with other medications. To free up pharmacists to perform that higher-value task, the board last year adopted a regulation to authorize pharmacy technicians to do the routine work. But the Office of Administrative Law subsequently ruled that legislation was needed to make the change.

AB 1244 ought to be an easy decision for lawmakers. But it is being opposed by labor groups that represent some pharmacists. They contend that technicians will make more errors than pharmacists, endangering the public, a charge that is refuted by the experience in the rest of the country. In fact, the unions simply want to maintain a system that amounts to featherbedding, imposing higher medical costs on the public.

The real weakness of the bill is its modesty. As a sop to opponents, it limits the number of technicians to one for every pharmacist and mandates that the state board register and establish training standards for technicians, requirements that limit AB 1244's potential cost-saving. If the Legislature really wants to help consumers, it will amend the bill to leave it to pharmacies to decide how many technicians, with what level of training, they need to give their customers the best service at the lowest cost.

Hospital Care Under Greater Scrutiny

A study Oct. 1, 1988 indicated that up to 27% of hospital patient deaths due to heart attack, stroke or pneumonia could have been prevented with proper care.

The study was conducted by Rand Corp. and published in the *Annals of Internal Medicine*. It analyzed patient deaths at 12 hospitals in the South and West operated by American Medical International of Beverly Hills, Calif., which had sponsored the survey.

Three doctors who examined the hospitals' records concluded that 14% of deaths due to heart attack were preventable, and two out of three agreed that 27% were preventable.

The study found that a relatively small number of errors caused most of the unnecessary deaths due to heart attacks. The survey concluded that "significant errors in management," such as inadequate treatment of chest pain, contributed to the preventable deaths.

With stroke patients, the study blamed errors in diagnosis and failure to perform appropriate tests. It faulted both diagnostic errors and treatment mistakes in pneumonia deaths.

In most cases of preventable death, the patients were elderly and suffered from less serious illnesses than those whose deaths were not preventable, the study found.

The consumer advocacy group Public Citizen April 23, 1991 released a report accusing the federal government of not enforcing a law prohibiting hospitals from "dumping" emergency-room patients who lacked health insurance or were on Medicaid. Patient dumping occurred when hospitals, not wanting to incur the costs of treating uninsured or Medicaid-insured patients, transferred them to other hospitals without providing treatment.

One percent of hospital patients were injured while receiving care because of negligence of health workers, according to a study published July 25, 1991 in the *New England Journal of Medicine*. The study found that fewer than 2% of such patients sued for malpractice.

The Health and Human Services Department June 10, 1992 said that it had found 102 hospitals with death rates for elderly patients that were significantly higher than what might be statistically expected. Many of the hositals were located in inner cities and the rural South.

By contrast, 59 institutions had lower-than-expected mortality rates for elderly patients.

The information was drawn from Medicare statistics for 1990. The department stressed that death rates, whether high or low, should not be the sole means of judging a hospital. Nevertheless, officials acknowledged that the high death rates constituted "quality problems."

Large hospitals in big cities tended to give better medical care than small-town hospitals, according to a survey in the *Journal of the American Medical Association* Oct. 7, 1992. The study found that big-city hospitals had lower death rates, offered more skillful treatment and were better organized than their rural or suburban counterparts. (The authors defined a big hospital as one having more than 100 beds.) The study looked at more than 14,000 elderly patients at 297 hospitals in five states.

The New York Times
New York City, New York, April 3, 1989

In New York as elsewhere, drug abuse and AIDS are creating chaos in urban hospitals — enough to threaten not only the quality of life but life itself. That forces urgent, painful decisions on strapped city and state governments. If the need for action is desperate, so is the need for careful planning and administrative ingenuity.

For some years city hospitals have suffered as more and more of the poor, lacking access to any other health care, use the emergency room as family doctor. Hospitals also suffer from a severe nursing shortage. But the twin evils of drugs and AIDS are pushing them to the brink.

Drug addicts are subject to diseases like pneumonia, hepatitis and tuberculosis that require hospital care. By far the most devastating is AIDS, now transmitted as commonly in New York by addicts' needle-sharing as by sex. On any given day, some 1,700 hospital beds, about 6 percent of the total, are occupied by AIDS patients, and a mayoral task force estimates that the figure will double by 1994. The group states: "The paralysis of New York's whole hospital system . . . has now become a disastrous but real possibility."

In response, hospitals are campaigning for more resources, and Governor Cuomo recently called for increases in health insurance reimbursements that would yield $193 million for hospitals to recruit more nurses. That's a sensible step. Hundreds of hospital beds currently are unusable because there aren't enough nurses.

The question of building more hospital space remains clouded. For several years, state officials have resisted, believing, with good reason, that improved hospital management could free up many beds. But that position becomes harder to maintain as the AIDS caseload grows. Both the mayoral task force and the foundation-supported Citizens Commission on AIDS argue for adding some 2,000 acute-care beds over the next four years.

There is broad agreement on the need for other space — nursing homes and other housing set up to offer some health services — to take the pressure off the hospitals. It's estimated currently that more than 100 AIDS patients in hospital beds on any given day do not need full hospital care, and their number is expected to grow rapidly. Additional hundreds of the aged are in hospitals for want of nursing homes. Thus the Mayor's task force calls for at least 1,500 new nursing-home beds and 2,500 more health-service housing units.

Health officials lament the difficulty of building such facilities. But Andrew Cuomo, the Governor's son and president of a nonprofit organization that has succeeded with housing for homeless families, recently negotiated $8.4 million in tax-exempt bond financing through the state's Medical Care Facilities Financing Agency for AIDS patient housing. It will cost only $225 per person per day to operate the 66-bed facility, including debt service on construction, compared with $700 per day in a hospital.

His example deserves emulation. New York's hospital crisis demands hard choices — and cost-effective compassion.

copyright © The New York Times 1989

The Providence Journal
Providence, Rhode Island, July 22, 1991

People shop for clothes, cars, houses and restaurants — why not hospitals? In Cleveland and Pennsylvania, employers and hospitals are cooperating to help patients do just that. They do so with a program that seeks to compare an area's hospitals with each other, in terms of the fees they charge and the services they deliver.

With costs of American medical care soaring, such comparisons offer another important way to understand what value patients receive for their money. These studies are just beginning in most areas, and results are not yet in. But the concept, in which hospitals are evaluated comparatively for their costs and the quality of their care, is eminently sound. The public at large, to say nothing of hospital management, needs to know what works and what doesn't. How better to find this out than by seeing how a city's hospitals stack up against each other?

Such studies, reports The New York Times, have earned the enthusiastic backing of major employers, who are interested in helping employees shop for high-quality health care as one way of controlling their spiraling health-insurance costs. If employees can determine which hospital has the best post-operative recovery record, say, or offers an outstanding unit for treating lung disease, they can better decide which hospital to choose.

Not only is employee health likely to benefit from such scrutiny, but employers expect their own insurance costs to drop. In the Cleveland experiment, in fact, several participating firms plan to offer incentives to employees who choose to use the hospitals that emerge with the highest ratings.

These experiments stress competition and quality control, both of which are keys to a stronger American medical care system. Between public and private hospitals, as between profit-makers and nonprofits, there are obviously great ranges in terms of costs, revenues, emergency room use, long-term patient care and other measurements. To be meaningful, the analysis will need to take such differences into account and weigh the data accordingly.

If such comparative cost-benefit studies are done for hospitals in Rhode Island, the findings are not given wide circulation. Perhaps the Hospital Association of Rhode Island, in the interests of increasing public understanding about a priceless (and often pricey) resource, could see if a parallel study might be undertaken here.

The Washington Post
Washington, D.C., March 16, 1991

THE DISTRICT of Columbia Hospital Association reports that, for the first time as a group, its member institutions operated at a loss in 1989. The reported loss of 1.6 percent is a bit less dire than it was made to seem: not all sources of income were counted; the survey included D.C. General, which is a municipal hospital and a special case; and not all private hospitals suffered equally. Some that are heavily burdened managed to do fairly well, suggesting that the system remains viable.

Still, the report is to be taken seriously—and it comes as no surprise. A similar pattern prevails nationally, particularly in big cities. Nor is it an accident or a result of neglect. The squeeze on the hospitals is the product of deliberate national policy, an effort by the federal government and other intermediaries to gain more control over health care costs, which now account for about one of every nine dollars Americans spend.

Hospitals understandably don't relish their role as collision point for the society's contradictory desires for more care at lower cost; they tend to feel victimized. But they tend also, in their discussions of the issue, to concentrate more on their faltering revenues than on their continuing costs. The current squeeze began with the federal decision in 1983 to go to a so-called prospective payment system under Medicare—in effect to take away from hospitals the power to set their own rates, saying instead that for a certain illness the government would pay only so much and no more.

Loose at first, that fee schedule has been steadily tightened and copied in varying degrees by private insurers and states in their reimbursement policies under Medicaid. All these cutbacks might have been fine except for one thing: there is also a seventh of the population with no health insurance, public or private. Thus the hospitals have been faced with rising bills for uncompensated care for which nobody is responsible.

All sides agree that, nationally, the system is approaching a point at which one side or the other—insurers or providers—must blink. The hospitals want the appropriate levels of government to pay more or to otherwise relieve them of the burden. The cost-controllers want the hospitals to take stronger action than many have so far to cut their costs; they insist there is more to be done (eliminating excess and duplicate capacity, changing staffing patterns, resisting unnecessary procedures) and that until this is made to happen, the cost problem won't be solved.

The D.C. association suggests that the pattern is somewhat different here—for example, that local occupancy rates are high and that the city has a large share of uncompensated care. That is doubtless true, but the D.C. institutions still have a heavier burden than they have met so far to show they have cut costs all they reasonably—not just conveniently—can. That's particularly so because some affected local institutions are still (barely) managing; why not the others?

The association mentions, as a goad, that its members constitute one of the largest elements in the local economy, so that about "one in every 20 working District residents is employed in a District hospital." But that is hardly unmixed news; this is not a jobs program. To suggest that at some level it be regarded as such is a kind of argument that does the hospitals' cause more harm than good. In making the case for help, they need to prove not that they're large—that's all too obvious—but that they're lean.

The Tennessean
Nashville, Tennessee, March 2, 1991

THE merger of Metro General and Meharry-Hubbard hospitals deserves a second chance.

Another chance may be on the way. Mayor Bill Boner announced this weekend that his administration will make its own evaluation of the proposed consolidation, which was shot down by the Metro Board of Hospitals Feb. 21.

Boner made it clear he intends neither to usurp the board's authority nor to endorse the measure.

A dispassionate look at the circumstances at this point should suit both sides of the issue.

The abrupt dismissal of the merger plan by the board was bitterly disappointing to supporters, including some of the Vanderbilt University Medical Center staff who had worked hard with Meharry officials for two years to build a workable plan.

Board members insisted they were persuaded by two late reports, one from the General staff and one from the Nashville Academy of Medicine, that disputed earlier reports that the merger would save money. Merger proponents just as adamantly persisted that the earlier studies are valid.

In any event, the bad taste left by the decision makes it virtually impossible for the two sides to find enough common ground to piece together a compromise.

It's been a long and difficult two years just to get the vote that left Meharry on the sidelines.

From Metro's perspective, the quest for a merger can't be abandoned. If there are savings to be had in merging a Metro facility that already needs to be replaced with a more modern hospital, further investigation is warranted. Putting health care dollars to their best use ought to be a priority.

From Meharry's view, the quest for consolidation must be pursued. Meharry needs more patients to meet its teaching needs. Its survival as an institution is at stake.

And, for both Nashville's and Meharry's sakes, leaders should be looking at how to save an historic black institution that has brought great distinction to this community.

At the very least, an analysis might show how to do just that, either with a merger or in some other type of partnership. Nashville has gone too far down the road of this merger to simply walk away from it now. Any time city officials spend in pursuit of finding more effective ways to manage services and the city's best resources is time well spent. ■

The Houston Post

Houston, Texas, June 2, 1991

NO SERVICE may be more critical to people than emergency medical care. The implementation of a "drive-by" policy at publicly funded hospitals could be the prelude to a public health crisis like the Houston area hasn't seen before. Here in the home of one of the world's most sophisticated medical facilities, tax-supported hospitals are wrestling with budget priorities and the number of beds needed for traumatic emergency.

City ambulances are being turned away at Lyndon B. Johnson Hospital because patient beds have been shut down. But the public perception has it that the hospital district has manufactured an emergency crisis as a ploy to get more funding than the recent 3-cent tax increase approved by Harris County Commissioners Court.

And the district surely hasn't done itself any favors with the taxpaying public by its decision to cut essential services like trauma care before doing away with proposed raises and job perks for certain administrators. This poor sense of priorities has caused many taxpayers to be more cynical than sympathetic.

That's too bad. Looking beyond the raises and perks, it just could be that the district is truly between a rock and a hard place. If it does not provide adequate trauma care while living within its budget, then it is destined to be criticized for failure to do its statutory job.

Can it do both?

Besides getting a leaner administration, the only way to live up to this budget mandate is to cut the number of beds available at both LBJ and Ben Taub hospitals, the latter considered one of the country's best trauma care centers.

There is no disputing the patient overcrowding at both facilities. And the district projects the numbers to keep on growing. In 1989, when LBJ first opened, the district's two hospitals had a total of 831 beds.

Today, because of the bed closures, there are 764. And let's not forget the larger number of those two numbers is lower than the 1,200 beds the American Public Hospital Association recommended for a city the size of Houston.

It's no secret that one way to "live within the budget" is to close off wings with beds. The annual per-bed cost at the two public hospitals is $211,000. Admittedly, this is big money. But is it really "saved" if it results in a policy requiring ambulances to drive by Ben Taub and LBJ because there is no room?

In such cases, the emergency vehicles must transport patients to private hospitals, which must in turn absorb the cost by charging higher treatment rates, while insurance companies jack up their deductibles and premiums.

How can the hospital district cope with this dilemma? The best the district could hope for at this point is one more penny increase in its tax rate, 4 cents instead of 3. The "extra penny" would mean another 43 beds.

Few would argue the district can control the number of people coming in for treatment. Should the current trend continue, the district and Commissioners Court must look beyond political accusations and solve this very human problem, even if takes another penny.

The San Diego Union-Tribune.

San Diego, California, March 24, 1991

Every year, 400,000 hospital patients in the United States contract a bloodstream infection, septicemia, which often leads to death. A promising new medication known as HA-1A has been developed to treat the ailment, but the federal Food and Drug Adminsitration has yet to approve it for regular use.

The FDA continues to review HA-1A, a genetically engineered antibody manufactured by Centocor Inc. of Malvern, Pa. Centocor submitted its marketing application in September 1989. A related medication manufactured by Xoma Corp. of Berkeley has awaited FDA approval since December 1988.

It is not as though the FDA does not have a mechanism in place to expedite approval of potentially life-saving drugs. It gave the go-ahead to such AIDS medications as AZT, dideoxynosine (DDI) and dideoxycytidine (DDC), even though their effectiveness is still under FDA review.

But HA-1A continues to wend its way through the FDA's review labyrinth — a process that regularly takes as long as seven years. A medication is first administered to a small test group of patients to ensure its safety. Then it endures several more phases of review to ascertain its effectiveness.

The FDA is apparently satisfied that HA-1A is safe; otherwise, Centocor would not have been permitted to supply the drug to small number of patients on a "compassionate use basis." The only reason we can think of that HA-1A is not more widely available is that the FDA remains unconvinced of the medication's efficacy.

But there is a large body of research suggesting that HA-1A is indeed an effective treatment. For example, an exhaustive study of hundreds of septicemia patients, conducted by the Department of Medicine at UCSD and several other institutions, found that patients using the drug had a 30 percent death rate within 28 days, compared with a 49 percent rate for those who did not take the medication.

What this means is that potentially thousands of Americans will die this year from septicemia who otherwise might have survived if HA-1A were available to them.

The Evening Gazette

Worcester, Massachusetts, June 9, 1991

The University of Massachusetts Medical Center proposal for salvaging Worcester City Hospital offers a glimmer of hope in what has been a dark era in the facility's 120-year history.

The UMass plan offers a scenario in which sub-acute services could survive in an area where they are critically needed. However, questions about funding, administration and past liabilities present a formidable challenge.

The plan would, in effect, create a health-care "mall" in the City Hospital buildings. The cornerstone of the services would be outpatient primary care provided by Family Health and Social Services Center — already well-established nearby and in critical need of room for expansion.

The mall approach, with the Worcester Health and Hospitals Authority or some other entity serving as landlord, allows for great flexibility. Other health-care services that might be established include emergency services, inpatient substance abuse therapy, geriatric care and psychiatric treatment.

The immediate challenge is to figure out a financing package. Reconstruction would cost $4 million to $21 million.

The administrative structure also would have to be modified. Expertise in administering sub-acute care would be crucial for the plan's success.

UMass has done a creditable job of devising a plan to make good use of the hospital buildings, but the toughest challenges lie ahead. Making the salvage plan work will require hard work, cooperation and commitment from everyone involved.

The Record
Hackensack, New Jersey, January 7, 1991

"We are in a crisis today because past administrations and legislatures failed to implement reforms. An extension now should provide a window of opportunity to forge real solutions."

That's Assembly Speaker Joseph Doria talking, and his subject is health care. Mr. Doria wants to extend for 15 months the controversial trust fund that pays hospital bills for those who can't pay themselves. The source of revenue for the fund, a 19 percent surcharge on all hospital bills, would also be extended — and increased.

Mr. Doria says he will not extend the fund without incorporating major reforms that should lower its cost. But he doesn't say what will happen when the 15 months are up. (Incidentally, by then next November's legislative elections would be over.) It is reassuring, at least, to see that New Jersey's health care crisis is finally being opened to public debate, and that a broad range of reforms is being considered.

An extension, at least for the short term, seems to be the only way out. What choice is there? The fund has already expired. If it isn't extended retroactively, urban hospitals will be threatened with bankruptcy, since they treat most of the patients who are unable to pay. But a lengthy extension of the fund would be a mistake, unless steps are taken for a permanent solution. There was a crisis when the fund expired two years ago. Then it was extended, and the crisis disappeared. Until now.

Some of the suggested ways to reform the fund are promising. One approach would be to reduce hospital bills by emphasizing cheaper outpatient and preventive care, and allowing the fund to cover those costs. That transition is harder to make than it sounds. If such a change can be carried off, the benefits would be enormous — in money saved, and in improved health care.

If Mr. Doria can come up with substantial reforms for the Uncompensated Care Trust Fund, then it is worth extending temporarily. But the problem of the 1 million people in New Jersey without health insurance is not going to go away. And neither is the fact that the fund's tax on all hospital bills is probably going up to 24.8 percent, further inflating health care costs. Some solution must be found.

A word must also be said about how this crisis has been handled since people realized, several years ago, that the trust fund was in trouble. The word is "badly." At this late date, there's a call for an audit of the fund to see how it is being used. Why wasn't an audit done before?

The state does not even know who the people in New Jersey without health insurance are. Why hasn't a demographic study of these people been done? That information, which was mandated by the Legislature before this crisis, would help in determining what kind of reforms would benefit the most people.

The San Diego Union-Tribune.
San Diego, California, September 1, 1991

Hospital emergency rooms are so overburdened that patients urgently needing treatment often must wait several hours before even seeing a physician. Many patients are in so much pain that they walk out of emergency rooms in desperation before receiving medical attention.

Those are the findings of new studies published in the Journal of the American Medical Association. They provide further evidence of the failure of the U.S. health system to provide basic medical care.

The studies were conducted at two public hospitals, one in Los Angeles and one in San Francisco. They found that the most seriously ill patients, such as those suffering heart attacks or gunshot wounds, were almost always treated immediately. But the rest of emergency patients, including many with serious conditions, endured waits ranging from 15 minutes to 17 hours. Of those patients, the 15 percent who left the hospital without being treated suffered from conditions no less serious than those who remained.

On a nationwide basis, researchers estimate that each year more than 1 million people in need of care leave emergency rooms before being seen by a doctor. The studies published in JAMA reported no deaths among the emergency room patients who left the hospitals untreated. But the researchers who conducted the studies are convinced that a broader survey would uncover instances where patients died needlessly after failing to receive emergency room care.

The overcrowded conditions in America's emergency rooms "challenge a fundamental assumption about emergency department care — that it will always be available in time of need," says Dr. Arthur Kellerman, chief of a study group at the American College of Emergency Physicians.

Authors of the emergency room studies offer a number of remedies to overcrowding and the lengthy waits for treatment.

Among other things, they call for universal health care coverage for all Americans, an increase in the sizes of emergency rooms and their nursing staffs, and a national initiative to emphasize preventive care so that emergency treatment is less necessary.

Implementation of these proposals would reduce much of the pressure on the emergency care system. But they also would carry a very expensive price tag and no one has proposed how to pay for them. In the end, the problems hampering emergency rooms are likely to be solved only when President Bush and Congress devise a comprehensive plan to overhaul America's beleaguered health system.

The TENNESSEAN
Nashville, Tennessee, September 24, 1991

STATE officials shouldn't get ahead of themselves in decreasing the number of beds in mental health hospitals.

The move toward fewer beds, while providing more community services to meet patients' needs, is appropriate. But the state must be sure that those community services are provided before turning patients out of hospital care.

In Nashville, the 330-bed Middle Tennessee Health Institute is due for changes. The Metro Airport Authority has decided to purchase land from the institution on Murfreesboro Road. Consultants have recommended relocating the hospital with fewer beds.

That's fine. But that cannot and should not happen before the state has adequate community services in place to meet the patients' needs. Without that, the premature shift away from hospital care is wrong and terribly dangerous.

Of course, community programs can provide a favorable alternative to hospitalization for many patients. But if those programs are not in place, or properly funded, reducing hospital beds is taking a step too soon.

There are 42,000 Tennesseans considered to have some type of mental illness. Currently about 1,500 of those receive hospital care, with 25,000 receiving some other type of services.

But that means that about 15,000 people receive no services at all. Many of those people suffering with mental illness are elderly and have difficulty caring for themselves. Others are teens and children who, with the right care now, could lead productive lives. Mental illness plays a devastating role in the lives of the homeless.

All those people need the care and attention a properly structured mental health care system can provide. Community programs can often provide it best.

Mental health advocates accept the fact that there isn't likely to be an increase in the $350 million provided for mental health services. But they also know that mental health officials can maximize the funding now available by shifting some of it to effective community service programs. Such a shift can't be made too swiftly.

Emphasizing community programs that work is a positive step, making it possible to decrease hospital care. But the state can't have one without the other. First things must come first. ■

THE ANN ARBOR NEWS
Ann Arbor, Michigan, January 9, 1991

Beyer Hospital in Ypsilanti is at a crossroads. Its status as an acute-care hospital is in jeopardy.

Beyer has been the subject of sale rumors since a purchase bid was made in December by Oakwood United Hospitals Inc. of Dearborn. Since then, Catherine McAuley Health System has made an offer to purchase Beyer as well as a corporation formed by Beyer Hospital doctors. Beyer is owned by United Care, Inc.

McAuley's plans for Beyer amount to an unfriendly takeover as far as the latter is concerned. In all likelihood, McAuley's plans don't include keeping Beyer as a facility that offers full in-patient services. The fear among Beyer staff, its supporters and community leaders is that the hospital's purchase by McAuley could mean a drastically downgraded facility.

With a total of 500 part-time and full-time employees, Beyer Hospital is an institution with deep roots in the community. It has served eastern Washtenaw County and western Wayne County since 1918.

Two of Beyer's strengths are its affordability and accessibility. Average day fees run $200-$300 less than McAuley; for intensive care, the rate is anywhere from $700 to $1,000 a day less than the Washtenaw County average.

The hospital has turned the corner financially and is now in the black. According to Administrator Mary Finn, Beyer has straightened out its finances because its medical staff got involved in helping the administration define what the hospital's goals should be.

Beyer is an excellent hospital for routine medical care and outpatient surgeries, and is continuing to improve in these generalized services. It also has a superb record of caring for Washtenaw County's indigent population. At Beyer, $1.5 million, or 5 percent of gross patient revenues, goes for uncompensated care; at the much bigger McAuley, about $12 million or 2.6 percent of gross patient revenues goes toward uncompensated care.

A takeover of Beyer by McAuley could mean a near monopoly on private hospital beds in the county; a bid by McAuley to purchase Saline Community Hospital is pending. Health consumers are not served by monopolies.

There is also concern over McAuley's commitment to a range of reproductive medical services. Catherine McAuley is affiliated with the Sisters of Mercy. If McAuley buys Beyer, the restrictions in place at McAuley will be applied to Beyer.

The Beyer doctors' proposal for buying the hospital and keeping it a full-service institution should be carefully considered by United Care officials. In this age of mega-institutions and exotic medical technology, there is still a role for a small community hospital. Beyer fills that role.

Beyer is a vital part of the community it serves, a major employer and an institution whose elimination or scaled-down status would be deeply felt. Keeping Beyer open should be a top concern of community leaders and users.

Ypsilanti and outlying areas want to keep the convenience and accessibility that Beyer Hospital represents. Its purchase by Catherine McAuley Health System could well mean the hospital many have come to know, love and depend on will cease to exist.

San Francisco Chronicle
San Francisco, California, March 25, 1991

TO SAY THAT our children constitute the future is to propound an authoritative, poignant truism. Any waste of young lives — any damage to them — tears in a specially painful way at the society we all inhabit.

That is why there is so much to lift the spirits in the news that doctors at Stanford University are now just months away from moving out of outmoded facilities and into a $100-million center — the Lucile Salter Packard Children's Hospital — that will provide "state of the art" care for youngsters with severe illnesses.

A major share of funds for the new hospital — $40 million — was contributed by computer billionaire David Packard and his wife, Lucile, who died of cancer in 1987 after devoting much of her life to children's health. The balance came from private donations and from Stanford University, which contributed $20 million.

Surely this is philanthropy of the highest sensitivity and intelligence. This is a gift that benefits not only the Bay Area, but the nation.

The new hospital will officially open in June, but it is worth commenting now on some of the facility's extraordinary and positive elements.

WHAT STRIKES home first is the strong humanistic focus provided in a high-tech environment. The feelings of patients and families have been given a substantive place amidst all the latest medical armamentaria.

The medical-surgical floor groups children by age, not by disease; nursing stations are scooped out so that small patients can see nurses as they talk to them, and beds for parents are built into each child's room.

The doors will be open, president Lorraine Zippiroli emphasizes, to "children next door and children everywhere." We warmly welcome this splendid, exciting hospital.

Chicago Sun-Times
Chicago, Illinois, March 25, 1991

Cook County Hospital's loss of accreditation was a disaster waiting to happen. But is building a new facility really the answer to dealing with the year-in, year-out problems of the hospital?

It's up to County Board President Richard J. Phelan and the County Board to put the hospital back into acceptable shape as soon as possible without losing $90 million in state and federal Medicaid and Medicare funds now in jeopardy.

Phelan has promised quick short-term repairs costing millions of dollars to correct numerous fire safety violations (as cited by the Joint Commission on the Accreditation of Healthcare Organizations in its action last Friday). But the County Board must look beyond emergency relief.

When it does, the desire of Phelan, a la George Dunne, to build another new hospital should be carefully examined. The former president's grand vision of a new County Hospital didn't come close to meeting the Chicago area's health needs.

What Chicago needs most are more neighborhood clinics for pregnant women, senior citizens and other poor people who can't get care at Fantus Clinic, a part of Cook County Hospital, because Fantus has six- to eight-week waits for enrollment.

Is a new $600 million hospital necessary when 14 general hospitals have closed in Chicago over the last five years, when Cook County has recently bought the shuttered 300-bed Provident Hospital and when hospital experts are predicting further closures?

"One need look no further than the number of hospital closings in our inner cities to know that medical care delivered in the ambulatory [outpatient] setting is the trend of coming decades," wrote Gerald M. Moss, dean of the University of Illinois College of Medicine, last April in a Sun-Times Forum.

So why does solving problems of the county's inadequate health system always revolve around the 90-year-old County Hospital, the county's equivalent of Humpty-Dumpty?

Will putting it back together, restoring accreditation, actually be a step toward improving health care to the poor? It has to be that at a minimum.

Lincoln Journal

Lincoln, Nebraska, July 15, 1991

What Dr. Charles Wilson told a University of Nebraska Board of Regents committee meeting in Kearney last week deserves earnest consideration by the university's Medical Center, and by all of us.

The Lincoln regent, himself a physician, criticized a joint program of the Medical Center and Chadron and Wayne State Colleges that allows students to enter medical school after only three years of undergraduate training. That runs the risk of producing doctors with a narrow background lacking in education in the humanities and social studies, Wilson warned. He said he'd rather see a year less of medical school than an abbreviated undergraduate education.

Good intentions underlie the shortcut for would-be doctors. It is intended to make medical training more attractive for state college students, in the hope that when they become doctors they will return to their rural and small-town areas to practice. The program has attracted 10 students in each of its first two years at Chadron, and five this year at Wayne.

Dr. Wilson has a good point, though. Skimping on studying the humanities shortchanges the doctors and their patients. More than ever in this age of high-tech medicine, society recognizes the value of physicians with well-rounded backgrounds. They need a sound base from which to address questions of ethics, quality of life, social values and other issues of a philosophical nature. A comprehensive education also stands to make them better citizens of the communities they serve. As the regent notes, when a year of college is lopped off, it's likely to be subjects such as the arts, literature, philosophy, history and economics that are sacrificed.

The Medical Center should think again about its shortcut program.

AKRON BEACON JOURNAL

Akron, Ohio, June 24, 1991

Nearly every hospital in Summit County is planning a major construction project. And the combined cost could exceed $165 million. Either directly through hospital fees or indirectly through premiums paid to health insurers, local consumers and local companies will pay the bill.

Yet it is impossible to say how much of this construction is really essential for the Akron area.

Even some hospital executives say that the community may over build — and that consumers may end up paying unnecessary costs at a time when decent health care is already unaffordable for many.

"We're spending money duplicating each other's services and we shouldn't be," said Al Gilbert, the president of Summa Health System, which runs Akron City Hospital and St. Thomas Medical Center.

A fundamental problem relates to the fact that hospitals attract patients by first attracting doctors. And hospitals attract doctors by building the best facilities and buying all the latest equipment.

Thus, while hospitals must compete — or risk violating federal antitrust laws — they don't always compete in ways that keep costs down. At times, the competition drives them on to greater spending and leads to higher costs for consumers.

A reasonable way to avoid that kind of unhealthy competition is through better regional planning. Because good planning is absent, the current building proposals have not been reviewed collectively to determine what they mean for the community when considered together.

Instead, a local health planning group, relying heavily on volunteers, is reviewing each project separately and making recommendations on each one to the Ohio Department of Health, which has final say over any new construction.

Last week, at a meeting of this health planning group, Summa's Gilbert challenged other hospital executives to agree to a comprehensive review of all current building proposals, except for the project at Children's Hospital Medical Center, where construction has started.

An executive at another hospital called Gilbert's challenge "at once a shrewd tactical move and a very serious call for what is needed in the community."

Indeed, it may be a tactical move, in that Summa has already scaled back plans for its expansion and it would be in Summa's interest for others to scale back their plans as well. And it would be understandable if Akron General Medical Center, which has gained final approval for a major renovation, objected to going back to the drawing board when its construction is so close.

But setting aside the competitive interests of any one hospital, the call for regional planning shouldn't be ignored.

The business and health professionals who are part of the local health planning group want better planning, too, but they currently have no authority to bring it about.

In some cities, top community leaders have taken a leading role in bringing about sensible hospital planning. That is needed here also.

There would be many details to work out. But clearly, the timing is right to set up a process for good hospital planning in the Akron area. Consumers need protection from the high costs of over building.

Chicago Tribune

Chicago, Illinois, March 5, 1991

The timing couldn't be worse for the Illinois Hospital Association to be urging Gov. Edgar and the General Assembly to change the way the state's Medicaid program pays hospitals to care for the poor. The governor already is being forced to cut current state spending, and faces a estimated shortfall of at least $1 billion in his fiscal 1992 budget. The hospitals' plan would cost the state an annual $150 million more.

But the hospitals have an urgent and compelling case. For years, Medicaid has paid them far less than the full cost of their services to the poor—now an average of about 79 percent. Reimbursement for outpatient care is even less—about 40 percent of actual costs. The state also has dragged out the time it takes to pay its hospital bills, a dirty trick often used by the Thompson administration to stretch the state budget. Currently, the state takes more than 80 days to pay its Medicaid bills.

These shameful Medicaid financing problems have a wide range of adverse side effects. In the last five years 22 Illinois hospitals have been forced to close; most were in poor areas and couldn't survive on the low level of Medicaid reimbursements. Other hospitals have had to make up for the inadequate Medicaid payments by increasing what they charge their privately insured patients. That in turn raises insurance premiums and costs to employers, who must eventually boost the prices of their products to cover employee health benefits—or cut the quality of the benefits.

What the Illinois Hospital Association is proposing is a major change in how Medicaid works. Currently, through a state program called "ICARE," hospitals contract to provide Medicaid patients with a total number of days of care per year at a negotiated price—a process that works in the state's favor against the hospitals, according to the association.

Instead, it wants to substitute a payment system based on the federal Medicare plan, which pays hospitals a flat fee for each patient based on the diagnosis of his ailment and the usual length of hospitalization required. This, at least in theory, gives hospitals a financial incentive to treat patients efficiently and discharge them quickly.

With a flat-fee system for Medicaid, hospitals would be paid about 97 percent of their actual expenses, the association estimates. The federal government, which matches state Medicaid contributions, would pay half of the extra $300 million a year this system is expected to cost, leaving the state's share at about $150 million. Several legislators have agreed to sponsor a bill incorporating the hospital association's proposals.

Of course Illinois must pay hospitals fairly for treating the poor. If the new governor can't squeeze the money into his new budget, the state will have to cut back on Medicaid services or begin to ration them—an intolerable solution that Oregon is trying to put into place. Or the governor will have to back down on his determination not to raise taxes.

Nationwide Nursing Shortage Seen

A government report Dec. 12, 1988 warned that a growing shortage of registered nurses could erode hospital care in the U.S. It recommended that federal funds be set aside to recruit and train new nurses, and provide better pay for nurses currently employed.

The report was presented Dec. 12 to Dr. Otis R. Bowen, secretary of Health and Human Services. It had been prepared by the department's Commission on Nursing.

The report blamed the nursing shortage on a greatly increased demand for nursing services, rather than on a decrease in the number of available nurses. It noted that the number of registered nurses in the U.S. had increased by about 5% since 1983, to a total of about 1.9 million.

However, demand for nurses had grown dramatically over the same period. In 1987, the study reported, 11.3% of nursing jobs had gone unfilled. In 1983, that figure had been 4.4%.

Dr. Carolyne K. Davis, the commission chairman, said that 10%-30% of the nation's hospitals reported that they had temporarily closed emergency rooms or intensive care units, and had delayed elective surgery, because of a shortage of nurses.

The commission attributed the increased demand to several factors, including hospital policies that released patients sooner (thereby keeping the patients who required the most care), the aging of the population, the spread of AIDS, the growing use of complex new technologies, and the fact that many hospitals had laid off less-skilled personnel in recent years and shifted their duties to registered nurses.

The panel also noted that nursing was becoming an unpopular profession. Enrollment in nursing schools had declined 26% since 1984, it pointed out. The commission blamed the decline on salaries that did not provide adequate raises, heavy workloads, a "negative public image," and increased career opportunities for women in other fields.

Los Angeles, California, July 10, 1988

That urgent cry isn't coming just from the too-demanding patient these days. Throughout the nation — and particularly in L.A. — hospitals are searching high and low for nurses. The dearth is so severe that Congress recently waived some visa restrictions on foreigners with the needed health-care skills. But there's another solution that would ease the shortage and offer jobs to Americans.

The American Medical Association is calling for a new training program open to high school graduates. They would study several months for positions involving simple hospital tasks, such as taking temperatures and keeping patients clean, and they would be under the supervision of nurses. They would have more training and responsibility than orderlies, but wouldn't have to go through the two years required to be a licensed vocational nurse. In addition to giving RNs more time for high-skill tasks, the entry-level caregivers would be a pool from which to develop future nurses.

It's a good idea, but some nursing organizations don't see it that way. They say this new category would undercut their profession and endanger patients. Instead, they think any money for training workers should go to boost nurses' salaries.

The safety issue is already a problem in hospitals strained by a lack of nurses. It's hard to believe that more hands on the job wouldn't improve that situation. And not all nurses are complaining. Some point out that apprentices would give full-fledged professionals more opportunity for management experience.

But probably the most compelling argument for this new kind of nurse — beyond filling the need — is financial. Lower salaries for work that takes less training and experience is a reasonable way to cut down on medical bills. The same money pressures have moved nurses into doctors' territory, as nurse practitioners become more common. And as the cost of a hospital stay continues to raise the pulse, any economizing that doesn't endanger the patient is worth seriously considering.

The Boston Globe
Boston, Massachusetts, June 27, 1988

If the American Medical Association has its way, one day soon hospital patients will no longer call a nurse to their bedside. Rather, they will call a registered care technologist.

This new category of health worker has been conjured up by the AMA as its answer to the nursing shortage. What the AMA seems to have in mind is an Edsel model of a nurse.

For many reasons this is a bad idea. It hints of an unrequited yearning to return to an era of modestly trained nurses who accepted their lesser place in the medical hierarchy. The AMA also seems to think it can find trainees among minorities willing to do menial work in hospitals and nursing homes. They might see it as the job opportunity it was for women a century ago. Today, nurses say such dead-end jobs drive them out of the field.

The RCT would be trained to provide fundamental bedside care – and no more. The role, the AMA says, would be a non-leadership one, in contrast to that of professional nursing. This "low tech" worker would give routine medicines, monitor blood pressure and be responsible for bathing, feeding and walking patients.

An "advanced" RCT would work in operating rooms, intensive care units and other specialized areas for the critically ill. This RCT would be schooled in "high tech" procedures.

Both types of RCTs would largely train in hospital programs that would be taught by physicians, as "diploma" nurse programs were in the past. This approach, the AMA concedes, was long criticized for being more akin to an apprenticeship than to traditional education; the trainees were exploited as low-cost workers. Organizations representing 2 million nurses nationwide oppose the AMA. An editorial in The American Journal of Nursing asks, "Why is it so difficult for these physicians to get beyond the antiquated notion that patient care is only a series of mechanical tasks?"

Nurses and physicians disagree on the cause of the nursing shortage. Physicians contend that professionalism is removing today's nurses from bedside care. Nurses argue that physicians fear the growing autonomy of nurses in deciding on patient care, as well as giving it, and in taking charge of nursing education and gaining upgraded salary status.

The RCT proposal is a poor prescription at a time when hospital patients, older and sicker than previous patients, need thorough nursing care rather than a technical attendant of limited skill.

AUGUSTA HERALD
Augusta, Georgia, June 28, 1989

Doctors attending the American Medical Association's annual policy-making convention in Chicago this week are responding to the nursing shortage crisis by debating a plan to establish a new type of lesser trained hospital worker to provide limited bedside care functions.

How would doctors like it if some organization with control over their affairs — say state government or universities — got together to consider a plan to graduate "lesser trained" physicians to meet a chronic doctor shortage?

Indeed, there is a chronic doctor shortage in many rural areas of the nation, including several communities in the Central Savannah River Area. But — wisely — no one is seriously considering lowering the standards of physician training to meet it.

The public should be wary of any plan that lowers the quality of nursing care. Well-trained nurses are no less necessary to good health care than well-trained physicians. Would you or your loved ones want to go to a hospital where today's high standards of nursing care have been replaced by lower standards?

To be sure, this is not the argument the AMA's "reformers" are making. They argue that their plan for so-called "registered care technicians (RCTs)" would free up skilled nurses to perform vital, highly technical patient-care management tasks.

The RCTs would handle such mundane chores as taking temperatures and blood pressure, monitoring vital signs, changing bandages, administering medication, and the like. These are the very jobs young nurses cut their teeth on. They are also the jobs that establish crucial nurse-patient rapport which is so important to successful treatment. And already much of this work is being done by nurses' aides.

The AMA plan would continue the trend of turning nursing into a low-paid, high-tech profession — taking nurses away from close human contact with their patients, which for many of them is the very reason they became nurses in the first place.

But there are other reasons many nurses leave the profession (and young, career-oriented women aren't getting in it): poor pay; long, disjointed hours; and better opportunities in other fields.

If the AMA is serious about wanting to end the nursing shortage it will consider plans to boost salaries, improve working conditions and allow nurses to do what they do best — provide personal care to patients; anything less is a "shortcut" that will worsen the crisis.

The AMA's time would be better spent addressing its own shortages instead of worrying about someone else's. It ought to be looking at ways to alleviate the surplus of doctors in well-heeled urban and suburban communities and directing physician resources to health-care starved rural areas.

The News Journal
Wilmington, Delaware, June 15, 1989

TIRED of hearing about the shortage of nurses? Brace yourself. You'll be hearing more about it in the next few years.

Nationwide, there'll be half as many nurses as needed by the year 2000 — a deficit of some 600,000 nurses. And Delaware, which already has a difficult time attracting enough nurses, will be hit just as hard as the rest, unless efforts are made now to forestall some of the problems.

Among those most concerned about the present and future nurse shortage is the state Department of Health and Social Services (DHSS), which employs about 300 registered nurses at its five residential facilities and in the Division of Public Health. Last summer, the state found itself in the precarious position of having 62 of its nursing slots empty — a dangerous situation regarding patient care and a tough situation for the nursing staff which was overworked. Since then aggressive recruiting has filled more than a third of those vacancies.

To avoid repetition of last summer's high vacancy rate, the department asked the University of Delaware to survey the attitudes and perceptions of licensed registered nurses in the state (there are 7,500, of whom 6,000 are employed). The results are in, and Secretary Thomas P. Eichler expects to use them to improve the recruiting and retention of nurses.

The survey showed that the state fails to attract and keep recent nurse graduates. Significantly more nurses in the 40-to-49 age group work for the state than in private-sector jobs. This raises the specter of a large number of retirements in the foreseeable future and many slots to fill.

Of the nurses working for the state, close to half indicated in the survey that they were likely to leave state employ. Among factors influencing a decision for a job change were benefits, child care, salary, condition of work site.

The state contends, with some justification, that its benefit package (vacations, holidays, health insurance etc.) is pretty good and in its new recruitment brochure carefully lists all the benefits.

Child day care is a problem all employers are hearing about; DHSS is looking into setting up day-care centers at two of its sites.

On salaries the state falls behind many private-sector facilities. State policy requires that salaries must be 15 percent off the market rate before adjustments can be made. Secretary Eichler wants that policy changed.

Currently state salaries for nurses fall about $5,000 behind those of nurses working elsewhere. That's unfair to the state's nurses and the state's patients who then get inadequate care because of understaffing.

Many of the state's buildings are old and have been allowed to deteriorate over the years. The General Assembly should heed the requests for capital improvement money. Better facilities will make for a pleasant work environment as well as for a comfortable place for patients.

Clearly DHSS is trying to put its best foot forward in looking for nurses. It also is helping employees to complete their studies for nursing degrees. This should improve the state's position relative to other employers.

But when all is said and done, there still remains the national nurse shortage. And that needs to be addressed by offering more student loans, providing career ladders for nurses and recognizing nursing as a profession that has real input into the care of patients.

THE KANSAS CITY STAR
Kansas City, Missouri, December 18, 1989

Nurses have already been missed. Hospital patients of the last few years already knew what a new federal study is reporting officially: There's a nursing shortage that is getting closer to dangerous.

Hospitals and nursing homes now have 137,000 vacancies. And the forces that caused them aren't abating by themselves. Unless intentional efforts are undertaken to educate and keep more nurses, the U.S. Department of Health and Human Services and the Commission on Nursing warn, the shortage will threaten the high quality of health care.

At the same time, beleaguered administrators at public hospitals like Truman Medical Center are caught in a double bind: tight budgets for staff salaries and the high cost of contracting with agencies for temporary employees. One unknown TMC must include in projecting next year's budget deficit is how difficult the current crisis might make it to hold the nursing staff. The more people leave, the more positions will have to be covered with expensive overtime and agency workers, driving up expenses even higher than now.

That's how ordinary people meet statistics. Moreover, it's one reason legislators and other leaders keep hearing changing numbers about the needs of TMC. The bad news of this year's budget won't necessarily be the same next year. It will be worse.

The American Nurses Association points to high-tech medical equipment, the growing aged population and similar changes on the patient side of the equation as part of the reason for the nurse shortage. But salaries also play a role.

There's a parallel with the teaching profession: Basic salaries are relatively low and they don't rise adequately with years of experience. Not surprisingly, in addition to calling for work on salary schedules, the report urges that nurses be given more representation on policy-making bodies. Both critically important vocations have historically been low in pay and short on power. They epitomize women's work.

Times have changed. It's just that a lot of institutions haven't caught up with it yet.

DESERET NEWS
Salt Lake City, Utah, May 12, 1989

Nurses are an integral part of health care and the system would collapse without them. It's a serious job. The demands are many, the stress high, the hours awkward and the work keeps getting more technical.

Just how much society owes to the many hard-working and oft-forgotten nurses in its midst should be remembered as the state prepares to observe National Nurses Week, beginning May 1. Sooner or later, most people will be in their care.

Will there be enough to go around? For several years, cries of doom and gloom have been raised about the shortage of nurses nationwide and in Utah — estimated to be 20 percent by 1990 — and about the growing crisis in health care as a result.

While some of those fears are becoming reality elsewhere, a curious thing seems to be taking place in Utah. According to nursing officials at Intermountain Health Care, the law of supply and demand has driven up wages, hospitals are trying to be more imaginative in meeting the needs of nurses and the shortage at IHC hospitals is only 3 to 4 percent.

Shortages are due in part to increasing needs, rather than a diminishing supply. And there is a relatively high turnover in the profession.

Nationally, a slow decline in the number of nursing graduates is projected through the year 2000. Fortunately, in Utah nursing remains an appealing career for young people. There are more applications at the University of Utah, for example, than there is room to accept them.

Starting salaries have risen to the point where they compare favorably with other professions. Men are beginning to enter the field, although they still make up only about 4 percent of the total in Utah.

Part of the nursing shortage is alleviated by heavy use of part-time workers, something that nursing is uniquely suited to offer. There aren't many jobs where a person can work one or two days a week or in the middle of the night or just on weekends.

IHC hospitals are trying to reduce the turnover by meeting other needs of nurses, such as providing day care for children of nurses. Except in this case, it is day or night care or on weekends. Traditional day care businesses don't offer help at the odd hours nurses are apt to work.

Utahns should take the opportunity to pay tribute to nurses and all they do. Anyone who has been in a hospital should have no trouble remembering one or more nurses with deep affection — who made the stay more bearable and recovery more rapid.

The Record
Hackensack, New Jersey, January 6, 1989

Why are the classified columns full of ads for nurses, laboratory technicians, and other highly trained health-care workers? Why are hospitals struggling to raise salaries and demanding higher reimbursement for patient care? The answer is a simple matter of supply and demand, according to a recent federal study: There aren't enough nurses to meet the care needs of an aging population, and not nearly enough now in training for future needs.

It will be a tough assignment for a new president and a new Congress, already burdened with budget problems, to find the money for nursing scholarships and to increase nursing compensation allowances under the Medicare program. That's what specialists are recommending.

But more than money is at issue. Recognition must be given to the fact that the delivery of health care has changed profoundly in the last decade, and so has the role of registered nurses on the health-care team. Faced with shrinking budgets and new federally imposed cost-cutting measures, hospitals have judged that nurses are their most cost-effective and versatile employees, and turned to using nurses in new ways. Nurses can do just about everything that needs doing on a hospital floor. Many community hospitals, trying to cut labor costs, have laid off practical nurses and aides and asked more highly trained registered nurses to do that work along with their own.

The cost crunch has also caused shifts in the structure of health-care delivery. Once, people were sent to hospitals simply to rest. Now, a patient must be very sick or need a complex procedure in order to be admitted.

Other patients are now cared for in clinics, as outpatients, or even at home. Registered nurses have the training to give these kinds of care. Practical nurses and aides generally don't.

High technology has also contributed to the shortage of RN's. As equipment, medications, and therapeutic techniques all rise to new levels of complexity, nursing staffs are called on for higher and higher degrees of specialization. Intensive care services suffer most severely from a deficit of nurses.

Normally, employees who are asked to take on new work loads or a more important role in an operation are compensated with a boost in status and better pay. Not so with nurses. According to Editorial Research Reports, the average starting pay of a head nurse in a community hospital is $26,000. The average maximum pay is only $36,000 — offering little incentive to make a lifetime career of hospital nursing! The numbers of graduating nurses are still inching up, but enrollments in nursing schools have dropped. That bodes ill for the future of health care.

New Jersey Health Commissioner Molly Coye has worked to upgrade the prestige of the profession. For the federal government, an ideal program to attract larger numbers of able nursing candidates would include a standardized educational requirement for nurses with college degrees. It would include opportunities for ongoing training and career enhancement. It would include a mechanism for giving nurses more decision-making opportunities in patient care. It would include nursing-school scholarships. And it would include a level of compensation consistent with enlarged responsibility.

The Boston Globe
Boston, Massachusetts, December 20, 1989

The Visiting Nurse Association of Boston reached a milestone this month when it recorded the 195,001st nurse's visit of 1989, the most in a year. The work of the association provides better health for thousands in the Boston area.

The association has been dispatching nurses to patients since 1886. The job has grown in importance during the past decade as medical technology has improved and the pressure to cut costs has intensified.

A visit with nurse Janet Roach to a patient in Dorchester shows the importance of the nurses' work. Two-year-old Johnny has a combination of ailments: a heart condition makes him weak, and a stomach disorder means he must be fed through a tube in his stomach. Johnny could stay in a hospital, at a cost of $700 a day. A few years ago that would have been the only option, but today feeding tubes have improved and he can stay at home, as long as a nurse comes by three or four times a week, at the bargain rate of $60 a visit. The result is a happy child, still confined to his crib for much of the day but alert and amused by a group of visitors.

Johnny is fortunate to have two grandparents living in the house who care for him while his parents work. All family members have been trained to manage the feeding tube, and when it sprung a leak, his grandfather made a temporary repair with a piece of tape.

Roach's 28-person caseload includes asthma sufferers, children of drug addicts, premature infants and a teen-ager with AIDS. "You get to know the patients," she says. "They are not just people in a bed." Because she sees them regularly, she is able to spot medical problems before they get out of hand. Her visits are subsidized by the much-maligned state Medicaid system.

This expansion of services is one reason that Medicaid costs increased in Massachusetts over the past few years. In Johnny's case, the new service provides him with competent medical care at a reasonable cost in a loving environment.

Not all the patients are as fortunate as Johnny in having an extended family living in the same house. For those living alone, the Visiting Nurse Association provides home health aides to prepare meals and help the patients care for themselves. For AIDS patients, workers with special training provide the services needed to treat this complex disease.

All these services come comparatively cheaply – $29 million provides for the needs of 12,000 patients. Sixty percent of the budget comes from the government. It is money well spent.

The Des Moines Register

Des Moines, Iowa, March 2, 1991

Offering nurses better educational opportunities, especially in training for work in rural Iowa where health care needs are most acute, should be a top priority. The closing of Drake University's nursing program, announced last month, is a sign that it's not.

Drake's program, which began in 1985, enrolls 83 students working toward bachelor's degrees and 126 students working toward master's degrees. Working nurses attend classes on nights and weekends to gain expertise in a nursing speciality or to become administrators or educators.

With the University of Dubuque phasing out its master's degree in nursing, the loss of Drake's program will mean the University of Iowa would offer the state's only graduate degree in nursing. As a result, fewer nurses will have the opportunity to expand their academic training. Some, disappointed at not getting a chance to advance their careers, may drop out of the profession.

Drake plans to close the program partly because the university was led to believe a state appropriation of about $250,000 for this school year, which has been whittled to $170,000, won't be continued in the next school year, says Richard Hersh, Drake provost. Drake is willing to continue the program with about half the current $500,000 annual budget, says Hersh. But the nursing faculty did not want to continue without enough money to allow the program to earn national accreditation in the near future.

Linda Brady, Drake's nursing division director, says a dependable $500,000 annual budget is critical to continuing to build a high-quality program. Part of the reason the state helped pay for the program this year is that lawmakers backed its goal of offering graduate nursing classes around Iowa to improve rural health care, she said.

That possibility — and a chance for nurses working in central Iowa to grow professionally — will be lost if enough money isn't found to allow Drake's nursing program to move ahead.

The Evening Gazette

Worcester, Massachusetts, April 25, 1991

The concerns voiced by students of Worcester City Hospital's nursing school are understandable. The school is expected to be closed when the hospital merges with the University of Massachusetts Medical Center this summer.

We sympathize with the students' desire to complete their training at the same place where they started it. If that's not possible, however, their dedication should help them meet the challenge imposed by the inevitable changes ahead.

The students should concentrate on finding acceptable alternatives to complete their studies — perhaps at Quinsigamond Community College or Worcester State College or at UMass. Officials at those institutions should help make the transition as smooth as possible. So should the Worcester Health and Hospitals Authority that oversees City Hospital.

The students say they want the current program continued even if it costs an estimated $300,000 for this one last class. That expectation is unrealistic.

Even if the money could be found, drastic changes at City Hospital would make proper training all but impossible there. With acute care eliminated, and the hospital assuming a new role,

instructors and lessons in bedside care would be lacking.

This is not the first time college students in Worcester were forced to switch schools. Hundreds of students of the former Central New England Colleges had to transfer when that institution went out of business in mid-term.

The nursing students at City Hospital will have a chance to complete this year's instruction and enough time to decide where to go next.

Even though the students addressed their pleas for help to the City Council, the politicians are in no position to offer assistance. Arrangements for City Hospital are out of their hands. That's just as well; decades of mismanagement and political meddling pushed the institution into bankruptcy.

At a time when bachelor's degrees are the preferred education for nurses, enrolling in a college or university program would be a blessing in disguise. Students at City's nursing school will be one year closer to that goal by transferring now.

We suggest the School of Nursing class of 1992 consider the changes as a challenge instead of a crisis, as an opportunity instead of a defeat.

ARGUS-LEADER

Sioux Falls, South Dakota, January 6, 1991

For almost two years, a dispute over ambulance service has divided Sioux Falls.

A lot has happened, particularly in the last 18 months, but not much has been resolved.

On Tuesday, city voters will go to the polls for an election that probably won't resolve the issue, no matter what happens. But the outcome will be significant.

Indirectly, the election pits Sioux Falls Ambulance against CareTraum Ambulance. Sioux Falls Ambulance has been the city's only provider of ground ambulance services since 1968; CareTraum is a relative newcomer trying to get a piece of the 911-emergency market.

Editorial

Voters will decide whether to repeal a city ordinance that bars CareTraum from the 911-emergency call system unless it receives emergency treatment privileges at local hospitals.

As explained on the ballot by the city attorney: "If Ordinance No. 100-90 is approved, an ambulance service may not be placed on 911 emergency response in the city of Sioux Falls unless it has emergency treatment hospital privileges from McKennan and Sioux Valley hospitals. If Ordinance No. 100-90 is disapproved, it will not go into effect."

In effect, a "no" vote is against the city ordinance and for CareTraum, the company that forced the election. A "yes" vote is for the ordinance and against CareTraum.

We recommend a "yes" vote, but not necessarily because we oppose CareTraum or support Sioux Falls Ambulance. We advocate a "yes" vote primarily because we are convinced that having two ambulance services splitting the community's limited market for emergency calls would not improve service.

If anything, ambulance service probably would deteriorate over the long term with two companies responding to calls. There just isn't enough business; in 1989, emergency calls averaged about eight a day.

CareTraum has desire and persistence, and its owners are assembling an impressive technological arsenal. But, overall, the company comes up short when the issue is broken down to equipment and personnel.

Sioux Falls Ambulance has eight vehicles, for example, and CareTraum has five. Sioux Falls Ambulance, which is owned and operated by Orlen Tschetter, also has a larger and better trained work staff.

We said 17 months ago that CareTraum deserved an opportunity to prove itself. It has had that. But it has failed to win the confidence of health-care professionals.

Sioux Valley and McKennan claim they will not allow their doctors to give patient-care instructions to CareTraum ambulance personnel at the scene or en route to their emergency rooms. CareTraum owners Jay and Jill Masur have been trying to force their way into the 911 market nonetheless.

CareTraum has a right to exist and compete for routine transfers and other ambulance business. But the company is not entitled to an automatic cut of half the 911-emergency calls.

The real issue is public safety, not competition. The best company should prevail in the scramble for 911 business.

Unfortunately, Tuesday's election is widely perceived as a big-guy, little-guy fight, with CareTraum playing the gutsy, little challenger about to upset the bully.

If the CareTraum side wins Tuesday, another election likely will follow in the spring. The second election would determine an initiated ordinance that would specifically allow CareTraum to respond to 911 calls.

We hope the second election does not come about. We hope the city and county commissions decide to create a franchising system under which bids are sought and one ambulance company — regardless of whether it's Sioux Falls Ambulance, CareTraum or some other company — is awarded the community's 911 business.

Regardless of whether franchising comes about, voters can help end the ambulance controversy for the better by voting "yes" on Tuesday.

Organ Transplant Issues Debated as Procedures Gain Wider Acceptance

Affluent white male kidney patients were more likely to receive kidney transplants than were women, blacks and poor people, it was reported Jan. 16-24, 1989. The findings were contained in a study conducted by Philip Held and a team of researchers at the Urban Institute and were published in the *Archives of Internal Medicine*.

In a survey of 15,000 dialysis patients, Held's team found that white patients were almost twice as likely to receive transplants as blacks, and that men were about one-third more likely to have transplants than women. In addition, the rate of transplants increased in direct proportion to the average family income in a particular geographic area. The disparities occurred despite the fact that blacks suffered higher rates of kidney failure than whites and in spite of a government program that paid the cost of most kidney transplant operations. (Dialysis, the alternative to transplants, was considered by most doctors to be less desirable because it imposed far greater restrictions on a patient's lifestyle.) The team's findings correlated with previous studies on kidney transplant rates. Explanations for the disparities ranged from a lower rate of kidney donorship on the part of blacks (many blacks were not able to accept transplants from whites because of mis-matching tissue) to a suggestion that some doctors failed to recommend poorer, black patients for transplants because they thought they could not afford to travel to a major transplant center or pay for expensive post-operative drugs.

The reluctance of Americans to commit organs and tissues for transplants after death was preventing thousands of Americans from receiving lifesaving organ transplants each year, according to a study released June 15, 1989 by Northwestern University's Annenberg Washington Program. The program said policy makers should consider instituting a program of rewards for donors.

Although many kinds of transplants had become medically routine and economically superior to alternative treatments, the study said, the number of people donating organs was far too low to meet the demand. Fewer than 50,000 Americans – less than 2% of the 2.2 million who died each year – donated tissues or organs of any kind, as opposed to the 5% of eligible people who donated blood in any given year.

As a result, to cite one example, the study estimated that at least half of the 30,000 Americans who began costly programs of kidney dialysis each year could have successful kidney transplants instead, at an ultimate saving to taxpayers of $200 million a year.

To encourage committing organs to donation, the study said, some professionals were now recommending a system that would make payments to the estates of those donating organs after death.

Surgeons at the University of Pittsburgh June 28, 1992 removed the liver from a baboon and implanted it into a terminally ill man. The man survived 71 days until dying Sept. 6.

It was reportedly the first time a baboon liver had been given to a human. Other animal organs had been implanted in humans at least 33 times since 1905. None of the operations had been successful.

The recipient was a 35-year-old man whose name was withheld for confidentiality. He was dying from hepatitis B, a virus that had destroyed his liver. He was unable to accept a human replacement because the virus would attack it as well. Baboon livers, however, were thought not to be susceptible to heptitis B.

The man's health took an unexpected plunge Aug. 28, when he went into shock an hour after undergoing an X-ray examination that involved manipulating his bile ducts with needles. Doctors suspected that the procedure had infected his blood with bacteria.

The patient's condition improved for a while, but he suffered a massive stroke Sept. 6 as doctors were trying to remove him from an artificial respirator. He fell into a coma and died that night.

At a news conference Sept. 8, the doctors said they had not identified the cause of the stroke. But they said an autopsy showed that the man had not rejected the baboon liver. They announced plans to perform a second baboon liver transplant.

SYRACUSE
HERALD·JOURNAL
Syracuse, New York, May 16, 1988

Maria DeSillers has financial troubles.

DeSillers is the mother of Ron De-Sillers, the 7-year-old who died last year after receiving three liver transplants.

The mother and son were cast into the national spotlight when the boy needed a liver transplant and President Reagan heard about the case. He called Ronnie and donated $1,000 to his medical expenses.

He wasn't the only one. Moved by the president's example, the contributions poured in — more than $500,000. An investigator, appointed by the court in Dade County where Mrs. DeSillers resides, is accusing the woman of spending $200,000 of the money on personal items such as jewelry, a used BMW automobile, clothes and furniture. DeSillers says some of the money was used to pay loans. The money spent on clothes and jewelry was necessary, she said, to help her look "professional" when she went out to raise money for the Ron DeSillers National Foundation.

The DeSillers case raises two issues. One is about the need for a more structured system of distributing organs in this nation. The other is the need for public accountability of money raised during special appeals.

While children were waiting for one liver, Ron DeSillers was able to get three and was waiting for a fourth before he died. Why? Because he had the support of President Reagan, which brought him media attention, and a mother who was a public relations specialist.

Organs should not be distributed based on publicity and links to the White House. Cases should be assessed according to need and risk. Ronnie, for example, was not a good risk after three failed transplants. In some cases, organs are given to people who happen to be on the right waiting list. Some patients have their names on several lists to cut the odds.

If a national or state distribution system were in place, organs could be distributed in a just manner. Potential recipients could be assured they would have just as good a chance of getting a liver, heart or kidney as the person who is promoted by a celebrity.

Since it is likely that special appeals — for organ transplant patients, orphans, the homeless, etc. — will continue, the recipients of the money or a representative should be required to deposit the money into a special bank account and make available a financial report detailing how the money is being spent.

Organ distribution and contributing to the needy are worthy endeavors. They should not be corrupted by promotional gimmicks or greed.

Pittsburgh Post-Gazette

Pittsburgh, Pennsylvania, August 28, 1991

Four years ago a federal computer network went on line to match donor organs to patients awaiting them. It was hailed as the answer to a particularly vexing problem — the unfair advantage enjoyed by rich foreigners who could afford the expensive medical procedures.

As far as that problem went, the United Network for Organ Sharing was an immediate success. Even before it went into operation, it adopted a policy that placed foreign nationals at the end of the waiting list and put them under the restrictions of a quota system.

To make distribution more fair, UNOS devised a plan based on medical urgency, tissue match and the patient's time on the waiting list as well as several other less-important criteria.

But even that careful screening system is being called into question now by the Transplant Recipients International Organization, whose members have seen the problem from the sharp edge of the surgeon's scalpel. The organization contends that the distribution system has evolved into a regional turf battle that doesn't guarantee that the sickest patients are getting top transplant priority.

The system allows transplant teams to attempt to find a matchable local patient before offering an organ for use anywhere in the country, no matter the patient's standing on the national waiting list. Thus, the recipients contend, a local patient may get an organ even though the needs of a patient in a distant state may be more acute.

That's a valid criticism, one that must be addressed by UNOS if it is to fulfill its humanitarian mission. Should the turf battle widen, there could be a backward trend toward pre-UNOS years, when an alarming number of organs transplanted were never offered on the national list.

With the exception of heart transplants, we agree with the recipients' organization that the national, rather than the local, picture must be examined when an organ is available. Viable for only four to six hours, hearts should be given local-recipient priority so none is wasted because of time lost in long-distance shipping.

Otherwise, the provision that gives priority to local patients can't be justified. An organ, donated with the best of intentions, should go to the person who needs it most, no matter where that person lives.

We recognize that a true national list — with no priority for patients in the area where the organ was donated and harvested — probably will lead to a decline in the number of smaller procurement centers, currently sustained by their local activity.

While that decline could, at least for a time, be accompanied by lesser procurement efforts at some of the smaller centers, the slack would be offset by increased faith in the fairness of the distribution system. And a strengthened faith will, in time, lead to increased donations, the only realistic answer to the frustrating problem of undersupply and over-demand.

The TENNESSEAN

Nashville, Tennessee, April 12, 1991

STATE House representatives took a step in the right direction this week with the adoption of legislation concerning organ donation.

The General Assembly has already approved legislation this year that allows people to indicate in a living will that they do not want to be kept alive with feeding tubes in the event of an irreversible coma.

Prior to this much needed change, Tennesseans could only indicate through a living will that they did not want heroic life sustaining treatment when death was imminent.

This week by a 79-10 vote, the House approved a bill that would allow people with living wills to indicate that they want to be kept alive by artificial means just long enough to donate their organs.

The bill still awaits action by the Senate.

Advances in medical science are convincing more and more people to sign living wills.

It only takes one case like the tragedy of Nancy Cruzan, who was kept alive in a vegetative state for years at great expense, to bring the message home. Too often, such heroic medical care only prolongs a family's suffering while it piles up enormous medical bills.

The legislation passed by the House takes the process one step further. Under it, people who are deliberately making a decision about their life through a living will can at the same time decide that they want to donate their organs.

With this nation's crying need for organs suitable for transplant, any means to increase organ availability is welcome.

The Senate should approve this legislation. It will not replace the organ donation approval now on Tennessee's driver's licenses. And it certainly won't force people into a decision that they don't want to make.

But it will give Tennesseans who have decided to have a voice in when and how their lives end a chance to help extend the life or the quality of life for another person. Certainly all lawmakers should recognize the merit and the goodness in that. ■

The Wichita

Eagle-Beacon

Wichita, Kansas, April 25, 1991

The greatest gift you can give to someone else won't cost you a penny, yet every year countless opportunities to offer that gift are wasted.

The gift is the donation of organs and tissue after your death. The waste comes from inaction, indecision and ignorance.

Almost all adult Americans know about organ and tissue transplants. And about half of those aware of the life-giving aspects of transplants say they're likely to donate their organs after death. Yet a huge number of these donations never get made.

It takes two steps to become an organ donor, and most people don't understand that. First, you have to complete an organ-donor card. In Kansas, that is as simple as signing the back of your driver's license.

But even with a signed donor card or driver's license form, family consent must be given after death. That's where the process often fails. Many people who are perfectly willing or even anxious to donate haven't talked it over with their families.

For anyone who's serious about donating organs and tissue, that's a discussion that shouldn't be put off.

Those who are worried about some of the implications of organ donation should be aware of a study of donor families. The study by Brandeis University shows:

Responding to the request for organ and tissue donation does not add to a family's grief. In fact, donor families say donation helps lessen the pain of a relative's death.

Families that give the go-ahead for organ donations say they do so for three reasons: to help someone else, because organs shouldn't be wasted and to bring something positive out of the death of a loved one.

Donor families say — overwhelmingly — they are willing to make the same decision again.

If you need some information about donor or tissue donation, or want to help spread the word, call Bob Randall at the Midwest Organ Bank, 262-6225, or Jana Konek at the Wichita Eye Bank, 688-3937.

The Oregonian

Portland, Oregon, September 21, 1992

Chad Cheriel, director of the Oregon Office of Health Policy, brought much-needed public oversight recently into the Portland hospital dogfight over who should do organ transplants.

St. Vincent Hospital & Medical Center, which wants to start a kidney transplant program, had argued it didn't have to undergo the state review required before hospitals can add expensive new programs. The hospital maintained that transplants were merely an extension of existing hospital kidney services and that a transplant program would cost less than $500,000 a year. A state certificate-of-need is required for any new medical service that costs more than $500,000 a year.

Cheriel's common-sense decision was that transplants would indeed be a new service and St. Vincent's own figures indicate the eventual cost would exceed $500,000 annually. So St. Vincent now must justify publicly why it should duplicate transplant services already available at Oregon Health Sciences University.

The same public accountability should be required of Legacy's Good Samaritan Hospital, which wants to begin heart transplants, either on its own or through a joint program with OHSU currently being discussed in private negotiations.

The ability of Portland-area hospitals to dance around the existing certificate-of-need process points up why that process should be revamped and strengthened.

State reviews were begun as one way to hold down skyrocketing health-care costs. Because of the quirky economics that affect the health-care industry, duplication of high-cost, low-volume medical services, such as organ transplants, doesn't drive costs down through competition. Instead, it drives overall medical costs up as hospitals try to recoup the cost of expensive machinery and personnel by charging more for the other services they offer.

Higher costs translate into a bigger tax bite to pay for such health programs as Medicaid and Medicare.

The Office of Health Policy unsuccessfully sought legislation last session that would have required state approval before a hospital could add any of a specific list of high-ticket medical services, including neonatal intensive care units, organ transplant programs, magnetic-resonance imaging scanners and open-heart surgery units. It also would have put a moratorium on adding any of those services until 1993. So it is no surprise that hospitals are rushing to add transplant programs now.

Hospitals have lots of reasons for wanting to start a transplant program. It raises the hospital's profile in a competitive market; it allows hospitals to hang on to transplant patients who need lots of post-transplant medical care; it allows staff surgeons and physicians to expand their expertise.

The public, however, has only two reasons for wanting more transplant programs: improved quality of care and lower prices.

Neither St. Vincent nor Good Samaritan has made a convincing argument that its entry into the transplant field will improve patient care or lower prices. OHSU's success rate and costs compare favorably with other kidney and heart transplant programs around the nation. Waiting lists for transplants are caused by a shortage of organs, not by a lack of doctors to perform them.

The public has a big stake in the outcome of Portland's transplant war. Its interests shouldn't be relegated to the sidelines.

THE INDIANAPOLIS STAR
Indianapolis, Indiana, March 7, 1991

A group of transplant experts tiptoed through a moral minefield last week and emerged to propose that "financial incentives" be used to encourage people to donate organs. Nothing so crass as dollars was discussed, only "incentives" and "benefits."

The startling proposition came during a conference sponsored by the National Kidney Foundation and attended by transplant coordinators, surgeons, attorneys and government representatives.

The conferees recommended that families donating organs from a newly deceased relative be paid burial expenses. A like amount would be paid to the estate or a beneficiary of a person who had previously declared he wished to be a donor. Payments would apply only to organs from cadavers, not living donors.

Isn't there a federal law banning the sale of human organs? There is indeed but the conference sidesteps that impediment with an awkward exercise in semantics.

The report stressed that the payments would be awarded for the *act* of giving an organ, not for the organ itself. It's not like selling blood, said one conferee, because there's no direct monetary benefit to the donor.

James Nelson, an ethicist associated with the Hastings Center, said the conference had taken precautions to avoid turning organs into commodities. Even so, he suggested, the proposal "trespasses on sensibilities."

Thank heaven there is still some sensibility remaining in a world that seems hell-bent on careening down slippery slopes. As for the trespasses, they can best be forgiven by reducing the conference report to ashes.

The Pittsburgh PRESS
Pittsburgh, Pennsylvania, January 14, 1992

Each day, as its science frontier is pushed back a litle farther, the medical comunity's ethics framework becomes a little more restrictive. As knowledge increases, so do the moral decisions that must be made to put the knowledge to work.

When Sarah Kelton, the world's youngest heart transplant, died Dec. 28, she raised once again the supply-and-demand issue that has bothered physicians since organ transplants were first begun. Sarah lived three months on a heart that was transplanted into her tiny body nine hours after she was born by Cesarean section 10 weeks early.

Her death left her doctors wondering, though, whether she should have been placed on the transplant waiting list so early. As one pointed out, the condition of a transplant-candidate fetus, in the safety of the womb, doesn't deteriorate. A child already born who needs a transplant, meanwhile, faces day-by-day deterioration.

Consequently, the United Network for Organ Sharing is considering whether a fetus, found to have a defect, should be placed on a transplant waiting list, giving it precedence over a child whose defect isn't

discovered until after a full-term birth.

And, it turns out, just that situation came to pass in Sarah's case. Placed on the list 10 weeks before term, she had priority over another baby who became a transplant candidate.

That baby, Joseph Christinis, wasn't placed on the list until four days after he was born and two days after Sarah was given the precious organ. Her placement on the waiting list while she was still in the womb had given her precedence and Joseph died without ever receiving a new heart.

Both babies had other medical problems, so there is no telling whether there would have been a reversal of fortunes if there had been a reversal of priorities. That's probably fortunate.

But their cases once again underscore the need for adoption of national transplant guidelines for fetuses. As long as the demand for organs outpaces the supply of donors, there will be life-and-death decisions to be made.

And, we think, it is better for all concerned that they be made in advance and followed fastidiously.

DESERET·NEWS
Salt Lake City, Utah, April 15, 1991

In some ways, medical science has come a long way in a short time when it comes to transplanting human organs. But in one important respect, such life-saving efforts often remain needlessly and tragically thwarted.

In the past 20 years, breakthroughs in surgical techniques, immunosuppressive drugs and tissue typing have translated into increasingly successful transplants of hearts, livers, kidneys, lungs, skin, corneas, bone, bone marrow, adrenal glands, ovaries, blood vessels and cartilage.

The big problem, however, is that not enough organs are being made available for such operations even though there are more than enough potential donors. As a result, the worst often happens and people die while waiting for an organ donation that never materializes.

The best potential donors are between the ages of 15 and 65 who were in otherwise good health but died suddenly and were declared "brain dead." Brain death is a condition in which brain function has permanently ceased but the heart and lungs can function with the use of artificial life supports.

This week the St. Petersburg, Fla. Times reported that of the estimated 30,000 brain deaths in the United States each year, only about 14 percent become donors.

Yet, if all brain deaths resulted in organ donation, there would be more than enough vital organs to accommodate all eligible recipients.

Among the groups trying to deal with this challenge is a national organization called the United Network for Organ Sharing. UNOS makes sure there are no special favors in selecting the recipients of a donation. Patients are put on a national waiting list. The hard-and-fast rule is: First come, first served.

For information on how to become an organ donor, call the United Network for Organ Sharing at (800) 24-DONOR.

THE DAILY GAZETTE
Schenectady, New York, September 10, 1992

He will be known only as the "first human to receive a baboon's liver." Having lost his liver to Hepatitis B virus, this unnamed 35-year-old was near death when researchers at the University of Pittsburgh gave him a liver taken from a baboon. For 70 days, the man and the baboon's liver worked together fairly well. But Sunday night, the man died.

Another example of science's failure to accept its limits, and stop fighting death when it is inevitable? Or is it Mother Nature's way of telling us, as some animal rights activists are bound to claim, that animals are not meant to be used as "spare-parts factories" for humankind?

Neither of the above. The transplant was actually a success. The experience should guide the Pittsburgh team to design better protocols for the next three baboon-to-human liver transplants they plan to perform.

On the surface, it may seem wrong to call a surgical operation a "success" when the patient died. After all, the operation was not primarily meant to test out a species-crossing procedure, but to help the patient live.

However, from all that is known about the liver

recipient's death, it wasn't caused by a faulty liver. The young man's body had accepted the transplant remarkably well: The baboon's liver had grown to three times its original size, and within days of the operation, it had taken over all the functions of a human liver. The death occurred due to some unrelated cause, most probably an infection in a blood vessel.

And that's why this operation was a success: It showed that unlike kidneys and hearts, it may be possible to transplant livers from human-like species into human beings. (One reason may be that the liver is different from other organs as it can grow after it is transplanted.)

Would that mean turning animals into spare-parts factories? When it comes to saving human lives, using animal organs is perfectly ethical. Medicine owes many life-saving breakthroughs to research involving animals. An even stronger case can be made for using animal organs where human organs wouldn't be suitable. (Baboon liver, for instance, is not susceptible to infection by the Hepatitis B virus.) Animals must be treated well, and without cruelty. But their use in (human) life-saving operations must go on.

Breast Implant Sales Halted

The Food and Drug Administration Jan. 6, 1992 called for a moratorium on the sale and implantation of silicone-gel breast implants, to give the agency time to review data on the devices' safety. The moratorium was expected to last at least 45 days. An FDA advisory panel had recommended in November 1991 that breast implants remain on the market while further safety studies were done.

FDA Commissioner David A. Kessler told a news conference that he had requested the moratorium because new information had come to light that cast doubt on the implants' safety. "We want surgeons to stop using these implants until this new evidence can be thoroughly evaluated," Kessler said.

The new information included additional reports from rheumatologists who reported seeing a growing number of autoimmune and connective-tissue disorders among implant recipients. In addition, the FDA had obtained access to documents that were currently under court seal in several implant lawsuits. The documents suggested that breast-implant manufacturers had had concerns about the devices' safety dating back to the 1970s.

About two million women had had silicone-gel implants inserted since they came on the market in the 1960s. Of that total, 80% had received the implants for cosmetic reasons and 20% for reconstruction of a breast following surgery for breast cancer. The FDA had not been given authority to fully regulate breast implants as medical devices until 1976. In the 1980s, the FDA had ordered manufacturers to conduct studies to prove that implants were safe, but the agency subsequently found that the data submitted by the manufacturers were insufficient.

"We still do not know how often the implants leak and, when they do, we do not know exactly what materials get into the body," Kessler said. "We still do not know how often the implants break, or how long they last."

Manufacturers and plastic surgeons said they would comply with the moratorium, although they insisted the implants were safe.

THE PLAIN DEALER
Cleveland, Ohio, January 12, 1992

The Food and Drug Administration, beset by voices of both panic and righteousness, acted wisely last week in requesting a moratorium on the use of silicone-gel breast implants.

The moratorium is to last until FDA and its advisory panel are satisfied they have enough data to decide whether the implants, used by at least a million women, are safe. That could be awhile. Having raised fears by its moratorium, FDA must resolve the matter speedily.

For now, acrimony over the safety of the implants, used for decades but suspected of causing serious illness in some women, has clouded fact and promoted hysteria. The FDA, entering the fray years' late, is smart to call a halt to the name-calling, and breast-implanting, while more data is gathered and assessed.

The implant manufacturers and plastic surgeons pushing the devices have been lax in doing the systematic studies needed to show whether the silicone implants are safe.

The implants had been used for years when FDA first got jurisdiction over their safety in 1976; the agency failed to require safety data from manufacturers until last year. Meanwhile, complaints about everything from leaks of the silicone gel, with suspected debilitating side effects, to botched surgery, mounted. (FDA also has collected complaints about saline-solution breast implants, but these are not covered by the current moratorium.)

Manufacturers insist there's plenty of evidence to show silicone implants are low-risk. An FDA panel that sifted through volumes of data disagrees: It found last fall that the four manufacturers whose silicone implants were still on the market had not proven their safety.

The halt in silicone implants does not mean FDA now believes the devices are unsafe. It just means the agency cannot ensure they are safe. The general rule of thumb should be that if the implants aren't causing problems, women need not worry. Indeed, silicone implants — sacs of silicone gel used to refashion or reconstruct breasts — have a huge cheering section among women. Satisfied customers appear by far to outweigh ones who have experienced trouble. Plastic surgeons cite fewer than 100 problem cases in the literature.

But the seriousness of some reported side effects — from possible autoimmune disorders to connective-tissue diseases and inability to do normal breast-cancer checks — merit thorough review and consideration.

The breast-implant controversy also illustrates the long-term costs of regulatory and industry lapses. If systematic, credible safety studies had been undertaken from the first year breast implants were used, scientists assessing their risks today would have a solid body of fact, instead of horror-story innuendo and anecdote, upon which to base their decisions.

The TENNESSEAN
Nashville, Tennessee,
January 11, 1992

WHATEVER new information is available on breast implants needs to be made public quickly.

Women who have implants, whether they've had trouble or not, need answers to make intelligent choices with their doctors.

Food and Drug Commissioner David Kessler set off a new debate on silicone breast implants this week when he called on doctors to temporarily stop using them until a panel could review new data about safety concerns.

Under the circumstances, Kessler had little choice, though he's been roundly criticized by both proponents and detractors of the implants.

A series of lawsuits claiming that leaking implants can cause immune disorders sparked much of the drive to get the implants banned permanently. Yet, just two months ago, an FDA advisory panel agreed that the silicone implants should be kept on the market. The American Medical Association and the American Society of Plastic and Reconstructive Surgeons both have vouched for their safety.

While there have been lawsuits filed by women who question the safety, there are testimonials as well from those women who have had no problems.

The sole concern should be those women who elect the surgery. Some scoff at surgical breast enhancement. About 80% of the implants are for cosmetic purposes. But who is to say that a matter of self-esteem for some women is not an important health issue.

About 20% of the implants are for women who lost their breasts to cancer. It's a matter of well-being as well as self-esteem at a difficult period for those women.

Certainly, there are other forms of surgery for enhancement, including a saline implant and reconstruction using other tissues from the body.

Yet, the only answer for women with silicone implants is to provide the information at hand. A 45-day moratorium isn't a ban, but it's a long time to be concerned about one's health.

Having raised the question, the FDA needs to provide the information in as timely and responsible a manner as possible. ■

The Washington Post

Washington, D.C., January 8, 1992

THE FOOD and Drug Administration has taken exactly the right step on the volatile and suddenly visible issue of safety in breast implants, calling for a 45-day moratorium on the use and distribution of the silicon gel devices while the FDA assesses new evidence as to whether they are safe. No one can reasonably accuse FDA commissioner David Kessler of jumping to his conclusion too quickly on this serious matter or of failing to give the implant makers a sufficient hearing; on the contrary, following prolonged and emotional November hearings on the subject, an FDA advisory panel ruled that the devices should continue to be available and that manufacturers should take steps to present evidence—so far, lacking—that they were safe and effective. Dr. Kessler changed the ruling Monday, he said in a press conference, after receiving new information about implants that "increases our concerns about their safety," including, apparently, court papers from two pending lawsuits. He offered a lengthy list of questions on which findings are still unavailable—how long the implants last, whether they are related to incidence of several diseases and whether the percentage of women whose implants harden and become painful is closer to 10 percent or 70 percent.

Why is there so little safety information on breast implants, which have been on the market since 1963 and have been implanted in nearly 2 million women? It's partly accident. Between 1963 and 1976, medical devices were unregulated. In 1976, a safety law was enacted, and existing devices were classified as either needing or not needing a retroactive safety check. A dispute developed over whether breast implants should be ruled "class 3"—which would have required the safety studies now being demanded—or "class 2," which would not. That dispute continued *through 1988*, at which point manufacturers were given an additional 30 months to prepare their case. This brings us to the present, and high time, too.

Much has been heard in this process about the importance of implants to women who want them, both the 20 percent who have reconstruction after breast cancer surgery and the remaining 80 percent whose breasts are healthy but who, for a variety of reasons, want them made larger. Some satisfied patients, and some doctors, complain that the public is overreacting to isolated instances of severe complication, which, while horrific when described, are rare. But that's just the point: Nobody knows for sure how rare they are, and nobody will until someone does the necessary studies. Nor have implant manufacturers responded to this process in a way that inspires great confidence. One, Dow Corning Wright Corp., shut down its telephone hot line last week after the FDA accused it of misleading callers on risk levels; another was quoted as observing that the moratorium would not prevent continued sale of implants abroad. The subject cries out for more study. Women who want implants should be able to have safe ones.

The San Diego Union

San Diego, California, January 10, 1992

The Food and Drug Administration's call for a voluntary moratorium on silicone gel breast implants is a prudent caution which plastic surgeons, manufacturers and women ought to heed.

On the basis of new information suggesting possible adverse side effects from implantation, FDA Commissioner David Kessler has concluded there no longer is sufficient cause to consider the procedure "100 percent safe," as one manufacturer previously claimed. However, it is important to recognize that there still is insufficient evidence that the gel implants pose a significant danger.

Of the more than 10,000 women a month who have been receiving silicone implants, about 80 percent have done so for purely cosmetic reasons. Based on the new information about the potential risks, candidates for cosmetic surgery and their physicians should defer the operation for the time being.

The other 20 percent of implant patients have the operation for reconstructive purposes, usually after breast cancer surgery. While the psychological need for implants must be considered, patients and their doctors would be wise to realize that many safety concerns remain unanswered.

There was a clear need for the FDA's warning. The agency has received about 2,500 reports of illnesses or injuries associated with the implants. Although these reports are anecdotal, they cannot be discounted. Frank B. Vasey, a University of South Florida rheumatologist, has linked implants to a connective-tissue disease which causes pain in the joints, general swelling, fatigue and some respiratory illness.

Kessler announced that the FDA also has obtained internal documents from a Dow Corning Corp. subsidiary, the major manufacturer of implants, which he said raises "substantial concerns" about implant leaks and ruptures. Other studies indicate the implants interfere with mammography exams for breast cancer.

Kessler will reconvene an expert panel on implant safety within 45 days to review the new data. All four manufacturers of silicone implants and leaders in organized medicine have pledged to cooperate with the FDA's review.

Surgeons say the great majority of women who have had breast implants express satisfaction. Kessler noted that if they are not experiencing difficulties, "there is no need to consider removing the implants."

All the same, it makes sense to call a timeout on implants until their safety can be clearly established.

Portland Press Herald

Portland, Maine, January 11, 1992

The Food and Drug Administration's moratorium on silicon breast implants pending further study makes good sense both for women and their surgeons. FDA Commissioner David A. Kessler, himself a doctor, underscored the need for caution when he said his agency "cannot assure the safety of these devices at this time."

Continuing to insert the implants while those 10 words hang over the devices invites potential health problems for women and possible litigation for their doctors.

At the same time, the FDA has a responsibility to conduct its study of silicone implants expeditiously. The devices are more than the stuff of Hollywood starlet jokes. They are an important physical and psychological aid for millions of women, particularly those having reconstructive surgery after breast cancer. Two million women have them now.

In addition, women considering the implants need the FDA's help in reaching fully informed decisions about any risk involved.

Meanwhile, let's be cautious not only about the implants, but about overreacting. So far, doctors suggest that, while silicone implants require regular monitoring, women with no symptoms of silicone leakage or scar tissue need not consider having them removed.

The FDA will reconvene an expert panel to review new data about silicone implants between now and Feb. 20. The sooner the better.

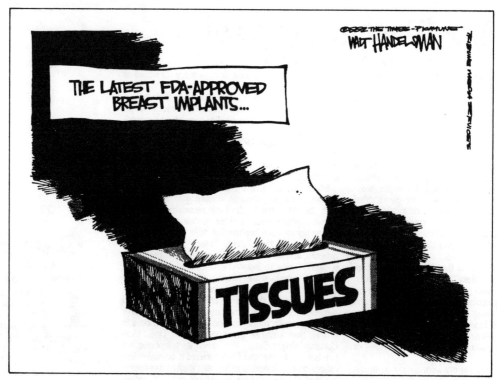

The Seattle Times

Seattle, Washington, January 15, 1992

AS more is learned about scientific disagreements among those involved in the manufacture of silicone gel breast implants, the decision last week by Food and Drug Commissioner David Kessler becomes clearer — and wiser.

Kessler ordered a moratorium on use of the implants while the FDA reviews available information, including new data from manufacturer's files, to determine whether they are safe for continued use.

Silicone gel implants have been in use for 30 years. As many as two million American women may have received the implants, 80 percent for nonmedical cosmetic reasons, the remainder for reconstruction after breast removal due to cancer.

Critics of the implants contend the silicone gel can leak and migrate to other parts of the body, causing inflammation or other serious side effects.

A consultant to the FDA said he was astonished by the lack of directly relevant scientific studies of silicone gel breast implants.

Reports this week revealed that implants were inserted in women before they were tested in animals and that subsequent animal testing may not even have been done in breast tissue.

Files of Dow Corning, the major manufacturer of the implants, show that company scientists argued — unsuccessfully — for studies that would assure the safety of implants.

Despite vigorous denials by Dow Corning, one conclusion is inescapable: Market demand, driven by women's desires and aided by willing plastic surgeons, was a far greater influence on company decisions than the nagging of their own cautious scientists.

The FDA moratorium is a welcome, if tardy, intervention on behalf of telling women the truth. It should lead, finally, to putting good science before good marketing.

LAS VEGAS REVIEW-JOURNAL

Las Vegas, Nevada, January 9, 1992

About 1 million American women have had silicon breast implants, most without complication — the Food and Drug Administration reports it has received only 3,400 complaints about the medical procedure. Yet on Monday, the FDA asked for a voluntary halt to the sale and use of the implants.

The move comes in response to recent information the agency has received about the safety of the devices. FDA chief David A. Kessler refused to label the implants dangerous, but critics claim growing evidence suggests they can rupture and cause auto-immune or connective tissue diseases. The American Medical Association and Dow Corning Wright, the largest manufacturer of the implants, dispute those contentions.

An FDA advisory panel will reconvene to examine allegations against the silicon implants and eventually make a recommendation about the future of the procedure.

While some of Kessler's melodramatic pronouncements needlessly scared thousands of women — "The FDA can not assure women of their safety at this time" — the agency's decision to stop short of an outright ban makes sense. It is the FDA's charge to keep the public informed about medical devices and procedures, and Kessler's announcement accomplished that. But a ban on silicon implants based on anecdotal evidence would amount to an arbitrary and capricious government intrusion.

CHICAGO Sun-Times

Chicago, Illinois, January 9, 1992

The Food and Drug Administration's request that plastic surgeons stop using silicone gel breast implants has touched off anguish and distress among the 2 million American women who have undergone the surgery.

Coming only two months after the FDA urged that the implants remain on the market pending further study, the reversal stirs fears of new data reflecting on the safety of the implants.

Without specifying the new data, the FDA says the evidence indicates the implants could cause autoimmune or connective tissue disorders.

That being the case, the FDA's call for a voluntary moratorium on these types of implants appears ambivalently weak-kneed.

Any evidence that justifies fanning new fears should have dictated a mandatory order.

Nothing in the FDA's warning casts doubt on the safety of saline-filled implants.

However, while the FDA reconvenes an advisory panel on the issue of silicone gel implants, doctors would be irresponsible not to obey the moratorium on gel implants, especially for the 80 percent that are not related to other medical problems.

The Record

Hackensack, New Jersey, January 7, 1992

THE Food and Drug Administration is right to ask doctors to stop using silicone gel breast implants until all of the information available on their effects has been thoroughly reviewed. The evidence to date suggests that major health risks are involved for some women who have had implants.

Fewer than one-quarter of the women who have the silicone gel implants do so to counter the effects of breast cancer or injuries. Most of the 150,000 implants done each year are done for cosmetic purposes. Women considering such unessential surgery shouldn't mind waiting a while longer until an informed decision can be made by the FDA. The agency has already received about 2,500 reports of illness or injury connected with the implants. About 2 million women have had them.

The new recommendation contradicts an FDA advisory panel that said last fall that the implants should stay on the market, even though their safety could not be guaranteed, because of the overriding public health benefits. That's questionable. There's no overriding public health benefit in having one's breasts enlarged. And women who are having reconstructive surgery after breast cancer have other options. There are implants available that are filled with salt water, instead of the rubbery silicone gel.

When potential risks are involved, there's no harm in waiting for a more definitive answer.

The Phoenix Gazette

Phoenix, Arizona, January 13, 1992

Is it science or bureaucratic paternalism that prompted the U.S. Food and Drug Administration to recommend that doctors stop using silicone gel breast implants until new safety information is assessed?

In November, an FDA advisory panel — the General and Plastic Surgery Devices Committee — recommended that the implants remain on the market while research into their safety continued.

The committee said manufacturers had failed to prove that the devices were safe — but there was nevertheless a compelling public health need to keep them available, particularly for reconstruction after breast cancer surgery.

The FDA should have followed the committee's advice. All that the current directive has done is frighten women who already have the implants and possibly discourage others from having needed cancer surgery because of the fear of disfigurement.

Although the moratorium is voluntary, if FDA Commissioner David Kessler's prediction that "all manufacturers and physicians will abide by it" comes true, the implants will quickly become unobtainable.

Dow Corning Wright, the largest manufacturer of silicone gel breast implants, said it was suspending shipment and sales of the devices. Less satisfactory implants filled with salt water will still be available.

The FDA says it has new concerns about the safety of the products as a result of a California lawsuit over a ruptured silicone implant that resulted in a $7 million federal jury award.

But evidence presented in lawsuits might or might not meet the standard of scientific validity.

About 1 million women in the United States have had implants in the past 30 years. Fewer than 1 percent of them have experienced problems. That's a record that beats many surgical procedures.

Questions abound. The FDA did not recommend a moratorium on silicone penile or testicular implants, joint replacements or insulin syringes that contain silicone materials. The agency's selectivity gives credence to feminists' charge that women are being subjected to a misguided effort to protect them from themselves.

No time limit was put on the moratorium, although Kessler said the agency would move as quickly as possible to settle the issue. Given the FDA's record of handwringing and delay, that is not cause for encouragement.

Until there is scientific evidence that the implants really are unsafe, the decision regarding their use should be left to patients and their physicians.

St. Petersburg Times

St. Petersburg, Florida, January 8, 1992

The Food and Drug Administration (FDA) moved Monday to halt the sale of silicone breast implants and their use by plastic surgeons in cosmetic and prosthetic surgery. The good news is that some 100,000 to 150,000 patients who might otherwise seek the procedure this year will be spared exposure to unknown medical risks. The bad news is that 2-million American women have already opted for a purely elective procedure that may pose serious health threats.

"The FDA cannot assure the safety of these devices at this time," said David Kessler, FDA commissioner. He requested that doctors and manufacturers wait until a panel of experts had studied new data before resuming the use of silicone-filled implants. Implants filled with a saline solution are not affected by the regulatory agency's request.

Kessler's list of belated FDA questions about silicone implants reveals a shocking disregard for product safety. He said the agency doesn't know how often the implants leak, what materials they release into the body, whether they increase the risk of cancer or whether crippling auto-immune and connective tissue diseases may be linked to their use. The FDA can't even say how long the implants should last and under what conditions they might rupture. Polyurethane coverings used on the devices pose another set of questions; again, the FDA has no answers for consumers.

Despite these critical unknowns, silicone implants have been manufactured and profitably marketed for 30 years. Women who trust their doctors — and why shouldn't they? — have been encouraged to accept the devices as a safe cosmetic option or as permanent prostheses after cancer surgery. Only recently have women learned that the presence of implants interferes with mammography, a life-saving tool in breast cancer detection.

Even now, Kessler is considering an ill-conceived proposal to keep implants on the market for women who have a "psychological" need for them. While the need may be real, it is based on women's false assumption that they are making a fully informed, safe choice.

Sadly, this is not the first time that elective health care options for women have been offered as harmless, only to be proved otherwise. The most obvious parallel is the Dalkon Shield, once touted as a highly effective, convenient option for birth control. As with silicone implants, women using the Dalkon Shield reported side effects for years before their complaints were taken seriously. How much damage could have been avoided? The question is destined to be repeated until the medical community and the FDA put the safety of women before the interests of those who profit from inadequately tested health care products.

Breast Implants Curbed by FDA

The Food and Drug Administration April 16, 1992 ended a moratorium on the insertion of silicone-gel breast implants that had been in effect since January. It said limited use of the devices would be permitted for women who agreed to participate in clinical studies on their safety. The action adhered closely to a February recommendation by an FDA panel.

Under the FDA's plan, silicone-gel implants would become available in three stages. In the first stage, women with ruptured or leaking implants would be able to obtain new ones. So would an estimated 9,000 women whose scheduled breast operations were put on hold by the January moratorium.

The second stage would provide implants to women who had an "urgent" physical or psychological need for breast reconstruction. Such patients included burn victims and women who had had surgery for breast cancer.

In the third stage, a few thousand women would be allowed to use implants for breast enlargement. But the number would be far lower than the estimated 100,000 women who had received the implants annually in the late 1980s for cosmetic reasons.

All women who got new implants would have to participate in follow-up studies conducted by both the FDA and manufacturers. In addition, the FDA planned to keep a permanent registry of recipients.

"We know more about the life span of automobile tires than we do about the longevity of breast implants," FDA Commissioner David A. Kessler said at a Washington, D.C. news conference April 16. "The data on failed implants that we've seen so far raises concerns." He added, "No one should think we are resuming business as usual. These are not approved devices, and any woman who wants one will have to be in clinical studies."

Rep. Ted Weiss (D, N.Y.), who in 1991 had spearheaded efforts to get the FDA to investigate silicone-gel implants, April 16 called the agency's decision "a reasonable compromise." "Any woman who now chooses implants will understand that she is participating in a massive experiment," he said.

The American Society of Plastic and Reconstructive Surgeons applauded the FDA's move. "This is the first sign that science, logic and compassion are being returned to the review process for these devices," said society president Norman Cale April 16.

Canadian Health Minister Benoit Bouchard April 16 announced a six-month extension of the existing moratorium on the use of silicone breast implants. More than 150,000 Canadian women had received the implants.

Bouchard's announcement came in response to a report by an independent committee set up to study the breast implant controversy, headed by Dr. Cornelia Baines of the University of Toronto. The minister rejected as potentially discriminatory the panel's key recommendation, a compromise that would allow women who needed reconstructive surgery and older women to continue using silicone implants. Of the two women in North America who had had implants since they first went on the market in the 1960s, 80% had them for cosmetic reasons.

Bouchard announced that the federal Laboratory Centre for Disease Control would conduct a $1 million epidemiological study of the health risks of breast implants. The government also commissioned a survey of women who had had the implants, to determine their experiences with the devices.

Winnipeg Free Press

Winnipeg, Manitoba, April 21, 1992

Health Minister Benoit Bouchard wants a Canadian solution to the nasty problem of breast implants. Nothing could be more Canadian than the thoughts of the committee he asked to think through the dilemma of health vs. well-being. The compromise it suggested — to allow silicone implants for breast reconstruction, but not breast enhancement — is unlikely to be improved upon through another moratorium. It is unfortunate that the health minister could not accept it or the several other good suggestions from Canadian experts.

The compromise solution is akin to the thoughts of a U.S. panel of experts made public in February. It is also the position the U.S. Food and Drug Administration has adopted. As FDA commissioner David Kessler acknowledged, continued disapproval of the gel-filled sacs to create bigger breasts is not a return to business as usual. Restoring approval of silicone breast implants for women who have lost breasts to cancer or other injuries is not risk-free but it is compassionate. It is not, as Mr. Bouchard suggests, unduly discriminatory. The distinction is made on product usage; the distinction is not drawn primarily between women.

The Canadian committee's other suggestion — to limit implants to women over age 40 — is more puzzling and more likely to be the sort of Charter violation that Mr. Bouchard wants to avoid. Physicians have used that age barrier in recommending other procedures, however. The health problems experienced by some women after breast implantation became evident very soon after surgery. Age will not protect women from unfortunate complications; nor should pain and discomfort be less regarded in older women.

The committee's other suggestion should not be hard to implement, but Mr. Bouchard is balking. The committee suggests that a national registry of women who have received breast implants would be helpful. The health minister wonders whether governments can force registration and sort out with provinces the jurisdictional questions. How foolish. How Canadian.

If anything should have been learned from the breast implant fiasco, it was the need to track health problems of people who have unusual devices placed in their bodies. The FDA has proposed that the makers of 35 kinds of devices be required to keep such registries. Instead, Mr. Bouchard will give Canadian women a toll-free telephone number. That's only slightly better than nothing.

The health minister has given himself and his officials another six months to craft a better Canadian policy. The department has badly mishandled the problems of implants for several years running. Mr. Bouchard was wise to appoint an independent committee. He would be wiser to heed its advice.

TULSA WORLD

Tulsa, Oklahoma, April 20, 1992

THE FOOD and Drug Administration faced a controversial question last week: whether to continue to allow silicone breast implants.

The decision and its background presented a classic case of how politics and greedy interests can influence decisions that are supposed to be based on scientific judgment and the public welfare.

The breast implants had been in use for more than a generation with a high percentage of satisfaction. There were, of course, some bad cases that could have been predicted in any extensive surgical procedure.

The decision was forced on the FDA by a publicity blitz backed largely by damage-suit lawyers. After a couple of successful lawsuits involving implants, the attorneys smelled more business if they could stir up controversy on the subject and encourage more claims.

There were a few horror stories of breast operations gone wrong. But thousands of women, fully advised of the risks, were willing to take their chances.

It was a tough one for the FDA. Satisfy the damage-suit hunters and the self-described "consumer" groups. Or satisfy women who wanted to choose for themselves whether to accept the small risk involved.

The FDA ducked. It banned the implants for cosmetic purposes, but allowed them to continue under certain conditions for women whose breasts had been removed or disfigured by accident or surgery.

The compromise doesn't make sense. But what can you expect when a supposedly scientific decision is made on such obvious political grounds?

AUGUSTA HERALD

Augusta, Georgia, April 22, 1992

Federal Food and Drug Administration Commissioner David Kessler finally defined under what conditions American women can have silicone gel breast implants: When they need reconstructive surgery following a serious illness or accident that causes severe deformity; and then only as participants in scientific studies designed to answer questions about safety.

Women can't have it for cosmetic purposes, even if they are fully apprised of the risks and are willing to be a part of the studies. Why not? If the surgery can be made available to some women under the new guidelines, why not to others?

As Augusta plastic surgeon, Dr. Randy Smith says, "If it is a good device, it should be available to all. If it is injurious, it ought not be available to anyone." And isn't it discrimination if it's not?

It seems silicone gel implants are being taken over by proponents of Political Correctness, using the FDA as their instrument of control. Implants for cancer patients are acceptable, but cosmetology patients who want breast augmentation are deemed frivolous, demeaning themselves and their gender.

But that's a social judgment, not a medical decision. Medical decisions should be left to doctors and their patients, not a federal bureaucracy. This is government meddling of the worst sort.

Let's not forget the case against silicone gel is shaky at best. It's been around for several decades and the Augusta area medical community, among many others, has enjoyed great success, with virtually no serious complaints.

This isn't surprising. An enormous body of evidence has built up over the years showing silicone gel implants to be safe, yet the FDA has chosen to respond only to recent anecdotal — not scientific — evidence indicating it might, in some cases, cause health-damaging side effects.

That's a small reed to rest the FDA's takeover of physicians' authority, but at least saline gels are still available for cosmetic breast surgery. But perhaps not for long. The FDA will take a "closer look" at them next year.

The Washington Post

Washington, D.C., April 20, 1992

TO EVALUATE the new Food and Drug Administration guidelines on breast implants, announced last week by FDA head David Kessler, it's important to compare the new formulas with the situation they replace. That situation was not the rosy one of free, fully informed consumer choice and painless, near-universal satisfaction portrayed by many plastic surgeons and implant manufacturers. Instead, women who thought they were in a position of making that free choice were in fact lacking crucial information that manufacturers had repeatedly failed to seek.

Basically, the new guidelines create a process by which every woman with implants becomes part of a comprehensive safety study on their effects. Women who want the devices for medical reasons (to reconstruct a breast they have lost) get priority in the trials over women who want to make their healthy breasts larger. These last were an estimated 80 percent of the previous market. But that may change in light of the case studies and unanswered concerns that have now been aired: whether implants interfere with mammogram detection of breast cancers, whether they leak silicone into the body and cause rheumatoid or autoimmune disease, whether and how often they cause hardness or loss of sensation. Women who already have the implants and have not experienced such problems are advised not to have them removed, but rather to contact a plastic surgeon and join a national registry so their experiences can become part of the data base.

To the criticism that the government is inappropriately interfering with women's freedom to have implants for any reason they like—cosmetic or otherwise—it's important to reiterate that the government is merely giving women the tools to make that calculation in the future. It wouldn't have been necessary if not for the repeated and long-term abrogation of this responsibility by those most directly responsible—manufacturers and doctors.

The FDA notes that fear of liability is a strong force *dissuading* manufacturers from aggressive investigation of possible safety problems such as implant ruptures; so is fear of losing customers. As for the doctors: In March, with the public furor at its peak, Wall Street Journal reporter Jane Berentson asked five plastic surgeons about possible implants. She wrote that "the medical care in these offices is accompanied by a healthy dose of salesmanship" and that, despite the public debate, none mentioned the mammogram or autoimmune concerns the FDA had raised. Many plastic surgeons testified in winter hearings that they are more responsible than that, but they can't and don't regulate their colleagues. In stepping in, the FDA filled a harmful gap.

Michigan MD Sparks Euthanasia Furor

A retired pathologist from the Detroit area, Jack Kevorkian, touched off a medical ethics controversy June 4, 1990, when he admitted that he had helped a woman to commit suicide by supplying her with a lethal dose of intravenous drugs.

Kevorkian told police that earlier that day he had driven Janet Adkins, 54, of Portland, Ore. to a suburban Detroit park in his van, where he hooked her up to a "suicide machine" of his invention by inserting an intravenous needle into her arm. Adkins had then pushed a button that released a fatal combination of drugs into her bloodstream, Kevorkian said.

Adkins left a suicide note stating that she had Alzheimer's disease and did not want to see the disease progress any further. Her husband, Ronald Adkins, said he supported his wife's decision.

Although Michigan did not have a state law prohibiting doctor-assisted suicide, many other states – including Oregon – did. Medical experts said the act also violated the American Medical Association's code of ethics, which prohibited doctors from actively helping their patients to die.

Kevorkian, an advocate of euthanasia, had long been regarded as a medical maverick. He had drawn criticism in the past for his suggestions that medical researchers perform experiments on death-row prisoners.

A state district judge in Clarkston, Mich. Dec. 13, 1990 dismissed murder charges against Kevorkian.

Kevorkian had been charged with first-degree murder Dec. 3, in connection with the death of Janet Adkins.

The judge, Oakland County District Court Judge Gerald McNally, ruled that prosecutors did not have a case because there was evidence that Kevorkian had planned or carried out Adkins's death. McNally noted that there was no specific law in Michigan prohibiting a person from assisting in a suicide.

Prosecutors in Oakland County said Dec. 14 that they would drop their case against Kevorkian. "This is an issue on which there is yet no societal consensus, and the legislature is the appropriate forum for dealing with those questions," said County Prosecutor Richard Thompson.

Thompson said, however, that he would seek to extend a temporary restraining order that had been in effect since shortly after Adkins's death that prohibited Kevorkian from using his suicide device.

Oakland County, Mich. Circuit Court Judge Alice L. Gilbert Feb. 5, 1991 issued a ruling barring Kevorkian from using the suicide device he had invented. Gilbert ruled that Kevorkian had "flagrantly violated" all medical standards and that "his real goal is self service rather than patient service."

Kevorkian Sept. 26, 1992 assisted a fifth person to commit suicide. The death occurred in Michigan. The deceased, Lois F. Hawes, a 52-year-old woman with terminal lung cancer, placed a mask over her face and turned on a canister of carbon monoxide.

Kevorkian assisted another suicide Nov. 23, 1992 and then two more Dec. 15. The deaths brought his total of aided suicides up to eight.

The woman who took her life in November was Catherine Andreyev, 46, a cancer patient. The two women who died in December were Marguerite Tate, 70, who had been suffering from amyotrophic lateral sclerosis, and Marcella Lawrence, 67, who had had heart disease, emphysema and a failing liver.

A few hours after Kevorkian aided the two women Dec. 15, Michigan Gov. John M. Engler (R) signed a law that made assisting a suicide a felony punishable by four years in prison and a $2,000 fine.

The law, which would take effect in 90 days, was a temporary measure that would expire after two years. It also created a state commission to study the issue of suicide.

A county prosecutor in East Lansing, Mich. March 5, 1993 said he would not bring charges against Kevorkian for assisting an elderly man in killing himself.

The Phoenix Gazette
Phoenix, Arizona, December 17, 1990

The case against a Michigan physician who invented a machine that enabled a woman to take her own life was weak legally and debatable morally.

Last year, Dr. Jack Kevorkian provided 54-year-old Janet Adkins, who was suffering from Alzheimer's disease, with a machine to inject herself with a lethal drug.

Oakland County prosecutor Richard Thompson charged the doctor with first-degree murder, citing a 1920 Michigan Supreme Court decision in a case in which a man who mixed poison and placed it near his wife at her request was convicted of murder.

However, as Kevorkian's attorney pointed out, Michigan has no specific law against assisting suicide. Clarkston District Judge Gerald McNally agreed and threw out the murder charge.

Admittedly, Kevorkian, a retired pathologist, has his own agenda as an advocate for doctor-assisted suicide. "What happens to me is immaterial. The time has come for this thing," he said.

In fact, it is nothing new for physicians to abide by the wishes of hopelessly ill patients who want to be permitted to die. Usually it is a private agreement between the patient or the patient's family and the physician.

The difference in this case is that the patient's illness had not yet reached the terminal stage. She purposely enlisted the physician's cooperation before the disease had robbed her of the ability to act in her own behalf.

Nor can it be argued that he took advantage of an irrational mind. It is hard to imagine a more deliberative act. The patient and her husband traveled from Portland, Ore., to Michigan because the state is one of the few that does not explicitly make it a crime to help someone commit suicide.

The medical profession will have to deal with the issue of whether physician-assisted suicides are ethical, or whether they infringe upon the Hippocratic Oath and its injunction "to do no harm."

But at this time, under Michigan law, and by ethically defensible standards, the doctor committed no crime.

Wisconsin ⚓ State Journal
Madison, Wisconsin, December 19, 1990

Janet Atkins believed she had a "right to die," even though she could still think, talk and play tennis up until the day Dr. Jack Kevorkian rigged up a suicide machine that gave her a lethal injection of drugs.

The parents of Nancy Cruzan believed their daughter had a "right to die," too. It was a right earned by spending seven years in a persistent vegetative state, curled up in a hospital bed, unresponsive to almost all stimulation.

Now that a Michigan judge has dismissed murder charges against Kevorkian, and a Missouri judge has given the OK to disconnect Cruzan from her life support, the ethical fog surrounding the issue of euthanasia may be lifted.

Clearly, both cases fall under the broad heading of "right to die," but that's where the similarities end. Atkins, 54, could have enjoyed months or even years more of productive life, because the Alzheimer's disease she so feared had not yet taken over her brain. Cruzan, 33, had been kept alive with chemical nutrition from a surgically implanted tube since the car accident left her oblivious to the world around her.

Atkins' brain functioned; Cruzan's did not. That distinction is crucial as the "right to die" debate is renewed — and as society searches for an ethically consistent answer to a related dilemma, abortion.

Two months ago in Iowa City, Iowa, an international conference of ethicists and philosphers debated a model Uniform Determination of Life Protection Act. It was written by Hans-Martin Sass, a Georgetown University professor who may have found an answer to the question, "When does human life begin?"

Sass suggests starting the life clock when the unborn baby is old enough to emit measurable brain waves. Sass pegs the moment at about 10 weeks after conception; some medical researchers put it at eight weeks. The beauty of Sass' proposal is its combination of scientific knowledge and ethical reasoning. Most states accept the cessation of brain waves as evidence of death; could not their inception become evidence of life?

That brings us back to the sad cases of Atkins and Cruzan. Atkins' decision to kill herself — with the morally repugnant assistance of Dr. Kevorkian — is a step too far. It is one thing to accede to the death of a woman locked in an irreversible coma; it is quite another to allow doctors to aid in premature suicides.

Cruzan's case was both helpless and hopeless; Atkins' case was neither. The difference between the two may help lawmakers codify the right to die so that in the future, such heartbreaking decisions can be made where they belong: in private.

CHICAGO Sun-Times
Chicago, Illinois, December 20, 1990

When Dr. Jack Kevorkian was sprung by a Michigan judge from a first degree murder charge in the "assisted" suicide of a woman with Alzheimer's disease, his lawyer, Geoffrey Fieger, said:

"[Kevorkian] stated for the whole world that there was a need for the terminally ill to die with dignity. This proves he was right."

Hardly.

What happened in the Michigan courtroom has to be narrowly construed, and in no way can it be judged to be a victory for Kevorkian's cause. The judge simply ruled that Kevorkian couldn't be tried because Michigan has no law against assisting in suicide.

Significantly, the judge noted that state legislatures and not the courts must address such right-to-die issues, including whether assisted suicide should be legal. And he urged the Michigan legislature to do so.

That's as it should be. As imperfect as they are, legislatures remain the best institutions a democracy has for reflecting whatever societal consensus there might be on such issues.

Meanwhile, nothing that happened in the courtroom changed the essence of what Kevorkian did: He hooked a woman—not in pain and apparently not close to the final stages of a terminal illness—to a machine of his making, and then watched while she pushed a button and died. Acting simultaneously in conflicting roles of euthanasia advocate and a professional healer, this physician helped someone who wasn't his patient, someone he barely knew, take her life.

If this was not a crime, it was certainly abhorrent.

Newsday
New York City, New York, December 5, 1990

The ghoulish case of Dr. Jack Kevorkian and his suicide machine is now about to be heard in that uncomfortable theater, a criminal courthouse. It doesn't belong there.

The prosecutor in Oakland County, Mich. has charged Kevorkian with first-degree murder for helping an Oregon woman who suffered from Alzheimer's disease, Janet Adkins, to kill herself. Last June, Kevorkian hooked her up to his homemade death machine. When Adkins pressed a switch, lethal chemicals dripped into her veins and she died — just as she had wished.

In Michigan, a statute says that murder by poisoning is first-degree murder. It was so in 1920, when a husband left poison by the bedside of his wife, who wished to die. State courts have since affirmed that application of the Michigan law.

Prosecutor Richard Thompson says he feels that to uphold the law as he is sworn to do — and to prevent his state from tacitly approving of suicide and of those who assist in it — he must prosecute Kevorkian.

But is a criminal trial the forum for sorting out the legal, moral, religious and ethical issues posed by this episode? Can — or should — a jury of 12 ordinary people speak for society in either condemning Kevorkian or sanctioning his conduct?

Certainly not. A criminal trial, with its guilty-or-innocent, black-or-white outcome, cannot assess the shades of gray in this case. Legislative bodies — elected by the people, with days, months and sometimes years to debate and shape laws — are far better equipped to perform that task.

Kevorkian is dangerous; he has advocated medical experimentation on death-row inmates and other unorthodox, unethical schemes. In the Adkins case, he was not a benevolent physician simply allowing a terminally ill patient to die in dignity. He helped put to death a woman who was not on the verge of death, and who was not suffering inordinately from her disease. He was wrong. Doctors should heal not kill.

But trying him for murder might result in an unpredictable outcome that could well prove the adage that bad cases make bad law.

The Times-Picayune
New Orleans, Louisiana, November 5, 1992

The question of doctor-assisted suicide got another public airing this week as proponents and opponents debated the controversial and emotionally charged issue before leaders of the American Bar Association.

Most of the emotion came from advocates who pleaded with the ABA's policy-making House of Delegates to approve a proposal encouraging the enactment of state laws "permitting voluntary aid in dying to terminally ill persons who request such aid."

But the panel overwhelmingly said no to the proposal, similar versions of which have been opposed by the American Medical Association.

The measure was introduced by Bert Tigerman, a Beverly Hills, Calif., lawyer who recounted the suicide of his brother-in-law, who shot himself after learning he had cancerous brain tumors. "These things should not have to happen," he said.

Also appearing in support of the proposal was television journalist Betty Rollin, whose book "Last Wish" told about aiding her mother's death.

"You have to rescue these people," she said. "This is an emergency, not a theoretical situation."

In contrast, attorney John Pickering based his opposition on a worrisome issue. "Once doctors have a license to kill, it becomes a duty to kill," he said. "There is a bright line between refusing medical treatment . . . and intentional killing."

Mr. Pickering's concern was echoed by Dr. Nancy Dickey, representing the American Medical Association. She said such legislation would tell older Americans they have a duty to die.

The phenomenon of physician-assisted suicide has become a topic of widespread interest in recent years largely because of Dr. Jack Kevorkian, who used "suicide machines" of his own design in assisting three of his patients to die.

Dubbed "Dr. Death," the 63-year-old retired pathologist has been suspended from practicing medicine and a grand jury has indicted him for murder in the two most recent cases. Michigan does not have a law specifically against doctor-assisted suicides.

The increasing number of aging Americans makes the final solution espoused by Dr. Kevorkian and others a poignant issue for our time. But to race down the path chosen by the former Michigan practitioner can be to slam the door on hope.

One of the women Dr. Kevorkian helped to die last October was suffering from a painful but not terminal pelvic disease. Perhaps she could have gotten relief had she sought another medical opinion. And many elderly people are known to suffer from depression, which, left untreated, could lead to suicide.

In cases where illnesses are deemed hopeless by doctors, elderly victims often resort to suicide as a way to end their lives with dignity. The decision by terminal patients that life is no longer worth living is one that deserves understanding and compassion, not condemnation.

But we agree with the ABA and AMA that a physician's options should not include playing an active part in a patient's suicide.

The Providence Journal
Providence, Rhode Island, November 5, 1991

When asked recently whether he intended to repeat the use of his famous suicide machine, Dr. Jack Kevorkian replied, "Of course I'll use it again." And then added for emphasis, "I'm a doctor!"

It is that latter phrase which concerns us on this morning when voters in Washington State are invited to legalize "physician-assisted" suicide. If this proposition should pass, Washington will not only possess the most open-ended euthanasia law in the United States, but in the whole world. Nowhere on earth, not even in the Netherlands, do physicians who help people kill themselves enjoy the sanction of the law. Washington's vote will be closely watched by other states.

To be sure, there are limitations in this instance: People must be terminally ill, and understand what they're doing, before doctors may dispatch them. But there are loopholes, too: Any physician — and that includes plastic surgeons, radiologists, psychiatrists and pathologists — would be eligible to participate. How long, we wonder, before optometrists and podiatrists?

The right to die is a complicated, emotional issue. There is no question that just as modern medical technology has prolonged human life, it has prolonged needless suffering as well. We believe that physicians should have the qualified right to make terminal patients as comfortable as possible — including the use of pain-killing opiates such as heroin — and to allow patients to die passively — to "turn off the machines" — when they are clearly beyond recovery.

There is a difference, however, between nature taking its course and physicians playing God. At some point, and especially for older people whose care is expensive and whose families are impatient, the right to die might easily be transformed into the duty to perish. And in Holland, physicians are tacitly permitted to decide if the "quality of life" is sufficiently bleak to mandate euthanasia without consulting the patient's family!

Dr. Jack Kevorkian, whose zealotry and vulgar self-promotion have concentrated public attention on this issue, recently "assisted" the suicides of two women who were clearly not terminally ill. It seems evident that physicians, who take an oath to sustain human life, now stand at an ethical crossroads; and that public policy on matters of life and death is not wisely decided by TV commercials and voter propositions.

The Hartford Courant
Hartford, Connecticut, August 21, 1991

Medicine does not cope with death and the wish to die as well as it does with treating illnesses and prolonging life. Yet the more that technology advances, the more complex becomes the debate over the right to die and euthanasia.

A controversial best-seller, "Final Exit," goes to the heart of the issue by describing how to commit suicide. It is a needed but potentially dangerous book — a commentary on society's gradual acceptance of the reality that many terminally ill people want to end their lives at a time and in a setting of their choosing.

The book contains detailed instructions on committing suicide and dealing with insurance and other matters. It also describes alternatives for the terminally ill, such as hospice care.

Author Derek Humphry, the executive director of the Hemlock Society, is right in arguing that many people do not want to drag out the dying process and face a death full of pain. The society he leads wants to take the issue out of the hands of judges, theologians, philosophers and reluctant doctors.

Mr. Humphry's critics are equally correct that a suicide manual could be misused by depressed or otherwise unstable people. There is also a fear that murderers might use the techniques.

But the bigger issue is how to better deal with dying. Doctors can prolong "life" well beyond the moment of natural death. It wasn't until the parents of Karen Ann Quinlan asked in 1975 that she be disconnected from her respirator that the right-to-die debate became public. Since then, courts have gradually accepted a patient's explicit request that heroic treatment be ended, or not started, and are now upholding a family's right to order a similar ending.

Many critics of the right-to-die movement claim that the other side's true goal is euthanasia. Should doctors or anyone else help terminally ill patients end their lives? Is there a profound difference between allowing patients to die by unplugging a respirator and giving them the means to commit suicide?

The fact that "Final Exit" is selling so well indicates that too many people don't trust medicine to help them face these issues. Death and dying should be discussed openly by doctor, patient and family. Reading the book could enhance such discussions.

THE SAGINAW NEWS
Saginaw, Michigan, December 29, 1992

Some people think Jack Kevorkian, Michigan's notorious "Dr. Death," is not in his right mind.

It does take an unusual bent of character to make helping people die your life's work.

So far, though, Kevorkian has proved himself quicker and smarter than the Michigan Legislature, faint praise though that is.

At practically the same time Gov. John Engler signed the bill outlawing, at least temporarily, the work Kevorkian does, he helped two more stricken women go on their final way with doses of carbon monoxide.

Stop me if you can, Kevorkian was saying. And no one could. The law itself doesn't kick in until next April, and who knows how many more willing suicides he'll have helped to kick off by then?

Kevorkian may never go to trial or to jail under the law. His attorneys plan to challenge the measure. Among their pertinent questions: How can the state prosecute someone for an action — assisting a suicide — the state hasn't decided is a crime yet?

But there's more, all arising from the Legislature's rush into an arena where angels of mercy as well as death fear to tread.

The assisted-suicide bill expires at the end of 1994. By then, Michigan is supposed to have the considered judgment of a panel of experts and interested parties, such as the Civil Liberties Union and Right to Life of Michigan, to help decide whether to maintain the ban.

Other legal and ethical events, however, may intrude before then.

It is always risky business to write legislation that, in effect, pertains to a single individual. There is no one else in Michigan advertising for suicide clients.

But there are many, many others in Michigan who must deal with the most difficult questions of life and death every day. Physicians and families alike come to a time when they must decide whether to continue painful or artificial measures, or to let nature take its own, more peaceful, course with a suffering patient.

"If a person chooses to have plugs pulled, the bill may make anyone who assists in that guilty of a felony," speculated Patrick Clarke of Ypsilanti, who serves on a State Bar medico-legal study committee.

Many people — although not necessarily a majority — feel revulsion at Kevorkian's practices. It will be different, however, when they find their doctor — or themselves — challenged under the Kevorkian bill.

Kevorkian has taken advantage of the absence of clear legal guidance on this issue. But the question of the time to die is a moral and ethical one not susceptible to strict legal resolution.

The state would do better to just stay out of it, and suffer the Kevorkians if it must. The potential alternative is unnecessary suffering for thousands of others. The Legislature should not wait for the first prosecution of a family doctor to pull the plug on a hasty, misguided bill. Then it can wait for the study commission's report.

The Salt Lake Tribune
Salt Lake City, Utah, December 21, 1992

The true danger of Dr. Jack Kevorkian, the "medicide" pioneer commonly known as "Dr. Death," was revealed, appropriately enough, by his own lawyer last week. Geoffrey Fieger said of his ghoulish client, "Dr. Kevorkian told me that he is held to a higher standard."

Evidently, that means "a higher standard" than the one adopted by Michigan lawmakers, who are outlawing assisted suicides in the wake of Dr. Kevorkian's death spree of the past 2½ years. The legislation was signed into law last Tuesday by Gov. John Engler, but it doesn't become effective until March 30 — which means Dr. Kevorkian has until then to practice his sinister brand of medicine legally.

The "higher standard" undercurrent of the assisted-suicide movement is the most chilling. The fear is that authority figures, including doctors, will use the legalization of euthanasia to decide who is worthy of living and who is not. The image of Nazi Germany comes to mind. The term "higher standard" thus becomes a red flag in this ethical debate, and it is no surprise that Dr. Kevorkian should be the one waving it.

The issue of assisted suicides for terminally ill patients is a serious one, and it has already received public airings in the United States. Voters in the state of Washington considered an assisted-suicide initiative in 1991; voters in California did the same last month. In both instances, they rejected the proposals by a 54%-46% margin, but it is clear that this is no longer an issue that merely hovers on the fringe of serious debate.

As the issue moves more toward mainstream discussion, however, Dr. Kevorkian is still firmly occupying the fringe. Last Tuesday, he facilitated the suicides of two more women, bringing to eight the number who have died with his help in the last 2½ years. Michigan officials tried to prosecute him for the first three deaths but couldn't because their state lacked an assisted-suicide law.

Michigan now has become the 28th state to outlaw the practice. Gov. Engler signed the bill the same day Dr. Kevorkian assisted in the carbon monoxide deaths of a 70-year-old and a 67-year-old. The timing was hardly coincidental; the governor wanted to make the point that he was responding specifically to the actions of Dr. Kevorkian, who seems to enjoy his jousts with the state.

Indeed, a *Los Angeles Times* profile of Dr. Kevorkian earlier this month quotes him as saying that "the stage is set for fun" in the wake of the Michigan Legislature's passage of its bill. The article contained other disturbing items about the 64-year-old bachelor, among them the charge that his assisted suicides have not been easy deaths. The county coroner who investigated the first six said the carbon monoxide poisoning "was probably less humane than the cyanide poisoning used in Auschwitz."

Whether Americans are moving closer to accepting the concept of assisted suicides, there clearly is no place on the landscape for a free-wheeling, one-man experimentation campaign like the one Dr. Kevorkian is conducting. The man is a menace and must be stopped. The new law that Gov. Engler just signed represents a high enough standard for the people of Michigan, without Jack Kevorkian invoking his own.

THE INDIANAPOLIS NEWS
Indianapolis, Indiana,
March 10, 1993

After two strikes, proposed living will legislation is out for this session of the Indiana General Assembly.

House Bill 1053 was defeated by a 52-48 vote this week. Last week the legislation failed to receive a 51-vote majority, on a 49-48 vote, with some members absent.

Because it was not defeated by 51 votes, the legislation was brought back for another vote.

This double defeat indicates that some members of the General Assembly are wisely taking a cautious approach to this proposal.

A number of doctors have warned that the legislation could be abused in favor of euthanasia, on grounds that the use of some language could be broadly interpreted. The legislation would change state law to permit a person to designate the withdrawal of medical care and food and water in cases of "incurable injury, disease or condition."

But that vague language can be applied to a wide range of medical problems from which people can recover and live productive lives for several more years.

Dr. Robert Heimburger is one of several doctors who have raised warning flags about the vagueness of the legislation.

He is a retired neurosurgeon and teacher at the Indiana University School of Medicine. "Many injuries, diseases and conditions are incurable, but are compatible with many more years of good quality life," he said in objecting to the legislation. "Examples are Parkinsonism, diabetes, Alzheimer's and even old age."

Other doctors have made the same point and have warned about potential abuse of living wills.

Dr. Heimburger and other physicians have recommended that any new legislation be written with the help of doctors who have dealt with this matter on a regular basis. That wisdom from doctors who have worked at the bedside of dying patients could be invaluable.

Meanwhile, it is comforting that so many members of the Indiana House of Representatives are wise enough to take a cautious approach to opening the door to death and closing any doors on life.

THE ARIZONA REPUBLIC
Phoenix, Arizona, February 8, 1993

JACK Kevorkian, Dr. Death to most, last week loosed his instrument of destruction on two more people, carrying out a lethal personal agenda in the name of humanity.

Two elderly people, both dying of cancer, ended their lives in Michigan with the help of the former pathologist and his "suicide machine." Dr. Kevorkian's death toll now stands at 11, and it is likely to increase as the window of opportunity for assisted suicides closes.

Dr. Death has practiced his trade in Michigan because that state has no law against assisted suicides. He was charged with murder on three occasions, but the cases were dismissed. Effective March 30, however, assisted suicide will be banned for 15 months while a commission studies the issue.

It is a law of questionable soundness, signed by Gov. John Engler in December only hours after two women, numbers seven and eight for the energetic Dr. Kevorkian, took their lives. Legal authorities predict that the law, which many think could have the unintended consequence of discouraging commonly administered treatment, will be ruled invalid as soon as it can be tested in court.

No law, however, is likely to deter the work of the Grim Reaper's disciple, Dr. Kevorkian, who proclaims that he is held to a higher standard. He seems certain to continue to play an active role in drawing the curtain on other people's lives.

Beneath the tawdry and offensive exploits of Dr. Kevorkian, however, are issues of enormous importance that need to be carefully assessed. Should people whose condition is beyond hope, whose human frailties entail the certainty of unrelieved pain, long endured and ending in death — should such people be allowed, with the help of their doctor, to end their lives? Should it be an established right, legal and God-given, to die at the hands of a physician when the quality of one's life has diminished significantly, suffering has become unbearable, but death is not near?

Surely, when extraordinary measures are required to sustain life and little chance exists that the sufferer will emerge from a vegetative state, an ethical argument can be made for medical restraint and early death. But the degree of certainty about death varies. Several of Dr. Kevorkian's "patients" were chronically ill, but not terminally ill — a difference that seriously clouds the right-to-die issue.

It is no secret that physicians, moved to mercy, have prescribed the means by which terminally ill patients could end their agony with dignity. In extreme cases, no rational person will judge them harshly for having done so.

But Dr. Kevorkian's gleeful pursuit of his mission of death makes a mockery of the medical profession. His grandstanding may in fact have inspired much-needed discussion of the individual's right to die and the need to prepare for that inevitability, but his actions extend beyond the parameters of medical ethics and social acceptability.

Dr. Death's career of arranging suicides should cease, even if, as one Michigan lawmaker thinks, the "only thing that's going to stop him is prison."

THE ☁ SUN
Baltimore, Maryland, March 11, 1993

In their haste to stop the spectacle of Dr. Jack Kevorkian's parade of assisted suicides, Michigan legislators may have created a bigger problem.

Until now, Michigan has had no law making it a crime to help in a suicide, thus making it possible for Dr. Kevorkian to assist in 15 suicides so far. Last month, new legislation was rushed into effect, which makes assisting a suicide a crime punishable by up to four years in prison and a $2,000 fine. It is a temporary measure while a commission studies the issue.

Meanwhile, the American Civil Liberties Union is requesting an injunction against the measure, and Dr. Kevorkian has vowed that, if the lawsuit fails, he will challenge the law's constitutionality by continuing with his suicides. This confrontation is producing more heat than light.

Physician-assisted suicide is a more complicated issue than Dr. Kevorkian or his opponents would have us believe. One Michigan medical group worries that physicians will be prosecuted if a patient uses prescription drugs to commit suicide. Other doctors, especially those who treat terminally ill patients, have legitimate fears about the widespread misunderstanding of pain medication. In advanced cases of terminal cancer, for instance, giving a patient enough medication to control pain can suppress vital signs like pulse and breathing. Under this law, some worry that a physician determined to keep a dying patient comfortable could be charged with assisting in a suicide.

However compassionate Dr. Kevorkian's intentions, virtually no one concerned about medical ethics condones his methods. Hard decisions about life and death are made between doctors and patients every day. But they should be made in the context of an established relationship, they should include more than one physician and they should be made in settings which can provide a system of ethical checks and balances. A free-lance suicide doctor is a tragedy waiting to happen.

Yet the widespread support for Dr. Kevorkian says something important. Too many people fear that their physicians will be more concerned about keeping them alive than about keeping them comfortable. If people could be assured their pain would be controlled, that they would be spared needless heroics, that their families would not be bankrupted by medical bills — in short, if the medical system worked as it should — physician-assisted suicide would not be an issue. The fact that a maverick pathologist can become a folk hero by helping people die is a sobering indictment of the health care system.

St. Louis ♞ Review

St. Louis, Missouri, February 19, 1993

The government of the Netherlands is using some mighty slick logic to maintain that euthanasia is still considered a crime in that country. They have produced a legal fiction, but the Dutch people are not being fooled. We should not be fooled either. Legalized killing of the terminally ill now has the protection of law in a nation of Western Europe.

While doctors who practice euthanasia are still technically committing a crime, the new Dutch law protects them from prosecution if they follow certain procedures. (There had been virtually no prosecution in euthanasia cases in recent years even without this law.) Only 11 percent of Dutch doctors say they would refuse to practice euthanasia, and about 80 percent of the population supports the current policy.

Many in the Netherlands say they personally oppose euthanasia but want to protect the right of others to choose it legally. That kind of reasoning has a familiar ring to it. It is the rhetoric of the so-called pro-choice position, now broadened to include the sick as well as the unborn. The use of terminology like mercy killing and assisted suicide also tends to make the concept more acceptable. The term euthansia, originally meaning easy death, is itself a euphemism for killing.

The current national attempt to control rising health-care costs no doubt colors our own view of the terminally ill and their care. A recent study of the cost of treating critically ill cancer patients has found that medical costs can easily top $100,000 for each year of life gained. That kind of information can act as a subtle type of conditioning, leading us to see people who are ill as an overwhelming burden to families and society. An increasingly materialistic society will naturally become less tolerant of those who cost too much and produce too little.

Of course there are many options between the bankruptcy of families and killing terminally ill people. The hospice movement and other creative means of assistance to the dying and their families help us answer the call to care for the weak.

Euthanasia is an act of desperation. With our rich tradition of faith and our rich material resources, we are not a desperate nation. The Dutch solution to the challenge of the dying diminishes them as a society and we should not follow their example. This question will certainly be argued in our own country in the coming years. We are called upon again to stand up for the sanctity of life.

The Salt Lake Tribune

Salt lake City, Utah, February 15, 1993

In this interconnected world, in which ideas and values spread quickly from one part of the globe to another, the Dutch have taken a dangerous step for the human family with their parliamentary approval last Tuesday of the world's least restrictive euthanasia law.

Even in the Netherlands, where a majority of the population and of doctors support a patient's right to request euthanasia, the ultimate step of approving the practice outright is too difficult to take. Euthanasia will still be technically illegal there, but last Tuesday's 91-45 vote approved a law that would protect doctors from prosecution if they followed strict guidelines in assisting a terminal patient's death.

The Dutch experience will surely be observed closely and warily in this country. Many Americans believe in a patient's right to euthanasia, but the population in general is not ready to embrace the concept. Voters of two states — Washington in 1991 and California in 1992 — rejected euthanasia initiatives, and more than half the states have outlawed the practice of assisted suicide, including Michigan, which aims to halt the continued "mercy killing" of Dr. Death, Jack Kevorkian.

As the debate continues in the United States, people on both sides of the issue are likely to find examples from the Dutch system to support their position. In fact, they already have, since a series of court decisions in the past decade have enabled Dutch doctors to practice euthanasia without fear of legal penalties.

A government study on the practice found that there were 2,300 euthanasia deaths in Holland in 1990 and 400 assisted-suicide deaths, accounting for nearly 2% of all deaths in the country that year. For euthanasia supporters, the study's positive number is that there were nearly 9,000 euthanasia requests that year, meaning that about two-thirds of them were refused and that doctors therefore handled such requests in a discriminating manner. On the other hand, it was reported that, in about 1,000 of the deaths, the patient had not made a recent request for euthanasia.

This is the statistic that alarms since it illustrates the danger of the Netherlands' initiative — the painful yet powerful position in which it places a doctor and the possibility that some doctors could abuse their new authority. It is the statistic that made Tuesday's events even more painful for prolife doctors in the Netherlands; one of them said the passage of the new law meant the abolition of the Hippocratic Oath in his country.

Certainly, the guidelines under the new Dutch law seem strict: The terminal patient must make the euthanasia request himself, of his own free will and in a lucid state, and he must make it over a period of time; the physician must consult with at least one other doctor and must document the case history for the government after the patient's death. Even so, it would be impossible to make rules that are airtight.

One benefit of the new law is that reporting of future euthanasia cases should be more complete than before, thus giving the rest of the world an accurate barometer of the Dutch experience. But the one development that will be most difficult to gauge is potentially the most chilling: "The great danger is that here we may get into a euthanasia mentality," as one pro-life doctor put it.

That is precisely the danger in the step the Dutch took for the world Tuesday — the blurring, over time, of the line between the sanctity of life and the preference for death.

DAYTON DAILY NEWS

Dayton, Ohio, March 1, 1993

Dr. Jack "Death" Kervorkian is a strange bird, but the idea that he is assisting suicides of people who really want to live gets off the main subject.

A right-to-lifer scrounged around the garbage of a Kervorkian assistant and came up with a paper. The paper is being interpreted as saying that Kervorkian client Hugh Gale (now deceased, of course) didn't want to be gassed with carbon monoxide because he said "take it (the mask) off" early on in the process.

The charge that Dr. Kervorkian doesn't follow the most rigorous procedures for gauging people's determination to end their suffering is not really and truly the case against him. And if Mrs. Gale — who was there — disputes the right-to-lifer's interpretation of the trash-can report, authorities should be slow in cooking this into some kind of homicide charge.

The real issue raised by Dr. Kervorkian is whether people who *really* don't want to keep living in agony have the right to get a friendly push through the Big Exit Door. How one answers that depends partly on one's moral view of suicide, partly on one's view of a physician's responsibilities, and partly on whether or not one has some incurable and unrelenting disease.

The Michigan legislature has made its decision, outlawing physician-assisted suicide. Courts will decide if the law stands. At least the law is at the heart of the matter. The law accepts the fact that some people want to be dead sooner rather than later, and says no, they can't be helped.

Now Dr. Kervorkian says, "It's my life against your (Michigan's) law." He threatens a hunger strike. Whether this is illegal — because it amounts to doctor-assisted suicide — remains to be seen.

Nancy Cruzan Dies After Life-Support is Cut Off

Nancy Beth Cruzan, 33, a comatose patient who had been the focus of a nationwide debate concerning her parents' efforts to have doctors remove the feeding tube that was sustaining her life, died Dec. 26, 1990 – 12 days after the tube was removed with the permission of a Missouri state court.

A probate court judge in Jaspar County, Mo. Dec. 14 ruled that the parents of Nancy Beth Cruzan had a right to remove a feeding tube from the comatose woman and allow her to die. The ruling marked an end to a landmark legal battle that had galvanized national attention over the question of whether it was ethical to terminate artificial feeding for patients who were terminally ill or in an irreversible coma.

The tube was removed by Cruzan's doctor, James Davis, at the Missouri Rehabilitation Center in Mount Vernon, less than two hours after the ruling was issued.

Cruzan, 33, had been hospitalized in a "persistent vegetative state" since being permanently brain damaged in a car accident in 1983. She had been sustained by a surgically implanted feeding tube that supplied a liquid diet to her stomach. Doctors said that once the tube was removed she would die within two weeks.

The Supreme Court in June 1990 had rejected an appeal from Nancy's parents, Lester and Joyce Cruzan, for the removal of the tube, ruling that there was no "clear and convincing evidence" as to what Nancy's wishes would be if she were mentally competent.

In August, the Cruzans had petitioned the local court for a new hearing, saying that three former co-workers of Nancy's had come forward with new evidence. The three testified at a probate court hearing in November that they had had conversations with Nancy in which she said she would never want to live "like a vegetable."

The state of Missouri, which had initially opposed efforts to cut off Nancy's feeding tube, had announced in September that it no longer had a "recognizable legal interest" in the case and would not oppose the Cruzans in court. (The lawyer appointed by the courts to serve as Nancy's legal guardian had supported the Cruzans' efforts to end her life.)

The Dallas Morning News
Dallas, Texas, December 27, 1990

Nancy Cruzan's death certificate will say she passed away on Wednesday. But for all intents and purposes, she left this life years ago. In 1983, when she was 25, Ms. Cruzan was seriously injured in an automobile accident. Her doctors said she was in a "persistent vegetative state" from which she never would recover. For eight years, she lay in a hospital bed, unable to communicate, subject to seizures and dependent on others for her every need.

Her grief-stricken family, knowing she never would want to be kept alive if only to exist as a vegetable, tried for three years to end her artificial feeding. Their struggle, which took them to the U.S. Supreme Court, ended two weeks ago when a Missouri judge finally found clear and convincing evidence of the woman's preference and authorized the family to discontinue the feeding. In the early hours of Wednesday, surrounded by her family, Nancy Cruzan got her wish.

As torturous as the last eight years have been to the Cruzans, their experience may help millions of other Americans. In the course of the litigation, the Supreme Court set out ground rules governing the decision to die. The justices said competent people have the right to refuse medical treatment, execute living wills and convey a durable power of attorney to others so that their wishes will be carried out if they become incompetent.

The ruling was one of the most historic decisions of the 1989-90 term. For the first time, the court acknowledged that the right to live free includes the right to die — specifically, that constitutional liberty includes a right to refuse medical attention even when that could prolong or save one's life. But the justices also went on to say that this is a right that can be exercised only if one takes appropriate steps in advance to make his or her preferences known.

Because Nancy Cruzan never had taken such specific steps, her family was left the difficult task of proving her wish. Their struggle prompted thousands of Americans to think for the first time about writing a living will. In recent months, requests for information about such documents have soared. And several weeks ago, President Bush signed legislation that will require hospitals and nursing homes to inform patients of their right-to-die options.

The suffering has ended for the Cruzans. But the possibility of a similar tragedy befalling thousands of other American families remains quite real. At least now, they may be better prepared to deal with it.

The Philadelphia Inquirer
Philadelphia, Pennsylvania, December 27, 1990

The reason why Nancy Cruzan died yesterday, 12 days after doctors removed her feeding tube, should be remembered. She died because *she* hadn't wanted to be kept alive year after year in a vegetative state. That's what she had told friends and relatives before the car crash that left her unable to see, hear, smell, feel or think. And when clear and convincing evidence of her intent became public this summer, Ms. Cruzan was finally allowed to die after years of legal wrangling.

As her family and friends mourn, they may feel consoled that, in effect, she had lost her life nearly eight years ago, when she slipped into a hopelessly comatose state somewhere between life and death. Her loved ones can also feel consoled that legislators, health-care organizations and individuals have reacted to the Cruzan case by working to reduce the number of people who end up in such straits without having earlier made sure that their wishes for care will be followed.

The starting point is to inform people about their constitutional right to refuse unwanted medical care. News coverage of the Cruzan case has accomplished that to a degree. This year, for example, hundreds of thousands of people contacted the Society for the Right to Die/Concern for Dying to receive information on how to avoid being kept barely alive beyond their wishes. This public awareness is sure to increase thanks to this year's budget bill, which requires the U.S. Department of Health and Human Services to conduct a public information campaign on the "right to die."

The same bill also requires that when hospitals, nursing homes and other care-givers admit patients, the patients must be informed of their legal rights to say no (in advance) to various categories of life-sustaining care. (A bill that would clarify the right to die was under consideration in the Pennsylvania legislature, but wasn't passed before the legislature adjourned in November.)

Thus the public tragedy of Nancy Cruzan is leavened by the certain decrease in the number of people who, against their wishes, will some day endure a similar fate. As her parents said this week, "Because of Nancy ... hundreds of thousands of people can rest free, knowing that when death beckons, they can meet it face to face with dignity, free from the fear of unwanted and useless medical treatment."

The Idaho STATESMAN
Boise, Idaho, December 30, 1990

Nancy Cruzan's death last week was greeted with the sadness and relief many people feel when one who is very ill or old dies.

Cruzan was unknown outside her circle of family and friends until an awful day seven years ago when an auto accident left her in a permanent vegetative state. The only thing keeping her alive was a feeding tube, which her parents sought to have removed to allow their daughter to die with dignity.

It was at that point that the rest of the world got involved in her life and in what eventually became a right-to-die vs. right-to-life cause celebre.

It's too bad we didn't know Cruzan before the accident. Then it would have been easier for us to know whether she would have wanted to live or die.

But we didn't know her. Only her family did.

That's why it's important to keep the family's role paramount in these difficult life-and-death decisions for comatose patients. The state's role must be secondary, used only to intercede when a patient has no family or guardian to act on behalf of the patient in accordance with his or her wishes.

There are an estimated 10,000 people around the country in a vegetative state like Cruzan's. We hope the families involved will be able to make painfully hard decisions about their loved ones in private consultations with their doctors, not the state.

Perhaps the Cruzan family's sad experience will enable families to do that without courtroom drama and interference by outsiders who seem more interested in advancing their own cause than doing what's best for one beloved individual.

The Oregonian
Portland, Oregon, December 31, 1990

Nancy Cruzan came to the end of her long death last Wednesday.

A Missouri state trooper had found the young woman, face down on the ground near her overturned car. That was Jan. 11, 1983, and he thought her dead. But life-support measures and later just a feeding tube brought her back to ... what? Life or what doctors call a "persistent vegetative state" and one doctor called "a living hell"?

Over these last eight years, Cruzan's parents watched their 25-year-old turn 33 and their own private hell turn into a public agony. For the last three years, the Cruzans fought all the way to the U.S. Supreme Court for the right to remove the tube that gave their daughter nutrition and water — and the barest vital signs.

Their child, mother and father testified, had said several times that if she faced life as a "vegetable" she would not want to live. Last June, the Supreme Court acknowledged a "right-to-die," but ruled that the Cruzans had not met Missouri's evidentiary standard of "clear and convincing evidence" that a patient held such views. With new testimony from Nancy Cruzan's old co-workers, a Missouri judge found that the Cruzans had met the evidentiary standard, the feeding tube was removed. Twelve days later Cruzan's life and her prolonged dying came to an end.

Despite all this — despite Nancy Cruzan's death, her parents' ghastly ordeal in hospital rooms and court

rooms, the despicable actions of those who stormed the hospital to try to reinsert Cruzan's feeding tube — the Cruzan case worked out about as well as any just and caring society could hope in an age of medical technological wizardry.

In acknowledging a right to die, the Supreme Court also acknowledged a state interest when someone — even a parent — asserts that right on behalf of someone else. Both are proper acknowledgments.

Modern medicine gives us an increasing capacity to make life-and-death decisions for others. It hardly seems unreasonable that our laws should guard against the casual use of these new powers. True, the government seems a crude participant in such delicate family matters, and its intrusions should be limited. But families can trample the rights and wishes of other family members just as easily as non-relatives can — and sometimes more easily.

In the end, the Cruzan case underscores this reality: The right to die, like other rights, comes with attendant responsibilities. In other words, if you do not want to live as a "vegetable" by extraordinary medical means, make those wishes clear while you're able. In Oregon, an individual can spell out decisions about life-sustaining measures in advance through a living will or by granting power of attorney for health care to his representative.

Again, not a perfect system, but perhaps the best available.

The Hartford Courant
Hartford, Connnecticut, December 27, 1990

After seven years in an irreversible coma, Nancy Beth Cruzan was allowed to die. Her death Wednesday brought sadness to the millions of people who followed her case. It probably also brought relief to the heartsick family, which fought for this young woman's right to die in peace.

Miss Cruzan had not written a living will or similar document before her 1983 automobile accident in Missouri, during which her heart stopped for 15 to 20 minutes.

In the 3½ years that her parents and sister struggled in courts to gain permission to disconnect her feeding tube, Miss Cruzan became a symbol in the debate over the right to die.

Two weeks ago, Jasper County Probate Judge Charles E. Teel reaffirmed his 1988 ruling that Miss Cruzan, who lay in a vegetative state, should be allowed to die. His original decision had been appealed to the U.S. Supreme Court by Missouri's attorney general.

In June, the high court said patients — conscious or comatose — had the right to avoid unwanted medical treatment if they had made their wishes known. At the same time, the court affirmed the Missouri law's requirement that "clear and convincing evidence" of a person's wishes be presented before the plug was pulled.

So it was up to the Cruzans to convince Judge Teel that the young woman held such a view. Three friends testified that Miss Cruzan had told them she would never want to live "like a vegetable." That was enough for the judge, who gave the parents permission to pull the feeding tube.

As humane as Judge Teel's decision was, the controversy is unlikely to end. Medical technology can keep someone "alive" even when the patient is, for all intents and purposes, dead. The Missouri ruling is not binding on other states, although the Connecticut Supreme Court came to a similar conclusion in the case of Carol M. McConnell of Danbury two years ago.

About 90 percent of Americans have left no treatment instructions. That includes Judge Teel, as well as the lawyer for the Cruzan family and the court-appointed lawyer for Miss Cruzan. Even so, most of the 6,000 deaths that occur daily in the United States are negotiated in private so that death-delaying technology is avoided, according to the American Hospital Association.

Congress, partly in reaction to the Cruzan case and the Supreme Court's affirmation of the right to refuse life-sustaining treatments, enacted legislation. By next November, most hospitals, nursing homes and other health-care facilities will be required to advise all patients of their right-to-die options.

But the wisest step for everyone is to consider the issue while still healthy. Think about this sensitive subject. Talk it over with your physician and family. Sign a clear letter of intent or a living will.

The Record

Hackensack, New Jersey, December 27, 1990

Nancy Cruzan has found peace at last. Death came to Ms. Cruzan yesterday in a Missouri hospital — seven years after she suffered severe, irreversible brain damage in an auto accident, and 12 days after removal of a feeding tube that was keeping her alive. Her death was a tragedy. It was also a release sought by her parents, her doctor, and her court-appointed guardian. They acted in the well-founded belief that they were doing what Ms. Cruzan, 33, would have wanted. And they provided a humane end to a story of great sadness.

Ms. Cruzan was driving home from work on Jan. 11, 1983, when her car went off the road and she was thrown into a ditch. Paramedics were able to restore her heartbeat. But neither they nor doctors who later treated Ms. Cruzan were able to repair the damage to her brain. She was put on a feeding tube, and she lingered for years in a state that few would consider life. She was comatose, her body rigid. Her hands and feet were constricted and bent, and her fingernails sometimes dug into her wrists. She suffered from seizures, vomiting, bleeding gums, and diarrhea. Doctors said she had no hope of recovery.

After four years, her parents asked a court for permission to remove the feeding tube. They had no doubt, they said, that they were doing what their daughter would have wanted. What they sought was not permission for a mercy killing, as some have charged. The issue was the right of a patient, or someone acting on behalf of a patient, to refuse unwanted medical treatment. And both the U.S. Supreme Court and the New Jersey Supreme Court have found that patients have a constitutionally protected right to refuse unwanted treatment.

In the Cruzan case, the U.S. Supreme Court found that there was insufficient evidence of Nancy Cruzan's wishes. At a later hearing, that evidence was provided. Three former co-workers testified that Ms. Cruzan had told them that she would never want to live "like a vegetable" on machines. Ms. Cruzan's physician termed her life "a living hell," and her court-appointed guardian said she should be allowed to die. So a local judge gave permission for the feeding tube to be disconnected. It was. And, despite the ill-advised efforts of protesters to break into the hospital on Dec. 18 and reconnect the tube, Ms. Cruzan died.

The story of Ms. Cruzan's ordeal has a special message for New Jersey. Virtually every state in the nation has a living will statute that allows people to sign legally binding documents directing that they do not want to be kept alive in a vegetative state with no hope of recovery. New Jersey does not have such a law. The Legislature should act. Until it does, there is a risk of the litigation and heartaches that have only now ended for the family of Nancy Cruzan.

The Des Moines Register

Des Moines, Iowa, December 27, 1990

The agony for the family of Nancy Cruzan should have ended long before her death in a Missouri rehabilitation center early Wednesday.

For three years Cruzan's parents had attempted to convince the courts that keeping their daughter alive in a vegetative state contravened what they felt was best, and what Cruzan herself would have wanted. Last June the U.S. Supreme Court prolonged the agony, saying the state of Missouri could continue life support until "clear and convincing" evidence was presented indicating that Cruzan would have preferred death.

Then earlier this month, a Missouri court ruled that such evidence did, indeed, exist. The feeding tubes were removed. The process that began eight years ago, when injuries from an automobile accident caused Cruzan permanent brain damage, was allowed to end. But what should have been a reflective and private time for Cruzan's family was not. Protesters marched outside the rehabilitation center. The terms, "killing," "execution" and "murder" were used.

The protesters argue that they are fighting to preserve the sanctity of life and that they feel a moral obligation to intervene in whatever way they can. They have every right to argue their point, of course. But their protest within shouting distance of Cruzan's bed was off the mark and out of line.

Cruzan's parents lost their daughter. They've grieved for nearly eight years. They have recognized that Cruzan's life didn't end Wednesday, but on the day of the accident that so severely damaged her brain. When medical treatment failed, and when doctors resigned themselves to maintaining a body in a permanent vegetative state, the Cruzans sought to allow natural death to occur. They did not commit murder. There was no execution.

In the wake of the Cruzan case, there will be calls for legislation. There will be more legal challenges, more protests outside of hospitals and hospices.

It is a murky area, as is evidenced by the inconsistent way lawmakers and judges have dealt with it. Living wills provide a partial answer in many cases. But in others, the outcome is better left with those best able to deal with it — caring family members and their doctors.

Lincoln Journal

Lincoln, Nebraska, December 28, 1990

In reflecting on the life — actually, two lives — and death of Nancy Cruzan, a line from *Twelfth-Night* unconsciously enters the process: *"Some are born great, some achieve greatness and some have greatness thrust upon them."*

In the manner of Dred Scott more than a century ago, although in far different circumstances, Nancy Cruzan involuntarily had a kind of awful greatness thrust upon her. But she never knew it.

Not in her most imaginative moments before the 25-year-old woman was an auto accident victim on Jan. 11, 1983, could Cruzan have imagined her fate would produce a landmark U.S. Supreme Court opinion. The June 25, 1990, holding has the potential of affecting hundreds of thousands of other people. It puts a permanent constitutional foundation under the "right to die" in beyond-hope circumstances.

Henceforth, Nancy Cruzan's name always will be associated with the Supreme Court's assertion — only Justice Antonin Scalia objecting — that people have a federal constitutional guarantee to refuse life-sustaining medical treatment.

Cruzan died Wednesday. Breathing ceased a dozen days after a feeding tube to her comatose-like form was removed. Not even the state of Missouri resisted once witnesses testified that Cruzan, when still a rational being, had said she wouldn't want to live "like a vegetable."

Doctors previously had speculated the helpless body could have been maintained for another 30 years, given a tube supplying water and nourishment. Nancy very likely would have outlasted her suffering, loving parents.

Because of the three-year Cruzan legal controversy, millions of Americans came to better understand the central, dramatic issue first raised in the 1976 case of Karen Ann Quinlan. Today 41 states and the District of Columbia — but not, alas, Nebraska — have laws outlining living wills. Even with them, experts estimate more than 90 percent of the adult population still is without a living will or has not executed a durable health care power of attorney. Maybe those numbers now will change.

In addition to the Supreme Court decision, the Cruzan case spurred Congress to pass a law (the Patient Self-Determination Act) requiring virtually all nursing homes and hospitals (as of November 1991) to inform patients of options under their respective state living-will statutes.

As noted above, Nebraska continues to be a last-gasp holdout against such a humane enactment. That is principally because of the opposition of the powerful Roman Catholic Church.

When another attempt is made next month to pass a law permitting death with dignity in hopeless or terminal situations, the Journal hopes Nebraskans will become involved in sufficiently great numbers to help sponsors finally carry the day.

The Union Leader
Manchester, New Hampshire, December 28, 1990

On the day after Christmas, Nancy Cruzan, a feeding tube that had kept her alive for eight years having been removed at her parents' request, died in the Missouri Rehabilitation Center. State and federal courts had only days before rejected injunction requests by anti-euthanasia organizations.

Nancy's death occurred only six months after opponents of passive euthanasia thought, mistakenly, that they had won a decisive legal battle. On June 25th, the U.S. Supreme Court ruled in a landmark decision capping three years of legal action that while competent adults may refuse all medical treatment, the parents of the then 25-year-old victim of a January 1983 car accident had offered **no "clear and convincing evidence"** that Nancy would have wanted to die.

But, back in Missouri courts, three former co-workers of Nancy Cruzan testified in November that they recalled conversations with her in which she said she never would want to live "like a vegetable" on medical machines, and her physician, who had opposed removing the feeding tube, changed his mind and testified that she should be allowed to die.

This newspaper most assuredly does not sit in judgment of Nancy's parents. Unless one has walked in their footsteps, it is impossible to appreciate their nearly seven-year ordeal. Rather, what concerns us most is the largely one-sided reporting on the outcome of the case, Big Media's portrayal of it as a great victory for the forces of compassion and the not-so-subtle insinuation that opponents of so-called mercy killing are insensitive, unyielding zealots.

Would that the issue were as simple as that caricature!

As with any controversy of this type, the court decision must hinge on the facts of the case —and opinions clash. Lower Missouri courts had ruled early on that Nancy's food and water should be cut off at the request of her parents because she was in a "vegetative state."

But her physician and nurses were opposed. The latter, who were closest to her on a continuing basis, testified that their patient was aware of her surroundings. In fact, one nurse tesified that Nancy, who was not on a respirator or any other life support system, clearly smiled when she told her a story.

On November 16th, 1988, the lower courts were overruled by the Missouri Supreme Court. Writing for the 4-3 majority, Judge Edward D. Robertson said they found *"no principled legal basis which permits the co-guardians in this case to choose the death of their ward. In the absence of such a legal basis for that decision and in the face of the state's strongly stated policy in favor of life, we choose to err on the side of life, respecting the rights of incompetent persons who may wish to live despite a severely diminished quality of life."*

At issue here, and one would not know it from much of what passed for news reporting at the time, or since, was **not** Nancy's "right to die." At issue was **whether her life should be taken.** Judge Robertson addressed that important distinction:

"Nancy is not dead nor is she terminally ill. This is a case in which we are asked to allow the medical profession to make Nancy die by starvation and dehydration. The debate here is thus not between life and death. It is between quality of life and death."

Also at issue was the attempt to confuse the provision of food and water with "medical treatment." Judge Robertson wrote for the majority that **"common sense tells us that food and water do not treat an illness, they maintain a life."** From abortion to euthanasia, at both ends of life's spectrum the "right to privacy" is being put forth as the rationale for taking a human life without the consent of that human life.

The Cruzan case itself is not nearly as important as what it may portend —a time when the state alone has the power to determine whether, based on its evaluation of the individual's "quality of life," he or she has the right to live. It would be a time when there is no longer a presumption that, in the absence of clear evidence to the contrary, persons of diminished capacity may wish to live.

It would be a time when the standard for determining who should live and who should die has nothing to do with morality and civil rights but is strictly a social or utilitarian one.

And that time may be closer than we think.

THE INDIANAPOLIS STAR
Indianapolis, Indiana, December 28, 1990

The agony for her family has ended but not the right to die debate for which Nancy Cruzan became an unwilling and unknowing symbol.

Her death is likely to spark demands for legislation giving third parties — usually families — the authority to discontinue life-prolonging treatment, including nutrition, for the hopelessly ill.

Just such legislation has been prepared for introduction next month in the Indiana General Assembly. The bill would revise the state's present living will statute so that the terminally ill would no longer be required to accept basic sustenance.

At present, Indiana law requires that all patients, with or without living wills, receive food and water.

Hospitals must provide patients with information on living will laws.

The proposed change "is designed to bring Indiana law into line with common law as handed down by the U.S. Supreme Court," said attorney Kristin Fruehwald, a member of the Probate Code Study Commission, which drafted the legislation.

The court ruled in June that individuals have the right to be taken off life support systems if they made clear before being incapacitated that it would be their wish. A later state ruling allowed Cruzan's parents to remove a feeding tube that had sustained her for eight years in a vegetative state.

Last fall Congress passed legislation, effective December 1991, requiring all hospitals and other health care institutions to provide written information about a patient's right under state law to control decisions regarding medical treatment.

All patients are to be provided information and forms necessary to make a living will. Institutions and agencies that do not comply can be denied Medicare and Medicaid funding.

John J. Curtin, president of the American Bar Association, supports the law, saying it will encourage a common effort "to develop educational initiatives and procedures that will respect and enhance individual choice."

Ironically, Curtin calls the legislation "the Nancy Cruzan Act." Yet Cruzan, brain damaged in an auto accident, arrived at the hospital in a comatose state from which she never recovered. Living will information and forms would not have changed her situation.

Contrary to some claims, the Cruzan case does not provide indisputable answers regarding the right to die. In many ways, it confounds the issue. What it does provide is anguished evidence that man must proceed with the greatest caution and humility when trying to define the sacred perimeters of life and death.

Supreme Court Upholds Concept of 'Right to Die'

The Supreme Court June 25, 1990 ruled that a person whose wishes were clearly known had a constitutional right to refuse life-sustaining medical treatment. But, in a 5-4 decision, the court held that states could require that comatose patients be kept alive unless there was "clear and convincing evidence" that they would not want to live under such circumstances.

The decision, in *Cruzan v. Missouri*, was the court's first ever in a "right-to-die" case.

In the decision, the court found that clear and convincing evidence as to her wishes was absent in the case of Nancy Cruzan.

According to news accounts, more than 10,000 Americans were currently being kept alive in vegetative states, and more than 40 states had laws allowing patients to specify their wishes in advance, or to designate a surrogate, if they became incompetent. Many of the states, however, excluded the right to refuse food and water from such "living wills."

Medical experts quoted in the *Washington Post* applauded the fact that the court had for the first time identified a constitutional right to refuse life-prolonging measures, including administration of food and water. But they expressed dismay at the court's decision that states could set stringent requirements of proof of the patient's wishes.

D. Joanne Lynn, a medical ethicist at George Washington University Medical School, called the ruling "a devastating opinion." "Most of us will face an illness that, at some point in time, will interrupt our competence and require that someone else make decisions for us. That someone now has their hands tied," Lynn said.

Although the court gave validity to living wills, it was estimated that fewer than 5% of adults now had them. Daniel Callahan, director of the Hastings Center for Medical Ethics, told the *Post* that it might be difficult for people to write living wills specific enough to cover all eventualities.

The court's emphasis on evidence of a person's wishes was protested by the American Medical Association. Nancy Dickey, an AMA trustee, said, "Written decisions made ahead of time are not the best way to make choices about health care which is changing all the time."

A spokesman for the American Academy of Neurology noted that the ruling left other states open to adopt less rigid rules than the Missouri standards upheld by the court, and he added, "This is where the battle must turn."

Some experts said that the decision meant that hopelessly ill incompetent individuals would have to be kept alive as long as possible, whatever the cost. The state of Missouri was paying $130,000 a year for Cruzan's care.

The ruling was hailed by organizations for the handicapped and by antiabortion activists. John Wilke, a president of the National Right to Life Committee, said, "No matter how profound a person's disabilities, he or she must not be deprived of the most basic care."

The Cruzan family's lawyer said June 25 that the family would continue to seek to have treatment discontinued and to "try to set her free from this hopeless condition she is trapped in. Not to do so would be to disregard the meaning of Nancy's 'lived' life."

The Phoenix Gazette

Phoenix, Arizona,
June 27, 1990

In the case of Nancy Beth Cruzan and her parents, there can be no happy ending.

Cruzan was injured in an automobile accident in 1983. She has been in a coma-like condition ever since, her care paid by the state of Missouri.

Four years after the accident, her parents, convinced their 32-year-old daughter would never improve and would not want to continue living in this condition, sought to have a feeding tube removed. The state of Missouri intervened.

By ruling that the state may require evidence of the patient's wishes, the court has certainly worsened an already agonizing situation for the family and friends of Nancy Cruzan.

However, lacking verifiable evidence of the patient's wishes on so fundamental a question as the preservation of her life, the court wisely determined that it is simply too risky to leave the decision to someone else.

"Not all incompetent patients will have loved ones available to serve as surrogate decision makers," Chief Justice William Rehnquist said. He was joined by Justices Byron White, Sandra Day O'Connor, Antonin Scalia and Anthony Kennedy.

The court affirmed the constitutionally protected right of a competent person to decide to die, but it said there must be convincing evidence of those wishes. Tragically, in the Cruzan case, the evidence does not exist.

The issue in this instance is not the patient's right to die, but the right of a family or legal guardian to order the death of another human being.

However heartbreaking for the family, the decision was necessary to protect the lives of those who are unable to speak for themselves.

THE
DENVER POST

Denver, Colorado, June 27, 1990

A HEALTHY person doesn't want to think about how it would be to lie in a vegetable-like state for seven years.

Nancy Cruzan may have thought about such unpleasant things, and even spoken to friends and family about them.

However, she never put her thoughts in writing before a terrible car crash robbed her of the ability to speak for herself. That omission has caused her family untold grief.

On Monday, the U.S. Supreme Court said the body of the 32-year-old comatose woman will remain on life-support systems indefinitely, because a Missouri law requiring "clear and convincing proof" that she would have wanted such measures discontinued is constitutional.

Although most states don't impose such a rigorous standard of proof, the high court ruling still means individuals must take responsibility for deciding such literal life and death matters while they are mentally competent.

If a person wants to end extraordinary medical treatment after brain-damaging injury or illness, the individual should draw up a living will that spells out when he or she wants these measures stopped. Colorado is among the 43 states that recognize living wills.

Even if a person's religious beliefs require the continuation of medical treatment, he or she should say so in writing.

To shirk this duty is to burden loved ones with painful decisions later, because 70 percent of Americans eventually will confront the choice of whether to sustain life-support systems for a family member.

Indeed, Monday's ruling really is a victory for people who believe an individual has a right to refuse medical treatment.

Eight of the nine Supreme Court justices think that a family has a right to unplug life-support systems of a loved one under some circumstances. They just don't agree on what those circumstances are, which is why Nancy Cruzan will remain hooked to a feeding tube.

That paradox is an injustice.

Ethically, the Cruzan family should have been allowed to disconnect the feeding tube that is sustaining their daughter's body.

These parents were not actively trying to help their daughter commit suicide, an action that would have been morally reprehensible. They simply were asking the doctors to step out of the way and let nature take its course.

It's sad the ethical dissent among the high court justices didn't allow the Cruzans to make that decision. Choices about medical treatment should be made by individuals and their families, and not by state legislatures.

Lincoln Journal

Lincoln, Nebraska, June 26, 1990

Let there be clarity about what a 5-4 majority of the U.S. Supreme Court said Monday in that body's first exploration of the "right-to-die" issue, the tragic case of Nancy Cruzan.

The majority did not declare constitutionally impermissible any state law which, under carefully determined and weighted circumstances, allows kin or guardians to approve of "pulling the plug."

But if a state does not have such an authorizing statute, or to the same effect, has enacted a law preventing withdrawal of life-sustaining procedures, then loved ones or guardians must stand down, regardless of their wishes. State policy prevails.

In some jurisdictions, political expression will result in laws which would invest in agonized steelworker Joe Cruzan and his wife Joyce the qualified power to allow their permanently comatose daughter to die, if artificial mechanisms are suspended. In other states, there will be no such measures, although the wishes of grieving relatives may still be quietly honored.

Several months ago Missouri's legislature tried to revise its law so Nancy Cruzan's surgically implanted feeding tube could be removed. According to Associated Press, intense lobbying led by the Missouri Catholic Conference beat back that amending. Parallel forces very likely would prevail as well in the Nebraska Legislature, were a comparable bill to be introduced here.

But now those same forces may have more difficulty once again preventing passage of a living will law in Nebraska. Although the point was not directly at issue in the Cruzan appeal, even the Supreme Court majority held that a competent person has a constitutional right to reject medical treatment for himself or herself.

That is the crux of the living will concept — a rational declaration of intentions and instructions dealing with future contingencies affecting the declarer's own health, without blocking state intervention.

If re-elected in November, Sen. David Landis should renew his leadership on behalf of a living will statute for Nebraska. On this issue, Landis continues to have more support from the public at large than is regularly reflected in legislative votes.

THE KANSAS CITY STAR

Kansas City, Missouri, June 27, 1990

The Supreme Court's decision in the Nancy Cruzan case indicates that in the issue of the right to die, the court wants the state in control.

Several important elements that need to be considered, however, keep the question open. The court acted specifically on the Nancy Cruzan case, not on the generic issue of terminating treatment. It made no distinction between nutrition and other kinds of treatment.

Eight justices from both sides did indicate that they believe a person has a right under the 14th Amendment to end unwanted medical care.

But the five justices who joined in the majority opinion, written by Chief Justice William H. Rehnquist, made it clear that the court would demand an irrefutable document showing a patient's wishes. Remarks to a friend are not the "clear and convincing evidence" that the majority of the court considered necessary.

At the least, the high court's ruling forces society to look at the question of when life-sustaining treatment should be ended for patients in coma-like conditions or with terminal diseases.

This means debating who should make the decision. It makes the Cruzan family's agonizing struggle personal to every other family that could confront similar nightmares.

This raises substantially the value of a living will. Most states have laws that let people authorize the termination of medical procedures in certain situations.

Besides Missouri, only in Maine and New York have the courts required the strict standard of "clear and convincing evidence" that a person has made such an authorization. Nonetheless, as with the familiar document dispersing material possessions, living wills that are properly written, witnessed and stored are the best safeguard that an individual's wishes will be carried out.

The American Medical Association estimates that 70 percent of Americans will be involved in a decision about life-sustaining treatment for themselves or a relative. The problem is not one that just happens to someone else.

The Record

Hackensack, New Jersey, June 27, 1990

The U.S. Supreme Court has offered solace to those who dread the living death made possible by medical technology. Justices found a constitutional right to refuse unwanted medical treatment. They endorsed living wills directing that treatment be terminated when hope of recovery has vanished. What the justices recognized is a right to die with dignity.

In the narrowest terms, the ruling Monday was a defeat for the family of Nancy Cruzan, 32, who has been in an irreversible coma since an automobile accident seven years ago. After doctors advised her parents that Ms. Cruzan could linger for 30 years in a vegetative state, they sought permission to disconnect the feeding tubes that keep her alive. But the Supreme Court upheld a Missouri law barring such steps without clear instructions from the patient.

The Missouri law, unfortunately, seems needlessly restrictive. Ms. Cruzan had once told a friend that she would not want to be kept alive if injury or illness left her unable to lead at least a halfway normal life. But such a verbal statement failed to constitute the "clear and convincing evidence" required by Missouri law. It's hard to believe anyone would choose to endure the shadow existence that Ms. Cruzan suffers.

But the court established a broad and important principle that virtually invites states to enact statutes far less restrictive than Missouri's. Justices found that constitutional guarantees of liberty extend to the freedom to refuse unwanted medical treatment. That freedom extends beyond mechanical respirators or surgery. It includes a right to reject artificially delivered food and water. The decision puts a clear burden on those who dread being kept alive by machines when there is no hope of recovery. They must set down their wishes in writing, in clear and detailed form and preferably in the presence of witnesses.

In New Jersey, the Assembly and Governor Florio face a burden as well. They should promptly approve legislation, sponsored by Sen. Gabriel Ambrosio, D-Lyndhurst, and passed by the Senate, that sets forth clear guidelines for so-called living wills. Although New Jersey's courts have recognized the validity of such documents, the absence of guidelines makes them easy to challenge. Many doctors, fearing lawsuits, have refused to honor living wills. Mr. Ambrosio's legislation is based on three years of hearings and study by a state bioethics commission. It is humane and thoughtful. It deserves enactment.

Modern medical technology has made it possible for people to live healthy and productive lives far longer than our ancestors would have dreamed possible. But it has also made it possible to keep a body functioning in a state that falls far short of what most people would accept as life. The U.S. Supreme Court, wisely, has recognized those concerns. It has restored a measure of control over the most personal of all acts, the act of dying.

The Des Moines Register

Des Moines, Iowa, June 27, 1990

The living will could take on considerable importance in view of the Supreme Court's decision in the Nancy Cruzan "right to die" case. The court said that in the absence of sufficient evidence of the comatose crash victim's desire to be freed from the feeding tube, the state's wish to maintain her life prevails. A living will presumably would have satisfied the court as to her wish.

Most states, including Iowa, have adopted living-will legislation. Concern for Dying, a New York-based organization that was formed to help promote the concept of death with dignity, has mailed out 8 million copies of its model living will.

It states that when reasonable expectation of recovery has passed, the signer directs "that I be allowed to die and not be kept alive by medications, artificial means or heroic measures. I do, however, ask that medication be mercifully administered ... to alleviate suffering, even though this may shorten my remaining life."

Wills geared to local laws are available in many states, including Iowa. Copies are available from the Iowa Bar Association, 1101 Fleming Bldg., Des Moines, Ia. 50309-4098.

LEXINGTON HERALD-LEADER

Lexington, Kentucky, June 27, 1990

It's hard to imagine a more cruel joke than the one the U.S. Supreme Court played on Nancy Beth Cruzan and her family.

Eight members of the court agreed that the terminally ill have a constitutional right to death with dignity. But four of those same justices turned right around and joined Justice Antonin Scalia in saying Missouri could deny that right to Nancy Beth Cruzan because her family did not present, to the Missouri Supreme Court's satisfaction, "clear and convincing evidence" that Nancy would not want her life artificially prolonged by medical technology.

Actually, it is irrational to call what Nancy has right now a "life." An automobile accident seven years ago left her in an irreversible "persistent vegetative state."

She is totally unaware. She has no cognitive brain function, although a functioning brain stem allows her to breathe. She is totally paralyzed, with atrophied and contracted muscles. She cannot swallow food and drink; she is fed through a tube in her stomach. Although there is absolutely no hope her condition will ever improve, she could "live" for 30 more years.

It is equally irrational for the state to assume Nancy Beth Cruzan would want to continue "living" in this manner. But that is the assumption the Missouri Supreme Court made.

She had told her family and friends verbally that she would not want her life prolonged by artificial means. In most states, that would be sufficient; courts would go along with her family's desire to remove the feeding tube and allow her to die with dignity.

But not in Missouri. It wants "clear and convincing evidence," presumably a living will. A person's wishes expressed to family and friends don't count.

So, along comes the U.S. Supreme Court. It says a competent person has a constitutional right to refuse life-sustaining medical treatment. It says qualified guardians can make that decision for an incompetent patient. It says it has no doubt that Nancy's parents are loving and caring and only want what's best for their child.

The court says all this; and then, it says Missouri can use the "clear and convincing evidence" argument to refuse the Cruzans' request. It's a decision that makes no sense. Either there is a constitutional right to death with dignity, or there isn't. If there is such a right, states should not be allowed to deny it by creating unreasonable legal barriers.

This ruling is a perverse reversal of the Greek myth involving Tantalus, who was doomed to spend eternity with food and water just out of his reach. Nancy Beth Cruzan and her family are being force-fed their living hell, with a merciful end always held just out of reach by our court system.

ST. LOUIS POST-DISPATCH

St. Louis, Missouri, June 26, 1990

Nancy Cruzan still lives — in a vegetative state and against what her parents testify were her wishes · – because of a cruelly stringent Missouri statute. Their hope of gaining permission to remove their daughter's life-sustaining treatment failed Monday when the U.S. Supreme Court declined to find in the Constitution a right to die that would supersede Missouri law. But another possibility remains; the court made it clear the Legislature could grant the Cruzans permission. Or, of course, the Cruzans could relocate to a state with more humane rules.

In its 5-to-4 ruling, the Supreme Court said no more than what was widely expected and is inherently reasonable: A state's interest in protecting life is sufficiently important that it may set a high evidentiary standard for proving that an incompetent person has, in fact, expressed a wish to be allowed to die when no hope of recovery remains. Missouri requires such a wish be proved by "clear and convincing evidence," a test that, unfortunately, Ms. Cruzan could not meet.

Last January, Attorney General William Webster pressed on the Legislature a bill that would have established an evidentiary standard Nancy Cruzan could meet, replete with elaborate safeguards to prevent any quick or heedless termination of life. But Sen. John Schneider of Florissant, and others unwilling to make any distinctions about the nature and quality of life under any circumstances, stopped it cold as a harbinger of euthanasia. Mr. Webster sat silent while it happened.

Now that Nancy Cruzan has been condemned to exist on a feeding tube for what physicians say could be 30 years or more, the Legislature, the attorney general and Sen. Schneider must revisit the issue. In 1991 the Legislature should revive the bill by Sen. Robert Johnson of Lee's Summit to modify Missouri's Living Will statute. It would establish a procedure to permit the family of an incompetent patient to petition a probate court to sanction withdrawal of life-sustaining treatment.

The terms of the bill are more than specific enough to rule out any abuse. A request for termination would have to be unanimous among immediate family members, could not be considered until the patient has been incompetent for three years and would have to be coupled with testimony by three independent physicians. A patient's wishes would have to be shown by a preponderance of the evidence, a slightly more lenient standard than the present rule of clear and convincing evidence, but certainly sufficient to preclude euthanasia.

The Supreme Court has, in effect, recognized the right to refuse treatment. The states must now write laws to make it meaningful for those who lose control over their destiny.

Arkansas Gazette

Little Rock, Arkansas, June 28, 1990

The United States Supreme Court has now said clearly, for the first time, that there is a right to die — that is, to refuse unwanted medical treatment. Nancy Beth ' Cruzan unknowingly won that battle for the rest of us, if not for herself.

While recognizing a person's right to refuse treatment, the court held that states have the authority to bar the removal of food, water or other life-prolonging treatment from permanently unconscious patients whose wishes are unknown or unclear. Miss Cruzan's sad life will continue — perhaps another 30 years, relieving her of all dignity and her family of all resources, tangible and otherwise.

Miss Cruzan, now 32, has been in a persistent vegetative state since a car crash in January 1983. She is kept alive in a Missouri rehabilitation center by a surgically implanted feeding tube. With no hope for their daughter's recovery, Miss Cruzan's parents sought to have the feeding tube removed. The state of Missouri resisted. The Missouri Supreme Court ruled against the family. That decision was upheld Monday by the Supreme Court in a 5-4 vote. The majority said the Constitution does not prohibit the states from preserving the life of an incompetent person unless a surrogate produces "clear and convincing" proof that the patient would have wanted to die rather than live in a vegetative state.

By tradition and common law, most states have permitted guardians to make the difficult decisions about patients in an irreversible state of coma, without requiring "clear and convincing" proof. It was widely believed that the family knew better than the state in such matters. But in a decision that pleased the "pro-life" movement, the Supreme Court Monday endorsed strong steps by state governments to preserve human life when an incompetent's family or guardian asks that life-sustaining medical technology be removed.

Some people, while still in control of their faculties, make a "living will," stipulating that they do not wish to be kept alive by extraordinary measures. The court's decision may encourage more of this. But most people, especially young people, will not be so far-sighted. They must rely on the vision of their state legislatures, and trust that it's better than Missouri's. Arkansas has a rather comprehensive right-to-die law. It provides not only for the living will, it says that a person can name a proxy to make the decision for him or her later, and if there is neither a living will nor a proxy, the law provides that certain relatives can be designated to make the decision. A move to another state, such as Arkansas, may be all that will help Nancy Cruzan now, but a family spokesman says it is too early to consider that option. A change in Missouri law is unlikely, considering the strength of the "pro-life" movement in that state. Indeed, the Supreme Court decision may result in more states following Missouri's example, making it more difficult to end these dreadful imitations of life. Once more, a majority of the Rehnquist court has encouraged government participation in the most personal of decisions. It is quite wrong, in general and in specific. A dissenting Justice John Paul Stevens spoke for Nancy Cruzan:

"The meaning and completion of her life should be controlled by persons who have her best interests at heart — not by a state legislature concerned only with the 'preservation of human life.' "

Omaha World-Herald

Omaha. Nebraska, June 27, 1990

A Supreme Court decision barring the withdrawal of feeding tubes from the hopelessly comatose body of Nancy Cruzan makes it more urgent for the Nebraska Legislature to pass living will legislation.

Like 95 percent of the U.S. population, Miss Cruzan had not set down in writing her wishes regarding life-sustaining treatment in the event that she became incapacitated with no hope of recovery. The court ruled that without such a statement, the parents of the 32-year-old woman couldn't end the treatment that maintains a semblance of life in her body.

The court ruling upheld Missouri law. But it came despite the testimony of Miss Cruzan's family and friends, who said the young woman had repeatedly expressed the wish not to be kept alive in such a state. She had not specifically said she wouldn't want nutrition or water in such circumstances, the court ruled, and therefore the artificial feeding and hydration must continue.

The ruling wrenches some of the most agonizing life-and-death decisions away from those who care most — the immediate family of the comatose patient — and gives the authority to the government. Doctors say that Miss Cruzan, who is one of about 10,000 patients in this country in a persistent vegetative state, could live another 30 years without regaining consciousness. Her care costs the taxpayers of Missouri about $125,000 a year.

At least 40 states have legislation recognizing living wills, and two other states allow people to designate someone to make medical decisions for them in the event they become incompetent.

Many states limit what the wills may require. Half the living-will states, including Missouri, permit life supports such as breathing equipment to be removed or withheld but prohibit the withdrawal of nutrition or water even if a living will specifically says that is the wish of the patient.

Nebraska laws do not recognize living wills, although some doctors and hospitals informally honor the expressed wishes of their patients as much as they can.

The decision in the Cruzan case had positive aspects. The court recognized the individual's right to refuse medical treatment. It approved of living wills and indicated that they are enforceable. Indirectly, it gave weight to the wishes of an incompetent patient so long as those wishes had been communicated in writing beforehand.

When the essence is gone but the shell of humanity is left, maintained by machines, tubes and monitors, a loving family should be making the final decisions. People who want to avoid having that decision taken away by the state should make their wishes known clearly, unequivocally and preferably in writing. And those expressions, whether referred to as a living will or something else, should be given official standing in the laws of all 50 states.

St. Louis ☙ Review

St. Louis, Missouri, June 29, 1990

Joe and Joyce Cruzan, parents of Nancy Cruzan, know what it means to watch and wait. They have watched Nancy, lying in a hospital, subsist in a persistent vegetative state for seven years. Giving up hope that she will recover, they have waited for her to die. Joe and Joyce also know what it means to fight. They have fought for the right to withdraw the feeding tube from Nancy knowing this will probably result in Nancy's death. It is this fight that took them to the U.S. Supreme Court.

Consistent with its stance on the protection of life and its legislation on living wills, the state of Missouri refused permission for the withdrawal of the tube. Even though the Cruzans testified that Nancy expressed a desire to avoid life-prolonging procedures, the Supreme Court felt these expressions were too vague in light of Nancy's present circumstances. The court's decision invoked the protection of personal liberty guaranteed Nancy by the 14th Amendment.

As fellow Missourians frequently interviewed in the newspapers and on television, Joe and Joyce Cruzan have become familiar and effective spokespersons for their cause. Our hearts go out to them when they describe their daughter's condition and their desire to end the frustration and anguish with which they have lived these last seven years. But when the television cameras show us Nancy Cruzan in her hospital bed then our reactions change. Her condition may be described as a "persistent vegetative state" but she looks vibrant and much like other patients. It is this appearance of normalcy that doctors tell us is misleading. If the feeding tube was removed Nancy would in all probability starve to death within a matter of days. In this case is feeding by tube to be considered medical treatment? This question remains unanswered.

The plight of Nancy Cruzan and her parents is real but not unique. There are many, many others who share this dilemma. USA Today states that of the 2 million people who die each year, 80 percent die in hospitals or long-term care facilities. Of those, as many as 70 percent die after decisions to forego life-sustaining treatment.

The Supreme Court considers such situations on the basis of legal principles and precedents. There is more at stake here than just one case. The justices are aware, however, that their decisions in this case will be applied countless times over in every one of our many states. There is a strong possibility that the potential abuses of a decision denying the patients' right-to-life and liberty could go way beyond anything envisioned here. Who is beyond the possibility of recovering? Is every claim that "she/he wouldn't want to be kept alive like this" to be given equal weight? These questions will become more difficult to answer as time passes and medical technology grows more sophisticated.

We are encouraged that the court responded to the challenges raised by these rapidly developing procedures with such a positive decision, affirming life and protective of the patient's rights.

The News Journal

Wilmington, Delaware, June 27, 1990

The issue of whether to ask that a loved one be allowed to die will always be heart-rending to any "surrogates," to use the judicial term used by the court.

"Surrogates" might include parents, spouses, children or other interested persons, as in the family of Nancy Cruzan, who has remained in a "persistently vegetative state" for seven years as a result of injuries suffered in an auto accident.

The U.S. Supreme Court Monday ruled 5-4 that the state of Missouri's requirement that persons like Nancy Cruzan must have provided "clear and convincing" evidence of their wishes in such circumstances was not unconstitutional, although many states do not, in fact, demand such a high level of proof of intention.

The majority finding, while leaving the family the agony of watching Nancy Cruzan linger in a "degraded" state so long, imposing on her parents a terrific burden in many ways, does address, for the first time, a constitutional "right to die."

That "informed consent" of the individual to refuse unwanted medical treatment, nutrition and hydration being defined as such treatment, should be honored, is implicit in the ruling.

Evidence of that consent apparently is satisfied by the concept of "living wills," now in force in various forms under laws of Delaware, Maryland and 39 other states and being considered in eight others, including New York and Pennsylvania.

Consent may be established in other ways in some cases. Those who would spare themselves and their families agony similar to that of the Cruzan family, however, will have "foresight," to make what Justice John Paul Stevens, in dissent, called "an unambiguous statement of their wishes while competent."

LAS VEGAS
REVIEW-JOURNAL

Las Vegas, Nevada, June 27, 1990

In another Supreme Court ruling with relevance in Nevada, the justices basically upheld right-to-die laws in 26 states, including Nevada, and the District of Columbia.

The Supreme Court did, however, draw clear limits concerning the rights of family members to make decisions for a dying person.

The case in question involved a 32-year-old Missouri woman named Nancy Cruzan who has been in a persistent vegetative state, unconscious, comatose and with almost no hope of recovery since an auto accident in 1983. The parents want Cruzan disconnected from her feeding tube so she can be allowed to die.

The court ruled there existed no "clear and convincing evidence" that Cruzan, while conscious, ever expressed an unambiguous wish to die should she find herself in a vegetative state. The court said a conscious patient does have the right to reject all medical treatment — but the family cannot automatically invoke that right if the patient is unable to speak for himself. Instead, the family must present clear evidence that the patient wanted to be allowed to die.

The ruling appears to reinforce Nevada's living-will law, which allows people to state their wish to be removed from life-support equipment if they find themselves in a vegetative state.

The ruling is relevant in the case of Kenneth Bergstedt, a long-suffering local quadriplegic who has sought court permission to have his respirator turned off. District Judge Donald Mosley has ruled that Bergstedt's appeal to be allowed to die falls within the spirit of Nevada's living-will statute, and the high court ruling reinforces that interpretation.

Again, the Supreme Court ruled correctly. Restricting the rights of families to order life support removed from a dying relative might not seem compassionate. But consider that not all families have the best interests of a relative in mind; they may, in some cases, simply seek to speed a person's death to hasten the award of an inheritance, for example.

But by upholding living-will statutes, the court allowed individuals to have a binding say in their own destinies.

ARGUS-LEADER

Sioux Falls, South Dakota, June 29, 1990

The potential value of documents called living wills became more evident than ever this week.

The U.S. Supreme Court ruled Monday that family members can be barred from ending the lives of persistently comatose relatives who did not previously make their wishes clearly known. By a 5-4 vote, justices blocked the parents of a Missouri woman, Nancy Cruzan, from ordering removal of tubes that provide her with food and water.

The ruling has particular relevance to South Dakota, one of only nine states that does not have a living will law. A living will is a signed, dated and witnessed document in which a person states in advance his or her desire regarding the use of life-sustaining medical technology.

Although South Dakota lacks such a law, two pieces of legislation take effect Sunday that will move the state forward in the sensitive area of death and dying. The bills were approved by the 1990 Legislature.

One of the new laws pertains to the so-called durable power of attorney. It will recognize the right of people to designate in advance someone to make medical decisions for them in case they become incompetent by illness or accident.

The other new law will merely put into the legal code procedures that commonly allow family members to make some care decisions for incompetent individuals.

Sen. W.R. Taylor, R-Aberdeen, said Thursday that with the two new laws, living will legislation is not particularly urgent. Taylor, a doctor, noted that South Dakotans can express their wishes in living wills, even though such documents lack official state recognition.

"South Dakota's in good shape," he said.

More accurately, South Dakota, with its two new laws, will be in better shape than it used to be. A living will law would still be a plus for the state.

One needs only to observe experiences such as the Cruzans' to see that the grief and uncertainty of an artificially prolonged death are more painful than sudden death.

Nancy Cruzan, 32, has lain in a coma-like condition for seven years. She was injured in an automobile accident in 1983 and has not spoken or acknowledged her parents' voices since then. Doctors say she could live for another 30 years in a "persistent vegetative" state.

Her parents, Joe and Joyce Cruzan, have said they will not waver in their attempts to allow their daughter to die with dignity.

Family members such as the Cruzans, not judges or doctors, should have the primary say in deciding whether the life of loved one should be prolonged. They know their loved one's desire better than anyone.

A living will law would not make deciding such life-and-death issues any easier. But it would give more legal clout to an individual's own desires.

The 1991 Legislature should add a living will law to South Dakota's legal code.

INDEX

A

ACQUIRED Immune Deficiency
  Syndrome—*See AIDS*
ADKINS, Janet
  Kevorkian euthanasia furor 190–195
AIDS (acquired immune deficiency
  syndrome)
  State plans overview 30–41
  Oregon plan rejection 42–45
  Disabled legislative gains 82–87
  US blood supply controversy 96–99
  Magic Johnson HIV announcement 100–105
  Medical personnel disclosure legislation
    106–109
  Immigration entry curb retention 110–113
  Amsterdam conference 114–117
  TB US rise 118–119
  Black Americans health debate 162–165
  US nursing shortage 176–179
AKRON (Ohio) Beacon-Journal, The
  (newspaper)
  Clinton family leave bill signing 64
  Disabled legislative gains 85
  Magic Johnson HIV announcement 104
  AIDS entry curb 113
  TB US rise 119
  Breast cancer debate 132
  Malpractice overview 160
  Hospital care scrutiny 175
ALBUQUERQUE (N.M.) Journal
  (newspaper)
  Infant mortality rate debate 70
  Breast cancer debate 131
ALCOHOL & Alcoholism
  Disabled legislative gains 82–87
ALZHEIMER'S Disease
  US overview 140–141
AMA—*See AMERICAN Medical Association*
AMERICAN Cancer Society
  Breast cancer debate 130–135
AMERICAN Medical Association (AMA)
  Breast cancer debate 130–135
  Medical costs debate 152–157
  Malpractice overview 158–161
AMERICAN Medical International
  Hospital care scrutiny 170–175
AMERICAN Red Cross
  US blood supply controversy 96–99
AMERICANS for a Sound AIDS Policy
  Medical personnel disclosure legislation
    106–109
AMERICAN Society of Plastic and
  Reconstructive Surgeons
  Breast implant curbs 188–189
AMERICANS With Disabilities Act (1990)
  Disabled legislative gains 82–87
AMERICARE
  Democratic reform proposal (1991) 22–25
ANEMIA
  Child vaccination debate 76–81
ANNALS of Internal Medicine
  Hospital care scrutiny 170–175

ANN Arbor (Mich.) News, The (newspaper)
  Infant mortality rate debate 70
  US blood supply controversy 99
  US cancer rise report 138
  Malpractice overview 159
  Pharmaceutical drug costs, quality debate
    167
  Hospital care scrutiny 174
ARCHIVES of Internal Medicine
  Organ transplant debate 180–183
ARGUS-Leader (Sioux Falls, S.D.
  newspaper)
  Catastrophic care legislation 9
  US nursing shortage 179
  Supreme Court right-to-die ruling 205
ARIZONA Republic, The (Phoenix
  newspaper)
  Democratic reform proposal (1991) 22
  State plans overview 39
  Child vaccination debate 80
  Nursing home debate 90
  AIDS entry curb 113
  US cancer rise report 139
  US mental health debate 147
  Kevorkian euthanasia furor 194
ARKANSAS
  Black Americans health debate 162–165
ARKANSAS Gazette (Little Rock
  newspaper)
  Democratic reform proposal (1991) 25
  TB US rise 118
  Medical costs debate 155
  Black Americans health debate 162
  Supreme Court right-to-die ruling 203
ASHEVILLE (N.C.) Citizen, The
  (newspaper)
  US mental health debate 145
  Medical ethics debate 151
  Black Americans health debate 165
ASPIRIN
  Heart disease studies debate 126–129
ATLANTA (Ga.) Constitution & Journal,
  The (newspaper)
  Medicaid congressional compromise (1991)
    12
  Clinton family leave bill signing 63
  Disabled legislative gains 87
  Medical personnel AIDS disclosure
    legislation 106
  EPA passive smoking report 125
  Breast cancer debate 134
  Black Americans health debate 163
  Pharmaceutical drug costs, quality debate
    168
AUGUSTA (Ga.) Chronicle and Herald
  (newspaper)
  Bush family leave veto 59
  US blood supply controversy 99
  AIDS entry curb 112
  US nursing shortage 177
  Breast implant curbs 189

B

BALTIMORE (Md.) Sun, The (newspaper)
  Oregon plan rejection 42
  Magic Johnson HIV announcement 102
  Medical personnel AIDS disclosure
    legislation 107
  EPA passive smoking report 125
  Kevorkian euthanasia furor 194
BASKETBALL
  Magic Johnson HIV announcement 100–105
BILLINGS (Mont.) Gazette, The
  (newspaper)
  Magic Johnson HIV announcement 104
BIRMINGHAM (Ala.) News, The
  (newspaper)
  Clinton family leave bill signing 65
BIRMINGHAM (Ala.) Post-Herald
  (newspaper)
  Catastrophic care legislation 6
  Heart disease studies debate 128
BLACK Americans
  Infant mortality rate debate 68–73
  Nursing home debate 88–93
  US cancer rise report 136–139
  Life expectancy negative statistics 162–165
  Organ transplant debate 180–183
BLADE, The (Toledo, Ohio newspaper)
  Clinton task force 52
BLOOD & Blood Products
  US safety controversy 96–99
BOSTON (Mass.) Globe, The (newspaper)
  State plans overview 36, 38
  Clinton task force 48
  Disabled legislative gains 84
  Medical personnel AIDS disclosure
    legislation 109
  Heart disease studies debate 127
  US mental health debate 143
  Medical costs debate 152
  US nursing shortage 176, 178
BOSTON (Mass.) Herald, The (newspaper)
  1988 presidential campaign proposals 20
  Disabled legislative gains 82
BOWEN, Otis R.
  US nursing shortage 176–179
BREAST Cancer
  Treatment debate 130–135
  Implant curbs 184–189
BUDGET, U.S.
  Catastrophic care legislation 4–9
  Clinton Medicaid order 14–17
BUFFALO (N.Y.) Evening News
  (newspaper)
  Catastrophic care legislation 8
  Medicaid congressional compromise (1991)
    12
  Bush family leave veto 58
  Breast cancer debate 131
  Medical costs debate 156
  Malpractice overview 159
  Black Americans health debate 162

BUSH, George Herbert Walker (U.S. president, 1989-93)
Medicaid congressional compromise (1991) 10–13
1988 presidential campaign proposals 18–21
Reform plan unveiling 26–29
Oregon plan rejection 42–45
Family leave veto 58–61
Disabled legislative gains 82–87
AIDS entry curb 110–113
Amsterdam AIDS conference 114–117
Malpractice overview 158–161
BUSINESS & Industry—See also related subjects; specific industry, company names
Bush reform plan unveiling 26–29
Bush family leave veto 58–61
Clinton family leave bill signing 62–67
EPA passive smoking report 120–125
US cancer rise report 136–139

C

CANADA
Medical costs debate 152–157
Breast implant curbs 188–189
CANCER—See also BREAST Cancer
EPA passive smoking report 120–125
US rise report 136–139
Medical ethics debate 150–151
CARTOONS
Tony Auth
Clinton task force 50
Magic Johnson HIV announcement 104
Supreme Court right-to-die ruling 204
Paul Conrad
Amsterdam AIDS conference 116
Walt Handelsman
FDA breast implant sales halt 186
Mike Keefe
EPA passive smoking report 124
Ranan Raymond Lurie
Clinton task force 54
Rogers
Organ transplant debate 182
Shelton
1988 presidential campaign proposals 21
Don Wright
Catastrophic care legislation 9
CATASTROPHIC Care
Congressional legislation 4–9
CENSUS, U.S. Bureau of the
Nursing home debate 88–93
CENTERS for Disease Control, U.S. (CDC)
Child lead poisoning test order 74–75
Medical personnel AIDS disclosure legislation 106–109
TB US rise 118–119
Breast cancer debate 130–135
US cancer rise report 136–139
Alzheimer's overview 140–141
CHARLESTON (W. Va.) Gazette (newspaper)
State plans overview 39
CHARLOTTE (N.C.) Observer, The (newspaper)
Bush reform plan unveiling 26
Medical costs debate 154
CHATTANOOGA (Tenn.) Times, The (newspaper)
Clinton task force 54
Clinton family leave bill signing 65
EPA passive smoking report 123

CHICAGO (Ill.) Defender (newspaper)
EPA passive smoking report 125
CHICAGO (Ill.) Sun-Times (newspaper)
Medicaid congressional compromise (1991) 13
Infant mortality rate debate 70
Child vaccination debate 77
Disabled legislative gains 85
Nursing home debate 90
Magic Johnson HIV announcement 104
Heart disease studies debate 129
Breast cancer debate 133
Alzheimer's overview 141
Hospital care scrutiny 174
FDA breast implant sales halt 186
Kevorkian euthanasia furor 191
CHICAGO (Ill.) Tribune (newspaper)
Infant mortality rate debate 73
Disabled legislative gains 83
Medical personnel AIDS disclosure legislation 107
Heart disease studies debate 128
Hospital care scrutiny 175
CHILDREN
Catastrophic care legislation 4–9
1988 presidential campaign proposals 18–21
State plans overview 30–41
Clinton family leave bill signing 62–67
Infant mortality rate debate 68–73
Lead poisoning test order 74–75
Vaccination debate 76–81
Disabled legislative gains 82–87
US cancer rise report 136–139
Malpractice overview 158–161
CHILDREN'S Defense Fund
State plans overview 30–41
CHRISTIAN Science Monitor (newspaper)
1988 presidential campaign proposals 18
Magic Johnson HIV announcement 103
CHRONICLE-Herald, The (Halifax, Canada newspaper)
Amsterdam AIDS conference 117
CIGARETTES—See TOBACCO & TOBACCO Products
CINCINNATI (Ohio) Post, The (newspaper)
Medicaid congressional compromise (1991) 11
Heart disease studies debate 126
CIVIL Rights
Disabled legislative gains 82–87
CLARION-Ledger, The/Jackson Daily News (Miss. newspaper)
Infant mortality rate debate 70
US blood supply controversy 98
CLARK, Barney (1921-83)
Medical ethics debate 150–151
CLEVELAND (Ohio) Plain Dealer, The (newspaper)
Clinton Medicaid order 15
Medical ethics debate 151
FDA breast implant sales halt 184
CLINTON, Bill (William Jefferson) (U.S. president, 1993-)
Medicaid order 14–17
Reform panel creation 46–55
Bush family leave veto 58–61
Family leave bill signing 62–67
AIDS entry curb 110–113
CLINTON, Hillary Rodham
Reform panel creation 46–55
COGNEX (drug)
Alzheimer's overview 140–141

COMMERCE, U.S. Department of
Medical costs debate 152–157
CONGRESS, U.S.
Catastrophic care legislation 4–9
Medicaid compromise (1991) 10–13
Democratic reform proposal (1991) 22–25
State plans overview 30–41
Bush family leave veto 58–61
Clinton family leave bill signing 62–67
Disabled legislative gains 82–87
Medical personnel AIDS disclosure legislation 106–109
AIDS entry curb 110–113
Malpractice overview 158–161
Pharmaceutical drug costs, quality debate 166–169
Breast implant curbs 188–189
CONSUMERS & Consumer Affairs
Pharmaceutical drug costs, quality debate 166–169
COURTS & Legal Profession
Medical ethics debate 150–151
Malpractice overview 158–161
CRUZAN, Nancy (1957-90)
Euthanasia debate 196–199
Supreme Court right-to-die ruling 200–205

D

DAILY Gazette, The (Schenectady, N.Y. newspaper)
Organ transplant debate 183
DAILY News (New York City newspaper)
TB US rise 119
Heart disease studies debate 128
DAILY Oklahoman, The (Oklahoma City newspaper)
Democratic reform proposal (1991) 23
Bush family leave veto 61
Heart disease studies debate 127
Malpractice overview 158
DALLAS (Tex.) Morning News, The (newspaper)
Disabled legislative gains 83
Cruzan euthanasia debate 196
DALLAS (Tex.) Times Herald, The newspaper
Infant mortality rate debate 72
Magic Johnson HIV announcement 100
Breast cancer debate 135
US mental health debate 147
Medical costs debate 157
DAVIS, Dr. James
Cruzan euthanasia debate 196–199
DAYTON (Ohio) Daily News (newspaper)
Clinton task force 55
AIDS entry curb 111
Kevorkian euthanasia furor 195
DeJESUS, Esteban (1951-89)
Magic Johnson HIV announcement 100–105
DENTISTRY
Medical personnel AIDS disclosure legislation 106–109
DENVER (Colo.) Post, The (newspaper)
Clinton Medicaid order 15
Clinton family leave bill signing 63
Child lead poisoning test order 74
Child vaccination debate 78
Magic Johnson HIV announcement 102
EPA passive smoking report 124
Malpractice overview 161
Supreme Court right-to-die ruling 201

DESERET News (Salt Lake City, Utah newspaper)
    Clinton task force 51
    Magic Johnson HIV announcement 101
    Malpractice overview 161
    Pharmaceutical drug costs, quality debate 166
    US nursing shortage 178
    Organ transplant debate 183
DES Moines (Iowa) Register, The (newspaper)
    Clinton Medicaid order 16
    Bush family leave veto 59
    Clinton family leave bill signing 64
    Child vaccination debate 79
    US blood supply controversy 96, 98
    Medical personnel AIDS disclosure legislation 107
    Breast cancer debate 135
    US mental health debate 144
    Medical costs debate 153
    Malpractice overview 161
    Pharmaceutical drug costs, quality debate 166–167
    US nursing shortage 179
    Cruzan euthanasia debate 198
    Supreme Court right-to-die ruling 202
DETROIT (Mich.) News (newspaper)
    State plans overview 34
    Clinton task force 47
    Amsterdam AIDS conference 115
    US cancer rise report 139
DIET—See NUTRITION & Diet
DISABLED Americans
    Clinton Medicaid order 14–17
    Oregon plan rejection 42–45
    Legislative gains 82–87
DOWN'S Syndrome
    Disabled legislative gains 82–87
DRUGS—See NARCOTICs & Dangerous Drugs; PHARMACEUTICALS
DUKAKIS, Michael S.
    1988 presidential campaign proposals 18–21

E

EDUCATION
    US nursing shortage 176–179
ELDERLY Americans
    Clinton Medicaid order 14–17
    1988 presidential campaign proposals 18–21
    State plans overview 30–41
    Oregon plan rejection 42–45
    Nursing home debate 88–93
    Malpractice overview 158–161
    Black Americans health debate 162–165
    Hospital care scrutiny 170–175
    US nursing shortage 176–179
El DIARIO-La Prensa (New York City newspaper)
    TB US rise 118
EMPORIA (Kan.) Gazette, The (newspaper)
    Democratic reform proposal (1991) 23
ENGLER, Gov. John (R, Mich.)
    Kevorkian euthanasia furor 190–195
ENVIRONMENTAL Protection Agency (EPA)
    Passive smoking report 120–125
ENVIRONMENT & Pollution
    US cancer rise report 136–139

EPA—See ENVIRONMENTAL Protection Agency
EQUAL Employment Opportunity Commission
    Disabled legislative gains 82–87
ETHICS—See MEDICAL Ethics
ETHNIC Minorities—See also BLACK Americans; HISPANIC Americans
    Organ transplant debate 180–183
EUTHANASIA
    Kevorkian furor 190–195
    Cruzan debate 196–199
    Supreme Court 1990 ruling 200–205
EVENING Gazette, The (Worcester, Mass. newspaper)
    State plans overview 38
    Child vaccination debate 76
    AIDS entry curb 112
    US cancer rise report 136
    Hospital care scrutiny 172
    US nursing shortage 179

F

FAMILIES United for Senior Action Foundation (Families USA)
    Nursing home debate 88–93
FAMILY Issues
    Bush leave bill veto 58–61
    Clinton leave bill signing 62–67
    Nursing home debate 88–93
FARGO (N.D.) Forum (newspaper)
    Medical personnel AIDS disclosure legislation 108
FDA—See FOOD & Drug Administration
FEDERAL Health Care Financing Administration
    Child lead poisoning test order 74–75
FLORIDA
    Medical personnel AIDS disclosure legislation 106–109
FOOD & Drug Administration (FDA)
    US blood supply controversy 96–99
    Alzheimer's overview 140–141
    Pharmaceutical drug costs, quality debate 166–169
    Breast implant curbs 184–189
FORT Worth (Tex.) Star-Telegram (newspaper)
    Catastrophic care legislation 4
    Medicaid congressional compromise (1991) 13
    Clinton Medicaid order 17
    Bush reform plan unveiling 28
    Oregon plan rejection 42
    Infant mortality rate debate 72
    Medical personnel AIDS disclosure legislation 109
FRANCE (French Republic)
    Amsterdam AIDS conference 114–117

G

GALE, Hugh (d. 1993)
    Kevorkian euthanasia furor 190–195
GAO—See GENERAL Accounting Office
GARY (Ind.) Post-Tribune (newspaper)
    Catastrophic care legislation 6
GAZETTE, The (Cedar Rapids, Iowa newspaper)
    State plans overview 40
    Clinton family leave bill signing 66

    US cancer rise report 137
    Medical costs debate 157
GENERAL Accounting Office (GAO)
    Medical costs debate 152–157
GLOBE and Mail, The (Toronto, Canada newspaper)
    Clinton task force 46
GRAND Rapids (Mich.) Press (newspaper)
    Clinton family leave bill signing 66
    Magic Johnson HIV announcement 104
    US mental health debate 144

H

HARTFORD (Conn.) Courant, The (newspaper)
    Clinton Medicaid order 15
    State plans overview 33
    Clinton task force 49
    Bush family leave veto 60
    Child lead poisoning test order 74
    Child vaccination debate 81
    Nursing home debate 88–89, 92–93
    Breast cancer debate 130
    Pharmaceutical drug costs, quality debate 168
    Kevorkian euthanasia furor 192
    Cruzan euthanasia debate 197
HARVARD University (Cambridge, Mass.)
    Nursing home debate 88–93
    Medical costs debate 152–157
    Malpractice overview 158–161
HASTINGS Center for Medical Ethics
    Supreme Court right-to-die ruling 200–205
HEALTH Affairs (journal)
    Medical costs debate 152–157
HEALTH Care Financing Administration
    Clinton Medicaid order 14–17
    Medical costs debate 152–157
HEALTH & Human Services, U.S. Department of (HHS)
    Clinton Medicaid order 14–17
    Oregon plan rejection 42–45
    Clinton task force 46–55
    Infant mortality rate debate 68–73
    Disabled legislative gains 82–87
    Nursing home debate 88–93
    AIDS entry curb 110–113
    Medical ethics debate 150–151
    Malpractice overview 158–161
    Hospital care scrutiny 170–175
    US nursing shortage 176–179
HEALTH Maintenance Organizations (HMOs)
    Pharmaceutical drug costs, quality debate 166–169
HEALTH United States
    Infant mortality rate debate 68–73
HEALTHY Start
    1988 presidential campaign proposals 18–21
HEART Disease
    Personality link/aspirin benefit studies 126–129
    Medical ethics debate 150–151
    Black Americans health debate 162–165
    Hospital care scrutiny 170–175
    Organ transplant debate 180–183
HEPATITIS
    US blood supply controversy 96–99
    Medical personnel AIDS disclosure legislation 106–109

HERALD News (Fall River, Mass. newspaper)
    Catastrophic care legislation 5
    Nursing home debate 91
    EPA passive smoking report 122
    US mental health debate 142
    Pharmaceutical drug costs, quality debate 167
HISPANIC Americans
    Nursing home debate 88–93
HIV (human immunodeficiency virus)—See AIDS
HMOs—See HEALTH Maintenance Organizations
HONOLULU (Hawaii) Advertiser, The (newspaper)
    US blood supply controversy 97
    AIDS entry curb 111
HOSPITALS
    Medicaid congressional compromise (1991) 10–13
    Medical costs debate 152–157
    Malpractice overview 158–161
    Black Americans health debate 162–165
    Pharmaceutical drug costs, quality debate 166–169
    Care scrutiny 170–175
    US nursing shortage 176–179
HOUSING & Homelessness
    Disabled legislative gains 82–87
    US mental health debate 142–147
HOUSTON (Tex.) Post, The (newspaper)
    Medicaid congressional compromise (1991) 11
    Infant mortality rate debate 68
    US blood supply controversy 96
    US cancer rise report 137
    Medical costs debate 154
    Pharmaceutical drug costs, quality debate 166
    Hospital care scrutiny 172
HUTCHINSON (Kan.) News, The (newspaper)
    Bush reform plan unveiling 28
    Clinton task force 49
    US blood supply controversy 98
    US cancer rise report 139
HYPERACTIVITY
    Child vaccination debate 76–81

I

IDAHO Statesman (Boise newspaper)
    Clinton task force 50
    Amsterdam AIDS conference 116
    Cruzan euthanasia debate 197
IMMIGRATION & Refugees
    AIDS entry curb 110–113
    Amsterdam AIDS conference 114–117
    TB US rise 118–119
INDIANAPOLIS (Ind.) News, The (newspaper)
    Child vaccination debate 76
    Magic Johnson HIV announcement 101
    US mental health debate 145
    Black Americans health debate 164
    Kevorkian euthanasia furor 194
INDIANAPOLIS (Ind.) Star, The (newspaper)
    Infant mortality rate debate 68, 71
    Child vaccination debate 77
    Malpractice overview 160
    Organ transplant debate 183

Cruzan euthanasia debate 199
INFANT Mortality
    US rate debate 68–73
INFLUENZA
    State plans overview 30–41
INSTITUTE of Medicine
    Malpractice overview 158–161
INSURANCE
    Catastrophic care legislation 4–9
    Democratic reform proposal (1991) 22–25
    Bush reform plan unveiling 26–29
    Breast cancer debate 130–135
    Malpractice overview 158–161
    Black Americans health debate 162–165
    Pharmaceutical drug costs, quality debate 166–169

J

JOHNSON, Earvin (Magic)
    HIV announcement 100–105
JOURNAL of the American Medical Association
    Nursing home debate 88–93
    Breast cancer debate 130–135
    Alzheimer's overview 140–141
    Black Americans health debate 162–165
    Hospital care scrutiny 170–175

K

KANSAS City (Mo.) Star, The (newspaper)
    Clinton task force 46
    Child vaccination debate 81
    US nursing shortage 177
    Supreme Court right-to-die ruling 201
KESSLER, David A.
    FDA breast implant sales halt 184–187
    Breast implant curbs 188–189
KEVORKIAN, Dr. Jack
    Euthanasia furor 190–195
KIDNEY Disease
    Organ transplant debate 180–183
KINGERY, John
    Alzheimer's overview 140–141

L

LABOR & Employment
    1988 presidential campaign proposals 18–21
    Bush reform plan unveiling 26–29
    Bush family leave veto 58–61
    Clinton family leave bill signing 62–67
    Disabled legislative gains 82–87
    Medical personnel AIDS disclosure legislation 106–109
    EPA passive smoking report 120–125
    US nursing shortage 176–179
LAS Vegas (Nev.) Review-Journal (newspaper)
    Medicaid congressional compromise (1991) 13
    Oregon plan rejection 44
    Clinton task force 52
    Medical personnel AIDS disclosure legislation 108
    FDA breast implant sales halt 186
    Supreme Court right-to-die ruling 205
LAS Vegas (Nev.) Sun (newspaper)
    Disabled legislative gains 86
    US blood supply controversy 99

LEAD Poisoning
    Screening of poor children 74–75
LEXINGTON (Ky.) Herald-Leader (newspaper)
    Bush family leave veto 61
    Supreme Court right-to-die ruling 202
LINCOLN (Neb.) Journal (newspaper)
    Medicaid congressional compromise (1991) 10
    Clinton Medicaid order 14
    US cancer rise report 136
    Black Americans health debate 165
    Hospital care scrutiny 175
    Cruzan euthanasia debate 198
    Supreme Court right-to-die ruling 201
LINCOLN (Neb.) Star, The (newspaper)
    1988 presidential campaign proposals 19
    State plans overview 35
    Clinton task force 48
    Nursing home debate 92
LIVER Disease
    Organ transplant debate 180–183
LOS Angeles (Calif.) Herald Examiner, The (newspaper)
    Catastrophic care legislation 4
    US nursing shortage 176
LOS Angeles (Calif.) Times (newspaper)
    State plans overview 30–31, 37, 41
    Oregon plan rejection 43
    Child vaccination debate 80
    Nursing home debate 89
    Heart disease studies debate 126
    US cancer rise report 138
    Black Americans health debate 164
LOUISIANA
    Black Americans health debate 162–165
LOUISVILLE (Ky.) Courier-Journal (newspaper)
    Clinton Medicaid order 16
    Clinton task force 51
    Magic Johnson HIV announcement 104

M

MALPRACTICE
    US overview 158–161
MAMMOGRAMS—See BREAST Cancer
MANAGEMENT & Budget, U.S. Office of (OMB)
    Clinton task force 46–55
MASSACHUSETTS
    1988 presidential campaign proposals 18–21
MEASLES
    State plans overview 30–41
MEDICAID & Medicare
    Catastrophic care legislation 4–9
    1991 congressional compromise 10–13
    Clinton streamlining order 14–17
    1988 presidential campaign proposals 18–21
    Democratic reform proposal (1991) 22–25
    State plans overview 30–41
    Oregon plan rejection 42–45
    Nursing home debate 88–93
    Medical ethics debate 150–151
    Malpractice overview 158–161
    Black Americans health debate 162–165
    Pharmaceutical drug costs, quality debate 166–169
    US nursing shortage 176–179
MEDICAL Ethics
    US debate, overview 150–151
    Kevorkian euthanasia furor 190–195

Supreme Court right-to-die ruling 200–205

MENINGITIS
Child vaccination debate 76–81

MENTAL Illness
State plans overview 30–41
Alzheimer's overview 140–141
US debate 142–147

MERCK & Co. Inc.
Child vaccination debate 76–81

MIAMI (Fla.) Herald, The (newspaper)
Catastrophic care legislation 7
Clinton task force 55
Clinton family leave bill signing 63
Disabled legislative gains 83
Breast cancer debate 131
Medical costs debate 155

MICHIGAN
Kevorkian euthanasia furor 190–195

MILWAUKEE (Wis.) Sentinel (newspaper)
Breast cancer debate 132

MINNEAPOLIS (Minn.) Star and Tribune
AIDS entry curb 113
Breast cancer debate 135

MISSISSIPPI
Black Americans health debate 162–165

MISSOURI
Cruzan euthanasia debate 196–199

MONTAGNIER, Luc
Amsterdam AIDS conference 114–117

MUSCULAR Dystrophy
Disabled legislative gains 82–87

N

NARCOTICS & Dangerous Drugs
Disabled legislative gains 82–87
US mental health debate 142–147

NATIONAL Academy of Sciences
Child vaccination debate 76–81
Alzheimer's overview 140–141
Malpractice overview 158–161

NATIONAL Basketball Association (NBA)
Magic Johnson HIV announcement 100–105

NATIONAL Cancer Institute (NCI)
Breast cancer debate 130–135
US cancer rise report 136–139

NATIONAL Center for Health Statistics
Infant mortality rate debate 68–73
Black Americans health debate 162–165

NATIONAL Citizens Coalition for Nursing Home Reform
Nursing home debate 88–93

NATIONAL Commission on AIDS
Medical personnel AIDS disclosure legislation 106–109

NATIONAL Institute of Drug Abuse (NIDA)
US mental health debate 142–147

NATIONAL Practitioners Data Bank
Malpractice overview 158–161

NATIONAL Right to Life Committee
Supreme Court right-to-die ruling 200–205

NATURE (magazine)
Alzheimer's overview 140–141

NCI—*See NATIONAL Cancer Institute*

NETHERLANDS, Kingdom of the
Amsterdam AIDS conference 114–117

NEW England Journal of Medicine
Child vaccination debate 76–81
Heart disease studies debate 126–129

Breast cancer debate 130–135
Medical costs debate 152–157
Hospital care scrutiny 170–175

NEWSDAY (New York City newspaper)
State plans overview 37
Oregon plan rejection 43
Clinton task force 51
Disabled legislative gains 82
Heart disease studies debate 129
Breast cancer debate 135
Kevorkian euthanasia furor 191

NEWS Journal, The (Wilmington, Del. newspaper)
Disabled legislative gains 86
Amsterdam AIDS conference 117
US nursing shortage 177
Supreme Court right-to-die ruling 205

NEW York City
TB rise 118–119

NEW York State
Malpractice overview 158–161

NEW York Times, The (newspaper)
Child vaccination debate 80
TB US rise 119
Hospital care scrutiny 170

NIDA—*See NATIONAL Institute of Drug Abuse*

NURSING
US shortage projection 176–179

NURSING Homes
US debate 88–93
Medical costs debate 152–157

NUTRITION & Diet
US cancer rise report 136–139

O

OMAHA (Neb.) World-Herald (newspaper)
1988 presidential campaign proposals 20
Nursing home debate 91
Heart disease studies debate 127
US cancer rise report 138
US mental health debate 142
Supreme Court right-to-die ruling 203

OPERATION Rescue
Kevorkian euthanasia furor 190–195

ORANGE County Register, The (Santa Ana, Calif. newspaper)
1988 presidential campaign proposals 19

OREGON
State plans overview 30–41
Plan rejection 42–45

OREGONIAN, The (Portland newspaper)
State plans overview 32, 41
Oregon plan rejection 43
Bush family leave veto 60
Clinton family leave bill signing 67
EPA passive smoking report 123
Black Americans health debate 163
Pharmaceutical drug costs, quality debate 168
Organ transplant debate 182
Cruzan euthanasia debate 197

ORGAN Transplants
Oregon plan rejection 42–45
Medical ethics debate 150–151
Debate & overview 180–183

ORLANDO (Fla.) Sentinel, The (newspaper)
Medical costs debate 155

P

PHARMACEUTICALS
Child vaccination debate 76–81
Nursing home debate 88–93
Amsterdam AIDS conference 114–117
Alzheimer's overview 140–141
Medical costs debate 152–157
Cost, quality debate 166–169

PHILADELPHIA (Pa.) Inquirer, The (newspaper)
Democratic reform proposal (1991) 25
State plans overview 33
Infant mortality rate debate 72
Child vaccination debate 77
US mental health debate 147
Black Americans health debate 165
Cruzan euthanasia debate 196

PHOENIX (Ariz.) Gazette, The (newspaper)
Clinton Medicaid order 14
Democratic reform proposal (1991) 24
State plans overview 39–40
Clinton task force 47
Clinton family leave bill signing 64
Infant mortality rate debate 69
FDA breast implant sales halt 187
Kevorkian euthanasia furor 190
Supreme Court right-to-die ruling 200

PITTSBURGH (Pa.) Post-Gazette (newspaper)
Catastrophic care legislation 7
State plans overview 36
Medical ethics debate 150

PITTSBURGH (Pa.) Press, The (newspaper)
Catastrophic care legislation 8
Disabled legislative gains 87
Heart disease studies debate 129
Organ transplant debate 181, 183

PLAY or Pay
Democratic plan (1991) 22–25
Bush reform plan unveiling 26–29

POLITICS
1988 presidential campaign proposals 18–21
Democratic reform proposal (1991) 22–25
Bush reform plan unveiling 26–29
Clinton task force 46–55
Bush family leave veto 58–61
Clinton family leave bill signing 62–67
Disabled legislative gains 82–87
Medical personnel AIDS disclosure legislation 106–109
AIDS entry curb 110–113
Amsterdam AIDS conference 114–117

PORTLAND (Me.) Evening Express (newspaper)
Breast cancer debate 131

PORTLAND (Me.) Press-Herald (newspaper)
Clinton Medicaid order 17
1988 presidential campaign proposals 21
AIDS entry curb 110
US cancer rise report 137
FDA breast implant sales halt 185

POVERTY & Welfare
Clinton Medicaid order 14–17
1988 presidential campaign proposals 18–21
Democratic reform proposal (1991) 22–25
Bush reform plan unveiling 26–29
State plans overview 30–41
Oregon plan rejection 42–45
Infant mortality rate debate 68–73
Child lead poisoning test order 74–75
Nursing home debate 88–93
TB US rise 118–119

US cancer rise report 136–139
Malpractice overview 158–161
Black Americans health debate 162–165
Organ transplant debate 180–183
PROVIDENCE (R.I.) Journal, The
(newspaper)
State plans overview 34
Child lead poisoning test order 75
EPA passive smoking report 120
Heart disease studies debate 127
Breast cancer debate 132
Medical costs debate 156
Pharmaceutical drug costs, quality debate
169
Hospital care scrutiny 171
Kevorkian euthanasia furor 192
PROZAC (drug)
Pharmaceutical drug costs, quality debate
166–169
PRYOR, Sen. David H. (D, Ark.)
Pharmaceutical drug costs, quality debate
166–169
PUBLIC Citizen
Hospital care scrutiny 170–175

R

RACE & Racism
Black Americans health debate 162–165
RALEIGH (N.C.) News & Observer
(newspaper)
Bush reform plan unveiling 27
Clinton task force 54
Child lead poisoning test order 75
Nursing home debate 93
Breast cancer debate 133
RAND Corp.
Hospital care scrutiny 170–175
RAPID City (S.D.) Journal (newspaper)
Bush reform plan unveiling 29
Infant mortality rate debate 71
Child vaccination debate 77
REAGAN, Ronald Wilson (U.S. president,
1981-89)
Catastrophic care legislation 9
RECORD, The (Hackensack, N.J.
newspaper)
State plans overview 37
Bush family leave veto 58
Clinton family leave bill signing 66
EPA passive smoking report 121
Hospital care scrutiny 173
US nursing shortage 178
FDA breast implant sales halt 187
Cruzan euthanasia debate 198
Supreme Court right-to-die ruling 202
REFUGEES—See IMMIGRATION & Refugees
REGISTER-Guard, The (Eugene, Ore.
newspaper)
Oregon plan rejection 45
Clinton task force 53
Clinton family leave bill signing 65
Infant mortality rate debate 73
Magic Johnson HIV announcement 102
Medical ethics debate 150
RELIGION
Medical ethics debate 150–151
RICHMOND, Tim (1955-89)
Magic Johnson HIV announcement 100–105
RICHMOND (Va.) News-Leader, The
(newspaper)
Magic Johnson HIV announcement 103

RICHMOND (Va.) Times-Dispatch
(newspaper)
EPA passive smoking report 121
RIGHT-To-Die Issues—See EUTHANASIA
ROANOKE (Va.) Times & World-News
(newspaper)
1988 presidential campaign proposals 21
Child vaccination debate 79
Heart disease studies debate 128
ROCKFORD (Ill.) Register Star (newspaper)
Catastrophic care legislation 7, 9
Bush reform plan unveiling 29
Clinton family leave bill signing 67
Magic Johnson HIV announcement 104
Amsterdam AIDS conference 116
EPA passive smoking report 120
Medical costs debate 157

S

SACRAMENTO (Calif.) Bee, The
(newspaper)
State plans overview 31
Medical personnel AIDS disclosure
legislation 109
Amsterdam AIDS conference 114
TB US rise 119
Malpractice overview 159
Pharmaceutical drug costs, quality debate
169
SAGINAW (Mich.) News, The (newspaper)
Bush family leave veto 60
Disabled legislative gains 87
Kevorkian euthanasia furor 193
St. LOUIS (Mo.) Post-Dispatch (newspaper)
Bush reform plan unveiling 27
State plans overview 41
Infant mortality rate debate 69
Child lead poisoning test order 75
Child vaccination debate 80
Disabled legislative gains 87
Amsterdam AIDS conference 116
Black Americans health debate 164
Supreme Court right-to-die ruling 203
St. LOUIS (Mo.) Review (newspaper)
Kevorkian euthanasia furor 195
Supreme Court right-to-die ruling 204
St. PAUL (Minn.) Pioneer Press & Dispatch
(newspaper)
State plans overview 38
EPA passive smoking report 124
St. PETERSBURG (Fla.) Times (newspaper)
State plans overview 35
Infant mortality rate debate 69
Disabled legislative gains 84
Amsterdam AIDS conference 115
EPA passive smoking report 121
Breast cancer debate 132
Alzheimer's overview 140
FDA breast implant sales halt 187
SALT Lake (Utah) Tribune, The
(newspaper)
Clinton task force 49
Alzheimer's overview 141
US mental health debate 146
Kevorkian euthanasia furor 193, 195
SAN Diego (Calif.) Union-Tribune, The
(newspaper)
State plans overview 31
Clinton task force 52
Child vaccination debate 79
Disabled legislative gains 84
US mental health debate 143

Pharmaceutical drug costs, quality debate
168
Hospital care scrutiny 172–173
FDA breast implant sales halt 185
SAN Francisco (Calif.) Chronicle
(newspaper)
US blood supply controversy 98
Malpractice overview 160
Hospital care scrutiny 174
SCHROEDER, William (1932-86)
Medical ethics debate 150–151
SCIENCE (magazine)
Alzheimer's overview 140–141
SEATTLE (Wash.) Times, The (newspaper)
Oregon plan rejection 45
Clinton task force 50
Clinton family leave bill signing 67
Child vaccination debate 78, 81
Alzheimer's overview 141
FDA breast implant sales halt 186
SEXUALLY Transmitted Diseases—See
AIDS
SMITH, Jerry (1943-86)
Magic Johnson HIV announcement 100–105
SOCIAL Security
Catastrophic care legislation 4–9
Disabled legislative gains 82–87
Nursing home debate 88–93
SOUTH Carolina
Black Americans health debate 162–165
SPINA Bifida
Oregon plan rejection 42–45
SPOKESMAN-Review, The (Spokane,
Wash. newspaper)
Medicaid congressional compromise (1991)
11
Magic Johnson HIV announcement 100
AIDS entry curb 111
SPORTS
Magic Johnson HIV announcement 100–105
STAR-Ledger, The (Newark, N.J.
newspaper)
Bush reform plan unveiling 28
Nursing home debate 90
Breast cancer debate 133
STATE, The (Columbia, S.C. newspaper)
Clinton task force 55
Infant mortality rate debate 69
Magic Johnson HIV announcement 103
US mental health debate 143
Medical costs debate 153
STDs (sexually transmitted diseases)—See
AIDS
SUICIDE
Kevorkian euthanasia furor 190–195
SULLIVAN, Louis W.
Oregon plan rejection 42–45
SUN, The (Vancouver, Canada newspaper)
Bush reform plan unveiling 27
SUPREME Court, U.S.
State plans overview 30–41
Disabled legislative gains 82–87
Right-to-die ruling 200–205
SYRACUSE (N.Y.) Herald-Journal
(newspaper)
Medicaid congressional compromise (1991)
10
Infant mortality rate debate 73
Disabled legislative gains 85
Nursing home debate 92
US blood supply controversy 98
Magic Johnson HIV announcement 101

US cancer rise report 138
Medical costs debate 154
Organ transplant debate 180

T

TACRINE (drug)
Alzheimer's overview 140–141
TAMPA (Fla.) Tribune, The (newspaper)
Democratic reform proposal (1991) 24–25
Disabled legislative gains 85
Medical costs debate 154
TAXES
Catastrophic care legislation 4–9
Medicaid congressional compromise (1991) 10–13
TB (tuberculosis)—SEE TUBERCULOSIS
TEEL Jr., Judge Charles E.
Cruzan euthanasia debate 196–199
TELECOMMUNICATIONS
Disabled legislative gains 82–87
TENNESSEAN, The (Nashville newspaper)
Medicaid congressional compromise (1991) 12
Clinton Medicaid order 16
Democratic reform proposal (1991) 22
Clinton task force 48
Disabled legislative gains 86
US blood supply controversy 97
US mental health debate 144
Hospital care scrutiny 171, 173
Organ transplant debate 181
FDA breast implant sales halt 184
TIMES-Picayune, The (New Orleans, La. newspaper)
Nursing home debate 93
Magic Johnson HIV announcement 103
Kevorkian euthanasia furor 192
TOBACCO & Tobacco Products
EPA passive smoking report 120–125
TRANSPLANTS—See ORGAN Transplants
TRANSPORTATION
Disabled legislative gains 82–87
TREASURY, U.S. Department of the
Clinton task force 46–55
TUBERCULOSIS (TB)
State plans overview 30–41
Oregon plan rejection 42–45
US rise 118–119

TULSA (Okla.) World (newspaper)
Medicaid congressional compromise (1991) 13
Clinton Medicaid order 17
Democratic reform proposal (1991) 23
Bush reform plan unveiling 29
State plans overview 33
Infant mortality rate debate 70
Child vaccination debate 78, 81
Nursing home debate 90
US blood supply controversy 99
Medical personnel AIDS disclosure legislation 108
Amsterdam AIDS conference 117
Breast implant curbs 189

U

UNION Leader, The (Manchester, N.H. newspaper)
Cruzan euthanasia debate 199
UNISYS Corp.
Malpractice overview 158–161
URBAN Institute
Organ transplant debate 180–183
USA Today (Washington, D.C. newspaper)
EPA passive smoking report 122

V

VACCINES & Vaccinations
Children's safety debate 76–81
VETERANS Affairs, U.S. Department of
Pharmaceutical drug costs, quality debate 166–169
VIRGINIAN-Pilot, The (Norfolk newspaper)
EPA passive smoking report 122
Breast cancer debate 134
US mental health debate 146

W

WADDELL, Tom (d. 1987)
Magic Johnson HIV announcement 100–105
WARNER-Lambert Co.
Alzheimer's overview 140–141
WASHINGTON Post, The (newspaper)
Catastrophic care legislation 6, 8

1988 presidential campaign proposals 19–20
Oregon plan rejection 44
Clinton task force 53
Bush family leave veto 61
Clinton family leave bill signing 62
US blood supply controversy 97
AIDS entry curb 112
Medical costs debate 153, 156
Hospital care scrutiny 171
FDA breast implant sales halt 185
Breast implant curbs 189
WASHINGTON Times, The (newspaper)
Catastrophic care legislation 5
State plans overview 40
Bush family leave veto 59
WHO—See WORLD Health Organization
WICHITA (Kan.) Eagle-Beacon, The (newspaper)
Clinton task force 47
Nursing home debate 91
US mental health debate 143, 146
Black Americans health debate 163
Organ transplant debate 181
WIGGINS, Alan (1958-91)
Magic Johnson HIV announcement 100–105
WINNIPEG (Manitoba) Free Press (Canadian newspaper)
Breast implant curbs 188
WISCONSIN State Journal (Madison newspaper)
EPA passive smoking report 123
Kevorkian euthanasia furor 191
WOMEN
Breast cancer debate 130–135
US cancer rise report 136–139
Malpractice overview 158–161
US nursing shortage 176–179
FDA breast implant curbs 184–189
WORLD Health Organization (WHO)
Amsterdam AIDS conference 114–117
WYDEN, Rep. Ron (D, Ore.)
Pharmaceutical drug costs, quality debate 166–169

Y

YALE University (New Haven, Conn.)
US mental health debate 142–147